© 2017 by Design Media Publishing (UK) Limited
Published in January 2017

Design Media Publishing (UK) Limited
Chase Business Centre
39-41 Chase Side
London N14 5BP
United Kingdom
Tel/ Fax: +44 (0) 20 8449 8974

All rights reserved. No part of this publication may be reproduced or transmitted in any form or by any means, electronic or mechanical, including photocopy, recording or any information storage and retrieval system, without prior permission in writing from the publisher.

ISBN 978-1-910596-78-4

Editing: Alena Lavdovskaya
Proofreading: Chen Zhang
Design/Layout: Muzi Guan

Printed in China

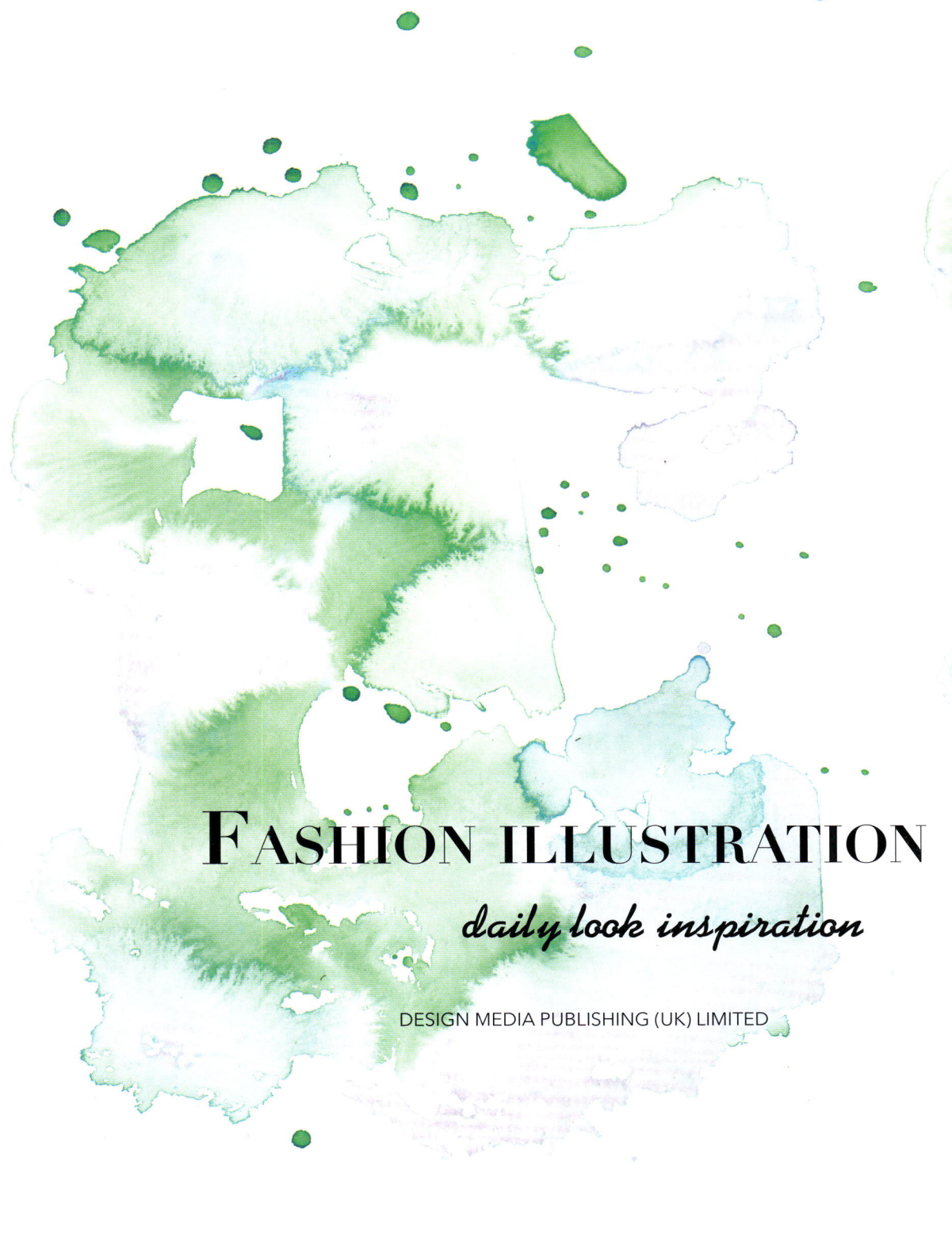

Fashion illustration
daily look inspiration

DESIGN MEDIA PUBLISHING (UK) LIMITED

CONTENT

Preface 006

Chapter One. Definition of fashion illustration 008

1.1 The functions of fashion illustration 008
Sketch
Effect drawing
Design picture
Fashion illustration

1.2 The distinctive art of fashion illustration 011

Chapter Two. The form of fashion illustration — Fashion models 012

Silhouette
Head
Hair
Body
Clothes
Shoes
Shading and colours

Chapter Three. The essence of fashion illustration 018

Chapter Four. Beauty of fashion illustration 024

4.1. The magic of colour 024
Monochromatic colour scheme
Complementary colour scheme
Analogous colour scheme
Black and white colour scheme

4.2 The treasure of fabrics 028
Transparent fabric
Soft fabric
Crisp fabric
Heavy fabric
Glossy fabric

4.3 The beauty of styling 030

4.3.1 Body figure and dressing tips 031
Inverted triangle
Triangle
Straight
Round
Hourglass

4.3.2 Symbolic meaning of different colours 033
Tips on styling 033

Chapter Five. The eye of fashion illustration —— accessories 034

5.1 The origin and significance of accessories 034

5.2 Drawing the texture of accessories 035

5.2.1 Jewel on a Dolce & Gabbana handbag

5.2.2 Texture of high heels

5.3 Drawing a Dolce & Gabbana handbag 036

Projects 038

Simple Chic
Cute and Sweet
Classic Elegance
Workday Outfits
Street Style
Gothic Myths
Ethnic Charm
Accessories

Index 254

Preface

Fortunately there's a true rise of fashion illustration over the past years on the world fashion arena. Big brands like Prada, Gucci, Valentino, Louis Vuitton, McQueen, Lancome make big collaborations with artists all over the world to capture their looks in a new way. Fashion magazines like Vogue, Bazaar, Numero, V, We are, Flair, Interview and many more start to use the illustrations on their pages on the regular bases. Web-resources and especially instagram gave the new breathe to the field and a great support for the successful return of the fashion illustration.

Hand-drawn, animated, realistic, stylized, beautiful, ugly, classy - the illustrated fashion is everywhere nowadays and gets a lot of well-deserved attention. Every day we find new names and artists, the quality of the image gets refined and brings the attention of clients. Many customers turn their attention to the imaginary world of the artist rather than just another beautiful photograph. Even photographers themselves collaborate with artists in the search of a new way of looking at fashion. It's like a new breath in the industry.

It's essential for a fashion illustrator to stay tuned and know what is going on in the arena of the world fashion. Looking daily at main portals like style.com and blogs like fashiongonerogue.com, trendland.net and others will help you to get the photoreferences and basic themes and knowledge of latest trends, as well as simply beautiful inspiration. Follow the once you admire on instagram to get the fresh insider's view and to know the latest real projects and collaborations. Study the works of masters, start to collect your illustrative library. I love to sit with a good book on a great master of the past - i have many, even very rare books with illustration of Rene Gruau, Antonio Lopez, Tony Viramontes, Erte, J.C. Leyendecker, Kenneth Paul Block and others. Don't miss the flea markets with old illustrated magazines. And simply just open your eyes widely, beauty is everywhere, you just have to see it.

When working on a show or backstage, I look around first, try to feel that atmosphere, breathe it in and try catch a model to pose for few minutes to get more details. I try to draw as fast as I can, free my hand and don't even look at the worksheet sometimes. This is for me the main goal of the reportage illustration - to get that motion in a drawing. I draw the final images from the photofererences, but those live sketches give me the understanding of how to make the final drawing and where to put accents on the final illustration.

Campaign images and editorial illustration are good to draw from the live model, to have an idea, set, styling, make up and hair-dresser. I 've overgrown the stage of drawing "from the head" or from the photo references. You need to work the same as photographers do. Have a strong

teamwork and lead the "drawing-session". Not every model can pose for a long time - so just take the photos from which you will do your illustrations. They just need to be your photos and the representation of your own goals in the illustration. I sketch a lot during the drawing sessions, but I also make tons of photos to draw the final image from.

My favorite tools today are pencils, markers and inks. Depending on the goal of the illustration I use different ones. I usually start to draw with the face, then basic contour of the body, then add the body colour, garment accents and fills. In the very end I add background. I love to draw fast and to keep the slightly unfinished touch. That brings live to the illustration and leaves a good space for the viewer's imagination.

Fashion illustration for me have always been a great passion and i'm very happy that it became a full-time story for me.

Great fields of work - from advertising images to editorials, reports on runway shows, event illustration, art projects - this is what is waiting for a brave one, who decides to dig into the profession. But behind a beautiful picture there's always a great hard everyday work, many challenges, searches, ups and downs. One who choses to become a fashion illustrator must have wide-open eyes, searching for beauty everywhere. This book collects over 200 fantastic fashion illustrations ranging from garments to accessories. Professional fashion illustrators, as much as those who love fashion and pursue their own style can find references and inspirations from this book.

Once you fall in love with fashion - it will never let you go.

Alena Lavdovskaya

Alena Lavdovskaya, The most famous Russian fashion illustrator, Drawing for all the glossy magazines&resources, such as Bazaar, glamour, Elle, Elle Decoration, SnC, In Style, vogue.ru and others. Among the famous clients are-Lancome, Jimmy Choo, Tsum department store. she join in fashion business from 2003, Nowdays she focused on illustratrated image of the store. she also a tutor and have personal f.i. workshops in Moscow and London. she is one of those illustrators who take it for a real profession and work with live-models to make a perfect unique picture.

Chapter One.

DEFINITION OF FASHION ILLUSTRATION

1.1 The functions of fashion illustration

Fashion illustration was created as a part of fashion design. It originated from fashion sketch that refers to the images created by designers and visually demonstrate the pose, style, colour, texture of the look. It can be referred to as sketch, effect rendering, design picture, illustration in different stages of the design process.

- The mind of designers could be changing by the second. A sketch helps capture and present the idea in a simple and efficient way. It is a best way for the recording of inspirations and design elements. See figure 1.1.1

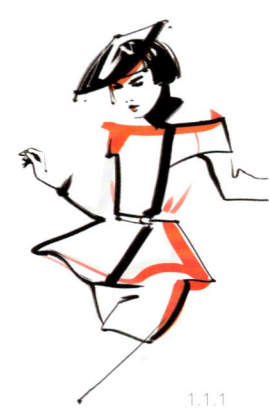

1.1.1

Figure 1.1.1:
Illustration by Katerina Murysina. A quick sketch with simple determined strokes to portray the pose and outfit of the model. Tinted lines in shades of the outfit indicate the overall colour scheme.

- Effect drawing is the dressed image of a concept design realized by the graphic means of colouring, styling, etc. It focuses on the reflection of design concept and the style, charm and characteristics of the garments on an accurate basis. Both the essence of the design and the structure of the clothing are required in this stage. See figure 1.1.2

Figure1.1.2:
Illustration by Mélique Street. In this piece of work, the model is posing accurately and the outfit presents a vivid structure. The costume is designed with a theme of 'lobster', adopting a classic black and red colour scheme. The styling ranges from elegant to youthful to enhance the captivating features of women from different ages group and different identities.

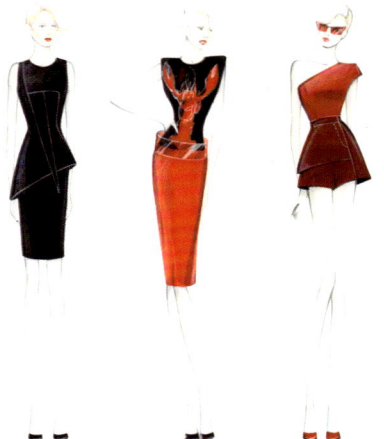

1.1.2

Design picture is used in the production process, it therefore needs to reflect the style, structure, size, texture, the technique used, and matching accessories, in some cases even details in the production procedure, to form a visualized, operable diagram. Illustrative text and sample fabric can be added when necessary. The main function of drawing is to convey the design intention to the patterner and provide a work basis of the whole production. It needs to be accurate and specific. See figure 1.1.3

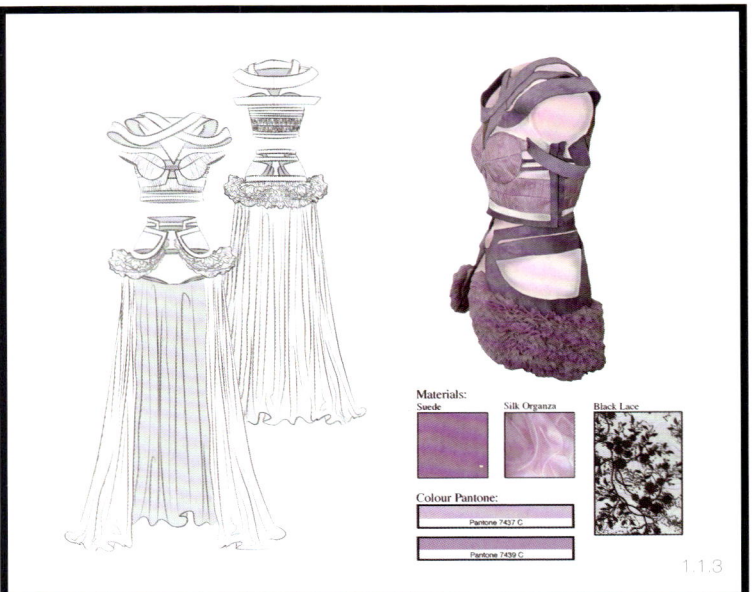

Figure 1.1.3:
Illustration by Rahel
Guiragossian

In the first years of its history, fashion illustration was more often used in posters and brochures to predict fashion trends and guide consumption as a means of campaign. Comparing to the realistic art form of photography, fashion illustration is an improvised means to record popular fashion somewhat between fashion design and illustrative art. It emphasizes drawing skills and visual impact, and it presents strong artistic quality and personal style. Special styling or colour details get enhanced in fashion illustration as with the help of rendering techniques and bold composition approaches. See figure 1.1.4

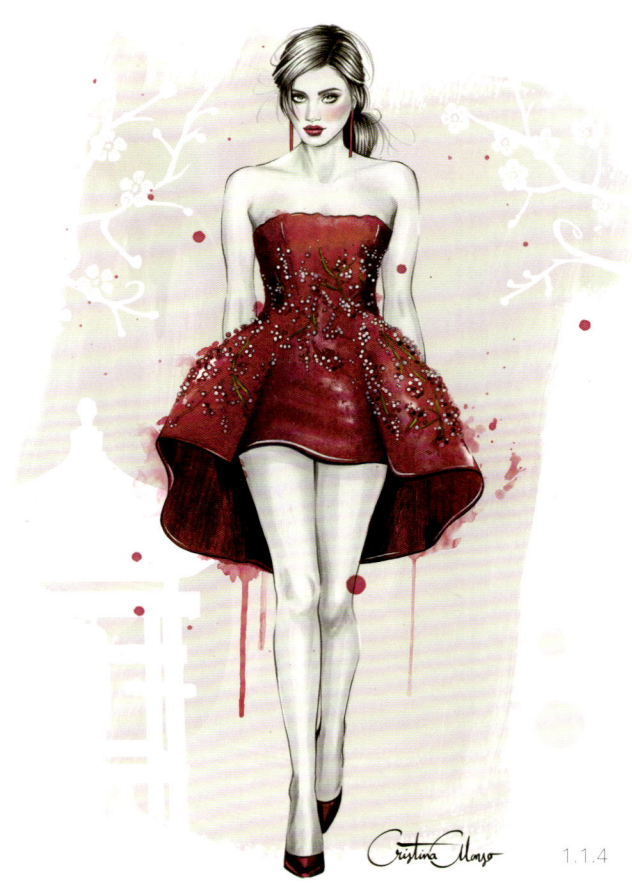

Figure 1.1.4: Illustration by Cristina Alonso. The work integrates the expressive forms of garment drawing and general painting and the details in the plain background indicates the cherry blossom theme of the outfit.

1.1.4

1.2 The distinctive art of fashion illustration

As early as 1672, Le Mercure Galant broadcast to the whole of Europe the stylish looks of French women through fashion illustration. People began to come in contact with this vivid, powerful form of costume display. Compared to other forms, fashion illustration is more straightforward in conveying the designers' intentions and it is highly personal and subjective. Realistic or exaggerated, fantasy or funny, figurative or abstract—the designers' emotions can be fully reflected in fashion illustration.

Nowadays, fashion illustration is no longer a branch of fashion drawing, but an art form itself, widely used in the design for artistic display, interior, general product, window display and etc. It has developed into a cross-disciplinary art form. See figure 1.2.1-1.2.4

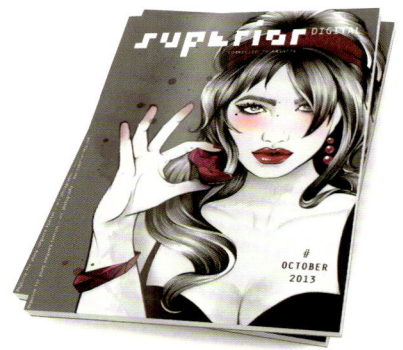
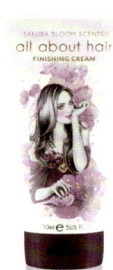
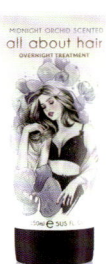

1.2.1   1.2.2

Figure 1.2.1-1.2.4: Illustration by Cristina Alonso. Fashion illustration is widely used in magazine covers, packaging design, interior decoration and product design.

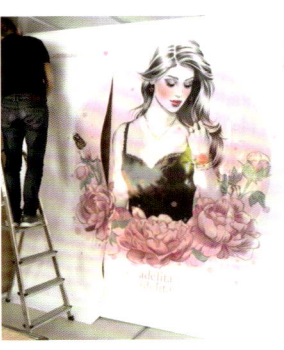
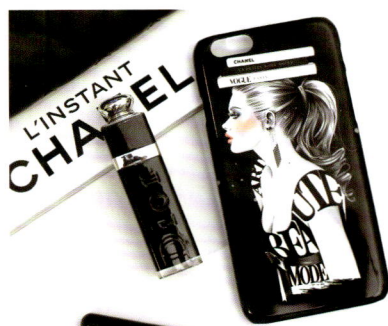

1.2.3   1.2.4

Chapter Two.

THE FORM OF FASHION ILLUSTRATION —— FASHION MODELS

Silhouette

Carole Wilmet usually draws from a picture and starts with a quick sketch of the silhouette. She tries to catch the right position as a whole and uses a 2H pencil to erase easily if she is not satisfied with something. She is more comfortable when she works on small drawings than on larger pieces, so she usually draws on A4 sheets of paper, hardly ever bigger than A3. When she is happy with the first sketch, she starts working on the details. See figure 2.1

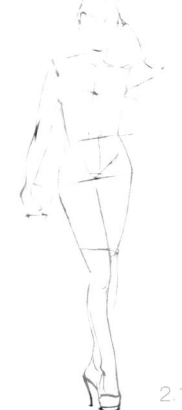

2.1

Head

Carole always starts with the head. She draws first a vertical line dividing the face in two. Then two horizontal lines, one for the eyes and one for the bottom of the nose, depending on the features of the model. It helps to put everything in place. She then draws roughly the eyes, the nose and the mouth and start adding some details and shading. See figure 2.2-2.4

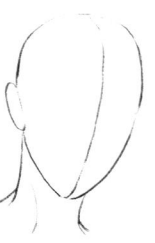
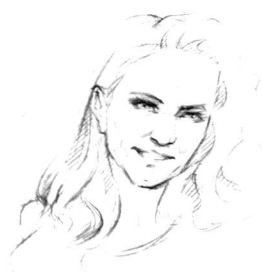

2.2 2.3 2.4

Hair

One of Carole's favourite part is the hair. They can be challenging, they don't always meet your expectations, but they're usually fun to draw. She draws lines that follow the locks and the volume of the head — lighter in the light areas and darker when they need more shadowing, depending on the light of the reference picture. Alphonse Mucha① was Carole's first art inspiration, and she thinks the way she draws hair is still somehow influenced by his work. See figure 2.5, 2.6

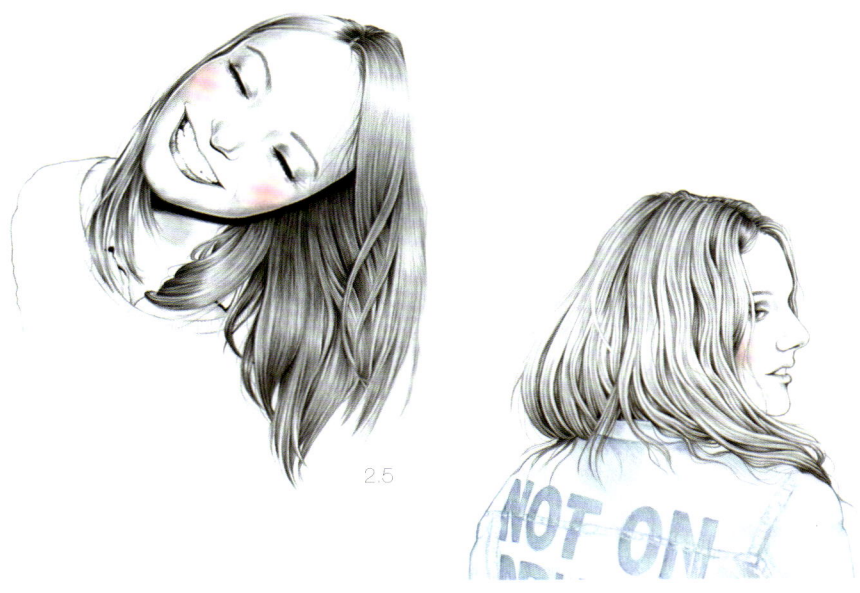

① **Alphonse Mucha**, Czech Art Nouveau painter and decorative artist. In his distinct style, Mucha combines sensational decorative lines, simple contour lines and lively watercolour.

Body

If the first sketch of the silhouette is good, drawing the body isn't the hardest part. Carole loves drawing arms and legs in plain lines, without too much shading. She often has fun with transparency, placing one leg on top of the other one to confuse the viewer and make him or her wonder which leg is which. It's a bit more complicated when models are drawn from a front perspective of course, but in any case, Carole is not fond of too much shading for the body. Keeping it light attracts the eye on the clothes and doesn't make the whole drawing look too heavy. See figure 2.7, 2.8

Clothes

Then Carole goes on with the body and clothes. Drawing clothes is very technical and doesn't really allow a lot of creativity, so Carole sometimes likes to work with inks and colours for this part as she feels more free to give her own interpretation of an outfit. She sees illustration as a way to express creativity, draw outfits or haircuts that she saw, liked and kept in mind. Being patient is an important key to draw clothes, especially when it comes to shading. It's important to look very closely at how the fabric folds and imagine how it moves on the model. See figure 2.9

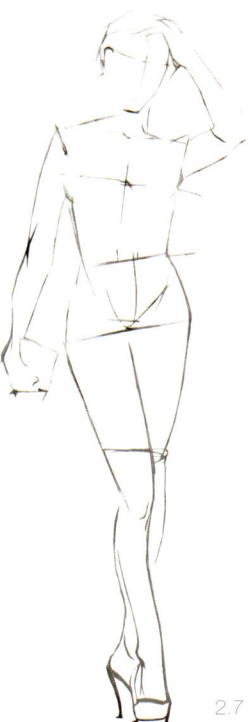
2.7

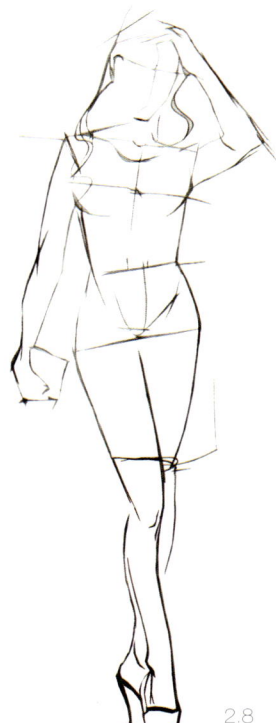
2.8

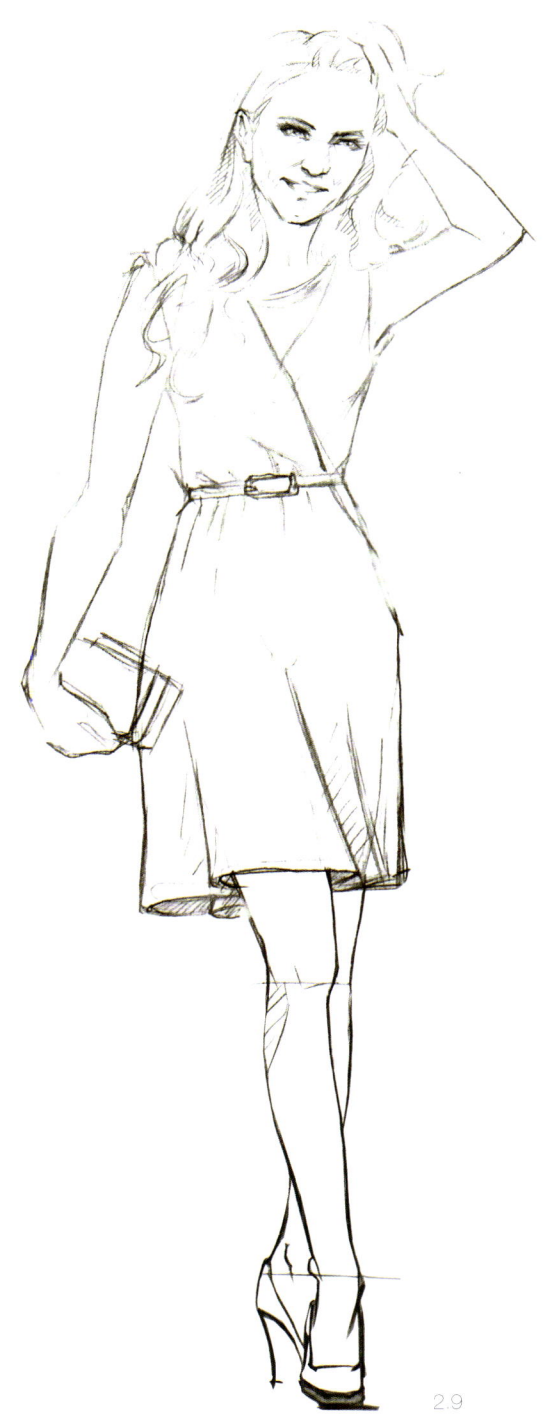

Shoes

Girls love shoes. Rather than buying shoes, Carole is more fond of drawing them. But it's not her favourite part in illustration either. Carole is much more interested in people, so she prefers drawing faces, expressions, looks, hair… for what they tell about one person. Feet tend to look weird in perspective and hands and feet are often a problem for art students. Carole likes it when shoes are treated as part of the composition, not just a form of accessories. When she draws shoes, she likes them to be clearly noticeable and have them being a key element the drawing. In some cases, a carefully drawn and detailed shoe can add so much depth to a drawing. See figure 2.10, 2.11

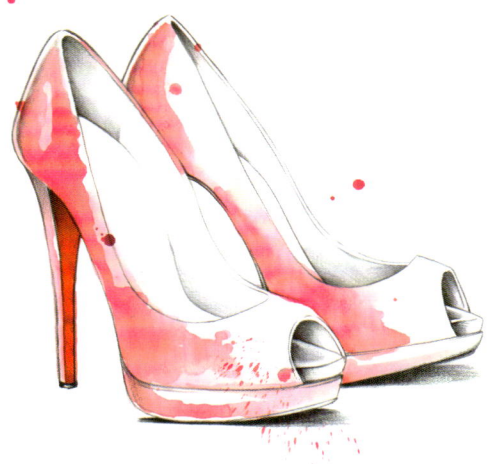

2.10

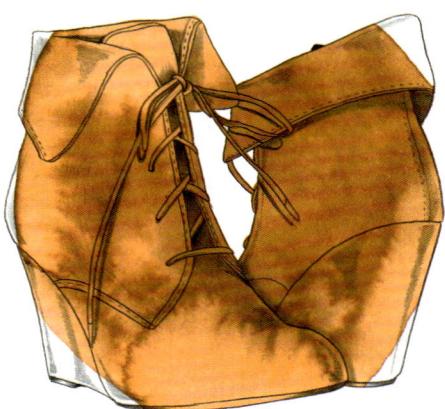

2.11

Shading and colours

When she is satisfied with every part of the silhouette, Carole looks at the shading as a whole as well and corrects it here and there. Add a bit more shading there, a bit more light over there... so that the drawing looks good. Then she can start adding colours. She usually uses watercolours or acrylics, directly on the drawing or sometimes also on another sheet. She then puts everything together on the computer. It really depends on what she has in mind and which technique is best to achieve the result she wishes for. See figure 2.12

—— Carole Wilmet [2]

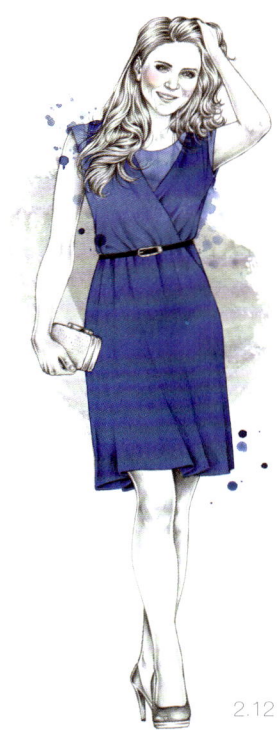

2.12

[2] **Carole Wilmet** started to work as a freelance illustrator in 2010. She's inspired by the everyday life and everyday people. In her work, she tries to catch a part of the 21th century life and of our usual habits, adding to them a touch of colourful inks.

Fashion and nature also influence her work a lot. Living in the country, trees, woods, flowers and fields are a very important source of inspiration for her illustrations and patterns. Her minimalistic and bright, yet sometimes sweet and pastel style gave her the opportunity to work for many brands in the fashion industry, including Armani, Diesel, Lancel... and for many magazines.

Since 2014, she runs her own brand of home decor, Wilde Things. She still lives in Belgium today, close to the Luxembourgish and French borders.

Chapter Three.

THE ESSENCE OF FASHION ILLUSTRATION

Making a truly unique fashion illustration takes quite some time and skills. Of course, one can make a spontaneous masterpiece. But it would be only after years of practice and will come from knowing the essences of a good illustration. What are those essences? It might seem very simple in theory, yet very complex in practice - composition, motion and position, the feeling, the atmosphere and of course the technical skills of using one's favourite materials and tools.

How to get a good composition in your illustration? It depends on the goal of illustration. When drawing a full-figure runway report an artist works with the photo reference or directly on a show. Here all you have to do - is to catch the flow of the garment, to get the right motion of the model and make her walk out of the piece of paper. See figure 3.1, 3.2

Figure 3.1:
A photo taken during the show, while figure 3.2 is the illustration made with the photo as reference. The texture of the fabrics, the floating motion of the train, as well as the expression of the model are all vividly captured in this picture.

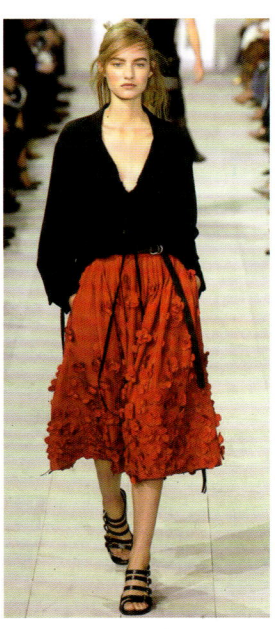 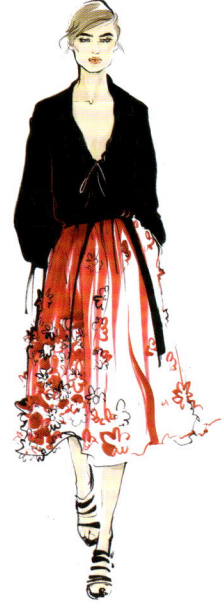

3.1   3.2

Next, you need to decide a central part of the look. Focus on that and leave the rest with an 'unfinished touch' – this creates space for the viewer's imagination and makes the picture more vivid. This can be done very simply - just don't fill in the contour completely and move your brush very quickly, so that it has the motion of the stroke. See figure 3.3

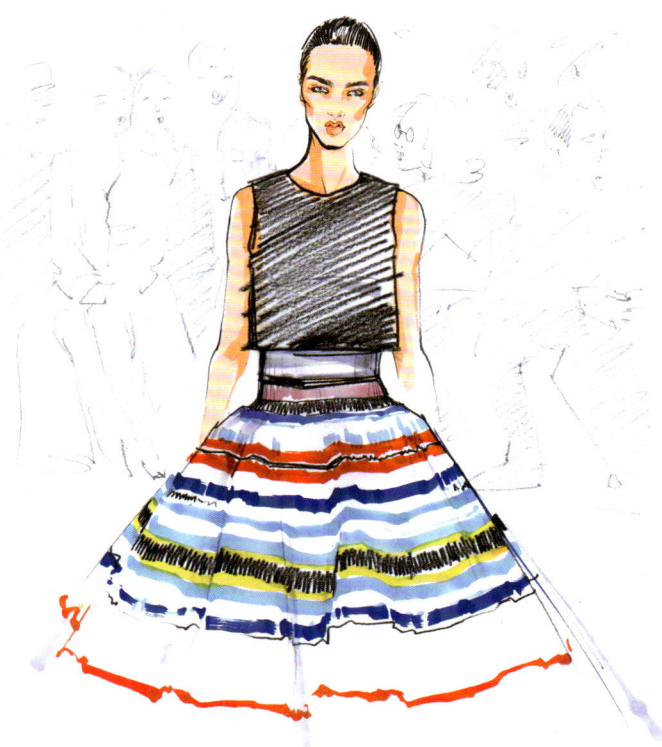

Figure 3.3:
In this illustration, the featured model is clearly portrayed while the background characters are roughly drawn with few strokes. It enhances the featured image and add a sense of depth to the picture.

It's very important to keep in mind the anatomically correct poses of the model, so that the motion feels natural. In cropped and close-up images an artist can play with composition. It can be centered and simple. In this case a model should have a very direct eye contact with the viewer. It also can be more strong & dynamic composition, when the parts of the body are cropped and the garments are flying away from the picture. This is more difficult to draw and it is recommended to work with the professional model and real styling to get the correct motion. See figure 3.4, 3.5

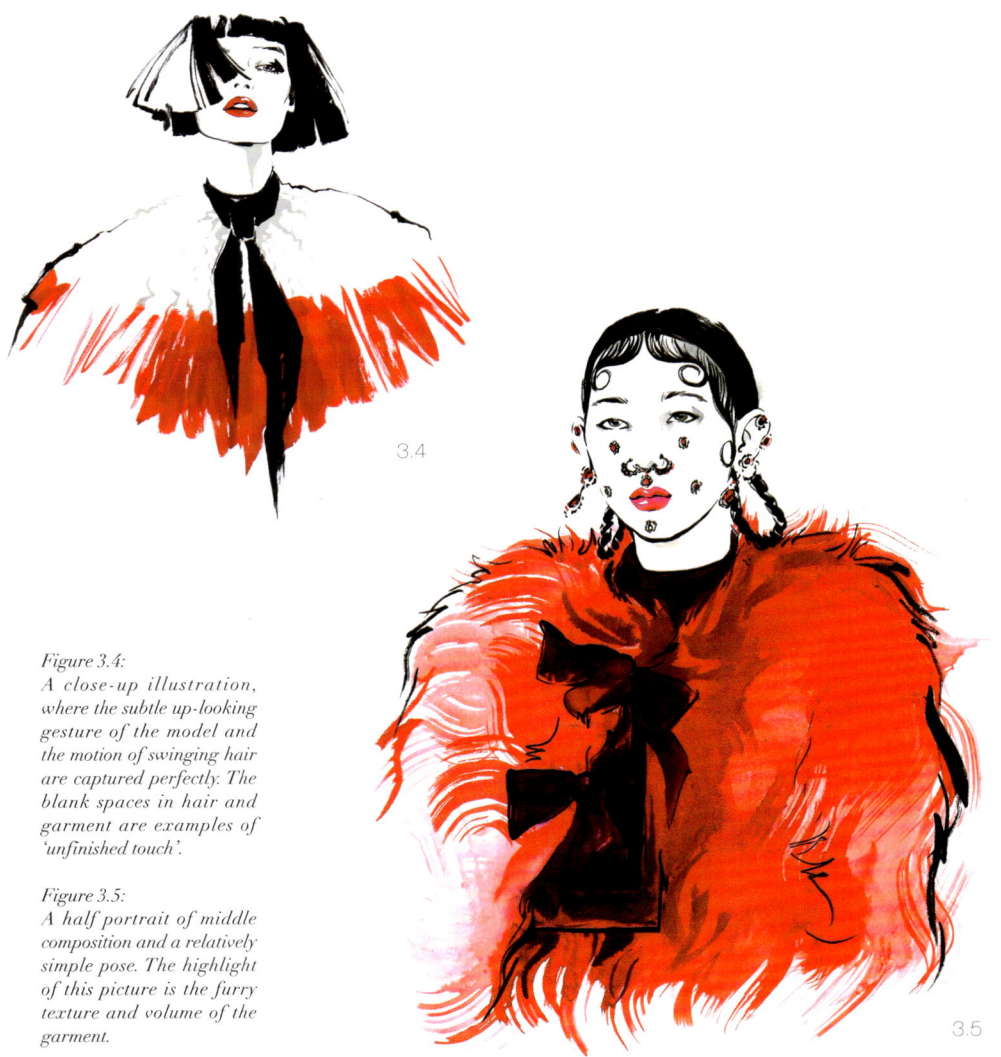

Figure 3.4:
A close-up illustration, where the subtle up-looking gesture of the model and the motion of swinging hair are captured perfectly. The blank spaces in hair and garment are examples of 'unfinished touch'.

Figure 3.5:
A half portrait of middle composition and a relatively simple pose. The highlight of this picture is the furry texture and volume of the garment.

The scene and the atmosphere of the illustration are the next level of work. Working backstage or sitting in the front row of the fashion show gives the feeling of the space and its vibes. It can be transferred into illustration by adding the quick line silhouettes on the background and some bits of interior and set. This will definitely give the image more lively and contagious. When making the illustration from real model in the studio, the illustrator can create the set himself/herself or add it later working with the photo references. See figure 3.6

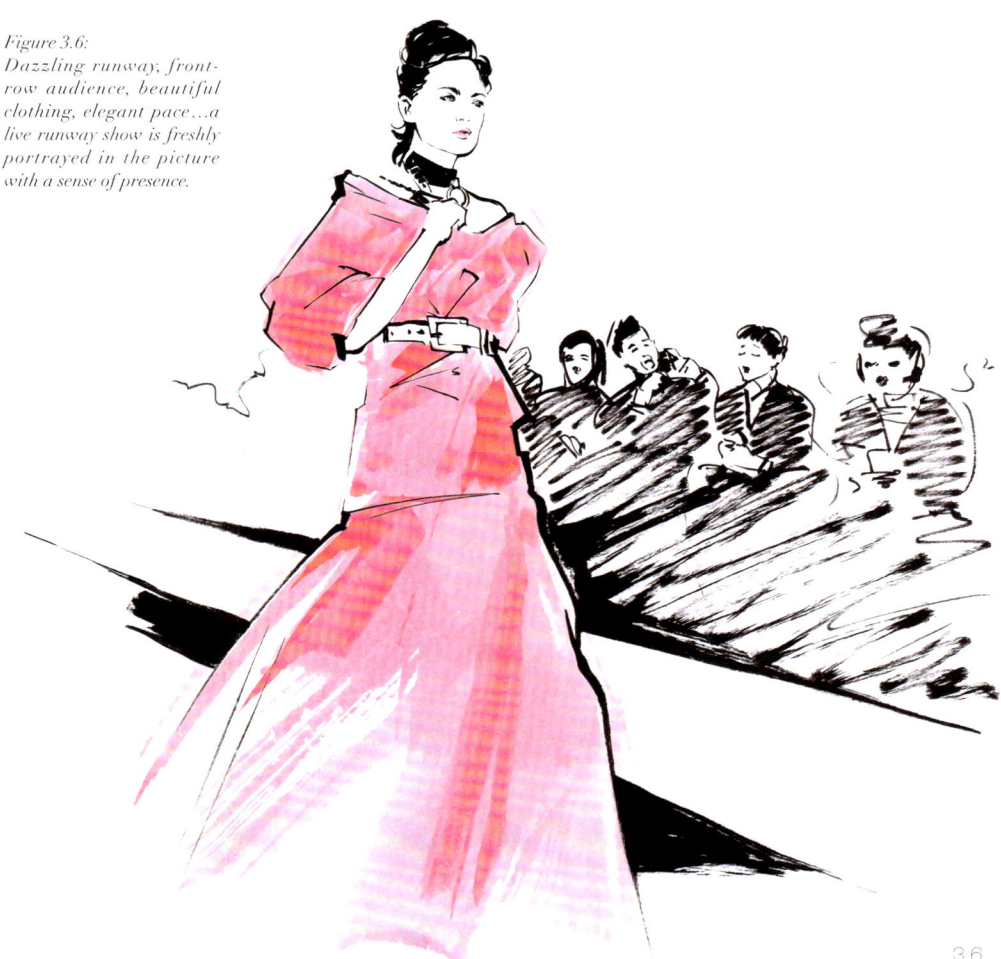

Figure 3.6:
Dazzling runway, front-row audience, beautiful clothing, elegant pace…a live runway show is freshly portrayed in the picture with a sense of presence.

In the end if you feel that there's something missing in the composition - then you can add the background. When drawing the runway report it's beautiful to draw the first row or the set. Do it with quick hand, just sketch it roughly, don't draw much details, so that the background doesn't contest with the main hero of the illustration. You can also add just one bold background colour - in this case it's good to make it bigger on one side behind the model and just some nice strokes on the other. This will add volume and finalize the composition of the worksheet. See figure 3.7

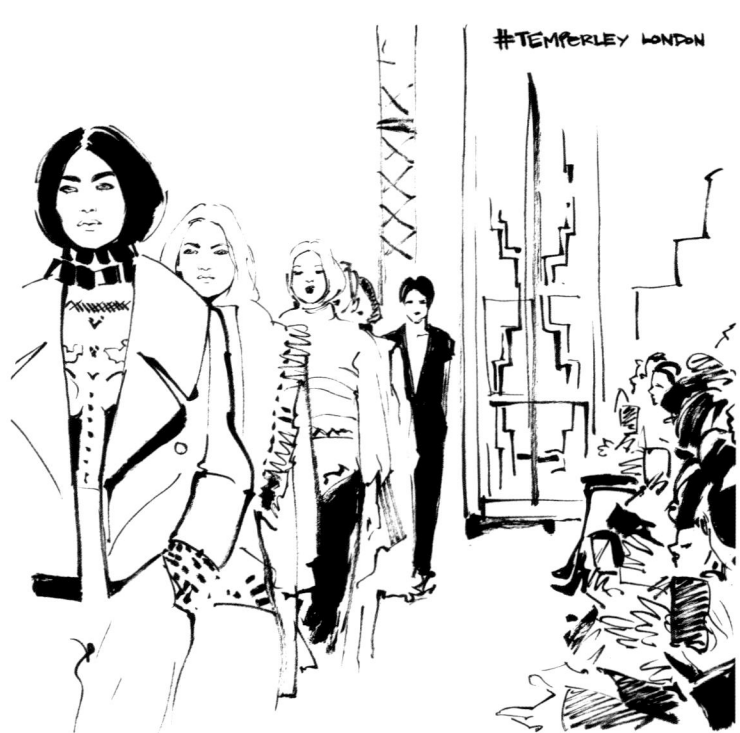

Figure 3.7:
The featured model is placed on the left of the picture, leaving enough space to create depth and background. Front-row audience and the background are roughly sketched comparing to the featured model, enhancing the sense of space.

To make good fashion illustrations, the illustrator needs to find his/her own materials and to get the best of it. It's important to learn and try new tools, but once you feel that it's 'yours' - stop searching and try to fell that pencil or marker or brush as a continuation of your hand.

Here are some tips for you to use to refine your brush skills.
• Its' good to have a pencil sketch of the pose and contour of your final image. Then you can add some skin tone by using a thick brush to fill the main tone of the body and then adding some 'shadows' with 1 or even 2 darker tones of beige to add volume.

• Once the body and face of your 'model' is done you can go ahead with the garments. The same technique works good for the bold coloured looks - do the fill with a big brush to get the main shape of the garmment, then add shadows wth darker tone.

• It's good to get the darker tone by adding the reflex colour, not just a black. Adding black might bring the muddy feeling of the overall of the picture.

• There's more trick with the printed garments-it's good to have some air in the illustration, so don't try to draw everything you see.

• Decide what is central to the outfit, draw it precisely and then let your brush flow and keep it little bit 'unfinished'.

—— Alena Lavdovskaya

Chapter Four.

BEAUTY OF FASHION ILLUSTRATION

4.1. The magic of colour

Colour is an essential element in fashion illustration. It tells the designers' attitude in a straightforward way and injects enormous vitality and emotion into the picture. It is therefore crucial to study the techniques in using colour in fashion illustration. As a basic subject in the art of painting, colour is also quite efficient in expressing emotion: forest green makes an outfit pure and refreshing; bright bold colours add a dreamy sense of fashion to the look; while orange wool overcoat stands for warmth against a cold winter day; flowing white-and-blue dress reminds of a gust of cool breeze by the sea. See figure 4.1.1

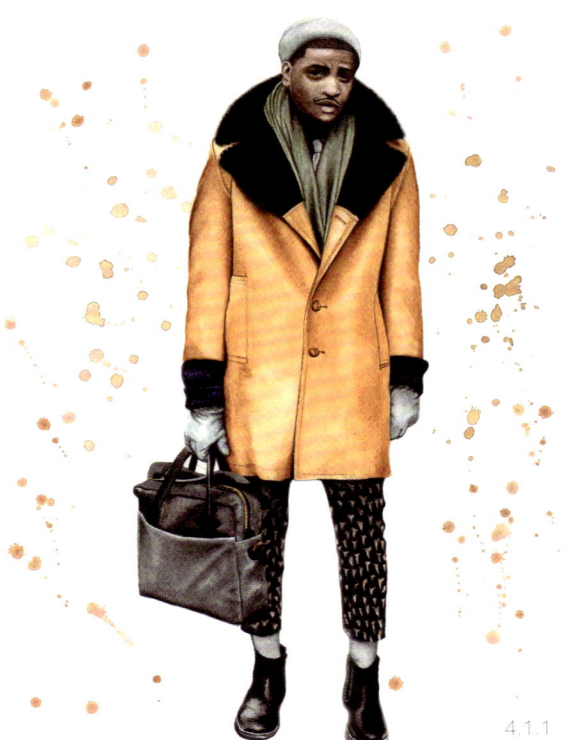

Figure 4.1.1: Illustration by Davide Morettini. Davide get inspired by street looks quite often. His works are mostly fresh and realistic. In this illustration, the model wears a warm yellow overcoat whose colour and texture are captured vividly; giving a comfortably warm and stylish impression.

Single colour indicates certain emotions, yet in everyday looks, there is usually more than one colour used. Matching different colours in different ways can result in varying visual effects. Below are a few common colour combinations.

- Monochromatic colour scheme. It means combining colours of similar hue yet different shades. Pink and fuchsia, vermilion and bright red are both examoles of this category. This creates a graceful, effect, which is suitable for elegant female images. It is essential to present a layered effect, taking garment, accessories, and makeup into consideration. It adds that vitalizing touch to the picture. See figure 4.1.2

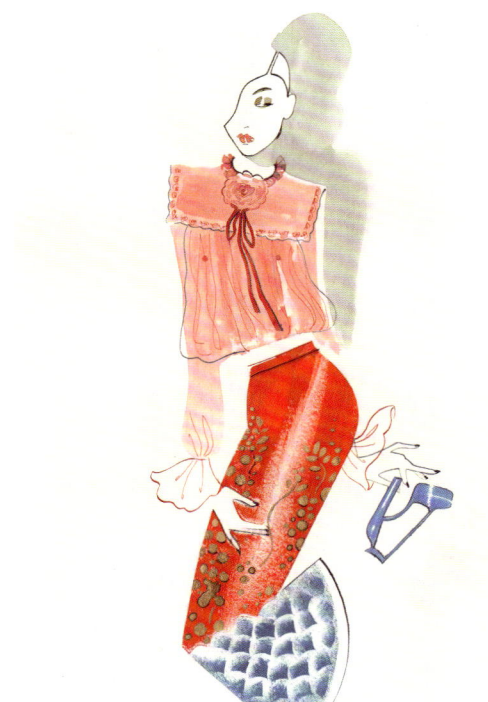

Figure 4.1.2: Illustration by Margot van Huijkelom. Airy vermilion blouse is matched with bright red silk skirt, presenting a balanced effect in weight and colour. There are interesting differences in details that come in a generally unified way.

4.1.2

- Complementary colour scheme. Contrasting colours like red and green, blue and orange, purple and yellow, of drastic visual impact gives a bold, passionate impression. This is often used for images of young women. And one thing to bear in mind the hierarchy of contrasting colours in their applied area to achieve a compatible result. See figure 4.1.3

- Analogous colour scheme. Groups of three colours next to each other within 90 degree on the colour wheel belong to this category, like red-reddish orange-orange, yellow-yellow green-green, and cyan-cyan purple-purple. There is no conflict between analogous colours and they can be matched and used in various combinations for a rich, monochromatic effect, which is suitable for images of all age groups and both genders. See figure 4.1.4

Figure 4.1.3:
Illustration by Samantha Hahn. The main colour is a pair of strong contrasting colours: yellow and purple. The dominant and secondary are clearly defined and surprisingly complementary since there is evident area difference between the two.

Figure 4.1.4:
Illustration by Natsuki Otani. This is an example of analogous colour scheme, where the shades change gradually from cyan in the trousers to the purple of shirt. The vey red coat highlights the whole look while the colour scheme generates a comfortable atmosphere.

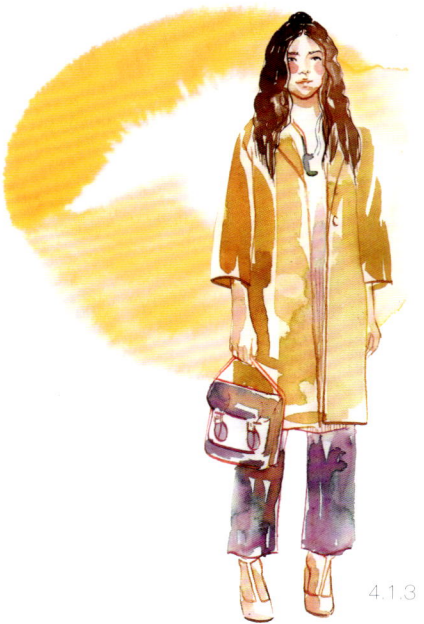

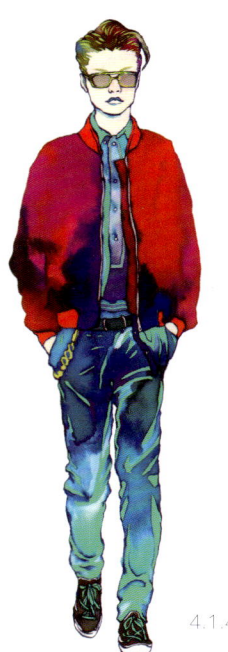

4.1.3   4.1.4

- Black and white colour scheme. The neutral colours of black, white and grey can go with basically any colour. It is a classic colour combination with an impression of being smart and professional. The little black dress look of Audrey Hepburn is also an influential example of the black and white colour scheme. When adding other colours to this scheme, there are a few tips to consider. White can brighten up dull tones, and black can enhance bright colours. Therefore, it is important to create a clearly defined system of primary and secondary colours, then adding black or white for that harmonious final effect. See figure 4.1.5

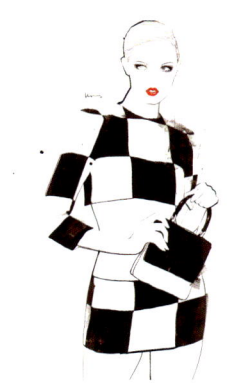

4.1.5

Figure 4.1.5:
Illustration by Floyd Grey. As in most of his works, this illustration by Floyd Grey is based on a black and white colour scheme. The model is elegant and smart and the tint of red lips adds life to the whole look.

Other than used for the clothing, some illustrators love to apply colours on the background or environment rendering. Bright vibrant colours for fantasy style; dark mysterious tones for quirky looks; light elegant shades for sumptuous effect. Applying background colours against the featured image enhances, highlights, and complements the whole picture. See figure 4.1.6

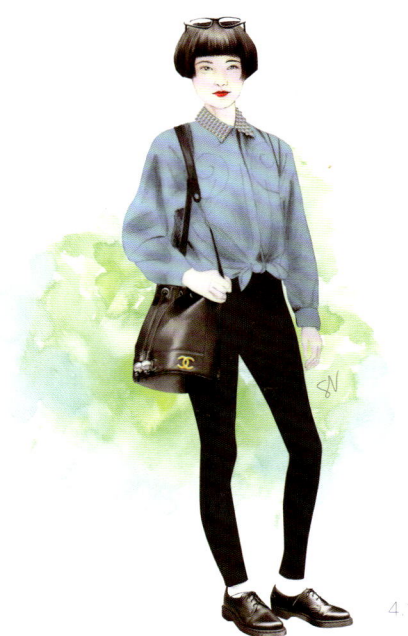

4.1.6

Figure 4.1.6:
Illustration by Sara Vera Lecaro. This is a casual look of jean shirt and black leggings, accessorized with sunglasses, bucket bag and shinny shoes. The illustrator uses fine, smooth outline to portray the comfortable outfit and the tint of light green in the background indicates the energetic season of spring.

4.2 The treasure of fabrics

Fabric is the carrier of clothing, the medium of designers' concept. There is a wide range of fabrics available in the clothing industry nowadays, from which the designers can choose according to season, function, and occasion of the garment. Airy or heavy, different types of fabrics match and present varying styles. Common clothing fabrics can be roughly categorized as follows:

- Transparent fabric

It creates artistic and romantic effect. Cotton, silk, synthetic fiber belong to this category, commonly used as chiffon, silk and lace. It is suitable for clothing of full shape and changing outline and transparent watercolour is recommended for portraying them. See figure 4.2.1

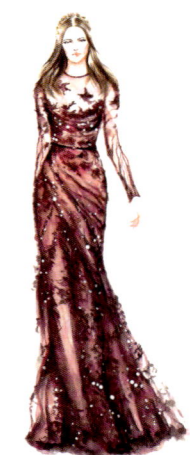

4.2.1

Figure 4.2.1:
Illustration by JiweiJW

- Soft fabric

Lightness and softness, also fine drapability, flowing smoothness are the features of this fabric. It mainly includes knitted fabrics of loose structure, silk fabrics, and thin hair cords. An ideal choice to reveal curves of the body. See figure 4.2.2

- Crisp fabric

It creates artistic and romantic effect. Cotton, silk, synthetic fiber belong to this category, commonly used as chiffon, silk and lace. It is suitable for clothing of full shape and changing outline and transparent watercolour is recommended for portraying them. See figure 4.2.3

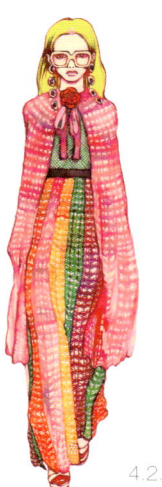
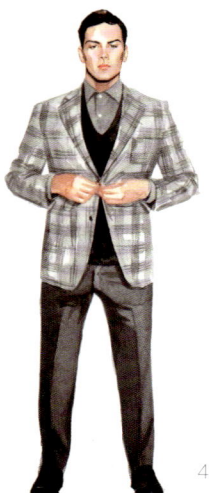

4.2.2   4.2.3

Figure 4.2.2:
Illustration by Natsuki Otani

Figure 4.2.3:
Illustration by Chidy Wayne

- Heavy fabric

Thick, strong textile of great thermal property, ideal for a stable styling effect. All types of thick wool and quilting fabrics have this volumetric feature of expanding impression. A great choice for quality garments like warm and elegant coats and overcoats. See figure 4.2.4

- Glossy fabric

Satin weave fabrics of smooth, reflective texture, mostly used in evening gown and stage wear with a strong dazzling visual effect. Glossy fabrics can adapt to different modeling purposes, perfect for both simple and dramatic designs. See figure 4.2.5

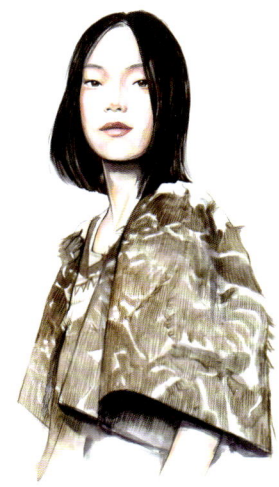

Figure 4.2.4: Illustration by Caroline Andrieu

4.2.4

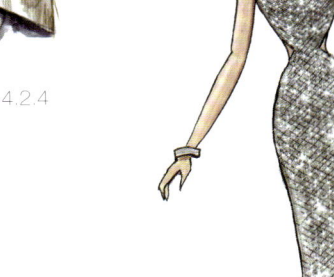

Figure 4.2.5: Illustration by Armand Mehidri

4.2.5

4.3 The beauty of styling

Clothing comes first in people's basic necessities. Though originated as a means to keep warm, clothing has become the voice of personal aesthetics. The quality of your outfit does not depend on the brand or the price of the garments, but whether the styling match with your objective situations: gender, figure, age, occupation, region, season, etc. The fittest is the best. And you will find useful guidelines in the relation between certain body figure and suitable clothing. See figure 4.3.1

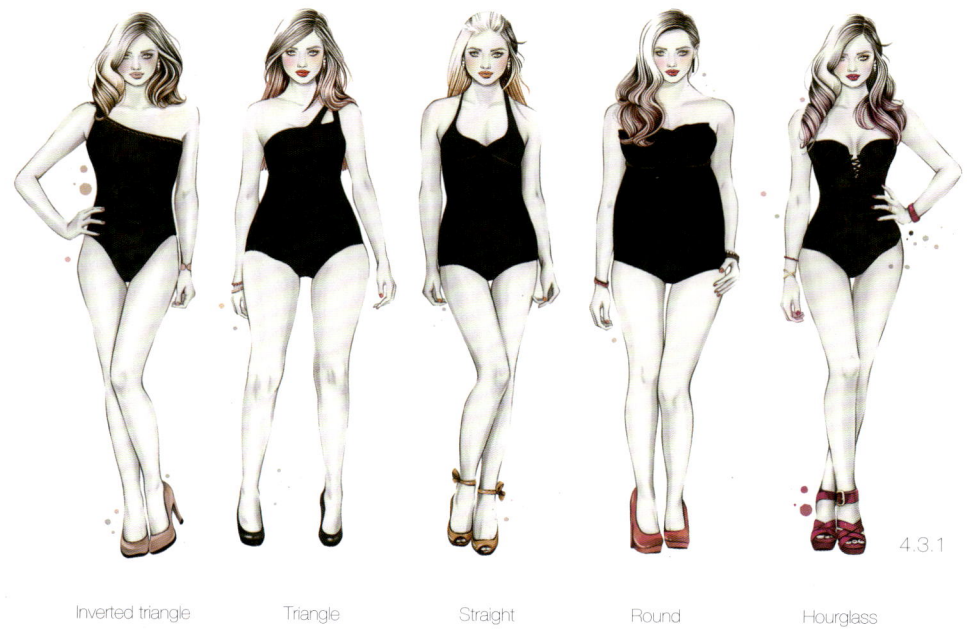

Inverted triangle Triangle Straight Round Hourglass

4.3.1

Figure 4.3.1: Common types of body figure. Illustration by Cristina Alonso

4.3.1 Body figure and dressing tips

• Inverted triangle. Featuring wide shoulder, slim waist, thin buttocks

A body of inverted triangle is perfect for men, but for women, it is relatively too strong and not feminine enough. Strapless items are suitable for ladies of this body figure. In terms of the choice of colours, coats and tops of simple colour scheme are preferable as bright bod colours will attract attention and amplify the size of the upper body. See figure 4.3.2

• Triangle. Featuring narrow shoulder, thick waist, large buttocks

Triangle body figure, also known as the pear shape. It is a common body type among sedentary people as the fat clusters around the waist, bottom and thighs. Such body figure resembles the shape of a pear, hence the name. Since it feels light on the top and heavy on the bottom, it is recommended to choose loose, layered tops, e.g. fluffy ruffles or laces, and skirt or trousers of simple design. Bright colours for the top attract attention and bring liveliness, while dark tones for the trousers or skirts give the impression of shrinkage, balancing the proportion of the whole body. See figure 4.3.3

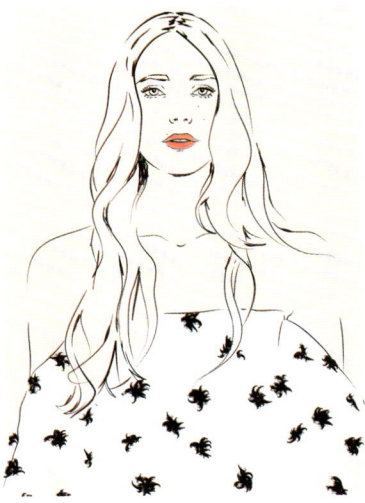 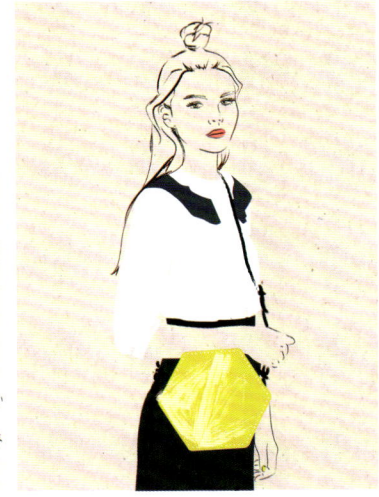

Figure 4.3.2, Figure 4.3.3:
Illustration by Paula Blanche

4.3.2　　　　　　　　4.3.3

• Straight. Featuring equal shoulder and bottom width, less obvious waist line
Most women of this body figure are rather thin, lacking obvious body curves. Playing with visual segmentation is a good way to build a fuller body shape. Smart, short tops and feminine skirts with higher waistline or waist belt used at higher position can visually divide the upper and lower body and dramatically enhance the beautiful waistline. Clothes with coloured high waistline are also a good choice. See figure 4.3.4

• Round. Featuring narrow shoulder, full waist and bottom lines
A round body figure is also referred to as the apple shape, with a fuller line at the waist and abdomen. It is essential to hide the abdomen and waist-tight clothing is not recommended. Tops with design details around the neckline are preferred as they attract attention and help ignore the waist and abdomen. Slender pieces with extending visual effect are suitable for the lower part. Dark tops of shrinking tone help make the upper body slimmer, while bright items of white, grey or 3D floral pattern stretch the lower body. See figure 4.3.5

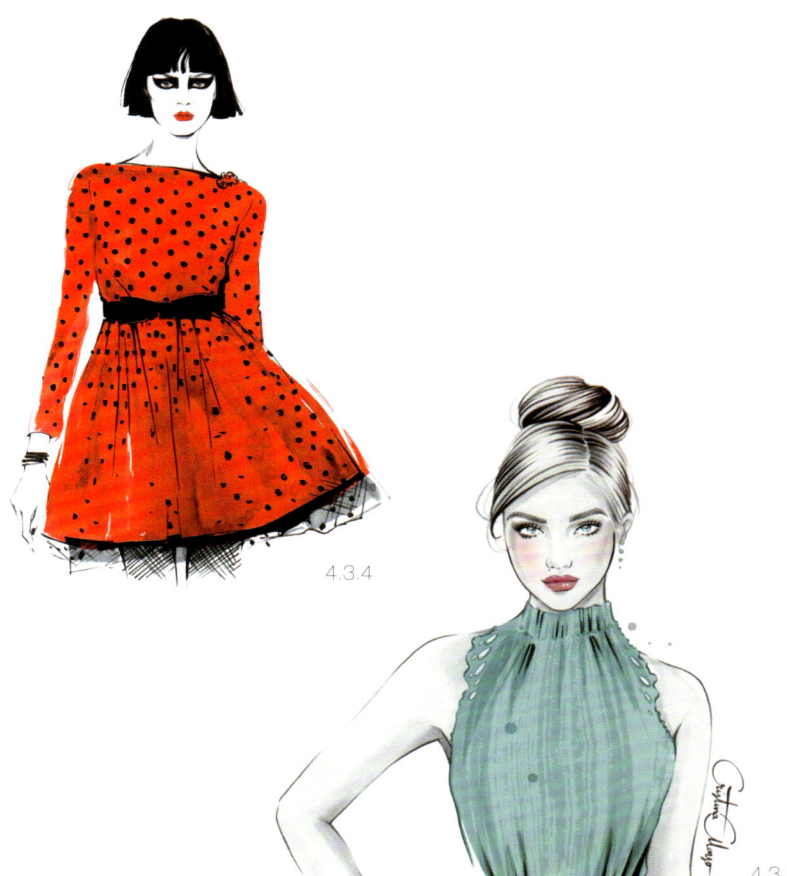

Figure 4.3.4:
Illustration by Alena Lavdovskaya

Figure 4.3.5:
Illustration by Cristina Alonso

• Hourglass. Featuring full breasts, slender waist and full bottom.
The hourglass body figure is basically the perfect shape for women. The range of suitable clothing is wider than for other shapes and clothing of simple designs are recommended, since they should enhance the figure, rather than distract attention from the beautiful body. See figure 4.3.6.

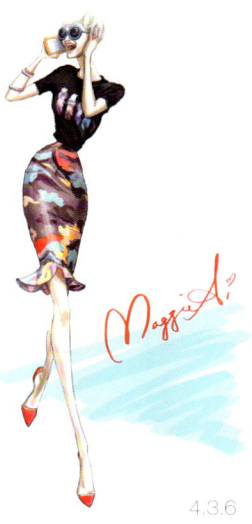

Figure 4.3.6:
Illustration by Maggie Ai

4.3.2 Symbolic meaning of different colours
Finding the right colours for one look is also important in fashion styling as colours can cast profound influence on people's mind and behavior. The principle of colour matching has been stated in the previous chapters, and below are the symbolic meaning of different colours to be used as a reference in styling practice.

Red: energy, passion, courage, hope, love, health, brutality
Orange: livelihood, richness, completion, future, friendship, generosity, positiveness
Yellow: wisdom, glory, gentleness, loyalty, hope, joy, brightness
Green: youth, nature, peace, happiness, sense, vigour, peace
Cyan: hope, strength, grace, crispness, intelligence, ethereality, elegance
Blue: confidence, eternity, truth, authenticity, silence, calm, freshness
Purple: magnificence, nobility, elegance, loneliness, mystery, pride, romance
Black: mystery, loneliness, darkness, solemnity, low profile, seriousness, presence
White: holiness, purity, selflessness, simplicity, freshness, honesty, cleanness
Grey: grace, taste, peace, prudence, simplicity, low profile, modesty

A few tips on styling:
• Don't run after the trends; find what's best for youself.
• Buy in items of classic design and pay attention to quality rather than quantity.
• Prioritize items of black, white, grey, beige colour scheme on your purchase list.
• Try out the magic of accessories.
• Establish your own style and optimize your personal image.

Chapter Five.

THE EYE OF FASHION ILLUSTRATION— ACCESSORIES

5.1 The origin and significance of accessories

Accessories complete a look. They come in a wide range of types and textures, covering shoes, bags, jewellery, glasses, hats, belts, etc. According to historic records, ancient humans wore coloured stone, shells and feathers to decorate themselves. It is the one of the earliest forms of aesthetic behaviour. People started to match accessories with clothes later in the human history, when the meaning of accessories changes from pure decoration to a symbol of honour, identity and social status, e.g. a king's crown accessorize him and stands for his mighty power. Accessories can also be the carrier of the wearer's beliefs, e.g. the crosses worn by Christians. It is generally the artistic record of social and cultural development in the human society.

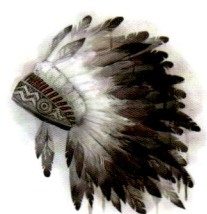

5.1.1

Figure 5.1.1:
Illustration by Carole Wilmet, Indian style feather headdress.

Accessories have developed over the years into an indispensable part of fashion styling. It is therefore an integral section in fashion illustration. Illustrators need to bear in mind however, that the accessories serve the clothing and enhance the whole look; and there should be clear hierarchy between them two.

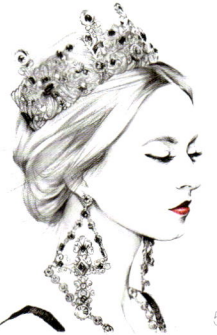

5.1.2

Figure 5.1.2:
Illustration by Ricoho

5.2 Drawing the texture of accessories

In the following pages, rising illustrator Ricoho [1] will introduce the techniques in presenting the texture of accessories and demonstrate the drawing procedure through a step-by-step tutorial.

5.2.1 Jewel on a Dolce & Gabbana handbag

Ricoho normally uses A4 watercolour paper for jewel illustration. He starts with a simple sketch of the jewel outline with 0.5 automatic pencil, mostly in straight lines. Then it is time to locate the light source, as it affects the brightness and weight of the jewel stones. The next step is to use a damp medium-sized watercolour brush and apply a thin layer of base colour, leaving out the highlight spots. When the paint dries, use a darker colour of the same tone for shadows. Lastly, mix the darker colour with brown, and use it to enhance the shadows. Highlight can be expressed via blank spots and use highlight pens if necessary. See figure 5.2.1.

Tip: it is about the control over the outline of shadow and highlight.

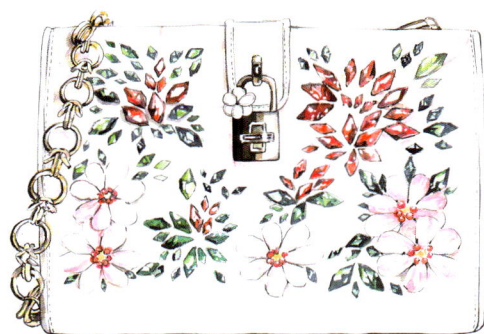

5.2.1

[1] **Ricoho**, rising Chinese illustrator, who won third place in the 5th Hong Kong original comic star competition and worked as ARTFIRE's online tutor and design director of MyFriday. Now Ricoho works as a freelance illustrator. He believes fashion illustration is a fantastic way to experience and express beauty and it is why he is so obsessed with it. According to him, adding one's own preference and understanding during the drawing process injects great personality into the work! To create a work of beauty that will be enjoyed by the audience is a wonderful thing itself.

5.2.2 Texture of high heels

Outline with 0.5 automatic pencil and leave the decorative white bead pieces for later, as they can be added with highlight pen. Since the shoe is black, the most difficult part in this illustration is to reflect depth and create a dimensional impression. The trick is using colours of varying concentration. Apart from the shoe body, a lighter black is used for the rest of the shoes. And one way to create this soft black is to add white colour into black paint, while the other is to control the moisture of the watercolour brush as higher level of moisture presents lighter colours. When the colours dry out, highlight pens can be used for embellished beads and sequins on the surface. Then scan and make detailed colour adjustment on the computer. See figure 5.2.2.

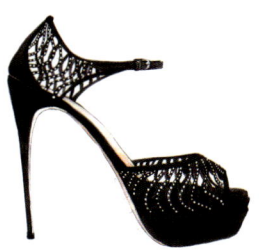

5.2.2

Tip: to gain control over the colour density.

5.3 Drawing a Dolce & Gabbana handbag

Step One. Draw first sketch. Use a 0.5 automatic pencil to draw the outline of the handbag in smooth lines. During this procedure, details give way to the overall proportion. Curved lines can be used to locate miscellaneous flower patterns. See figure 5.3.1

Step Two. Fill in the sketch. Add detailed outline of the handbag to the first sketch and pay attention to the weight of the lines. It is necessary to be aware that a sketch is in fact a completed black and white draft, which requires much patience to get a clean finish. See figure 5.3.2

Step Three. Apply base colour. Take loose watercolour with a brush and apply base colour on the draft. See figure 5.3.3

Step Four. Enhance the contrast. Use a darker colour on top of the base colour to fill in the shadows and leave out the brighter sections. Then add shades where the flowers border each other with an outline pen to bring out the detailed outline. See figure 5.3.4

Step Five. Finish the details. Add bright spots to the flowers with highlight pens. Strengthen shadows on the handbag and complete finer details, e.g. yellow cross lines. See figure 5.3.5

—— Ricoho

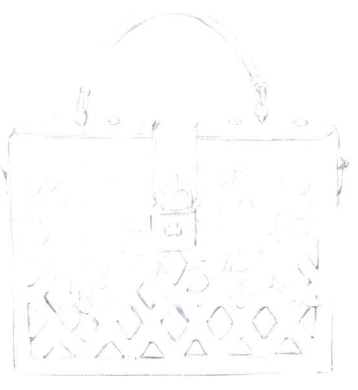

5.3.1

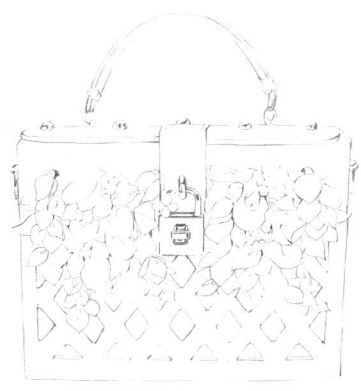

5.3.2

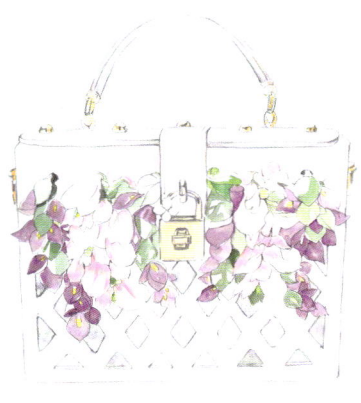

5.3.3

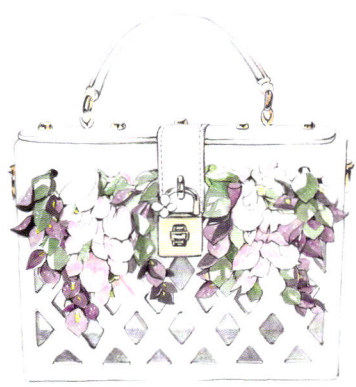

5.3.4

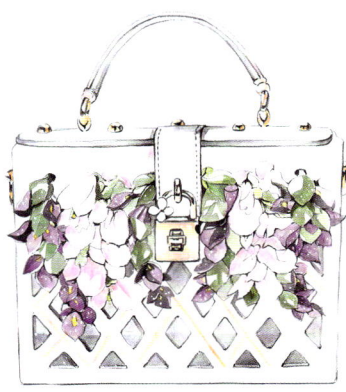

5.3.5

Prada-Million Dollar Girl

Personal work. Digital Fashion Illustration by Floyd Grey, with minimal black and white colour.
Illustrator: Floyd Grey Country: Malaysia

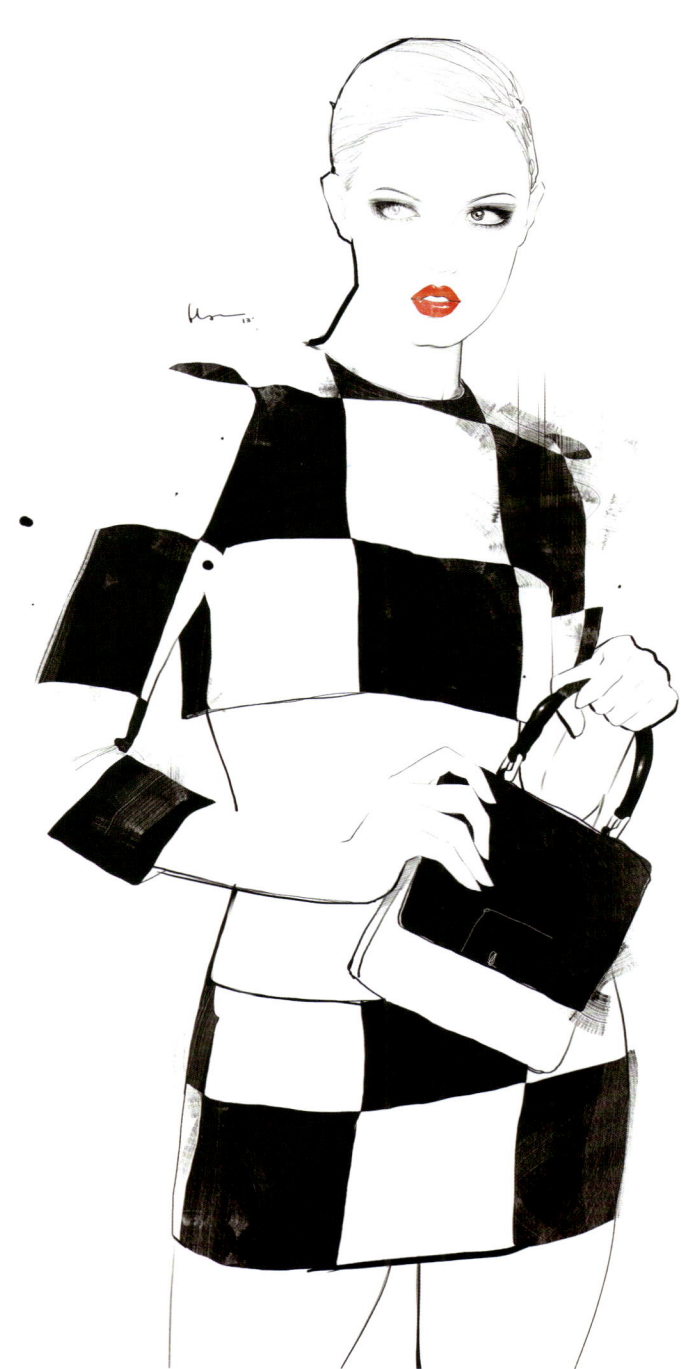

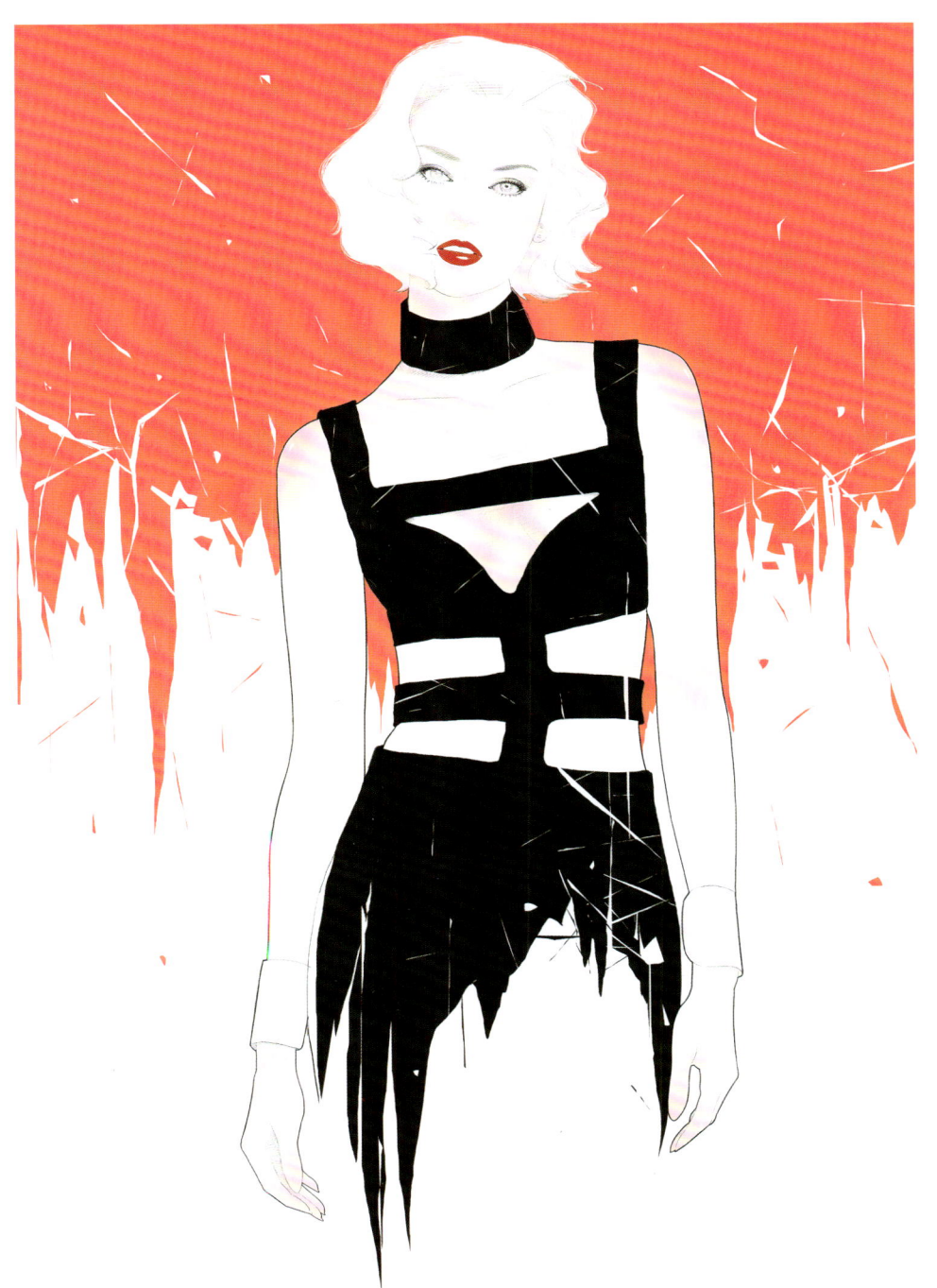

Personal work, digital fashion illustration by Floyd Grey done with paint effect background to emphasize the model and the dress.
Illustrator: Floyd Grey Country: Malaysia

Morden Black Skirt

Ralph Lauren

This fashion illustration is inspired by the model Fei Fei Sun for Vogue US February 2014.
Illustrator: Paula Blanche Country: Chile

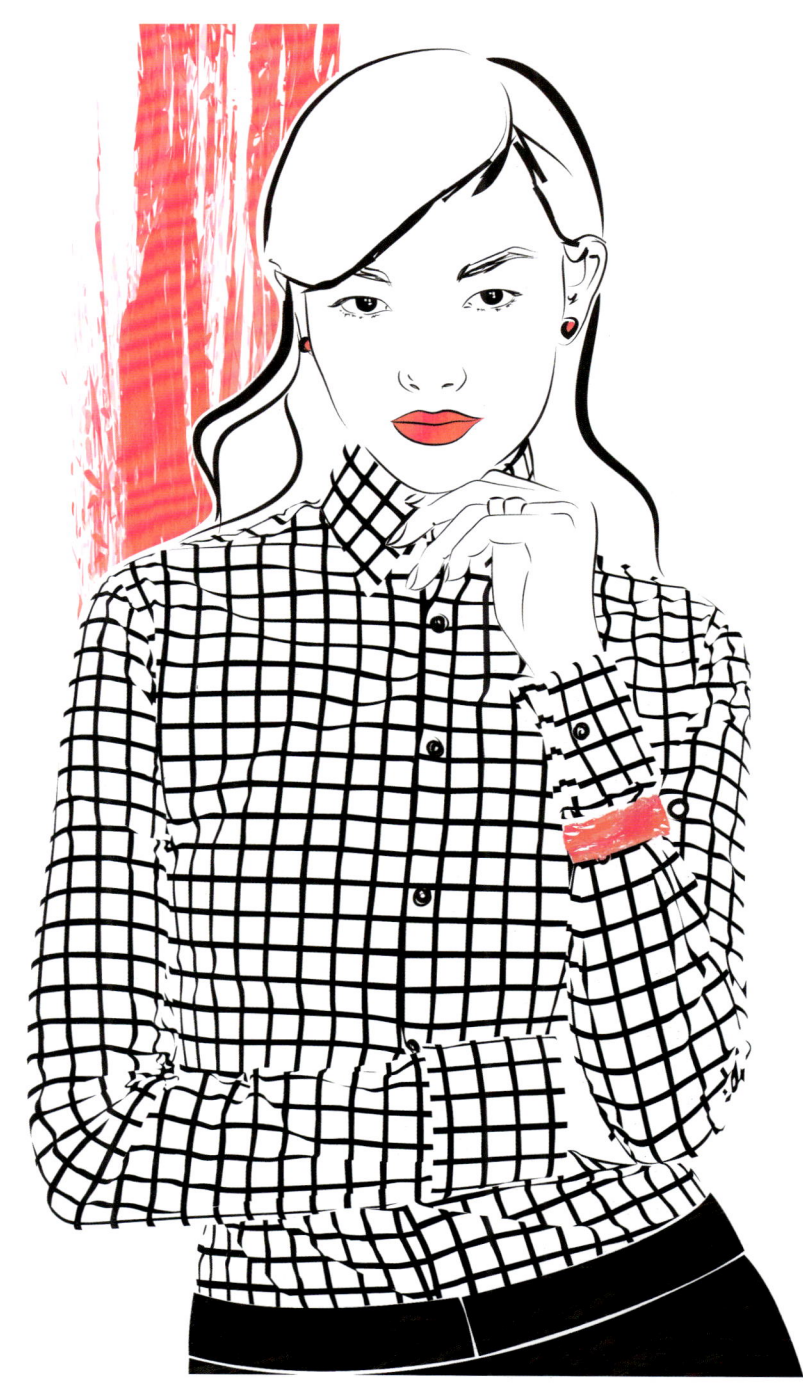

040 ✂ Simple Chic

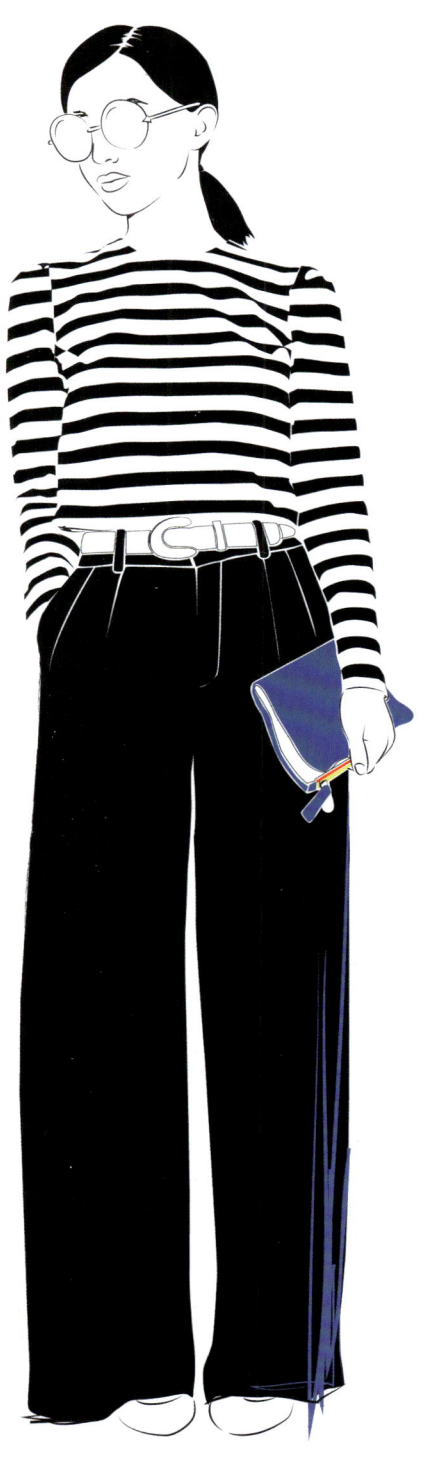

This fashion illustration is inspired by the blogger Nicole Warne, May 2013.
Illustrator: Paula Blanche Country: Chile

Asos and Zara

Striped Dress

This fashion illustration is inspired by the model Xiao Wen in simple striped outfit.
Illustrator: Paula Blanche Country: Chile

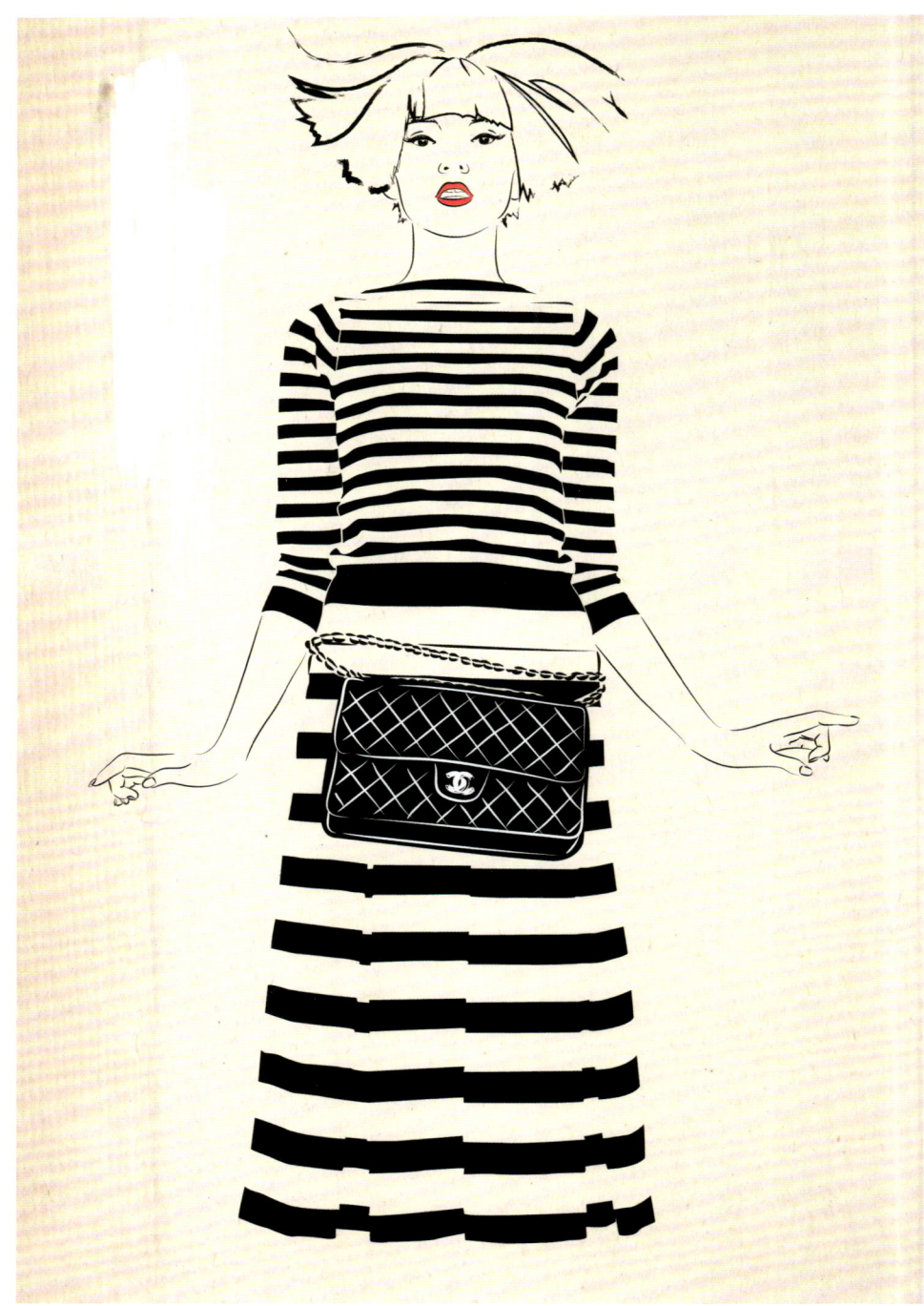

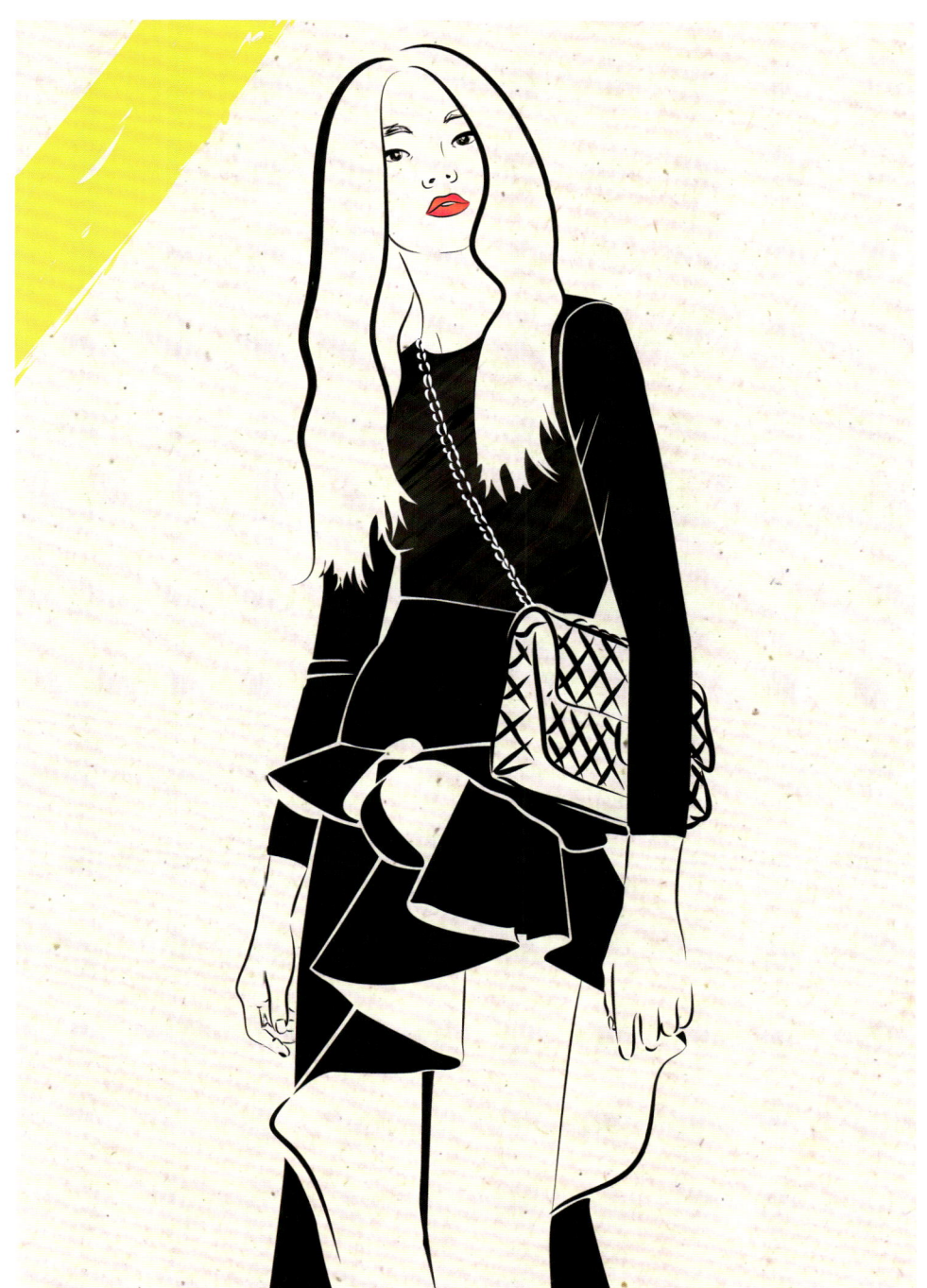

This fashion illustration is inspired by the model Xiao Wen and Chanel handbag.
Illustrator: Paula Blanche Country: Chile

Black Minimal Dress

Chloe Resort

This fashion illustration is inspired by Vogue China, January 2014.
Illustrator: Paula Blanche Country: Chile

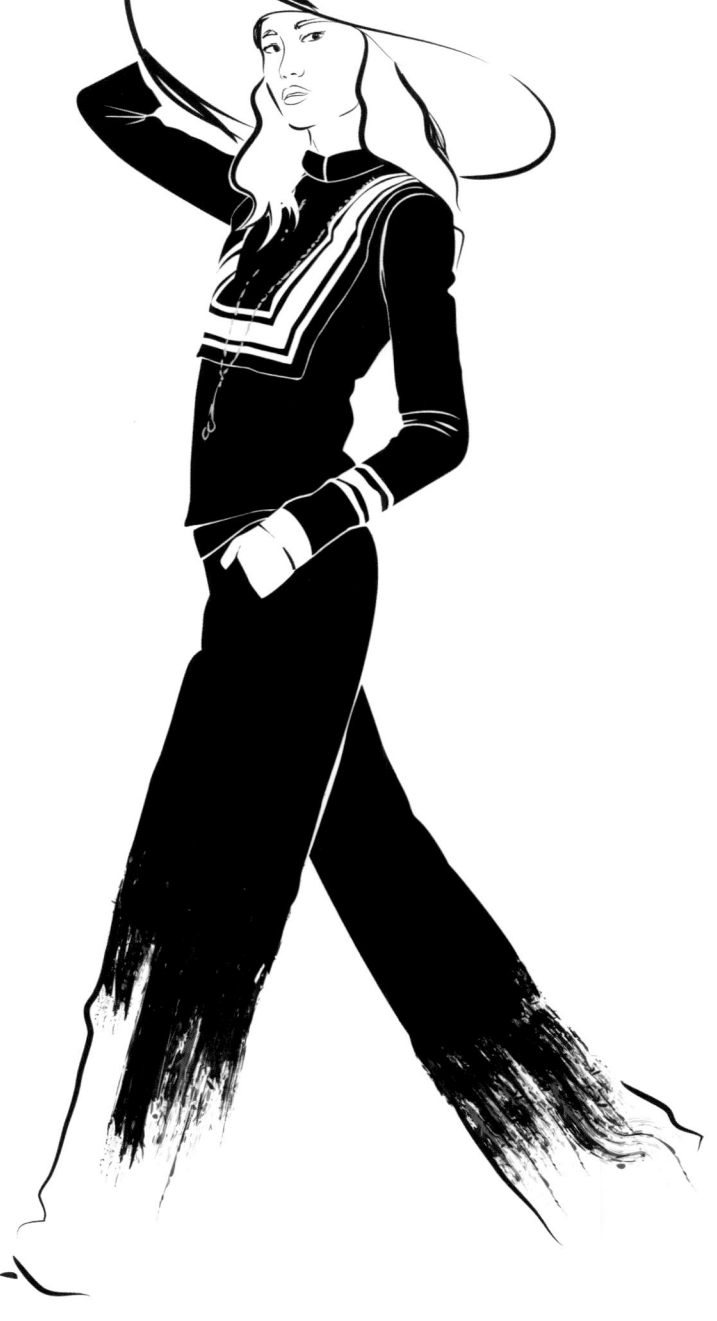

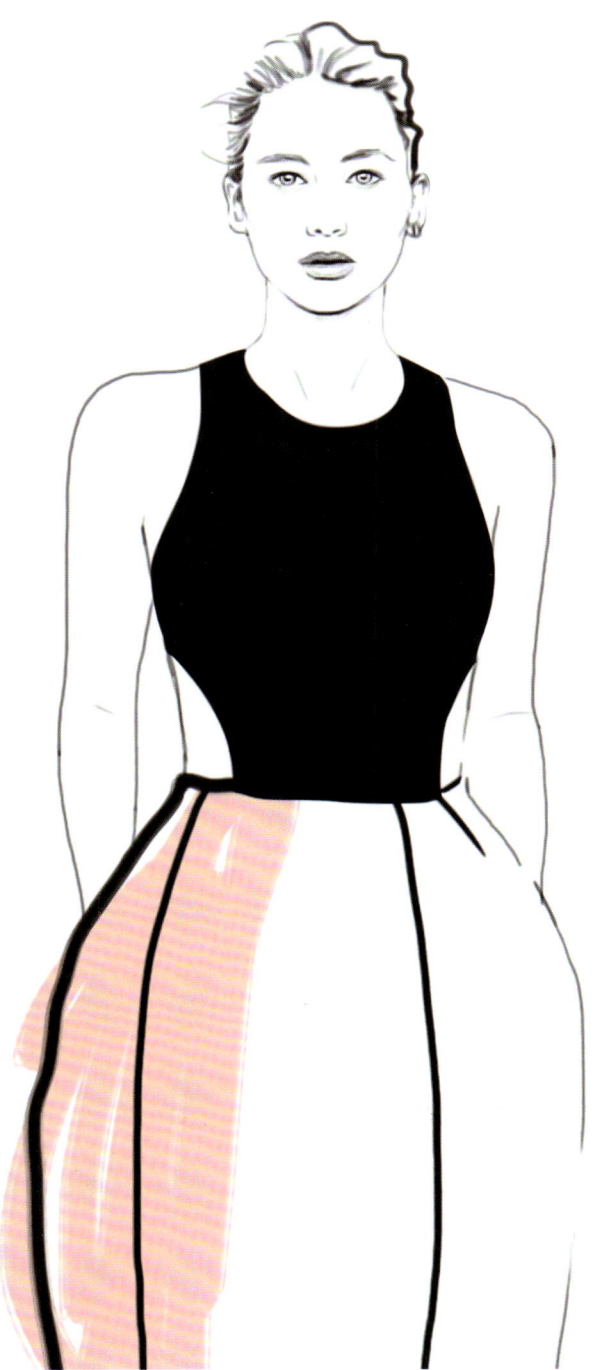

This fashion illustration is inspired by the actress Jennifer Lawrence wearing a Christian Dior dress.
Illustrator: Paula Blanche Country: Chile

Christian Dior

Celine

Editorial project for Japanese fashion magazine, 'Commons & sense' based on Celine runway looks.
Illustrator: Nicole Jarecz Country: USA

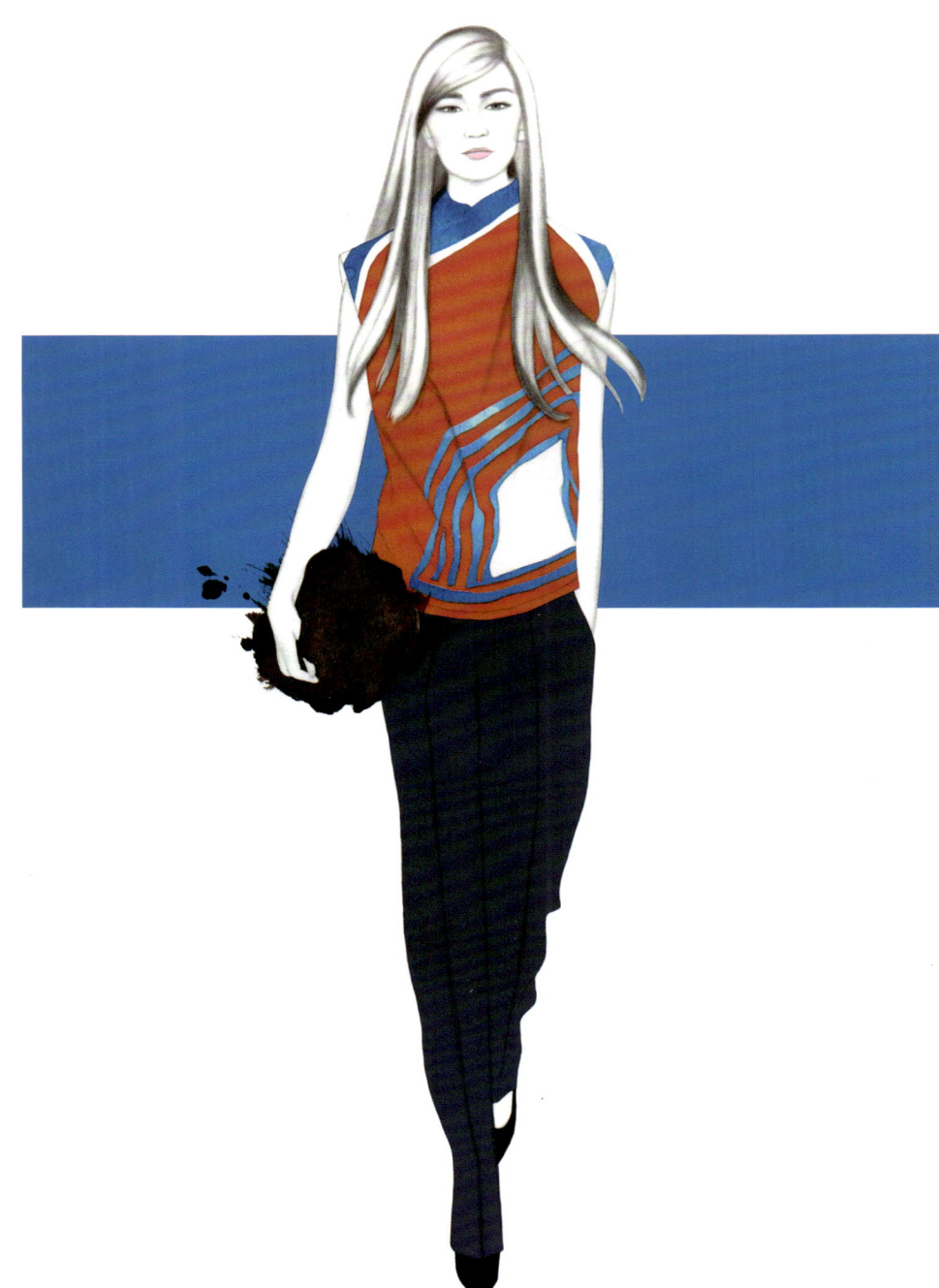

046 ✂ Simple Chic

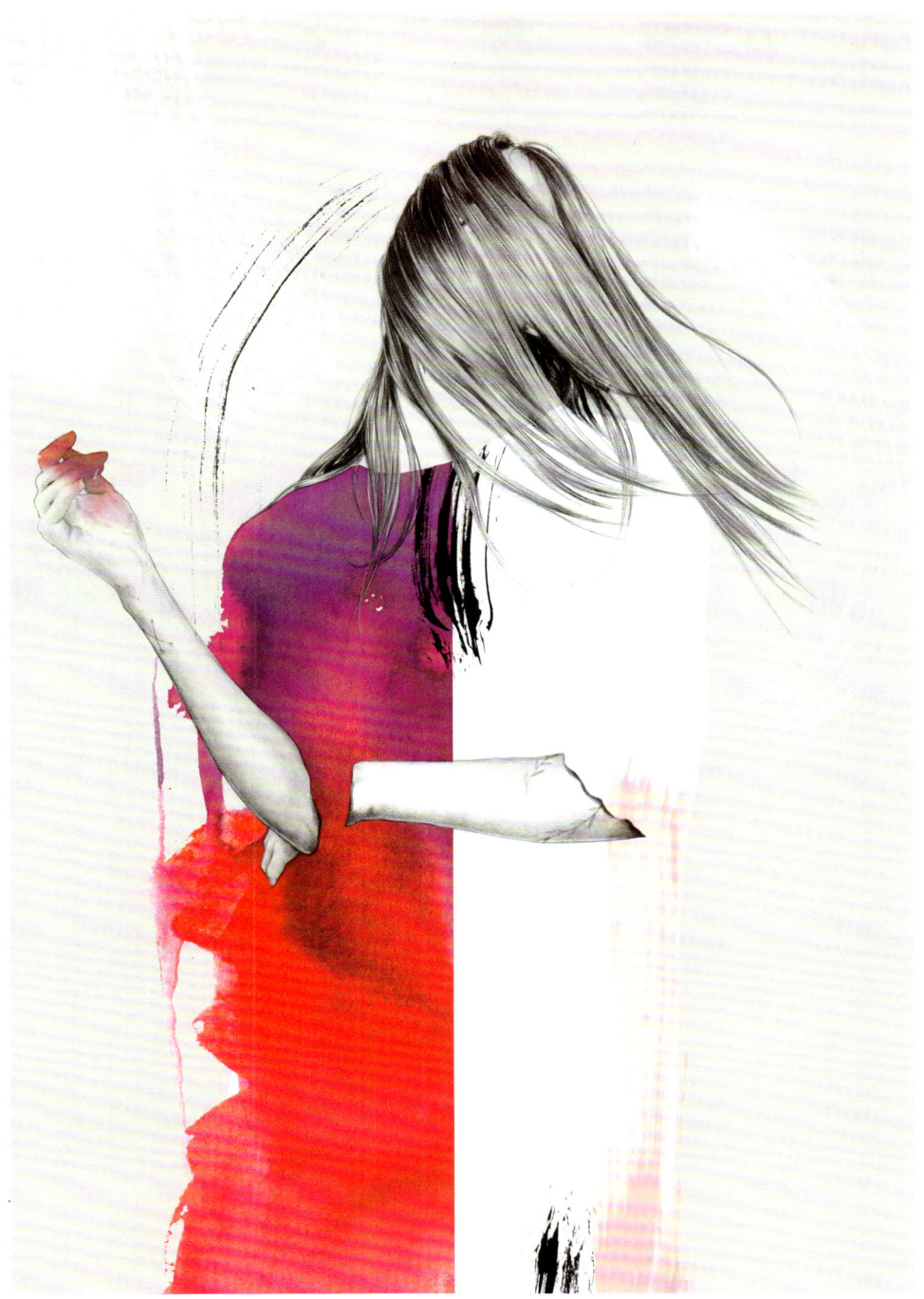

Part of a fashion editorial for Urban Outfitters, dress inspired by Jil Sander.
Illustrator: Esra Roise Country: Norway

Jil Sander

Giorgio Armani

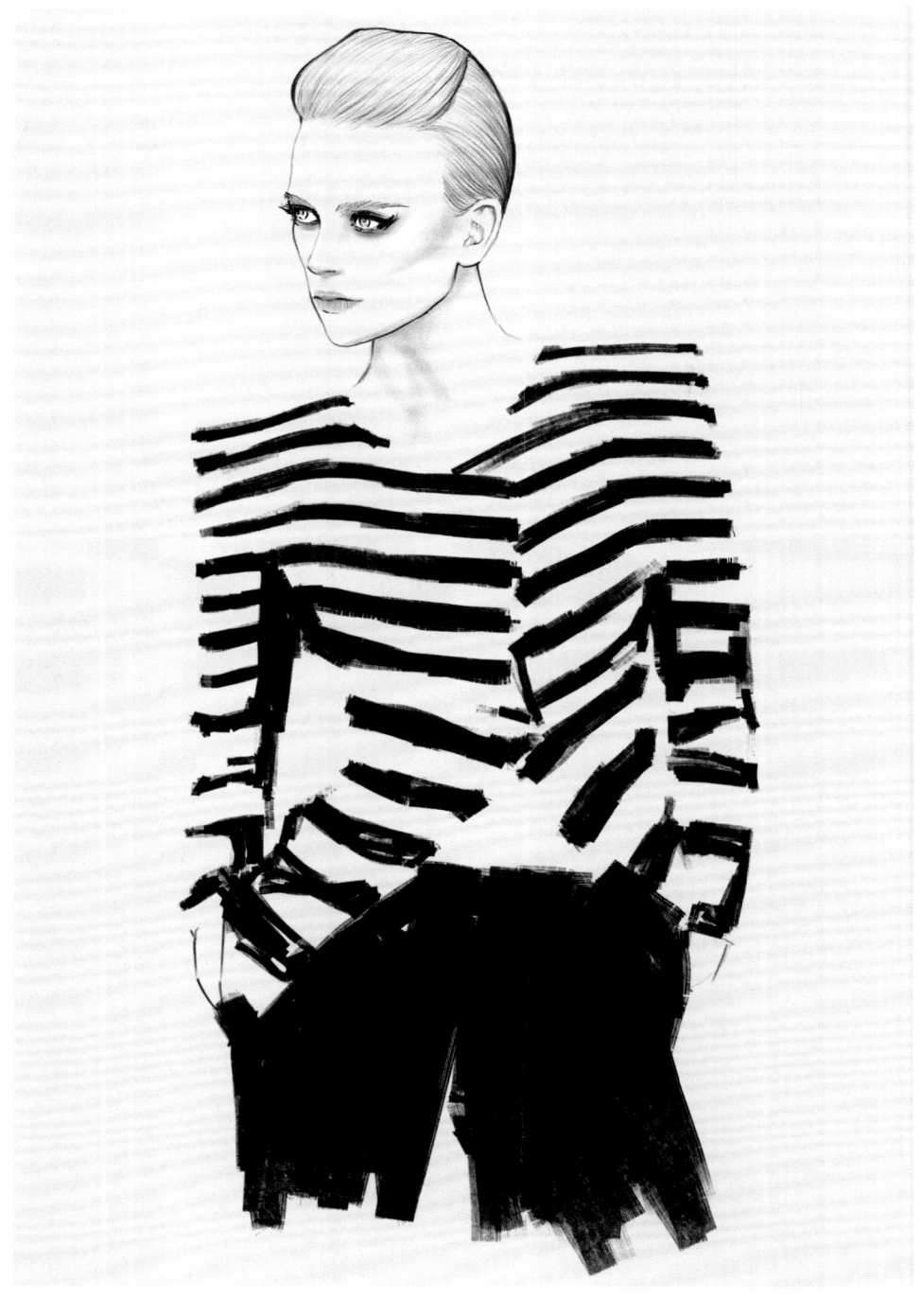

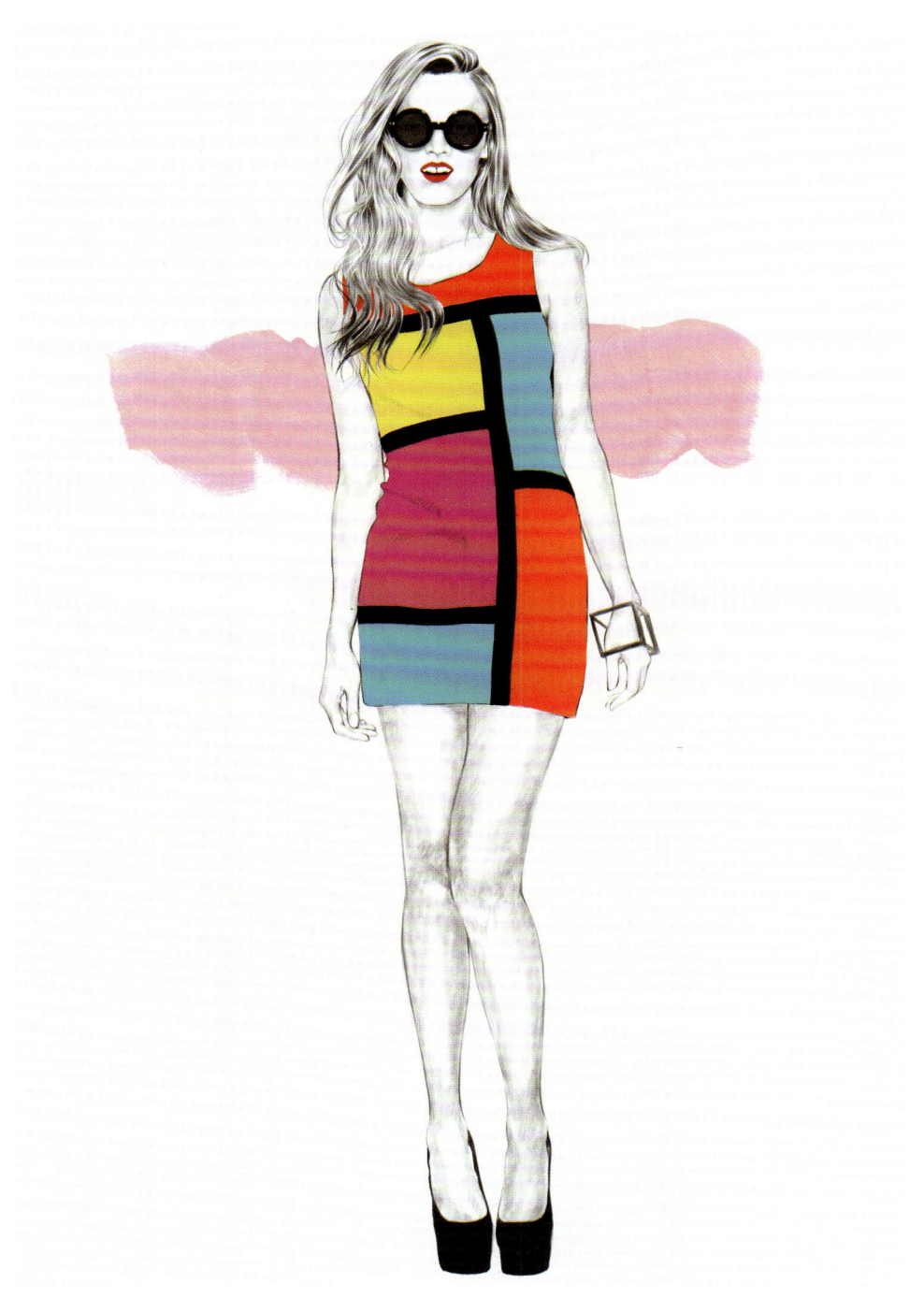

Leilia Goldkuhl for Shopcalico.com, created in Adobe Photoshop CS3 with pencil and watercolour splatter brushes.
Illustrator: Will Bayum Country: Malaysia

Colour Block Dress

Dior SS 2015

Personal work, Runway moment at Dior show. Paris' Haute Couture fashion Week SS 2015.
Illustrator: Alena Lavdovskaya Country: Russia

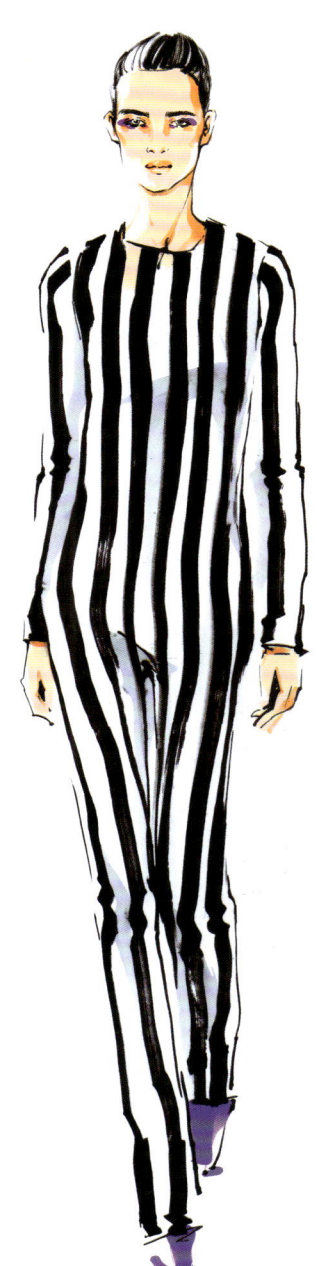
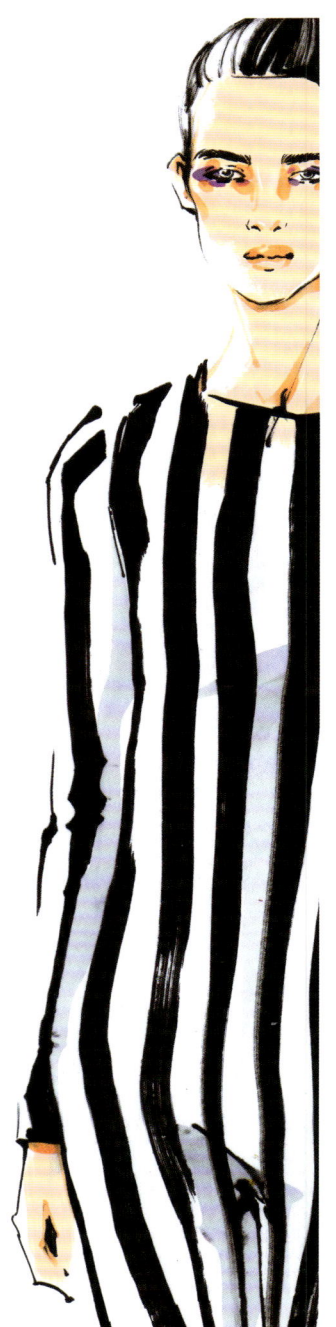

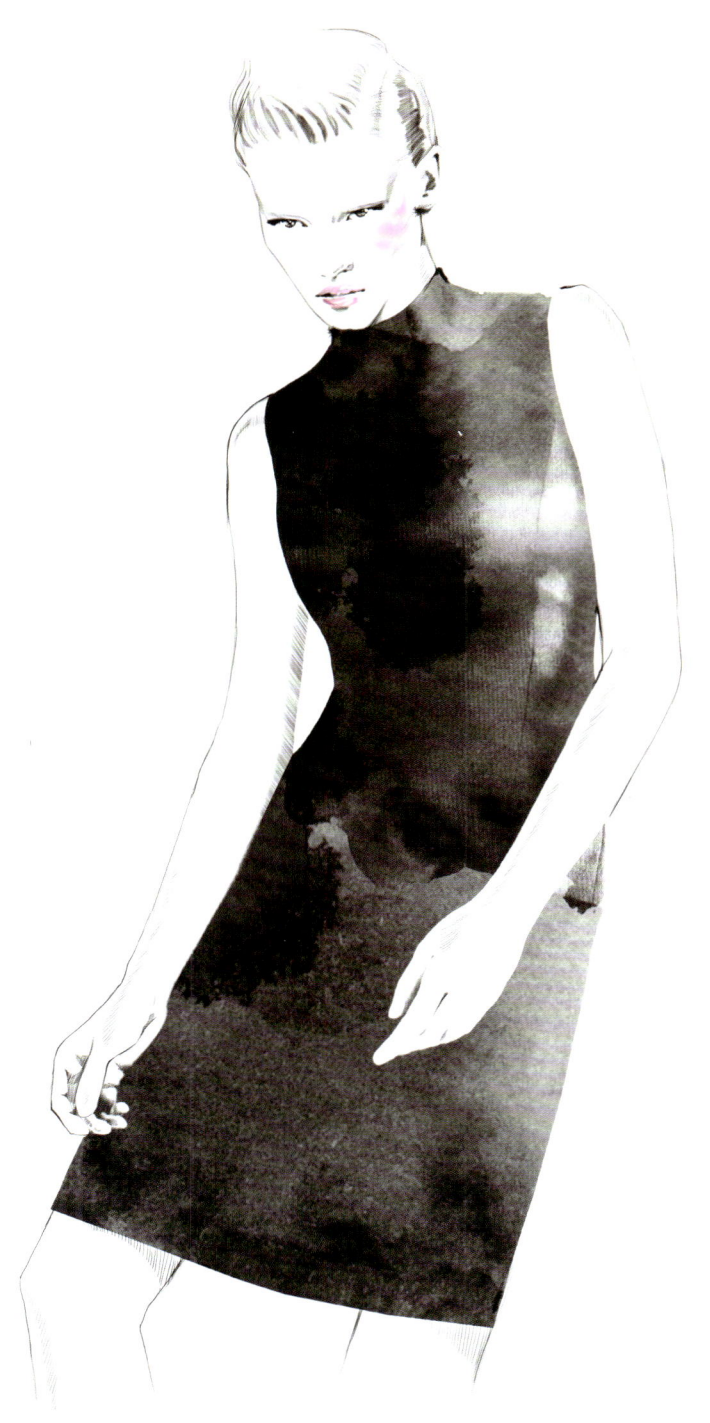

Classic little black dress with lace watercolour texture.
Illustrator: Svetlana Ikhsanova Country: Russia

Little Black Dress

Dior RTW FW 2015

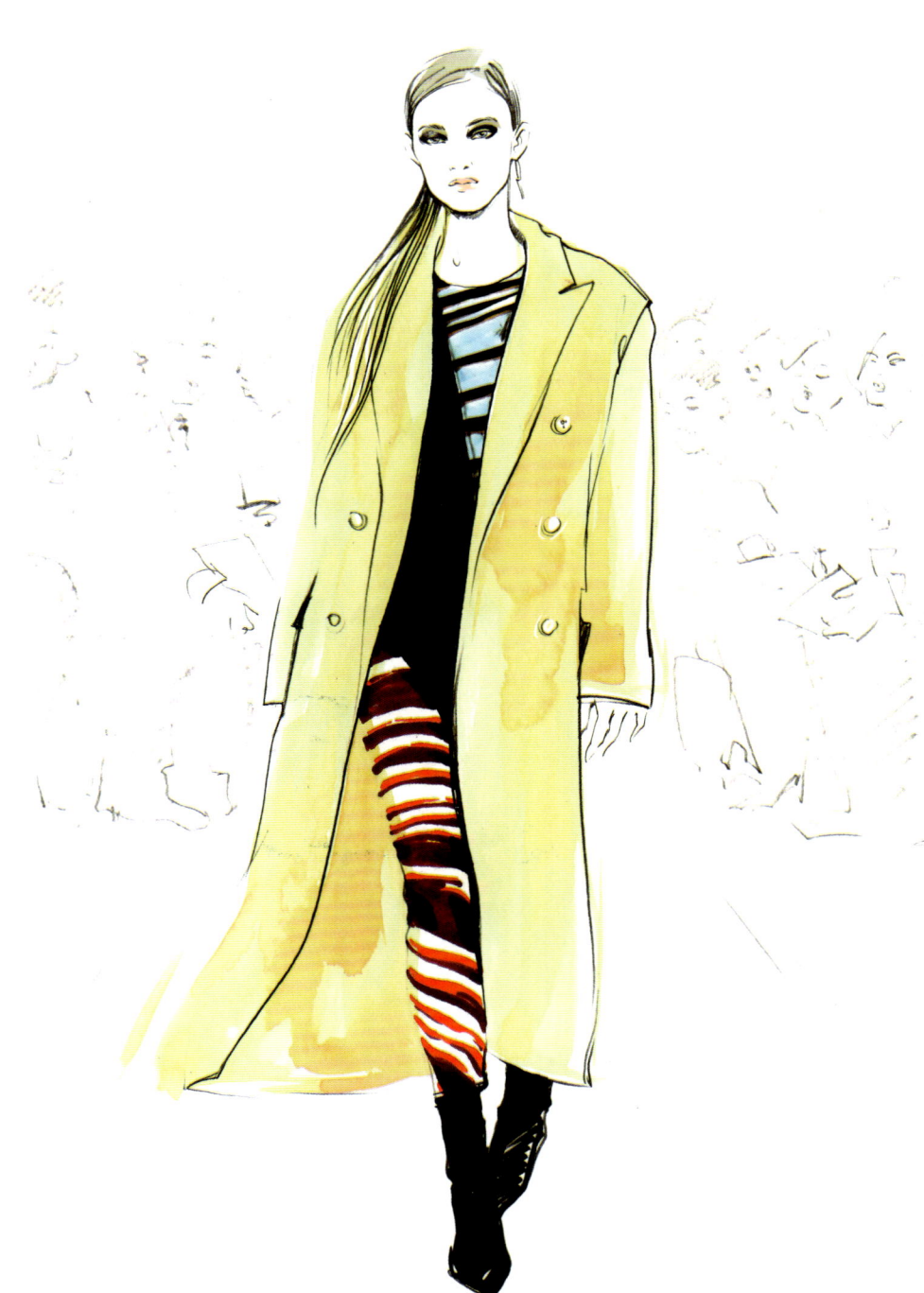

Runway moment at Dior show, Paris Fashion Week RTW FW 2015. Editorial work for vogue.ru. Illustrator: Alena Lavdovskaya Country: Russia

Editorial work for vogue.ru. Runway moment at Dior show. Paris Fashion Week RTW FW 2015.
Illustrator: Alena Lavdovskaya Country: Russia

Dior RTW FW 2015

Kenzo RTW FW 2015

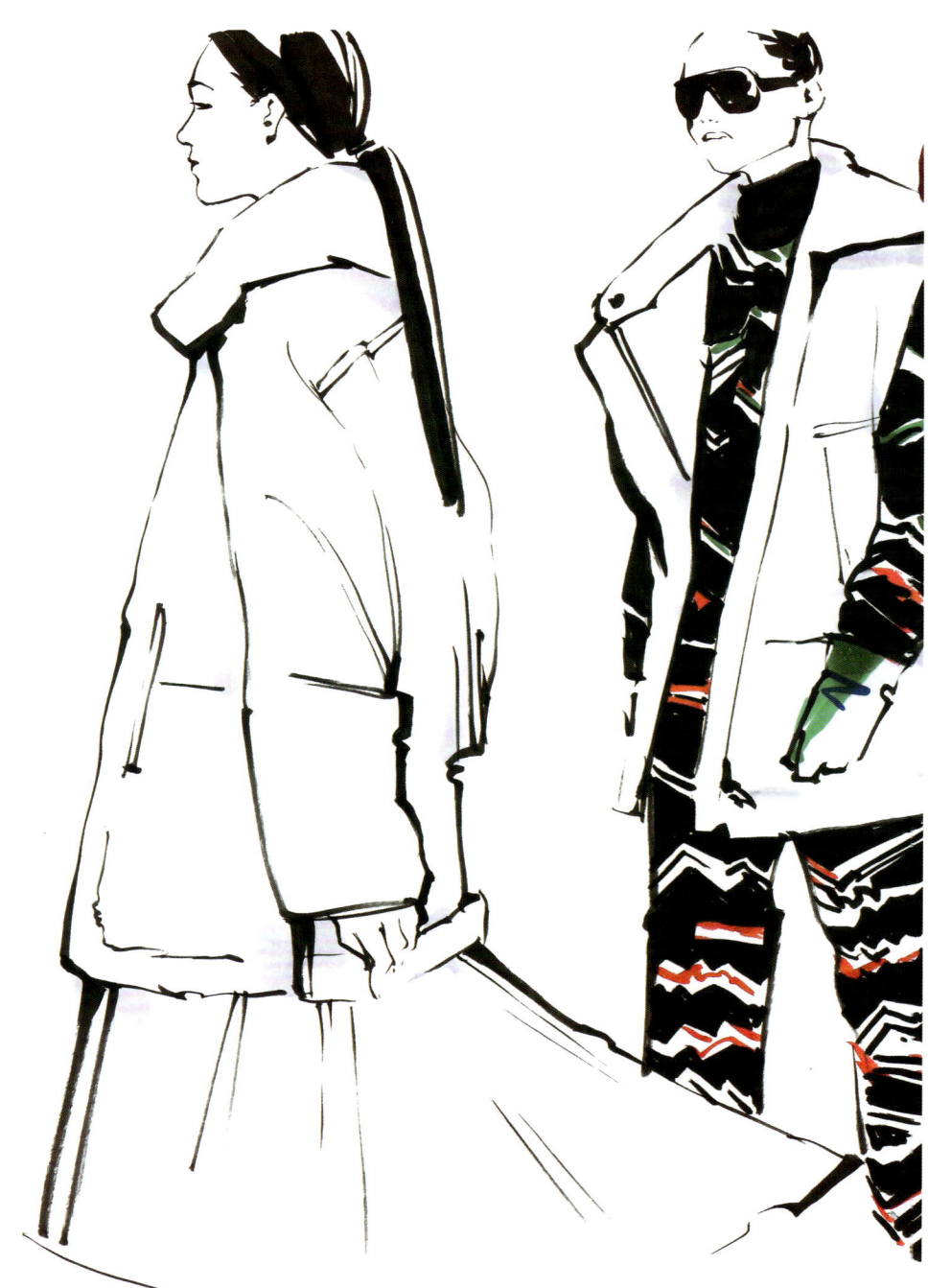

Personal work. Runway moment at Kenzo show, Paris Fashion Week RTW FW 2015.
Illustrator: Alena Lavdovskaya Country: Russia

Editorial work for vogue.ru, runway moment at Derek Lam show NY Fashion Week RTW FW 2015.
Illustrator: Alena Lavdovskaya Country: Russia

Derek Lam RTW FW 2015

Lanvin RTW FW 2015

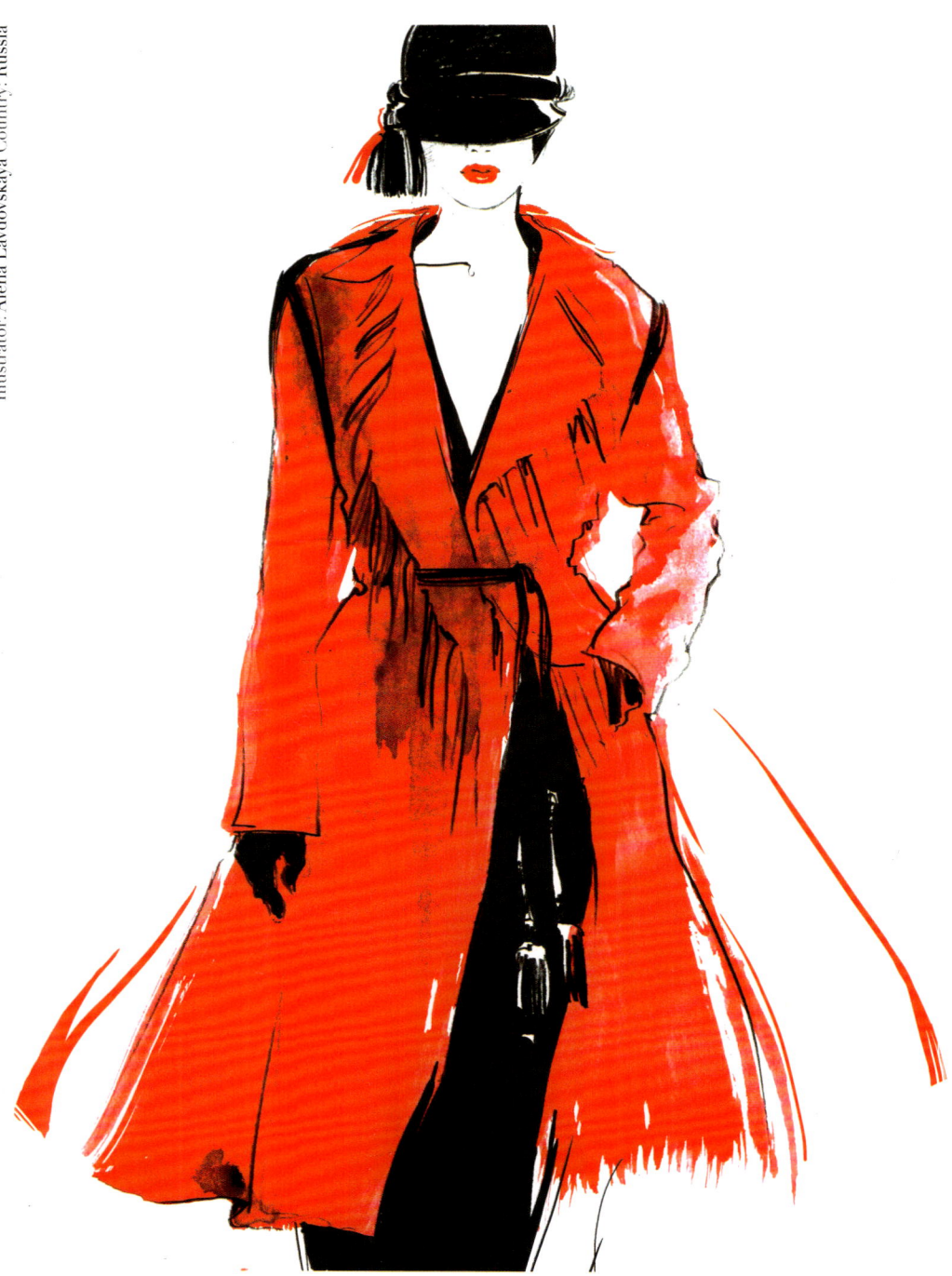

Editorial work for vogue.ru. Runway moment at Lanvin show, Paris Fashion Week RTW FW 2015. Illustrator: Alena Lavdovskaya Country: Russia

056 ✂ *Simple Chic*

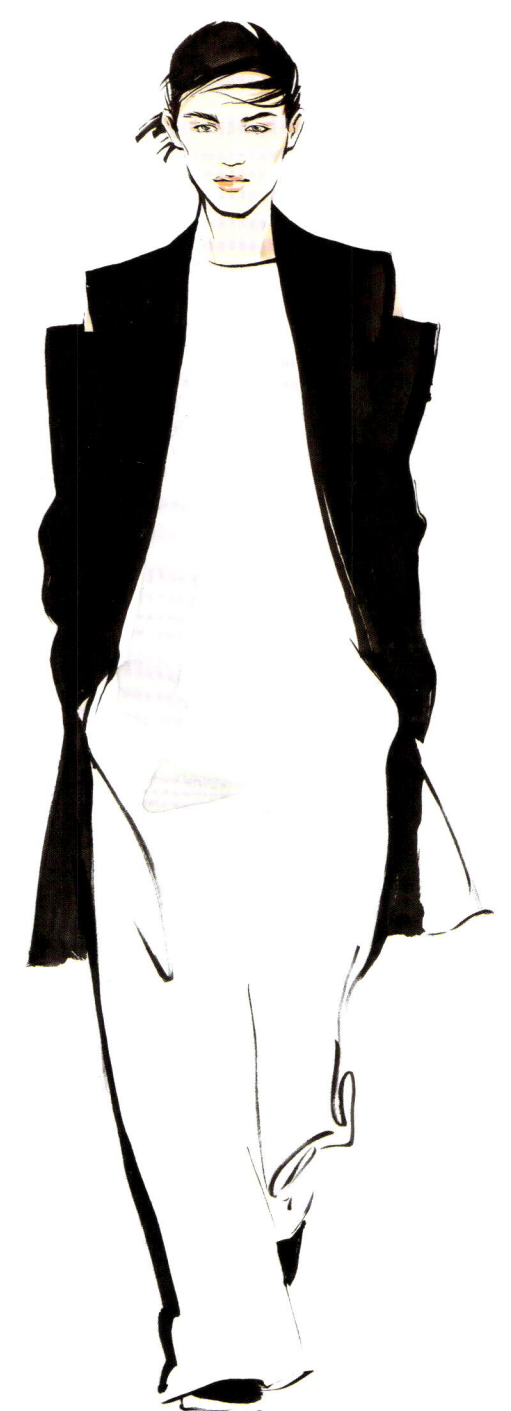

Runway moment at Vera Wang show, NY Fashion Week RTW FW 2015. Editorial work for vogue.ru. Illustrator: Alena Lavdovskaya Country: Russia

Vera Wang RTW FW 2015

The Coat SK

This fashion illustration is a personal order, inspired by The Coat SK.
Illustrator: Mariana Marchè Country: Ukraine

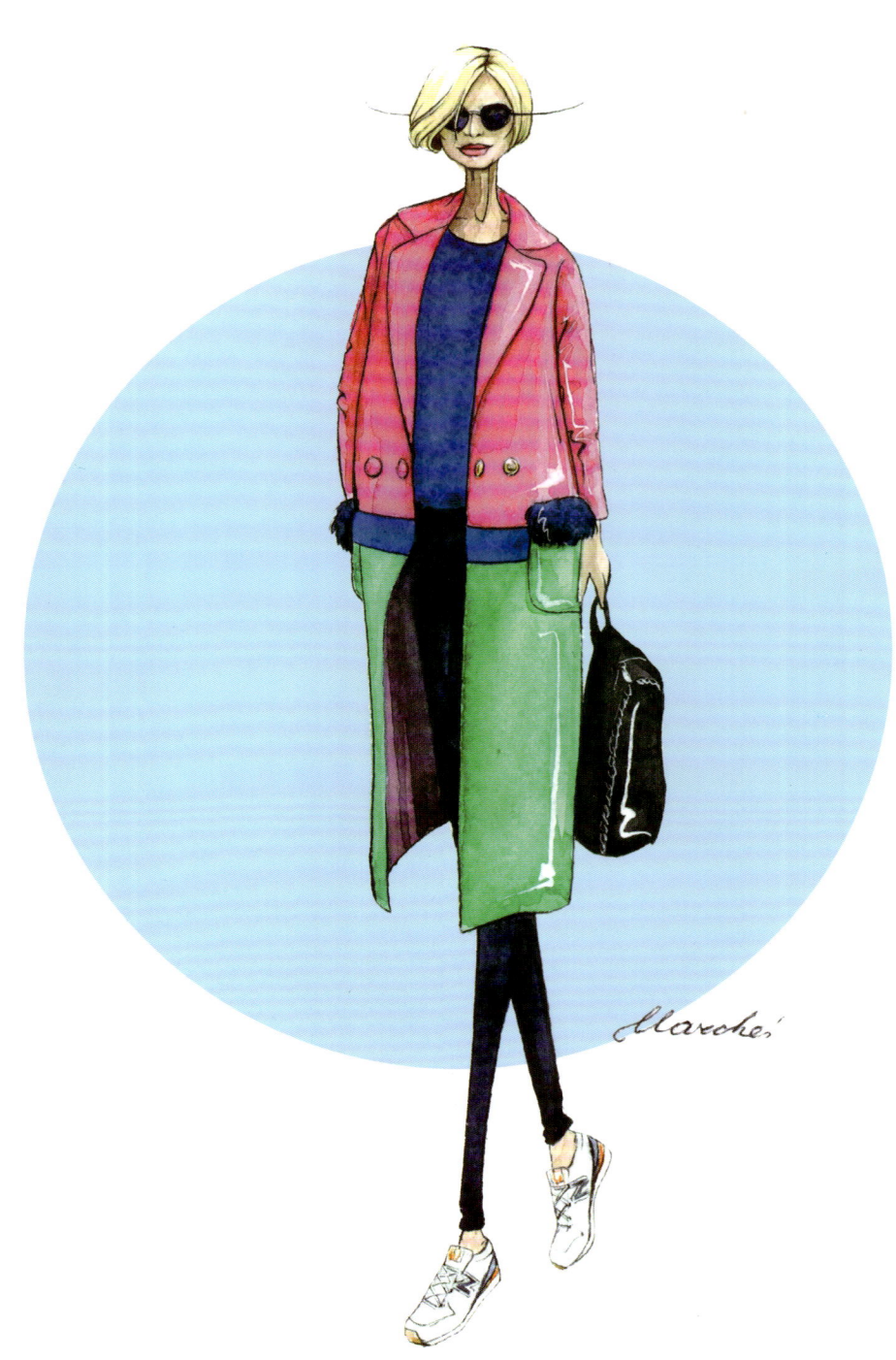

Simple Chic

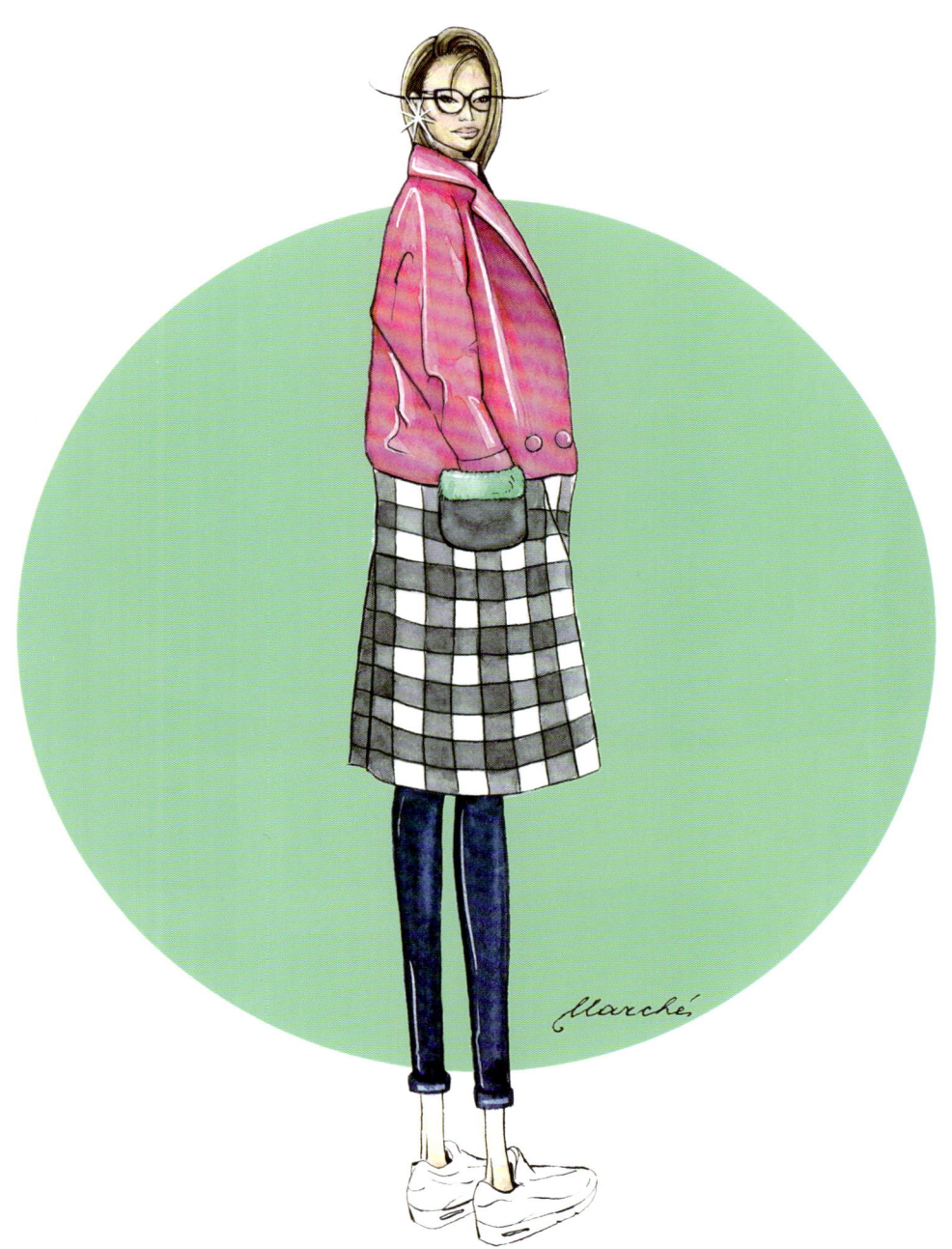

This fashion illustration is inspired by popular Ukrainian brand The Coat SK.
Illustrator: Mariana Marché Country: Ukraine

The Coat SK

Chanel Pre-Fall 2016

This illustration is inspired by Chanel pre fall 2016.
Illustrator: Nina Mid Country: Greece

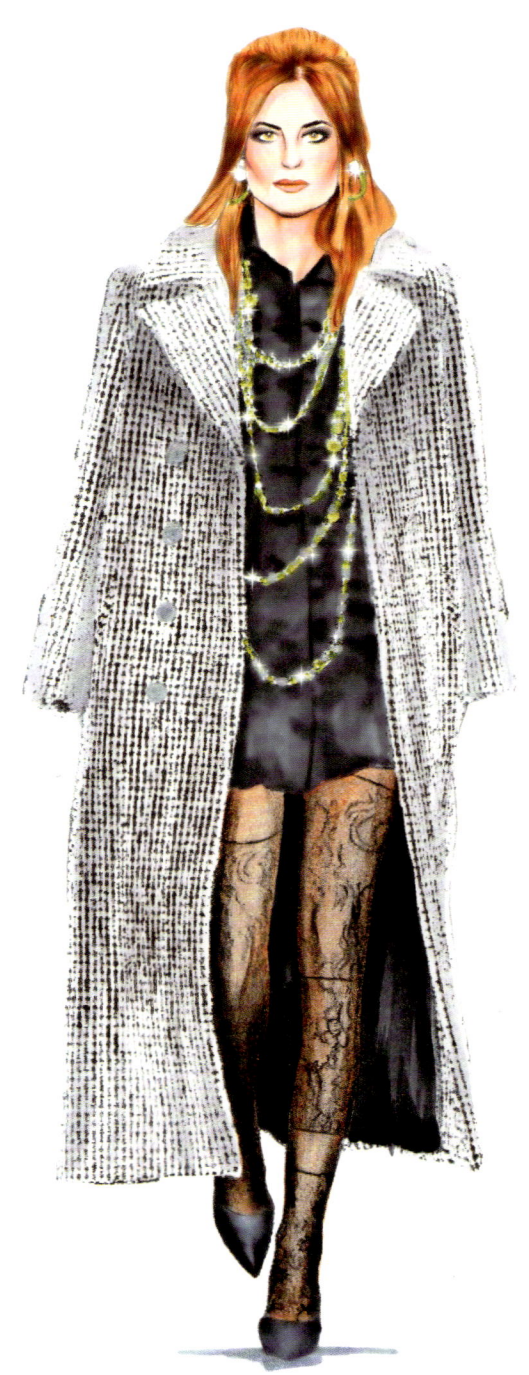

Simple Chic

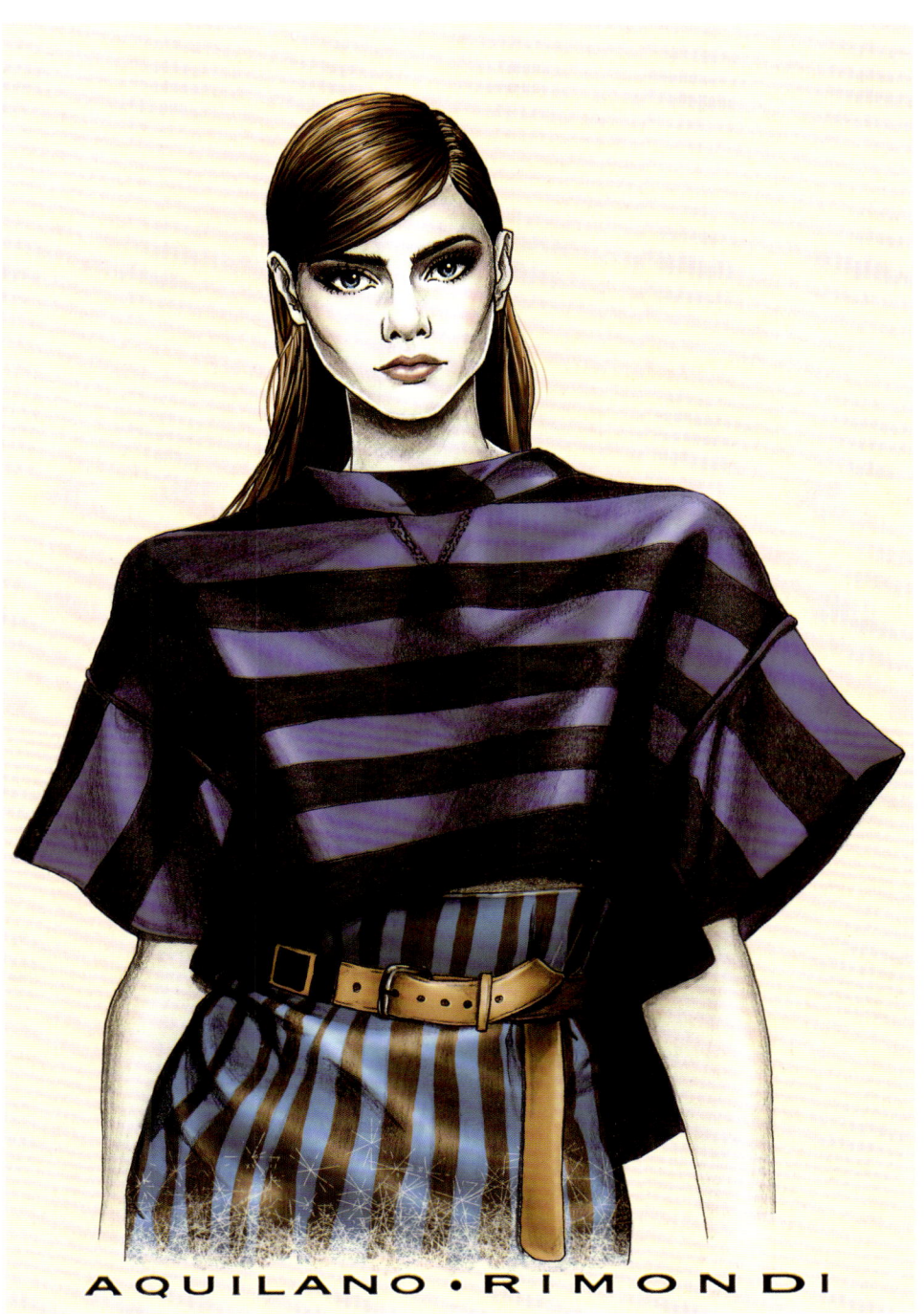

Fashion illustration from the Aquilano Rimondi Spring Summer 2014 collection. Done in paper and painted in Photoshop CS5.
Illustrator: Tania Santos Country: Portugal

Aquilano Rimondi SS 2014

062 / Simple Chic

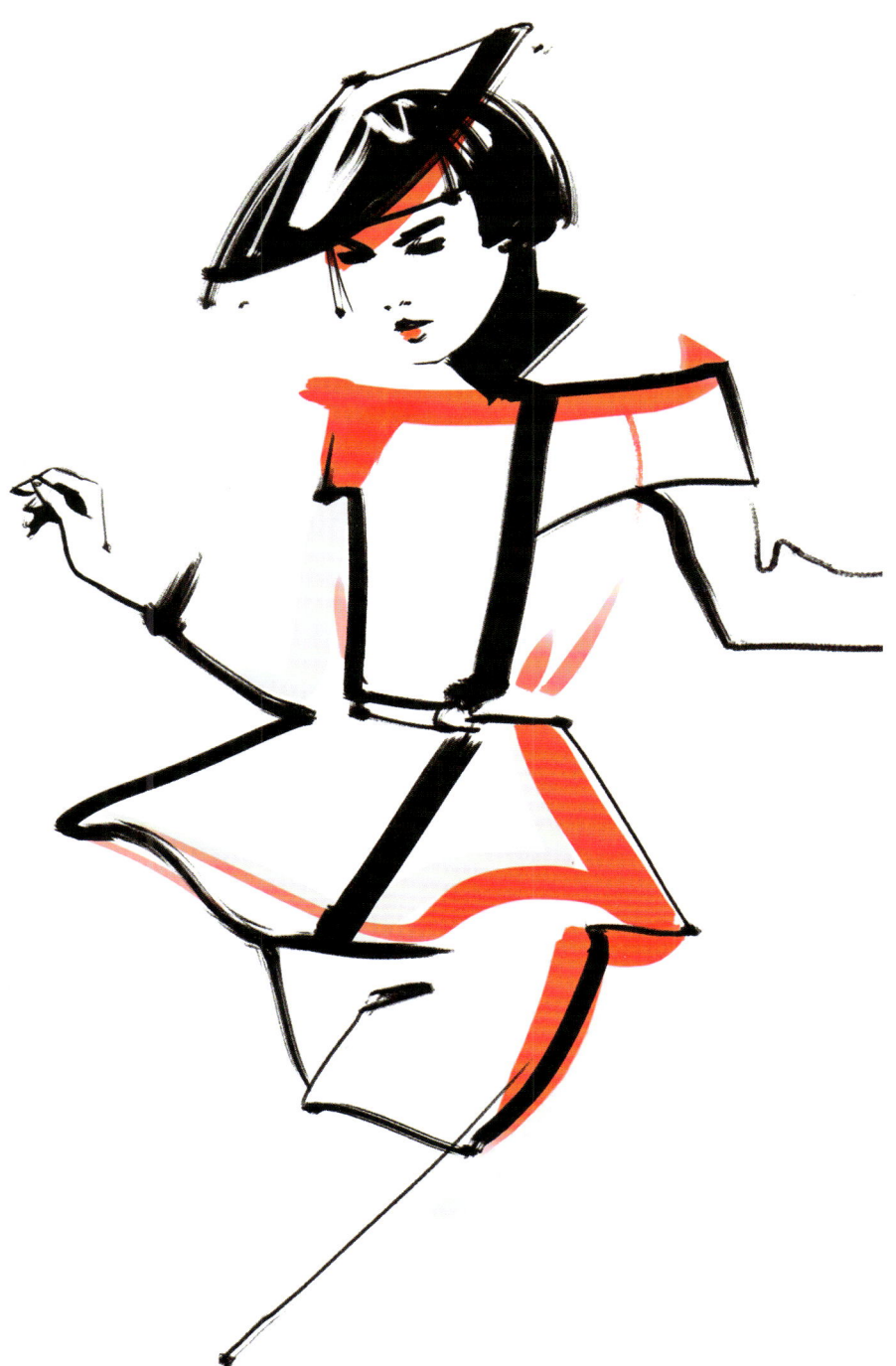

This fashion illustration is inspired by L'Wren Scott last collection in spring 2014.
Illustrator: Katerina Murysina Country: Russia

Oriental Spirit in L'Wren Scott SS 2014

L'wren Scott SS 2009

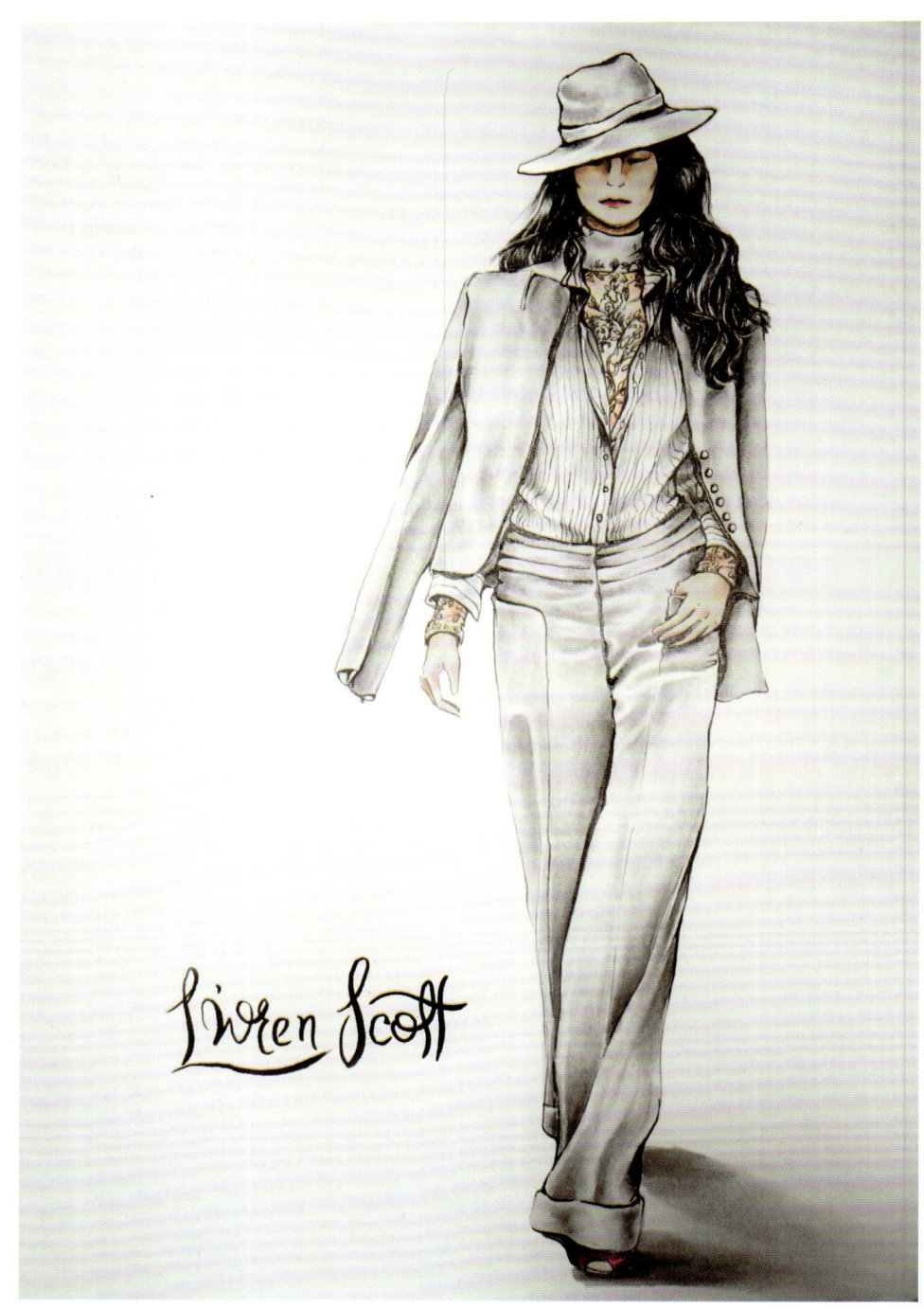

Inspired by L'wren Scott 2009 SS collection. Wear in the style or time you want, and be unique.

Illustrator: Kiara Tan Country: China

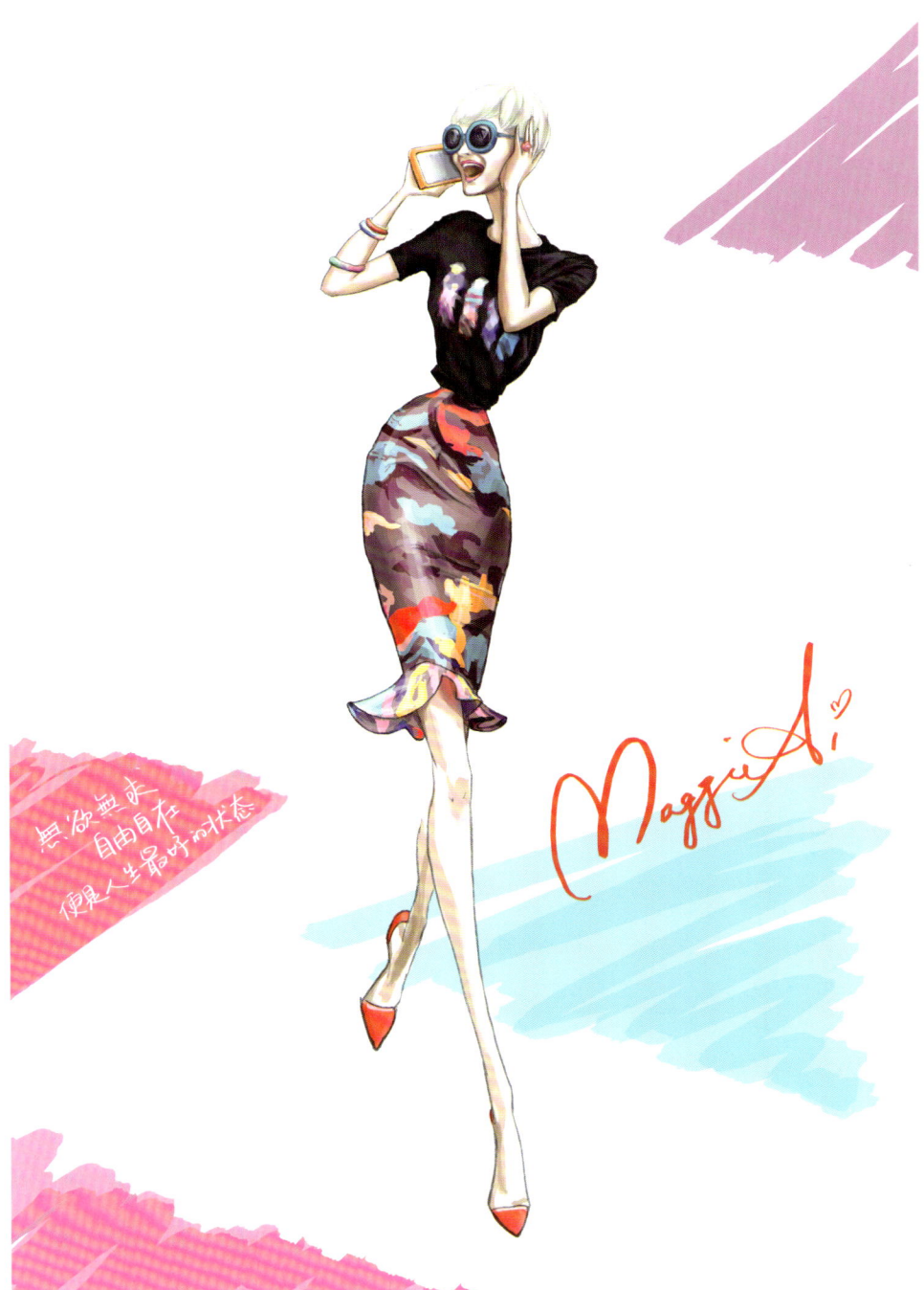

无欲无求
自由自在
便是人生最好的状态

To create a bright, stylish elegant female image with a crisp and motional colour scheme.
Illustrator: Maggie Ai Country: China

Stylish Fishtail Skirt

Dolce and Gabbana

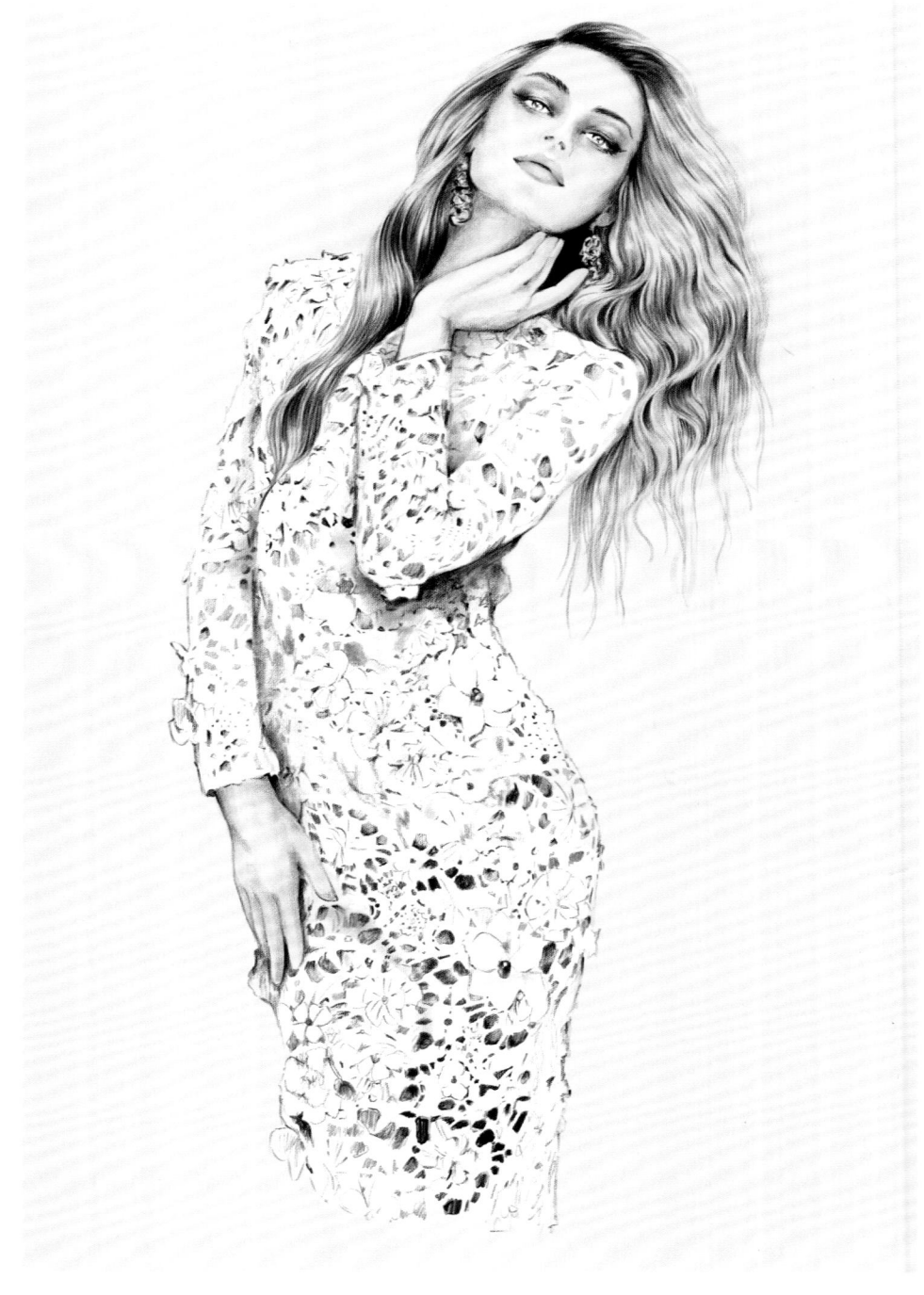

Jessica Stam Wearing Dolce & Gabbana flower dress for Harper's Bazaar Australia March issue 2012, created in Adobe Photoshop CS3 with pencil brushes.
Illustrator: Will Bayum Country: Malaysia

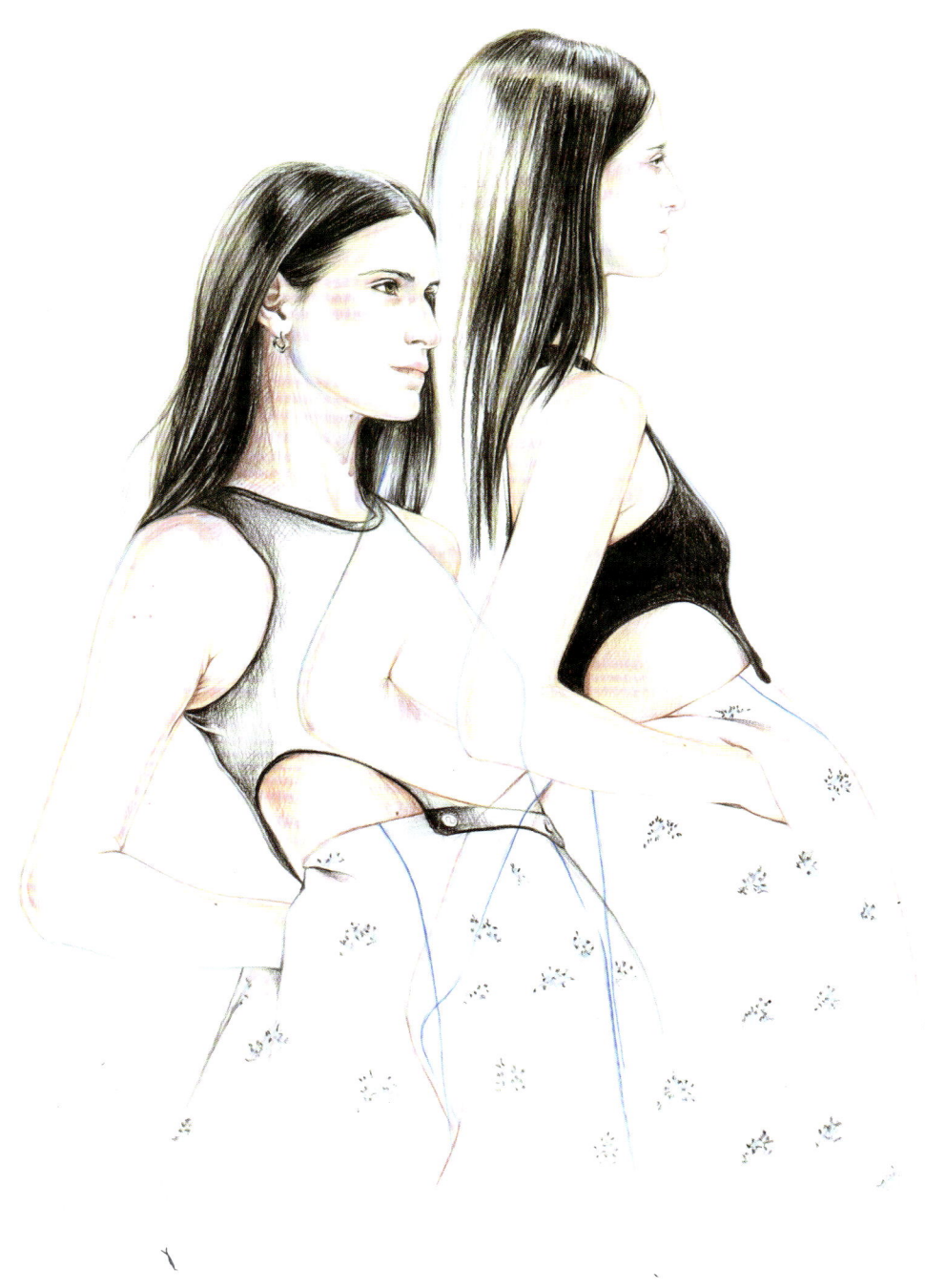

Model Daiane Conterato for Christian Dior couture spring 2015 collection. colour pencils.
Illustrator: Caroline Andrieu Country: France

Christian Dior

Fendi Girl 1

This fashion illustration is inspired by Fendi 2015 Resort collection.
Illustrator: Katerina Murysina Country: Russia

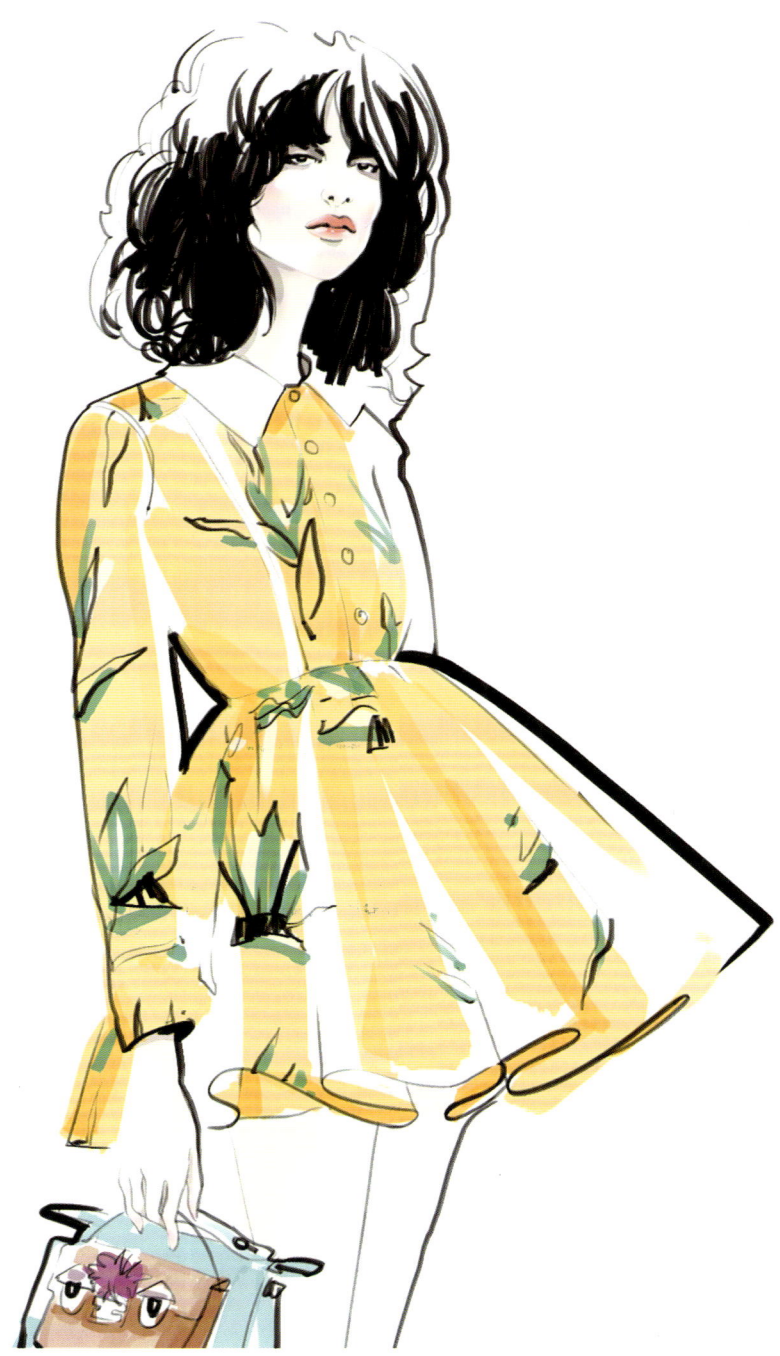

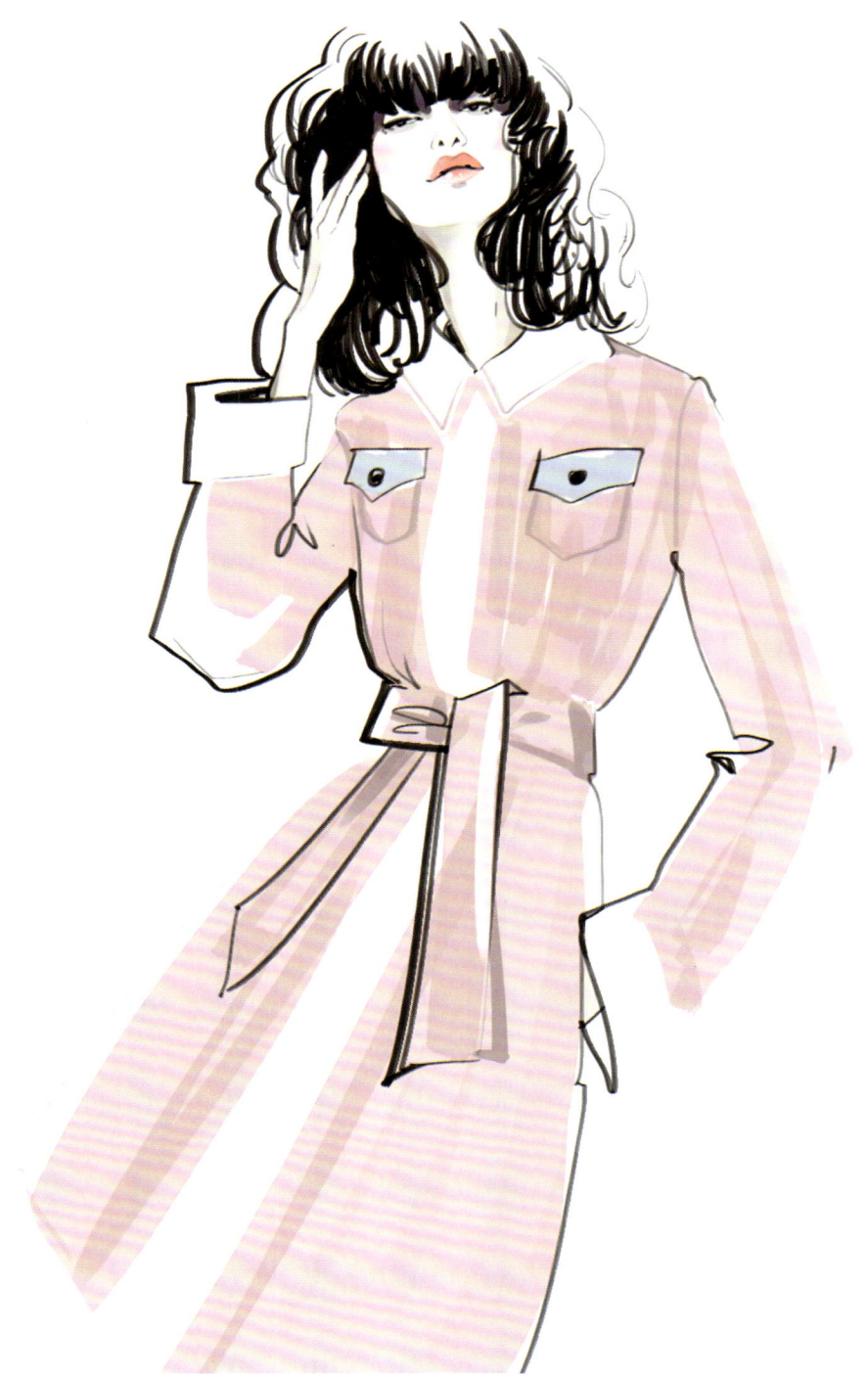

This fashion illustration is inspired by Fendi 2015 Resort collection.
Illustrator: Katerina Murysina Country: Russia

Fendi Girl 2

Stars and Stripes Printed Dress

Reinterpret Picture Caitlin Ricketts. Pencil, Pen, colourpencil on paper and digital work. Illustrator: Mina K Country:South Korea

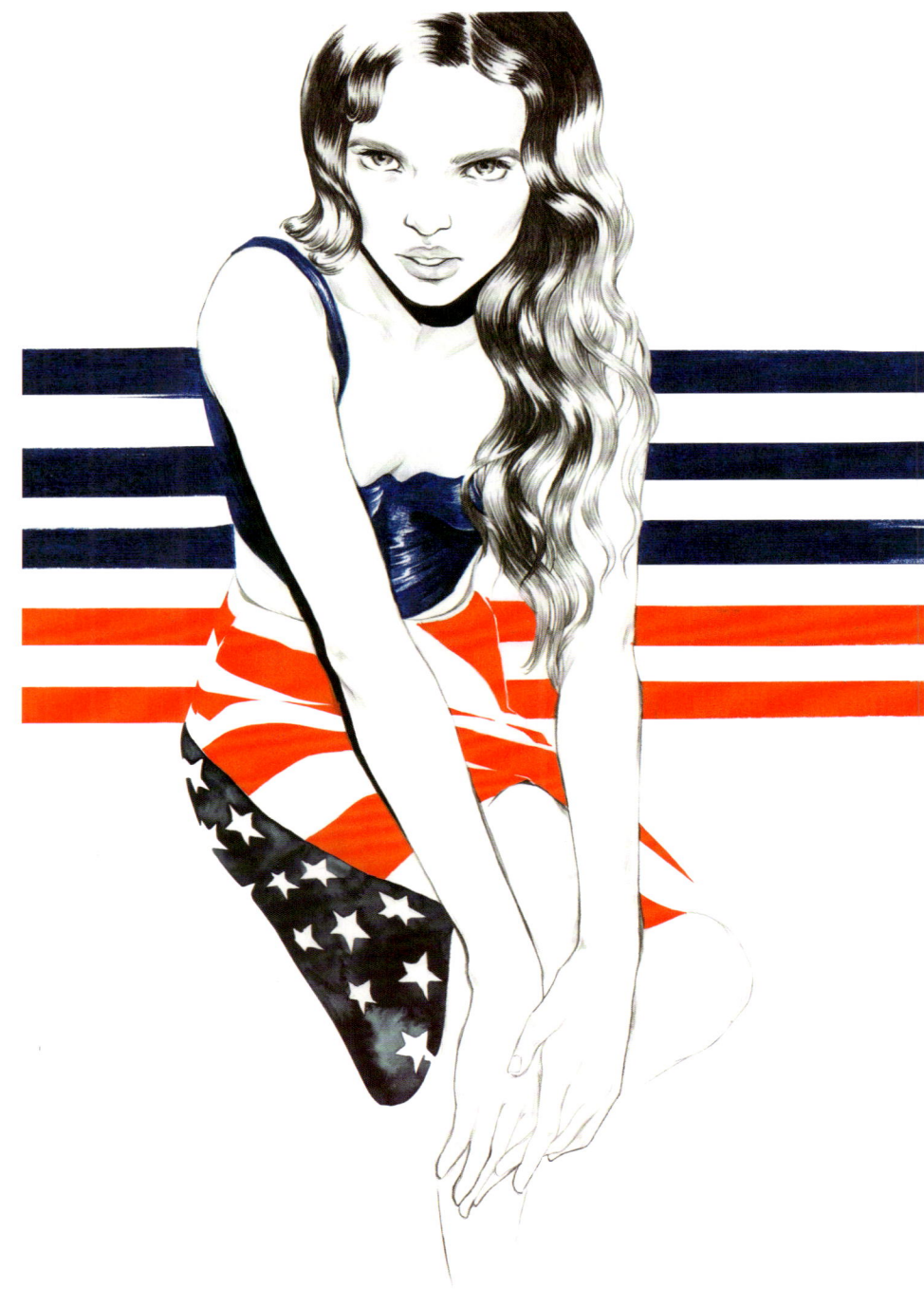

Dress is by Prada SS 2011. Reinterpretation fashion photograph and add the flowers around the lady.
Illustrator: Mina K Country: South Korea

Prada SS 2011

Pepe Jeans London

This fashion illustration is inspired by the portrait of the 'It girl' Alexa Chung.
Illustrator: Paula Blanche Country: Chile

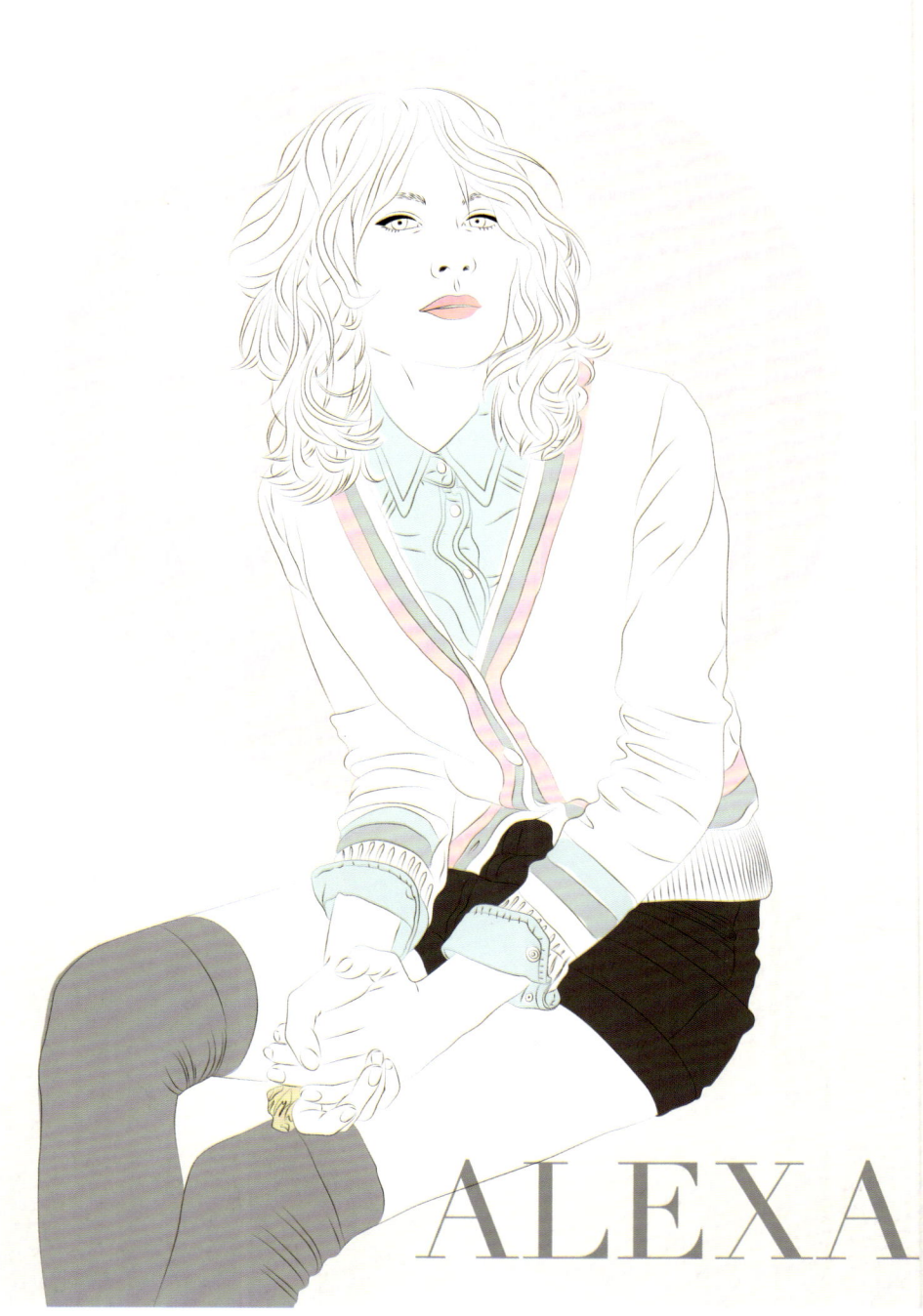

ALEXA

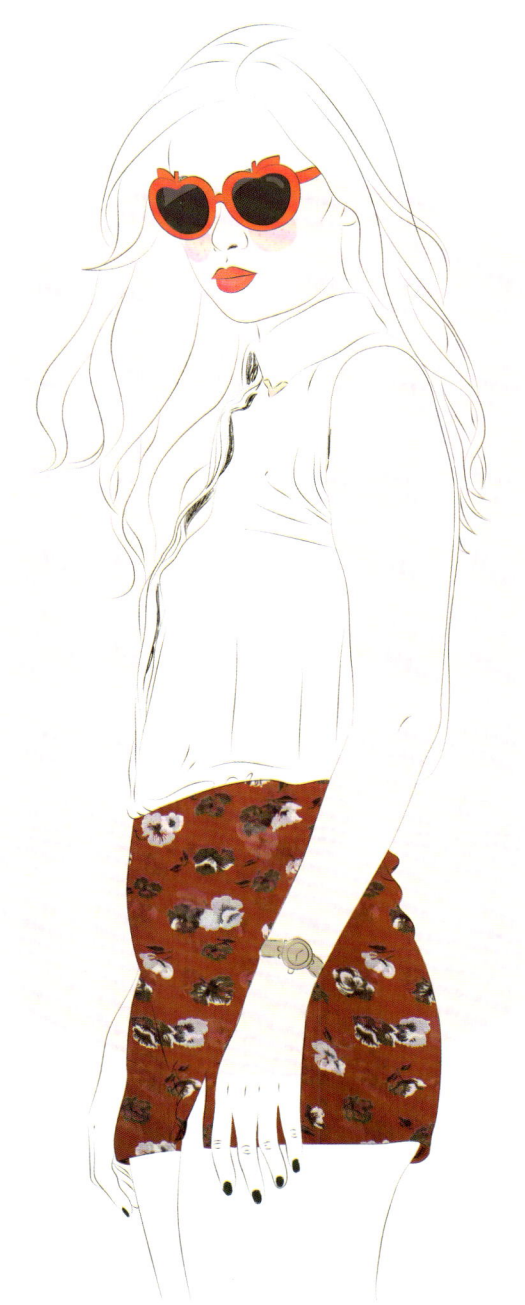

This fashion illustration is inspired by the Hong Kong blogger Mayo.
Illustrator: Paula Blanche Country: Chile

Mellow Mayo Outfit

Alix Bancourt Outfit

This fashion illustration is inspired by the French blogger Alix Bancourt.
Illustrator: Paula Blanche Country: Chile

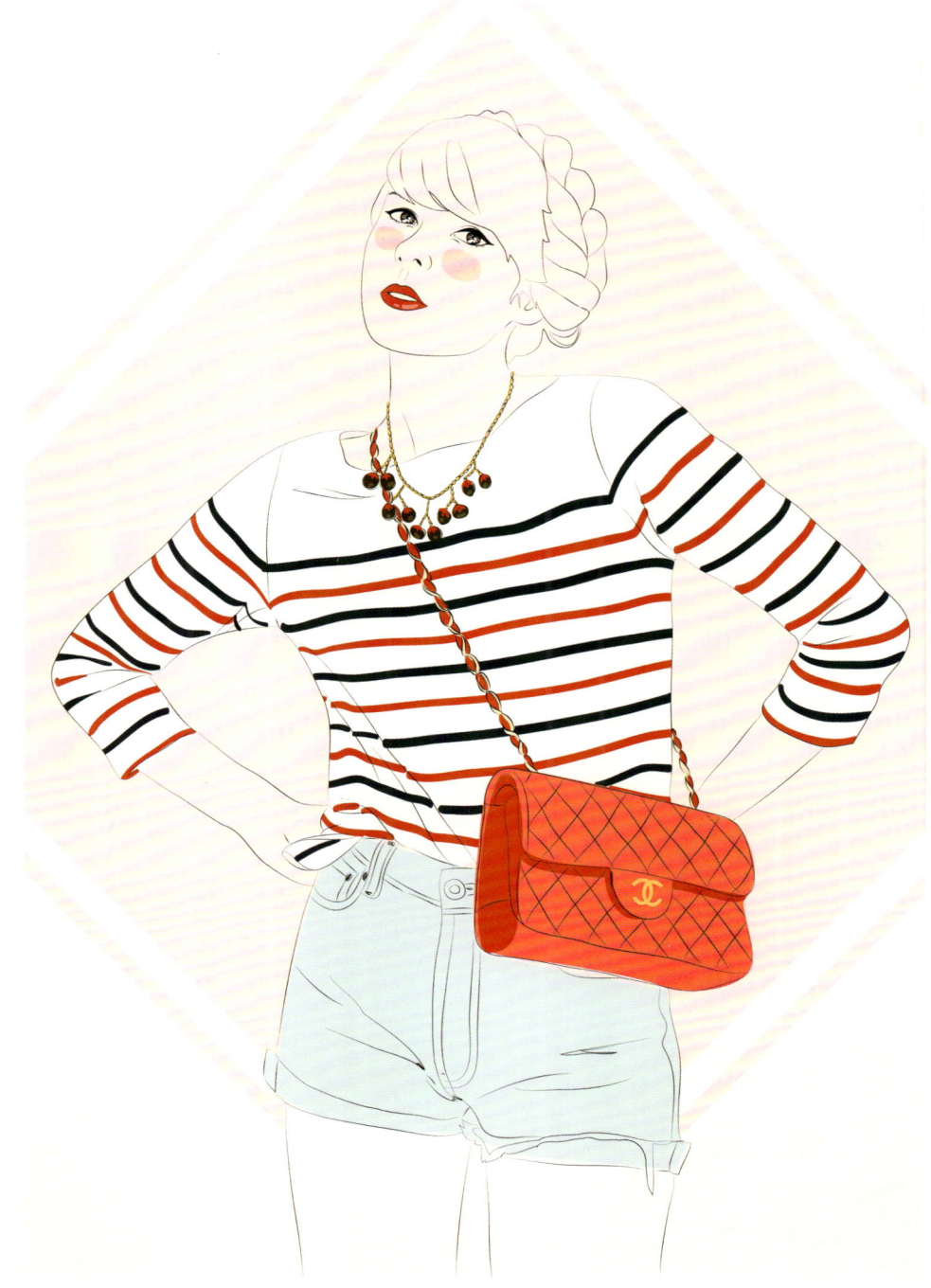

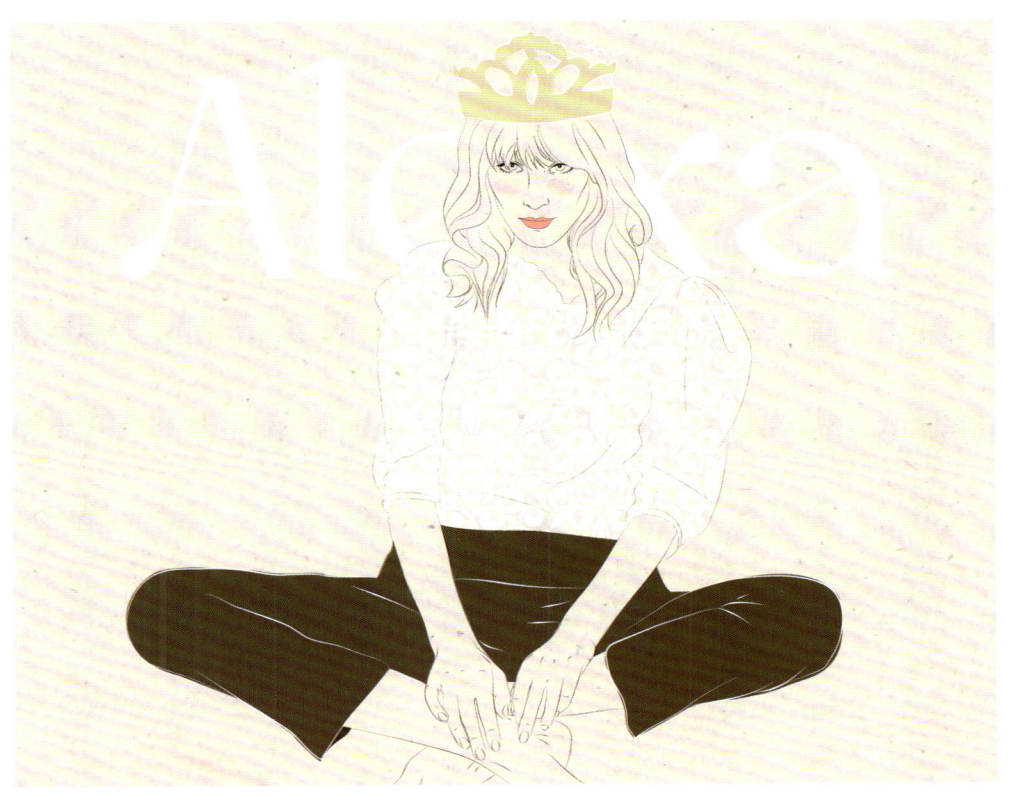

This fashion illustration is inspired by the portrait of the 'It girl' Alexa Chung.
Illustrator: Paula Blanche Country: Chile

FRAY I.D

Miu Miu

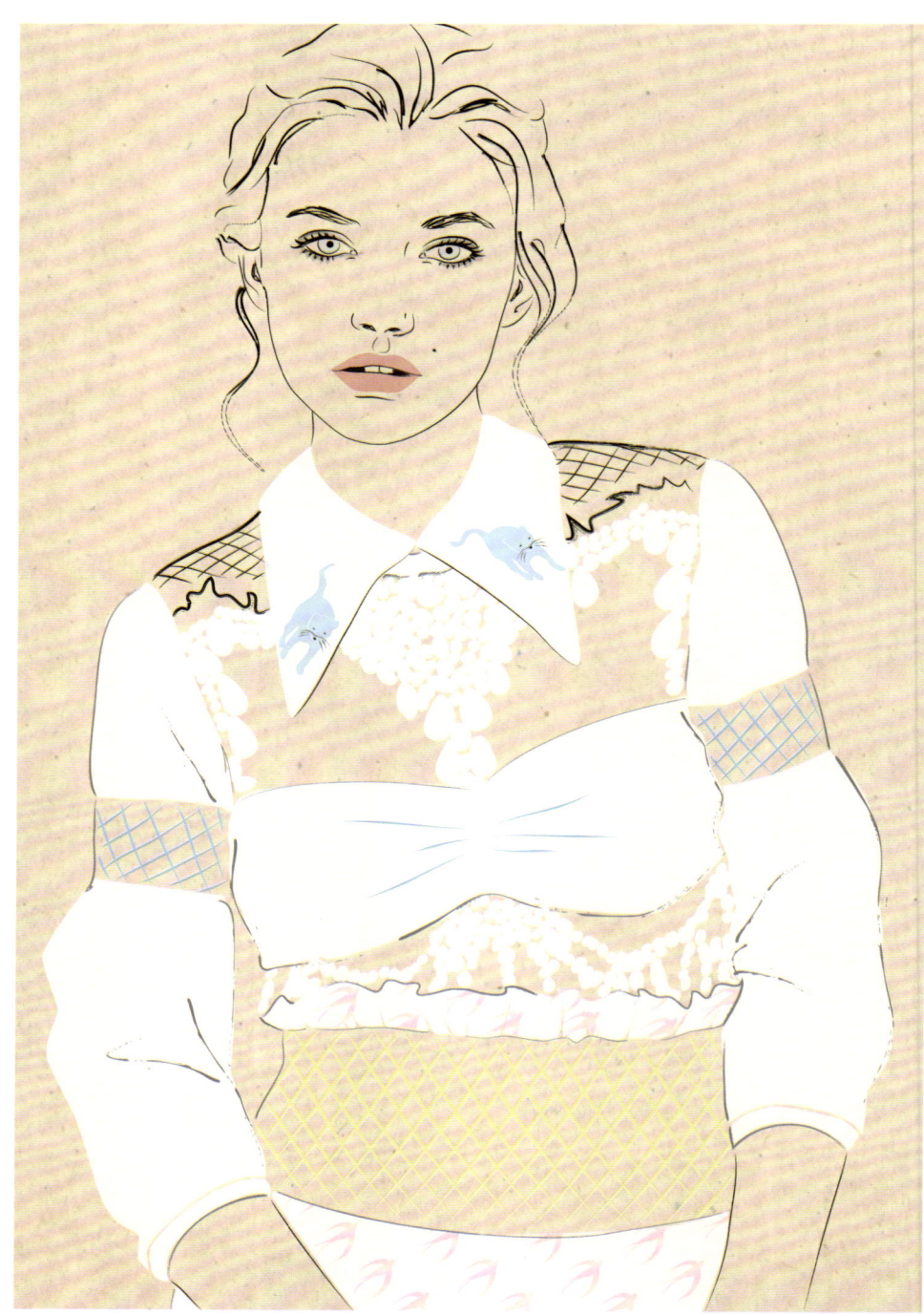

This fashion illustration is inspired by the actress Imogen Poots wearing a Miu Miu dress.
Illustrator: Paula Blanche Country: Chile

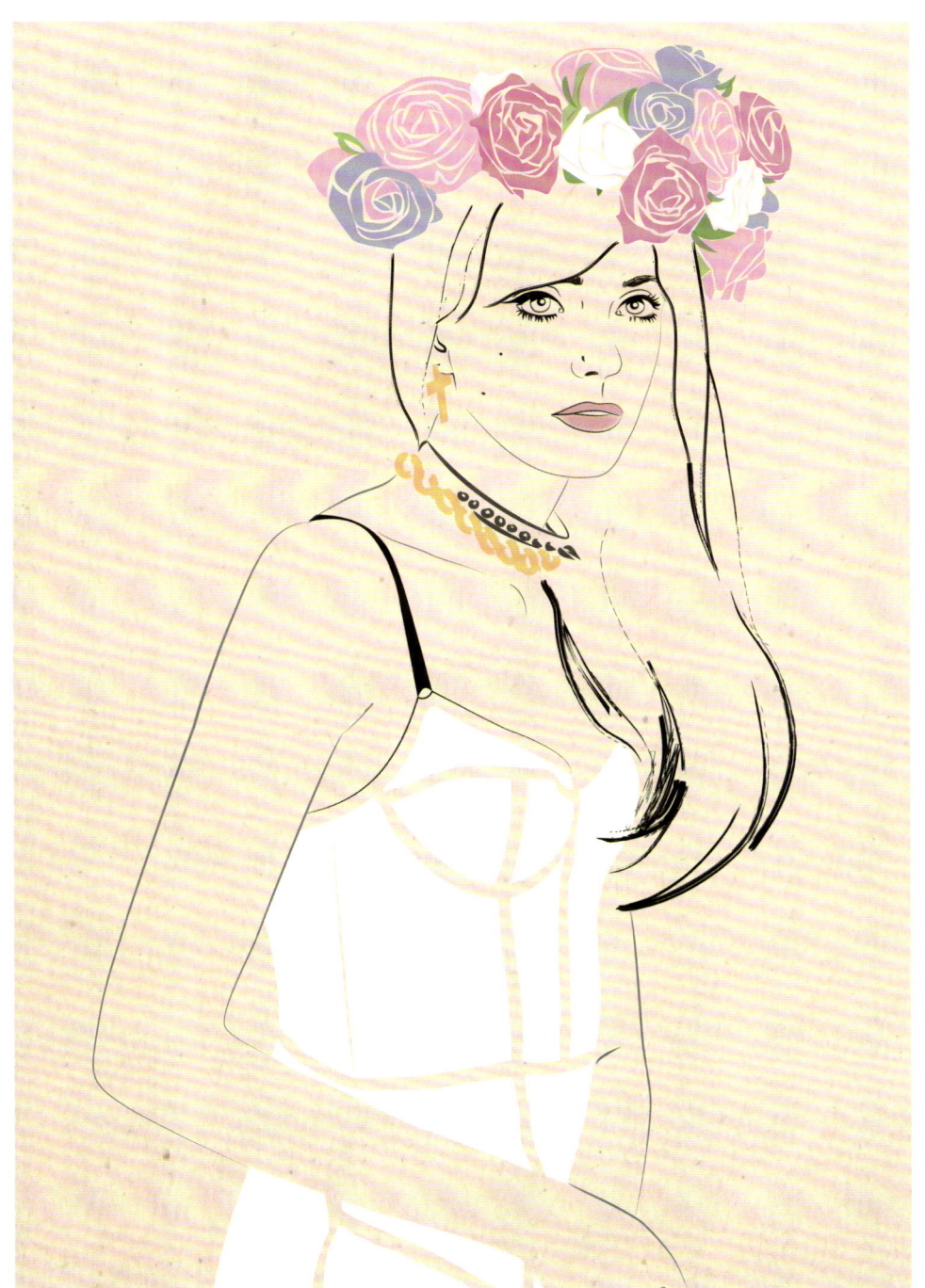

This fashion illustration is inspired by the actress Stacy Martin.
Illustrator: Paula Blanche Country: Chile

Maria Francesca Pepe

The Whitepepper

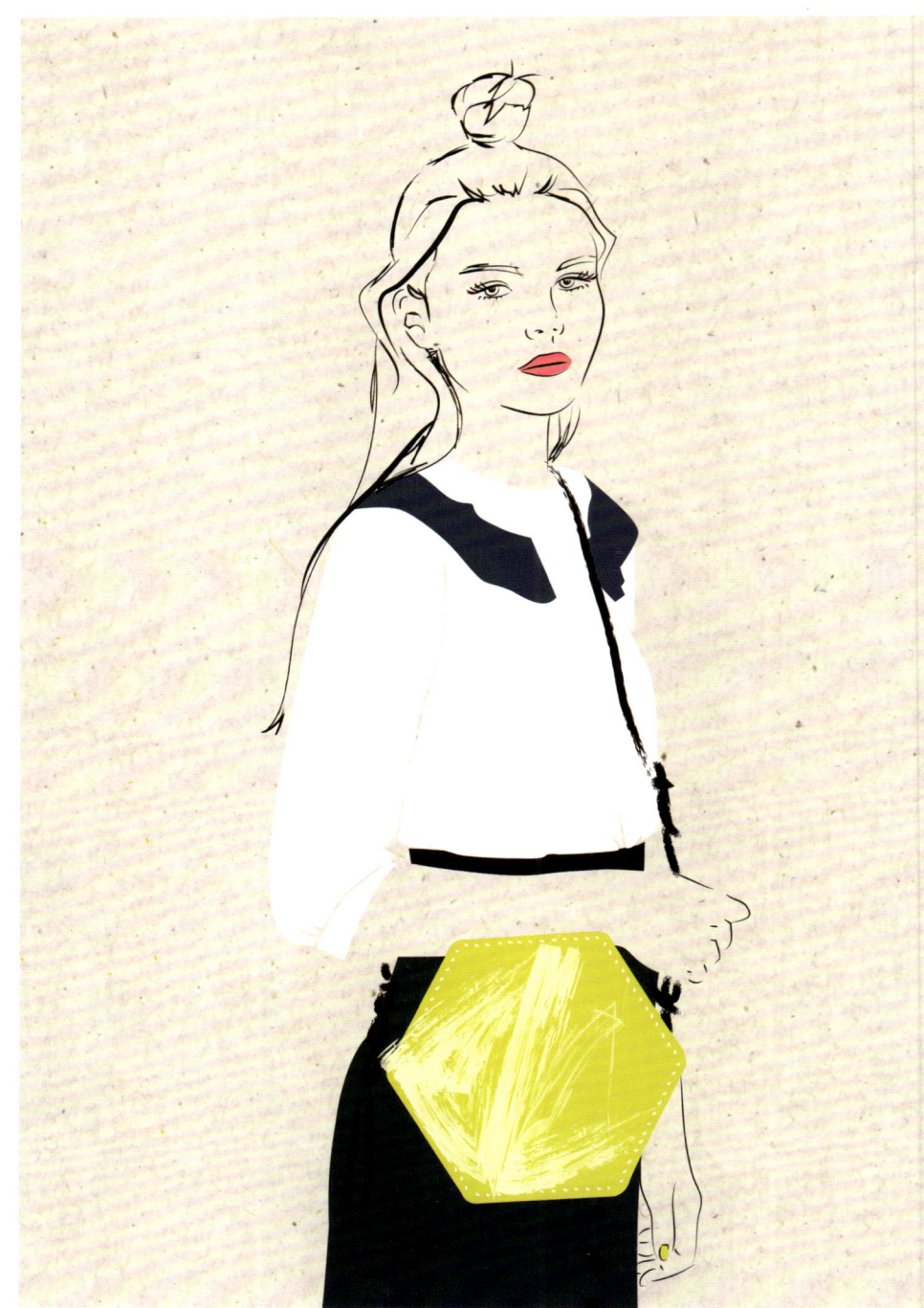

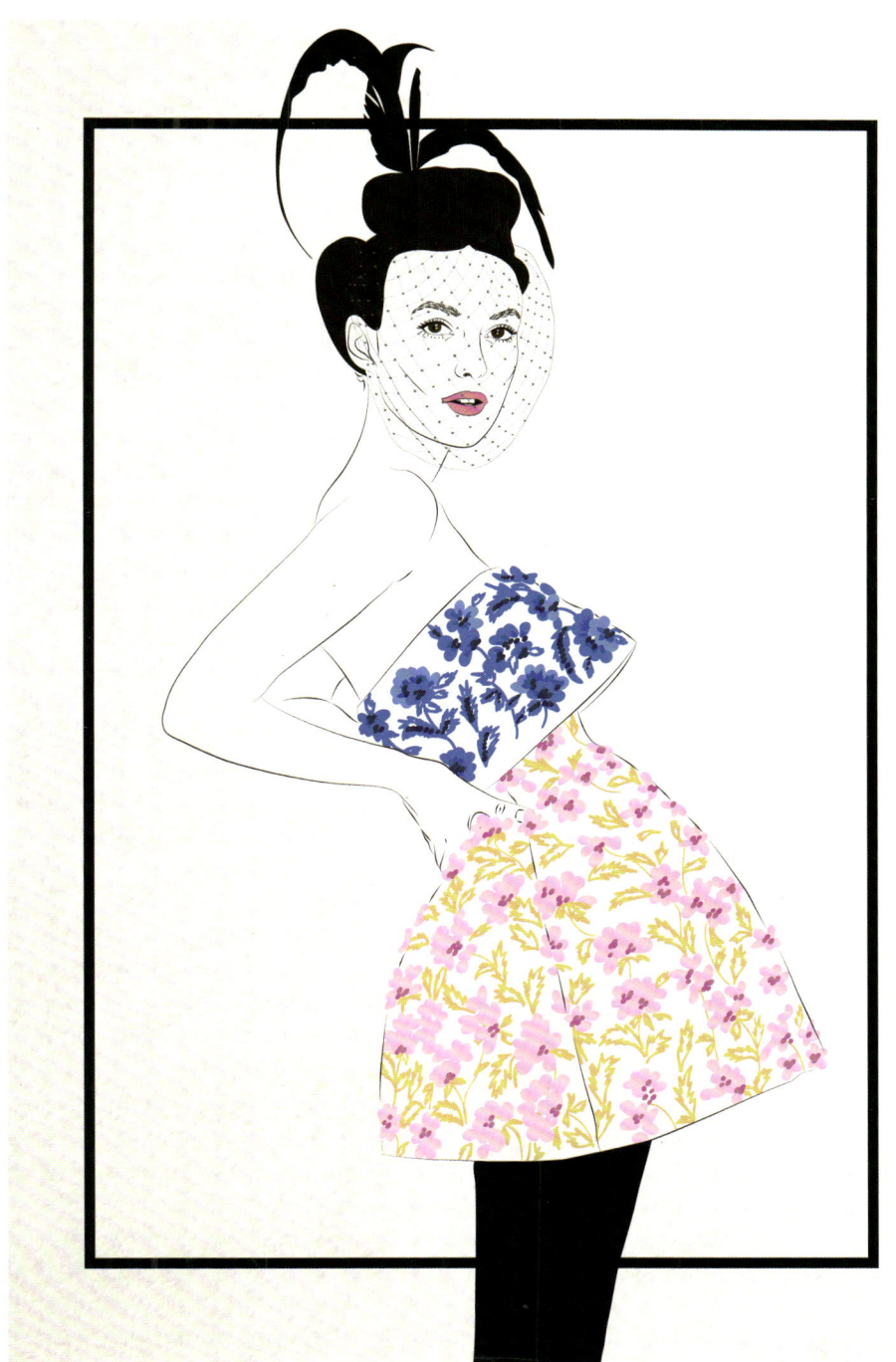

This fashion illustration is inspired by the actress Keira Knightley wearing a Christian Dior dress.
Illustrator: Paula Blanche Country: Chile

Christian Dior

Miu Miu RTW FW 2015

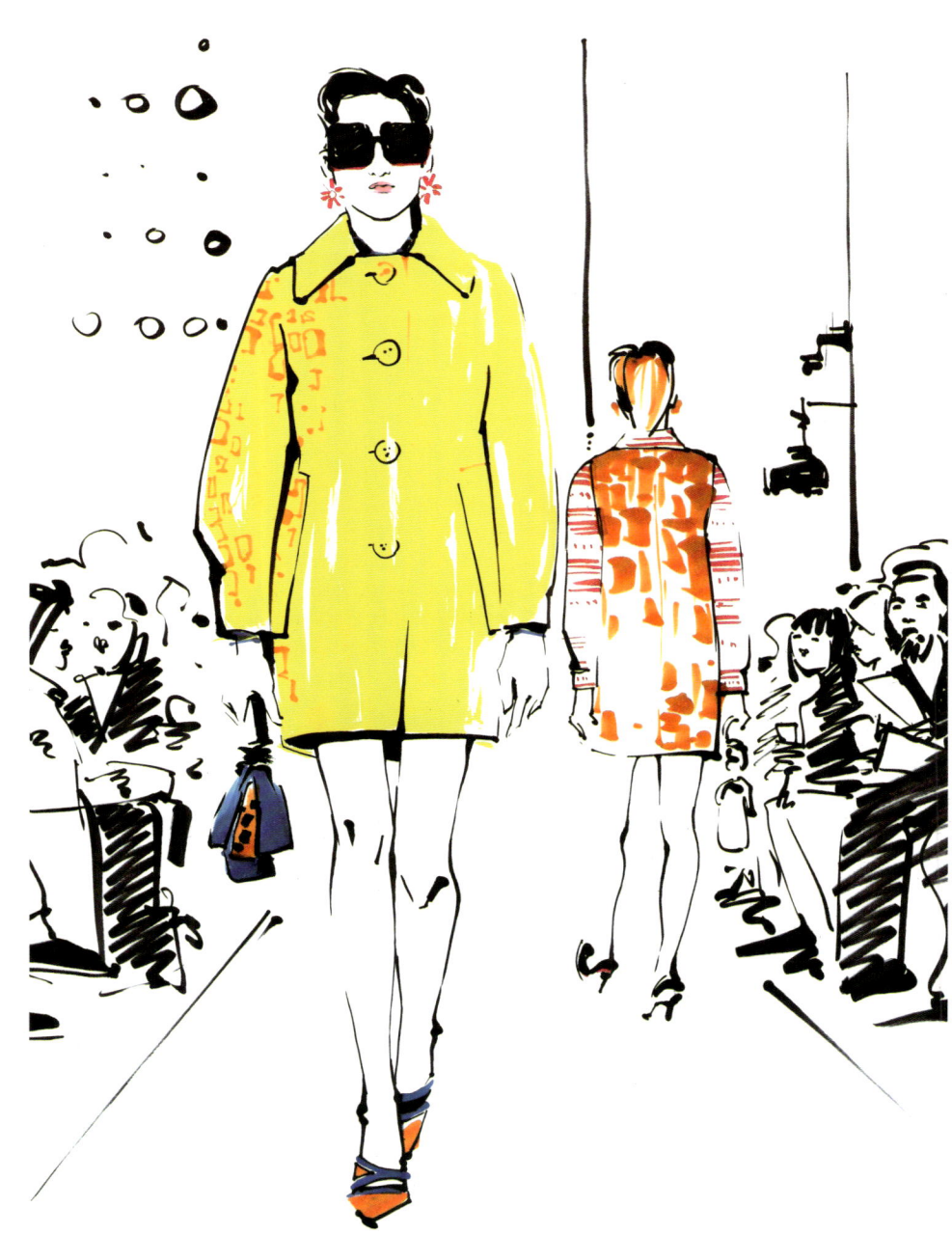

Personal work. Runway moment at Miu Miu show. Milan Fashion Week RTW FW 2015.
Illustrator: Alena Lavdovskaya Country: Russia

Personal work. Backstage moment at Rochas show. Paris fashion week RTW FW 2015.
Illustrator: Alena Lavdovskaya Country: Russia

Rochas RTW FW 2015

Chanel SS 2015

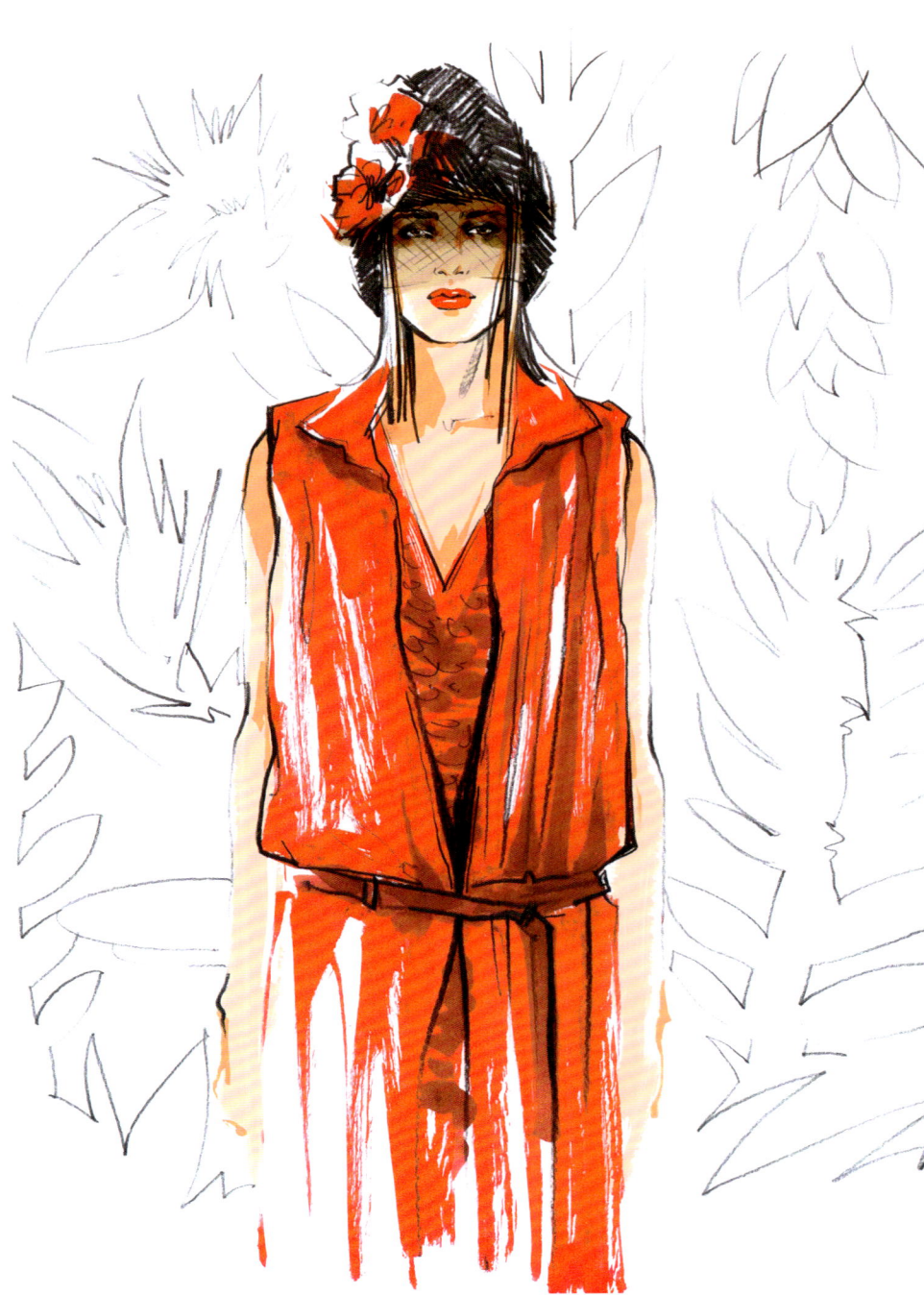

Personal work. Close up moment at Chanel show, Paris' Haute Couture Fashion Week SS 2015.
Illustrator: Alena Lavdovskaya Country: Russia

Cute and Sweet

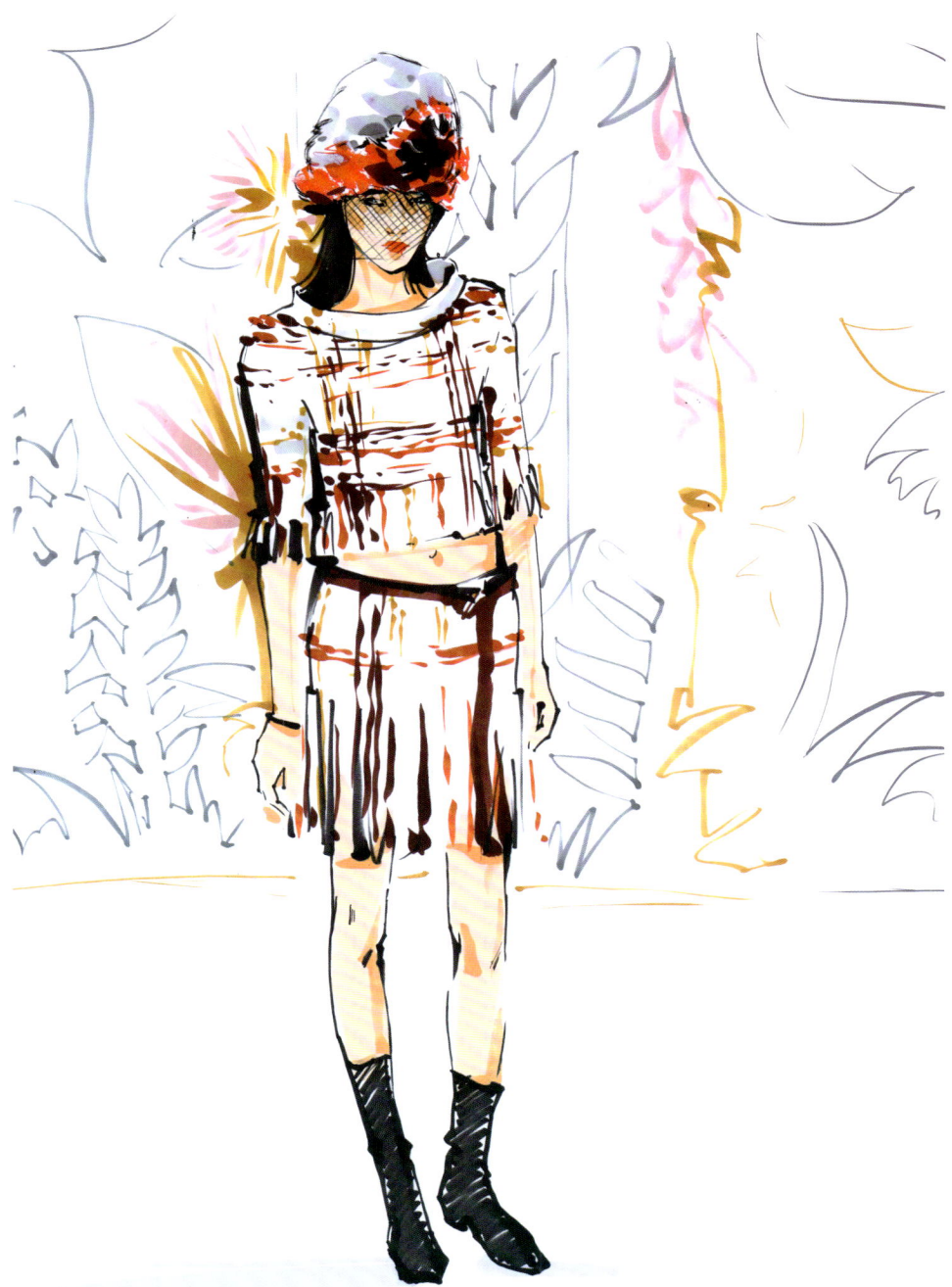

Personal work. Runway moment at Chanel show, Paris' Haute Couture fashion Week SS 2015.
Illustrator: Alena Lavdovskaya Country: Russia

Chanel SS 2015

Chanel RTW FW 2015

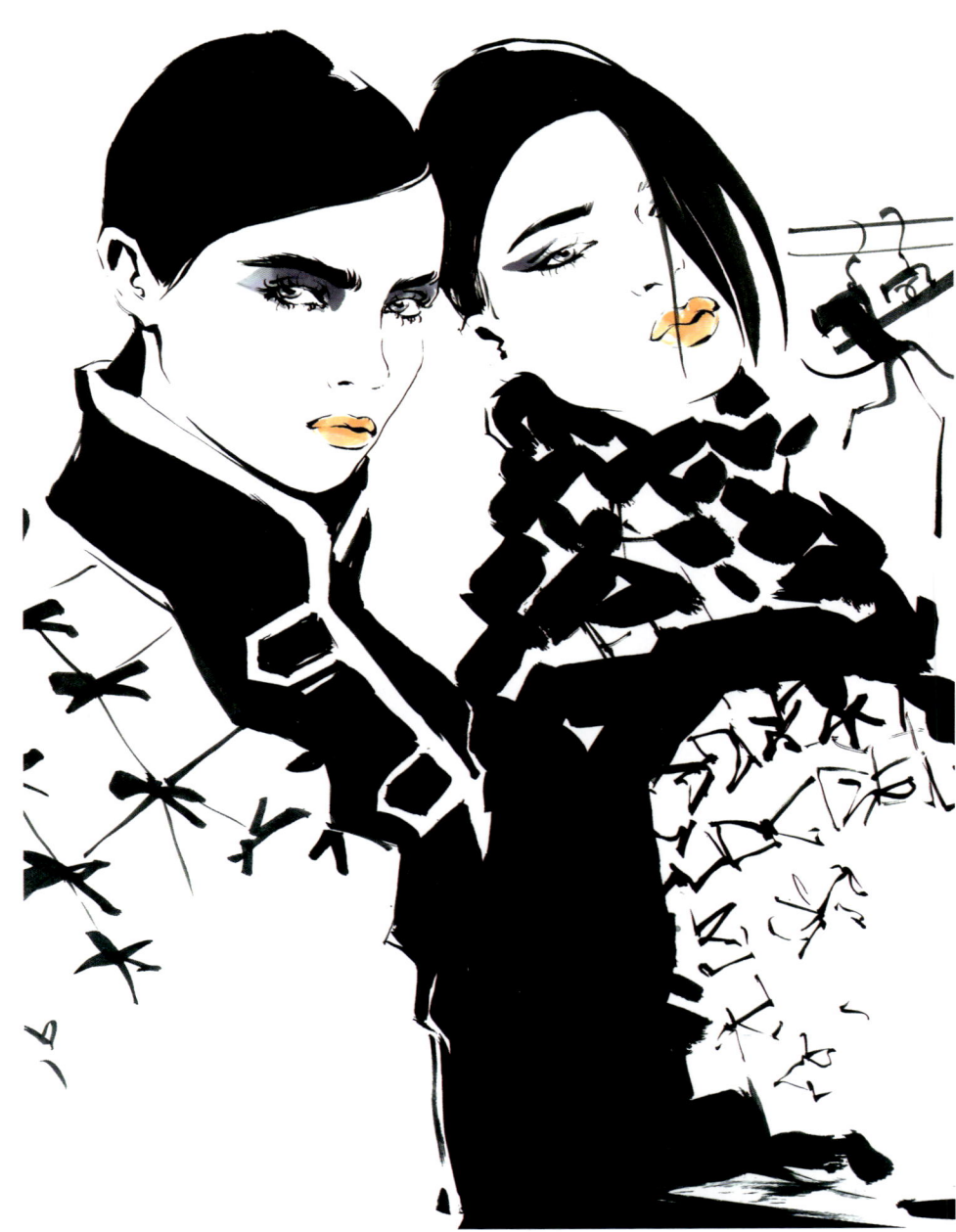

Editorial work for vogue.ru. Backstage moment at Chanel show, Paris Fashion Week RTW FW 2015.
Illustrator: Alena Lavdovskaya Country: Russia

084 >° Cute and Sweet

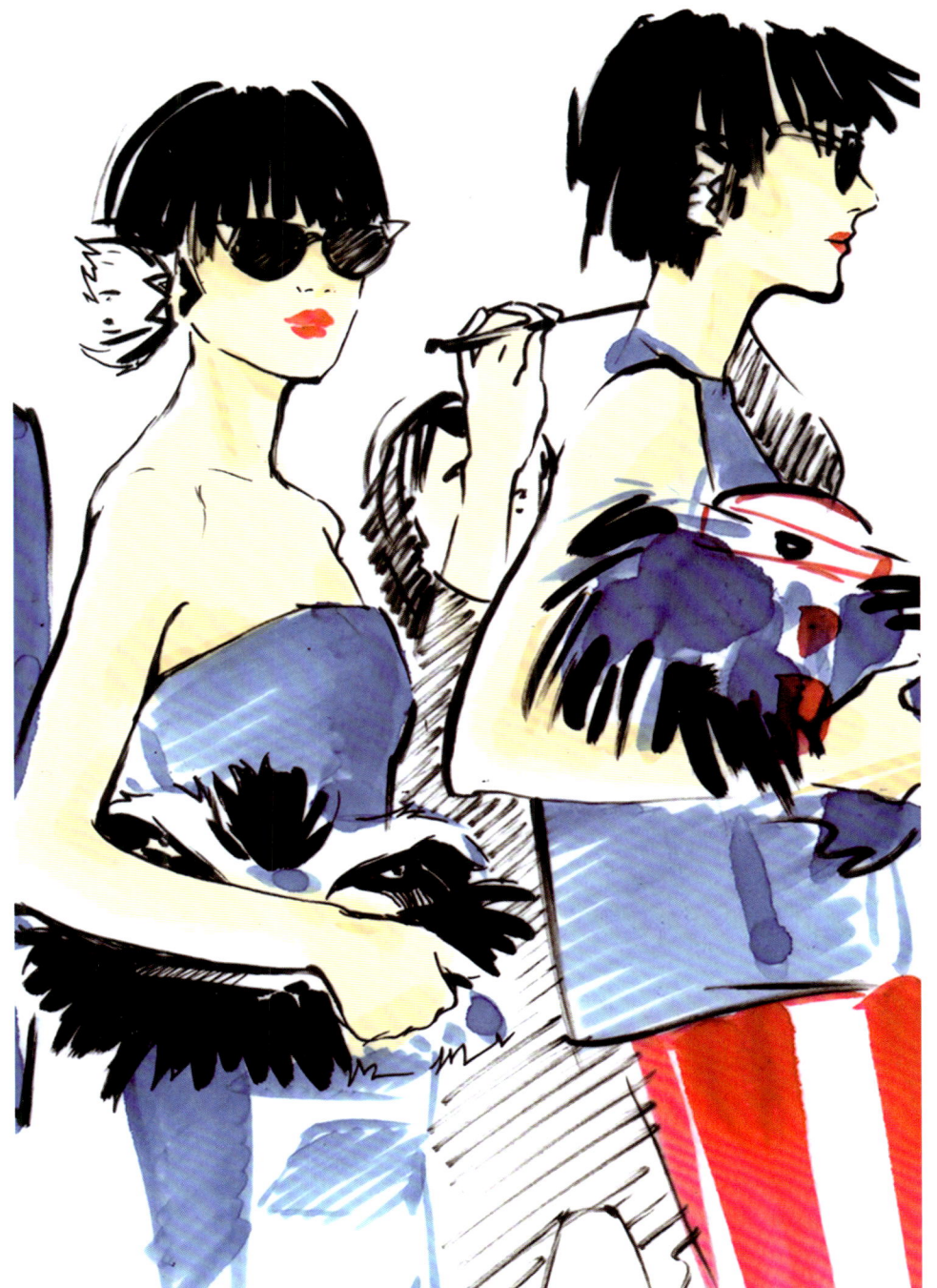

Comics 'Vasilisa's dairy' for dochkimateri.com, backstage moment at Fendi show, Milan fashion Week RTW SS 2015.
Illustrator: Alena Lavdovskaya Country: Russia

Fendi RTW SS 2015

Rodarte

Model Mariana Santana for Rodarte fall 2014 collection. Colour pencils on Ingres paper.
Illustrator: Caroline Andrieu Country: France

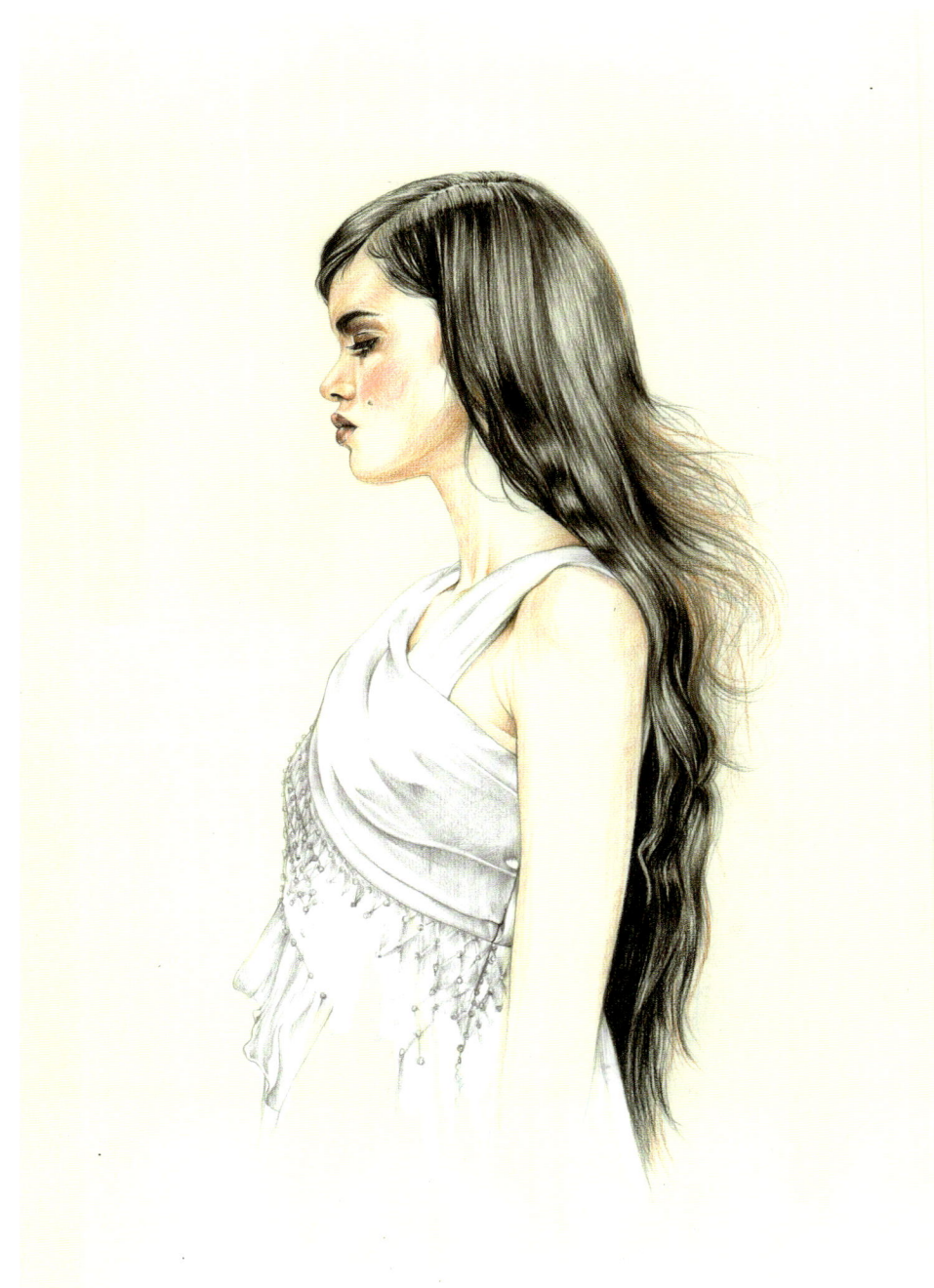

086 — Cute and Sweet

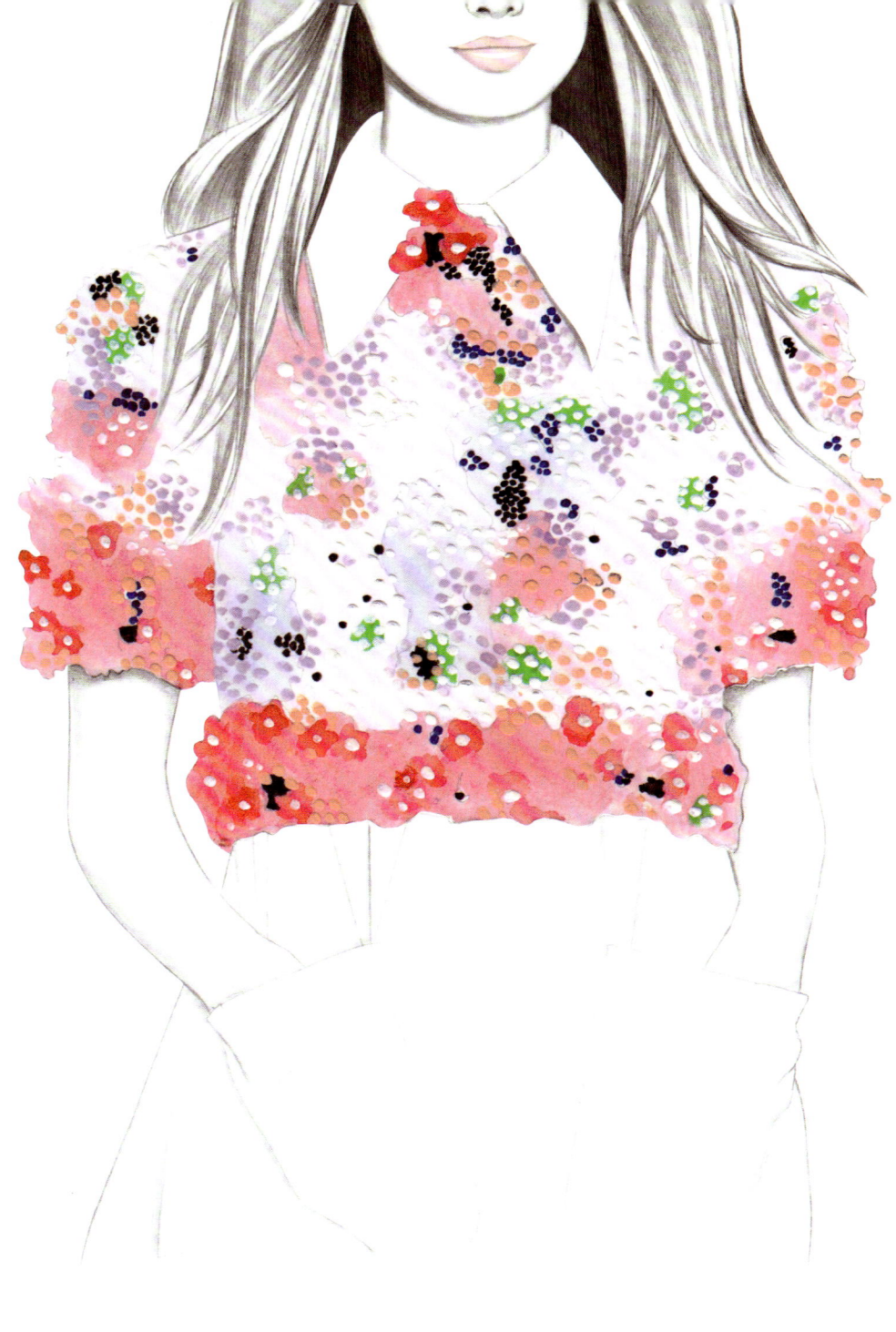

Personal project using gouache and graphite, with emphasis on the texture and grain.
Illustrator: Nicole Jarecz Country: USA

Chanel

Jill Stuart SS 2016

Jill Stuart is always the queen of femininity, the illustrator captured some of her flowing looks with pops of magenta and silky fabrics for The CFDA during NY Fashion Week.
Illustrator: Samantha Hahn Country: USA

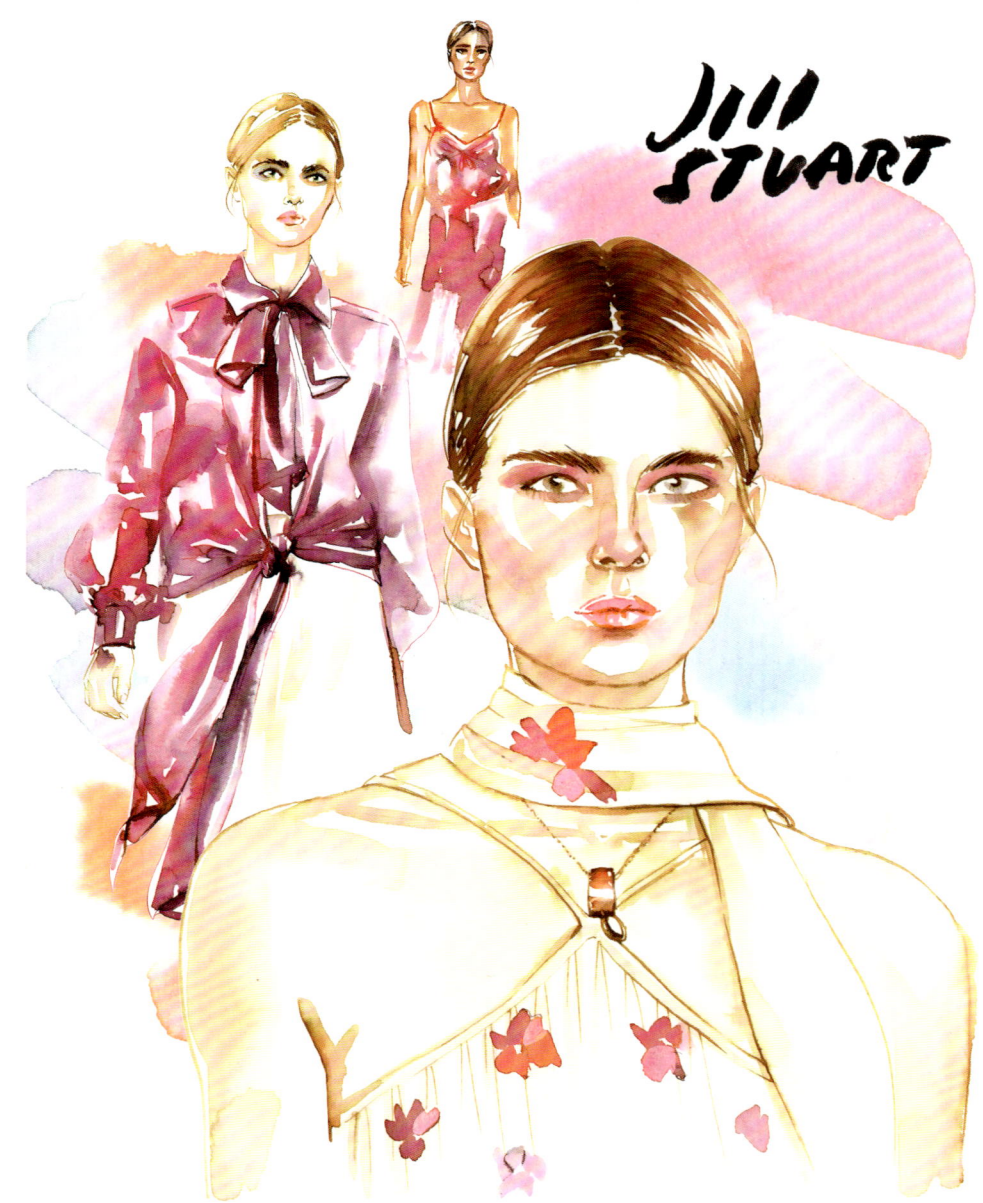

Cute and Sweet

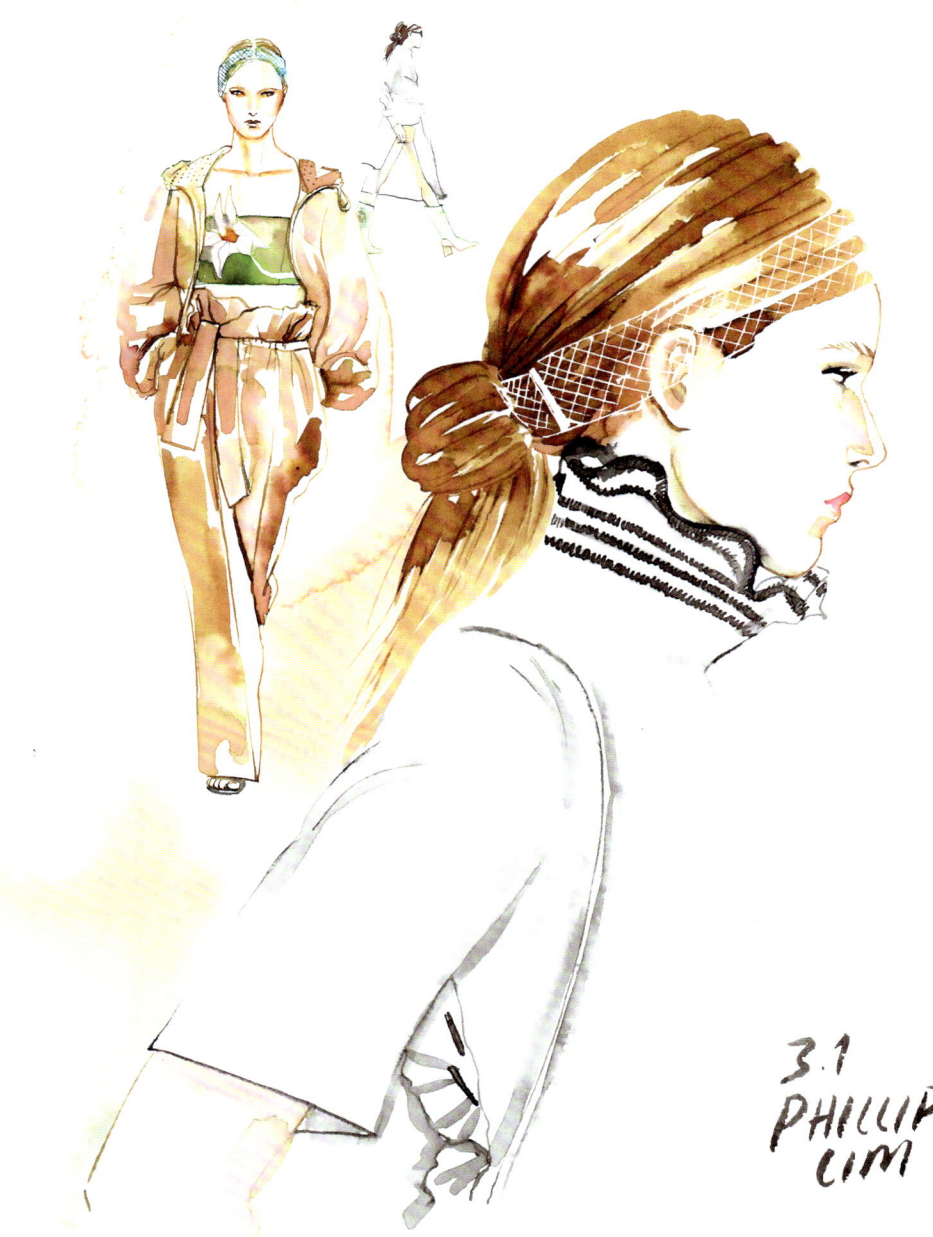

3.1 PHILLIP LIM

Phillip Lim had an amazing collection with irresistible charm.
Illustrator: Samantha Hahn Country: USA

Phillip Lim SS 2016

Proenza Schouler

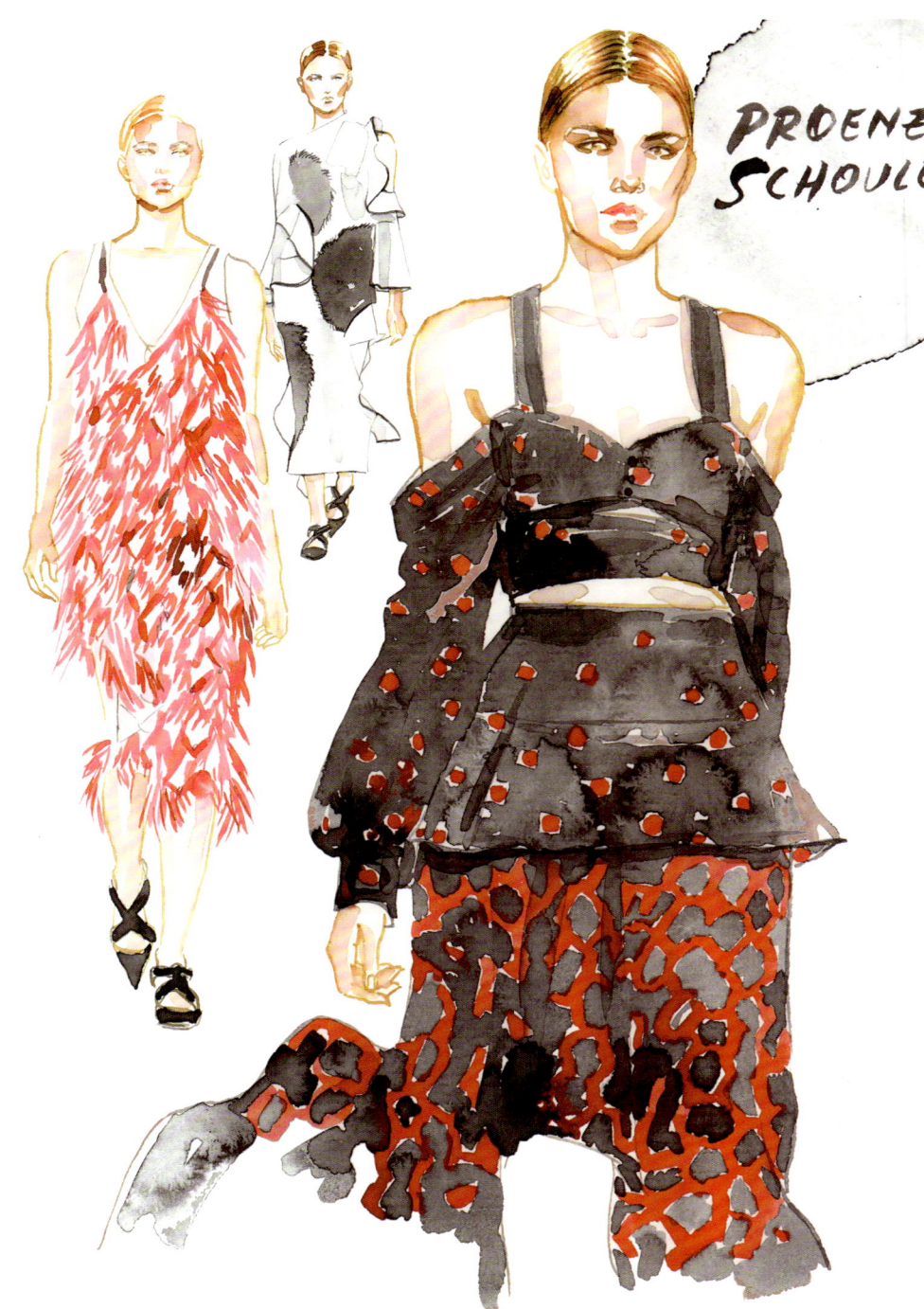

Proenza Schouler is always a crowd favourite. Their incredible textures and paired down palette of white, black and red were stunning and inviting to capture.

Illustrator: Samantha Hahn Country: USA

Cute and Sweet

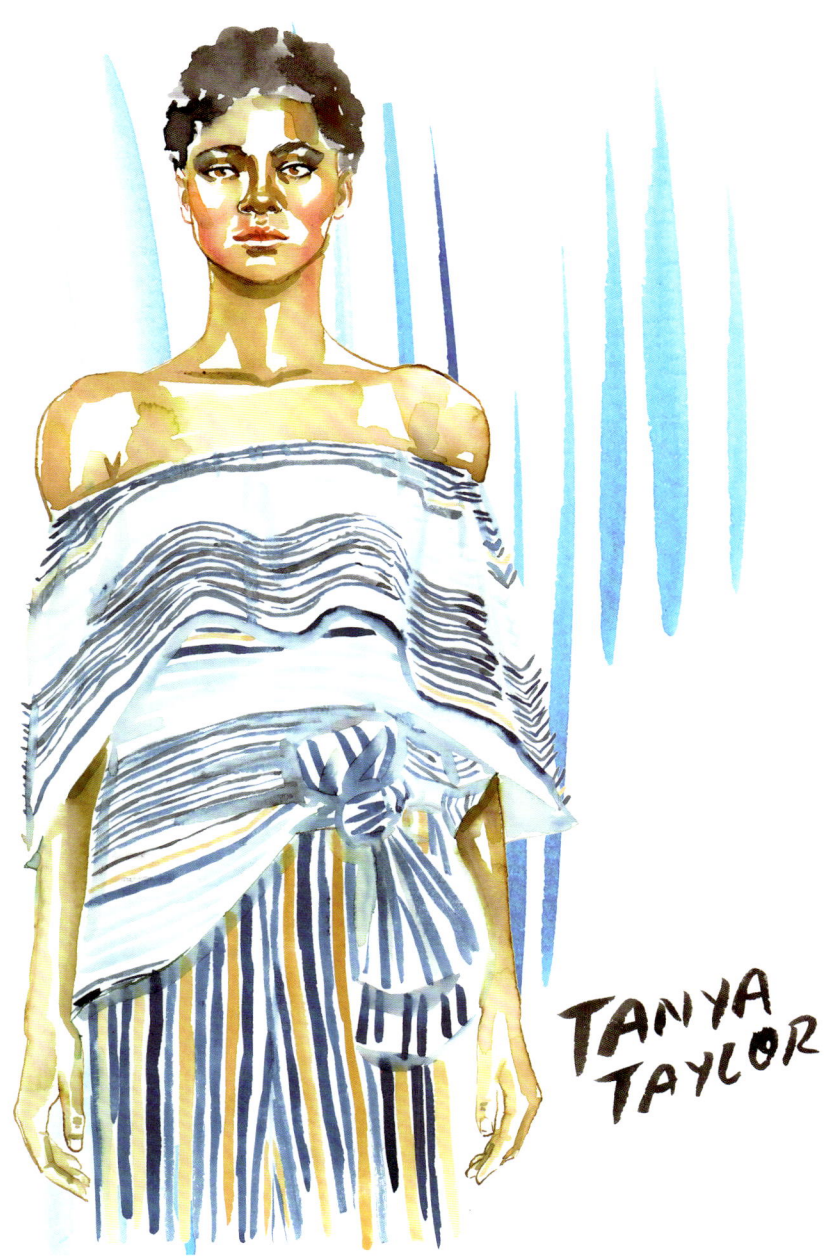

Tanya Taylor is an up and coming designer who has been accepted into The CFDA. Samantha loved her SS16 collection, especially this stripy look with that gorgeous colour palette. Samantha illustrated this look during her collaboration with The CFDA during NY Fashion Week. Illustrator: Samantha Hahn Country: USA

Tanya Taylor SS16

Dolce & Gabbana RTW Fall 2011

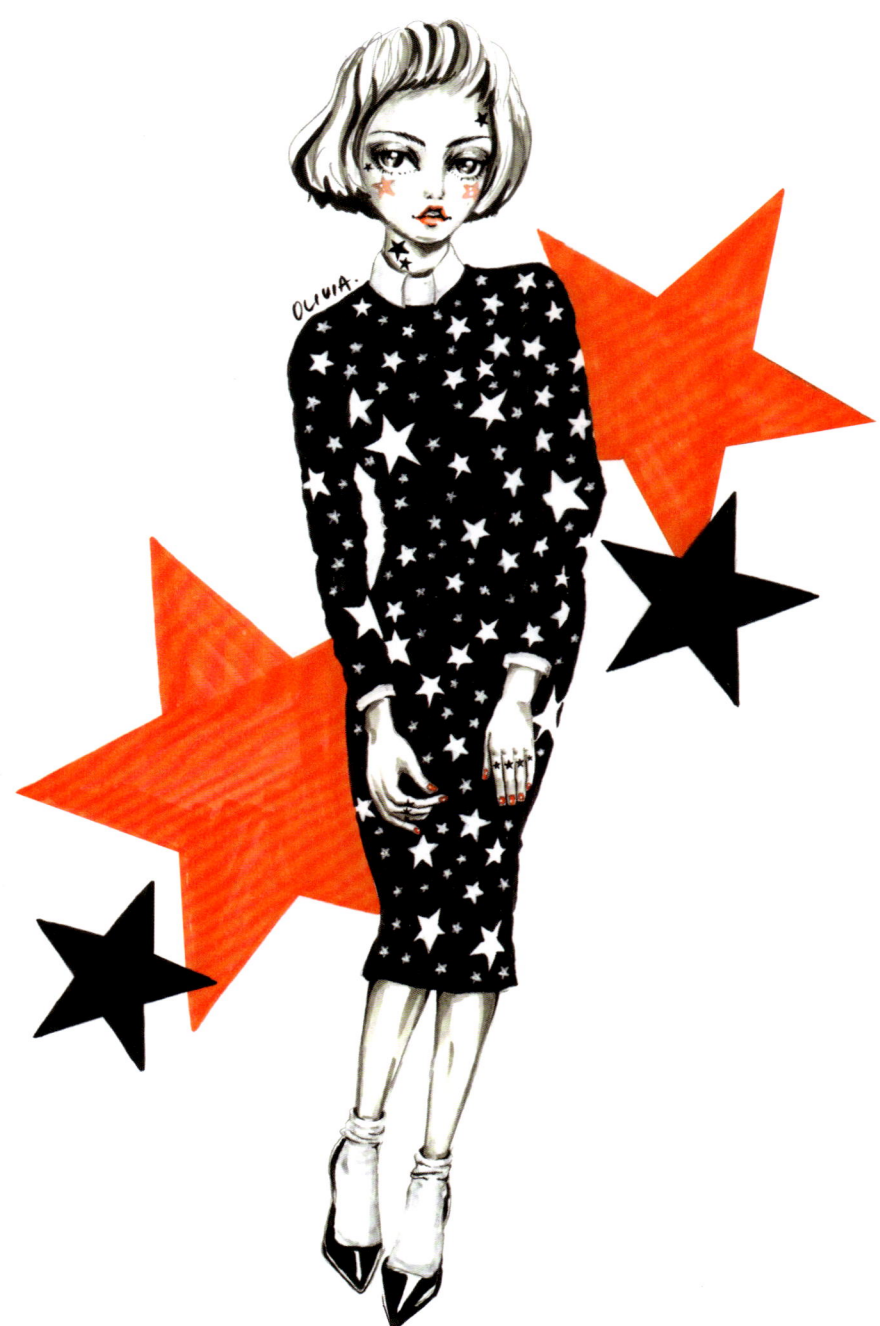

This illustration is inspired by V Magazine fashion editorial, girl wearing Dolce & Gabbana Fall 2011 RTW collection.
Illustrator: Olivia Au Country: Hong Kong, China

092 × Cute and Sweet

#SIMONE ROCHA

Backstage moment at Simone Rocha show, London Fashion Week RTW FW 2015. Editorial work for vogue.ru.
Illustrator: Alena Lavdovskaya Country: Russia

Simone Rocha RTW FW 2015

Giambattista Valli Spring 2014

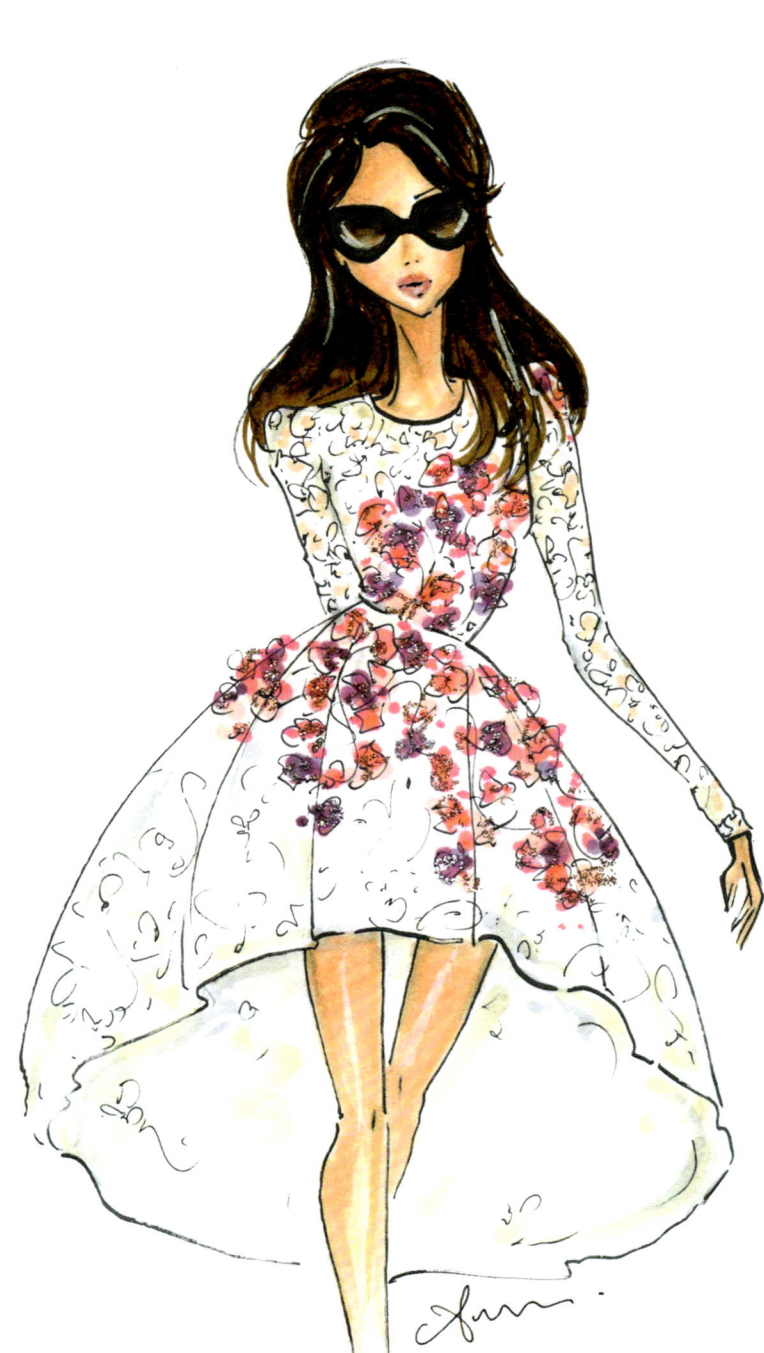

This illustration was inspired by Amal Clooney wearing a dress by Giambattista Valli from the Spring 2014 Haute Couture collection.

Illustrator: Anum Tariq Country: USA

094 ✂ *Cute and Sweet*

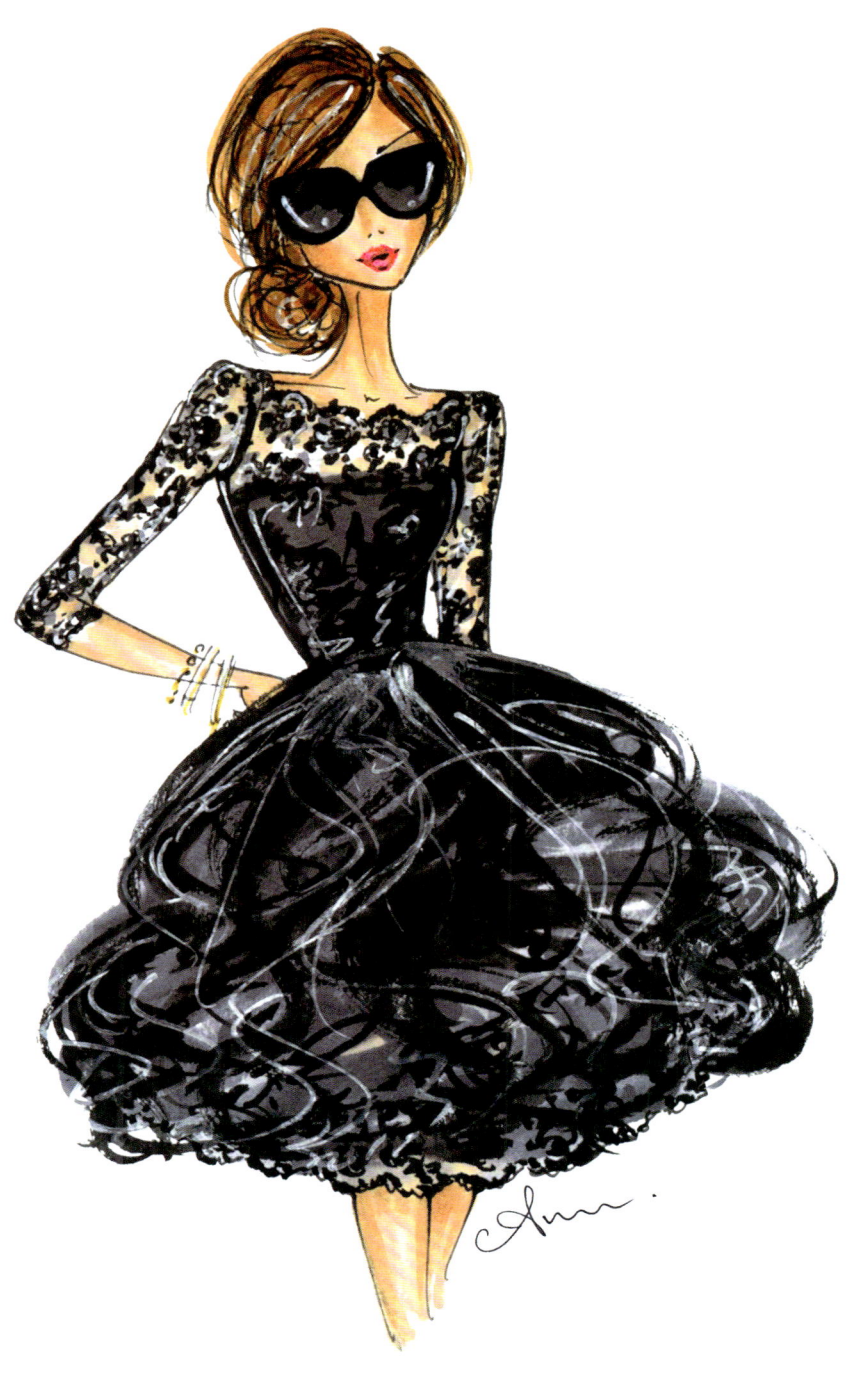

This illustration was inspired by a lace ruffled dress worn by actress Emma Stone.
Illustrator: Anum Tariq Country: USA

Oscar de la Renta 2015

Zuhair Murad Fall 2015

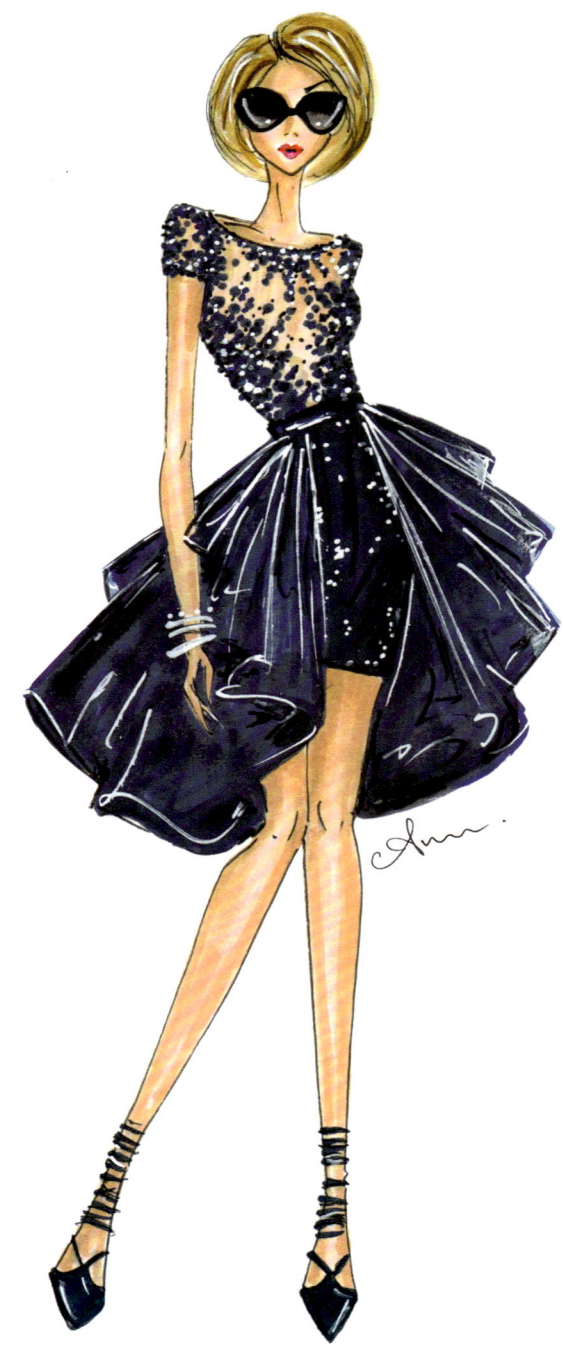

This illustration was inspired by a look from the Zuhair Murad Fall 2015 Ready-to-Wear collection.

Illustrator: Anum Tariq   Country: USA

Cute and Sweet

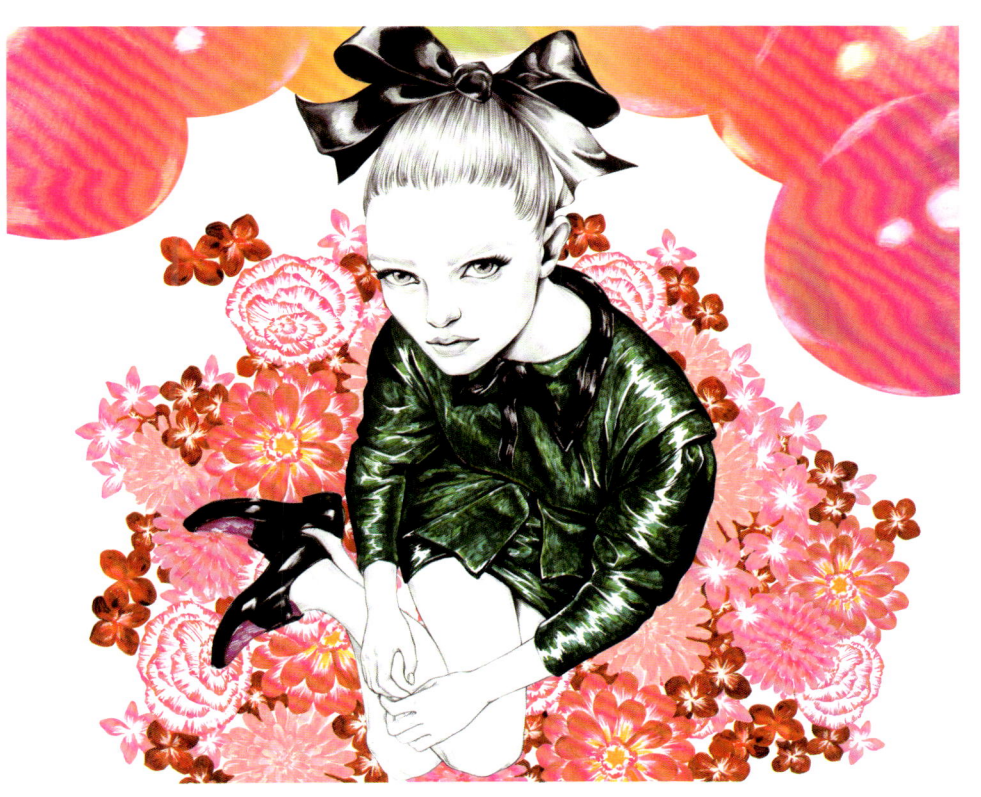

Reinterpretation of Fashion photo graph and add the flowers on the floor, balloons. Pencil, pen, ink, colour pencil, watercolour, marker on paper and digital work.
Illustrator: Mina K Country:South Korea

Coloured Shiny Dress with Shirts Collar

Chanel SS 2014

This fashion illustration is inspired by Chanel SS 2014 collection.
Illustrator: Mariana Marchè Country: Ukraine

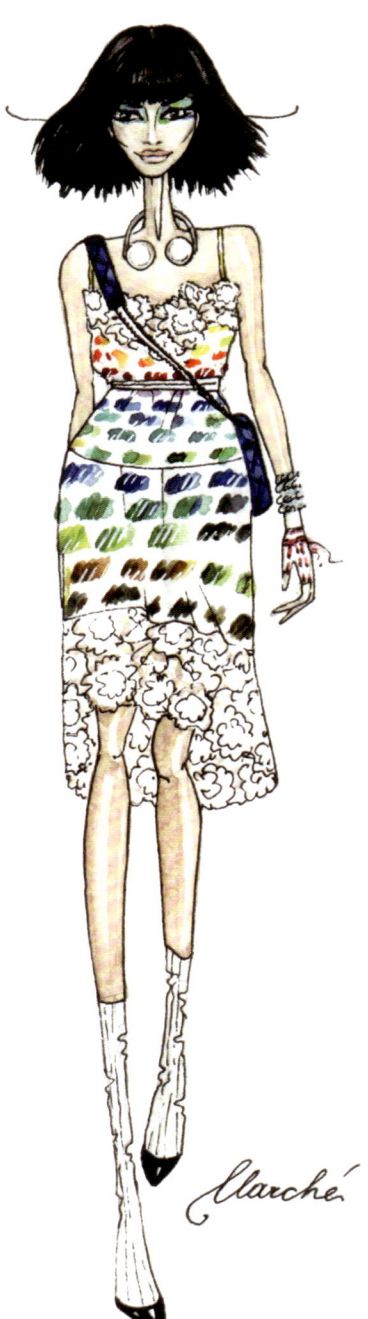

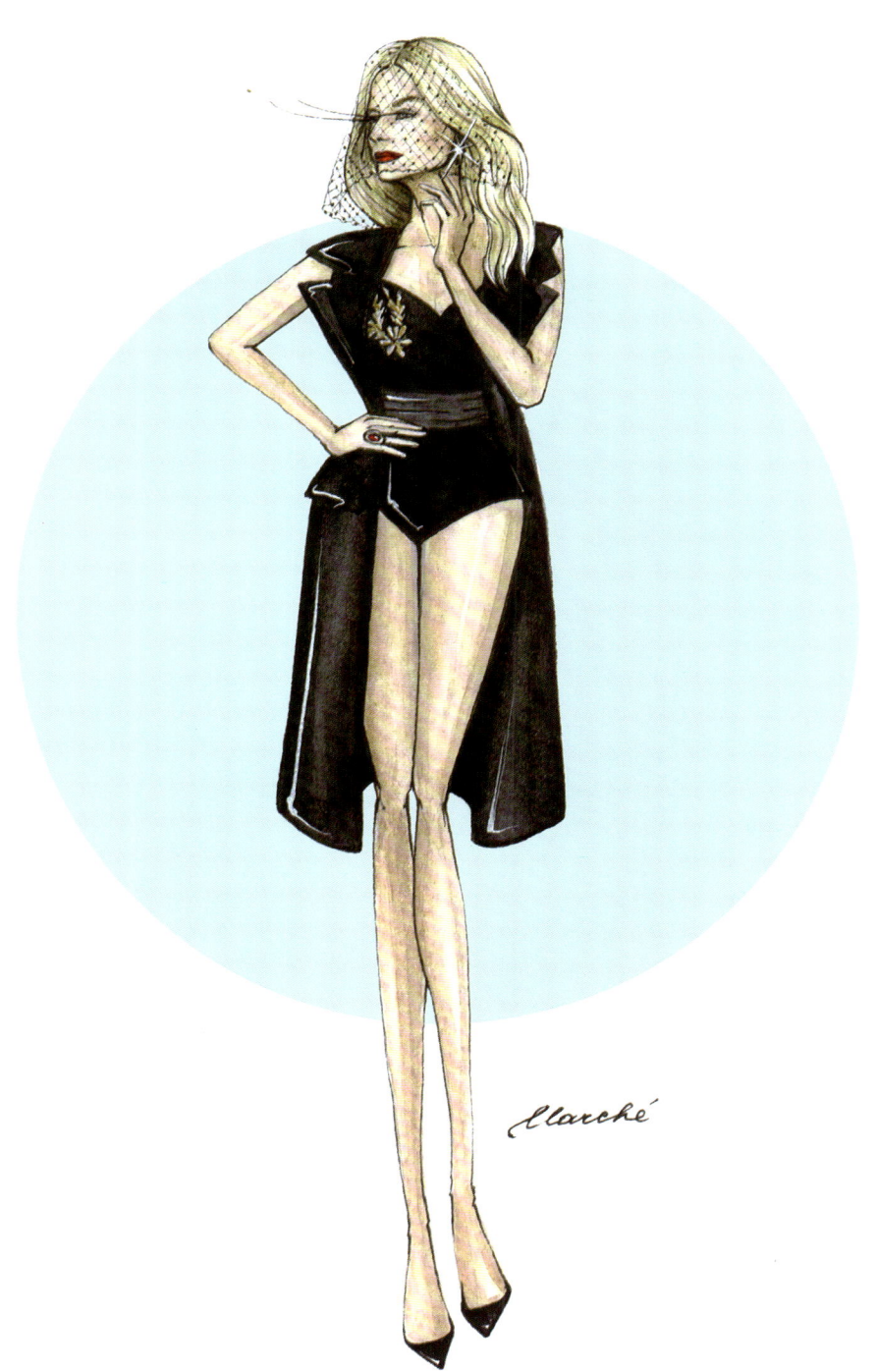

This fashion illustration is a personal order of girl with a veil.
Illustrator: Mariana Marché Country: Ukraine

Girl with a Veil

Marchè Resort 2014 Collection

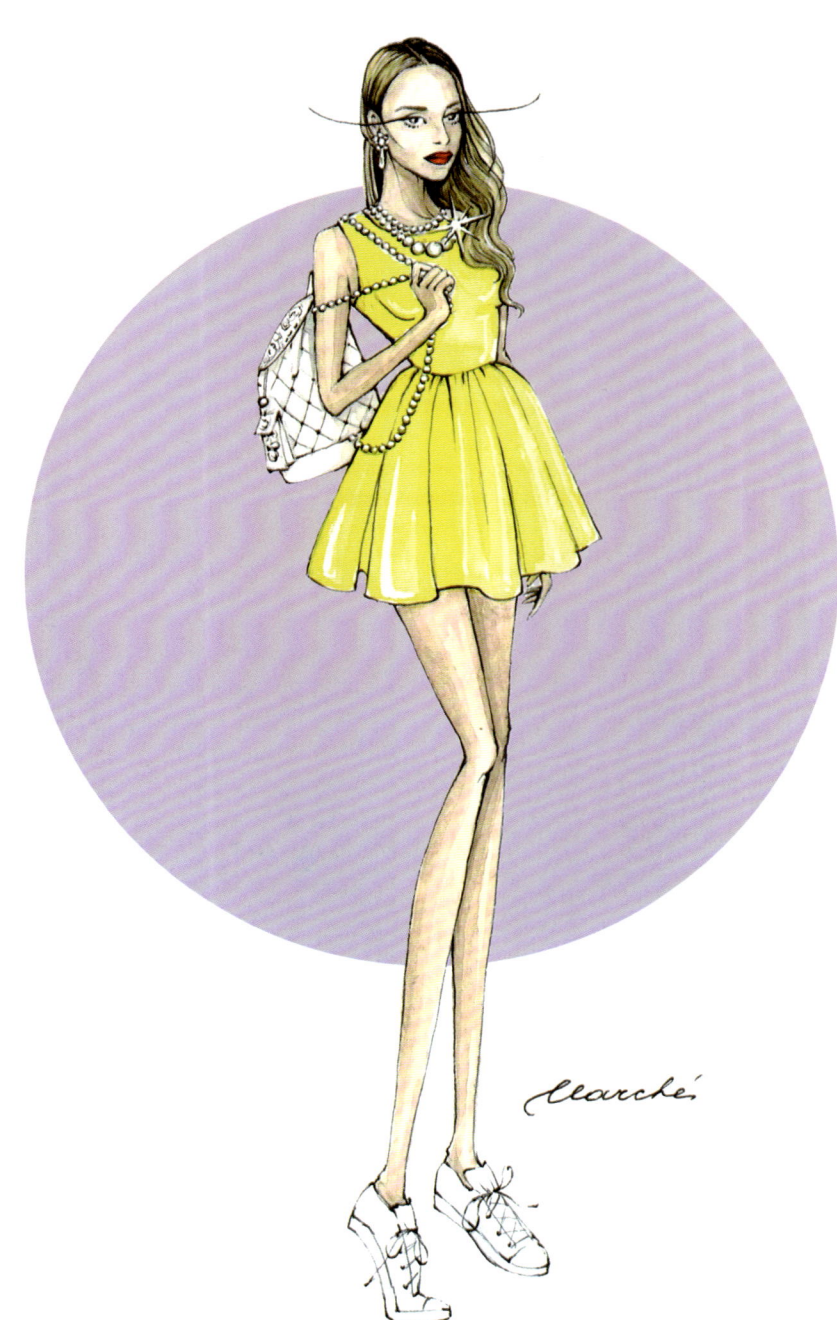

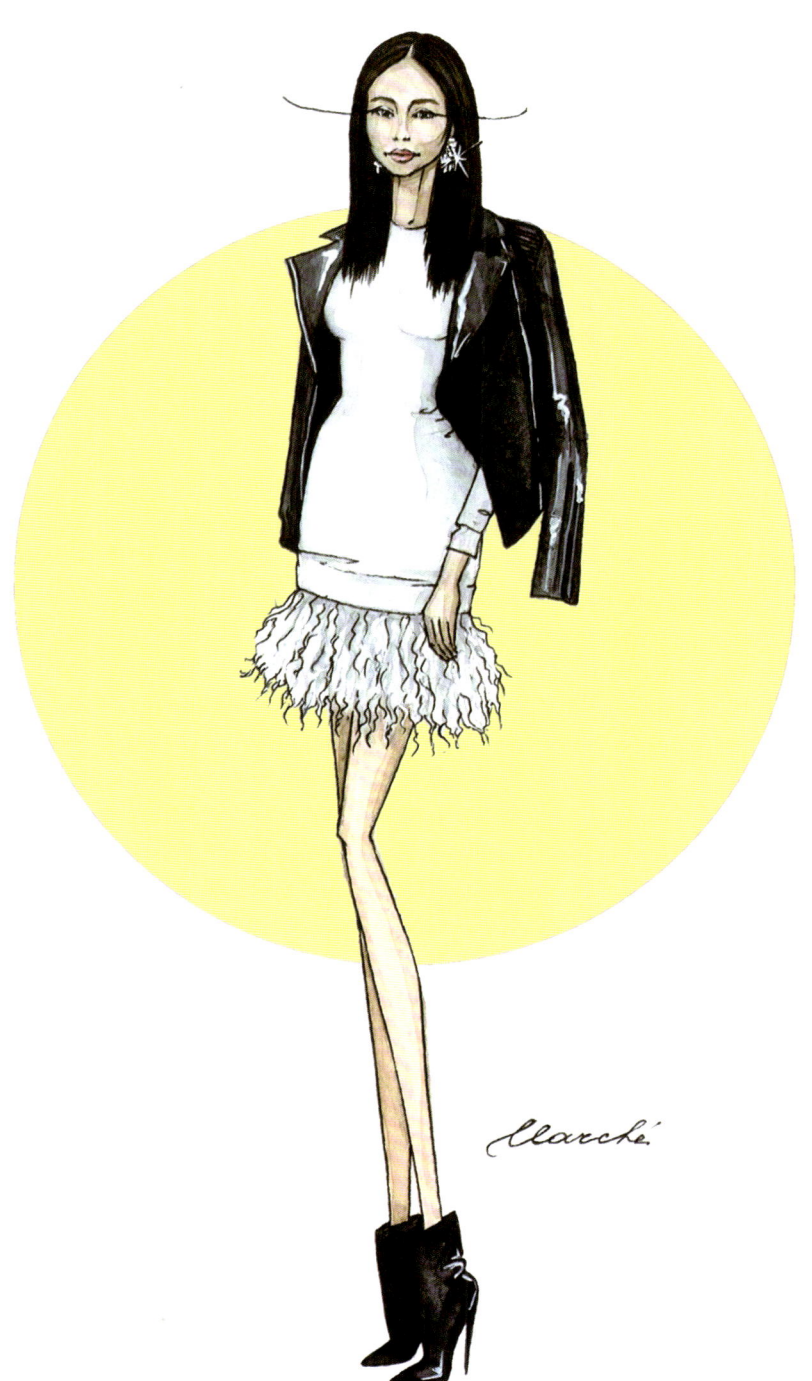

This fashion illustration is a girl from Paris, her looks are always bright and it is always interesting to illustrate.

Illustrator: Mariana Marchè Country: Ukraine

The Coat SK

Diane von Fürstenberg SS 2016 Collection

A beautiful look with unique butterfly embroidery by Diane von Fürstenberg Spring/Summer 2016 collection. The illustration was commissioned by Harper's Bazaar Arabia for March 2016 issue.
Illustrator: Veronica Kensky Client: Harper's Bazaar Arabia Country: Russia

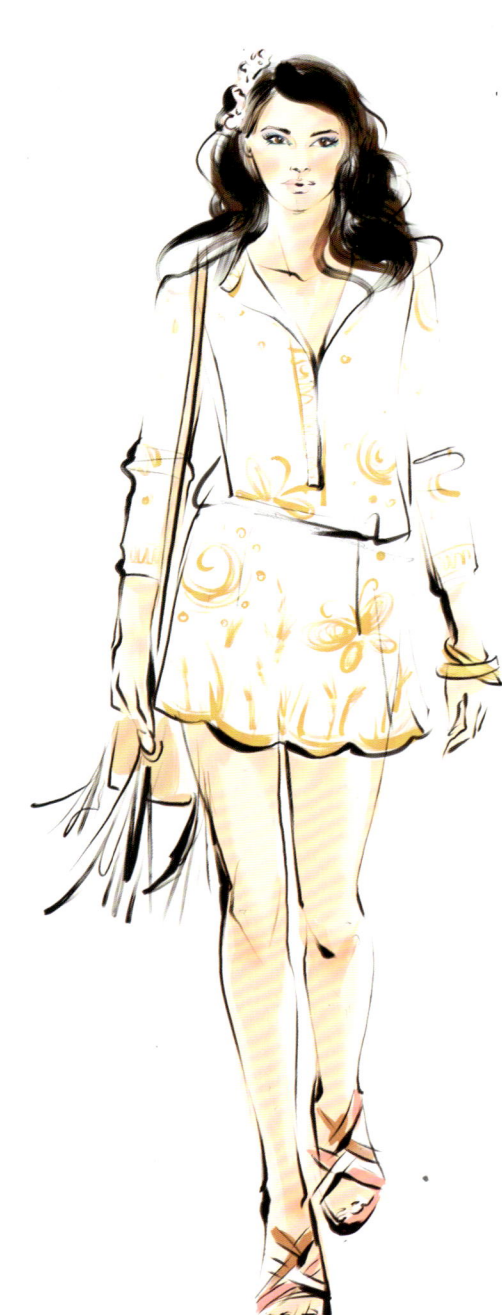

Cute and Sweet

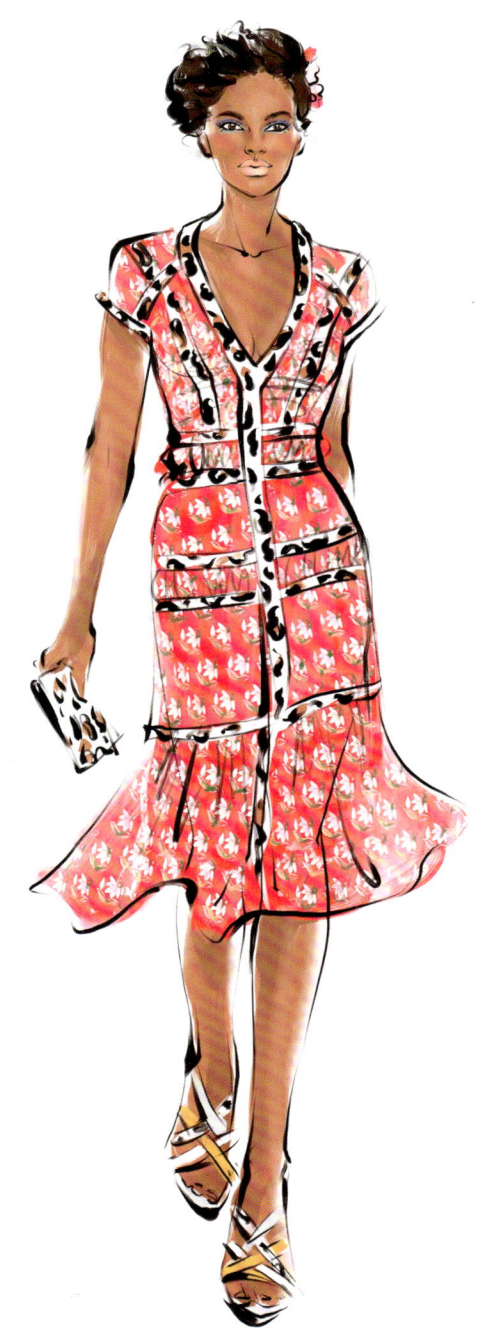

The bright look by Diane von Fürstenberg Spring Summer 2016 collection. The illustration was commissioned by Harper's Bazaar Arabia for March 2016 issue.
Illustrator: Veronica Kemsky Client: Harper's Bazaar Arabia Country: Russia

Diane von Fürstenberg SS 2016 Collection

Print Coat with Plant Pattern

The fashion illustration is made from scratch digitally in Photoshop by watercolour technique.
Illustrator: Mateja Kovac Country: Croatia

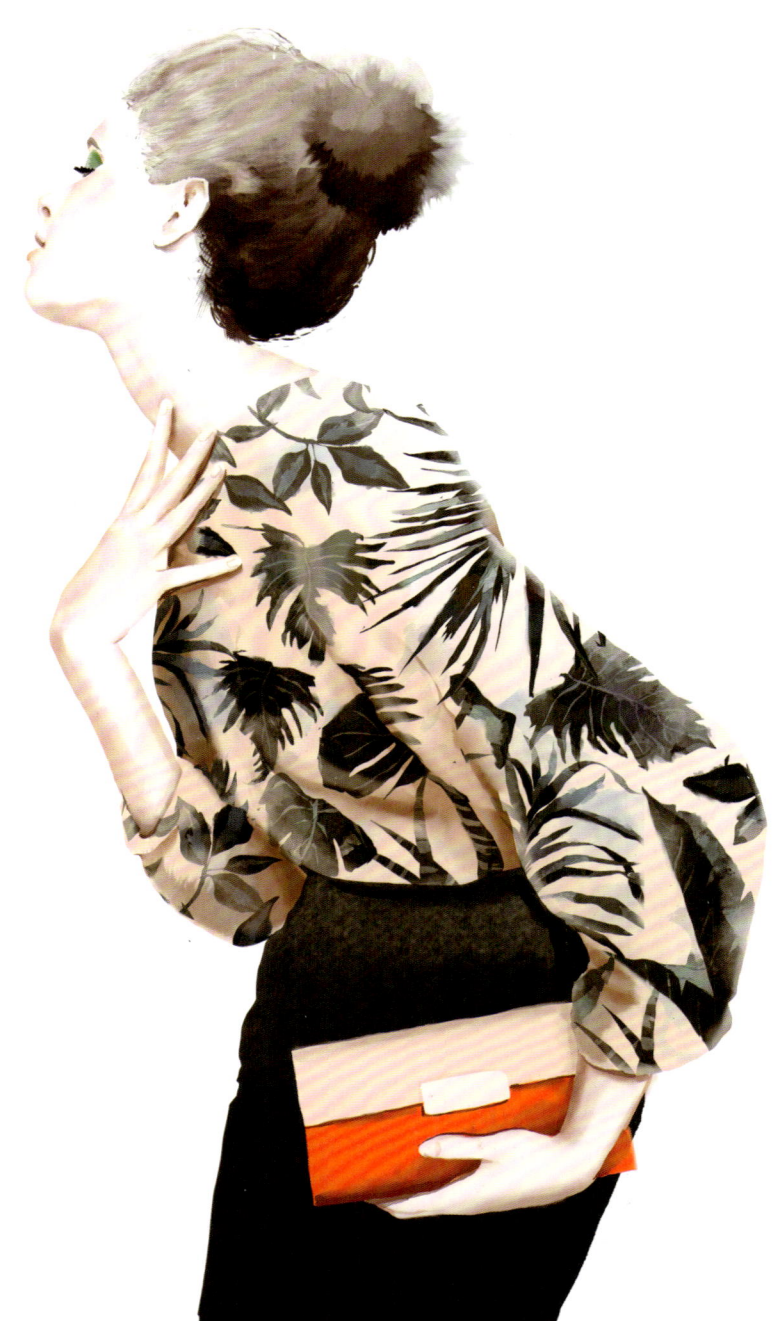

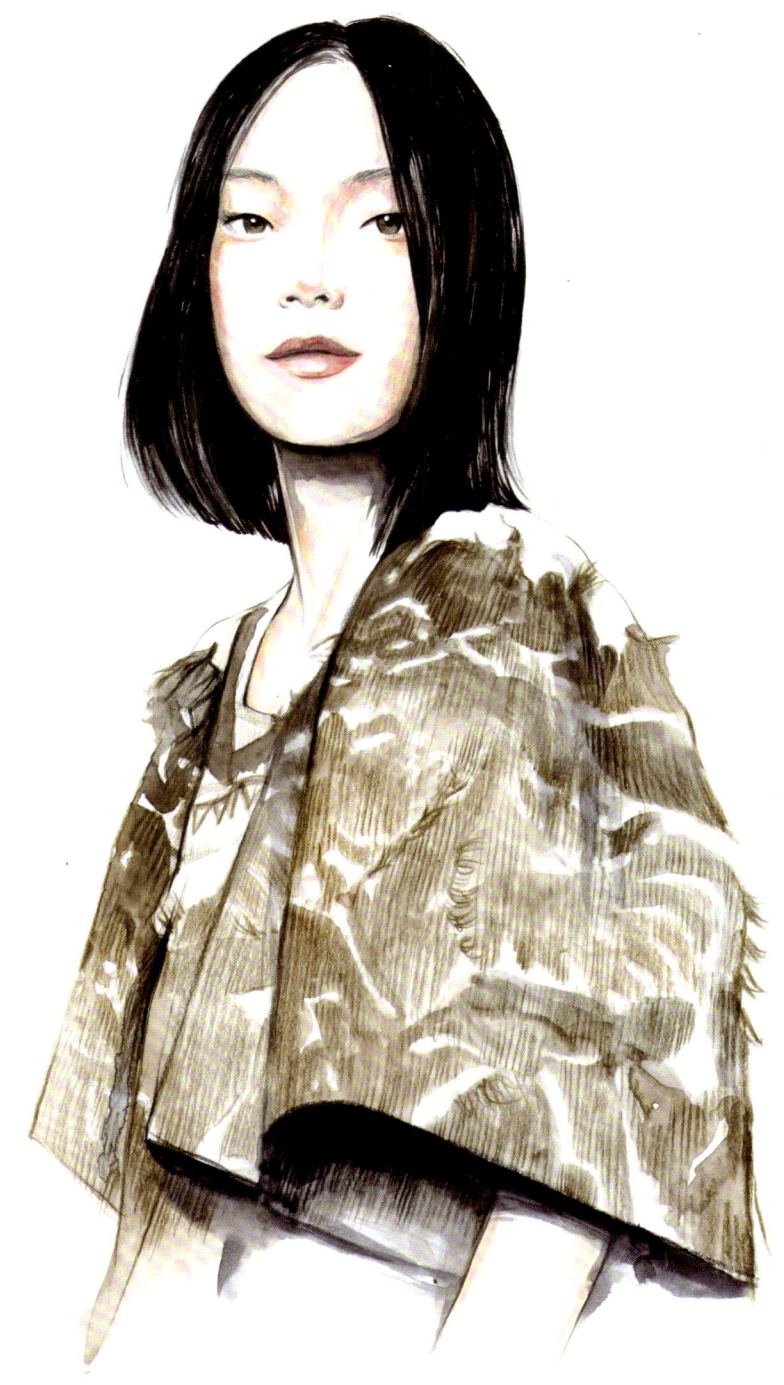

Model Xiao Wen Ju for Chloé spring 2015 collection. Watercolour.
Illustrator: Caroline Andrieu Country: France

Chloé

Elie Saab SS 2014

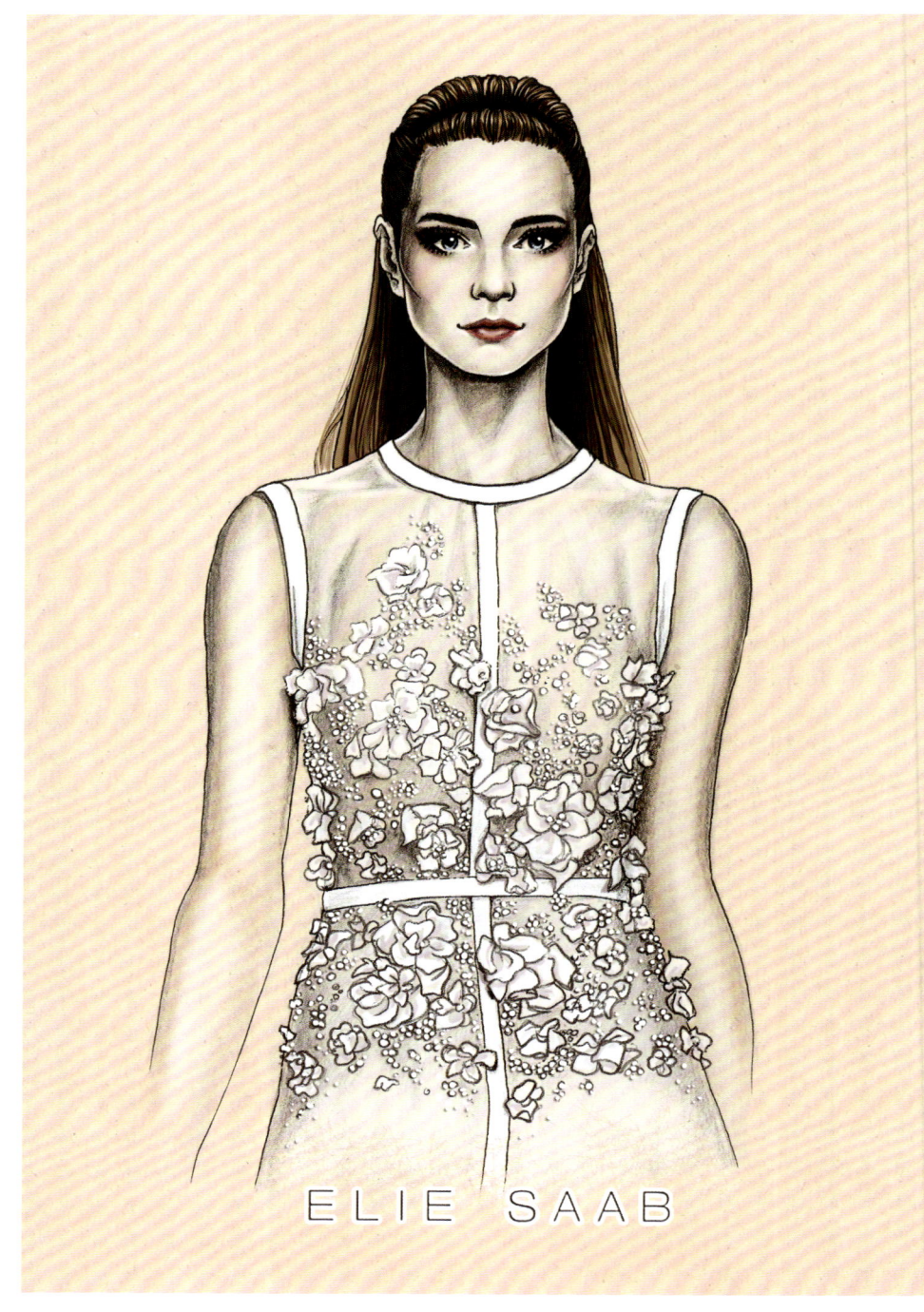

Illustration from Elie Saab Spring Summer 2014 collection. Done on paper and painted in Photoshop CS5.
Illustrator: Tania Santos Country: Portugal

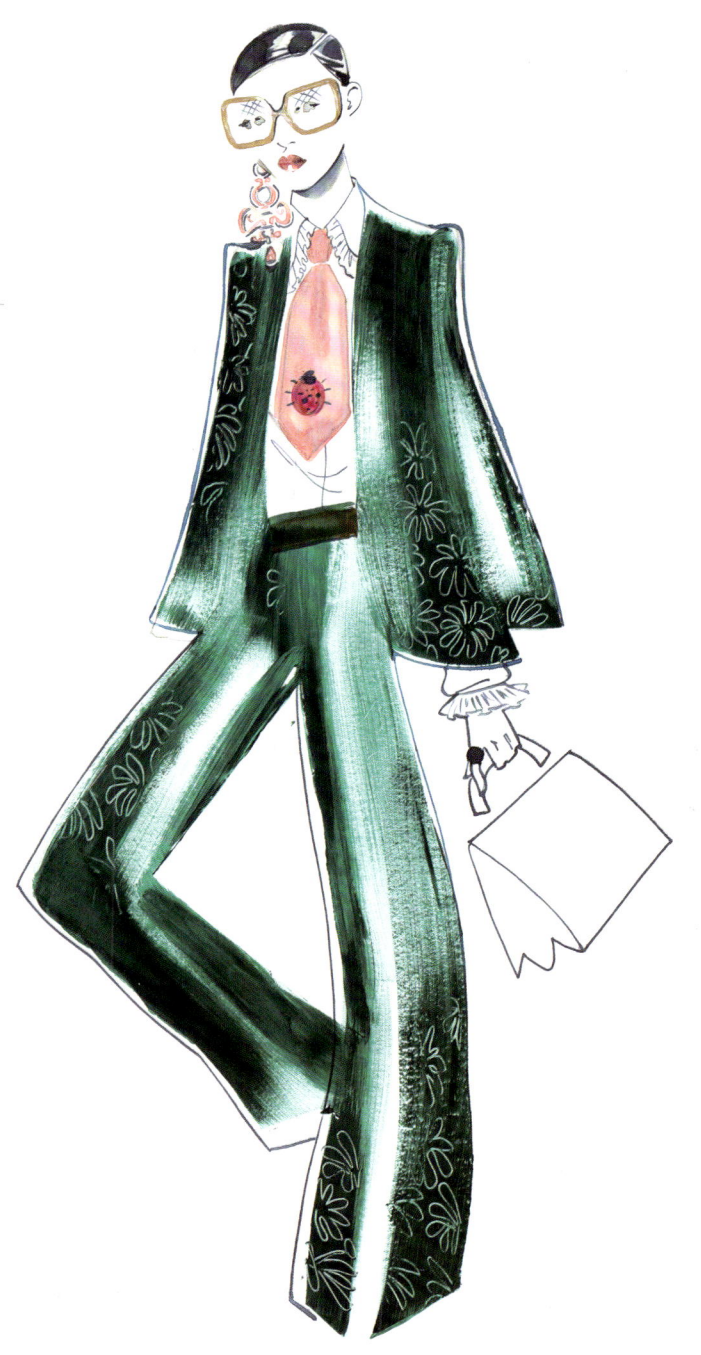

Mixted technique illustration for fashion week October 15. Gucci collection summer 2016.
Illustrator: Margot Van Huijkelom Country:France

Gucci Suit

Dolce & Gabbana Fall 2013

Illustration of a dress designed by Mélique Street and inspired by the Dolce & Gabbana fall 2013 collection.
Illustrator: Mélique Street Country: Italy

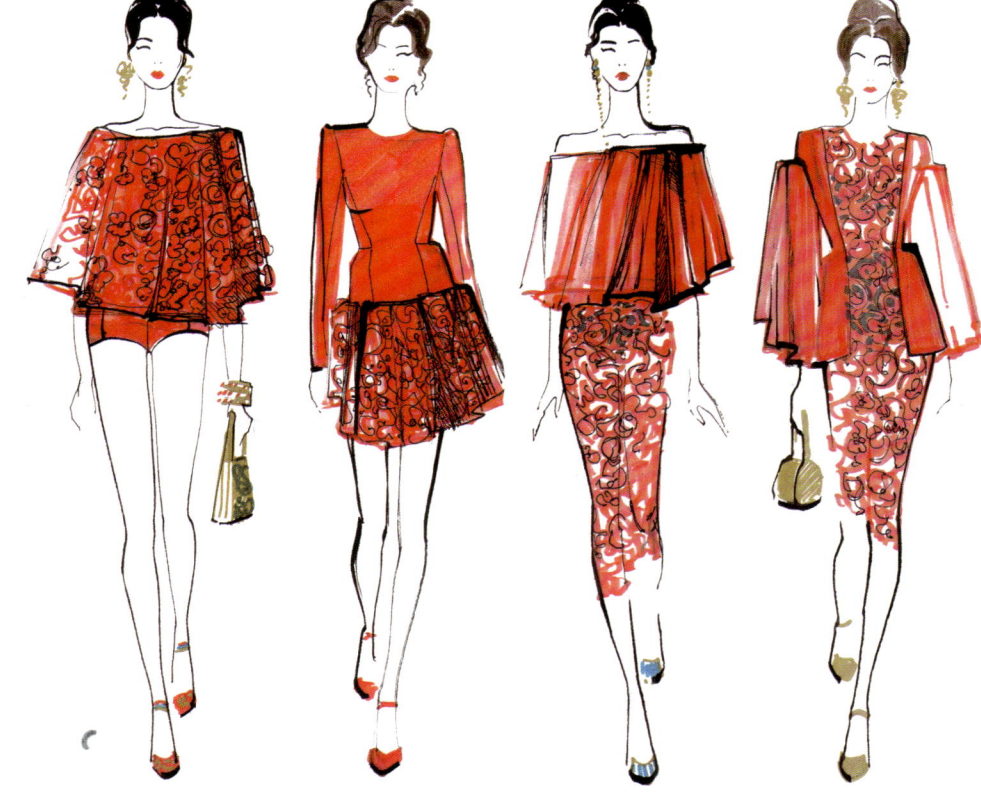

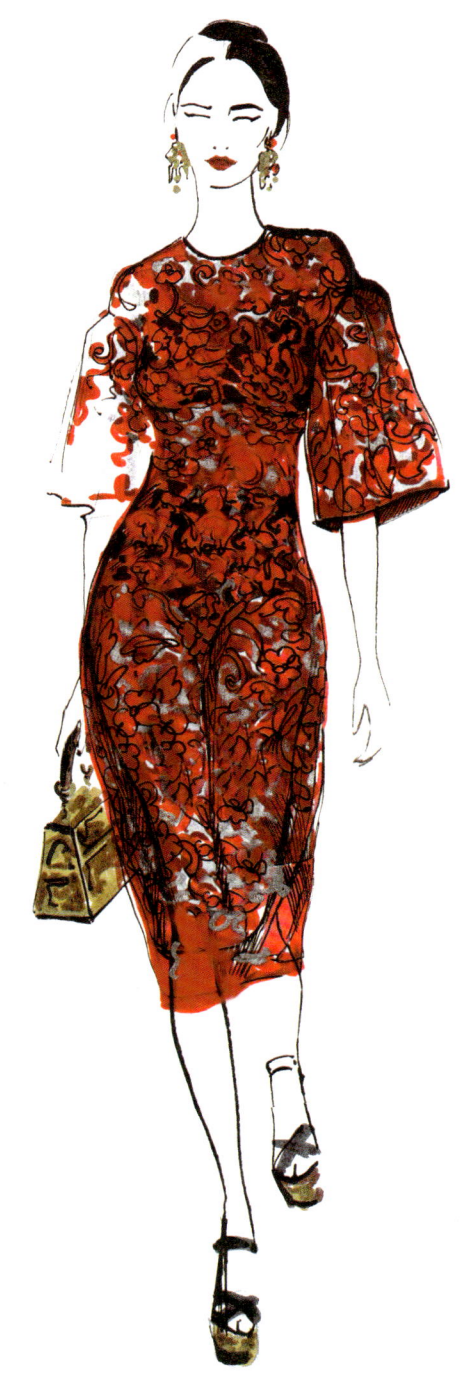

Illustration from the Milan Fashion Week with a figurine wearing a dress from the Dolce & Gabbana fall 2013 collection.
Illustrator: Mélique Street Country: Italy

Dolce & Gabbana Fall 2013

Pink Suit

Inspiration comes from Diana Enciu's outfit. A nice look suitable for early spring.
Illustrator: Maggie Ai Country: China

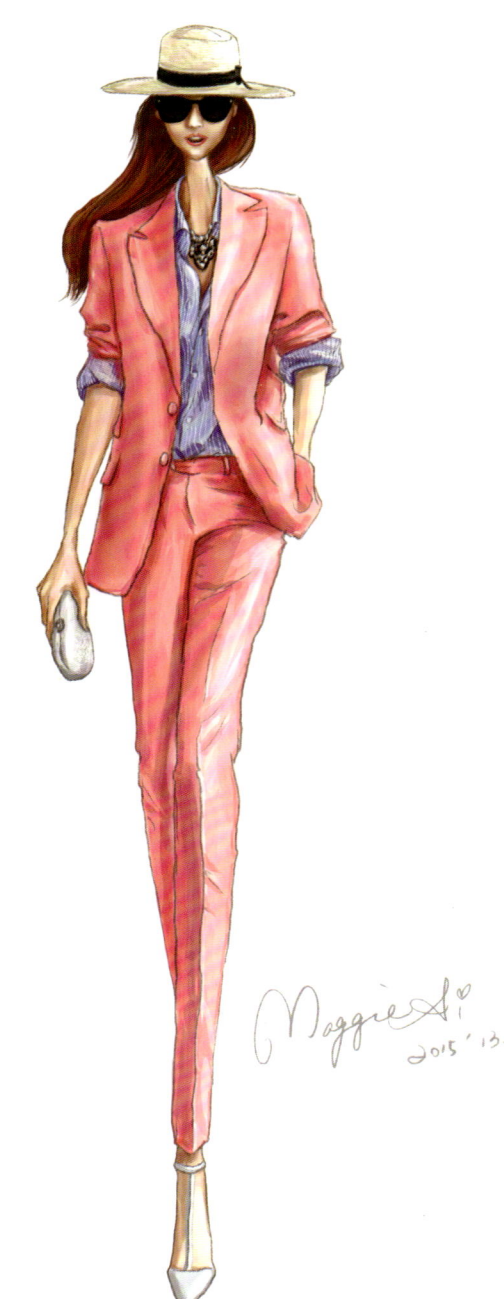

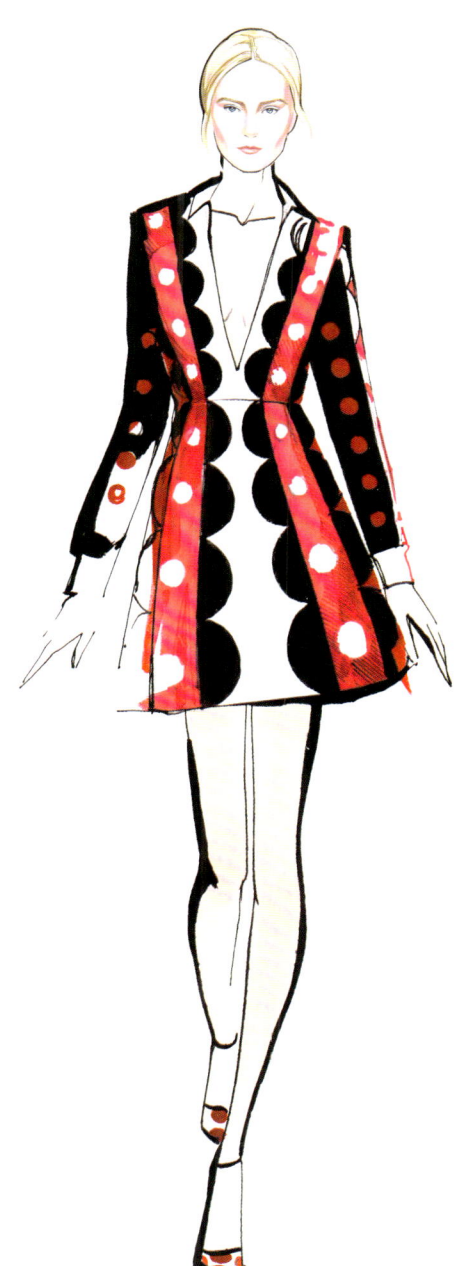
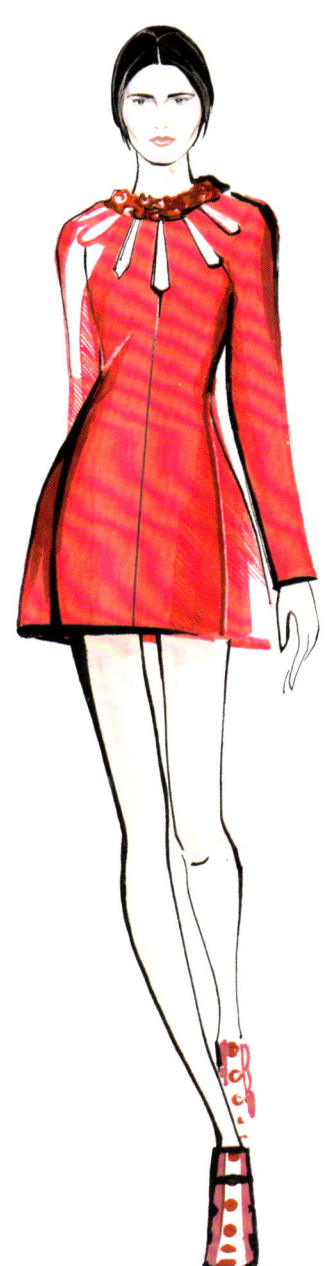

Illustration from the Paris Fashion Week featuring Harleth Kuusik and Iana Godnia wearing dresses from the Maison Valentino winter 2014 collection.
Illustrator: Mélique Street Country: Italy

Maison Valentino Winter 2014

Frozen Kingdom FW 2013-2014

Watercolour: Fashion Illustration for Fall Winter Collection of Russian designer Ksenia Knyazeva. Represented watercolour print 'Frozen Kingdom', which was the base of Capsule Collection.
Illustrator: Irina Kaygorodova Country: Russia

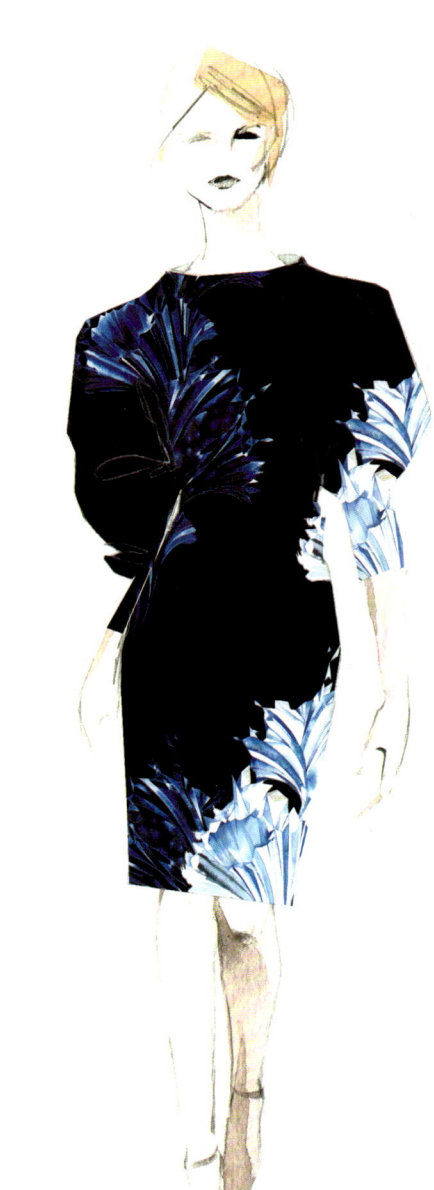
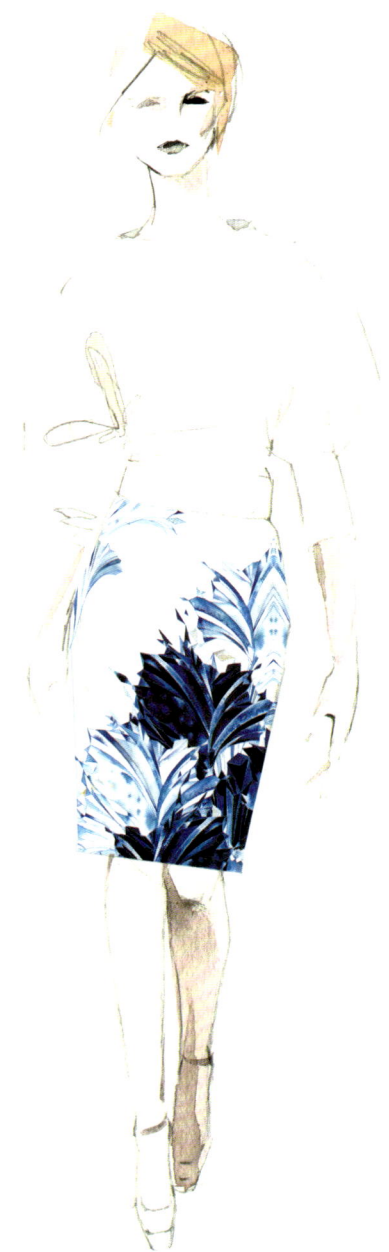

112 — Classic Elegance

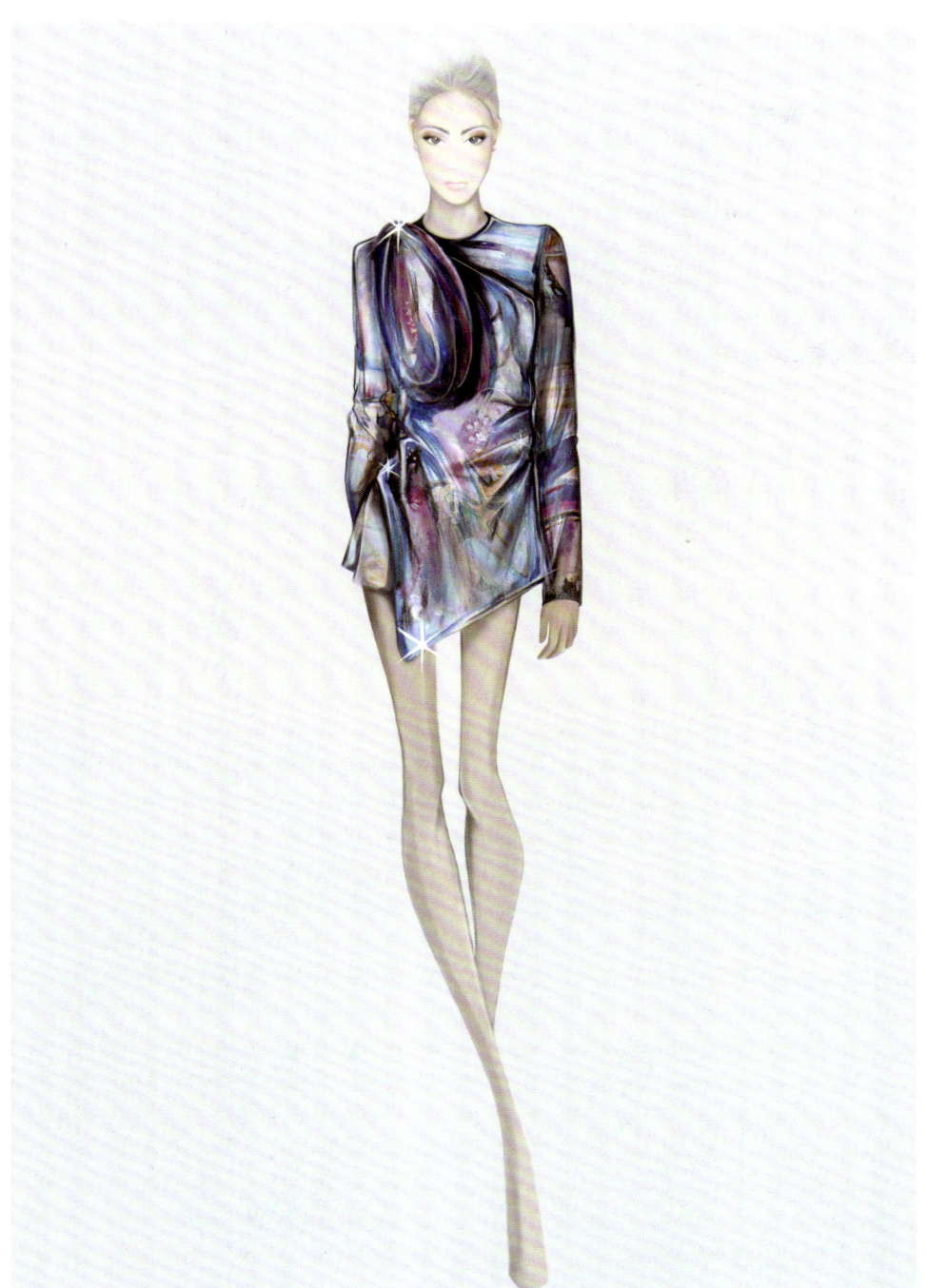

Illustration of unconventional bow dress that steps away from the ideal beauty such as the conventional proper bows and draping. Print Inspired by Paul Guiragossian's painting.
Illustrator: Rahel Guiragossian Country: Germany

Bow Dress from Rahel Guiragossian Collection

Dior 2015

The concept of this editorial is based on the realistic representation of the rich materials, where some of the individual collections are made emphasizing the diversity of combined textures, colours and details.
Illustrator: Mateja Kovac Country: Croatia

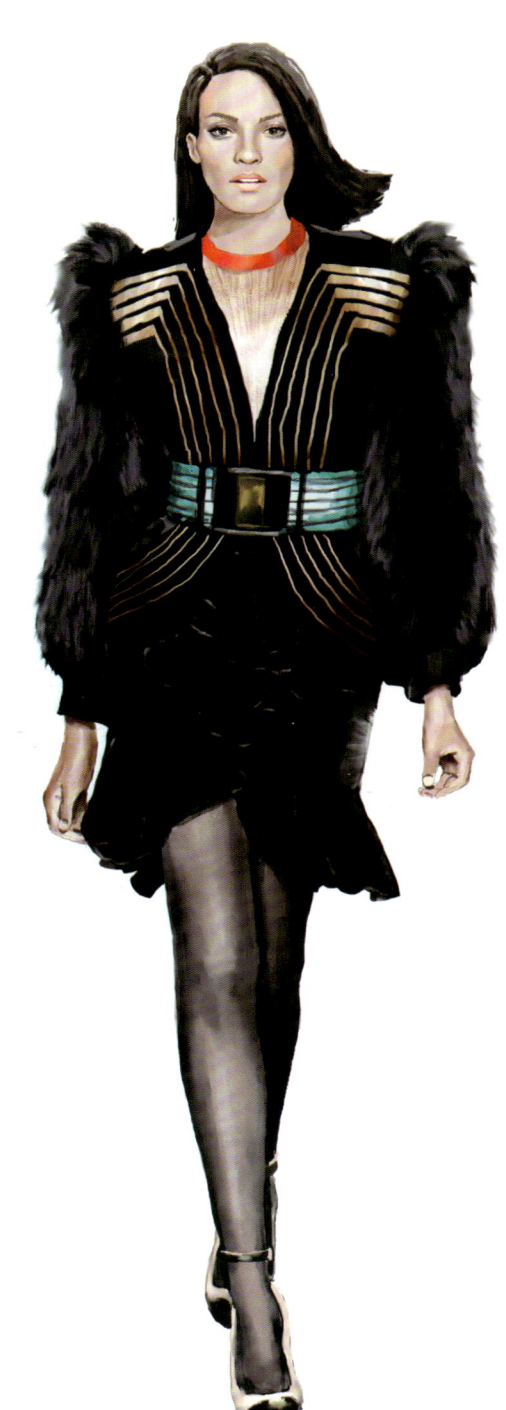

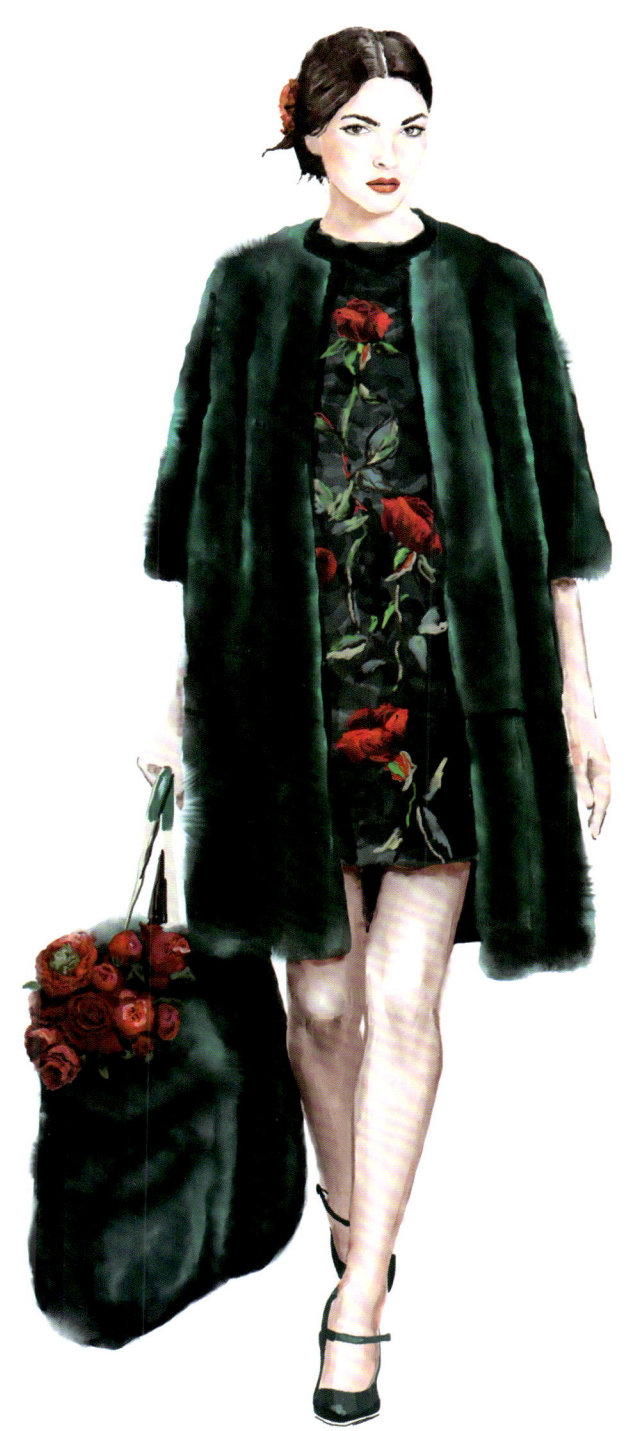

This work inspired by Dolce Gabanna, editorial work for Rouge magazine.
Illustrator: Mateja Kovac Country: Croatia

Dolce Gabanna

Giambatista Valli

Editorial work for Rouge magazine, aiming to reflect the texture of the clothes.
Illustrator: Mateja Kovac Country: Croatia

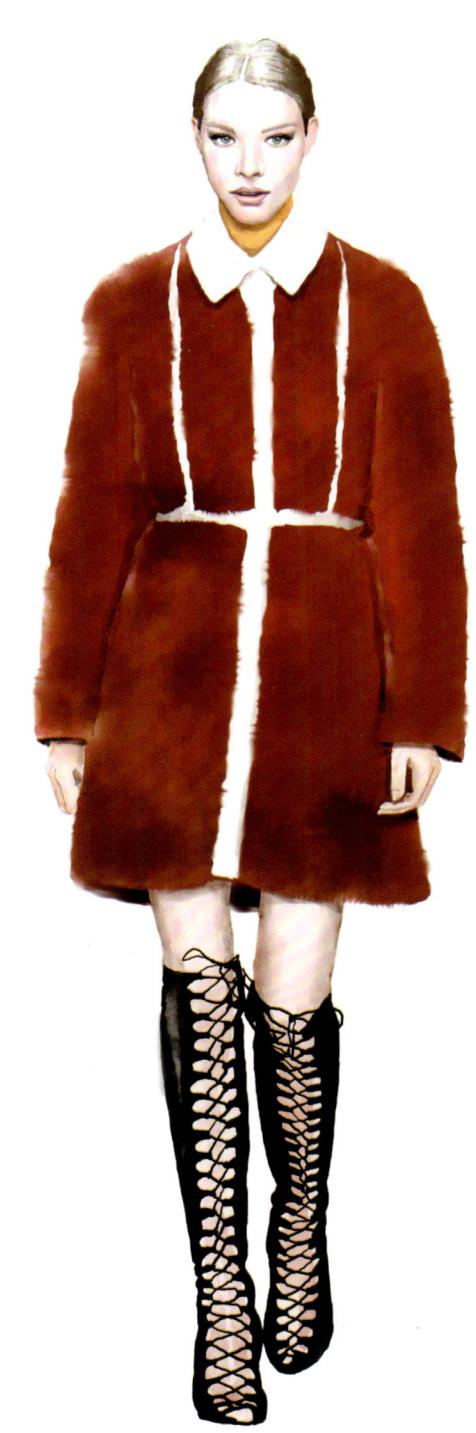

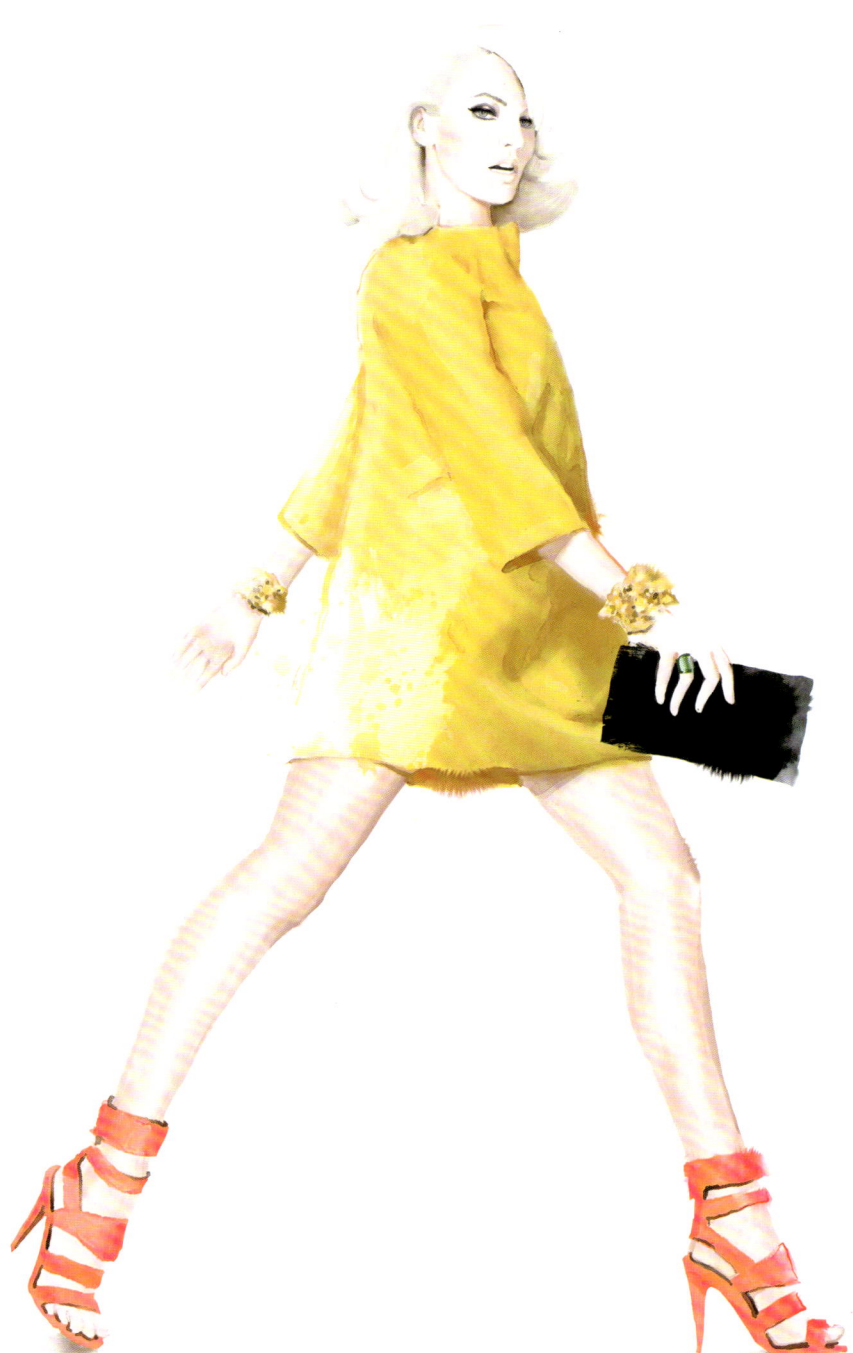

Through this work, the illustrator aims to portray the natural beauty of the woman, realistic proportions, sensuality, and the grace in movements taken after the old masters of fashion illustration.
Illustrator: Mateja Kova Country: Croatia

Elegant Yellow Dress

Ports

Editorial work for Rouge magazine. The work aims to reflect the texture and details of the clothes.
Illustrator: Mateja Kovac Country: Croatia

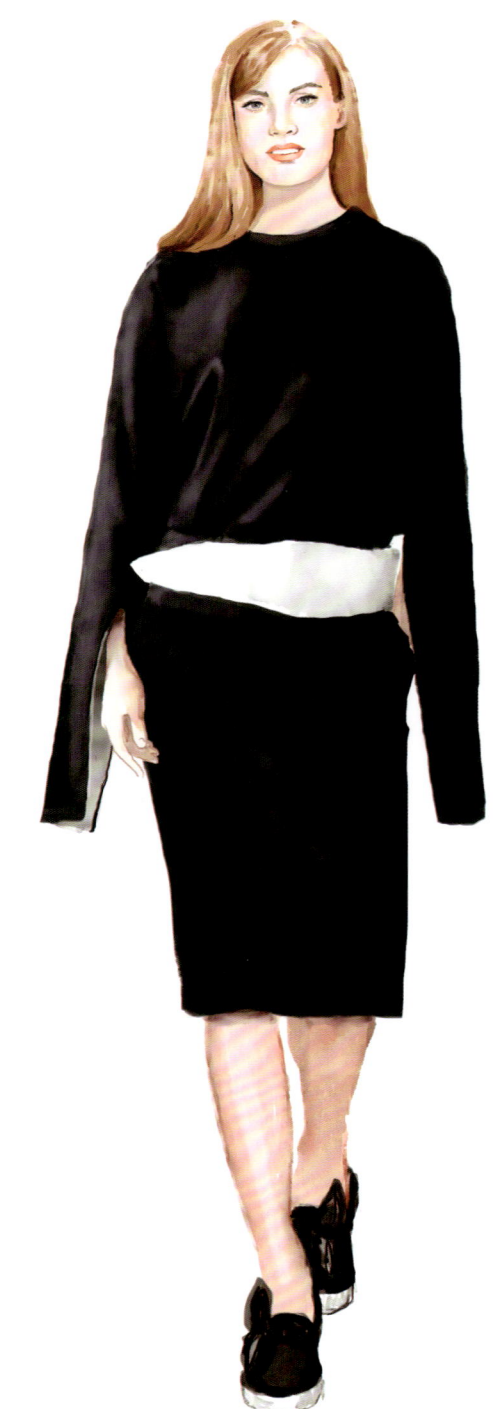

Classic Elegance

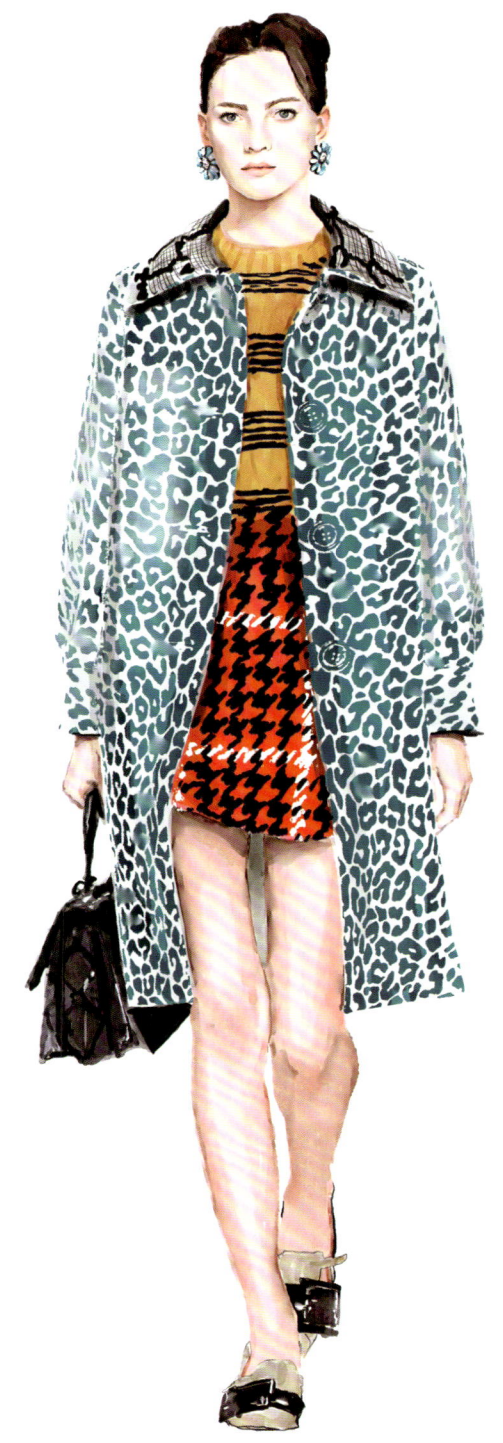

This work inspired by Miu Miu, editorial work for Rouge magazine.
Illustrator: Mateja Kovac Country: Croatia

Miu Miu

Prada

This work inspired by Prada, editorial work for Rouge magazine.
Illustrator: Mateja Kovac Country: Croatia

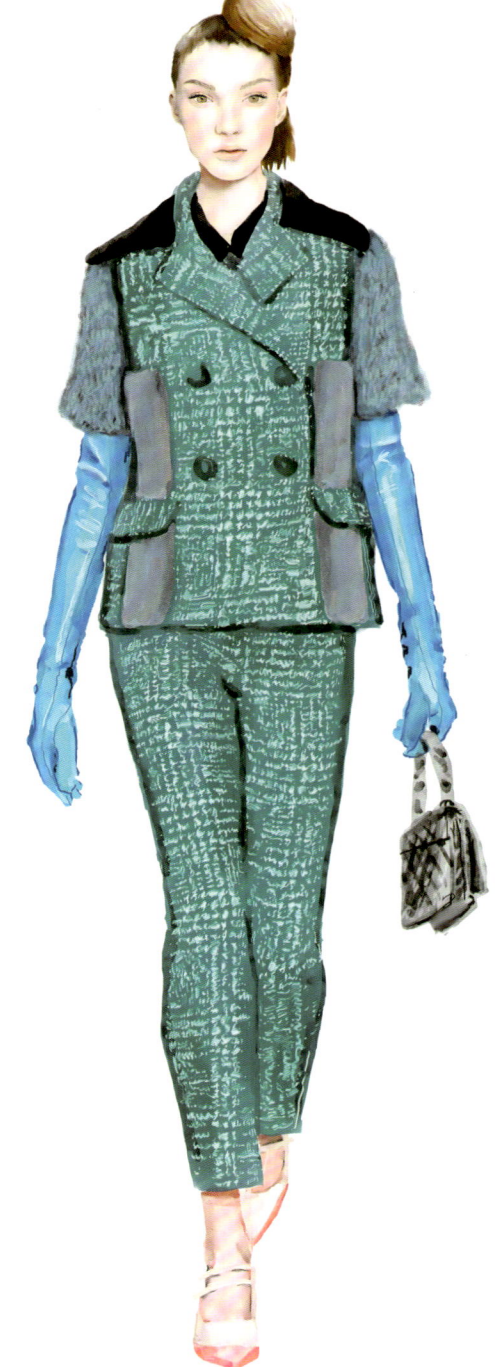

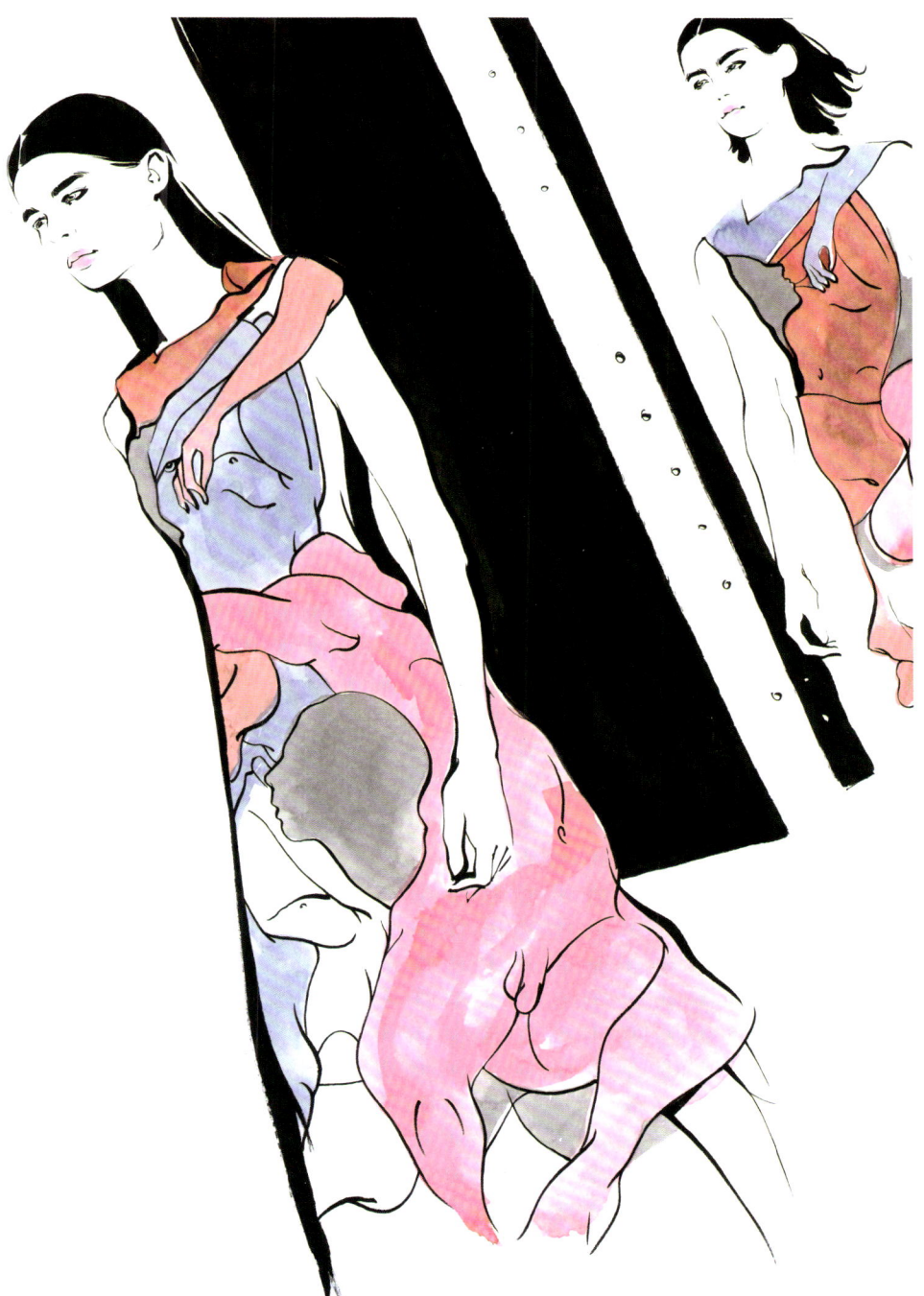

Editorial work for vogue.ru. Runway moment at Christopher Kane show, London Fashion Week RTW FW 2015. Illustrator: Alena Lavdovskaya Country: Russia

Christopher Kane RTW FW 2015

Chanel RTW FW 2015

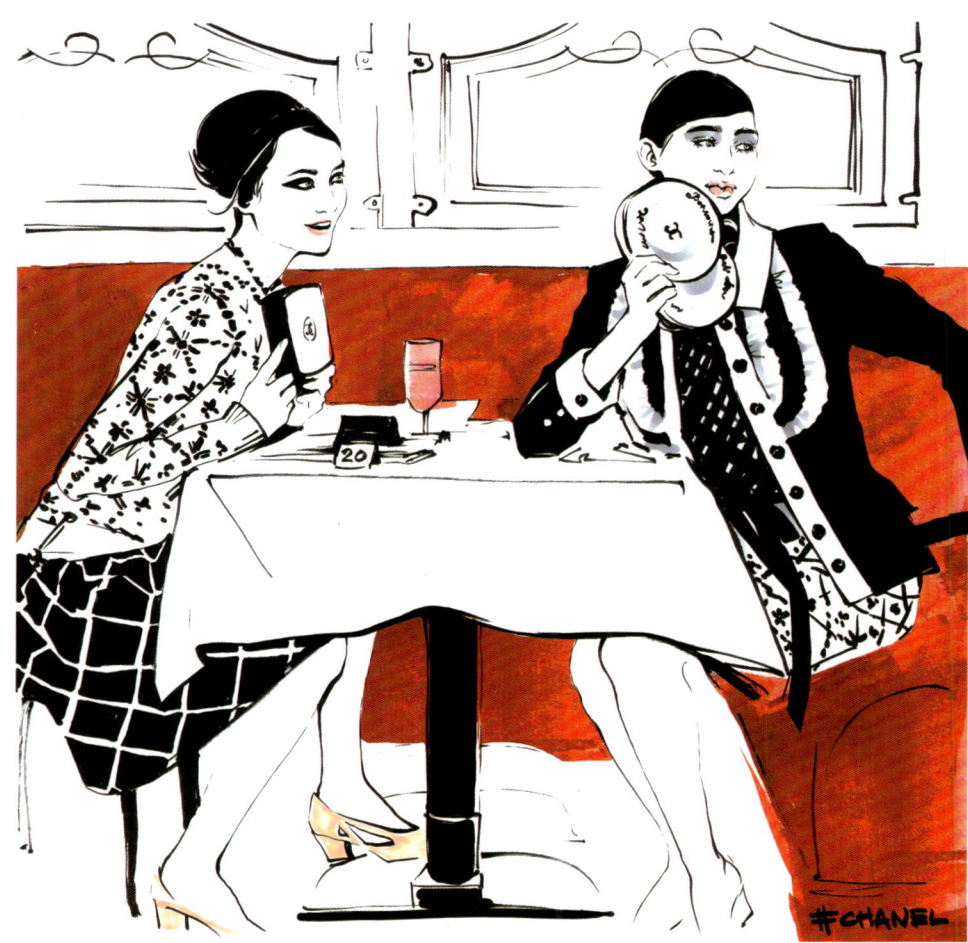

Runway moment at Chanel show, Paris Fashion Week RTW FW 2015. Editorial work for vogue.ru
Illustrator: Alena Lavdovskaya Country: Russia

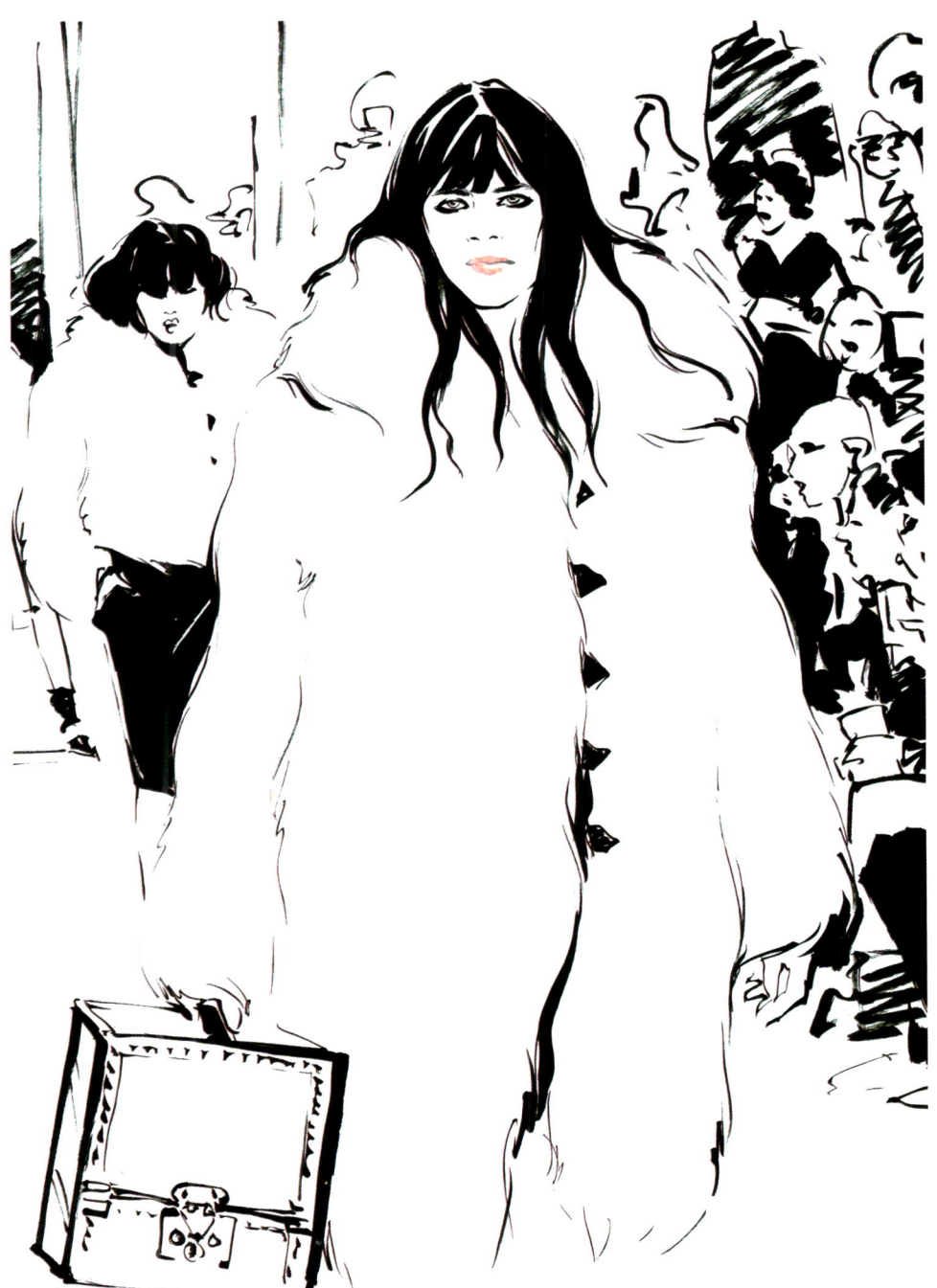

Editorial work for vogue.ru. Runway moment at Louis Vuitton show, Paris Fashion Week RTW FW 2015.
Illustrator: Alena Lavdovskaya Country: Russia

Louis Vuitton RTW FW 2015

Delpozo Autumn Winter 2016-2017

In this work, the illustrator highlighted the contrast between the simple shape of the dress and the decorative elements of the style. Tools used are, charcoal pencil, ink, watercolour and digital finishing.

Illustrator: Natsuki Otani Country: Japan

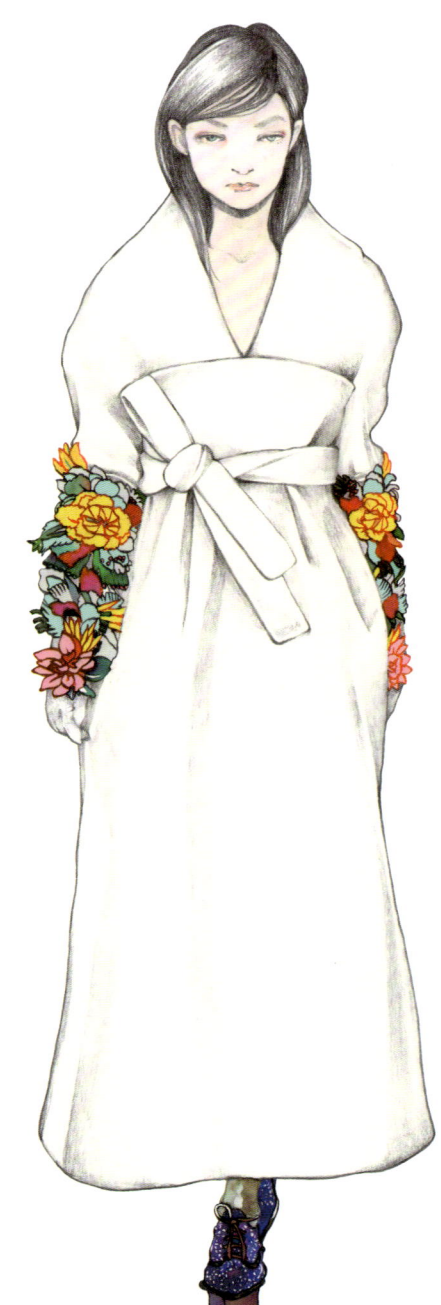

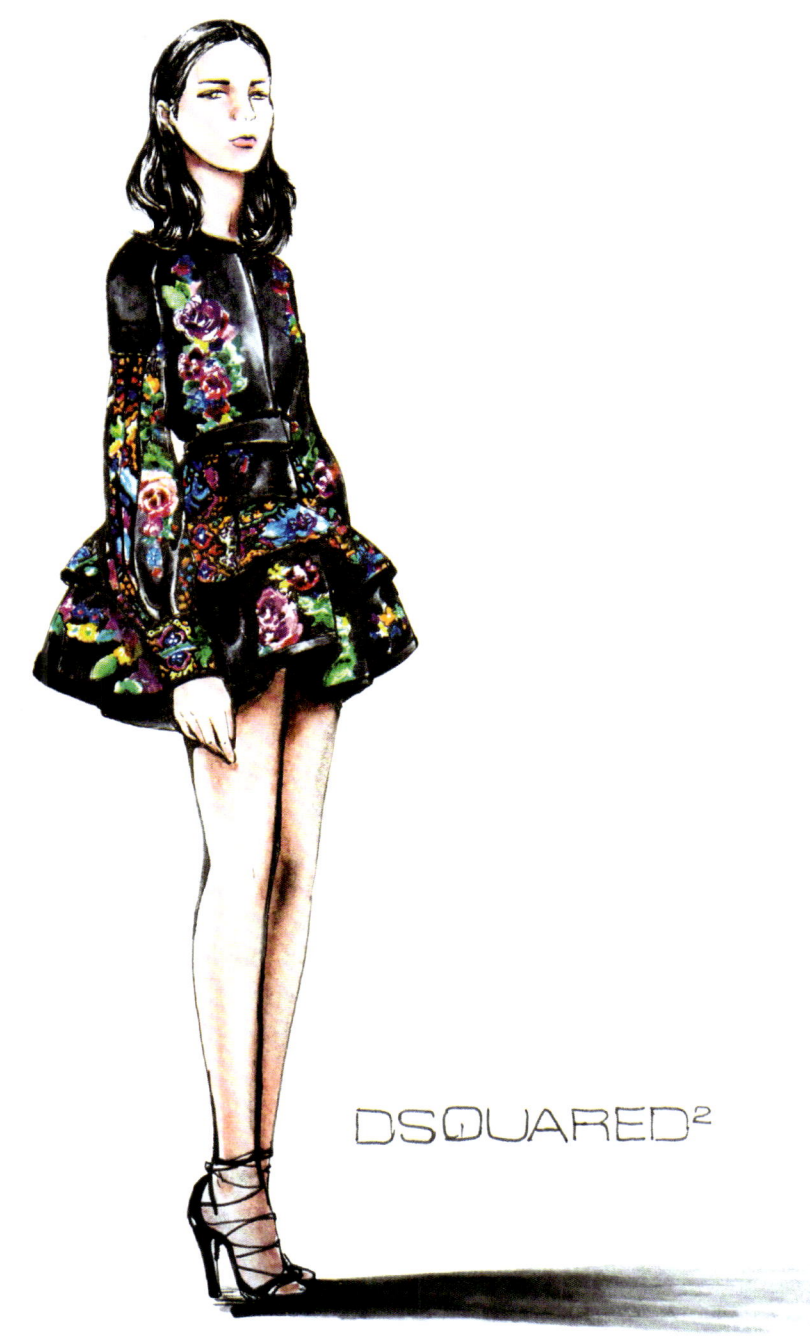

Inspired by Dsquared2 2015 Pre-Fall collection. Floral print is always a solution when you can not decide what to wear for the day.
Illustrator: Kiara Tan Country: China

Dsquared2 2015 Pre-Fall

Delpozo FW 2015

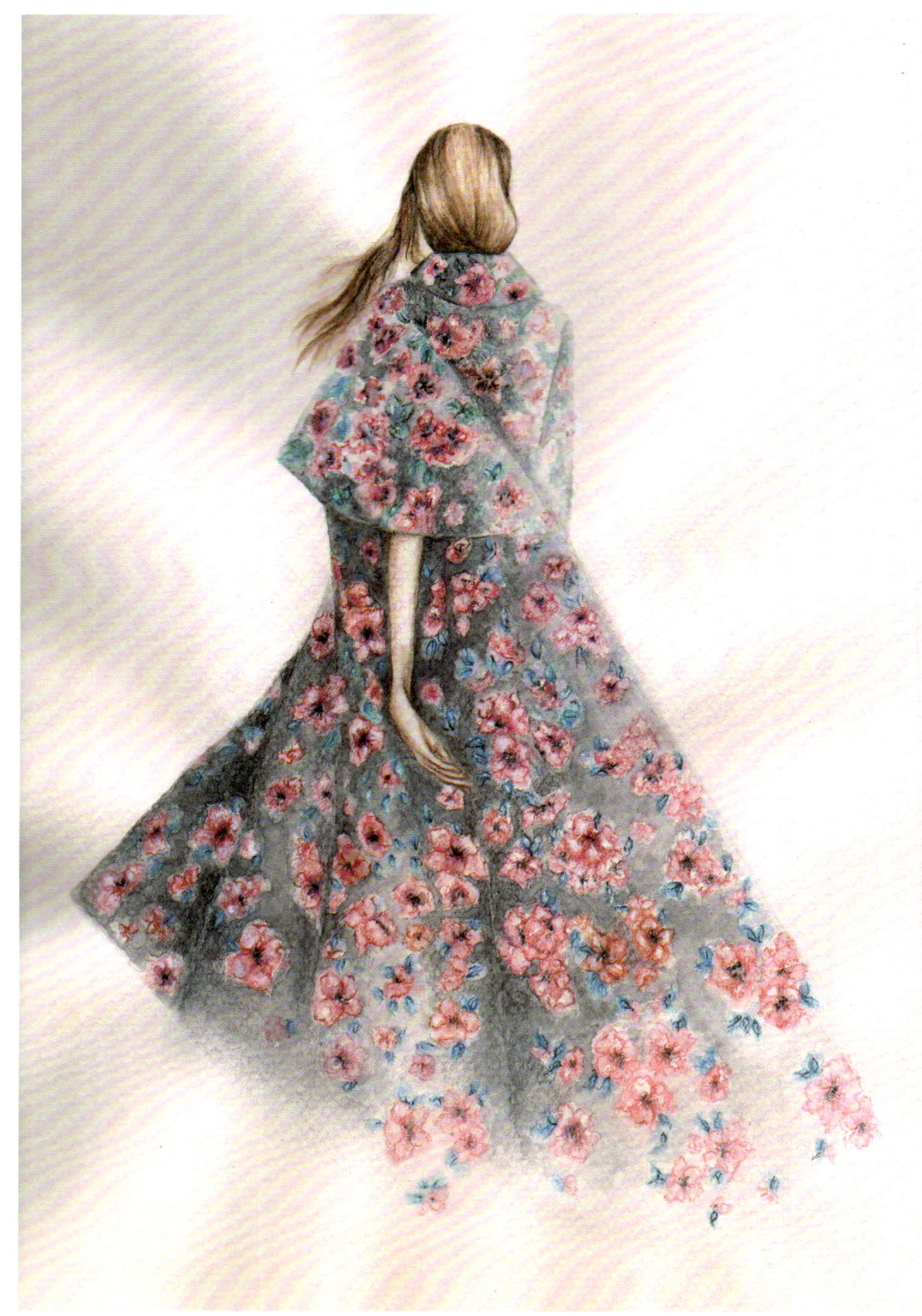

Illustration made in watercolour and pastel inspired in a magazine picture of the look.
Illustrator: Natalia Zamora Country: Colombia

Illustration made in watercolours of the author's favourite look of the collection.
Illustrator: Natalia Zamora Country: Colombia

'Freedom Ballerina' Marc Jacobs FW 2015

Little Black Dress

Watercolour, ink and pencil on high quality Fabriano paper.
Illustrator: Alicia Malesani Client: TIME OUT Hong kong Country: Spain

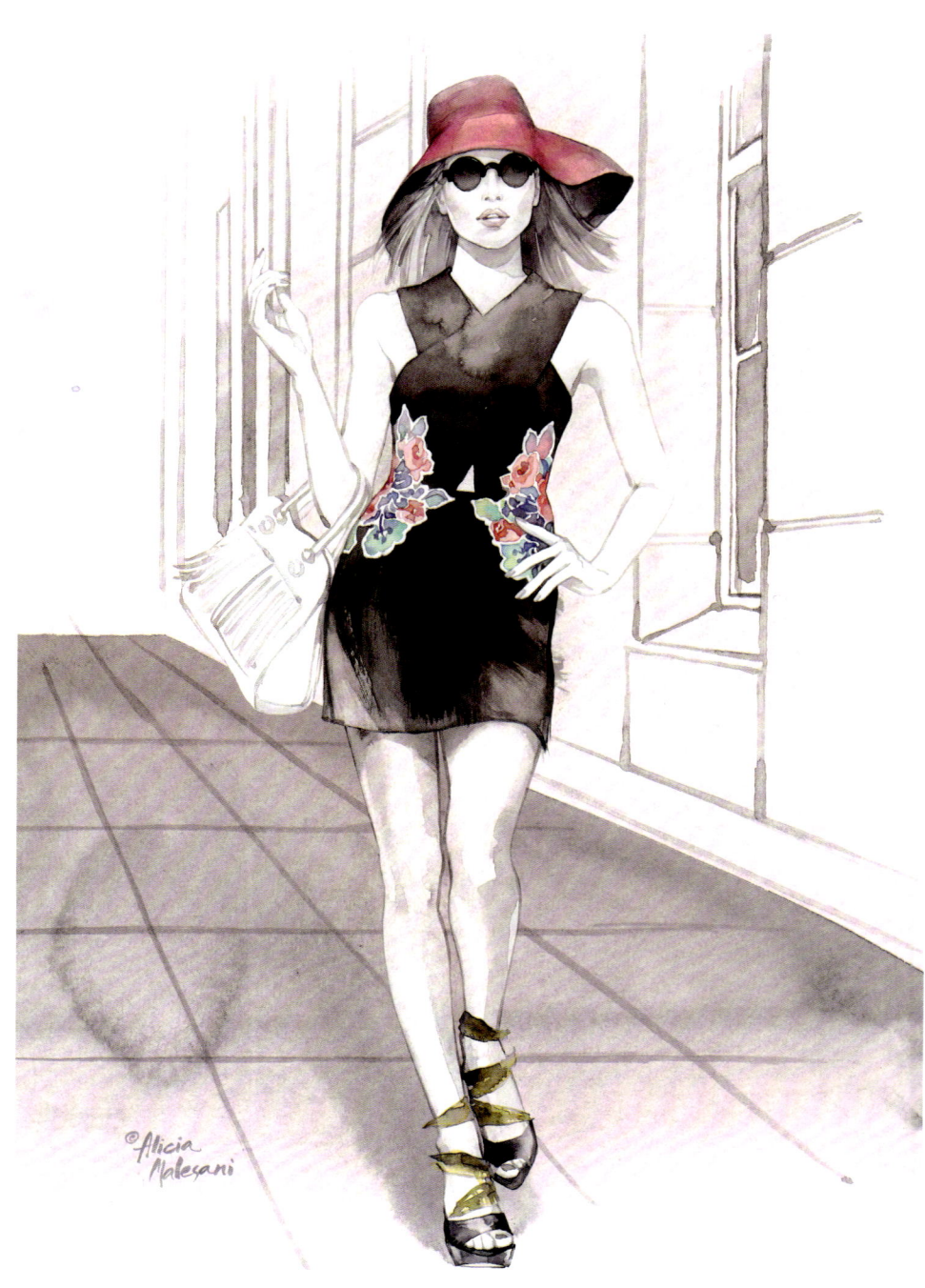

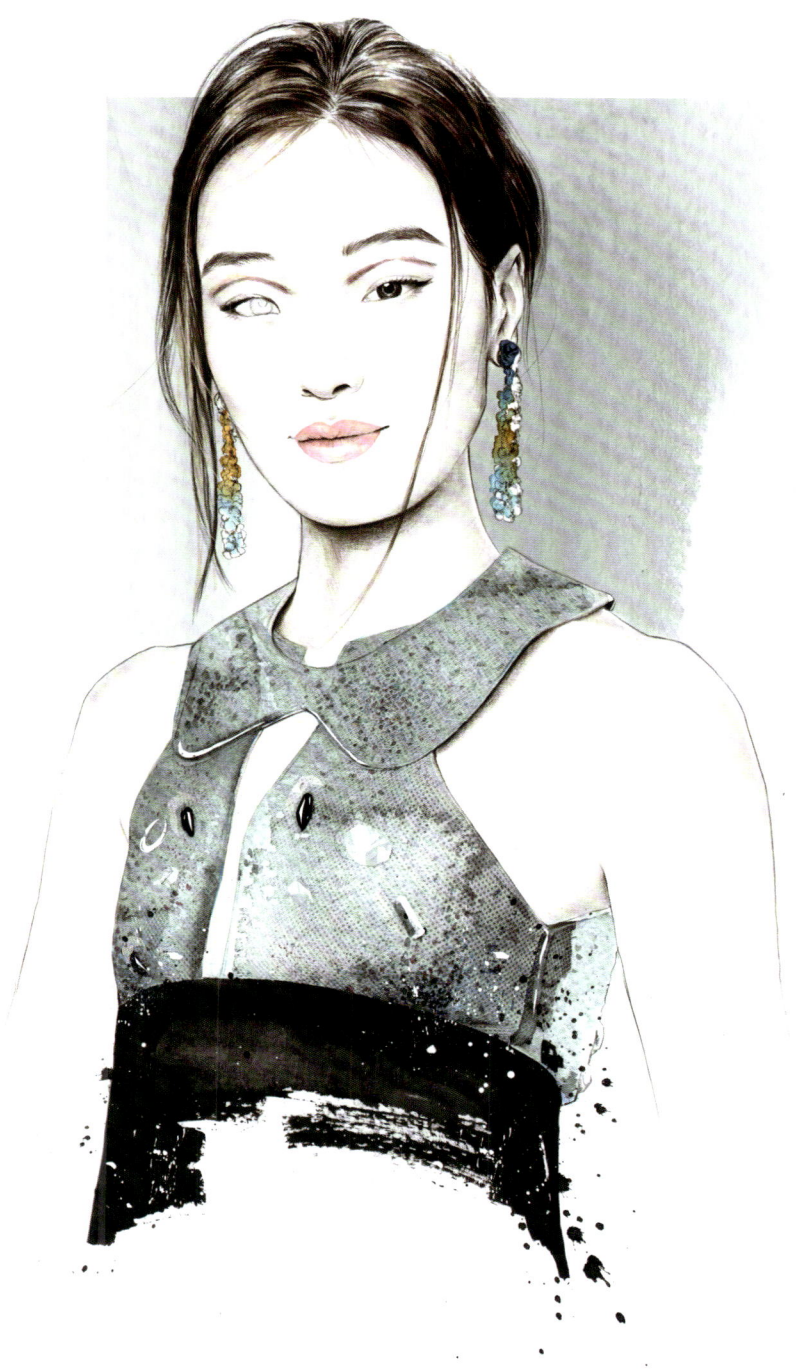

Beauty editorial for Vogue Nippon spring trends, use pencil, ink and digital.
Illustrator: Esra Roise Country: Norway

Prada Sleeveless Shirt SS 2015

Black and White Woman

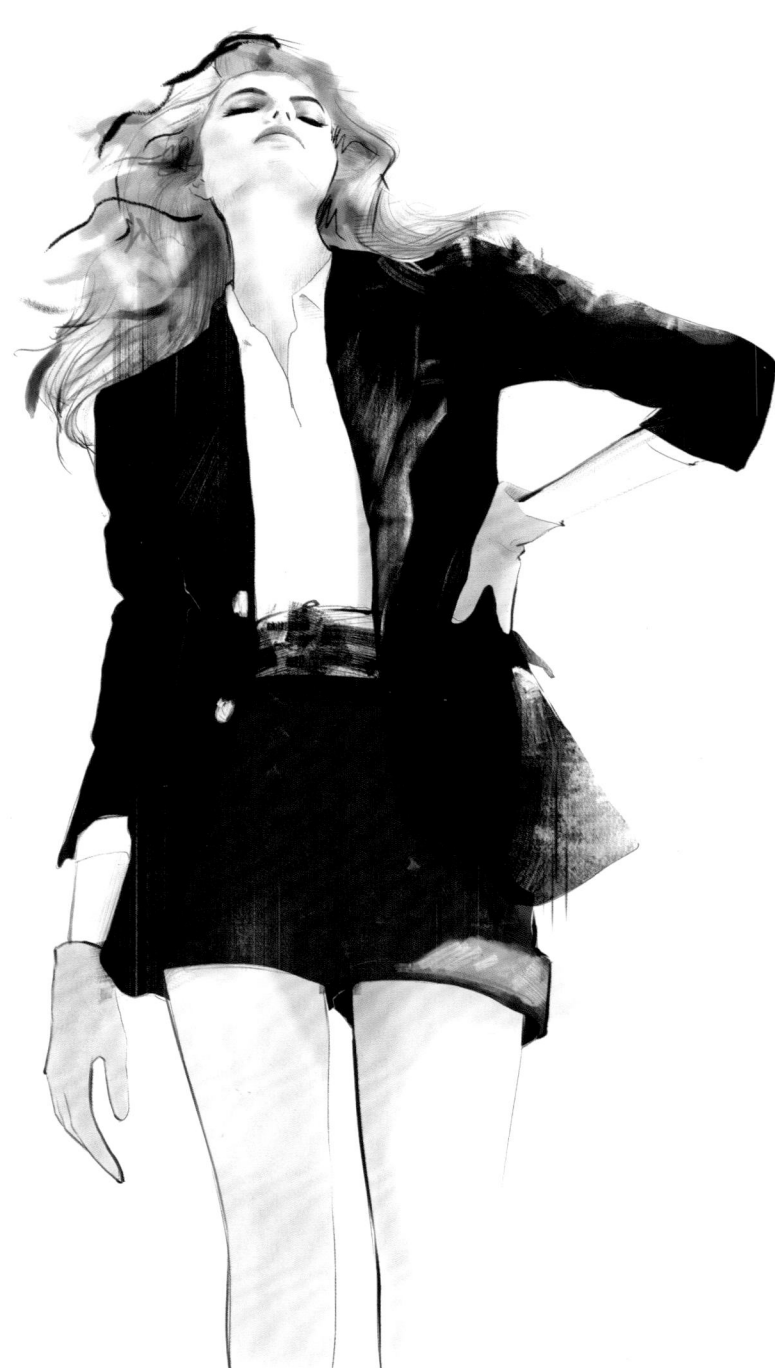

Personal work. Digital fashion illustration by Floyd Grey, with powerful strokes and dynamic effect.
Illustrator: Floyd Grey Country: Malaysia

Editorial for Vanity Fair Magazine, Spain. Watercolour, ink and pencil on high quality Fabriano paper.
Illustrator: Alicia Malesani Client: Vanity Fair Magazine Spain Country: Spain

Work Look for Men

Work Look

Editorial for Redbook Magazine USA. Watercolour, ink and pencil on high quality Fabriano paper.
Illustrator: Alicia Malesani Country: USA

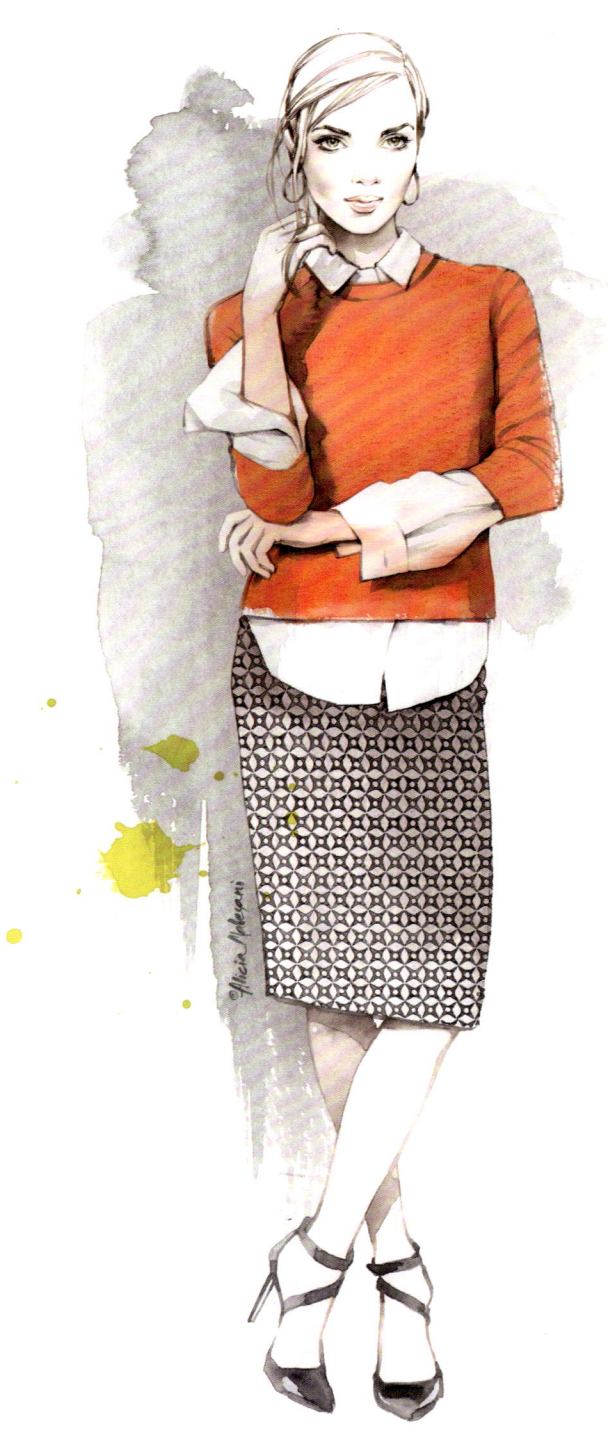

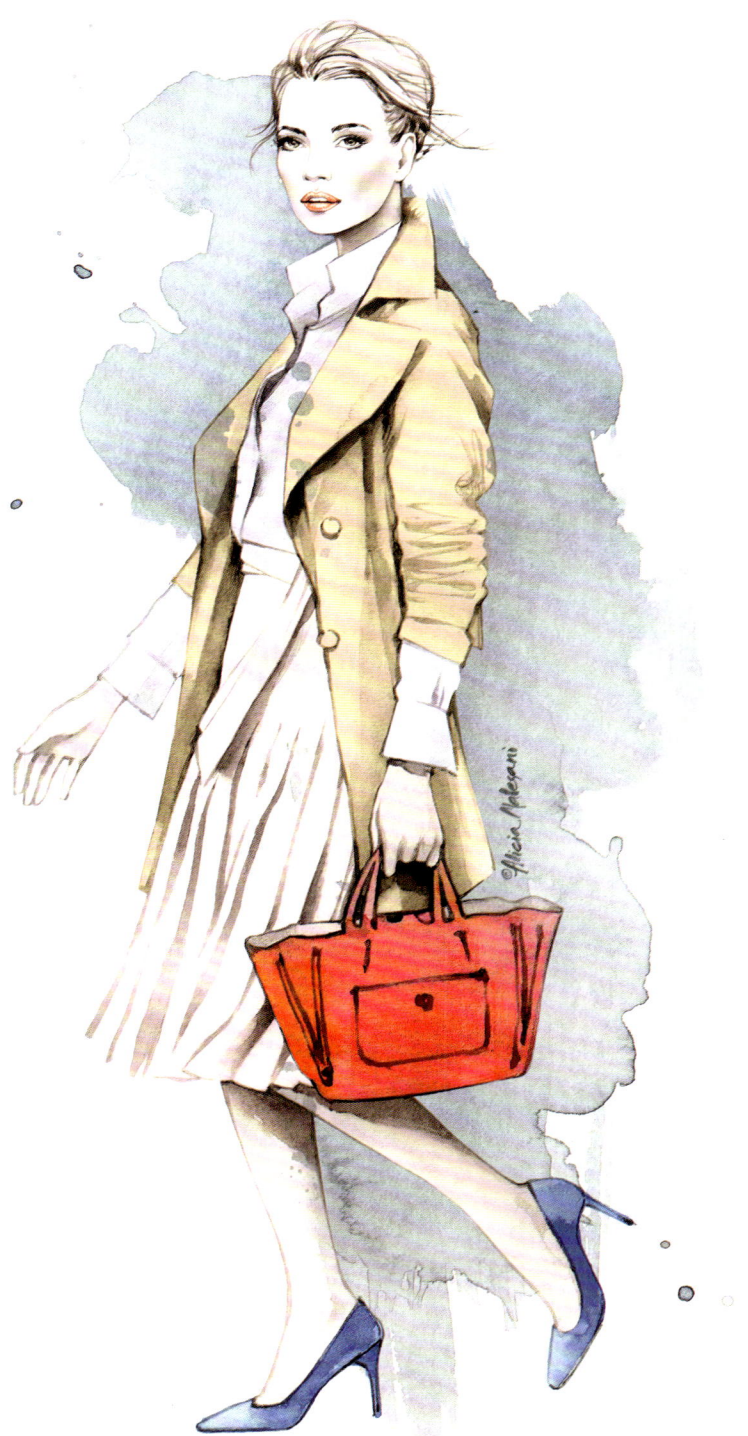

Editorial for Redbook Magazine USA. Watercolour, ink and pencil on high quality Fabriano paper.
Illustrator: Alicia Malesani Client: Redbook Magazine USA Country: USA

Smart Suit

Tailored Suit

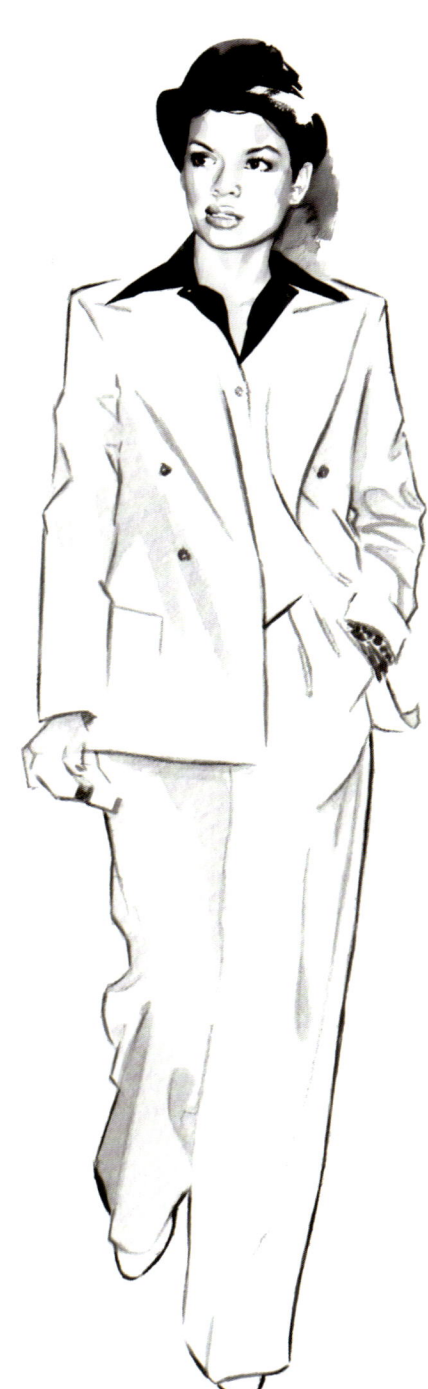

An illustration of Bianca Jagger for a chapter of a fashion book talking about fashion icons.
Illustrator: Chidy Wayne Country: Spain

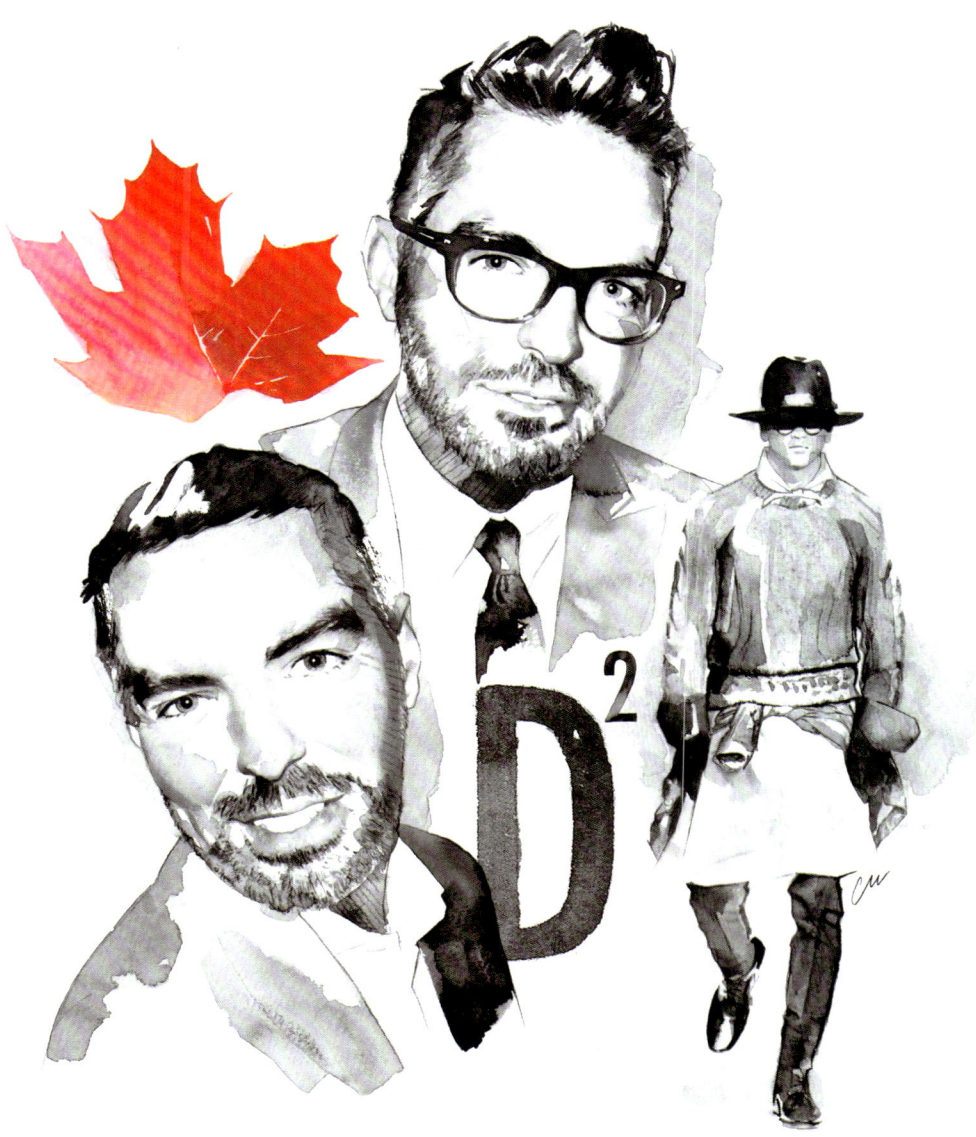

Illustrated composition of Caten brothers and their fashion brand Dsquared2 for the fashion book Trendy.
Illustrator: Chidy Wayne Country: Spain

Dsquared 2

Emidio Tucci

Illustrated model wearing Emidio Tucci for El Corte Inglés.
Illustrator: Chidy Wayne Country: Spain

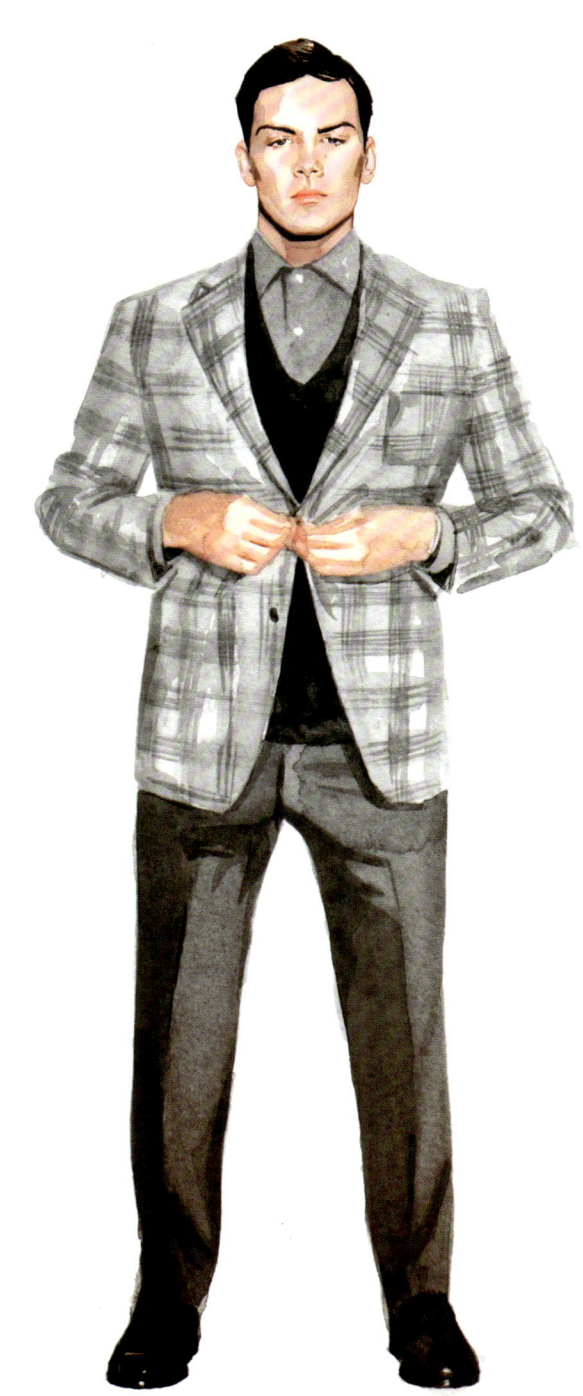

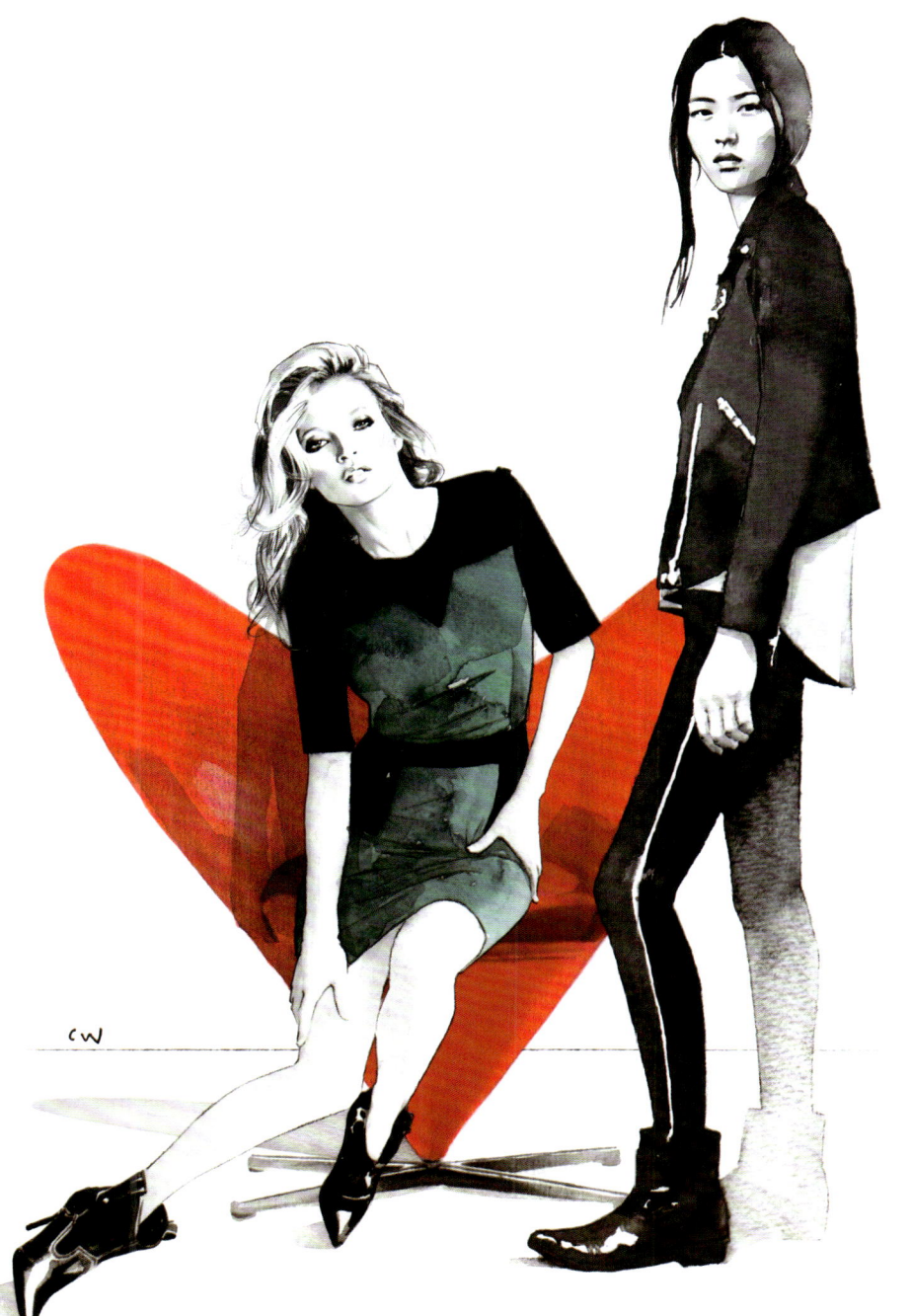

Suit of simple style and comfortable design, shifting freely between work and life.
Illustrator: Chidy Wayne Country: Spain

Office Lady Look

Textured Suit

Personal project using graphite, found textures, and Photoshop.
Illustrator: Nicole Jarecz Country: USA

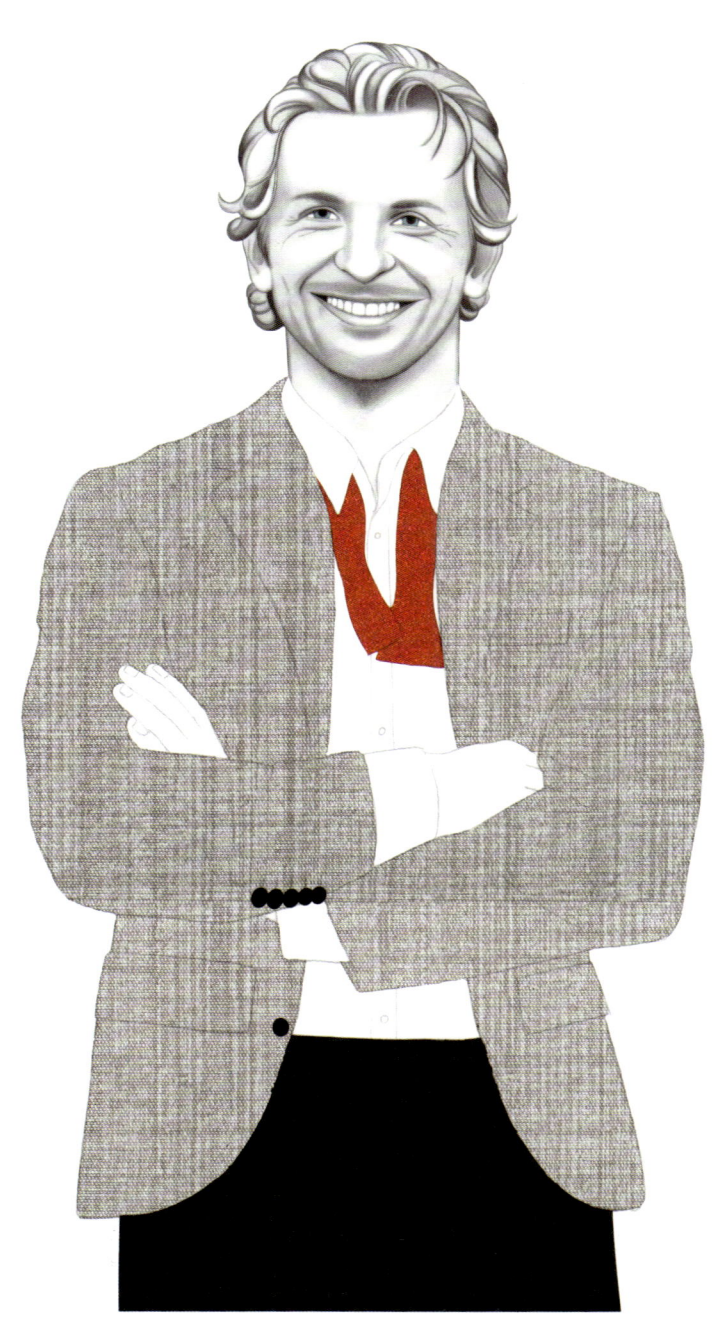

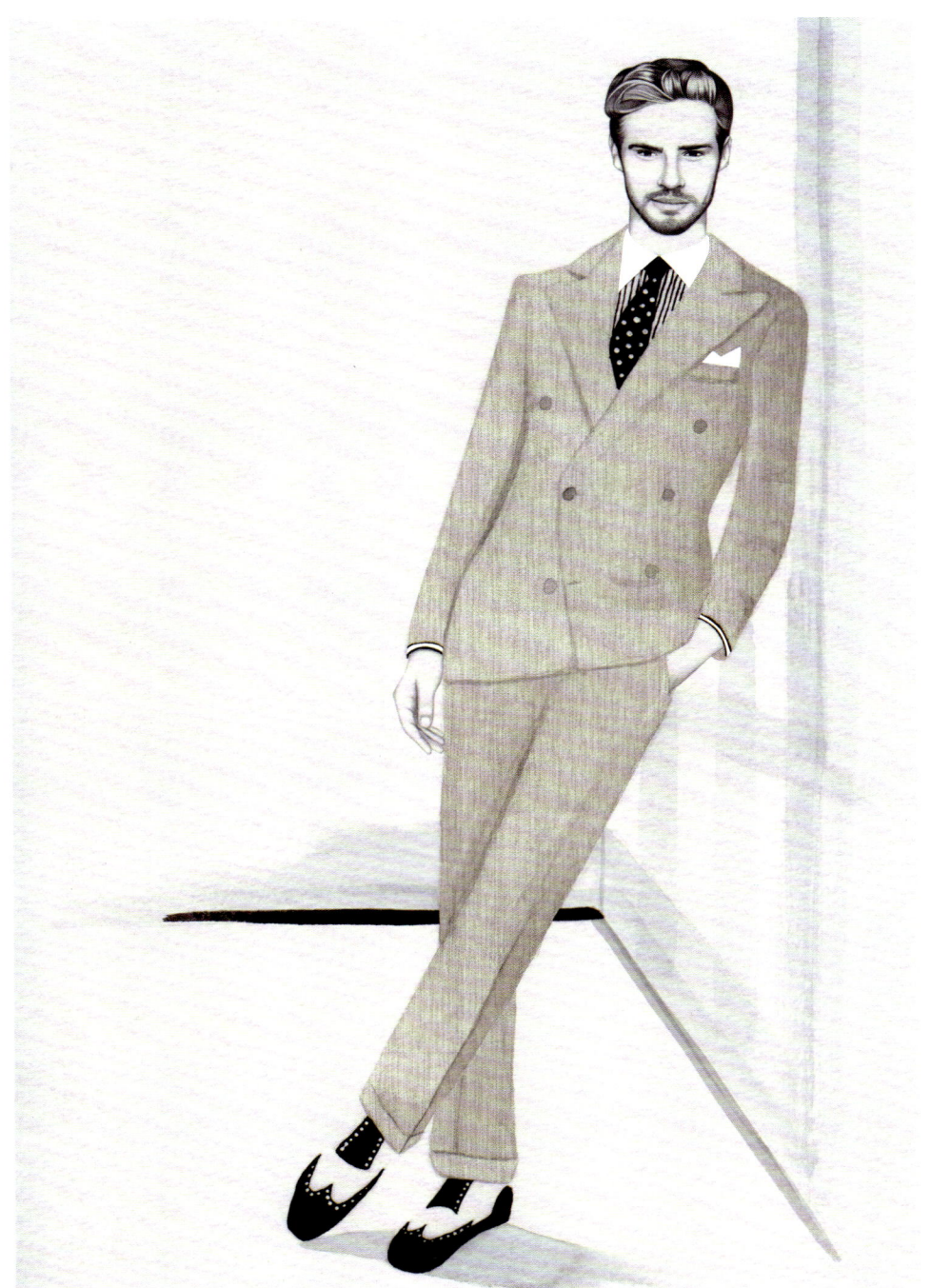

Personal project using graphite, gouache, found textures and watercolour.
Illustrator: Nicole Jarecz Country: USA

Ralph Lauren

Dior

Personal project using graphite, ink and found textures.
Illustrator: Nicole Jarecz Country: USA

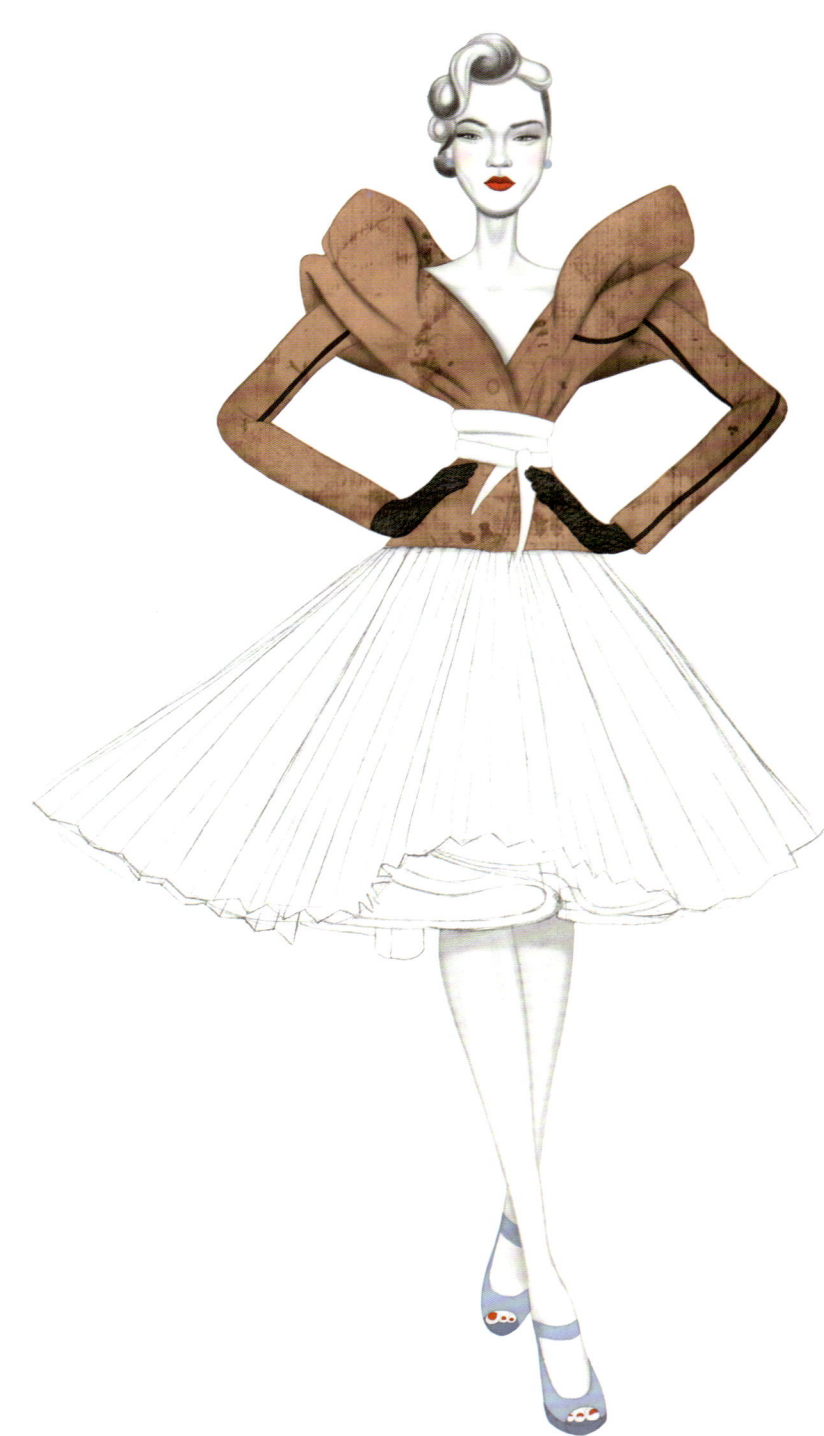

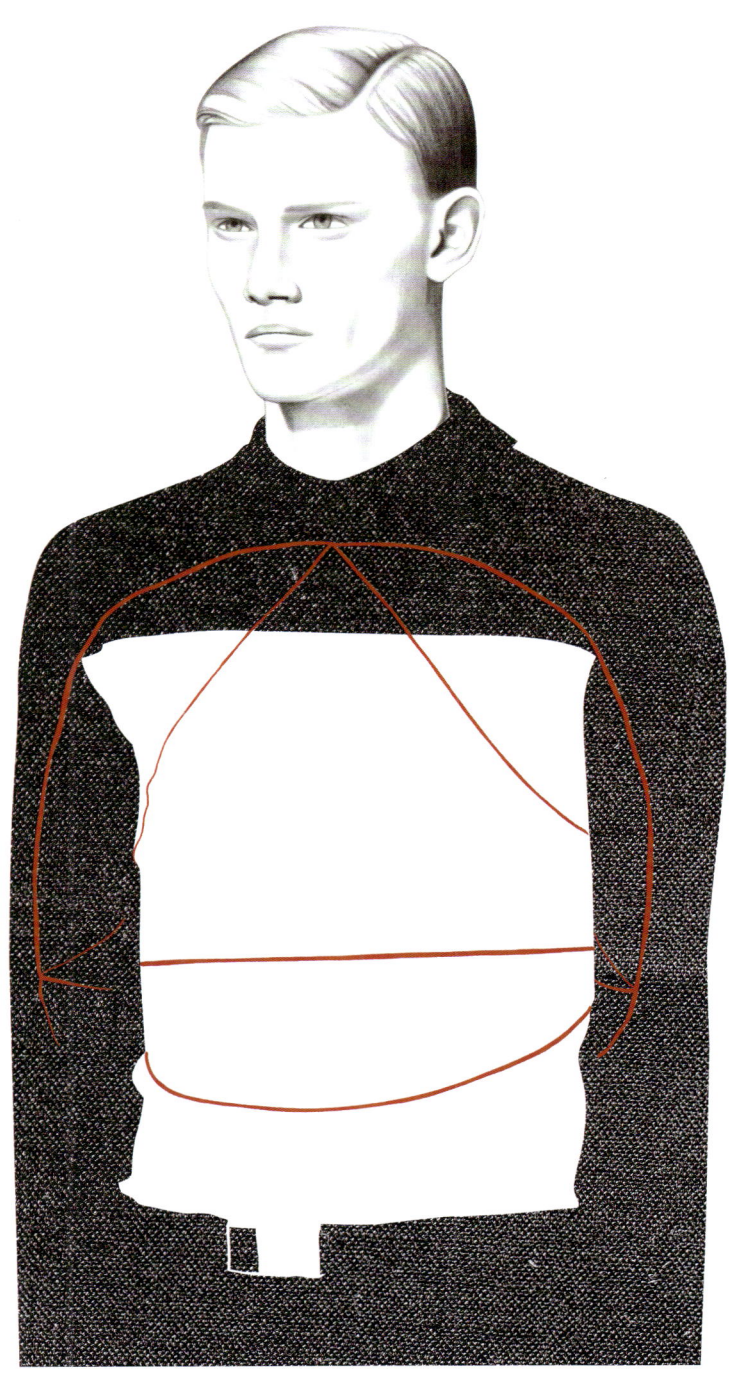

Personal project based on Dior menswear fashion.
Illustrator: Nicole Jarecz County: USA

Dior

Sophie Theallet SS 2016

Sophie Theallet's collection was beautiful and feminine, the illustrator loved this strong look with a clean and flattering silhouette, beautiful textures and gold sheen.

Illustrator: Samantha Hahn Country: USA

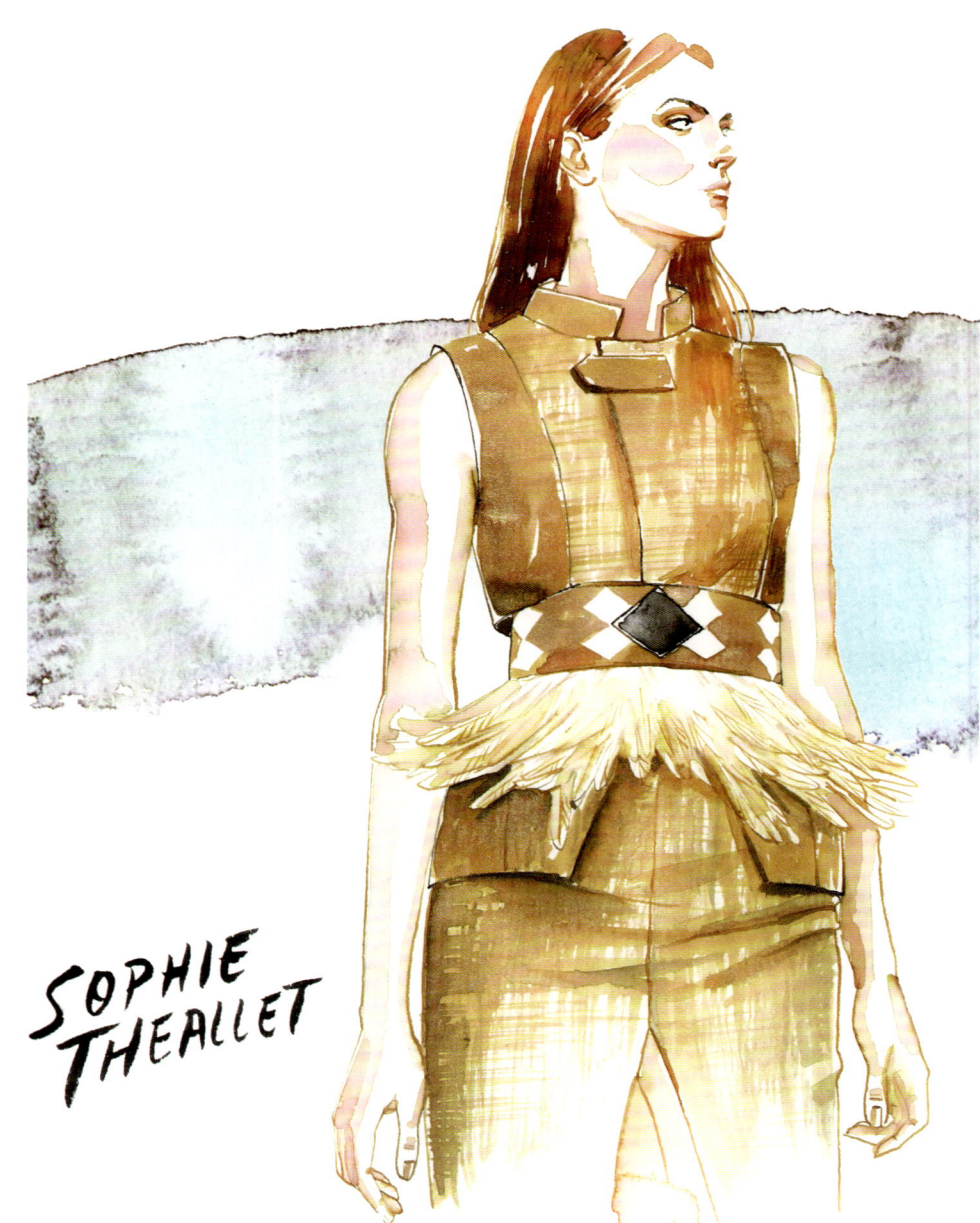

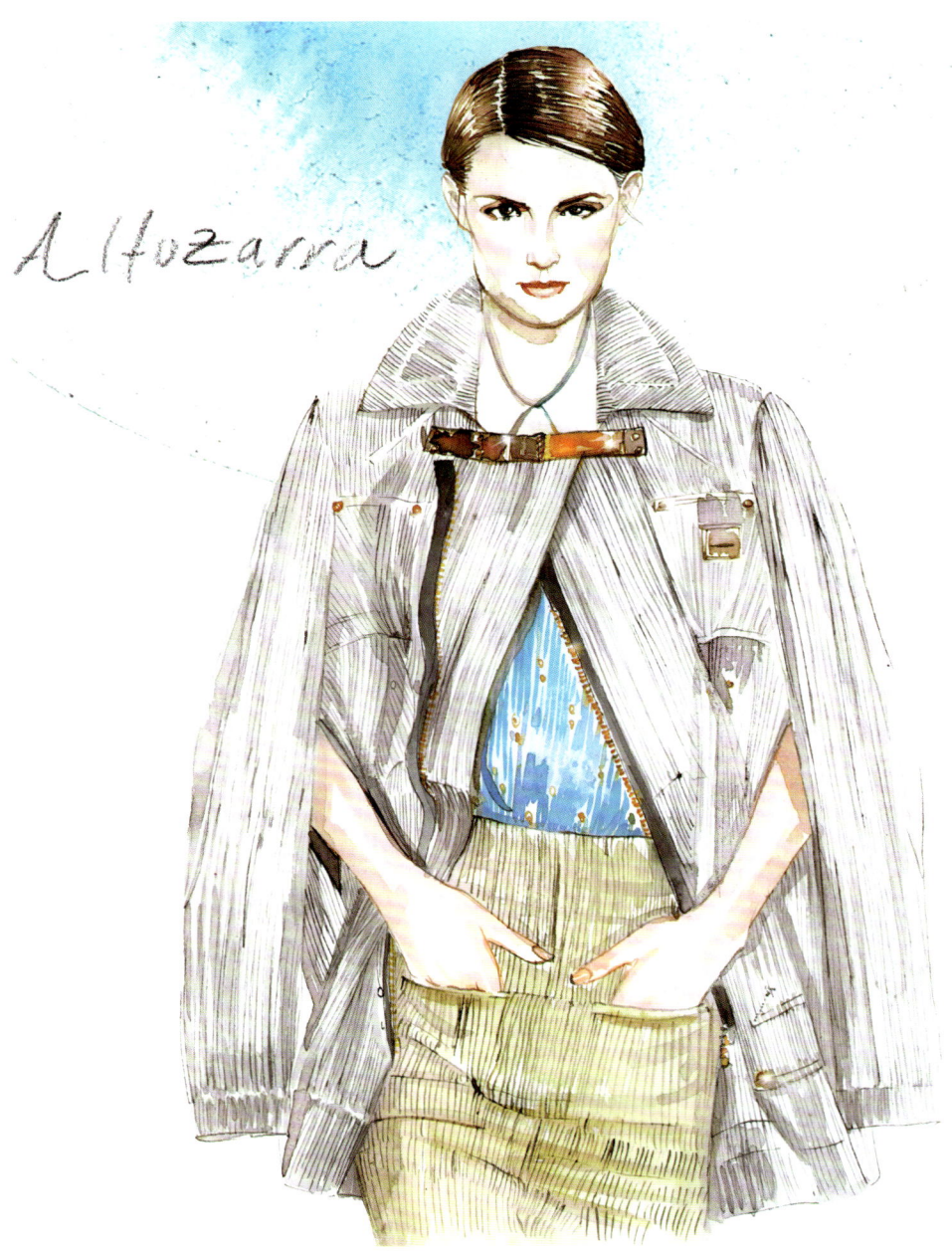

Altuzarra is amazing at creating looks that could be worn at work, a party or anywhere else.
Illustrator: Samantha Hahn Country: USA

Altuzarra

Saint Laurent RTW FW 2015

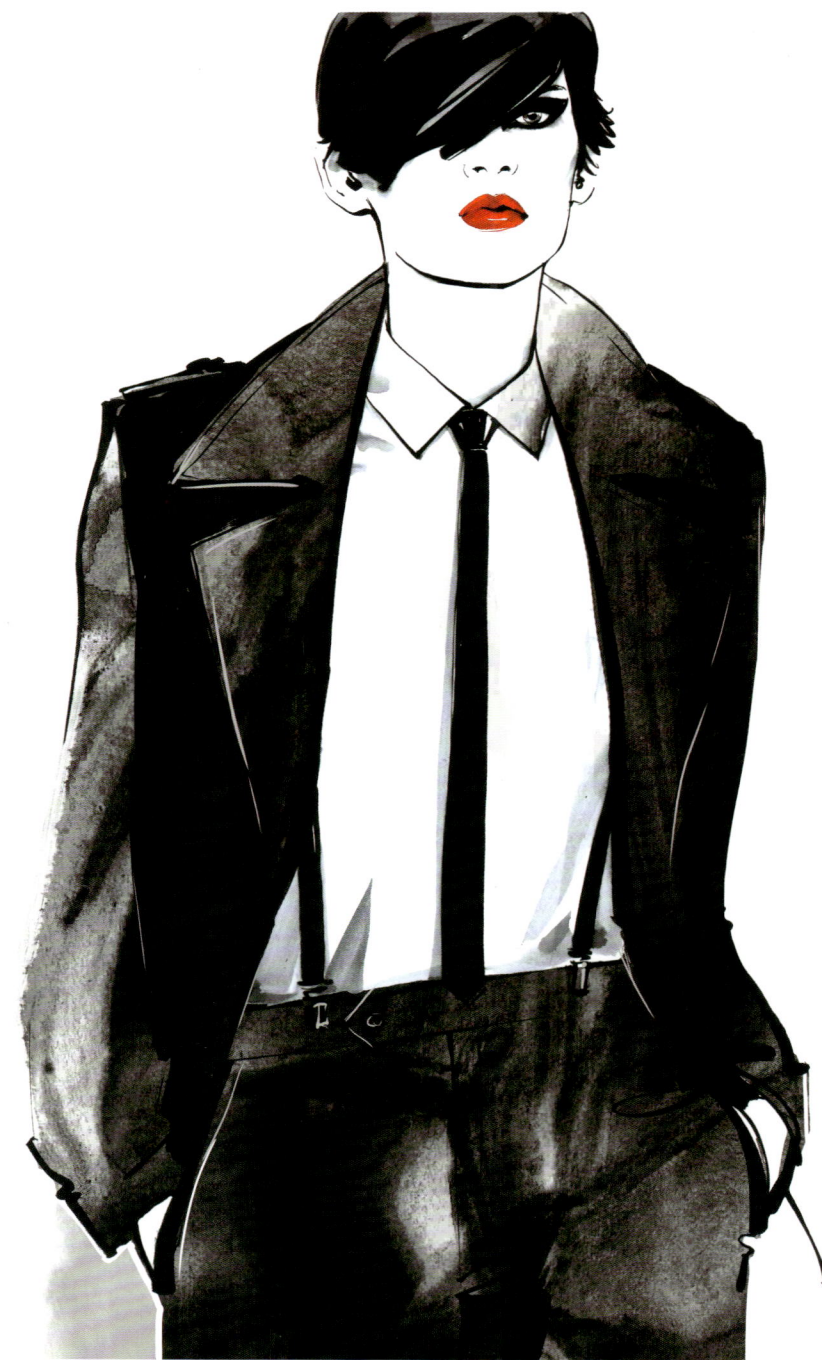

Close up moment at Saint Laurent show Paris Fashion Week RTW FW 2015, Editorial work for vogue.ru.
Illustrator: Alena Lavdovskaya Country: Russia

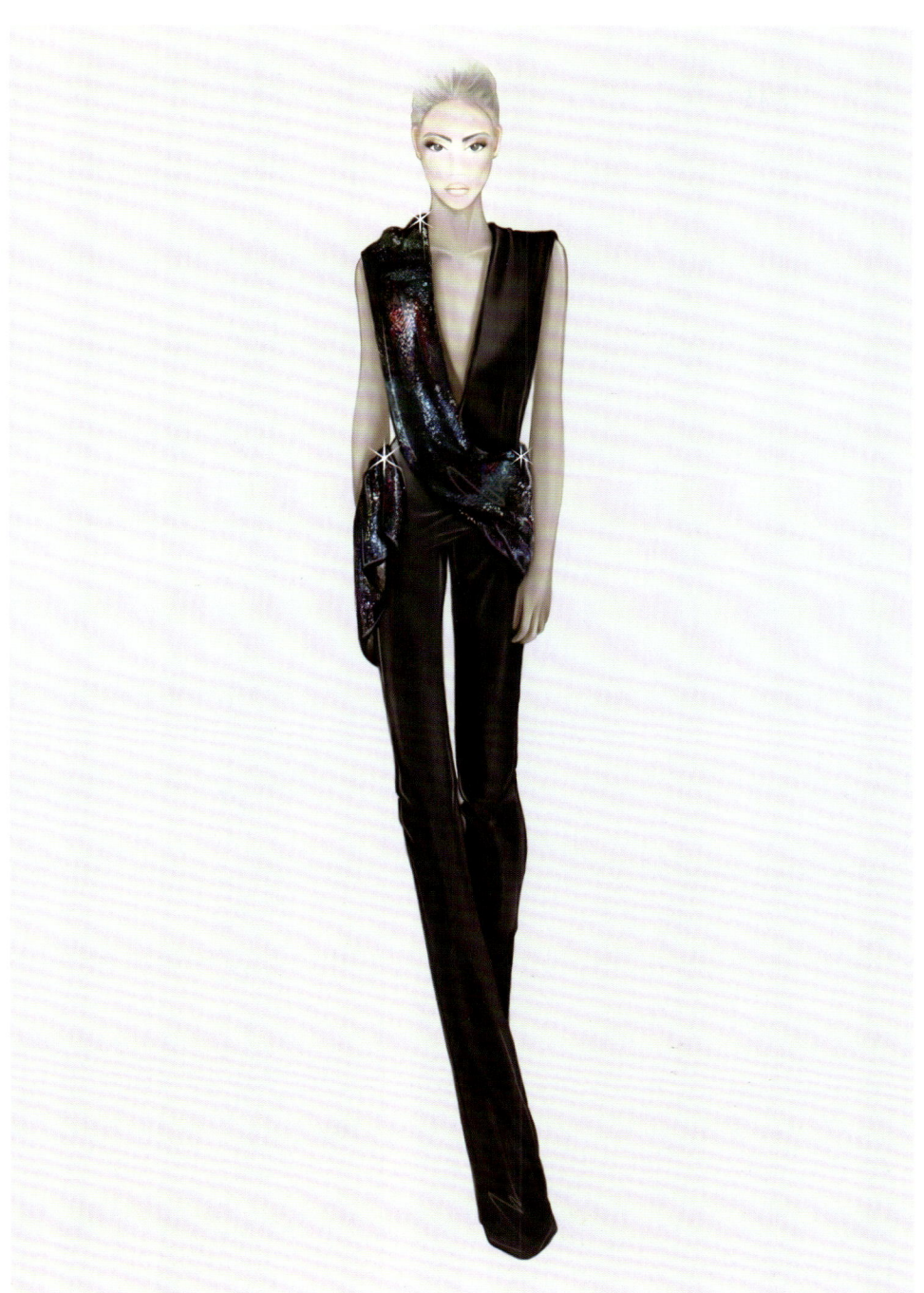

Illustration of jumpsuit inspired by menswear overall. Sequins freely draped around the body to merge the feminine and masculine aspects.
Print inspired by Emmanuel Guiragossian's abstract painting.
Illustrator: Rahel Guiragossian Country: Germany

Jumpsuit from Rahel Guiragossian Collection

Balenciaga Look

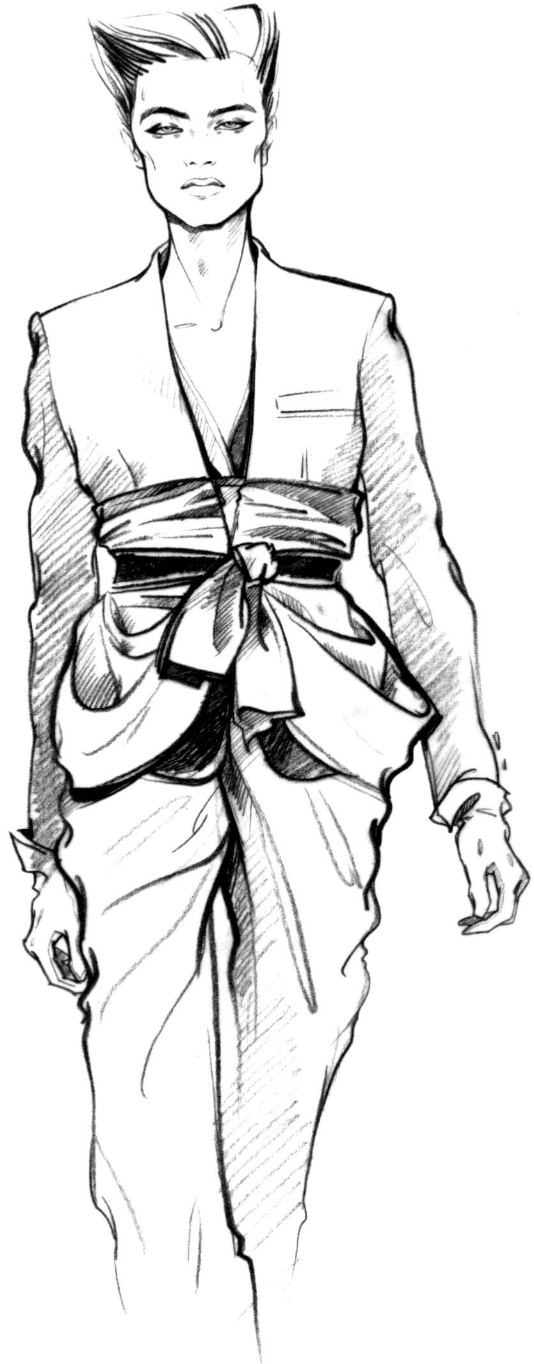

Sketch for TSUM department store's campaign with pencil.
Illustrator: Alena Lavdovskaya Country: Russia

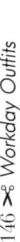

Sketch for TSUM department store's campaign with pencil.
Illustrator: Alena Lavdovskaya Country: Russia

Lanvin Look

The Coat by Kate Silchenko

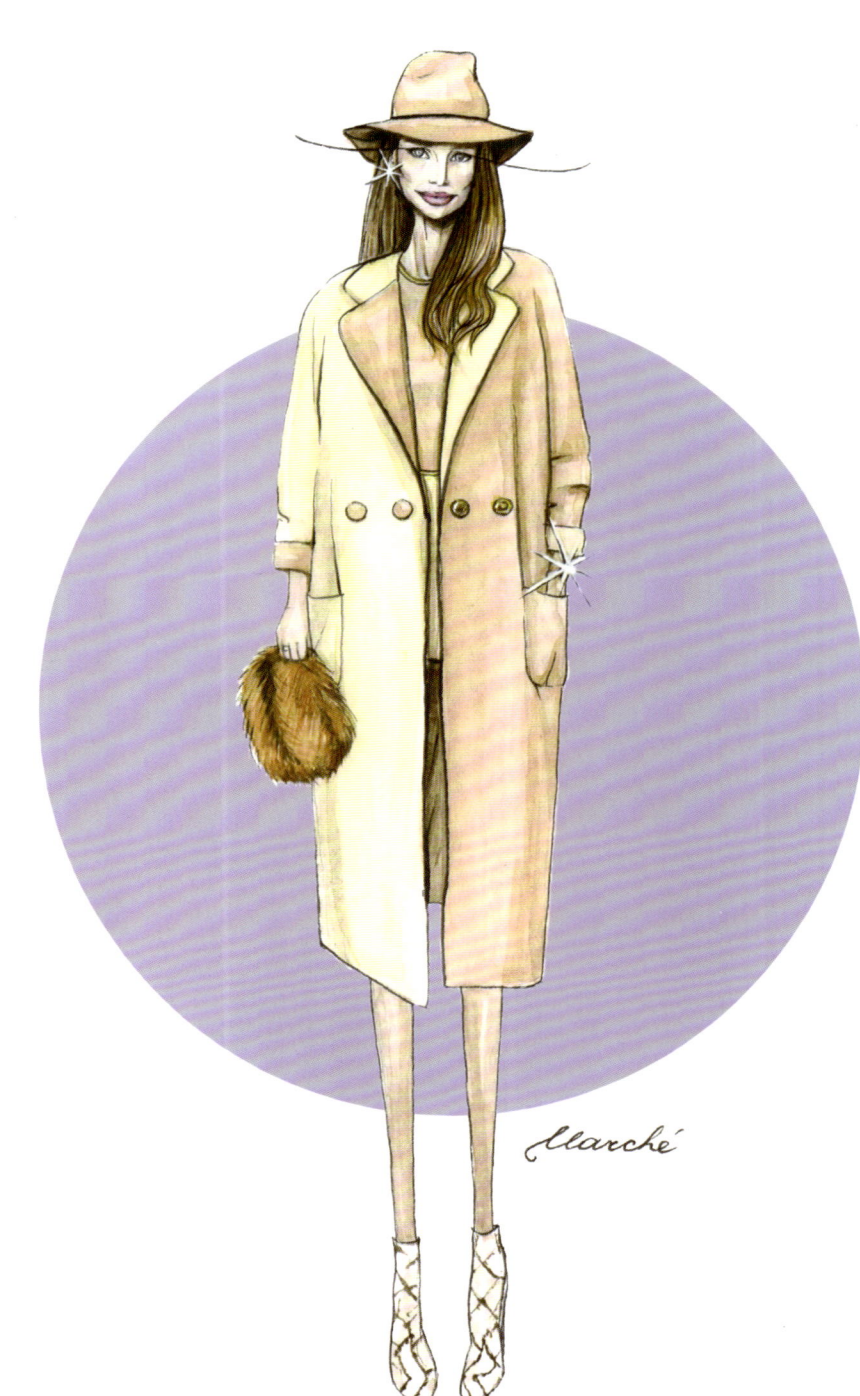

This fashion illustration is inspired by Ukrainian designer Kate Silchenko and her The Coat.
Illustrator: Mariana Marché Country: Ukraine

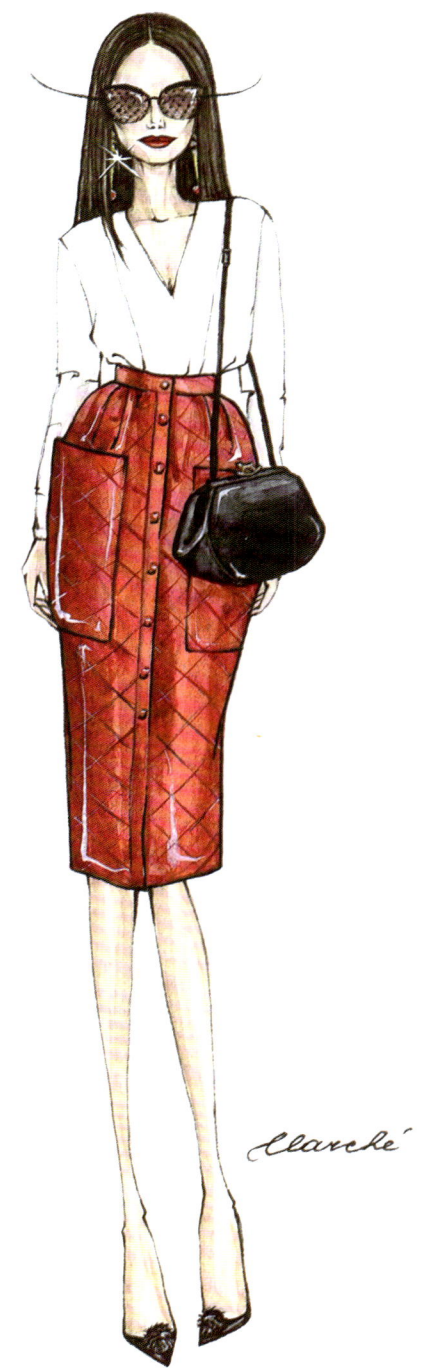

This fashion illustration is inspired by a Ulyana Sergeenko look.
Illustrator: Mariana Marchê Country: Ukraine

Ulyana Sergeenko Total Look

Halston Heritage 2016 Resort

Inspired by Halston Heritage 2016 Resort collection.
Illustrator: Kiara Tan Country: China

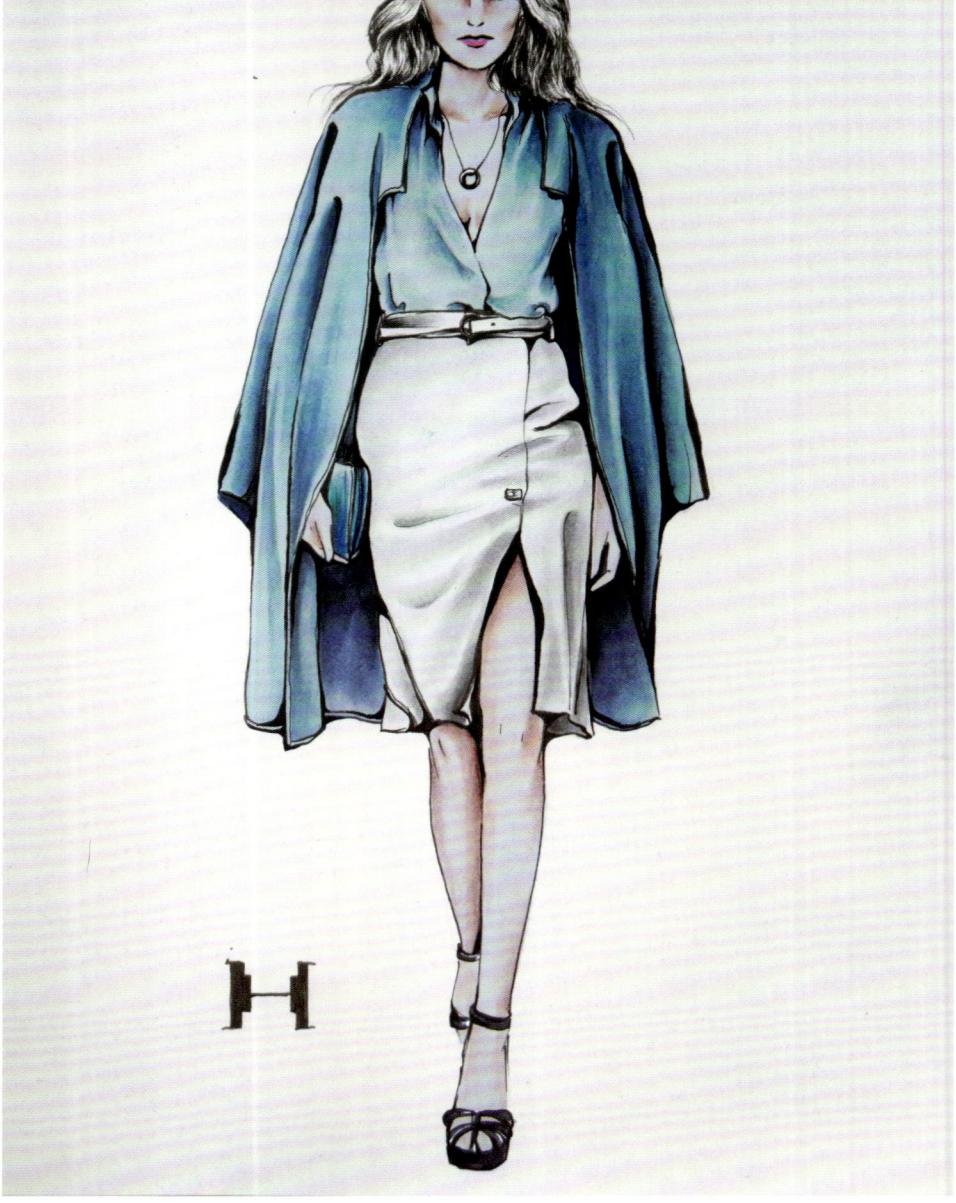

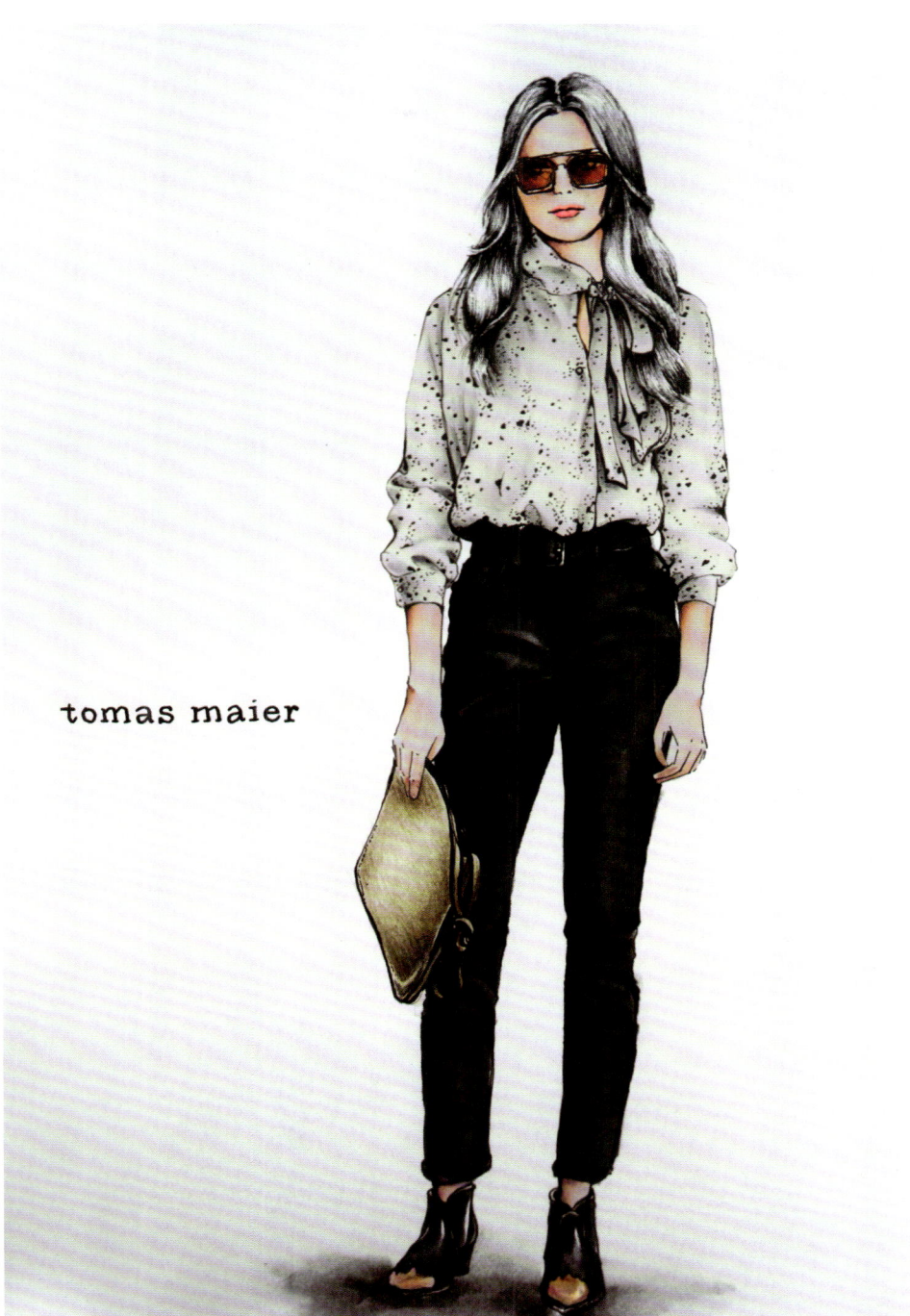

tomas maier

Inspired by Tomas Maier 2016 FW collection. The smart way is to wear something 'casual but designed'.
Illustrator: Kiara Tan Country: China

Tomas Maier 2016 FW

Chloé

Model from Chloé fall 2013 collection. Pencil & digital.
Illustrator: Caroline Andrieu Country: France

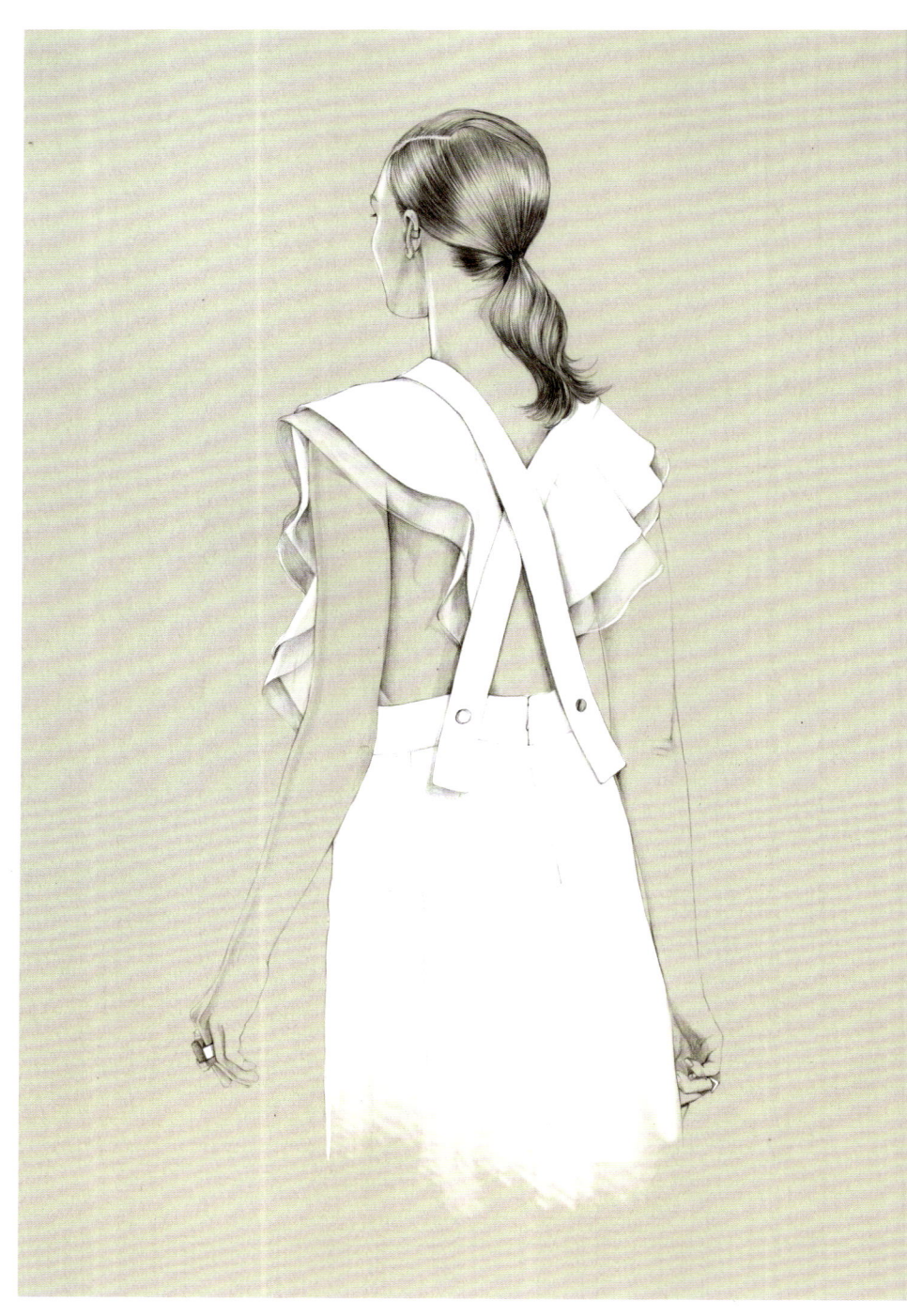

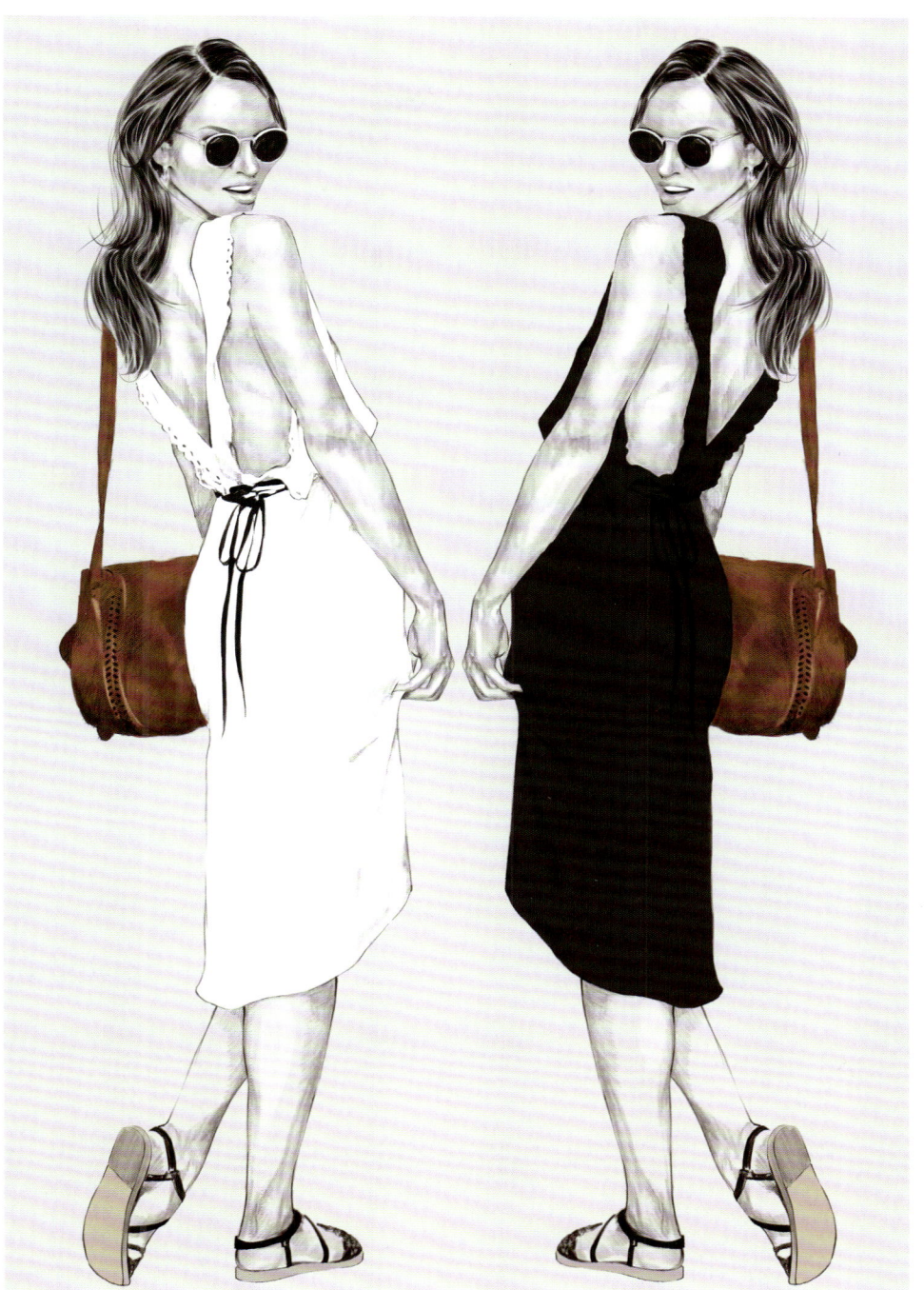

Candice Swanepoel, New York fashion week street style created in Adobe Photoshop CS3 with pencil brushes.
Illustrator: Will Bayunn Country: Malaysia

Candice's Street Style Dress

Burberry Fall 2014

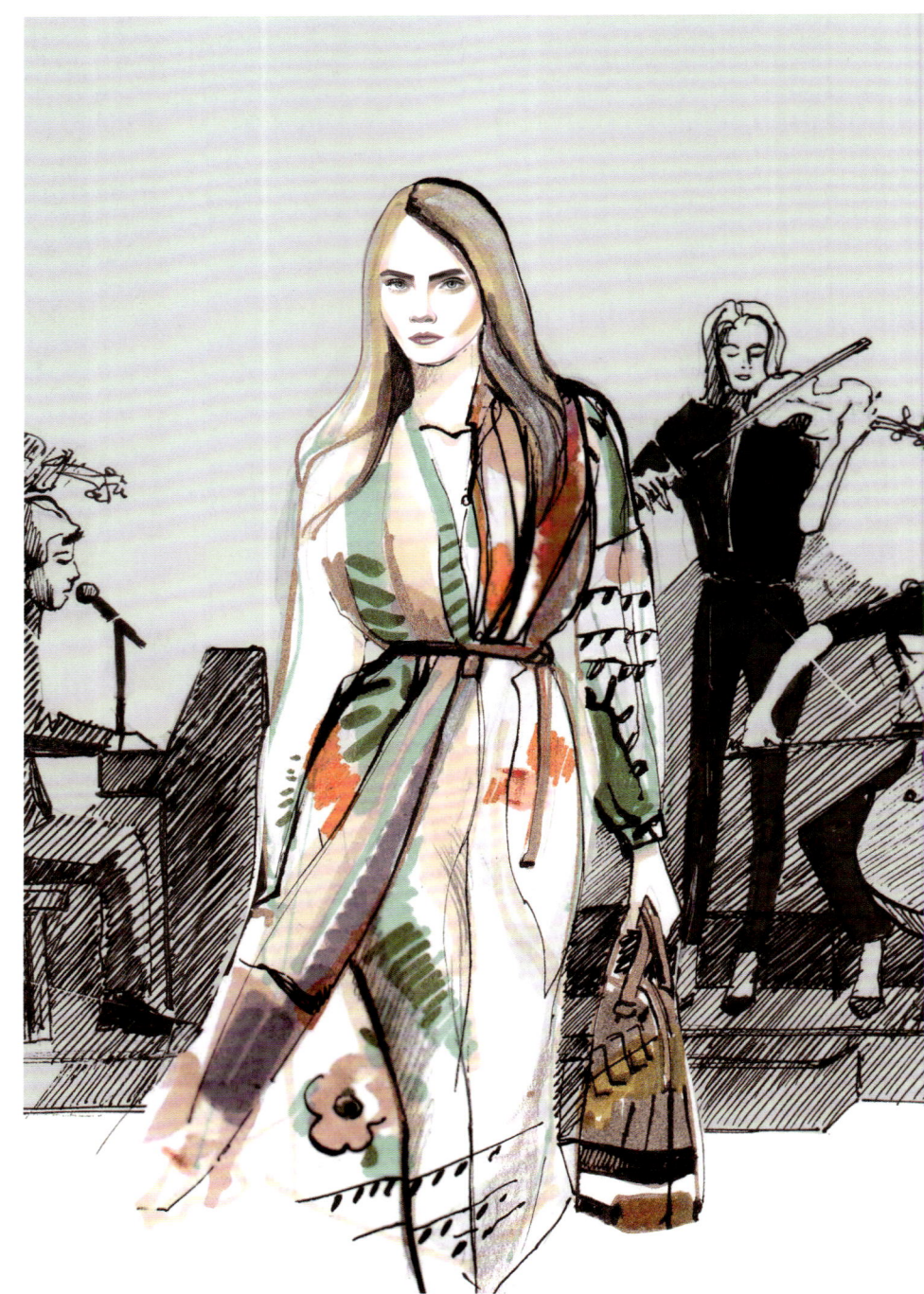

Illustration from the London Fashion Week featuring Cara Delevingne wearing a dress from the Burberry fall 2014 collection.
Illustrator: Mélique Street Country: Italy

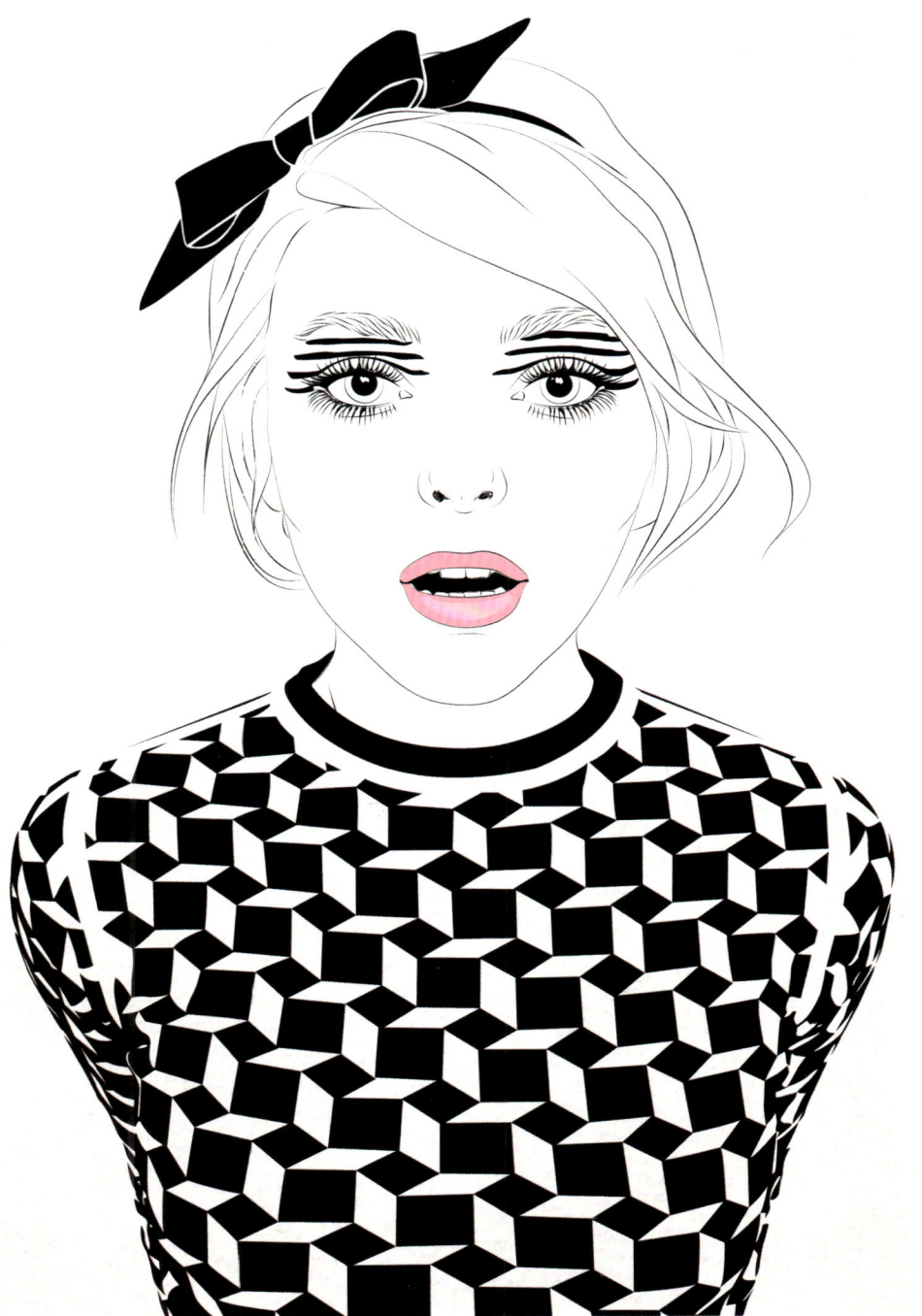

This fashion illustration is inspired by the actress Anna Sophia Robb for teen Vogue, February 2013.
Illustrator: Paula Blanche Country: Chile

Geometrically Patterned Sweater

Haider Ackermann

Series of illustrations for an article in Rouge Magazine about new rebel fashion trends, based on a collection by Haider Ackermann. Pencil and ink on paper. Illustrator: Carole Wilmet Country: Belgium

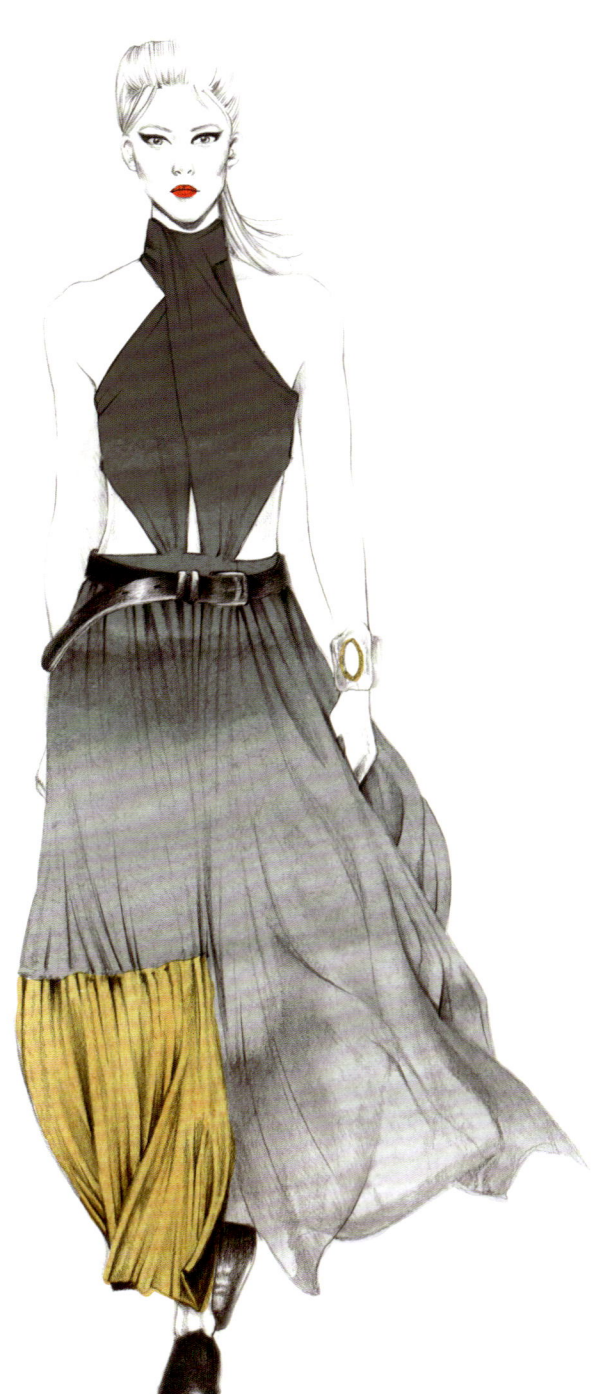

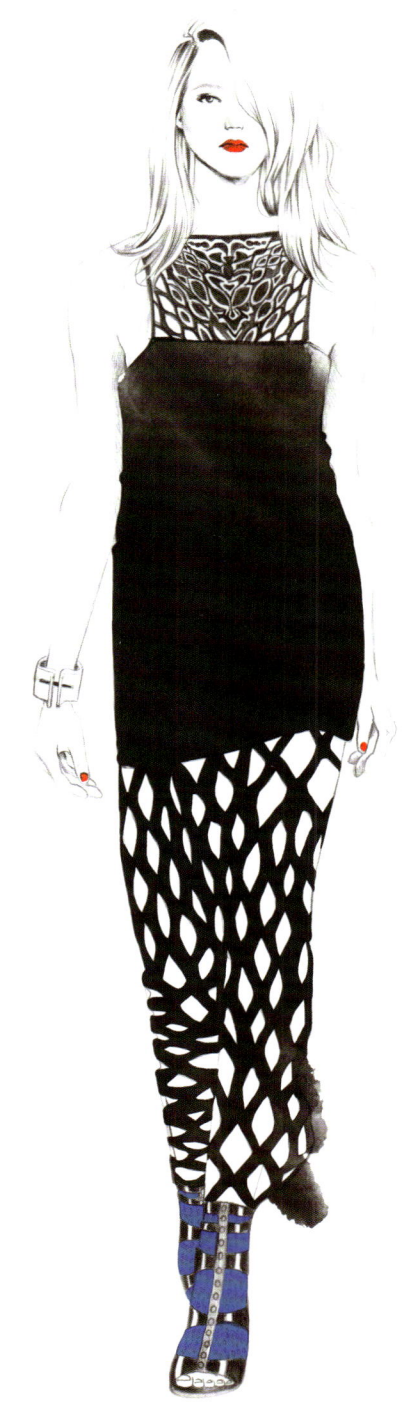

Series of illustrations for an article in Rouge Magazine about new rebel fashion trends, based on a collection by Emilio Pucci. Pencil and ink on paper.
Illustrator: Carole Wilmet Country: Belgium

Emilio Pucci

Versace Total Look

This fashion illustration is inspired by rapper Rick Ross.
Illustrator: Mariana Marché Country: Ukraine

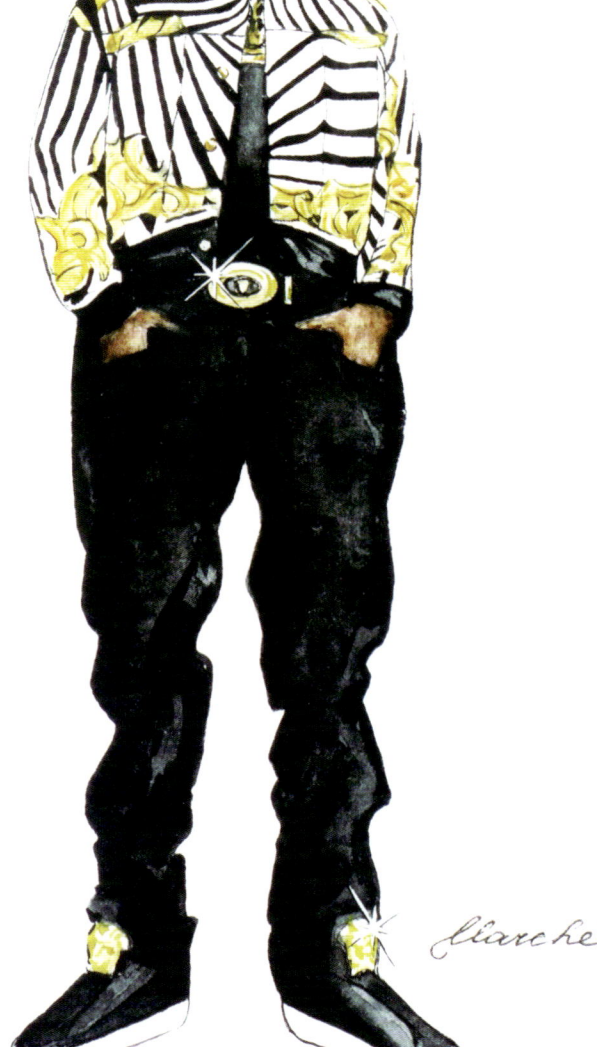

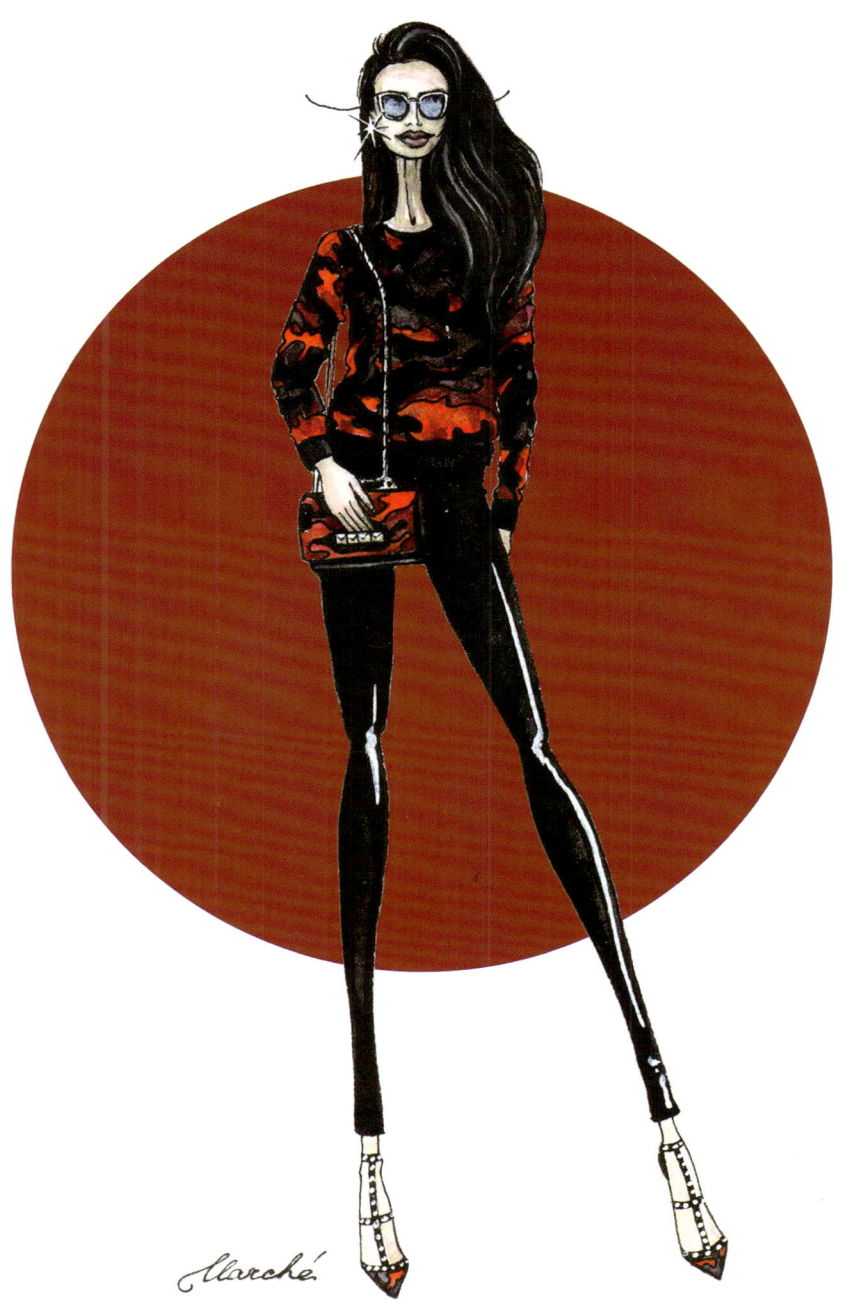

This fashion illustration is inspired by Ukrainian street style.
Illustrator: Mariana Marchè Country: Ukraine

Valentino Street Style

Balmain SS15

This fashion illustration is inspired by beautiful Liu Wen and Balmain 2015 Spring collection.
Illustrator: Katerina Murysina Country: Russia

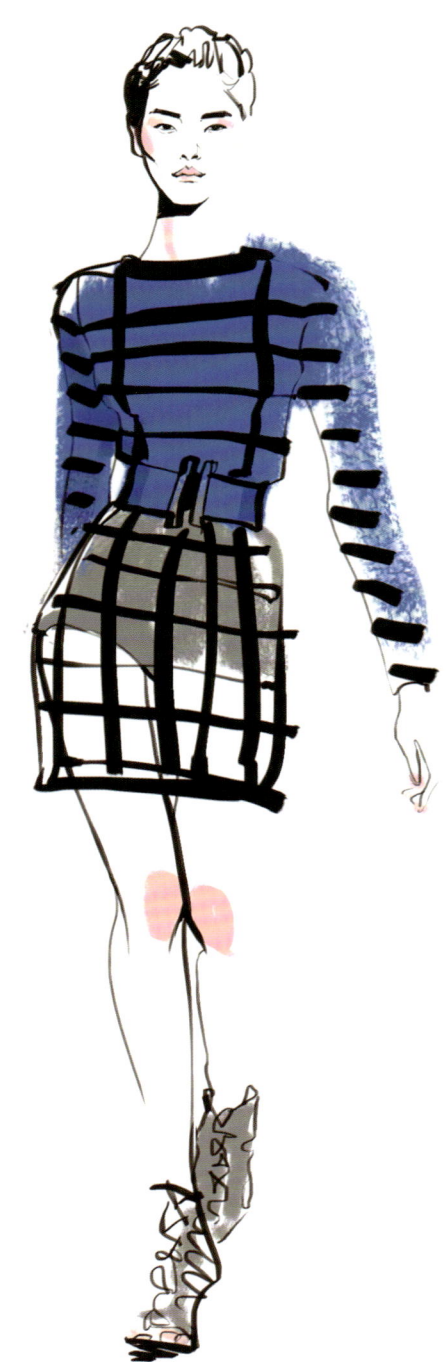

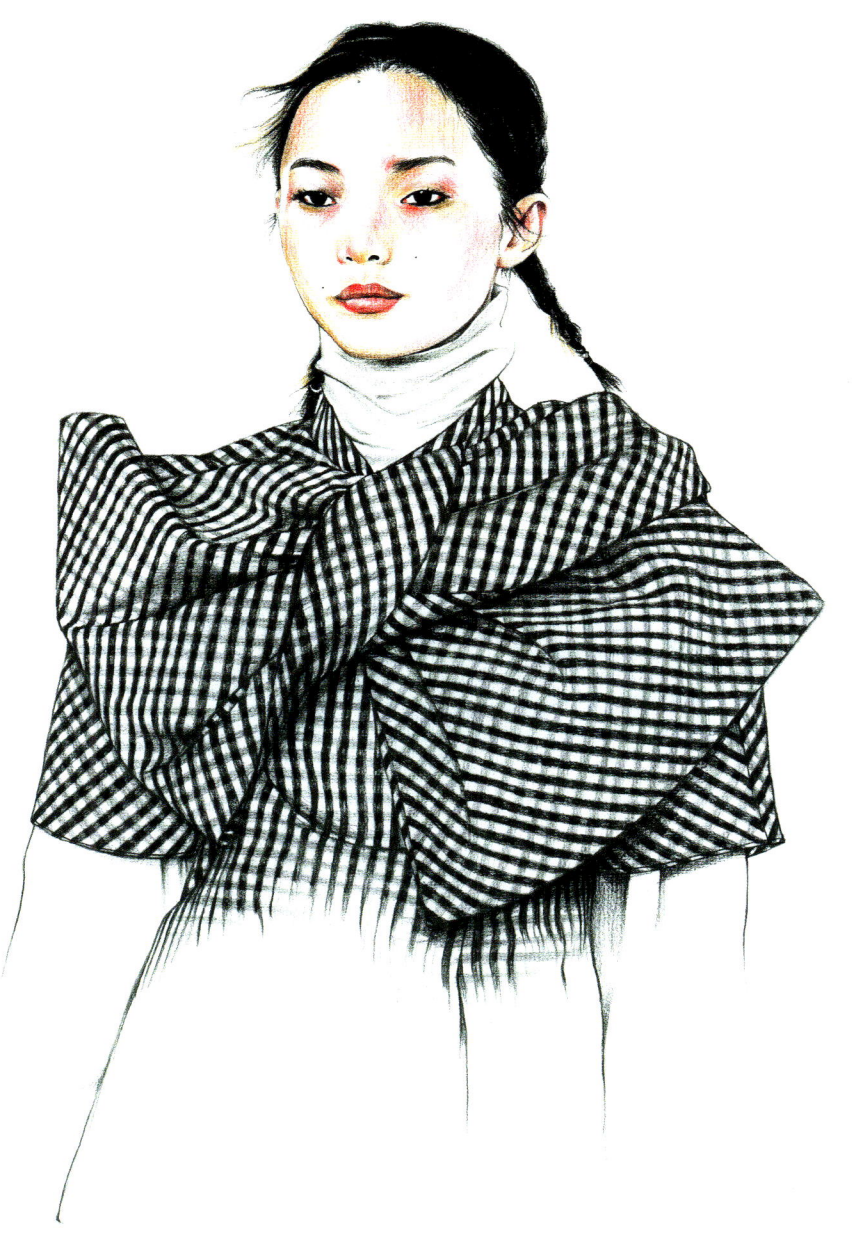

Xiao Wen Ju for Marc by Marc. Marc Jacobs fall 2014 collection. Colour pencils on Ingres paper.
Caroline Andrieu Country:France

Marc by Marc Jacobs

Prada

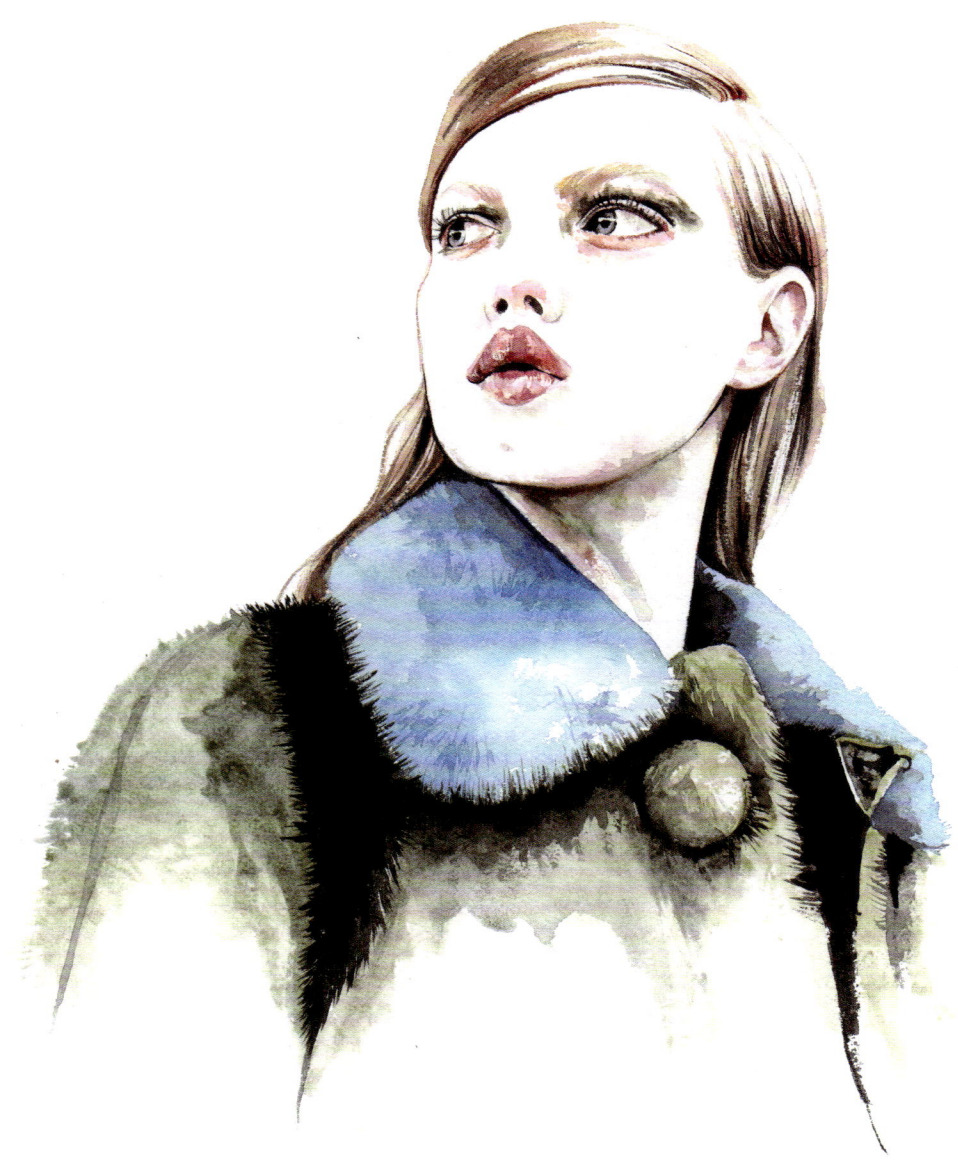

Model Lindsey Wixson for Prada spring 2014 collection. Watercolour. Caroline Andrieu Country: France

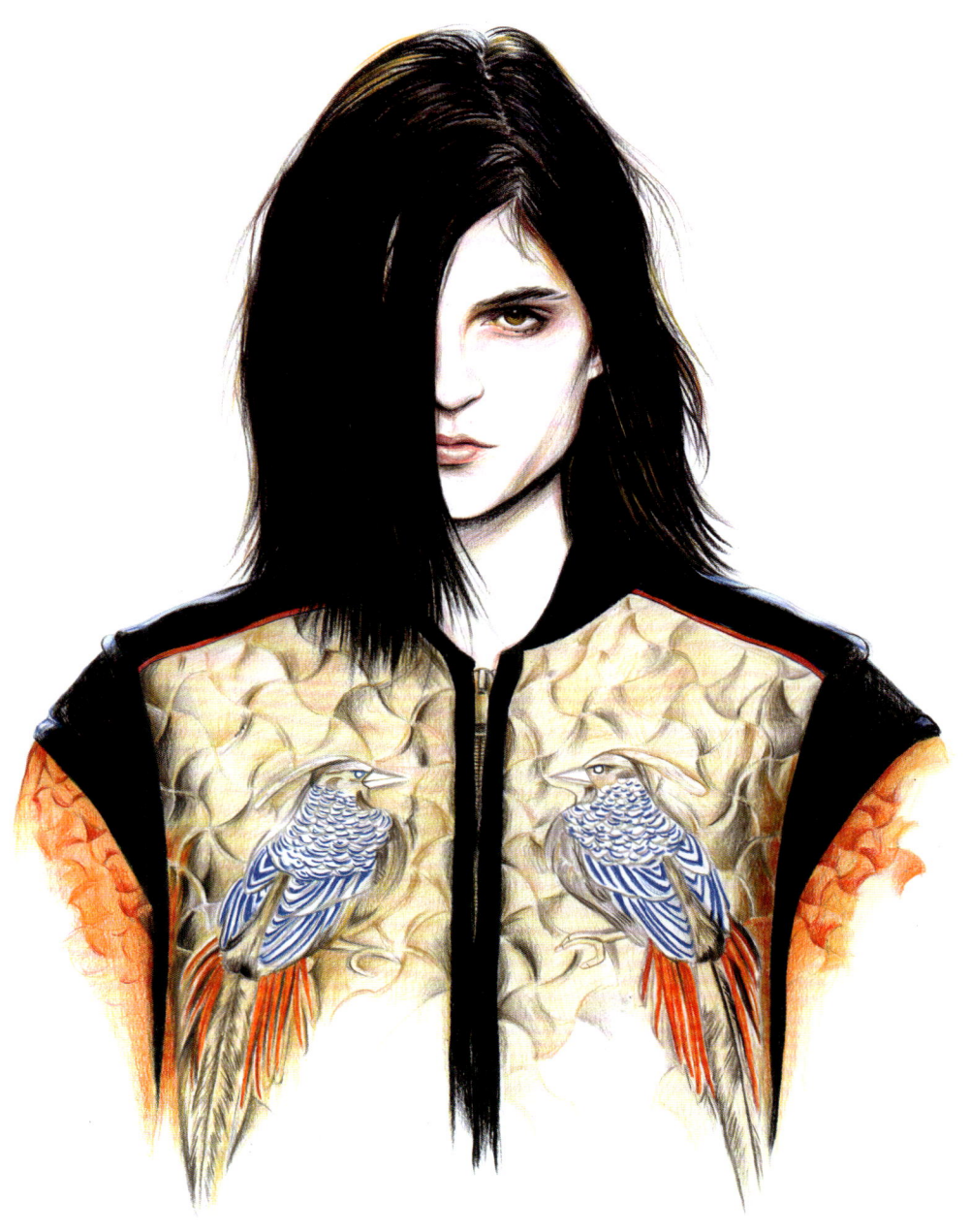

Model Kel Markey for Proenza Schouler fall 2012. Colour pencils.
Caroline Andrieu Country:France

Proenza Schouler

Street Style Fashion Outfit in Red

Example of street style fashion outfit in red.
Illustrator: Davide Morettini Country: Italy

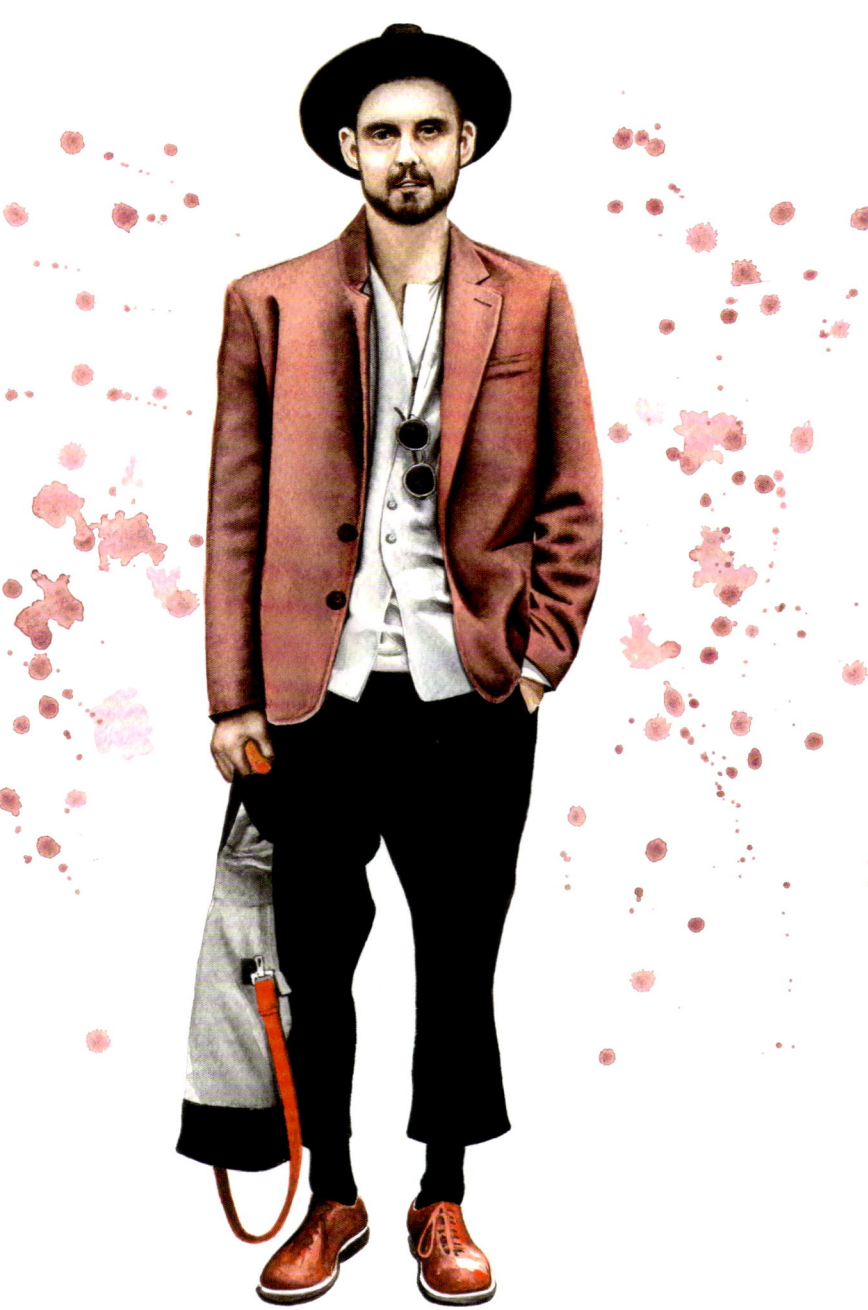

Example of street style fashion outfit in green.
Illustrator: Davide Morettini Country: Italy

Street Style Fashion Outfit in Green

Street Style Fashion Outfit in Yellow

Example of street style fashion outfit in yellow.
Illustrator: Davide Morettini Country: Italy

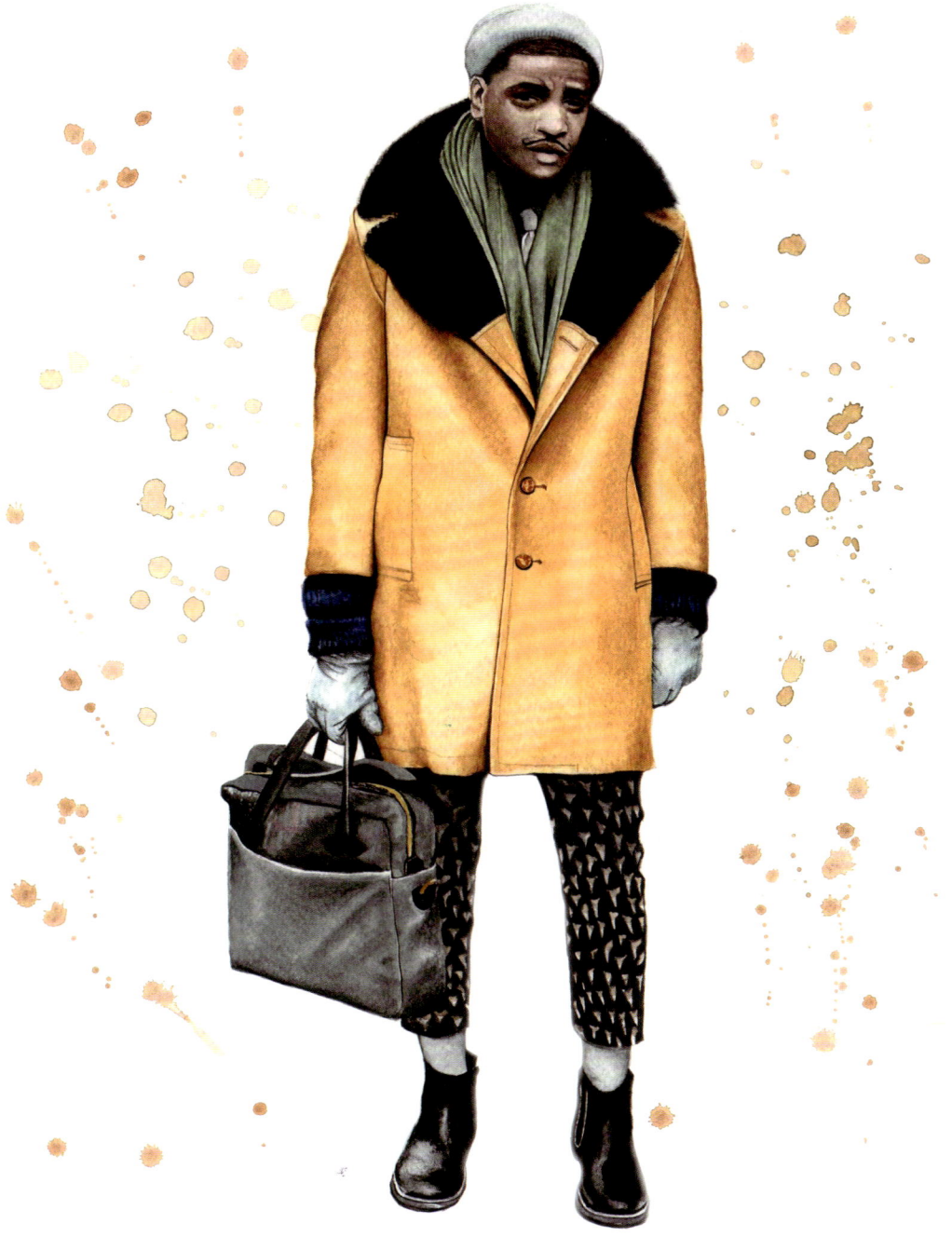

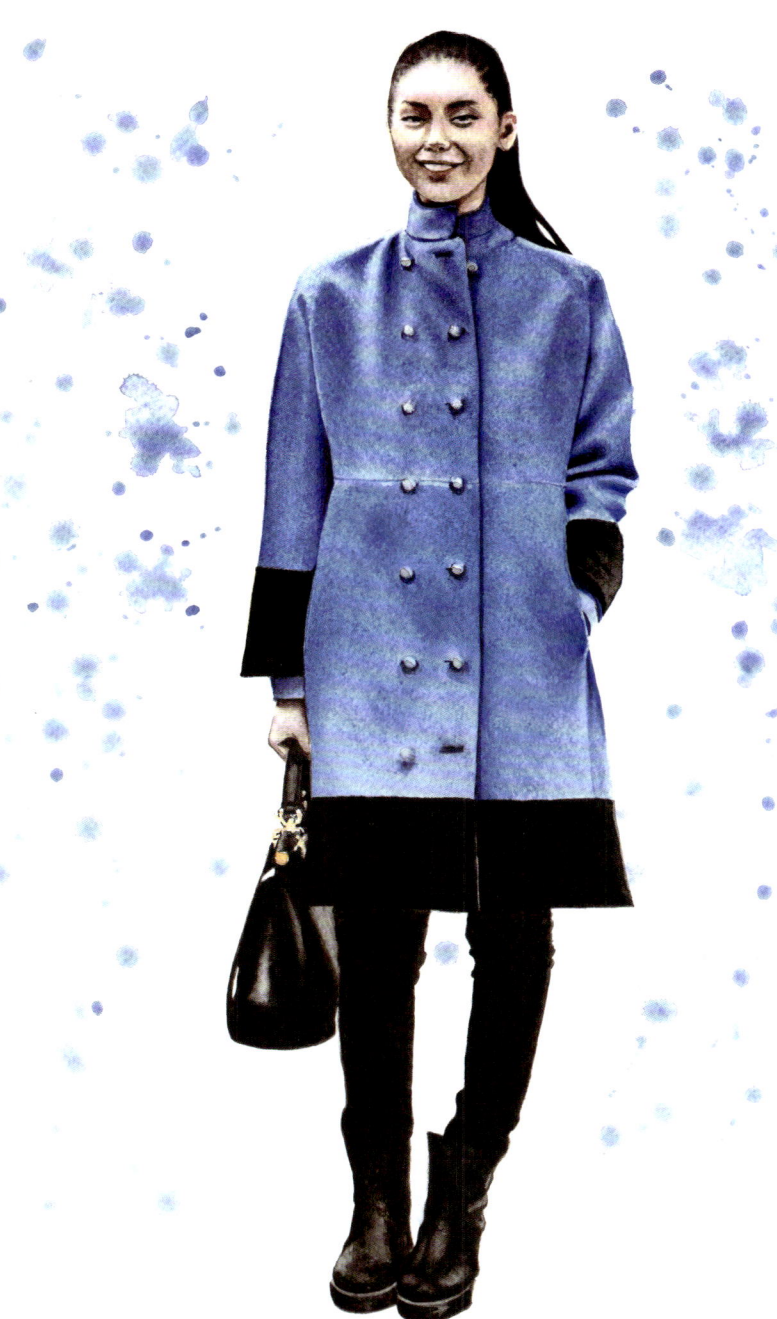

Example of street style fashion outfit in blue.
Illustrator: Davide Morettini Country: Italy

Street Style Fashion Outfit in Blue

Jason Wu SS 2016

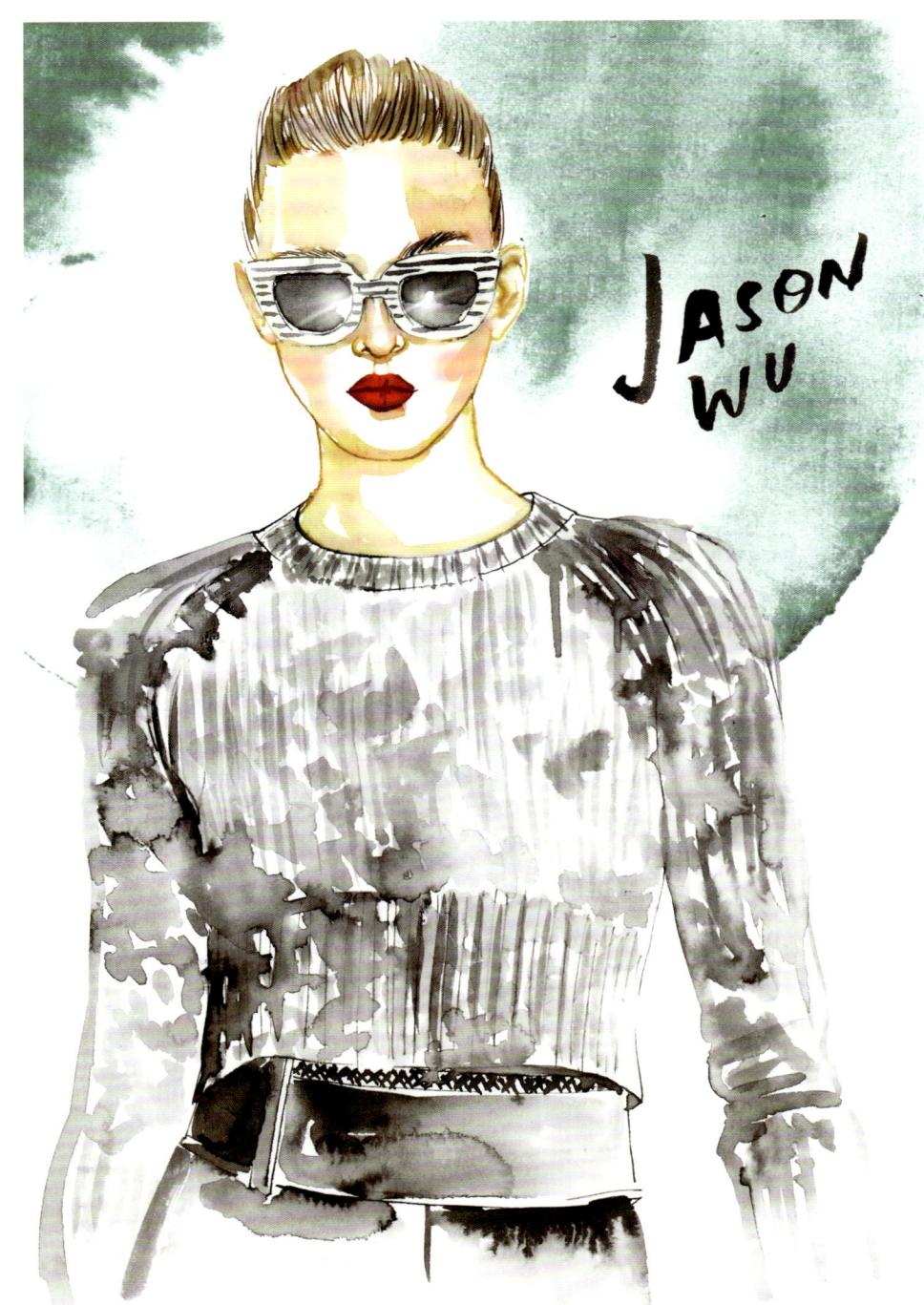

Watercolour: A stunning look with bold sunglasses and red lips from the Jason Wu show.
Illustrator: Samantha Hahn Country: USA

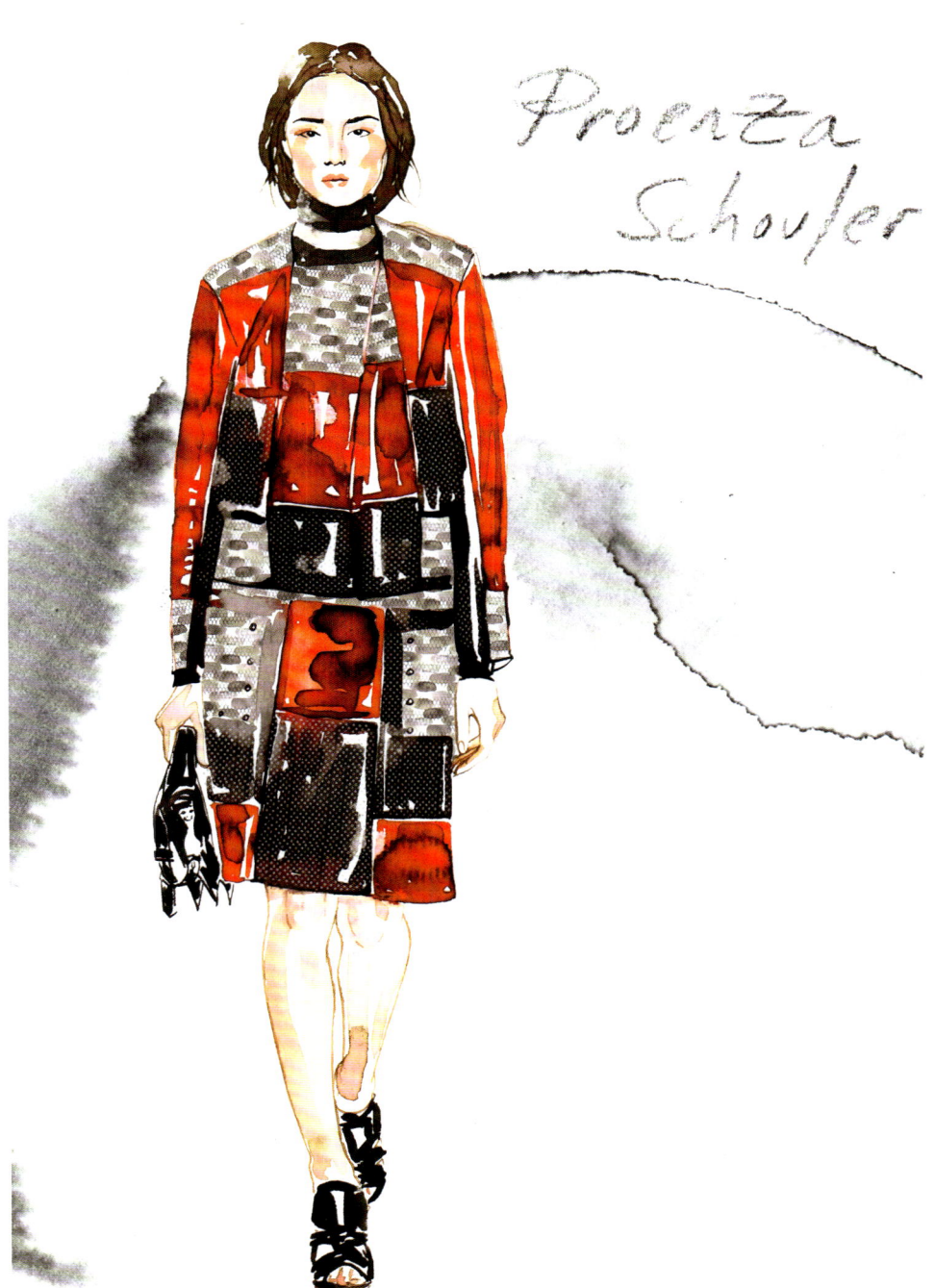

Proenza Schouler employs gorgeous textures and a paired down palette of white, black and red.
Illustrator: Samantha Hahn Country: USA

Proenza Schouler SS 2013

Chris Benz SS 2013

The illustrator went backstage before the Chris Benz presentation to capture the beauty and fashion looks and to really check out the vibe of the show before painting the favourite aspects of the collection.

Illustrator: Samantha Hahn Country: USA

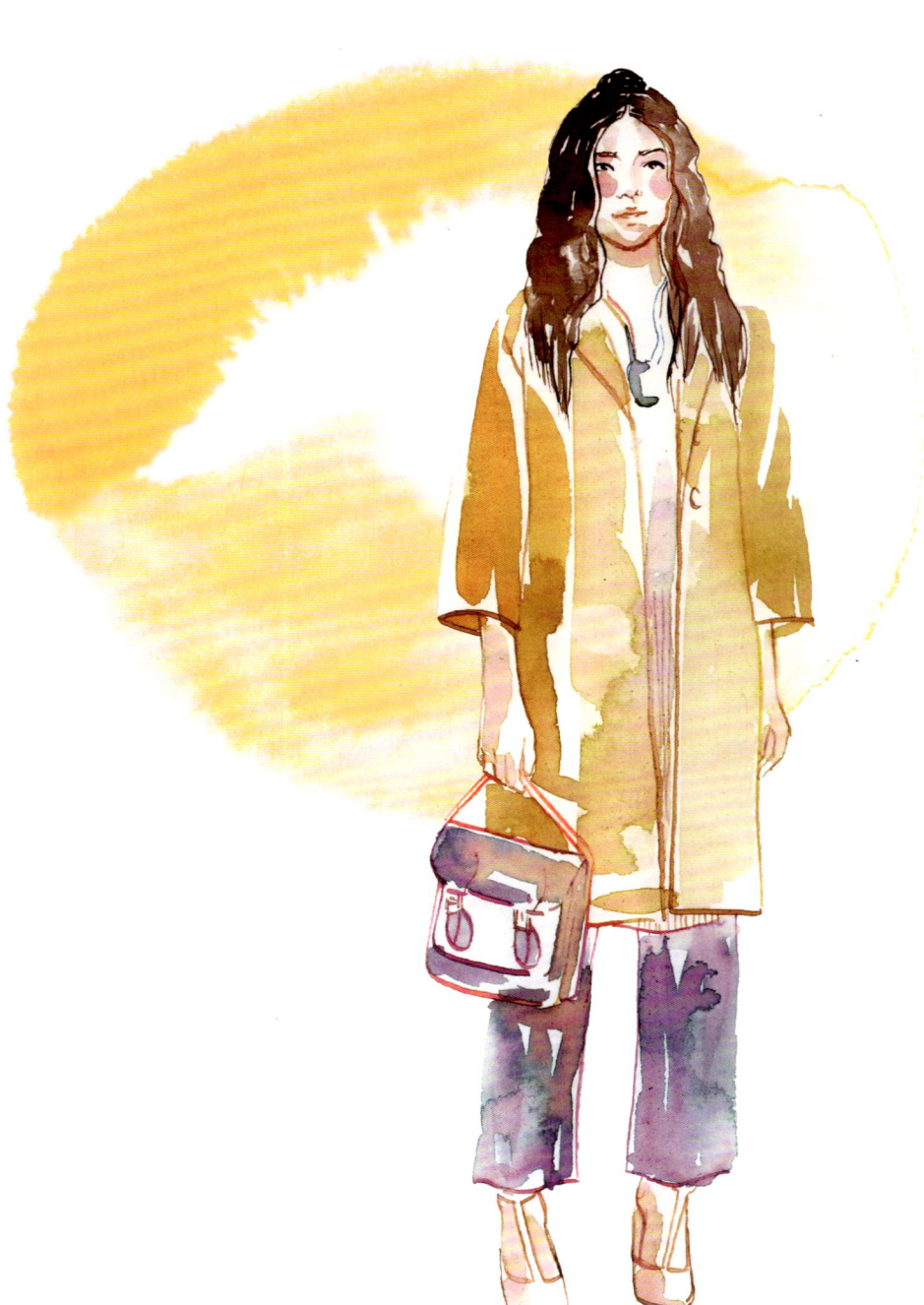

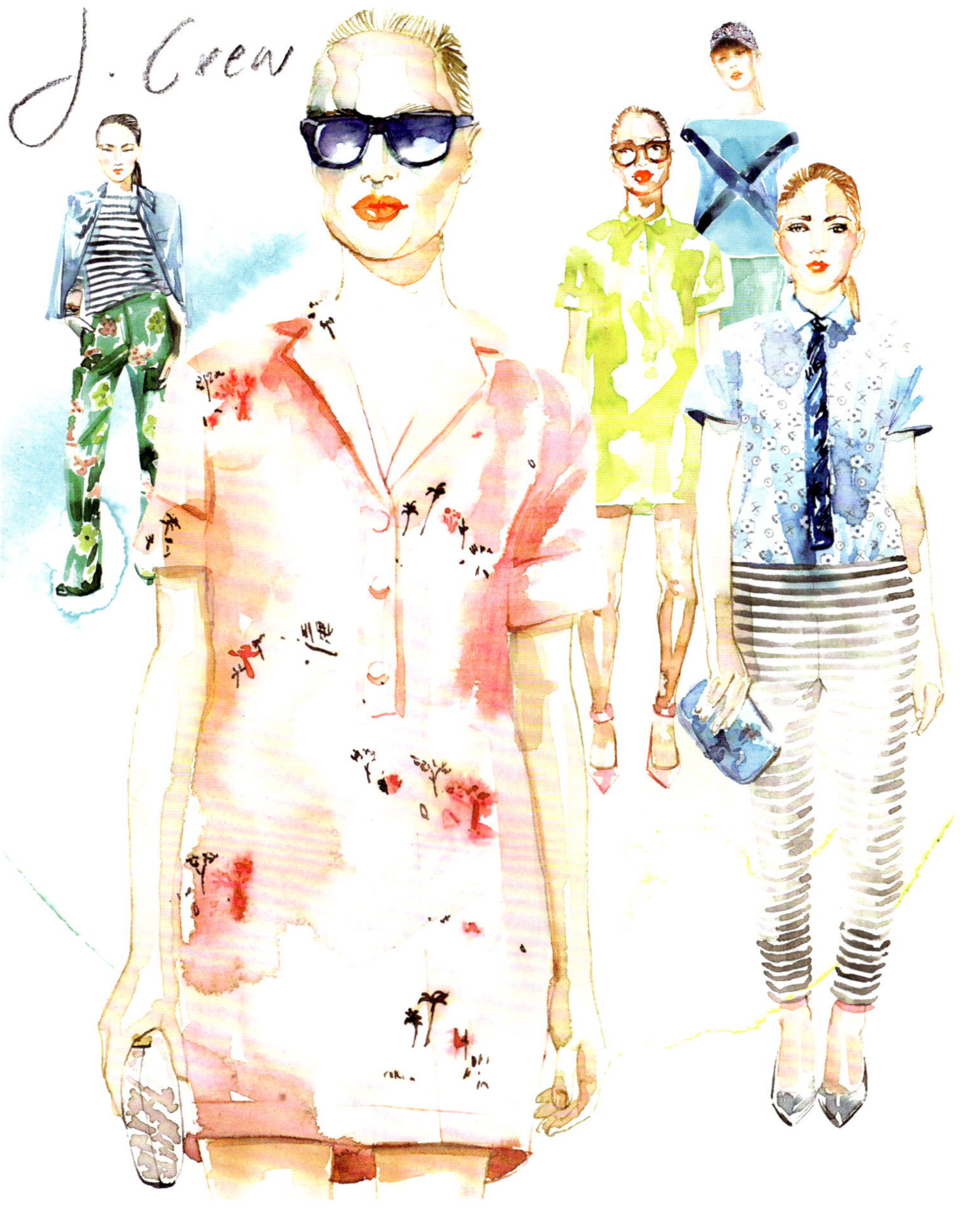

J.Crew

JCREW had a presentation and their looks are perfect for the daily life.
Illustrator: Samantha Hahn Country: USA

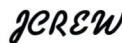

Céline FW 2013

Editorial for Pudder agency on fall fashion where the illustrator picked out personal favourites from the runway. Inspired by Céline FW 2013
Illustrator: Esra Roise Country: Norway

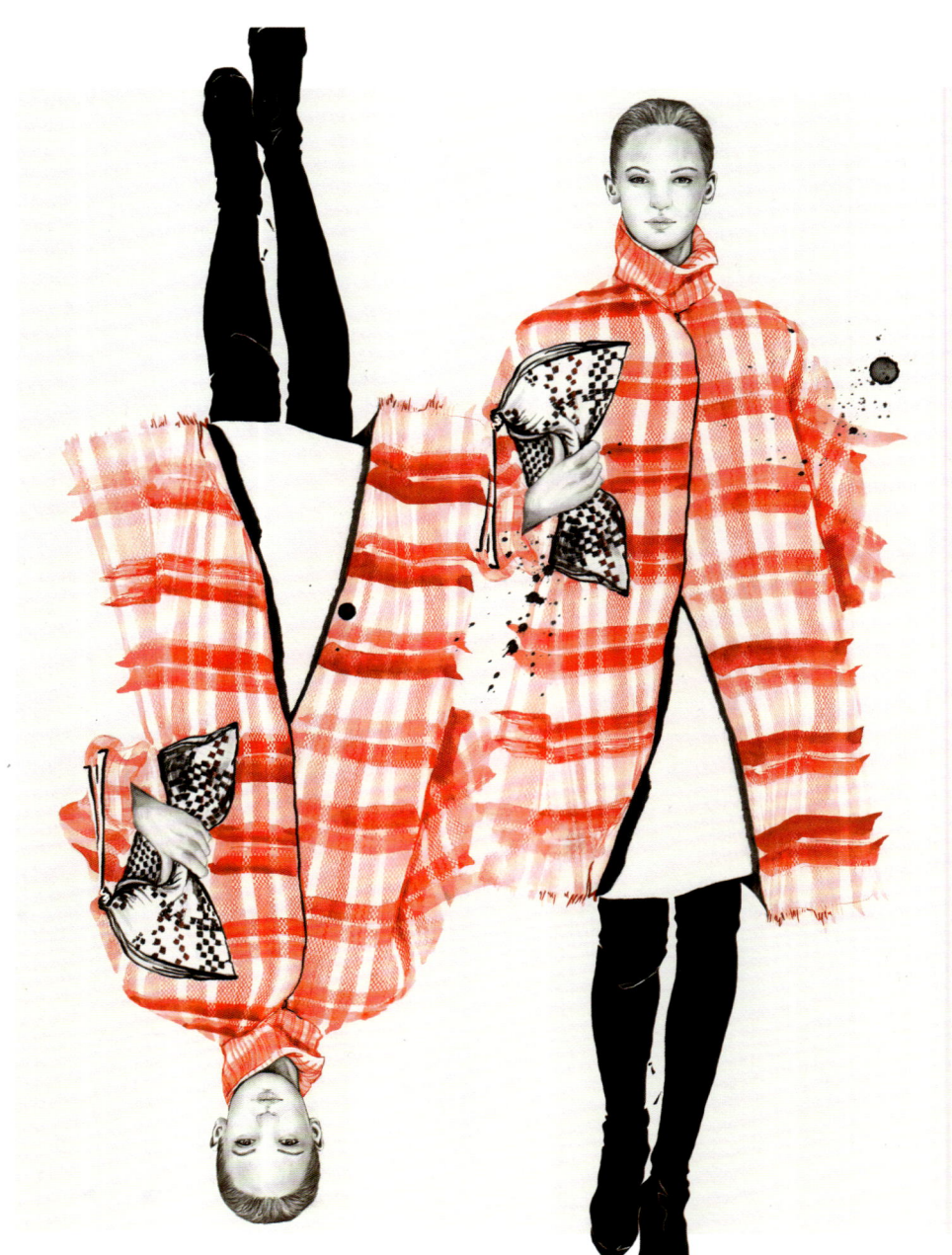

Personal work, inspired by the an earlier Céline FW collection.
Illustrator: Esra Roise Country: Norway

Céline

Fendi AW 2012

Fashion illustration inspired by model Kirsi Pyrhonen wearing Fendi AW12.
Illustrator: Esra Roise Country: Norway

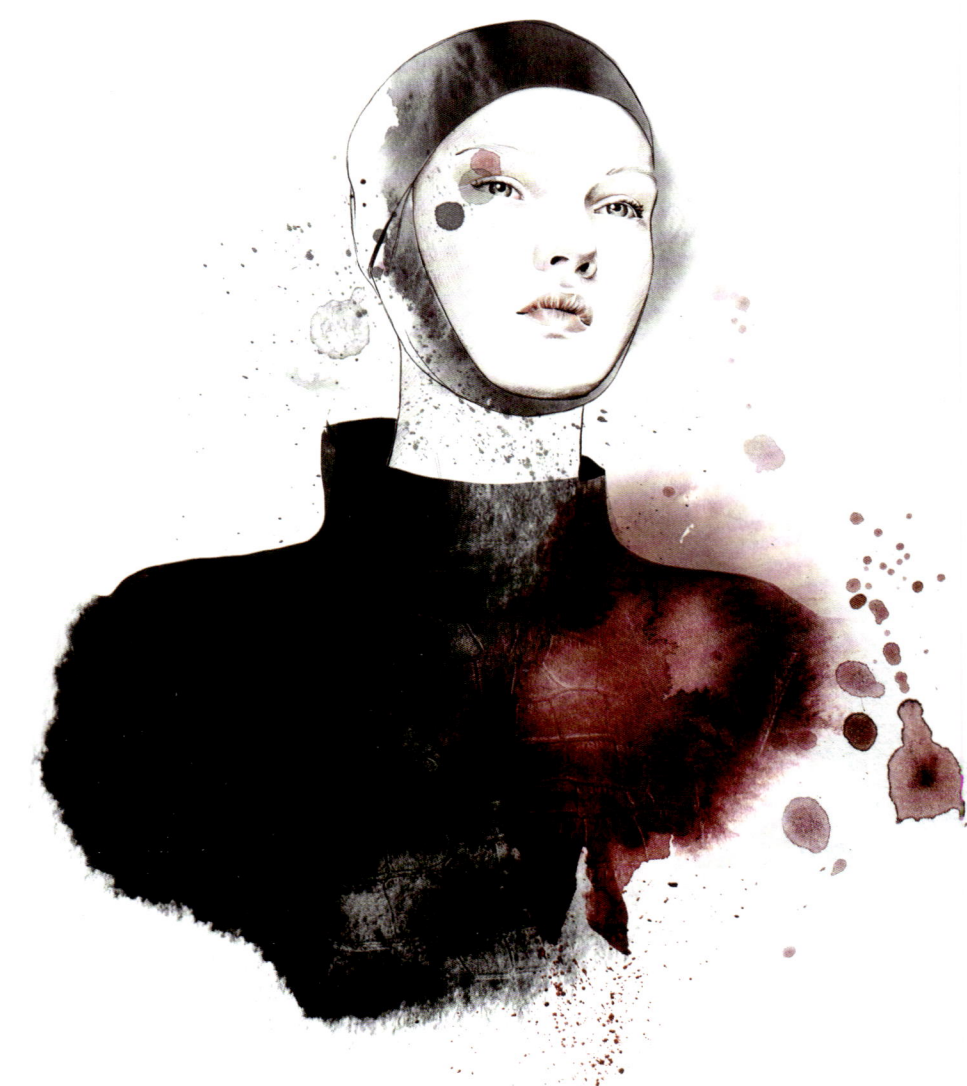

Fashion illustration inspired by model Kirsi Pyrhonen wearing Lanvin AW 12.
Illustrator: Esra Roise Country: Norway

Lanvin AW 2012

Céline AW 2013

Personal project for solo exhibition 'ByOne' in Oslo, Norway where the theme was femininity in fashion. Inspired by Céline AW 2013.
Illustrator: Esra Roise Country: Norway

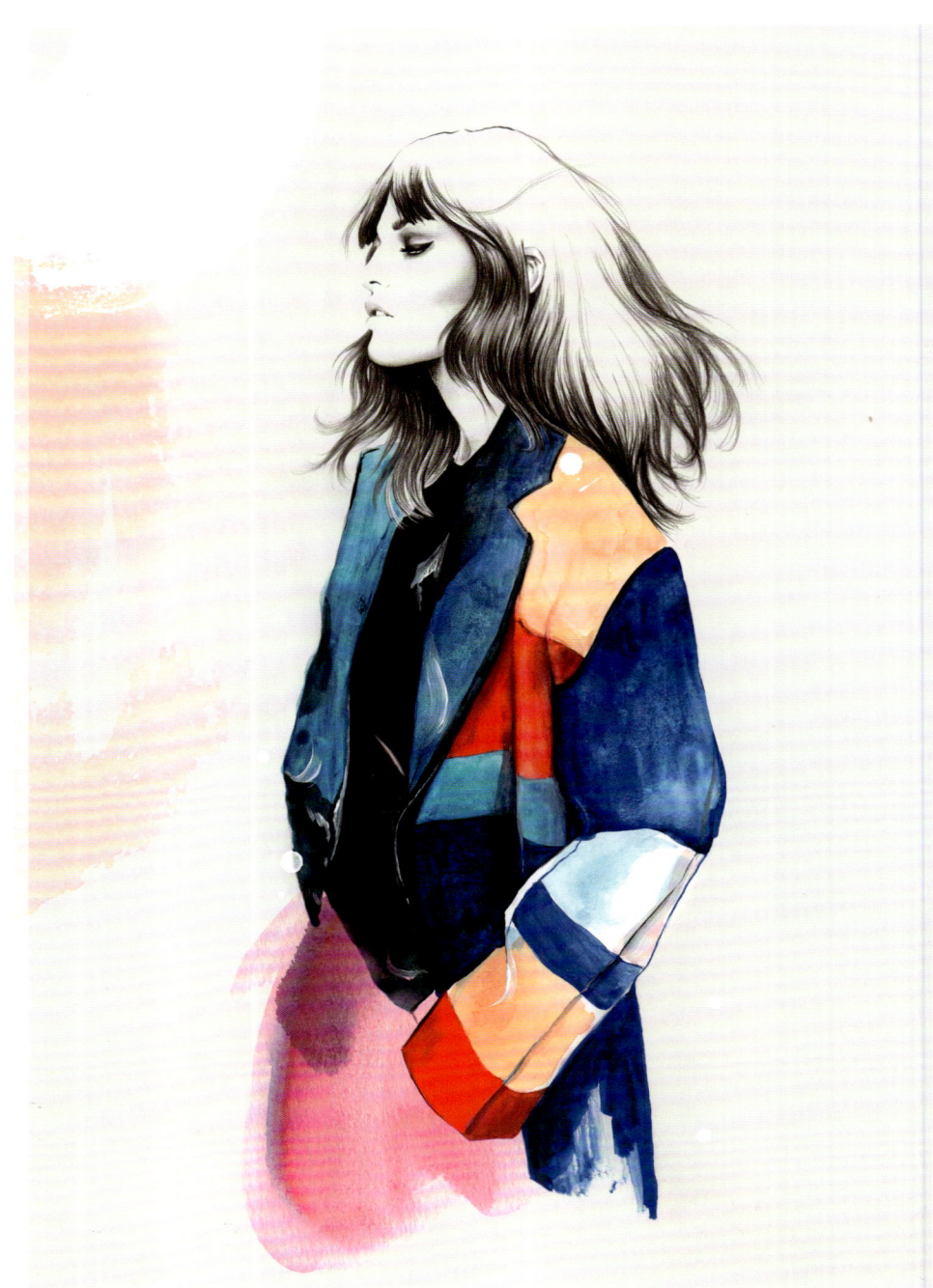

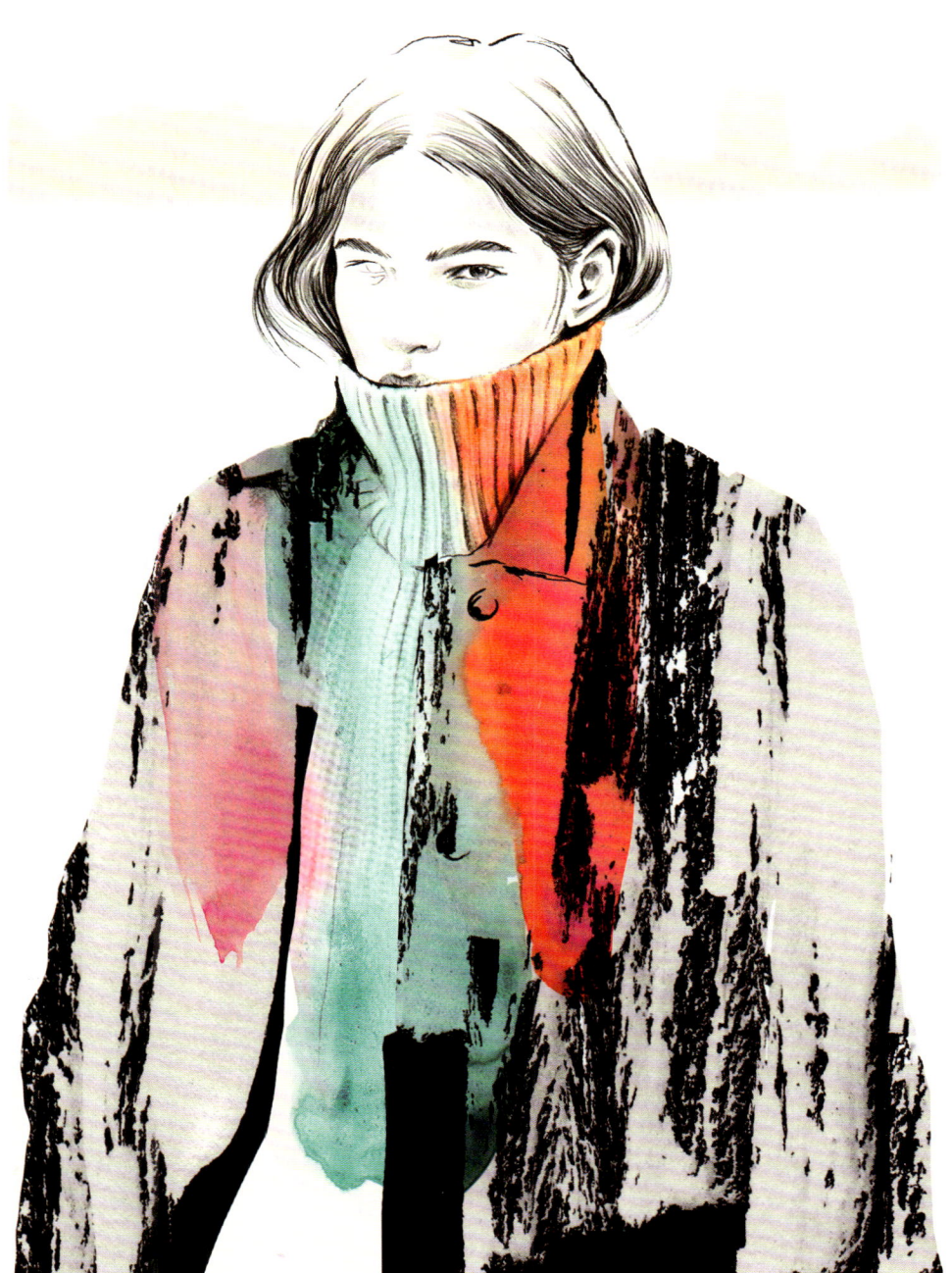

Winter Coat, pencil ink, mixed media. Fashion illustration inspired by L'officiel.
Illustrator: Esra Roise Country: Norway

L'officiel

Loewe AW 2015

Fashion illustration inspired by Loewe AW15.
Illustrator: Esra Røise Country: Norway

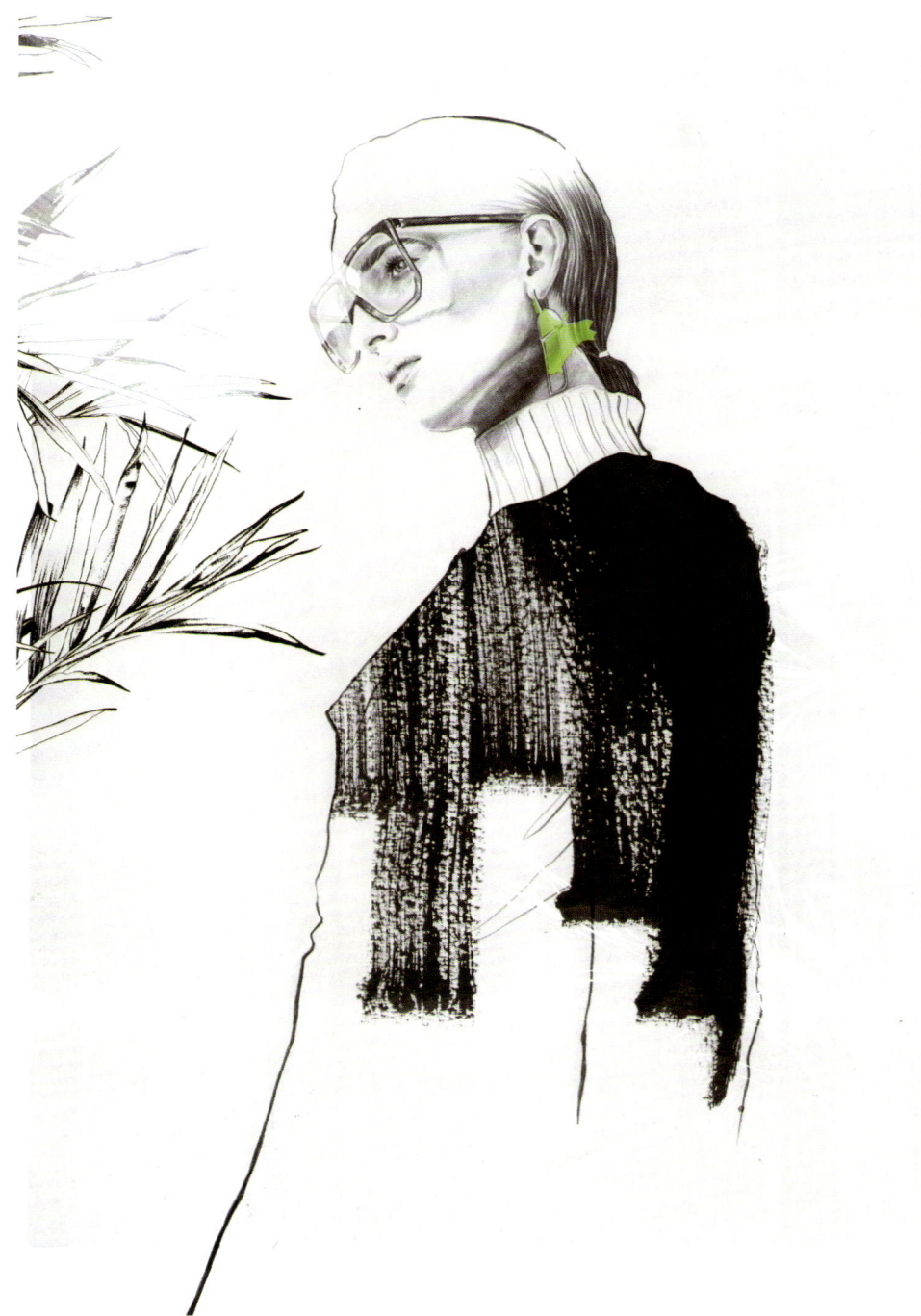

Personal project for solo exhibition 'ByOne' in Oslo, Norway where the theme was femininity in fashion. Inspired by Alexander Wang RTW 2014.
Illustrator: Esra Roise Country: Norway

Alex Wang Turtleneck

Celine Furry Sweater

Fashion illustration inspired by model Karoline Bjornlyke wearing Céline AW 2012 furry sweater.
Illustrator: Esra Roise Country: Norway

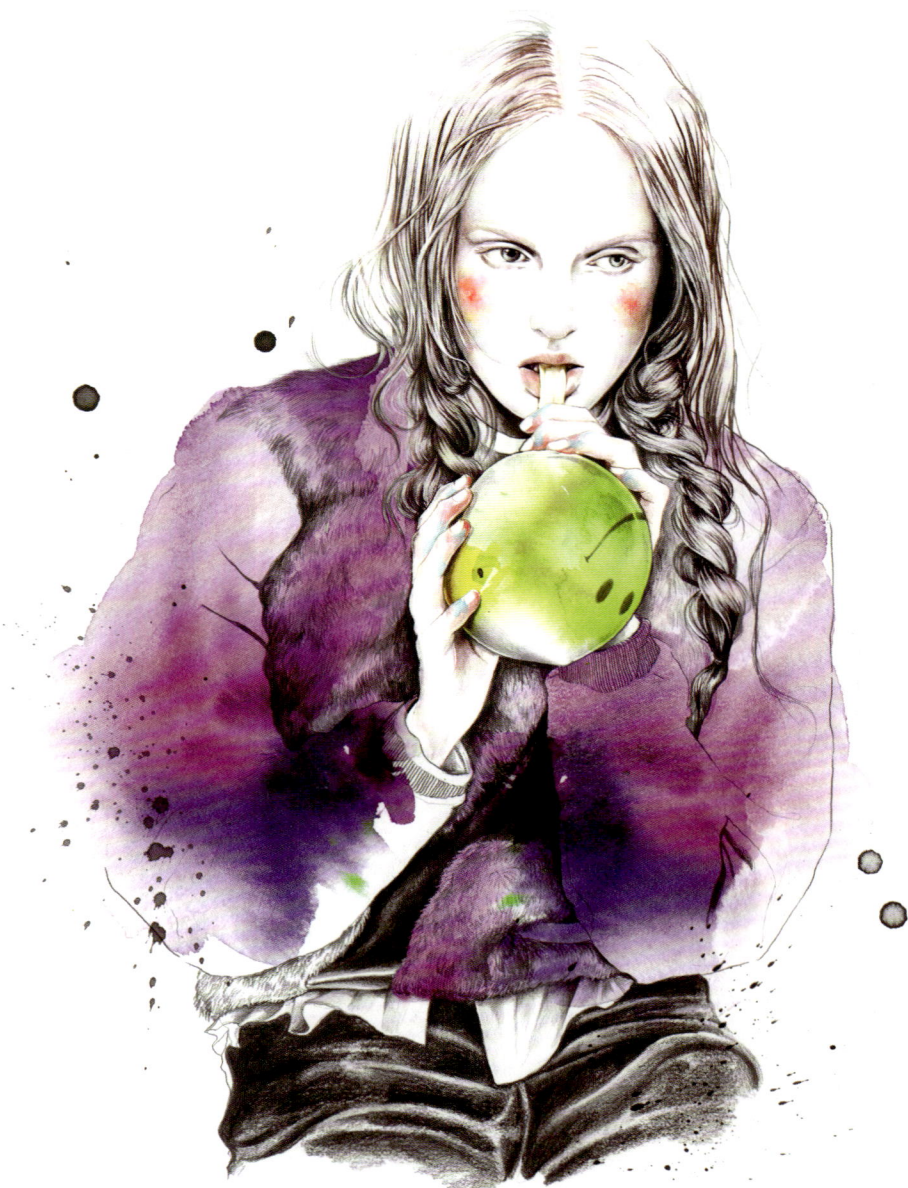

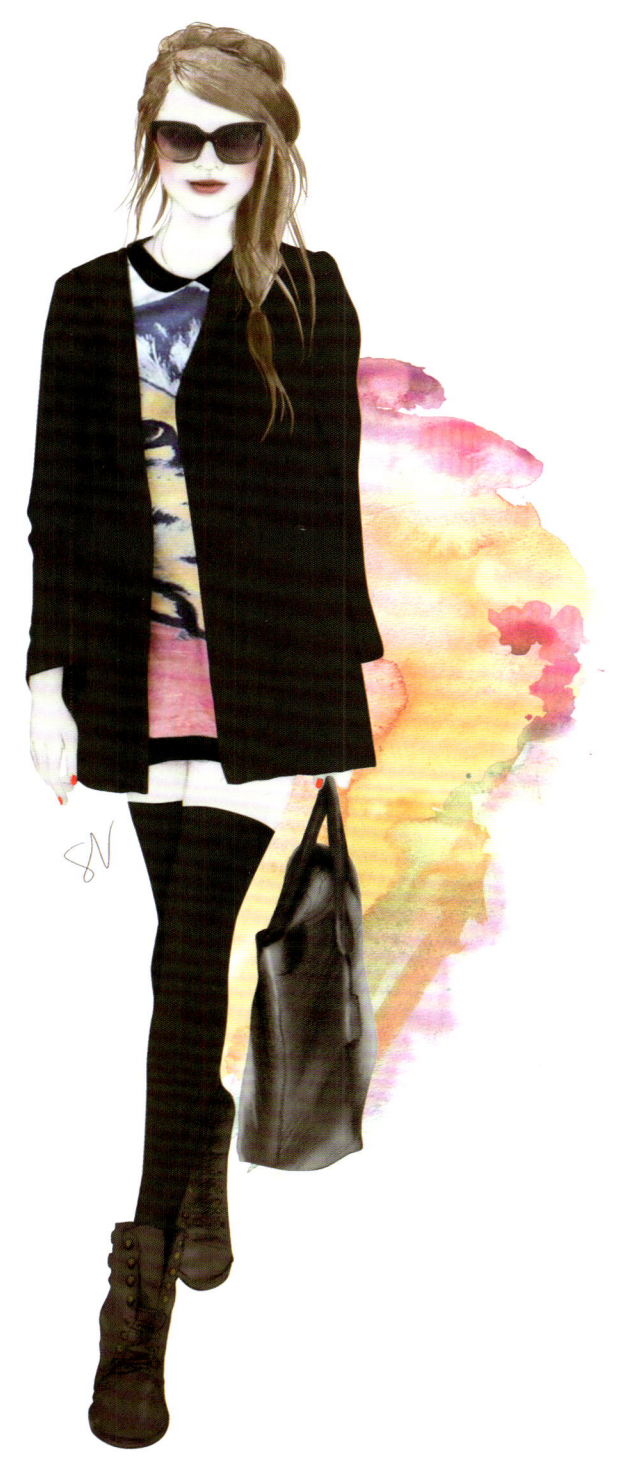

Russian red hair fashion model, with vintage style. She dresses trendy all the time. The illustration was supposed to have all the details as the original reference.
Illustrator: Sara Vera Lecaro Client: COSAS Magazine Country: Ecuador

Vintage Look

DKNY

Commissioned illustration series for fashion editorial about street style and fashion influencers at Ecuador Fashion Magazine COSAS.

Illustrator: Sara Vera Lecaro Client: COSAS Magazine Country: Ecuador

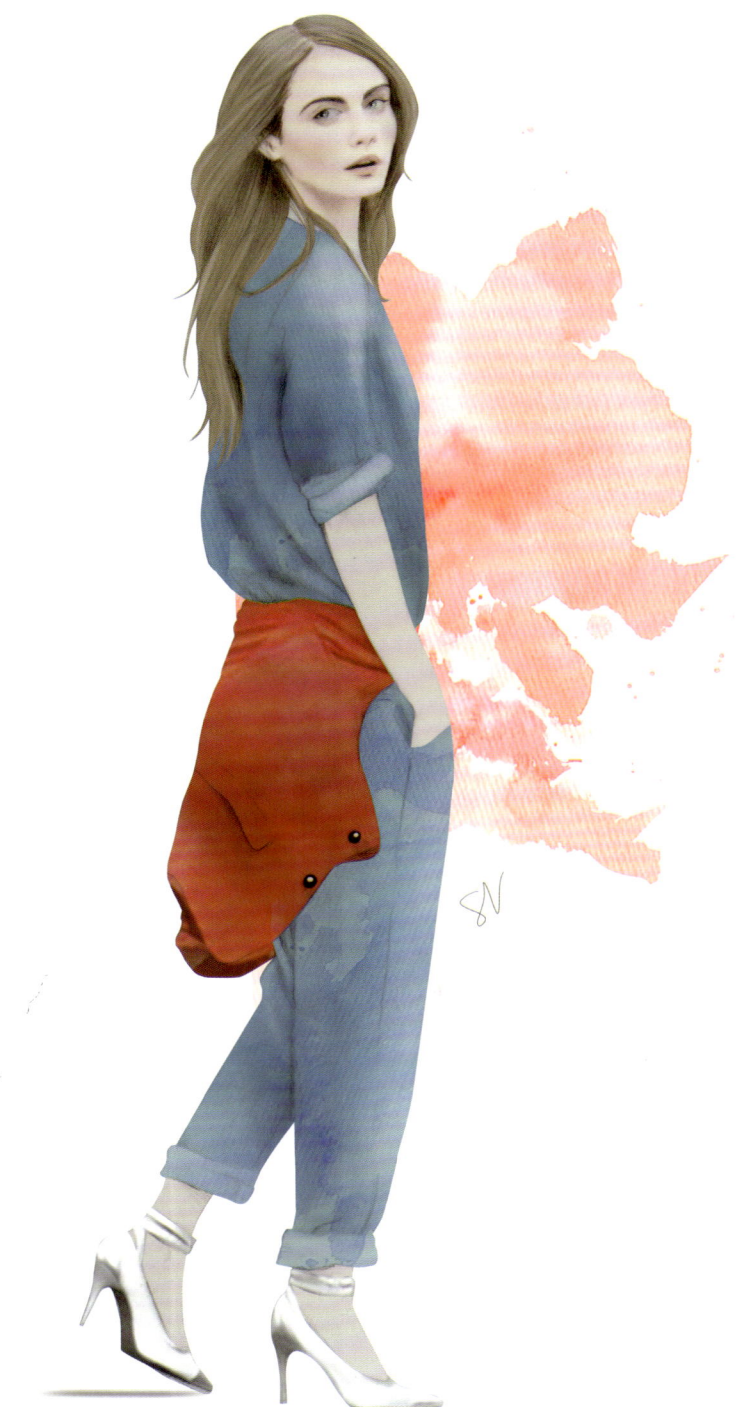

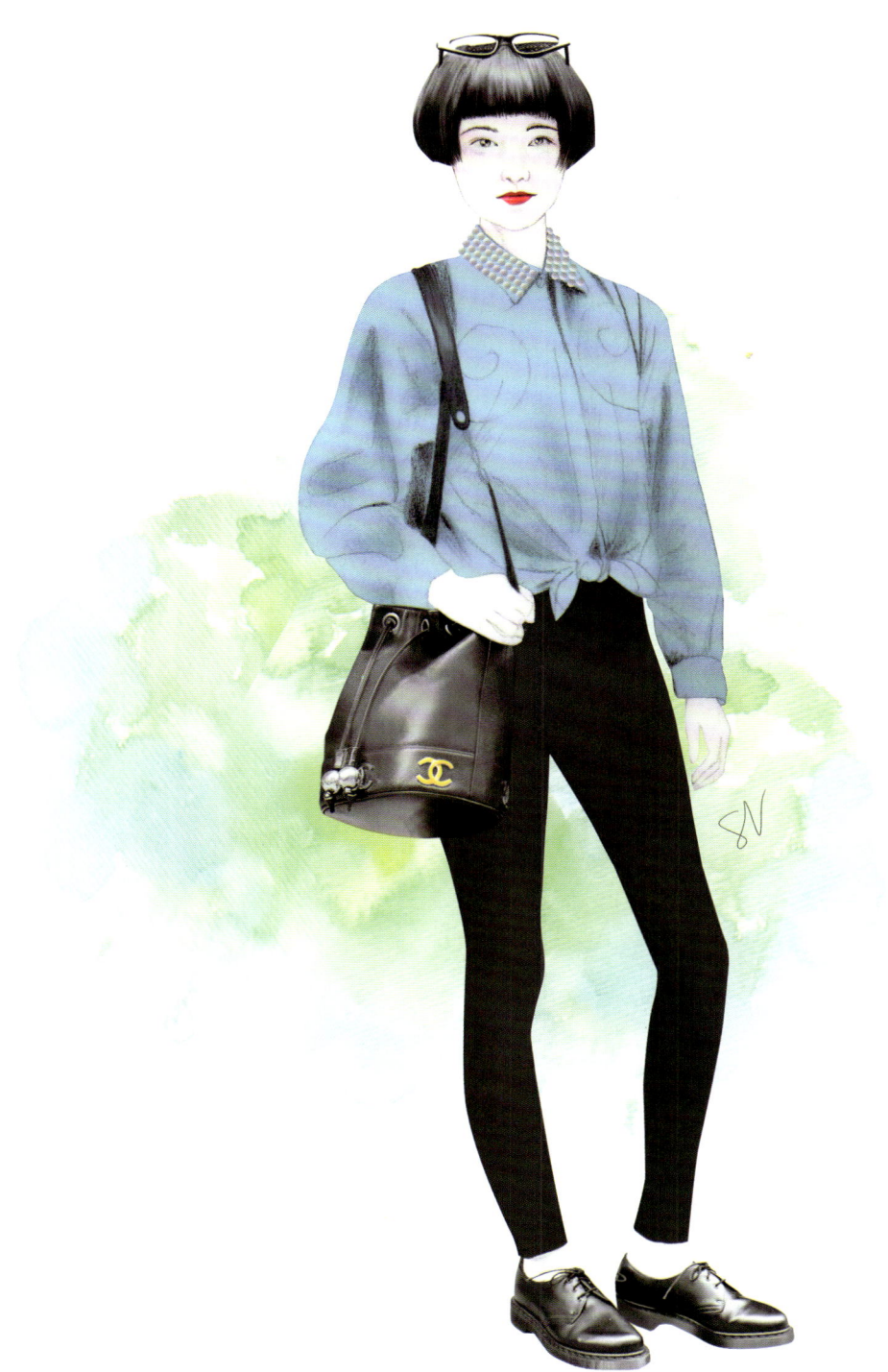

The illustration was supposed to be realistic specially in the bag and shoes. Illustrator: Sara Vera Lecaro Client: COSAS Magazine Country: Ecuador

Street Style Look and Chanel Bag

Prabal Gurung RTW FW 2015

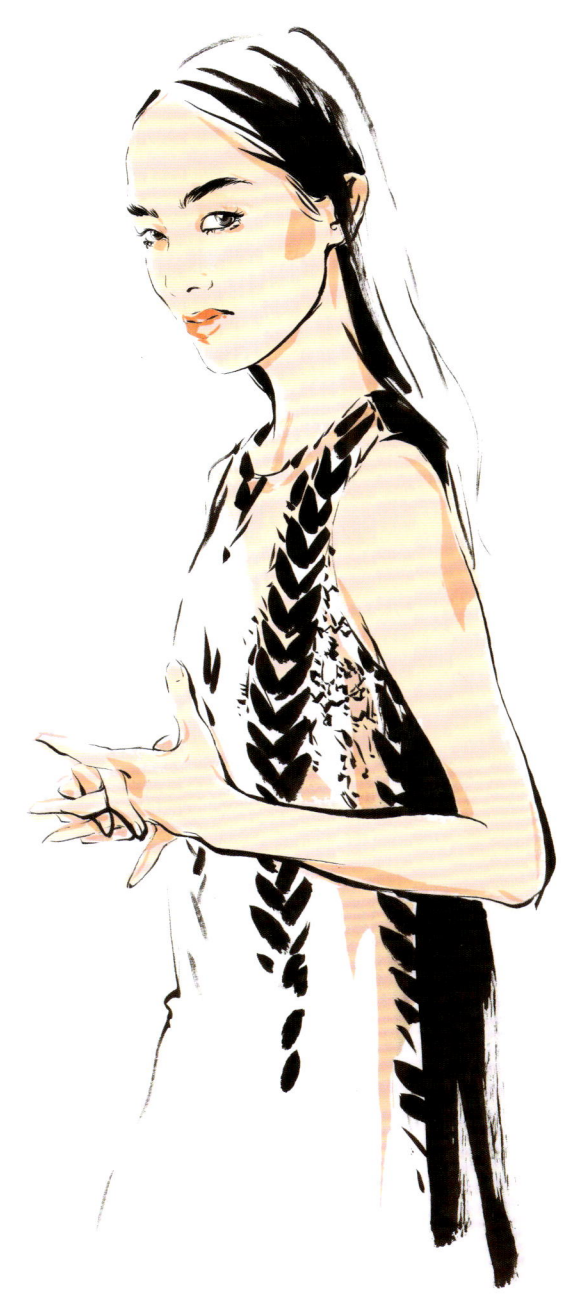

Backstage moment at Prabal Gurung show, N.Y. Fashion Week RTW FW 2015. Editorial work for vogue.ru
Illustrator: Alena Lavdovskaya Country: Russia

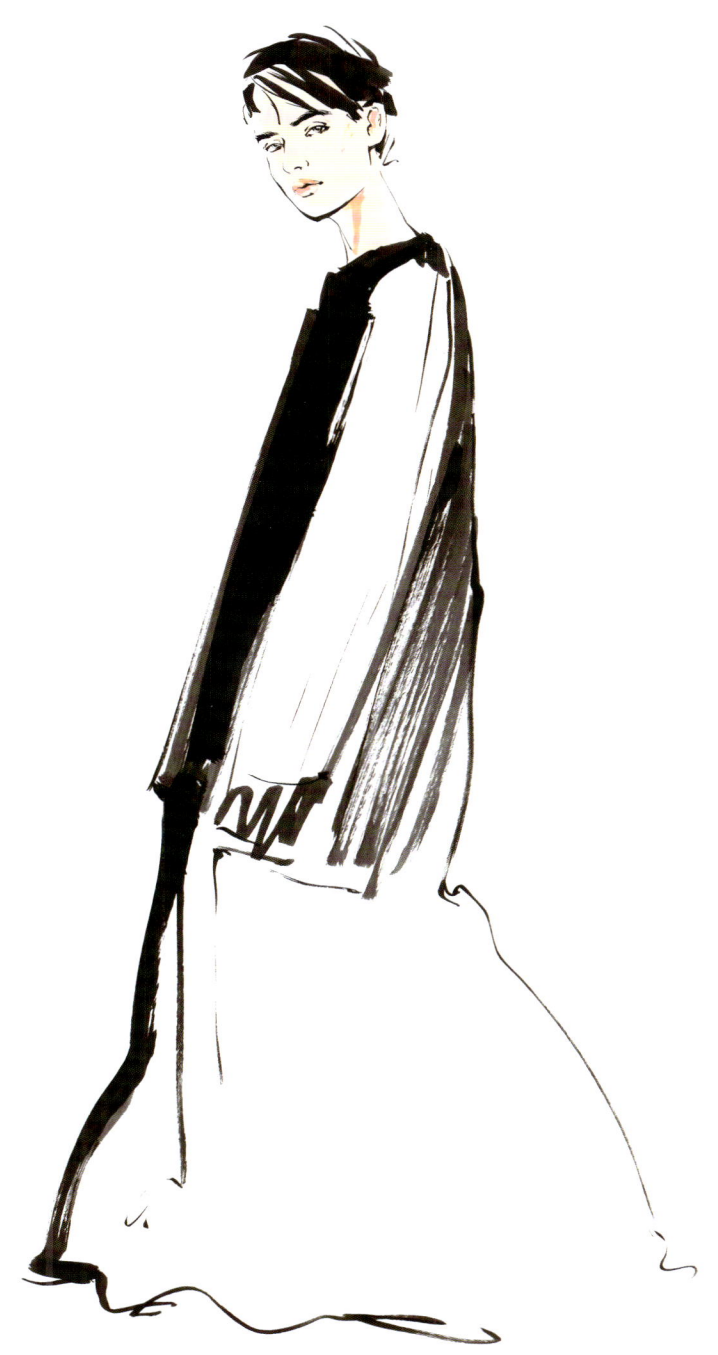

Backstage moment at Vera Wang show, N.Y. Fashion Week RTW FW 2015. Editorial work for vogue.ru
Illustrator: Alena Lavdovskaya Country: Russia

Vera Wang RTW FW 2015

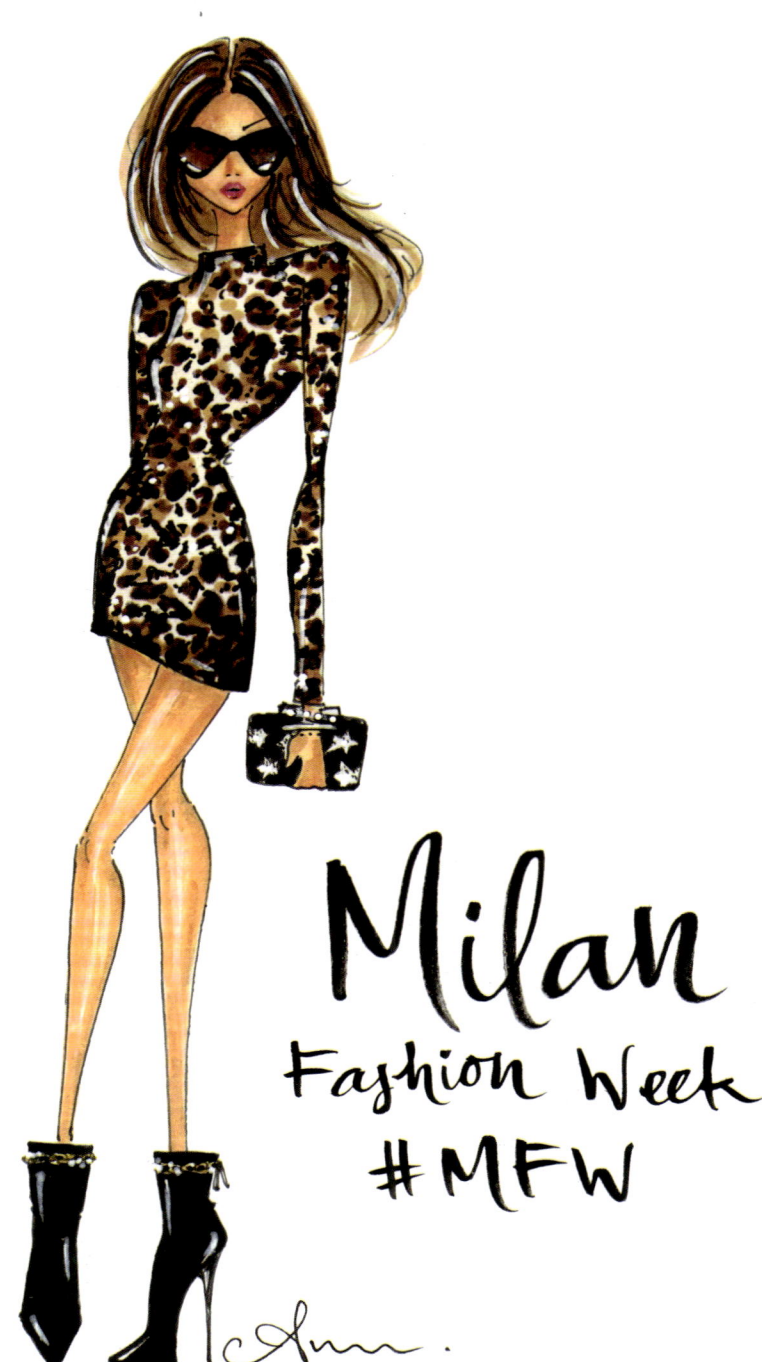

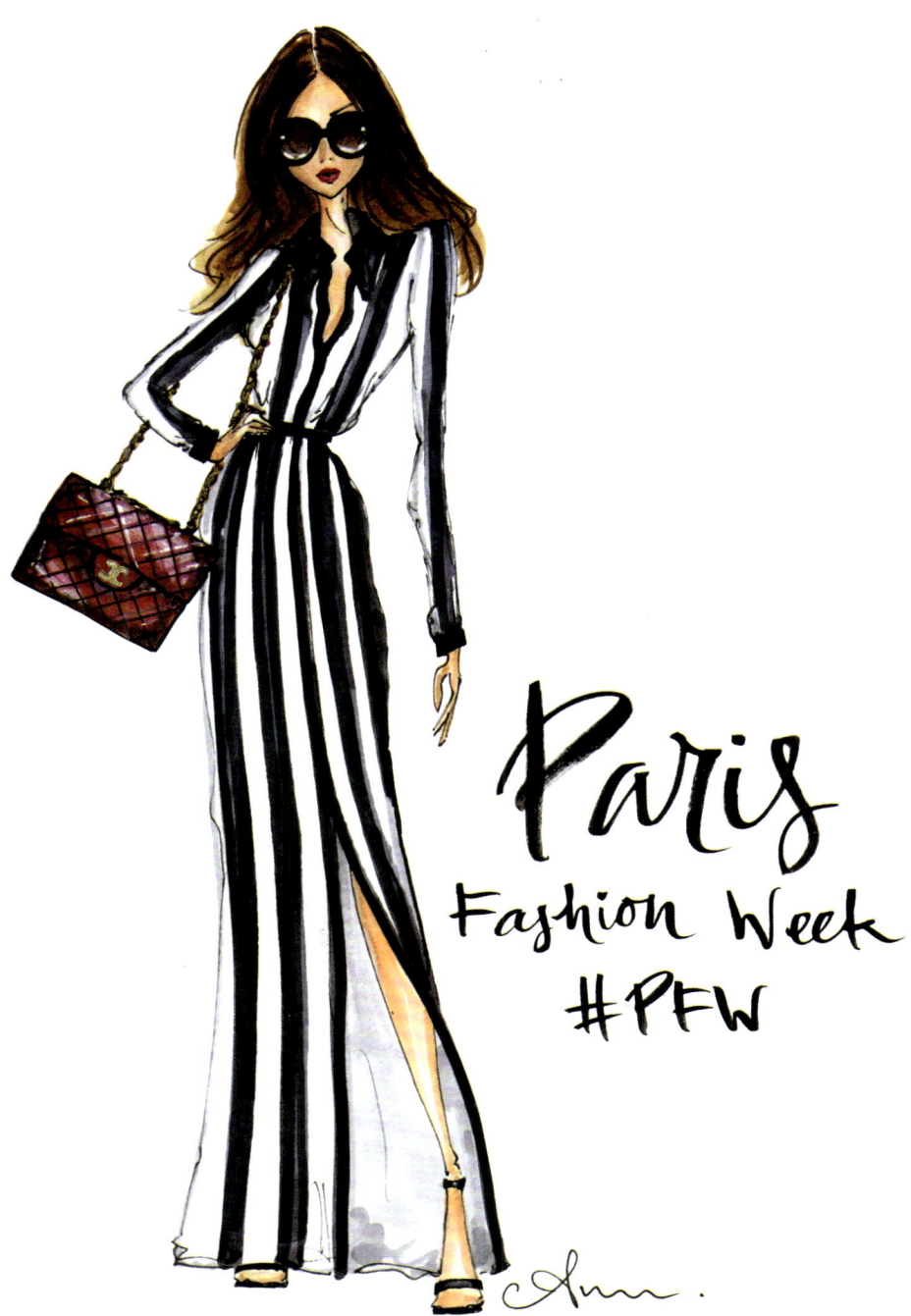

Dunhill SS 2016

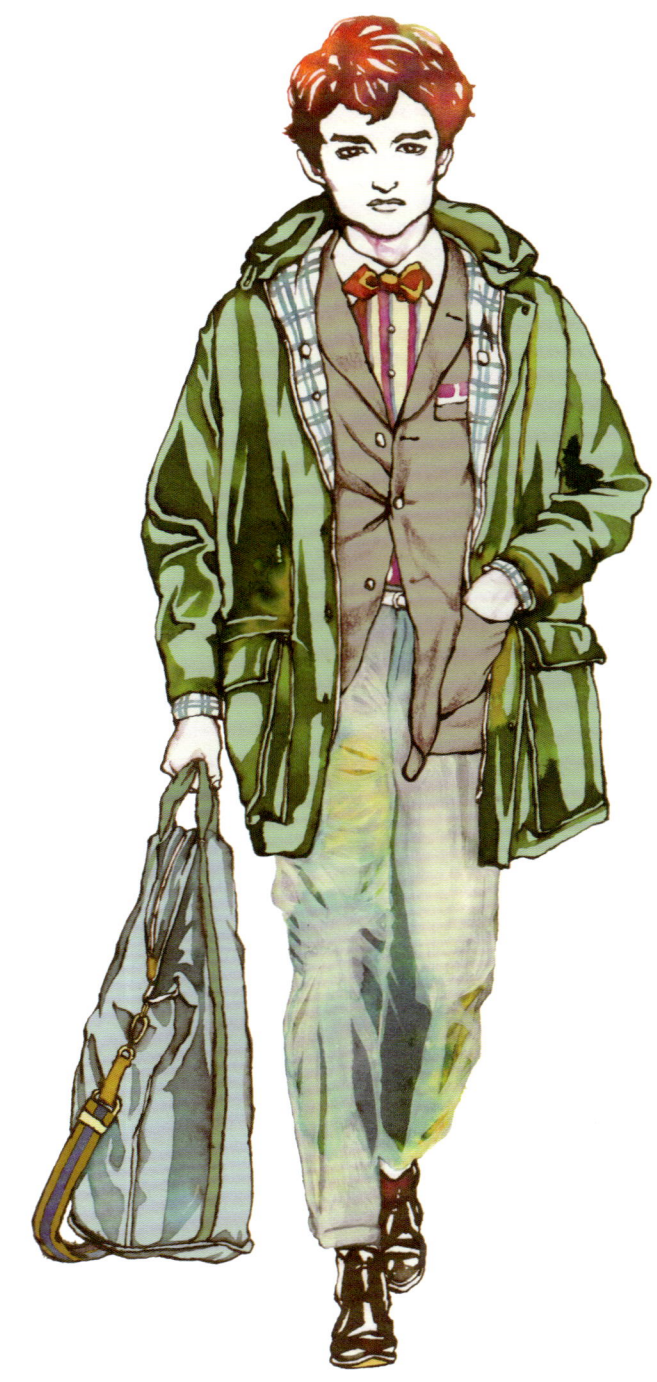

Colourful inky style fashion illustration, using ink, coloured pencil, gouache then digitally finished.
Illustrator: Natsuki Otani Country: Japan

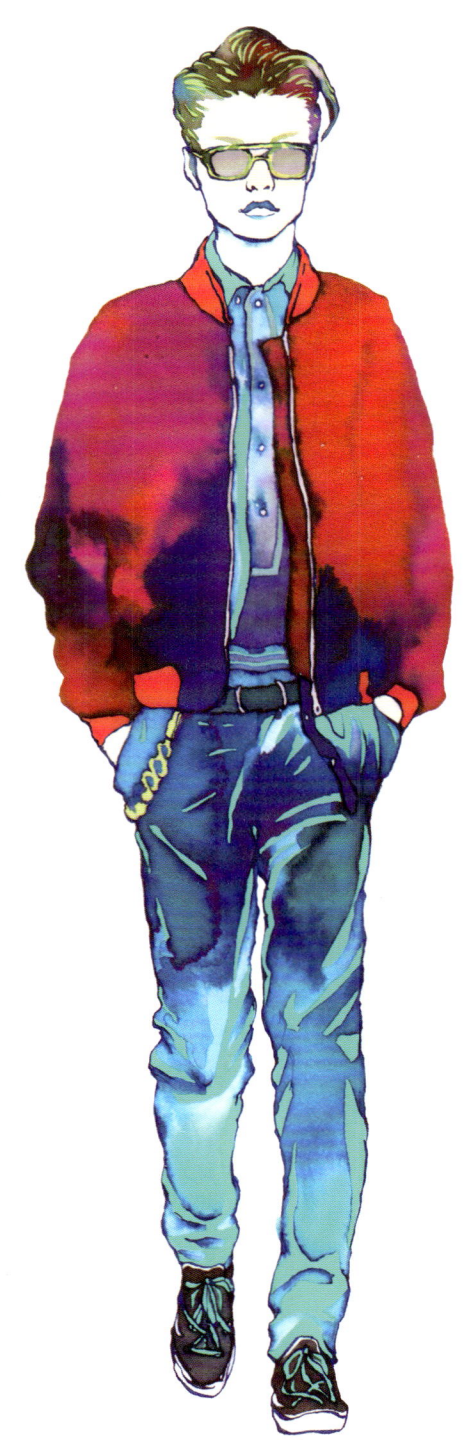

Colourful inky style fashion illustration, using ink then digitally finished.
Illustrator: Natsuki Otani Country: Japan

Katie Eary SS 2016

Shorts

Pencil, watercolour, ink and airbrush on paper. This illustration was commissioned by Wall Street Journal. This particular one was about how to wear shorts.

Illustrator: Mia Marie Overgaard Country: Denmark

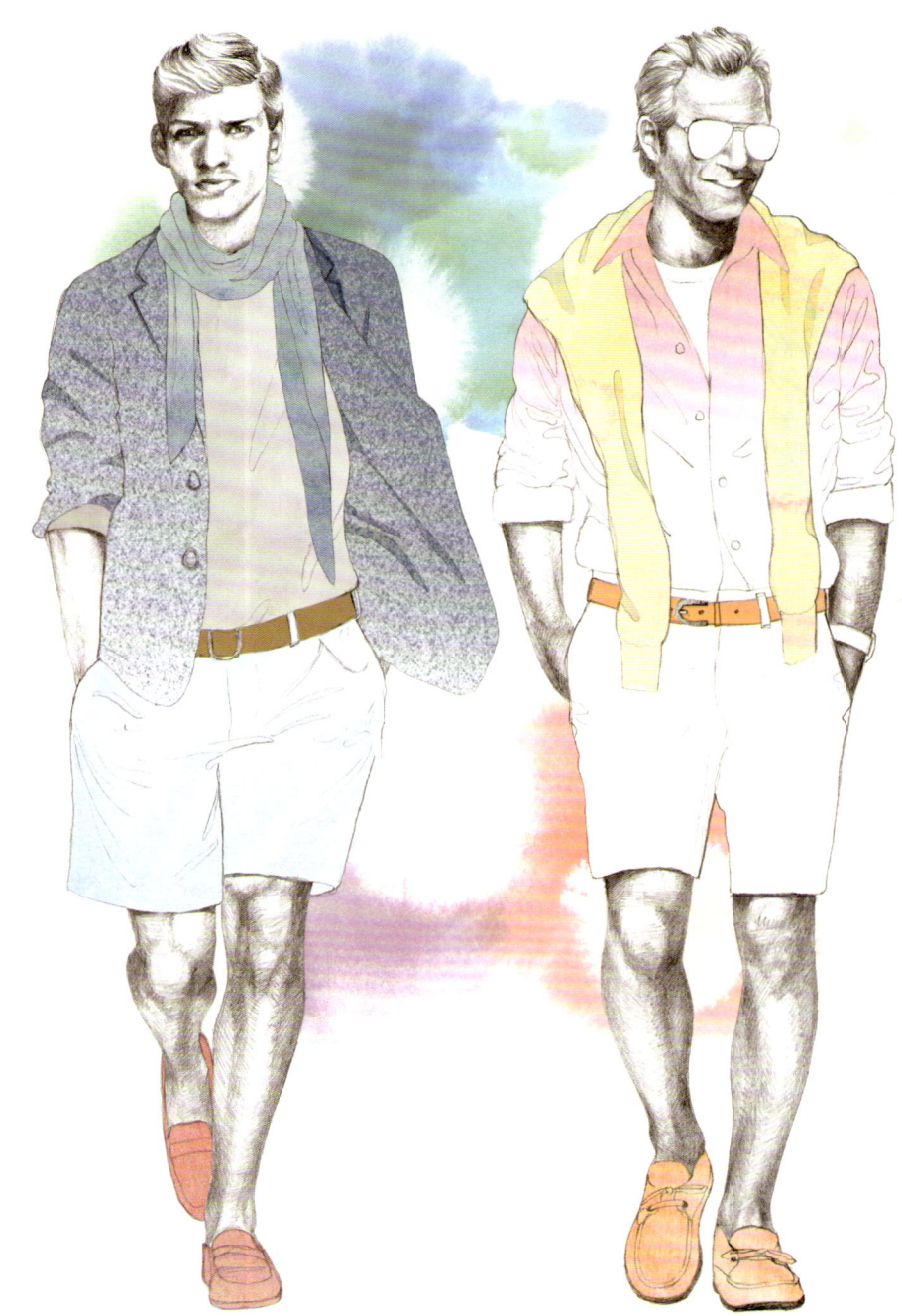

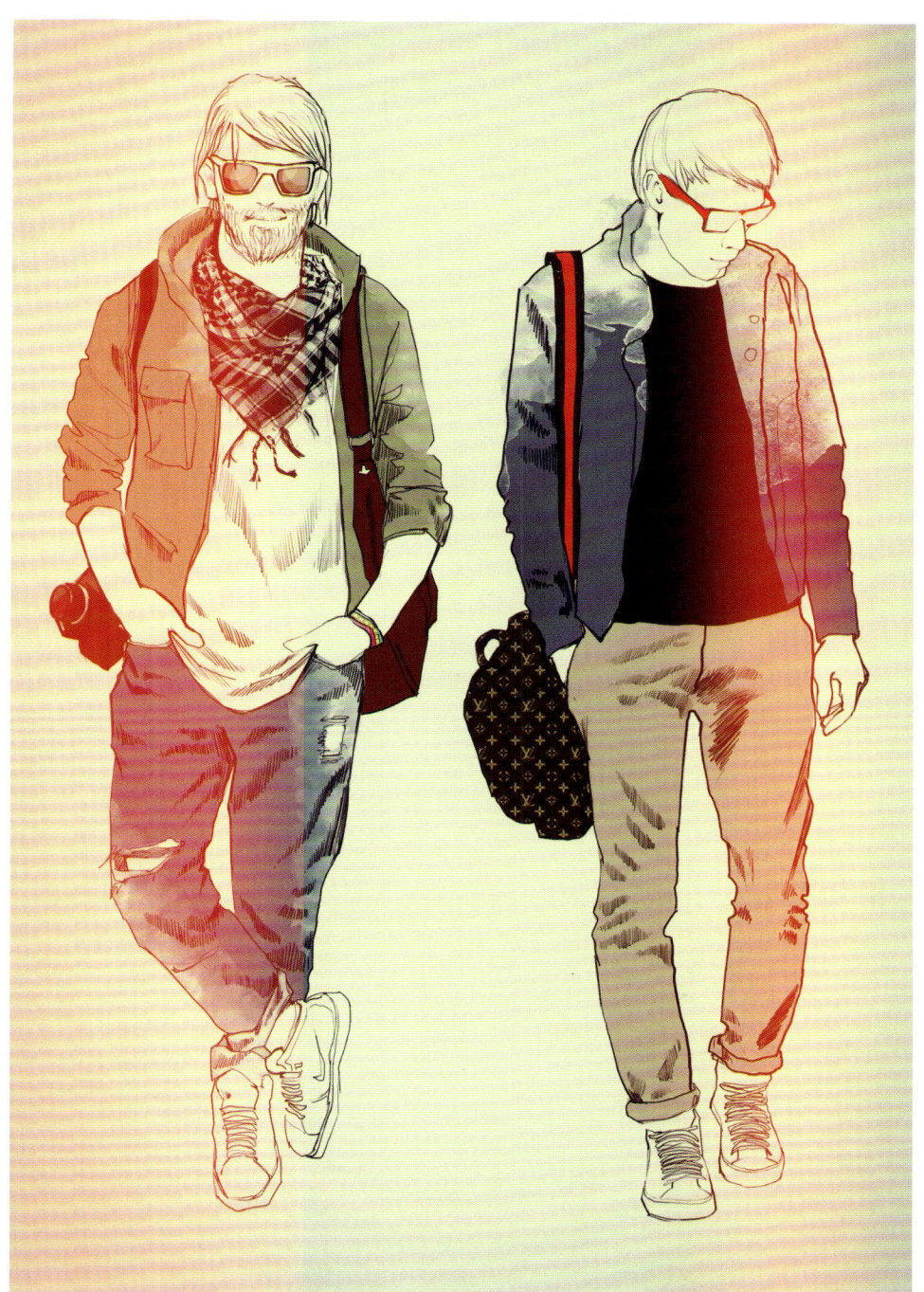

The idea was to illustrate Russian young middle class representers with their different looks in their casual life.
Illustrator: Svetlana Ikhsanova Country: Russia

Casual Look

Rag & Bone RTW FW 2015

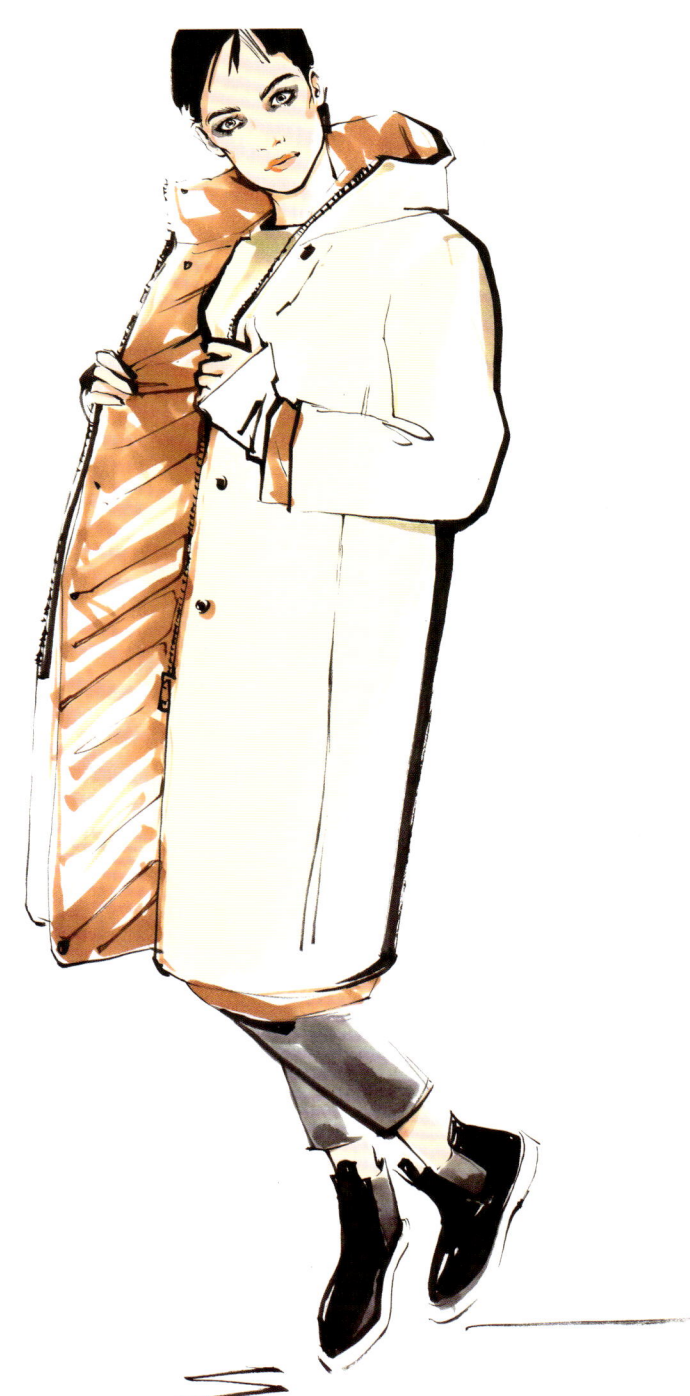

Editorial work for vogue.ru. Backstage moment at Rag & Bone show, NY Fashion Week RTW FW 2015.
Illustrator: Alena Lavdovskaya Country: Russia

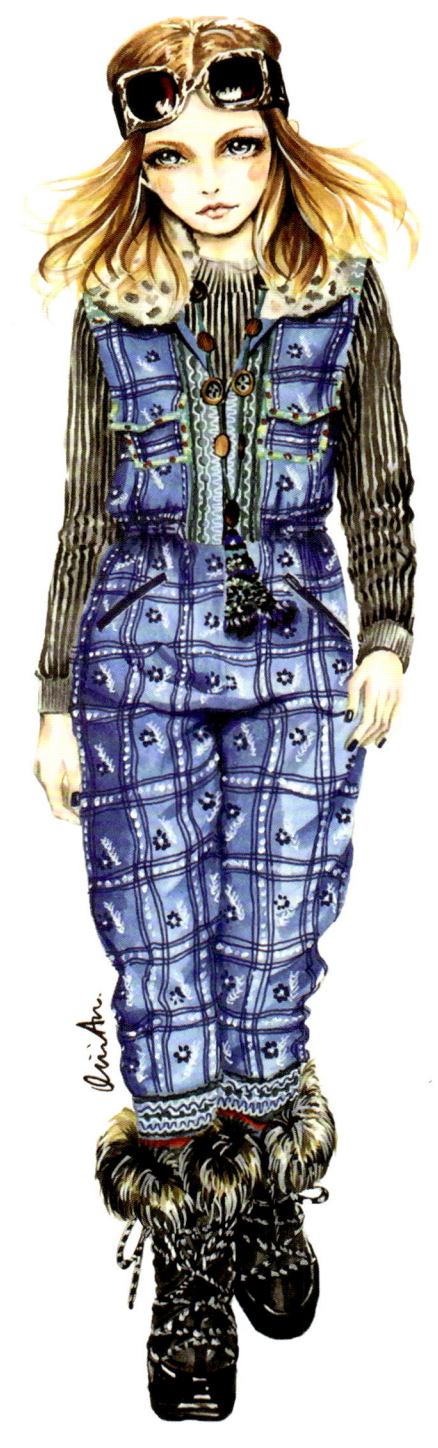

This illustration is inspired by Anna Sui Fall 2015 RTW collection.
Illustrator: Olivia Au Country: Hong Kong, China

Anna Sui Fall 2015 RTW

Peaks of London

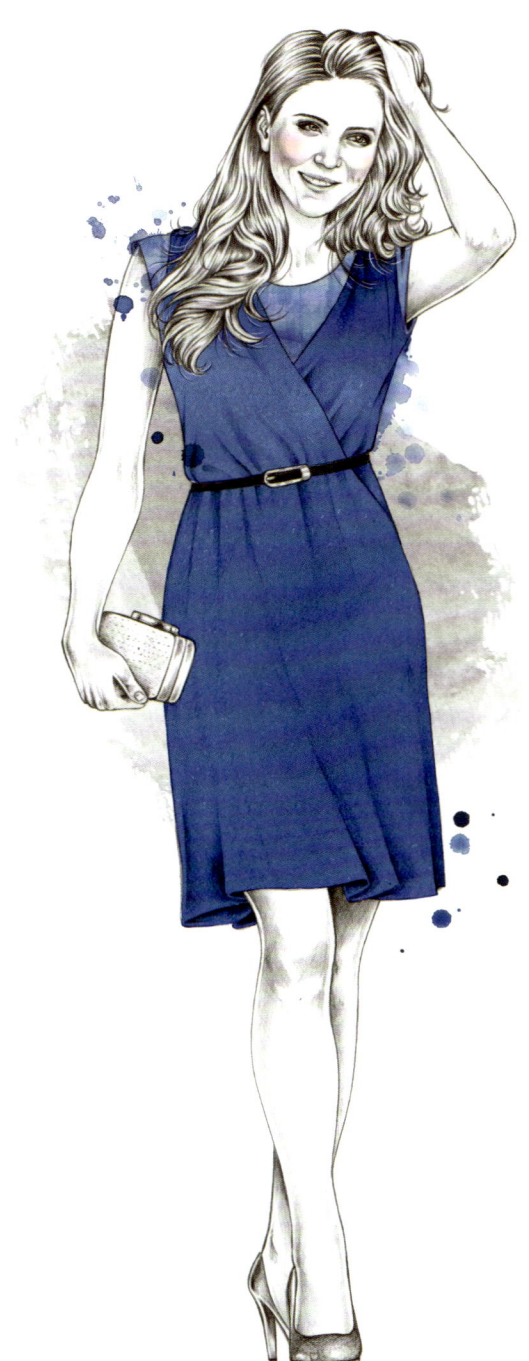

Illustration for British brand 'Peaks of London', inspired by Kate Middleton wearing one of their beautiful dresses. Pencil and watercolour on paper.
Illustrator: Carole Wilmet Country: Belgium

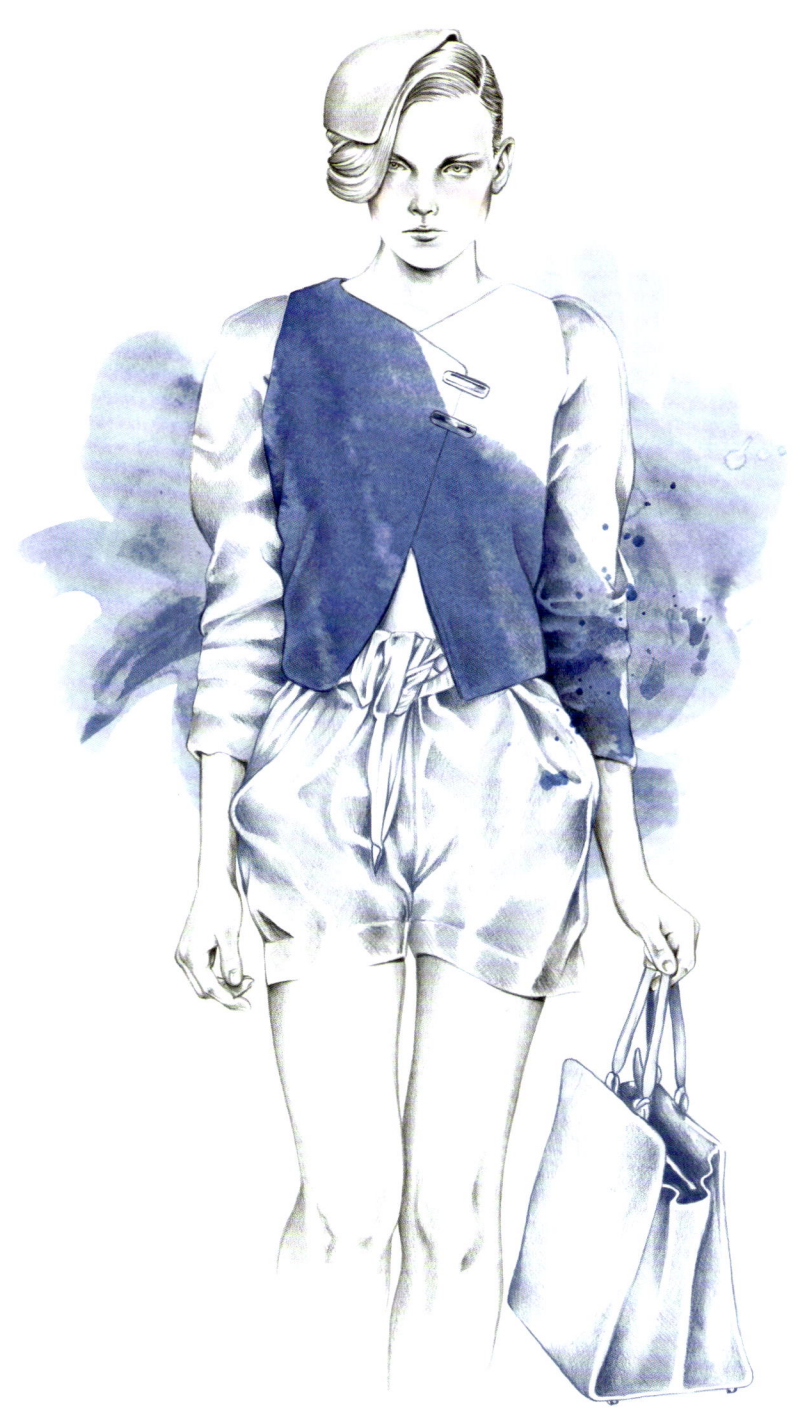

Illustration for Armani's Facebook page based on Giorgio Armani Womenswear Collection for Spring/Summer 2013. Pencil and watercolour on paper.
Illustrator: Carole Wilmet Country: Belgium

Armani

2014 RTW Pelin's Girl

Watercolour paint, hand-drawn with marker and pencil.
Illustrator: Pelin Ozelmas Country: Turkey

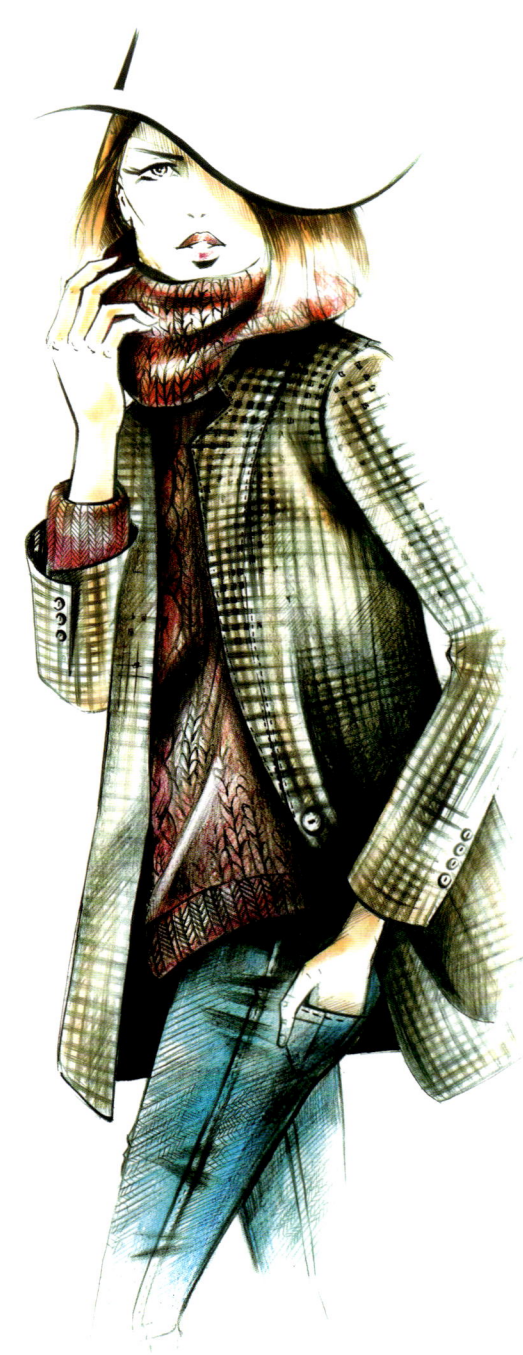

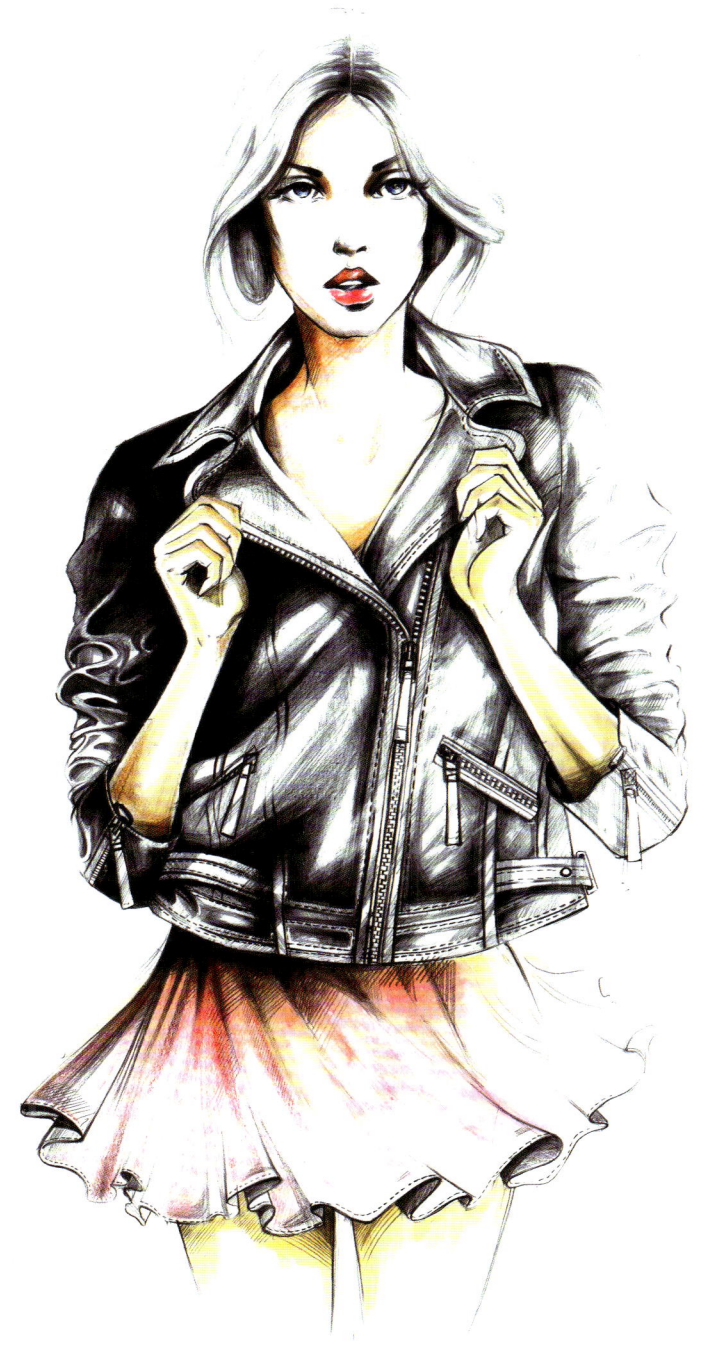

Dry paint, hand drawn, marker, and pencil.
Illustrator: Pelin Ozelmas Country: Turkey

2014 RTW Pelin's illustration

Christian Dior AW 2013 Collection

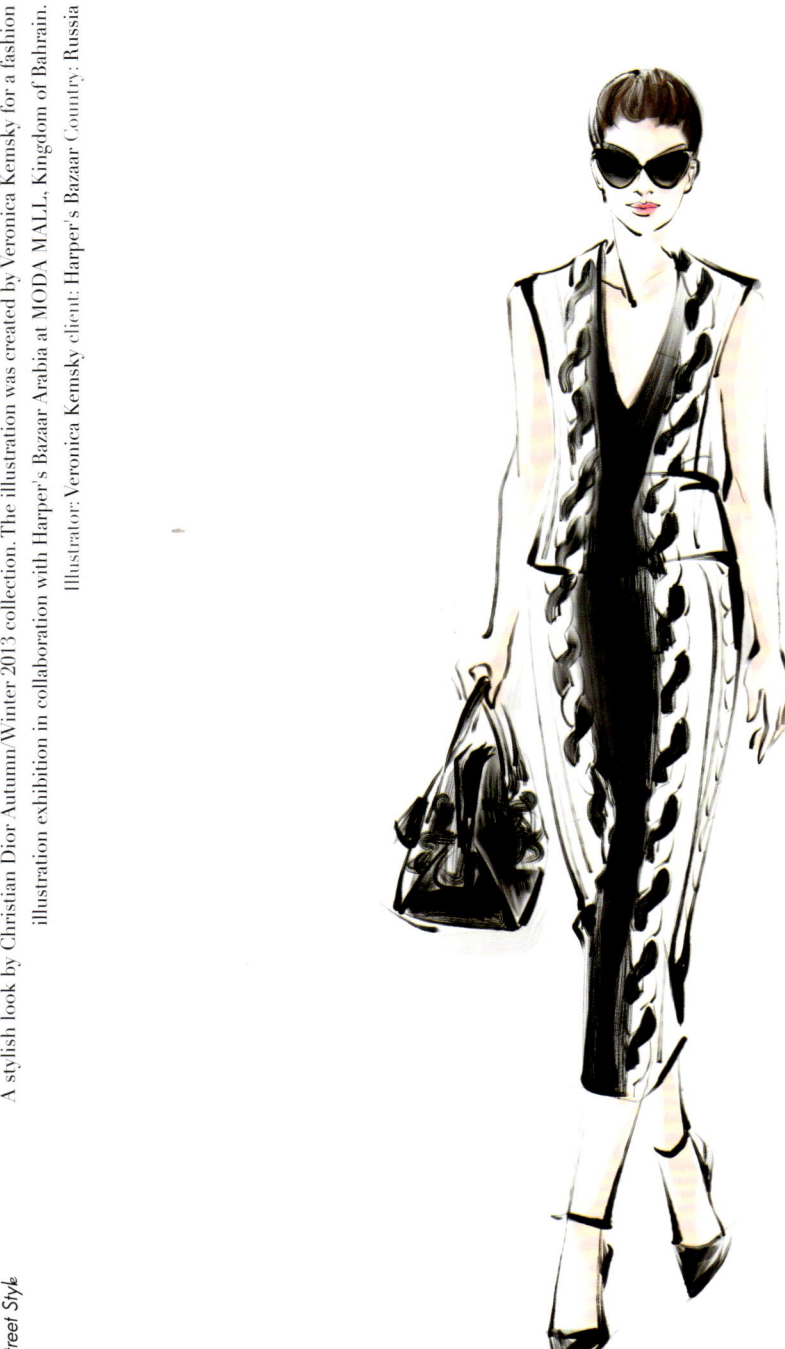

A stylish look by Christian Dior Autumn/Winter 2013 collection. The illustration was created by Veronica Kensky for a fashion illustration exhibition in collaboration with Harper's Bazaar Arabia at MODA MALL, Kingdom of Bahrain. Illustrator: Veronica Kensky client: Harper's Bazaar Country: Russia

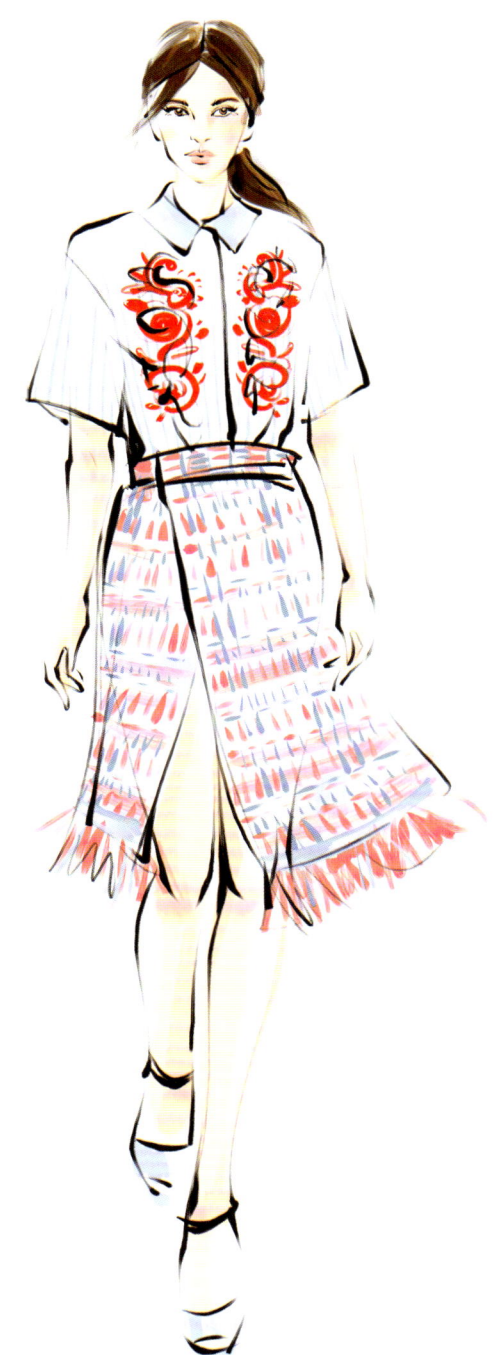

A folk style look by Tory Burch Spring Summer 2016 collection. The illustration was commissioned by Harper's Bazaar Arabia for March 2016 issue.
Illustrator: Veronica Kensky client: Harper's Bazaar Country: Russia

Tory Burch SS 2016 Collection

Vika Smolyanitskaya FW 2016-2017 collection

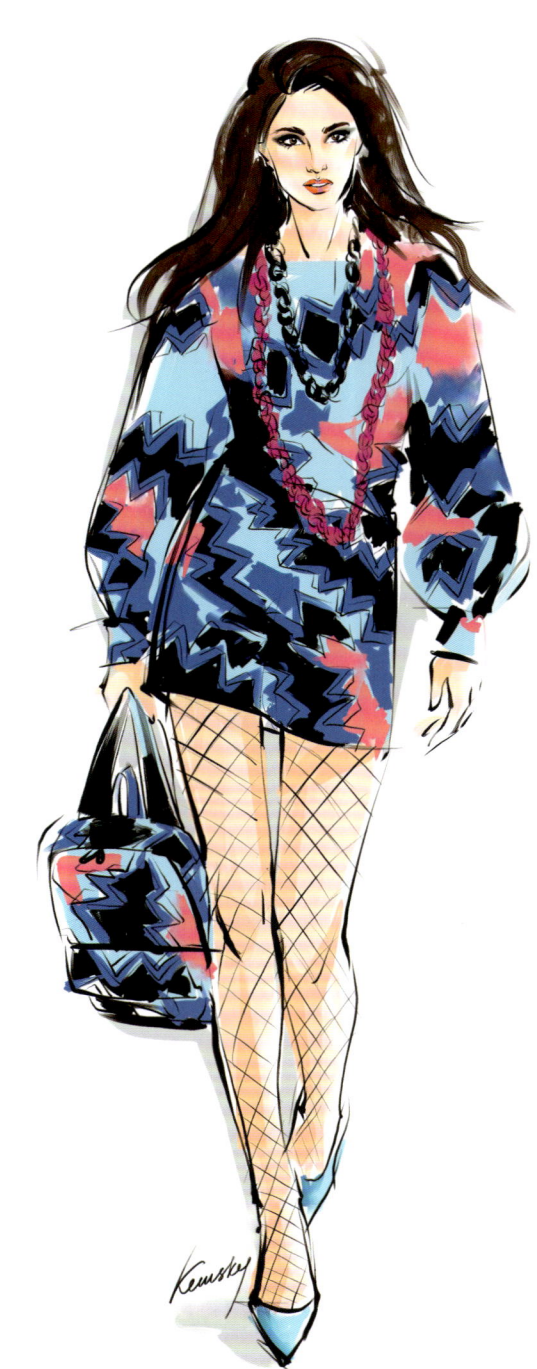

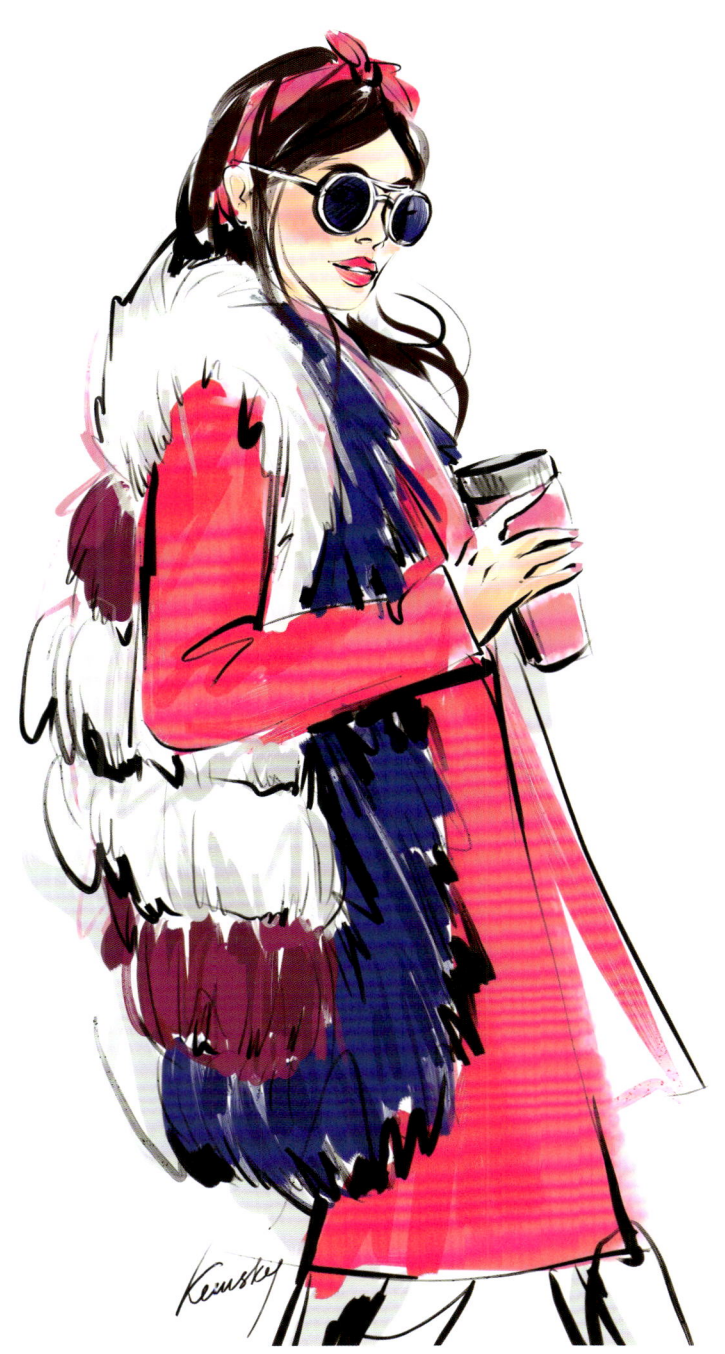

A Street Style look illustrated by Veronica Kemsky special for the 32nd season of Mercedes-Benz Fashion Week Russia.
Illustrator: Veronica Kemsky Client: Mercedes-Benz Fashion Week Russia Country: Russia

Street Style Look

Dries Van Noten

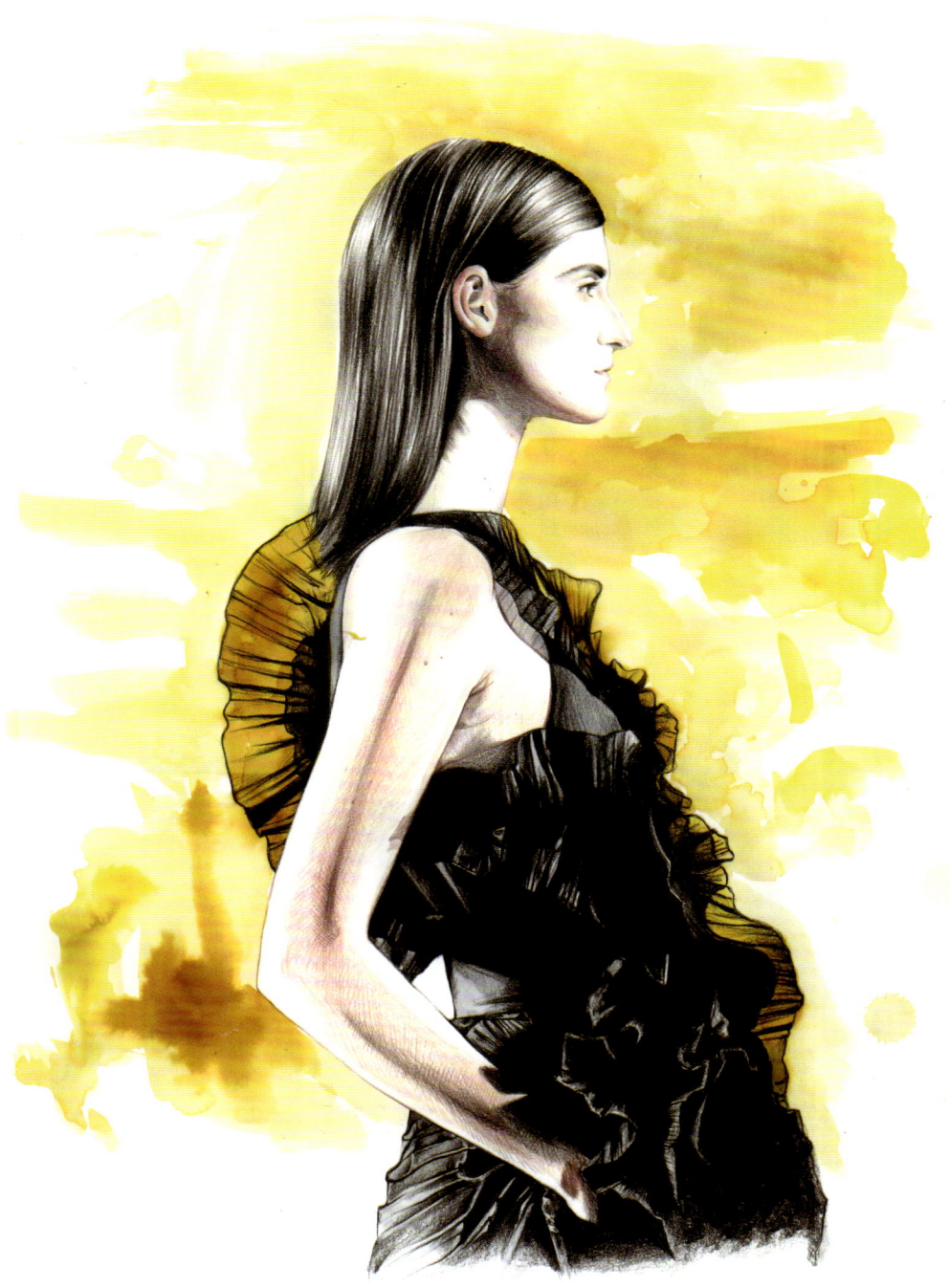

Model Daiane Conterato for Dries Van Noten spring 2014 collection. Coloured ink and pencils.
Illustrator: Caroline Andrieu Country: France

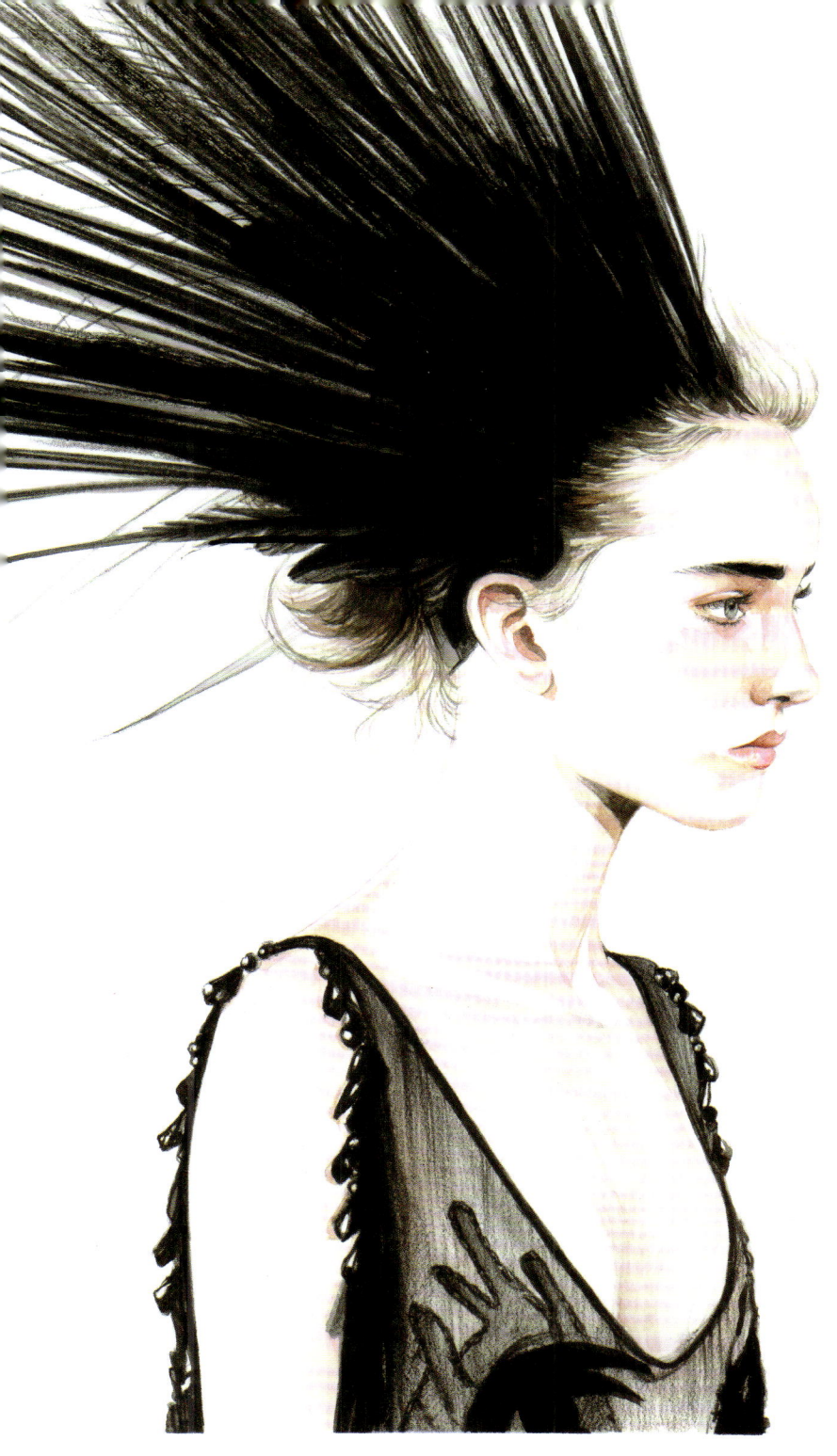

Model Clementine Deraedt for Louis Vuitton spring 2014 collection.
Illustrator: Caroline Andrieu Country: France

Louis Vuitton

Saint Laurent RTW FW 2015

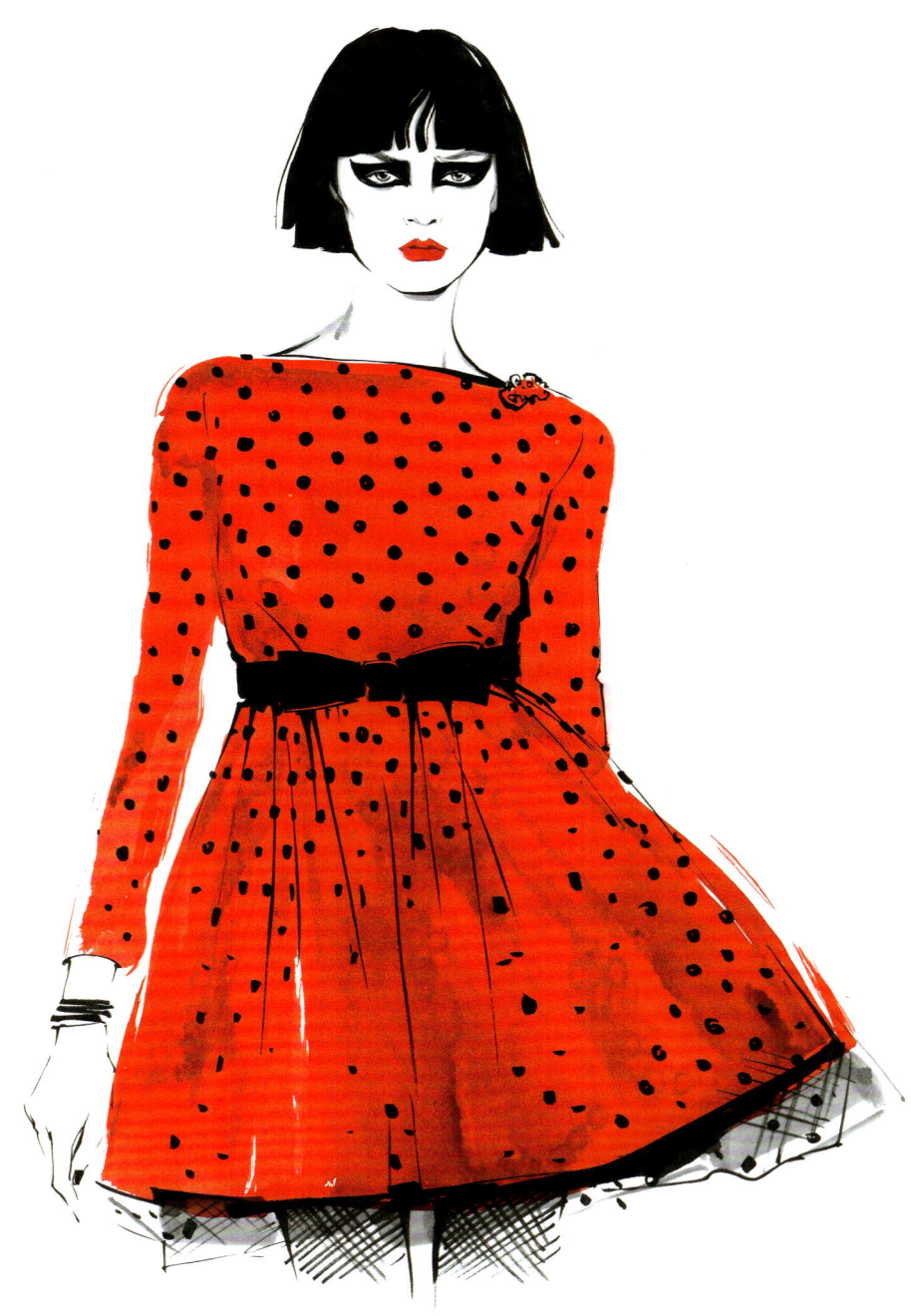

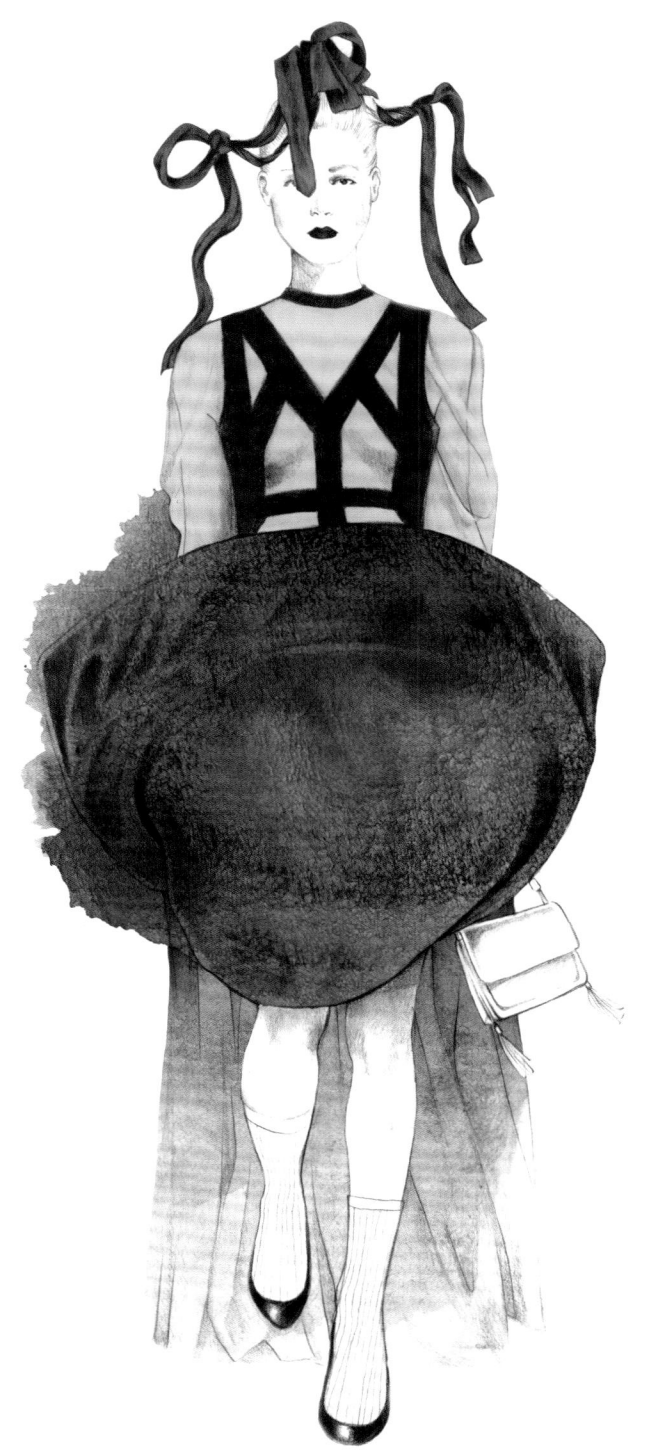

Series of illustrations for an article in Rouge Magazine about new rebel fashion trends, based on a collection by Comme des garçons. Pencil and ink on paper.
Illustrator: Carole Wilmet Country: Belgium

Comme des Garçons

Alexander Wang Fall 2015 RTW

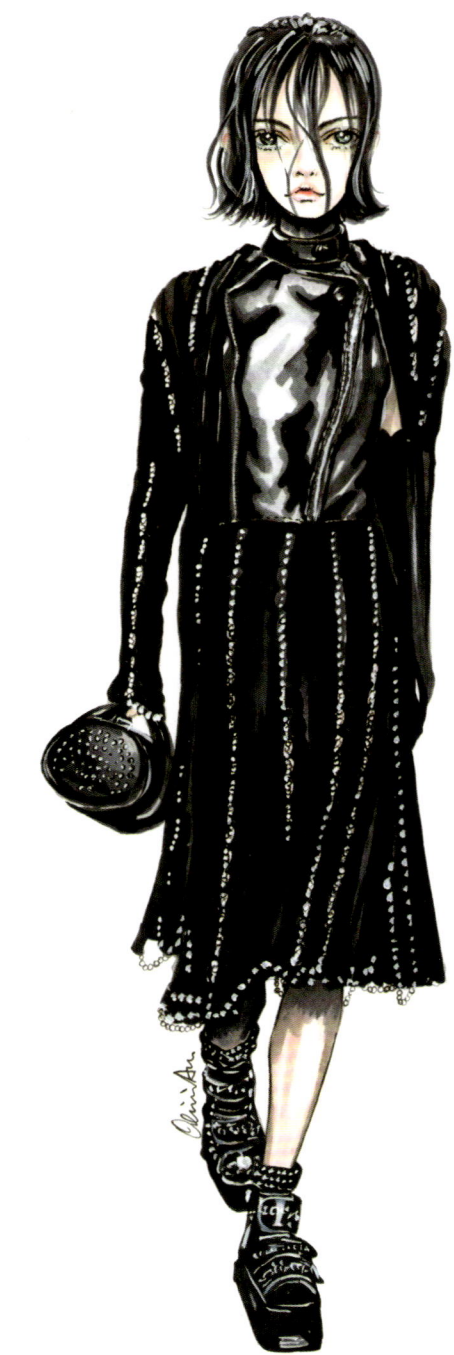

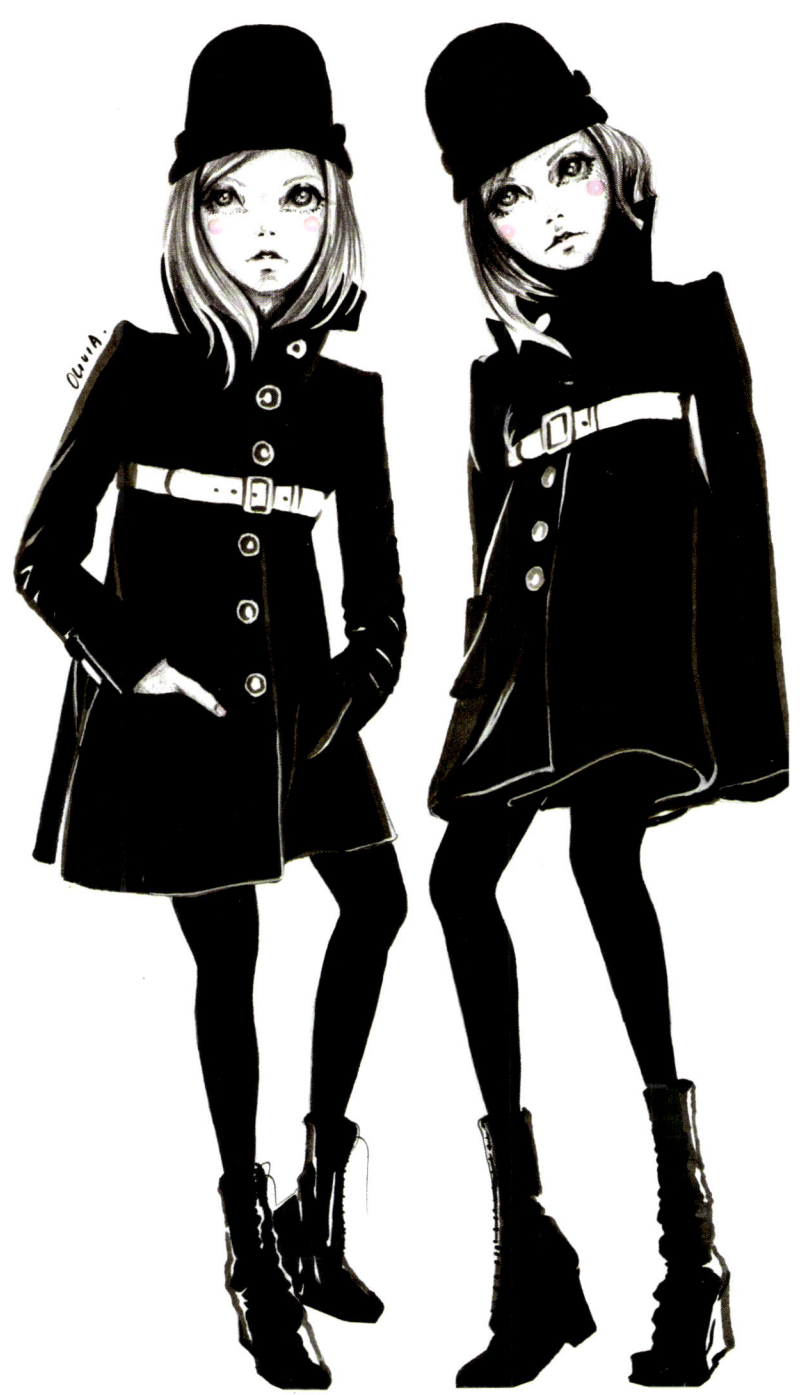

This illustration is inspired by Vogue UK 2006 editorial, girls wearing Balenciaga Fall 2006 RTW collection.
Illustrator: Olivia Au   Country: Hong Kong, China

Balenciaga

Dries Van Noten

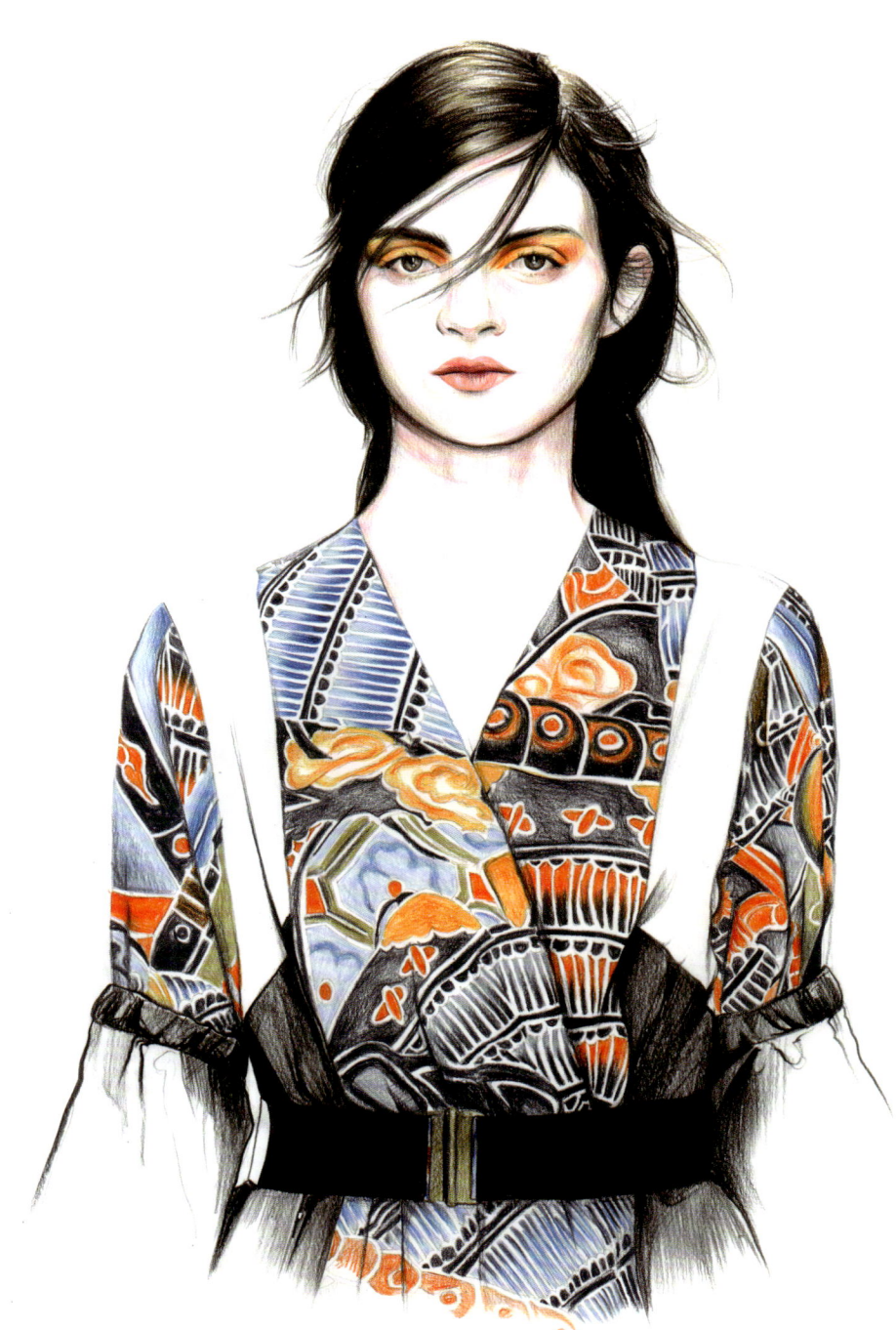

Model Magda Laguinge for Dries Van Noten fall 2012 collection. Colour pencils.
Illustrator: Caroline Andrieu Country: France

208 ✄ *Ethnic Charm*

This illustration is inspired by Viktor & Rolf Spring 2015 Haute Couture collection.
Illustrator: Olivia Au Country: Hong Kong, China

Viktor & Rolf Spring 2015

Gucci Blouse

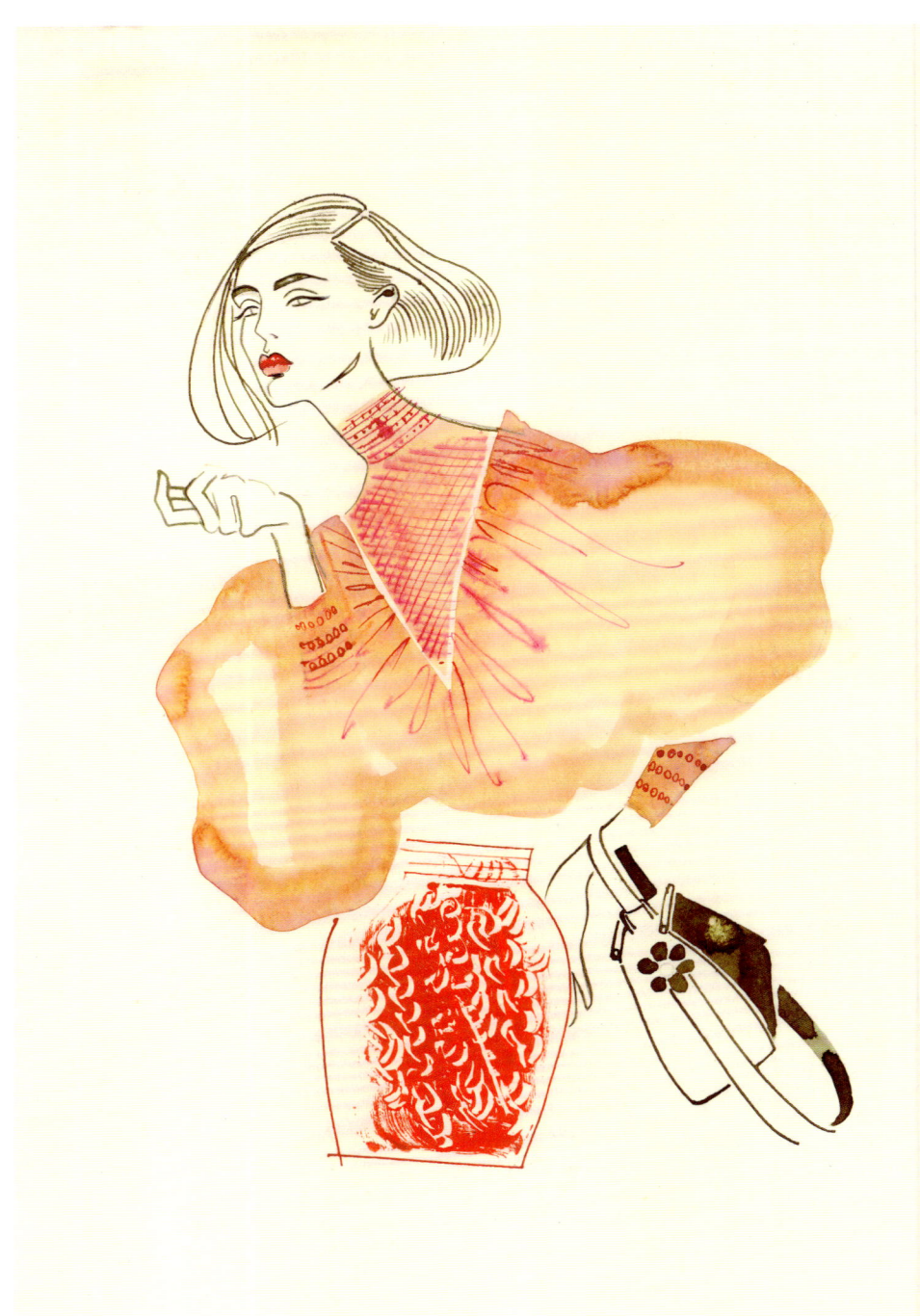

Mixtes Techniques; Illustration Fashion week October 15, Gucci collection summer 2016.
Illustrator: Margot Van Huijkelom Country: France

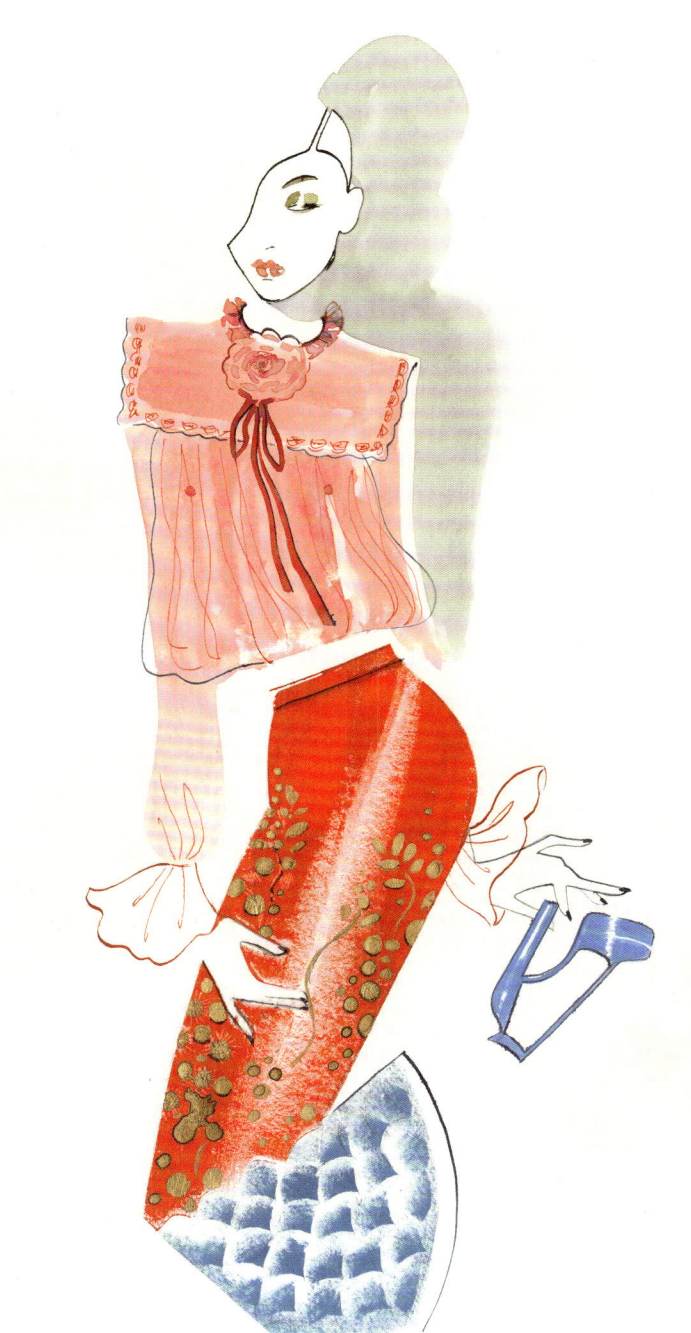

Mixtes Techniques: Illustration for fashion week October 15, Gucci collection summer 2016.
Illustrator: Margot Van Huijkelom Country: France

Gucci Summer 2016

Gucci SS 2016

Colourful inky style fashion illustration, using ink and coloured pencil, then digitally finished.
Illustrator: Natsuki Otani Country: Japan

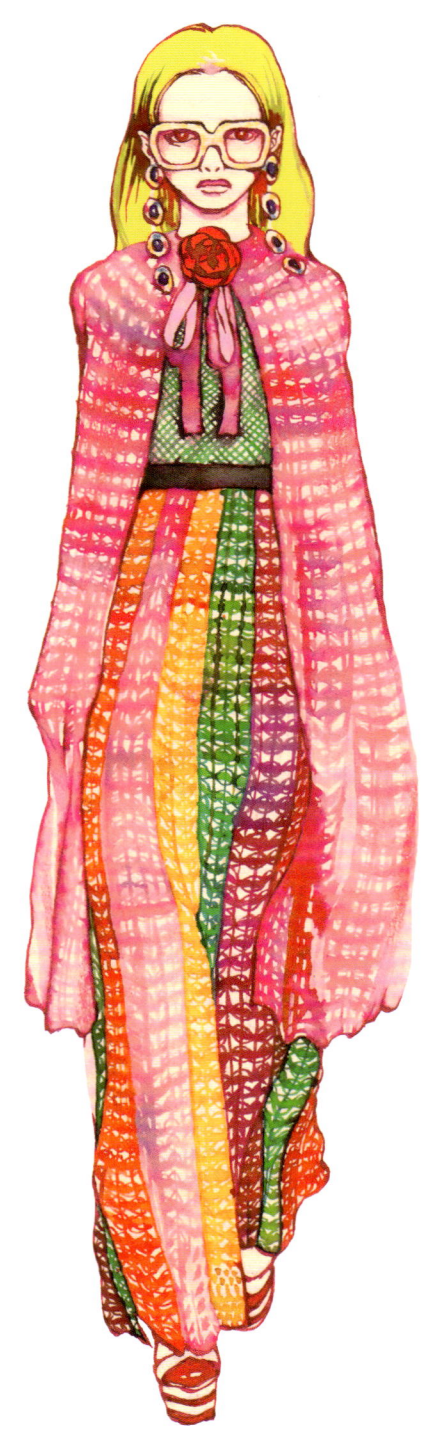

Ethnic Charm

This illustration is inspired by Prada Spring 2015 RTW collection.
Illustrator: Olivia Au Country: Hong Kong, China

Prada Spring 2015 RTW

Alexander McQueen

Series of illustrations for an article in Rouge Magazine about new rebel fashion trends, based on a collection by Alexander McQueen. Pencil and ink on paper. Illustrator: Carole Wilmet Country: Belgium

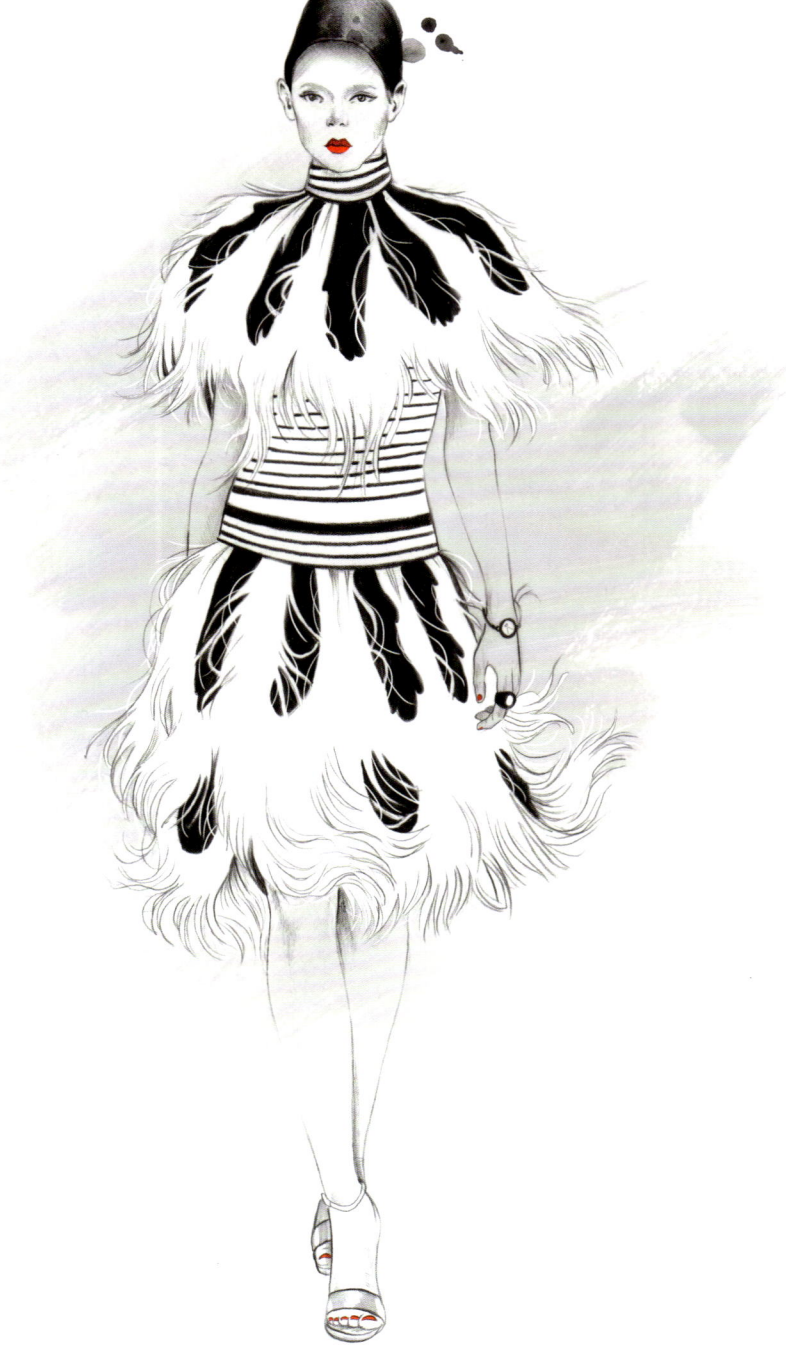

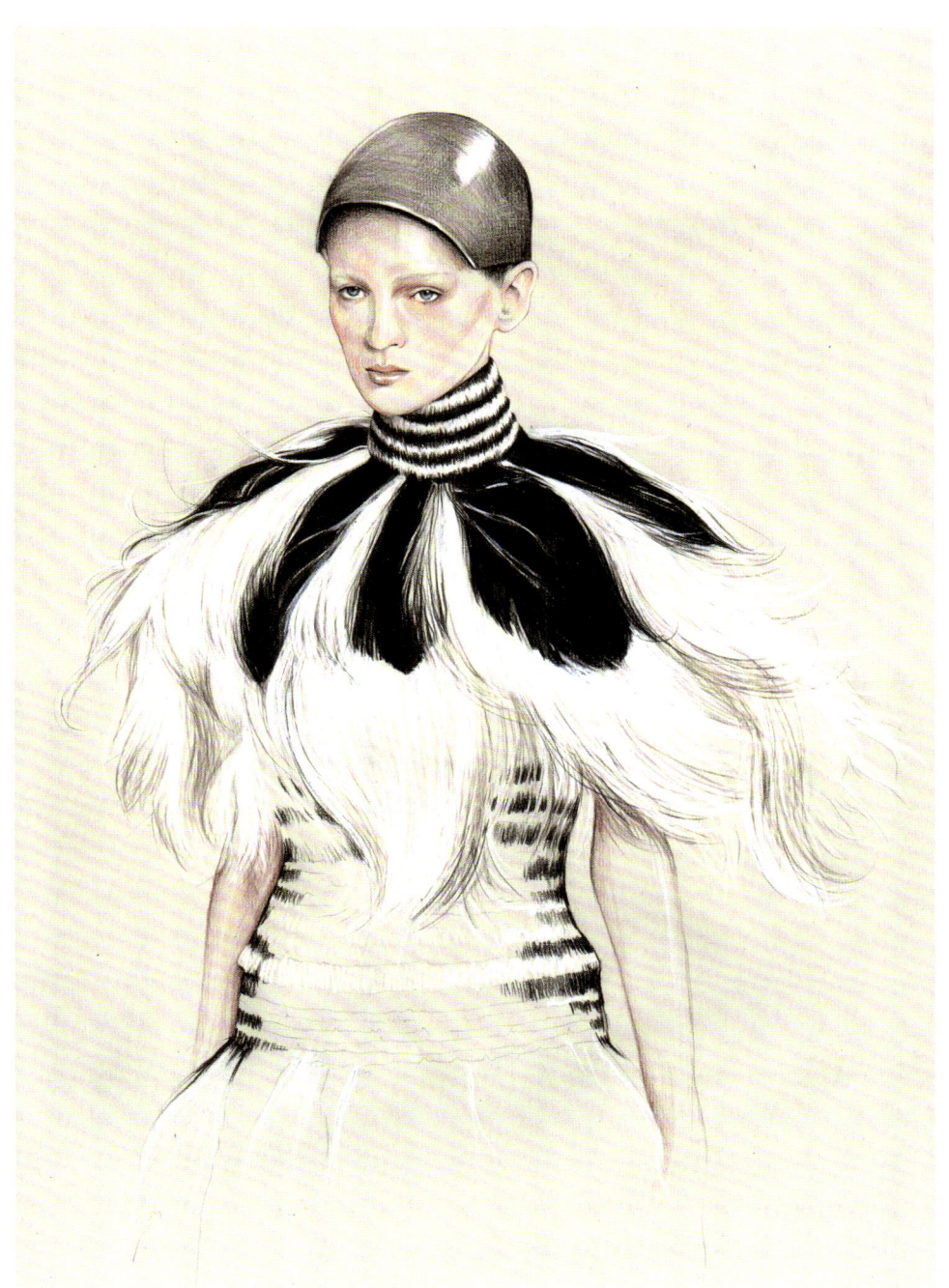

Model Nastya Sten for Alexander McQueen spring 2014 collection. Colour pencils on Ingres paper.
Illustrator: Caroline Andrieu Country: France

Alexander McQueen

Jeremy Scott RTW FW 2015

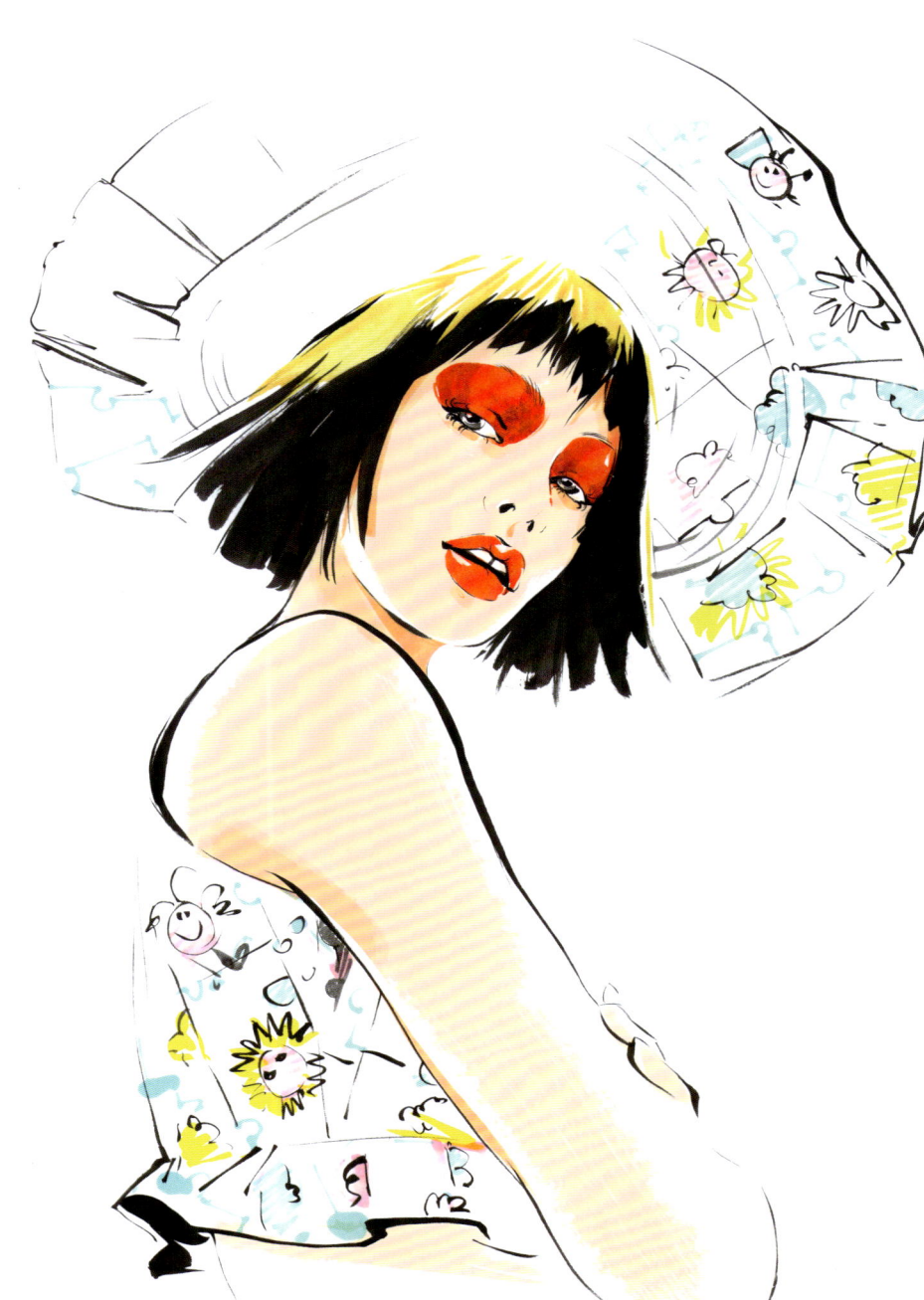

Backstage moment at Jeremy Scott show, NY Fashion Week RTW FW 2015. Editorial work for vogue.ru. Illustrator: Alena Lavdovskaya Country: Russia

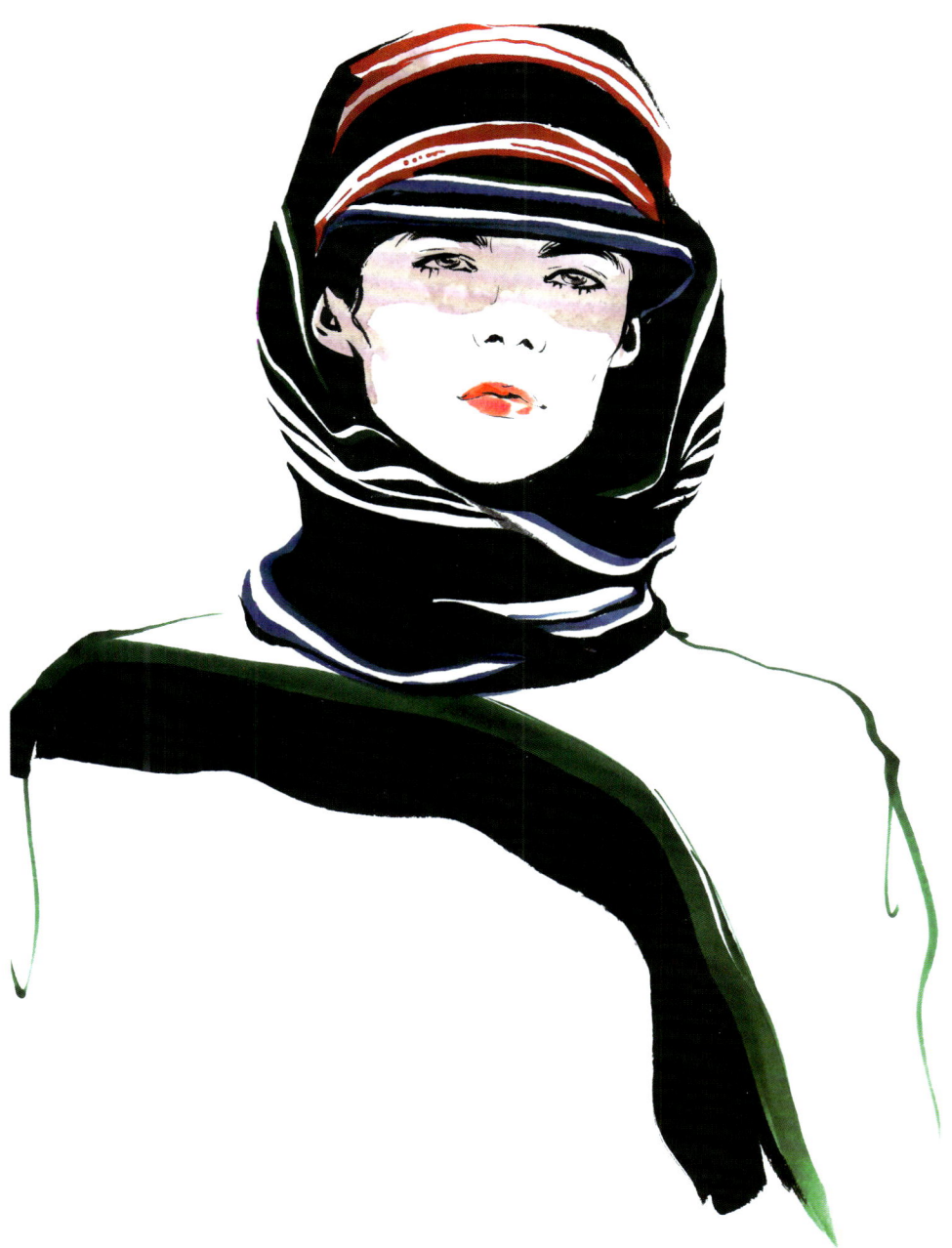

Close up moment at Kenzo show, Paris Fashion Week RTW FW 2015. Editorial work for vogue.ru.
Illustrator: Alena Lavdovskaya Country: Russia

Kenzo RTW FW 2015

GiambattistaValli SS 2015

Fashion illustration inspired by GiambattistaValli SS 2015 collection.
Illustrator: Esra Roise Country: Norway

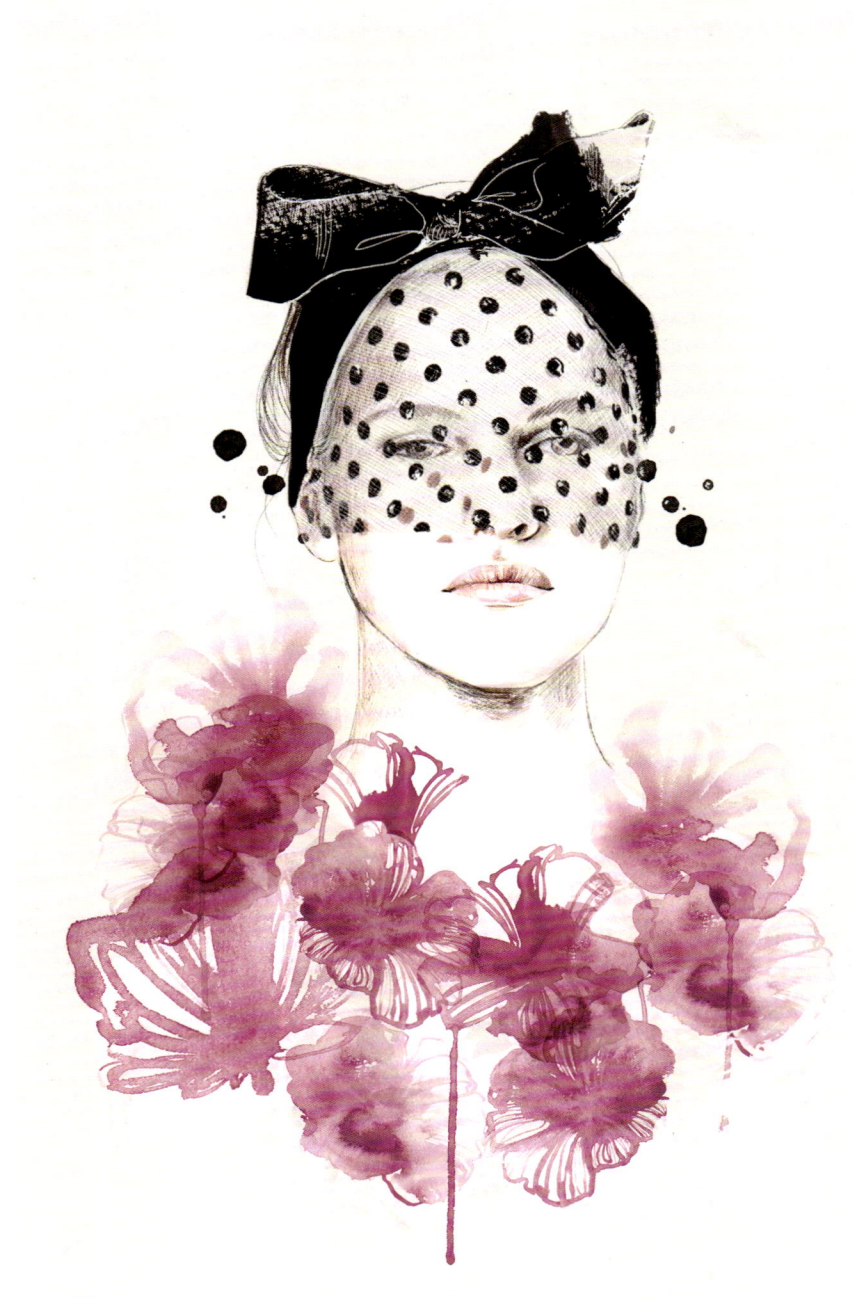

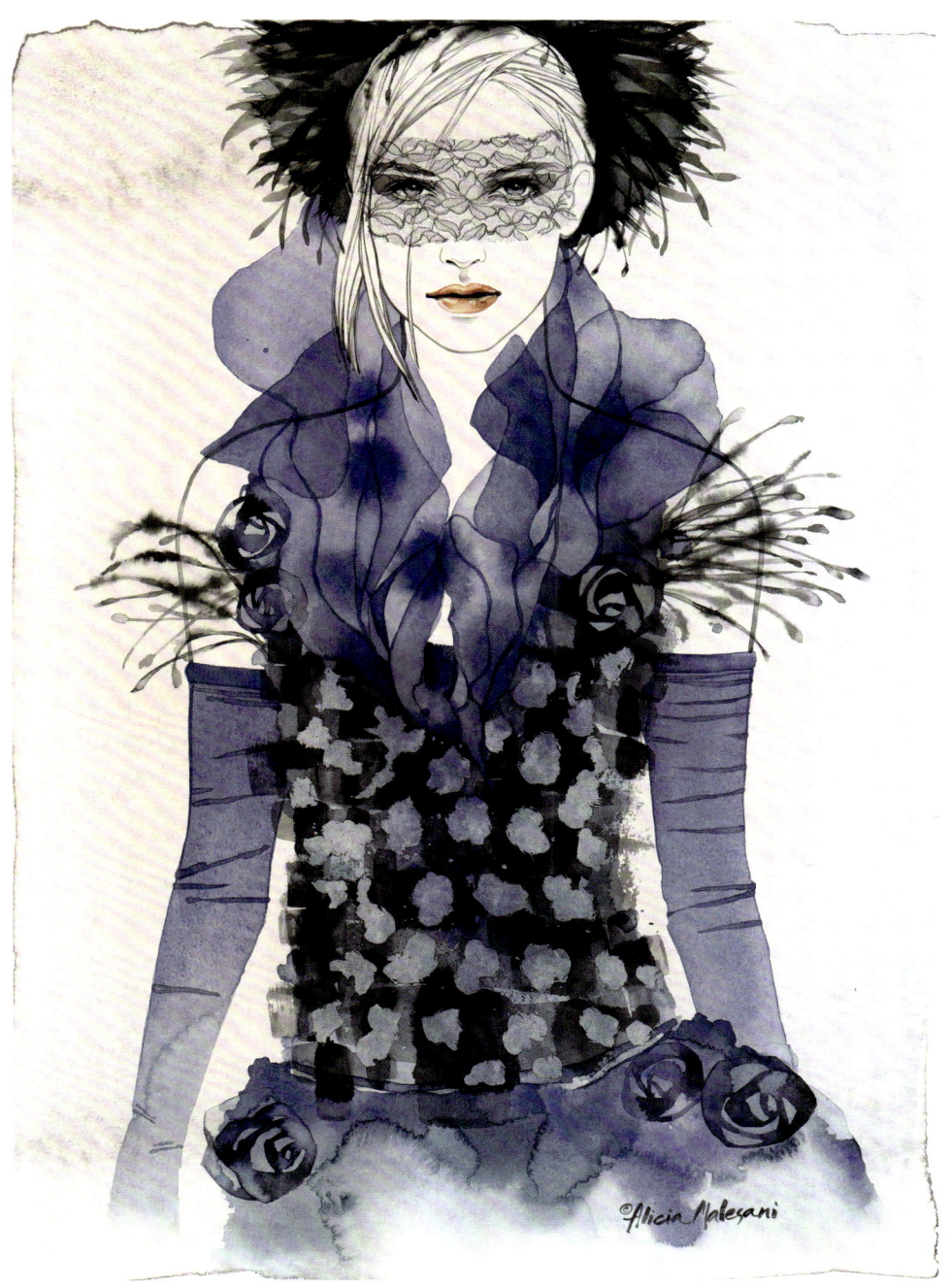

Personal Project. Watercolour, ink and pencil on high quality Fabriano paper.
Illustrator: Alicia Malesani Country: Spain

Chanel Hat

Lovely Hat

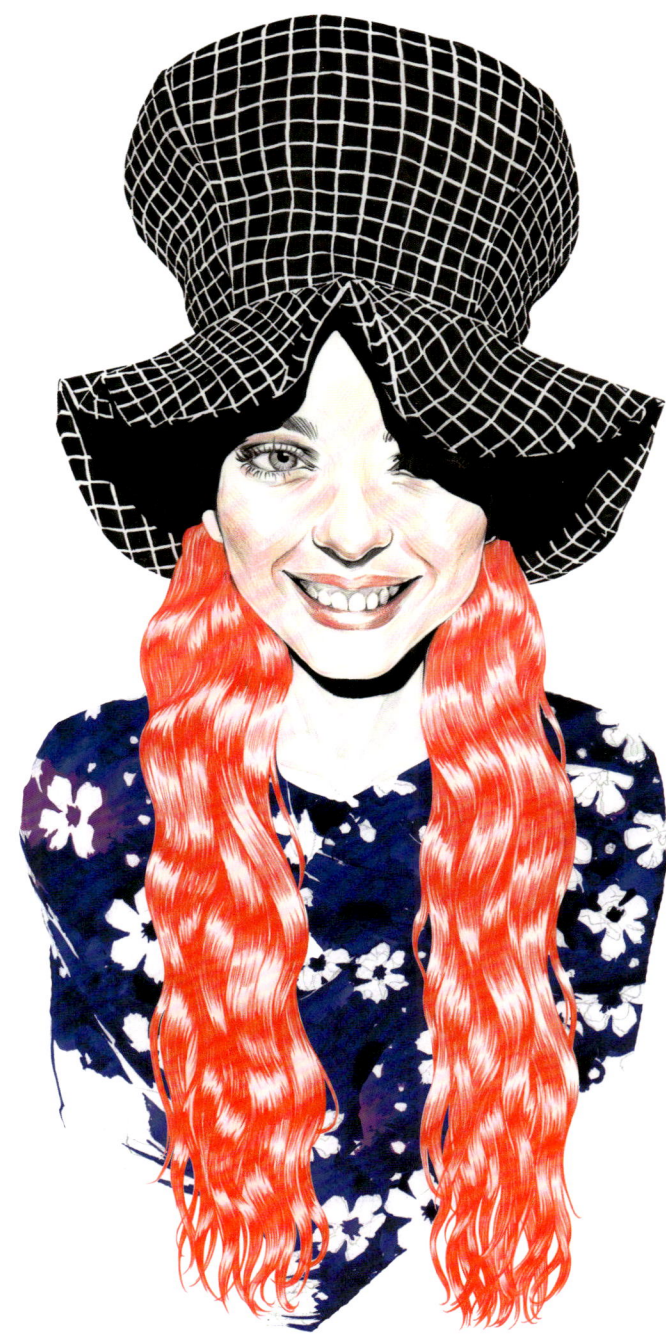

Reinterpretation of Photo by 'The CobraSnake'. Pen, Pencil, Colour pencil, watercolour, ink on paper and digital work.

Illustrator: Mina K Country: South Korea

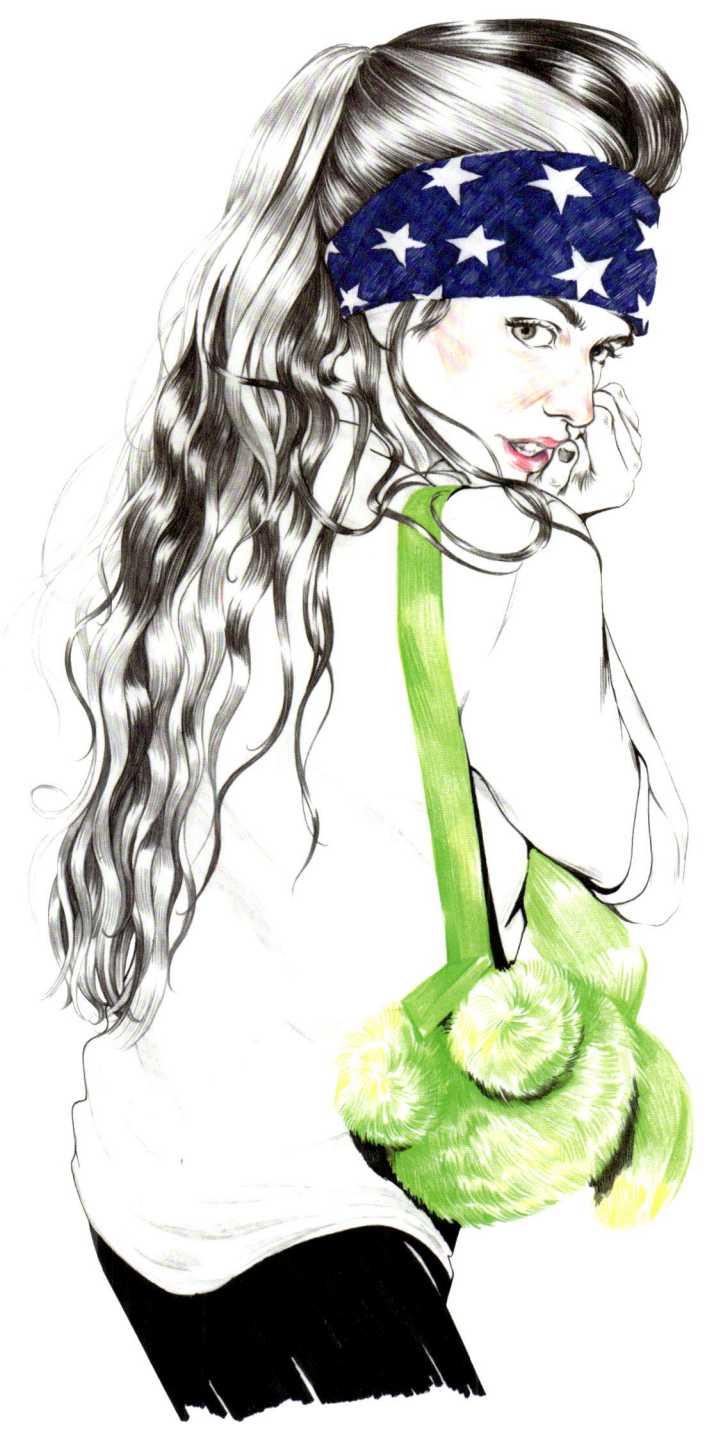

Reinterpretation of Photo by 'The CobraSnake'. This work focused on the performance of the girl's hair ribbon and stuffed bags.
Illustrator: Mina K Country: South Korea

Hair Ribbon

Cute Rabbit Ears

Reinterpretation of Photo by 'The CobraSnake'. Cute rabbit ears ornaments strengthen sweet personality degrees.
Illustrator: Mina K Country: South Korea

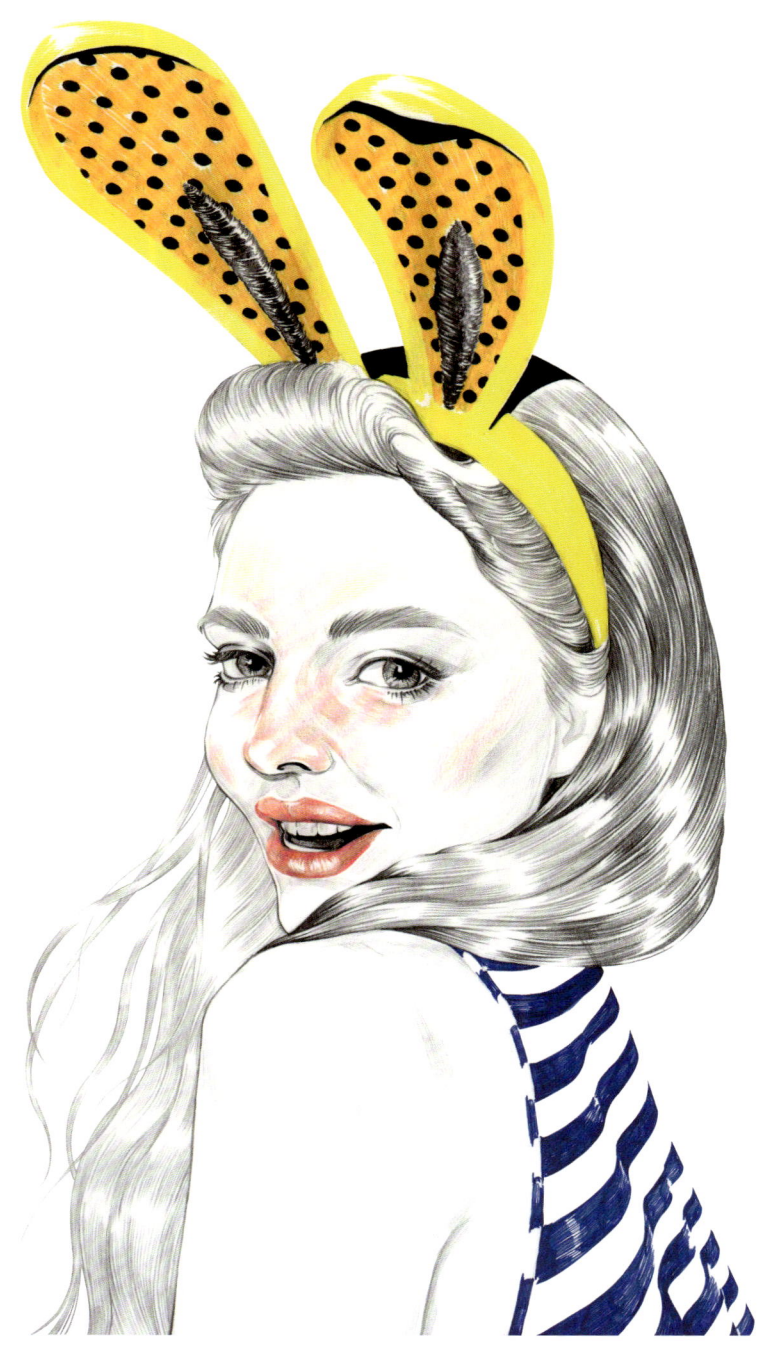

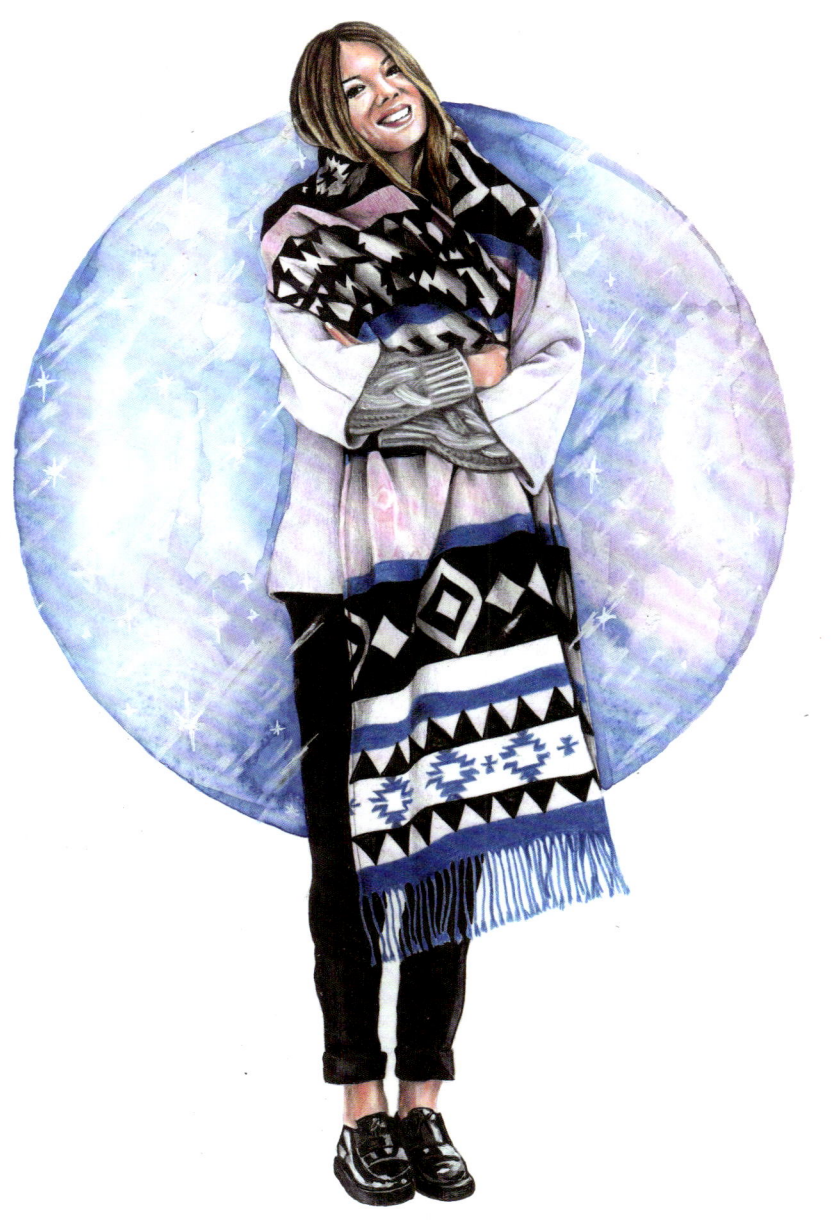

Inspiration from scraf and coat of Pinko, using coloured pencil and watercolour.
Illustrator: Kaznakova Olga Country: Russia

Pinko

LV Earring

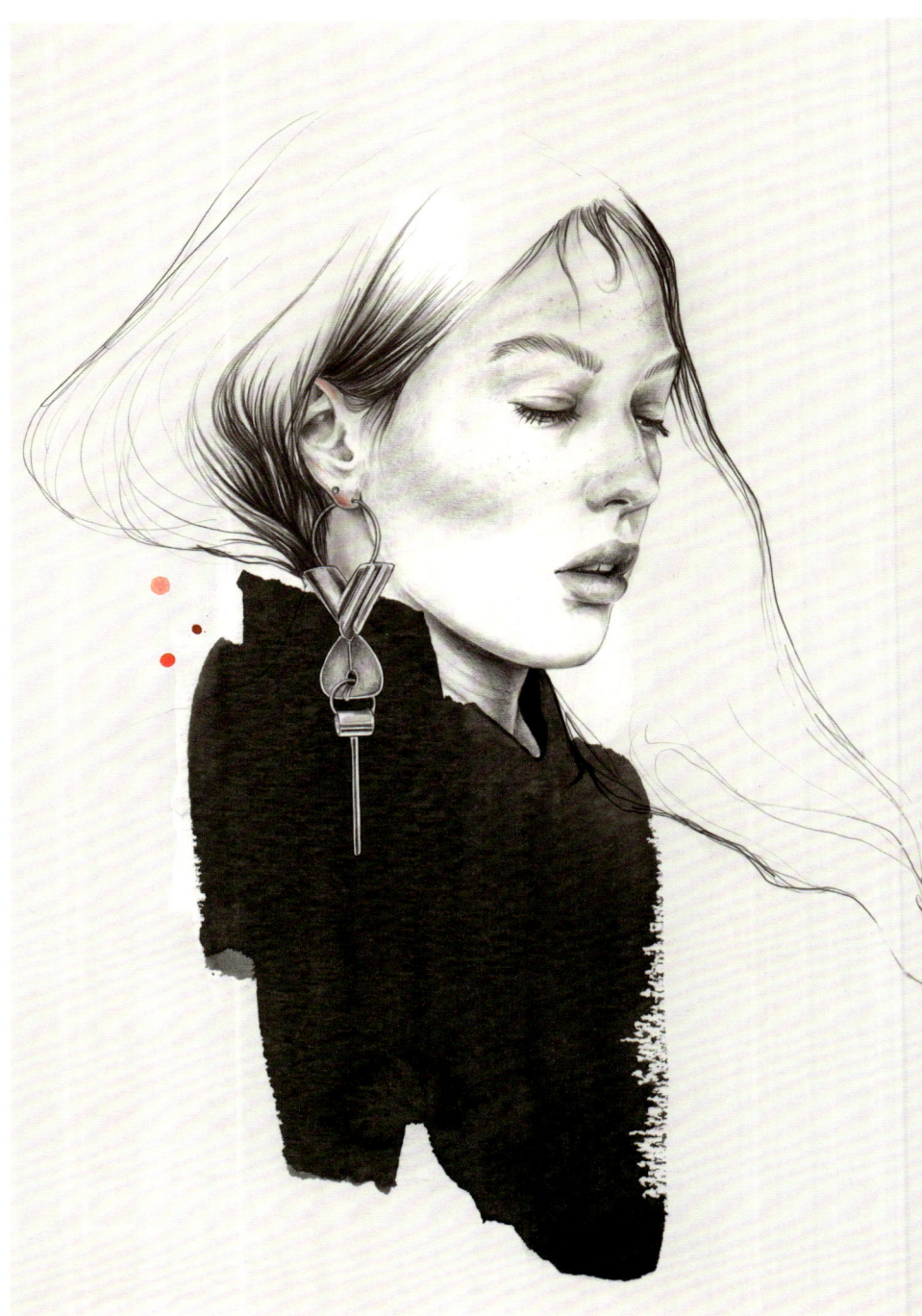

Personal project for solo exhibition 'ByOne' in Oslo, Norway where the theme was femininity in fashion. Inspired by LV AW 2014. Illustrator: Esra Røise Country: Norway

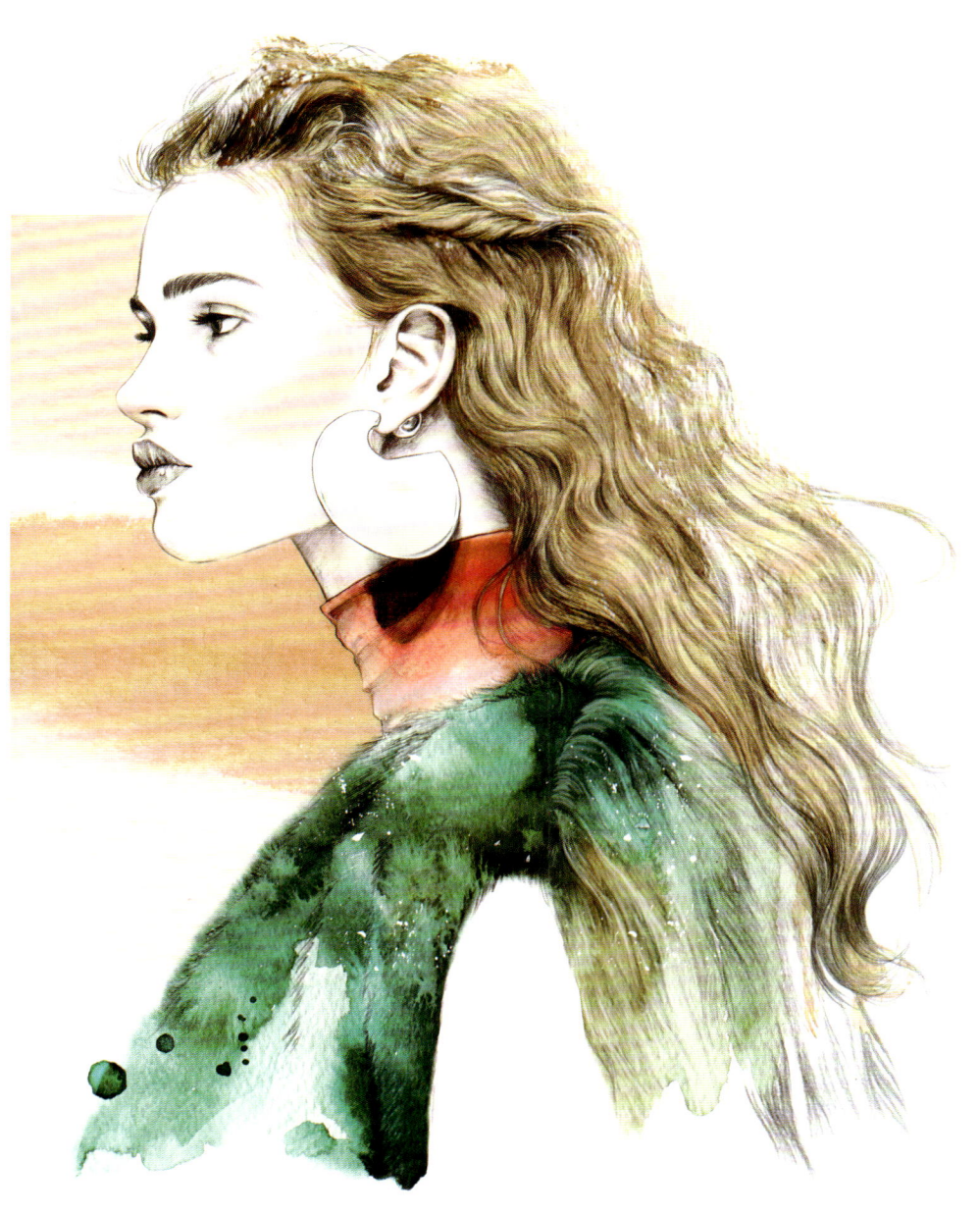

Beauty editorial for Vogue Nippon jewellery trends, using pencil, ink and digital.
Illustrator: Esra Røise Country: Norway

Marni Earrings AW 2015

Gold Necklace

Reinterpretation Photo by Txema Yeste for Numero China magazine. The Bold and gold necklace is vintage product and the Crab Claws necklace is creatures by Moe Nagata. Illustrator: Mina K Country: South Korea

Reinterpretation of fashion photograph. Exaggerated gold earrings.
Illustrator: Mina K Country: South Korea

Gold Crush

Dolce and Gabbana

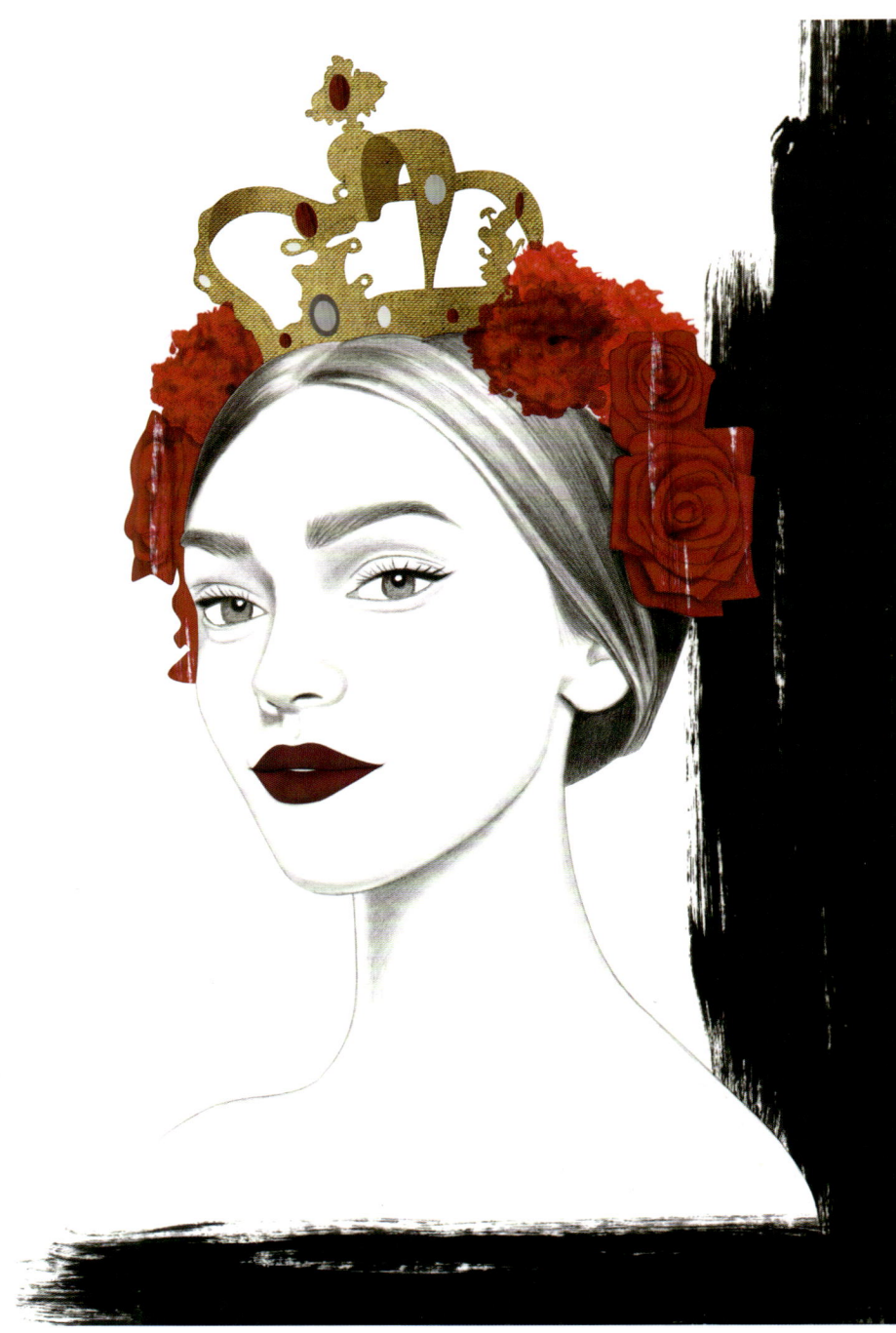

Inspired by Dolce and Gabbana. Personal project using graphite, found textures and watercolour.
Illustrator: Nicole Jarecz Country: USA

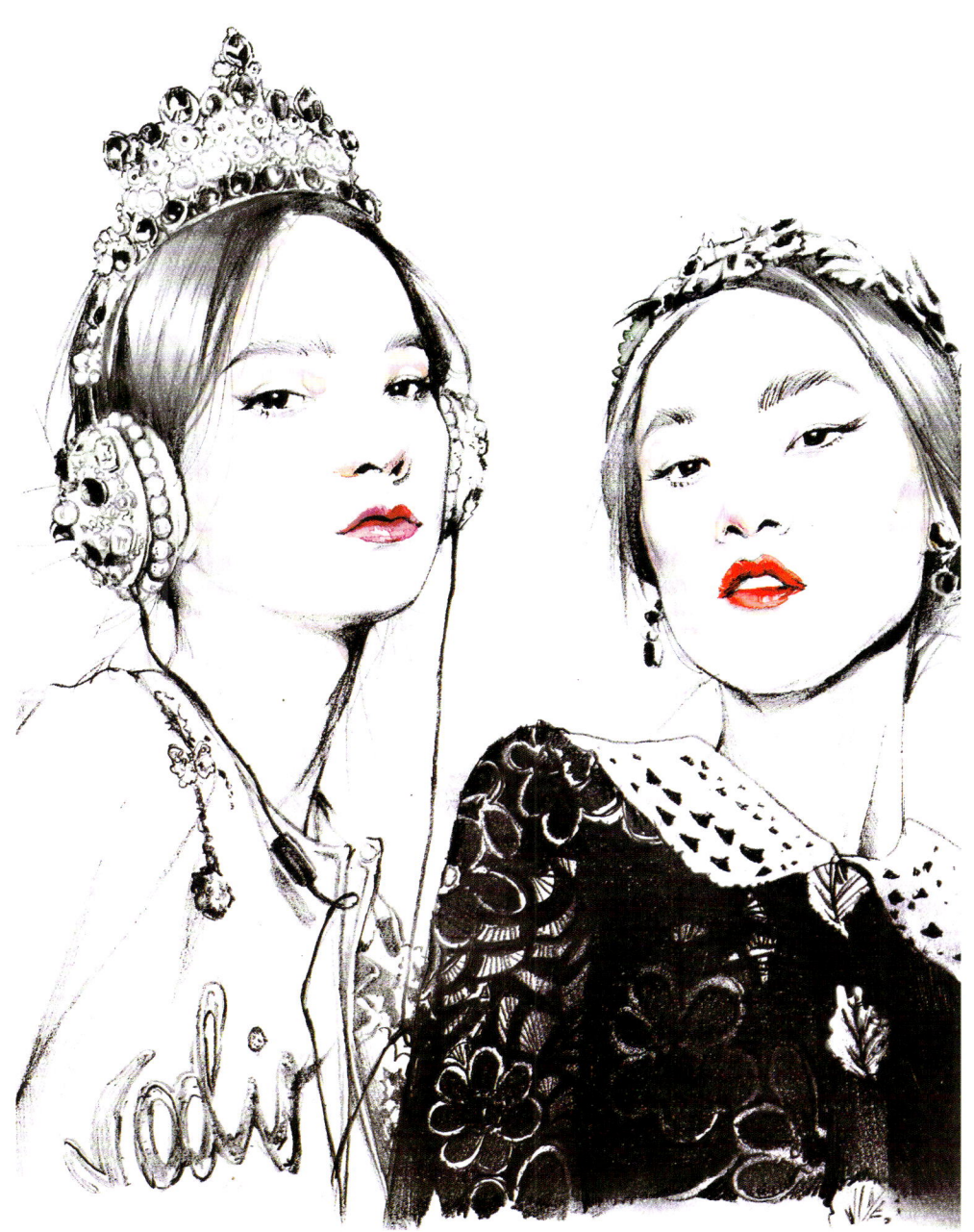

Illustration inspired by the backstage of Dolce & Gabbana winter show.
Illustrator: Ricoho Country: China

D&G Backstage

Tassel Earring

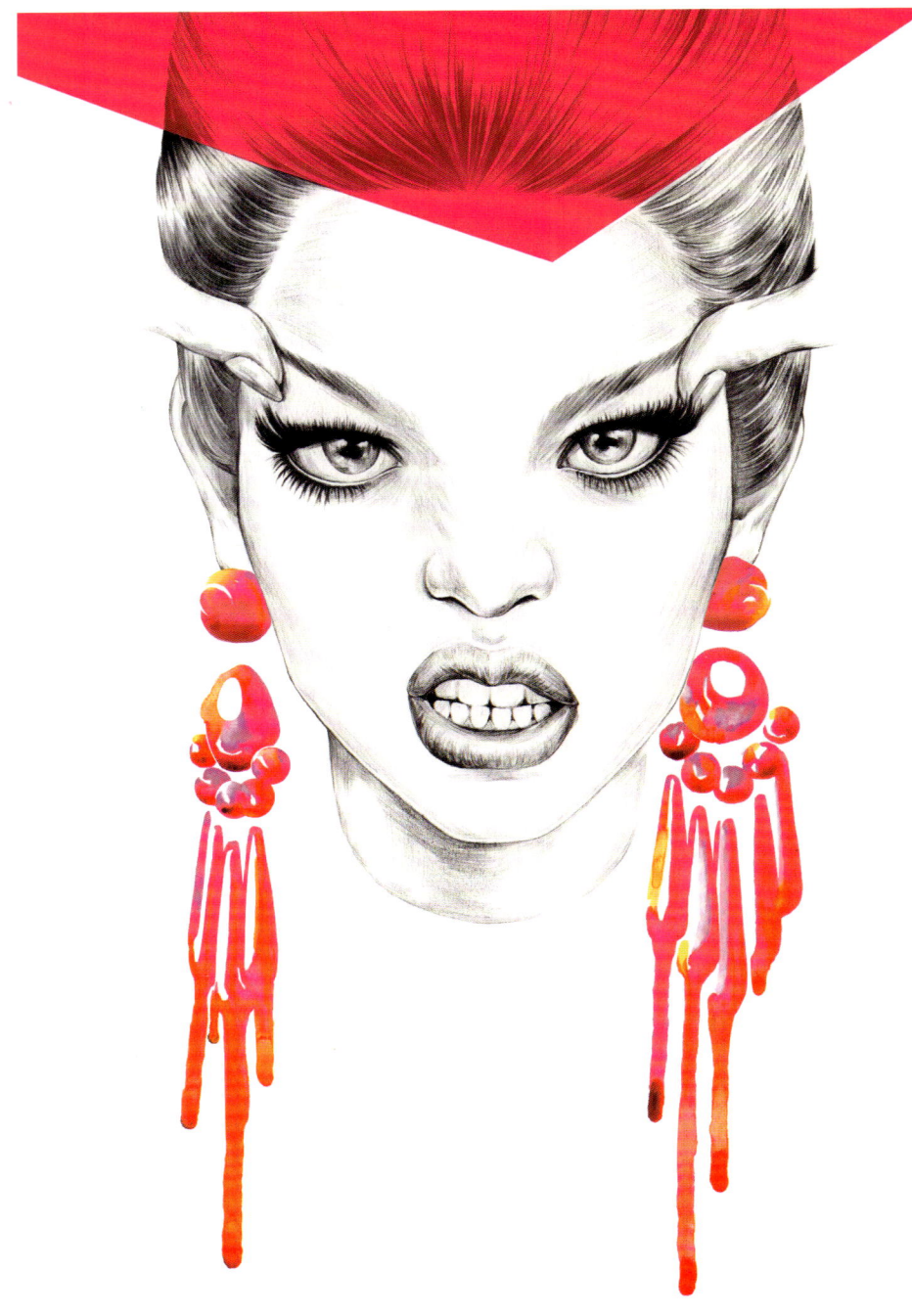

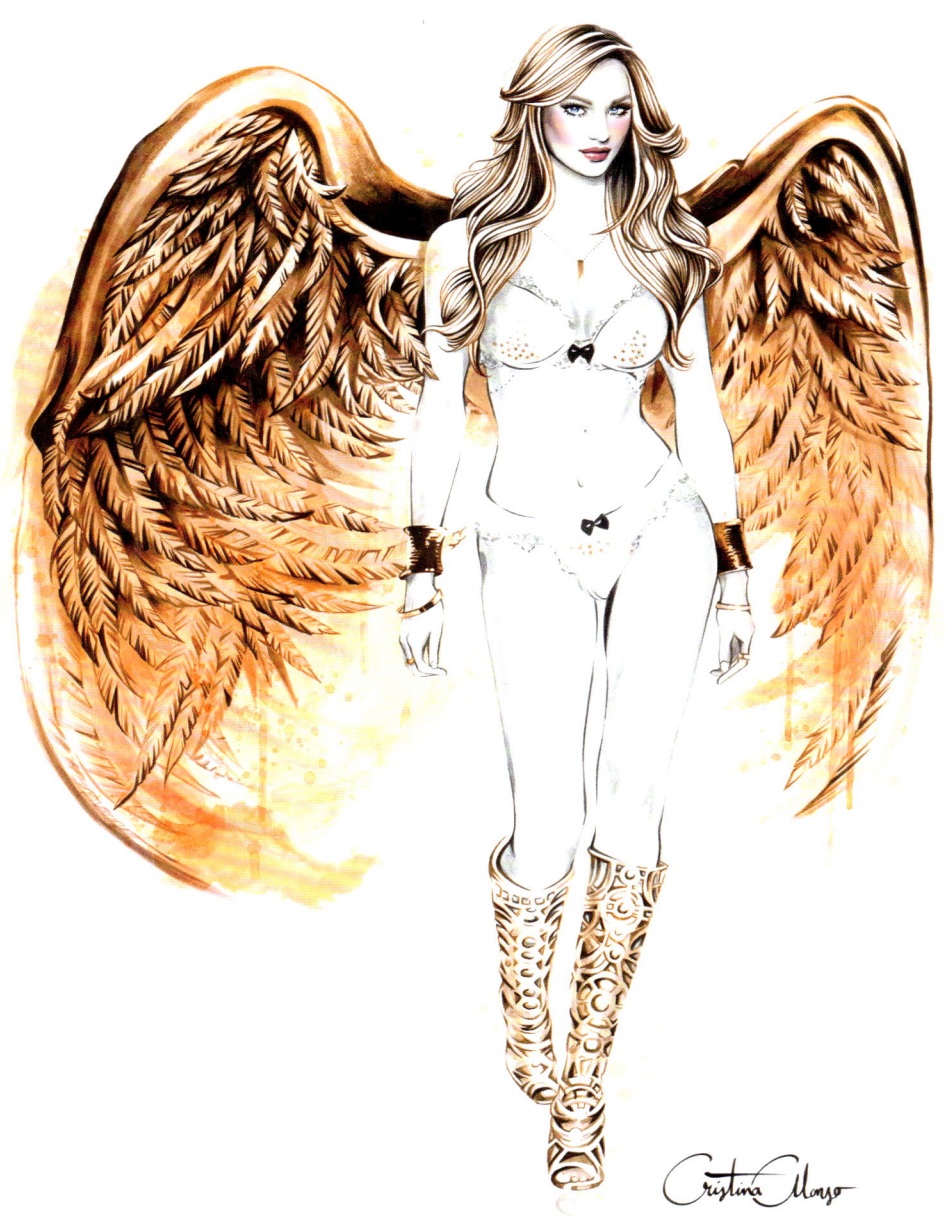

Fashion illustrations inspired by the homonym look by Victoria's Secret Fashion Show 2014 and model Candice Swanepoel.
Illustrator: Cristina Alonso Country: Spain

Victoria's Secret

Everyday Shoewear

Project description: Illustration made for Hillcrest shopping mall marketing campaign, spring 2015. The fashion illustrations are made from scratch digitally in Photoshop by watercolour technique.

Illustrator: Mateja Kovac Country: Croatia

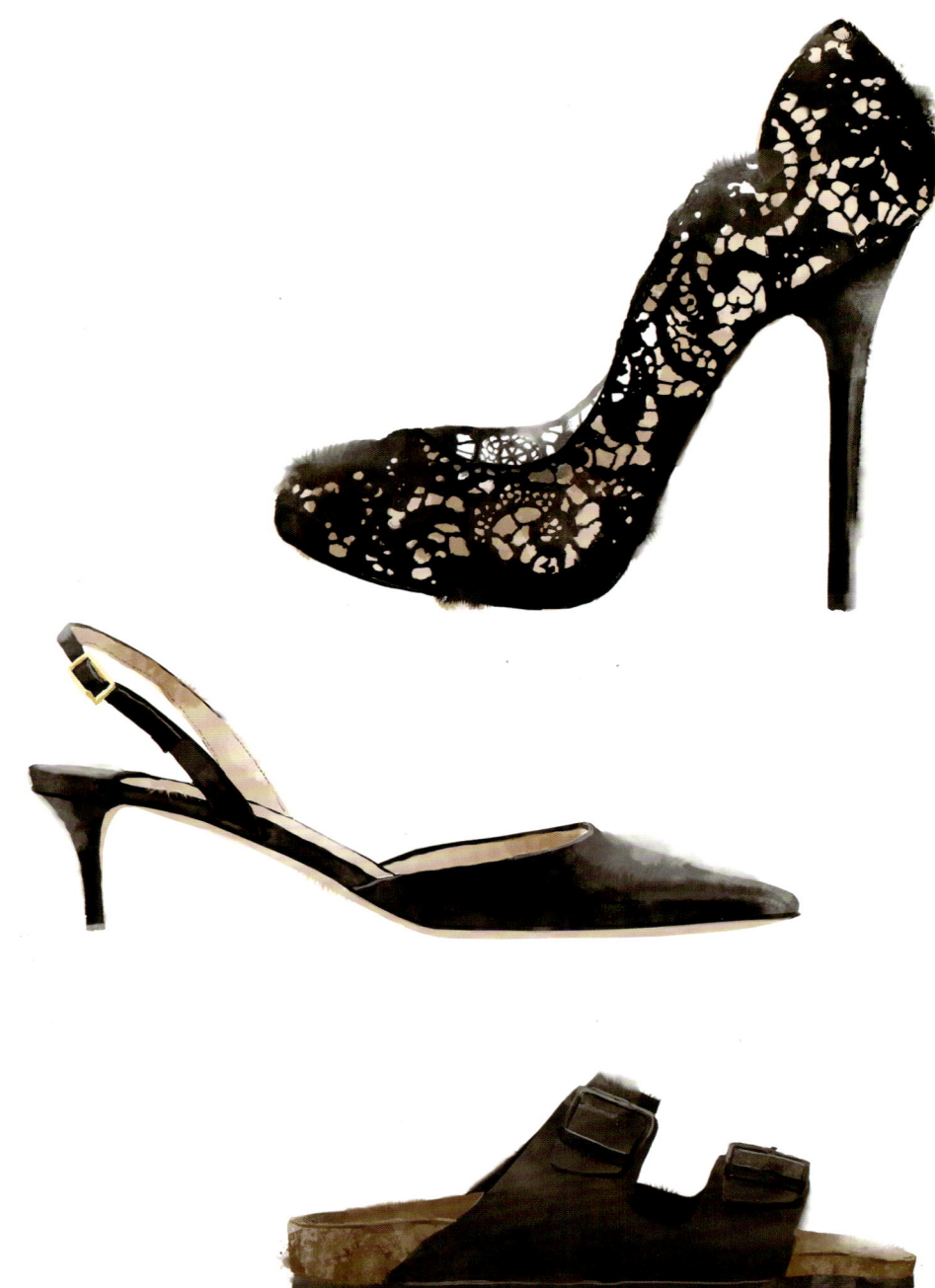

232 ✂ Accessories

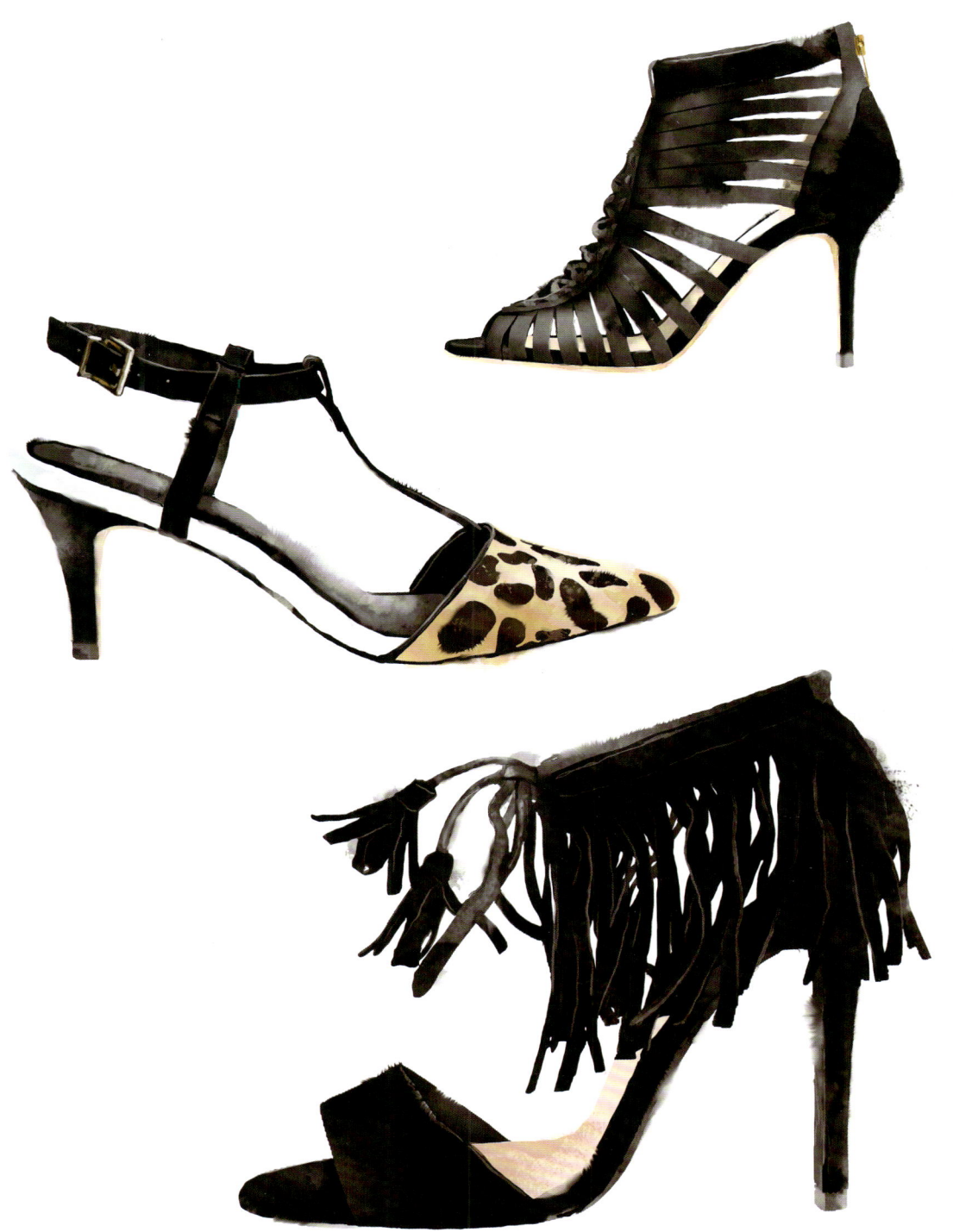

Floral Shoes

Flower-inspired shoes painted with watercolours.
Illustrator: Barykina Anastasia Country: Russia

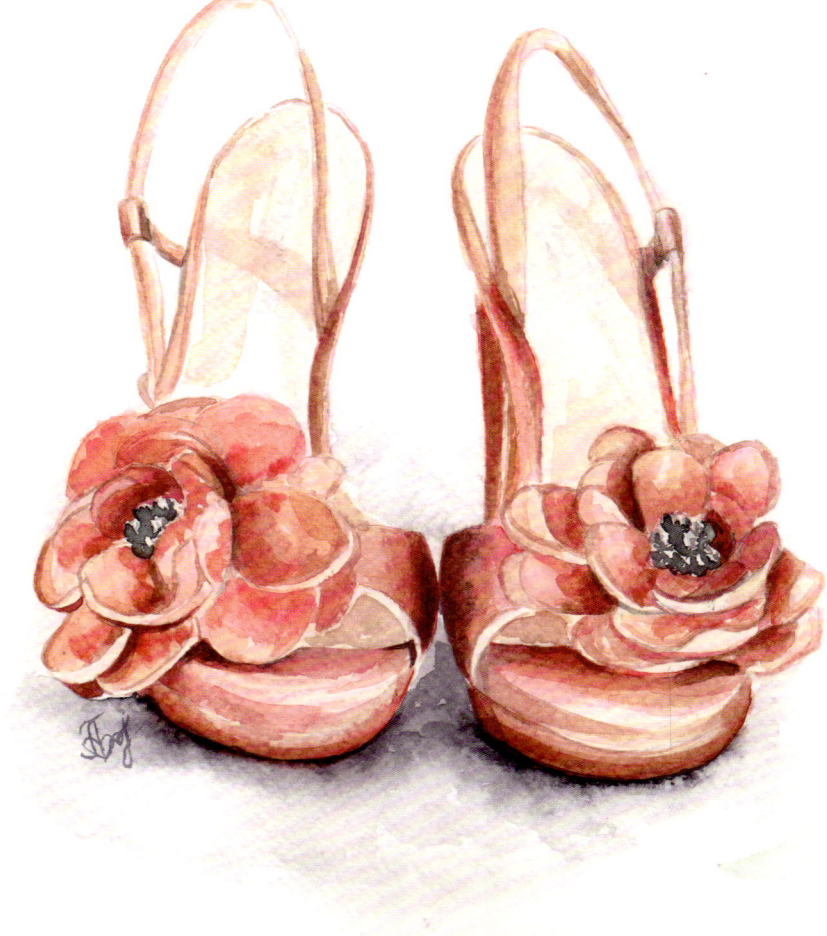

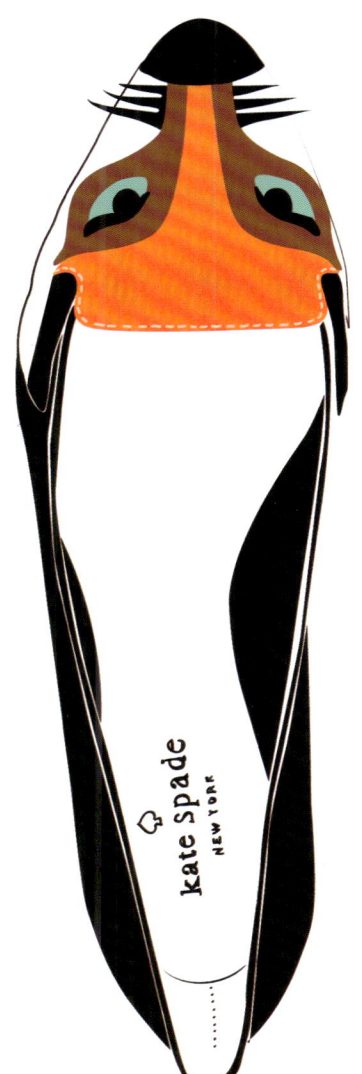
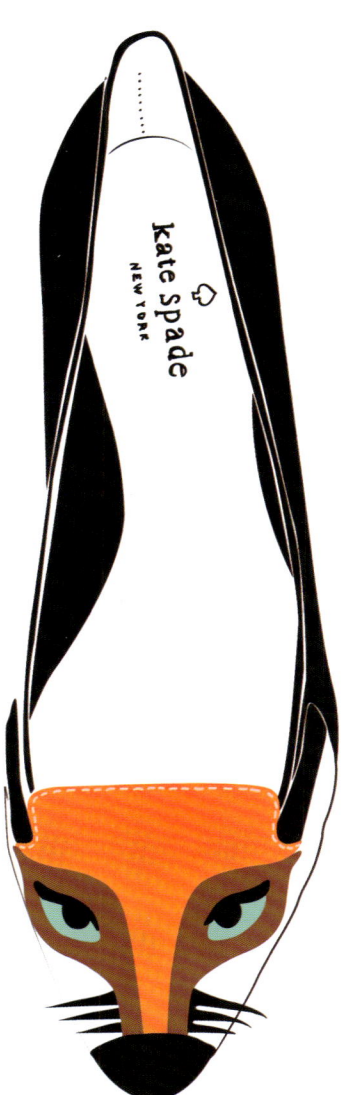

This fashion illustration is inspired by the beautiful Kate Spade foxes shoes.
Illustrator: Paula Blanche Country: Chile

Kate Spade Shoes

Balenciaga

Inspired by Balenciaga. Personal project using graphite and watercolour.
Illustrator: Nicole Jarecz Country: USA

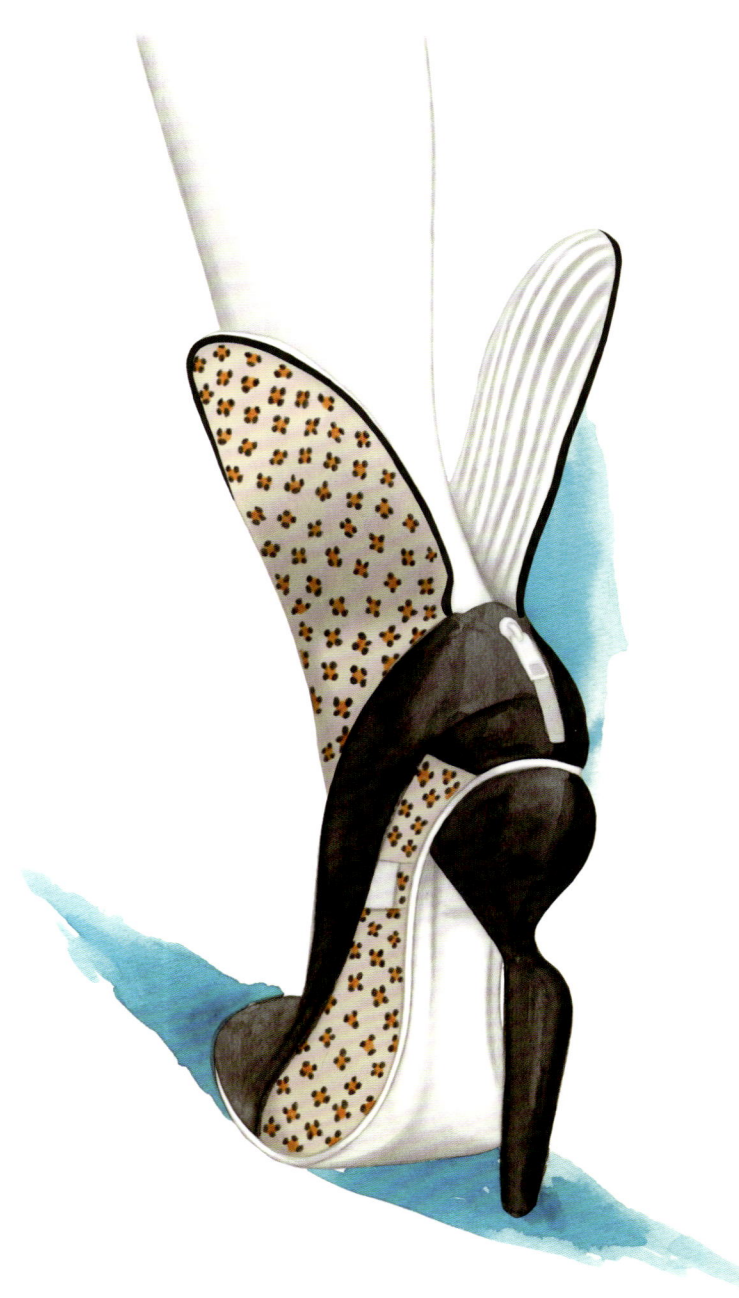

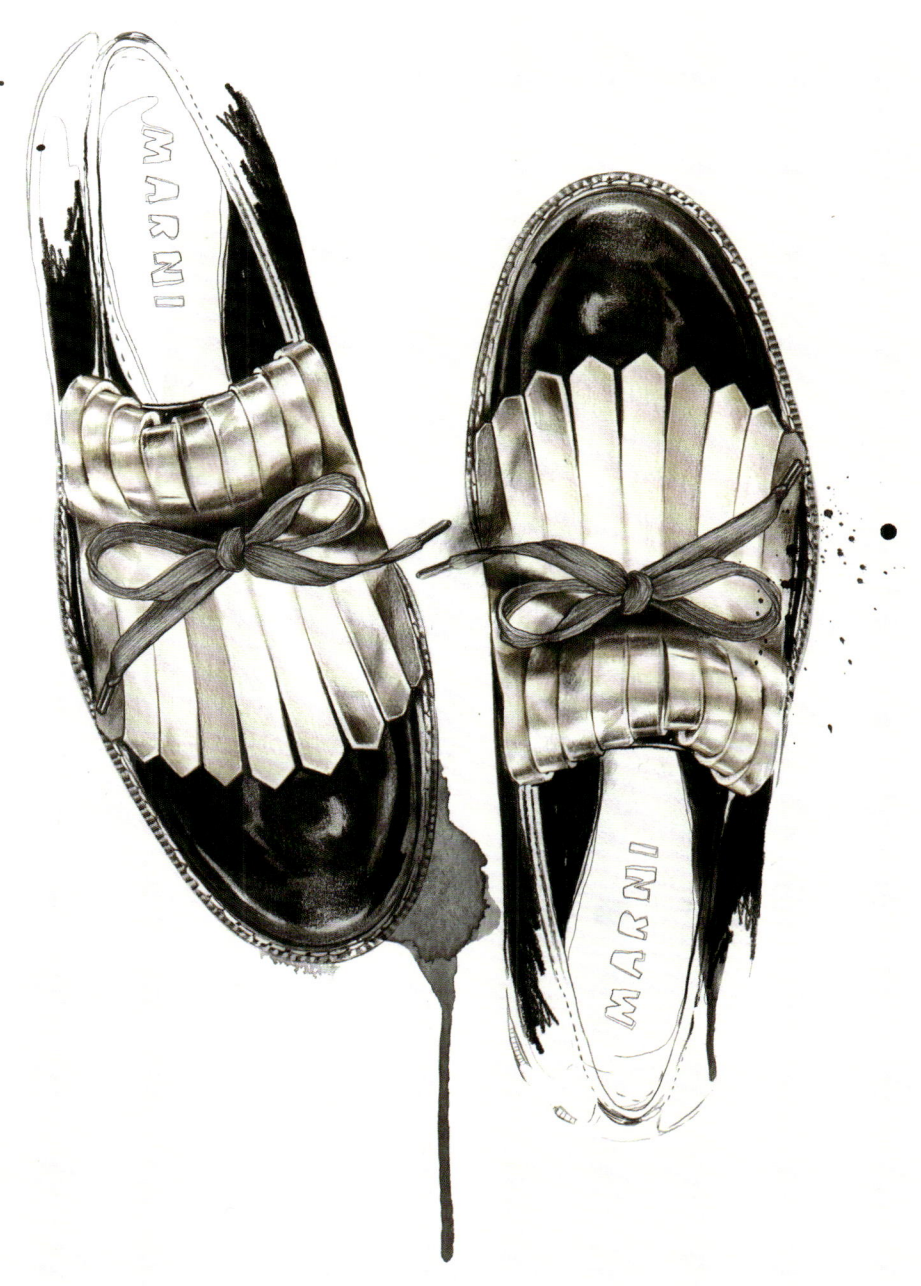

Editorial for Pudder agency on fall fashion where I picked out personal favorites from the runway. Inspired by Marni AW 2013
Illustrator: Esra Røise Country: Norway

Marni Brogues

Herve Leger SS 2013

The illustrator went backstage before the Chris Benz presentation to capture the beauty and fashion looks and to really check out the vibe of the show before painting favourite aspects of the collection.
Illustrator: Samantha Hahn Client: New York Magazine Country: USA

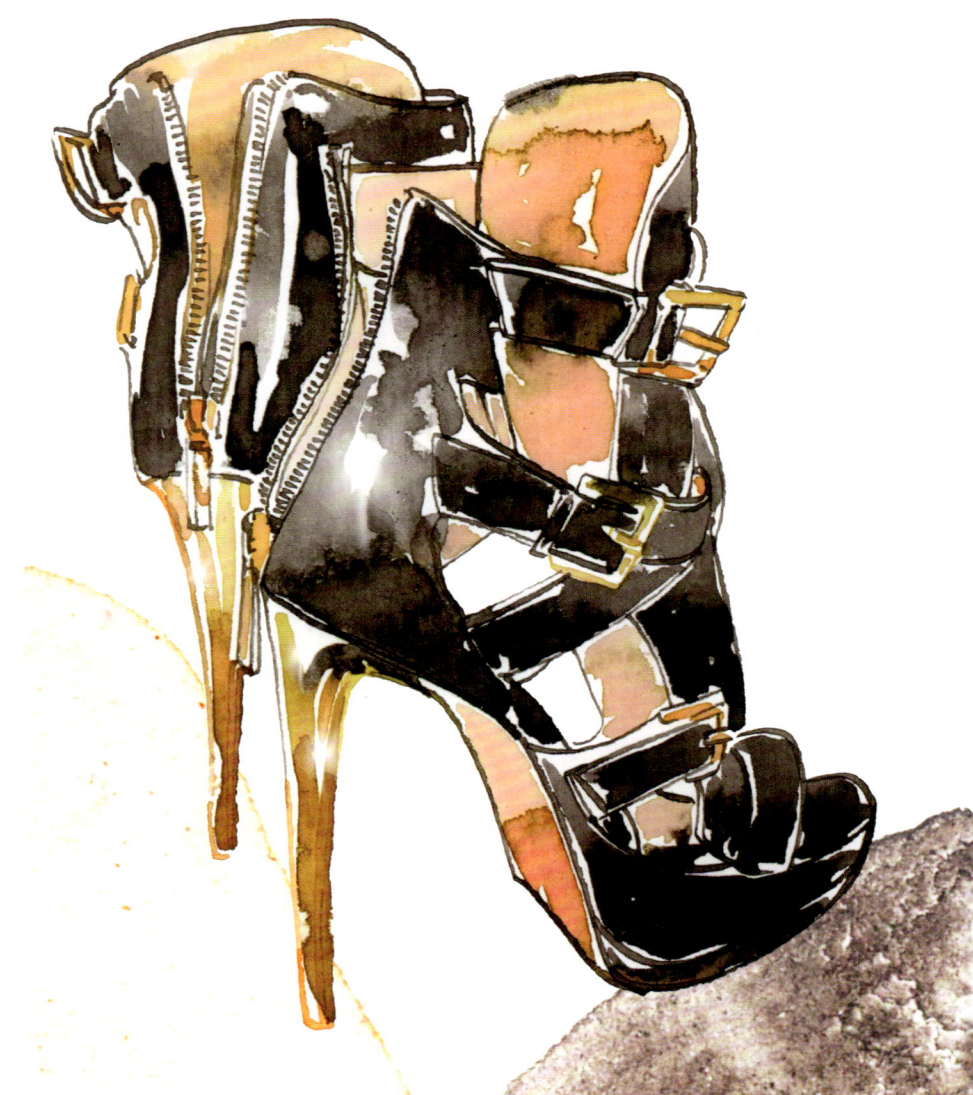

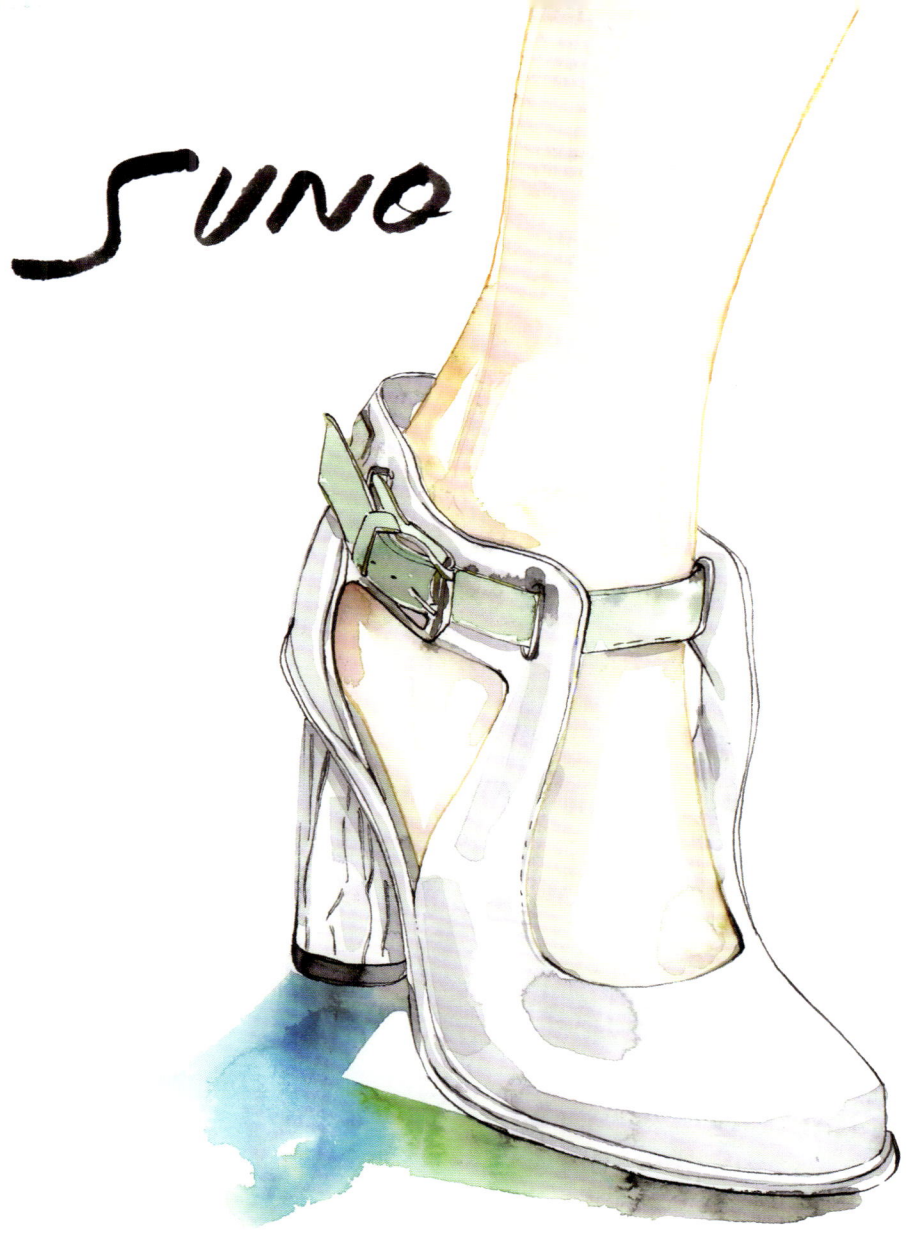

New York Fashion Week SS 2016 was when Suno launched their first shoe collection.
Illustrator: Samantha Hahn Country: USA

Suno SS 2016

Vivienne Westwood's Pirate Boots

As part of a personal project looking at the history of designer; Vivienne Westwood; Willa created a series of catwalk illustrations looking at how the pirate boot has evolved throughout Westwood's career.

Illustrator: Willa Gebbie Country: UK

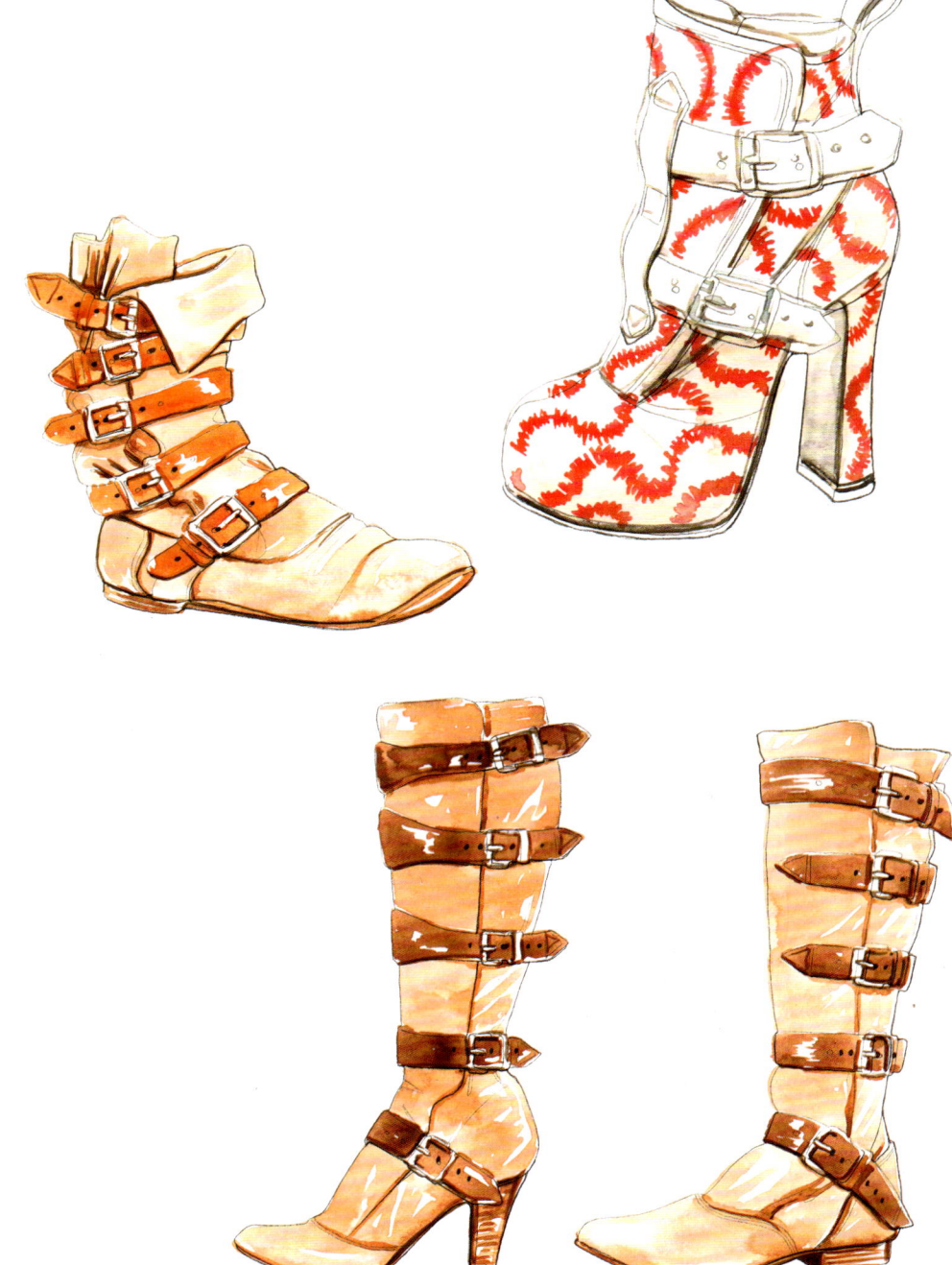

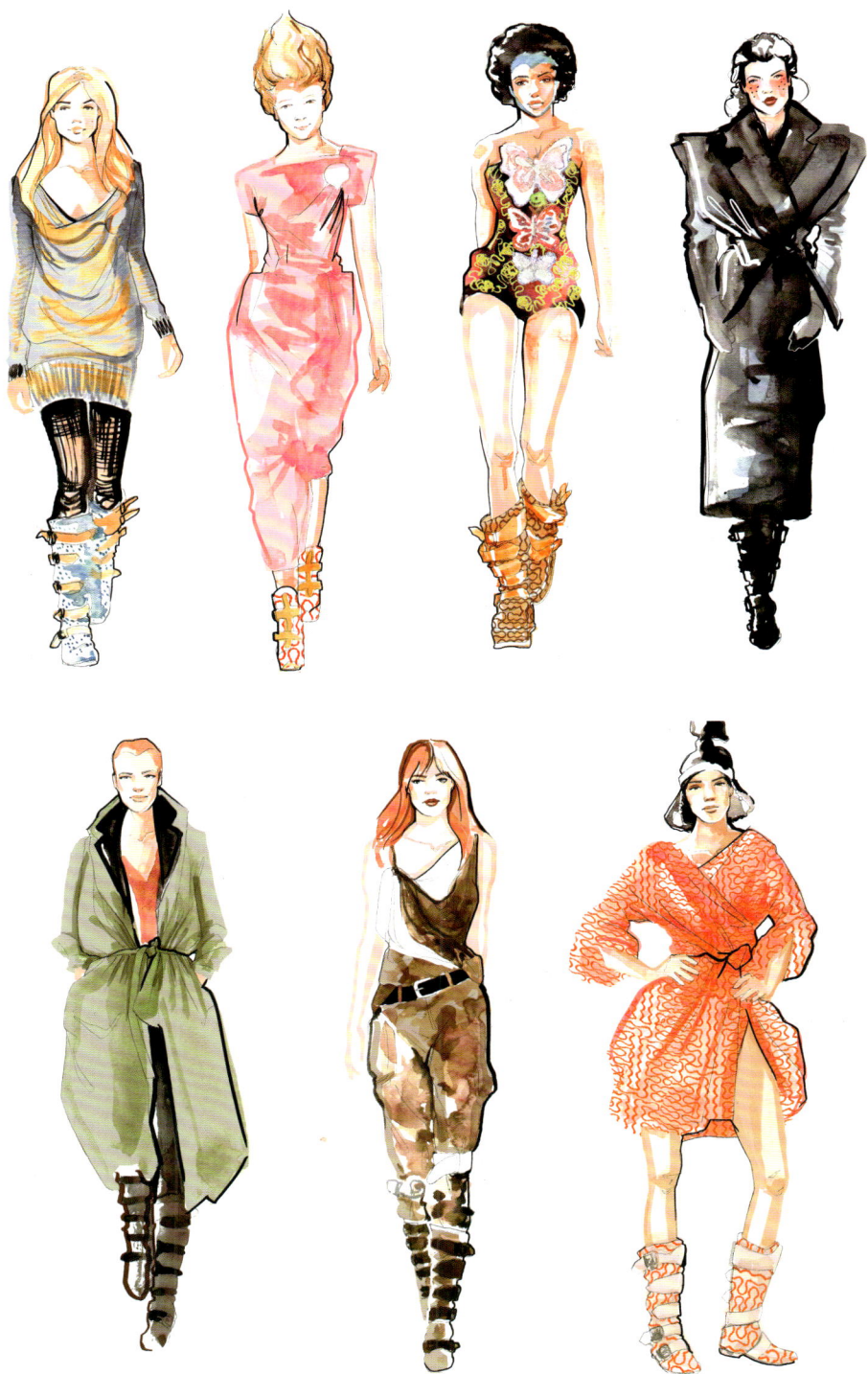

Butterfly Gladiator Sandal

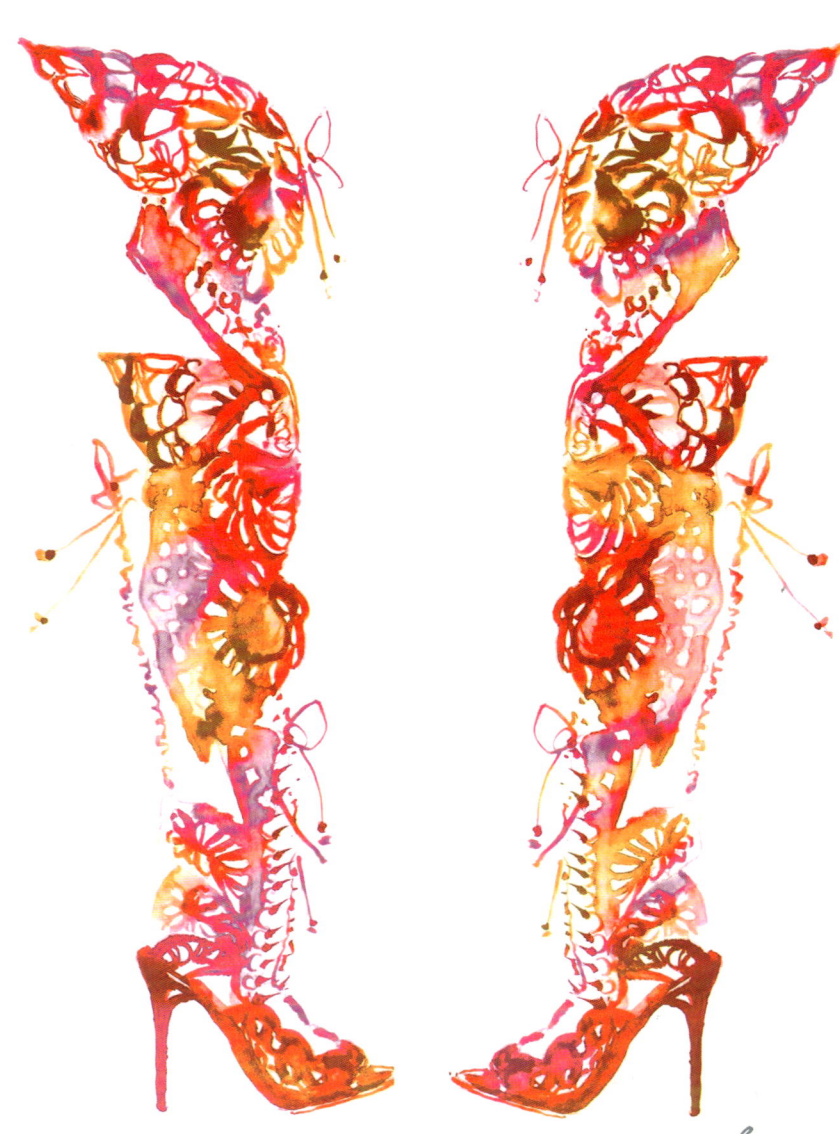

Sophia Webster 'Athena' Butterfly Gladiator Sandal, 2015. Materials use Watercolour on card, digital refinement. Illustrator: Stephanie Dellaportas Country: Australia

Christian Louboutin 'Impera' lasercut pumps, 2015. Created with watercolour on card and digital refinement. Illustrator: Stephanie Dellaportas Country: Australia

Lasercut High Heels

Watercolour Heels

Illustration of high heels, using pencils and watercolour. Inspired by popular brands of Dolce & Gabbana etc.
Illustrator: Ricoho Country: China

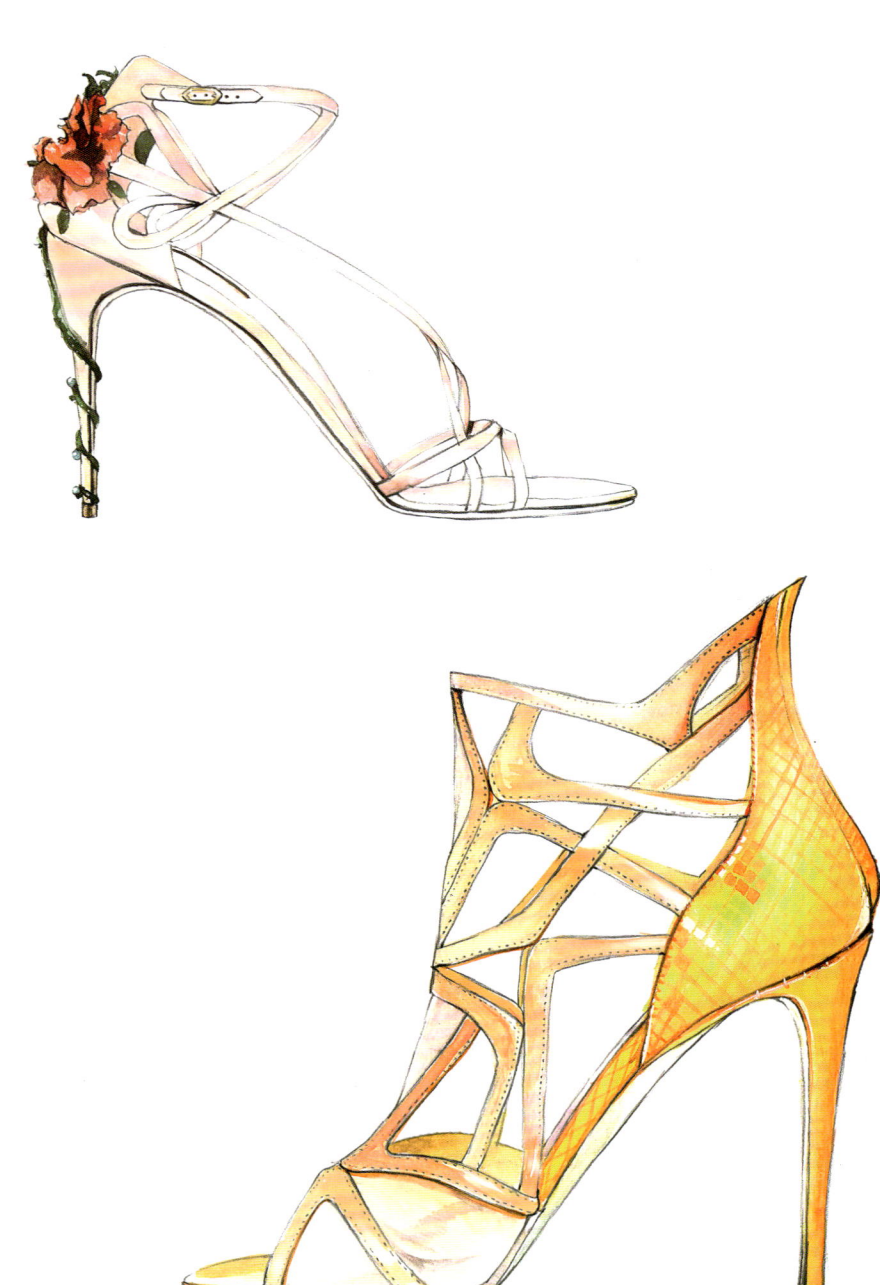

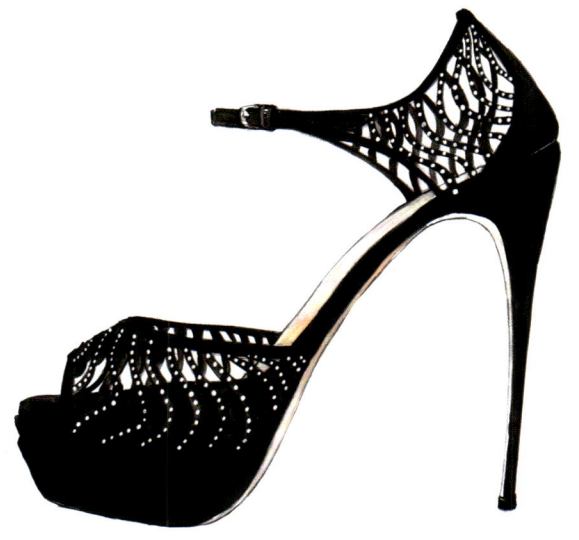

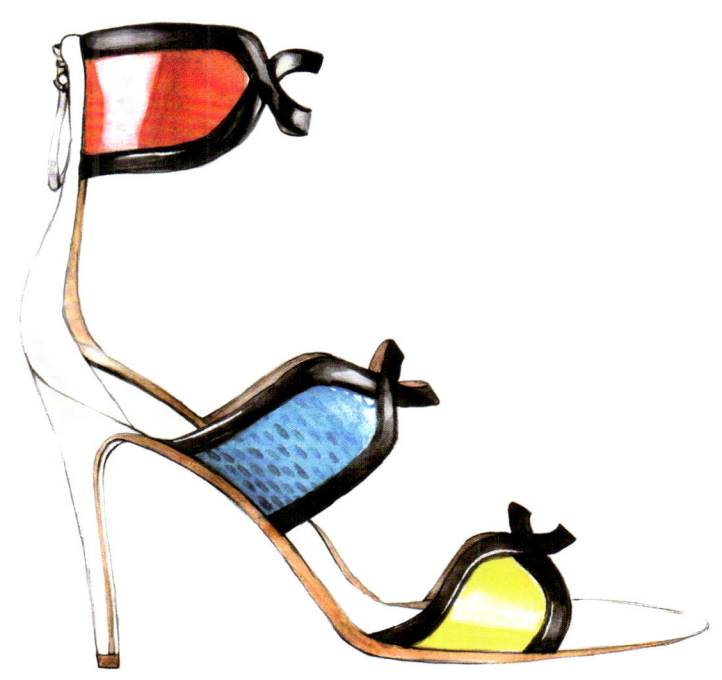

Illustration inspired by black Brian Atwood and Aquazzura high-heeled shoes, finished with pencils and watercolour.
Illustrator: Ricoho Country: China

Stylish High Heels

Blumarine Handbag

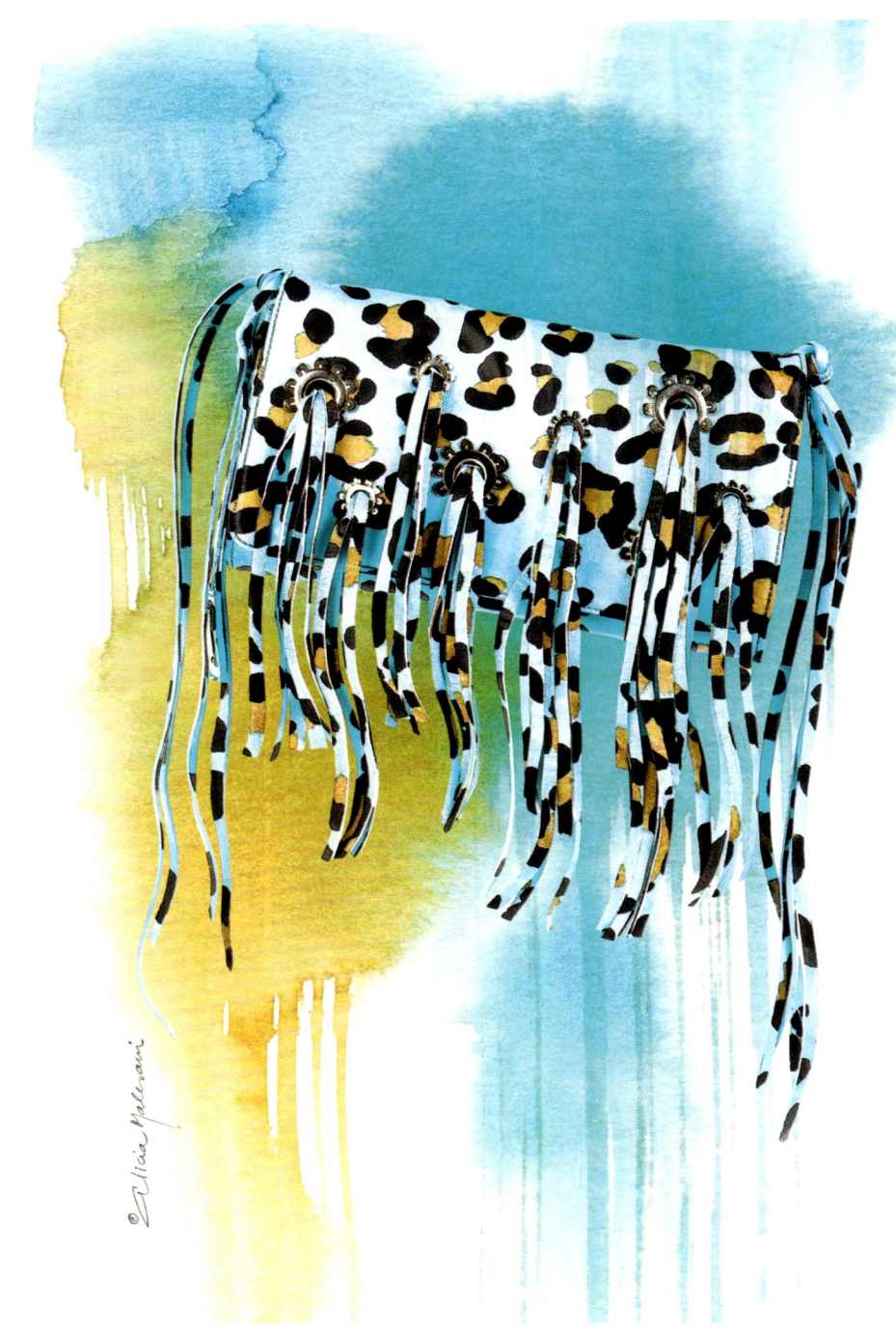

Harper's Bazaar Magazine (Spain). Watercolour, ink and pencil on high quality Fabriano paper.
Illustrator: Alicia Malesani Country: Spain

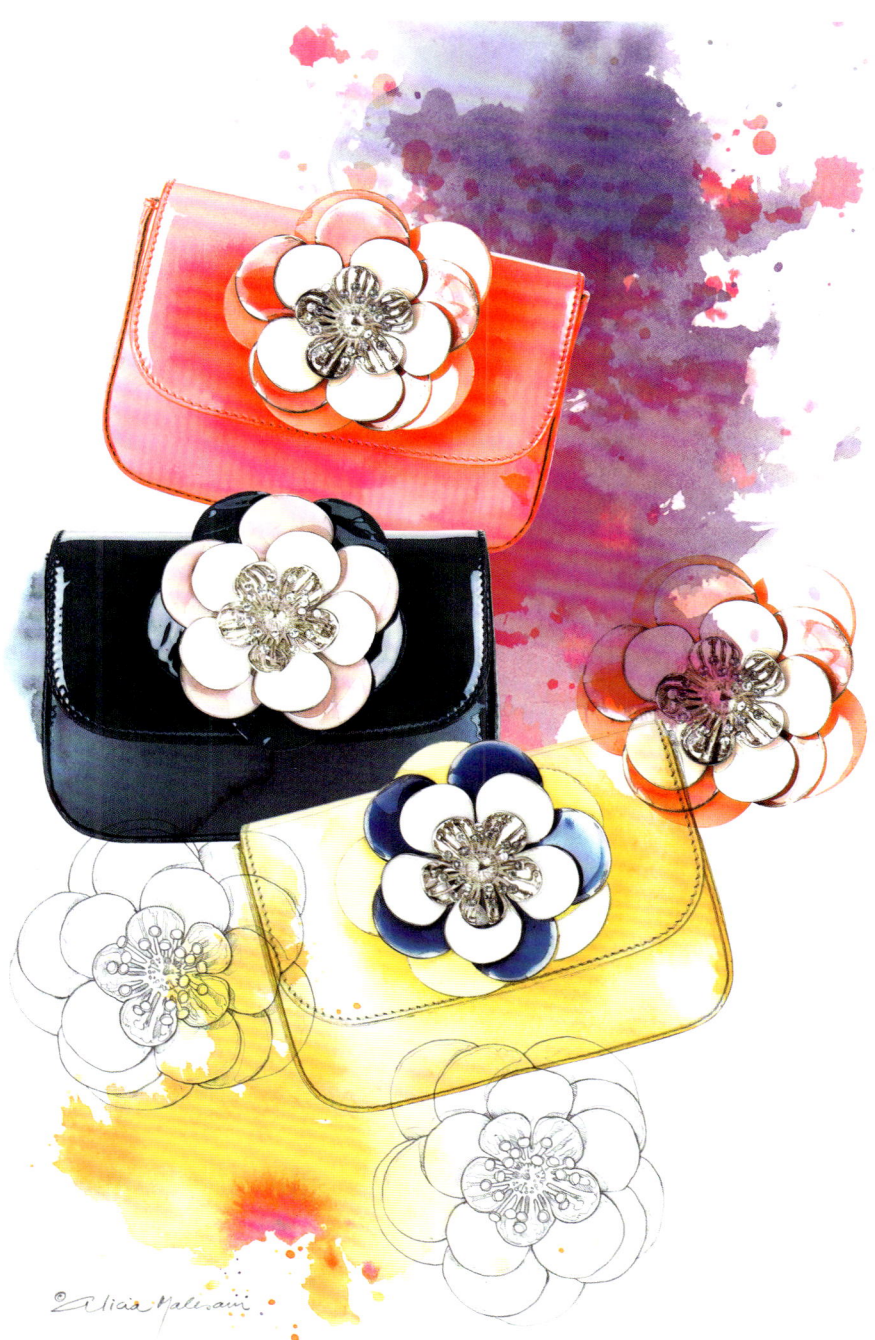

Harper's Bazaar Magazine (Spain). Watercolour, ink and pencil on high quality Fabriano paper.
Illustrator: Alicia Malesani Country: Spain

Miu Miu Clutch

Prada Clutch

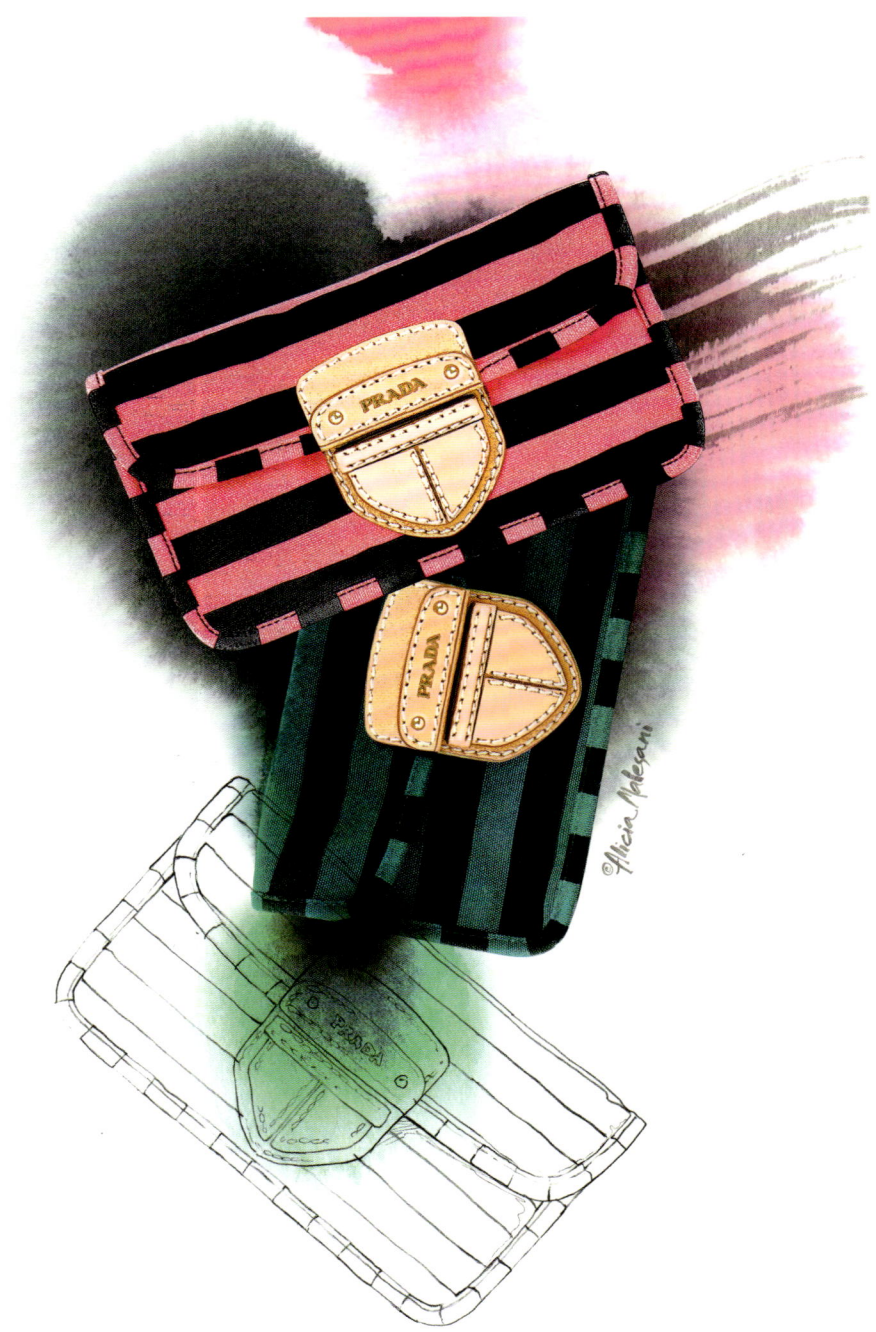

Harper's Bazaar Magazine (Spain). Watercolour, ink and pencil on high quality Fabriano paper.
Illustrator: Alicia Malesani Country: Spain

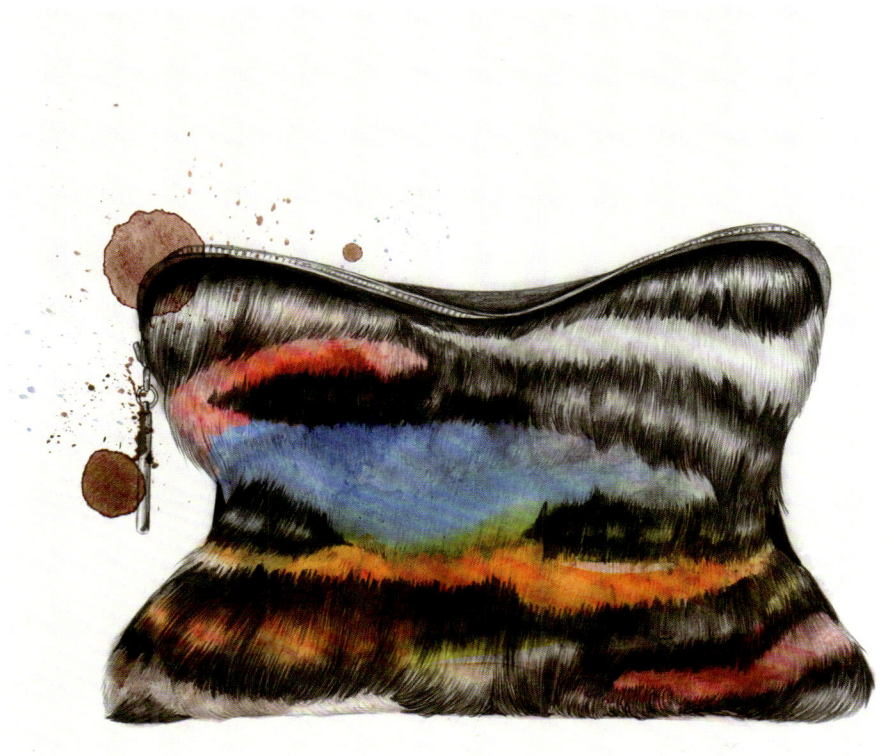

Editorial for Pudder agency on fall fashion where the illustrator picked out personal favourites from the runway. Inspired by 3.1. Phillip Lim AW 2013.
Illustrator: Esra Roise Country: Norway

Phillip Lim Furry

Everyday Bags

Illustration made for Hillcrest shopping mall marketing campaign, spring 2015. The fashion illustrations are made from scratch digitally in Photoshop by watercolour technique.
Illustrator: Mateja Kovac Country: Croatia

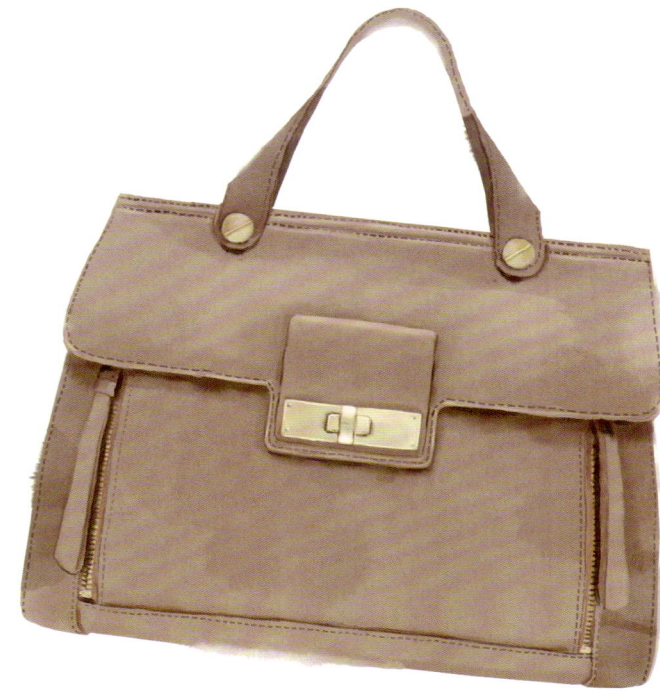

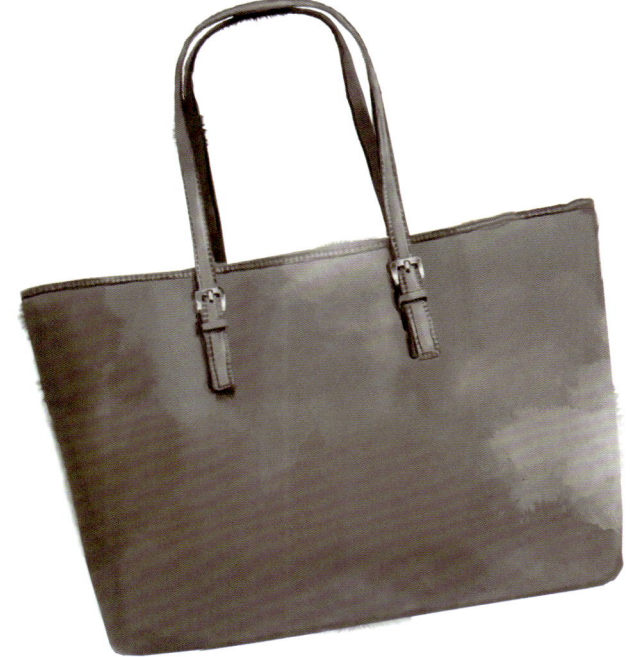

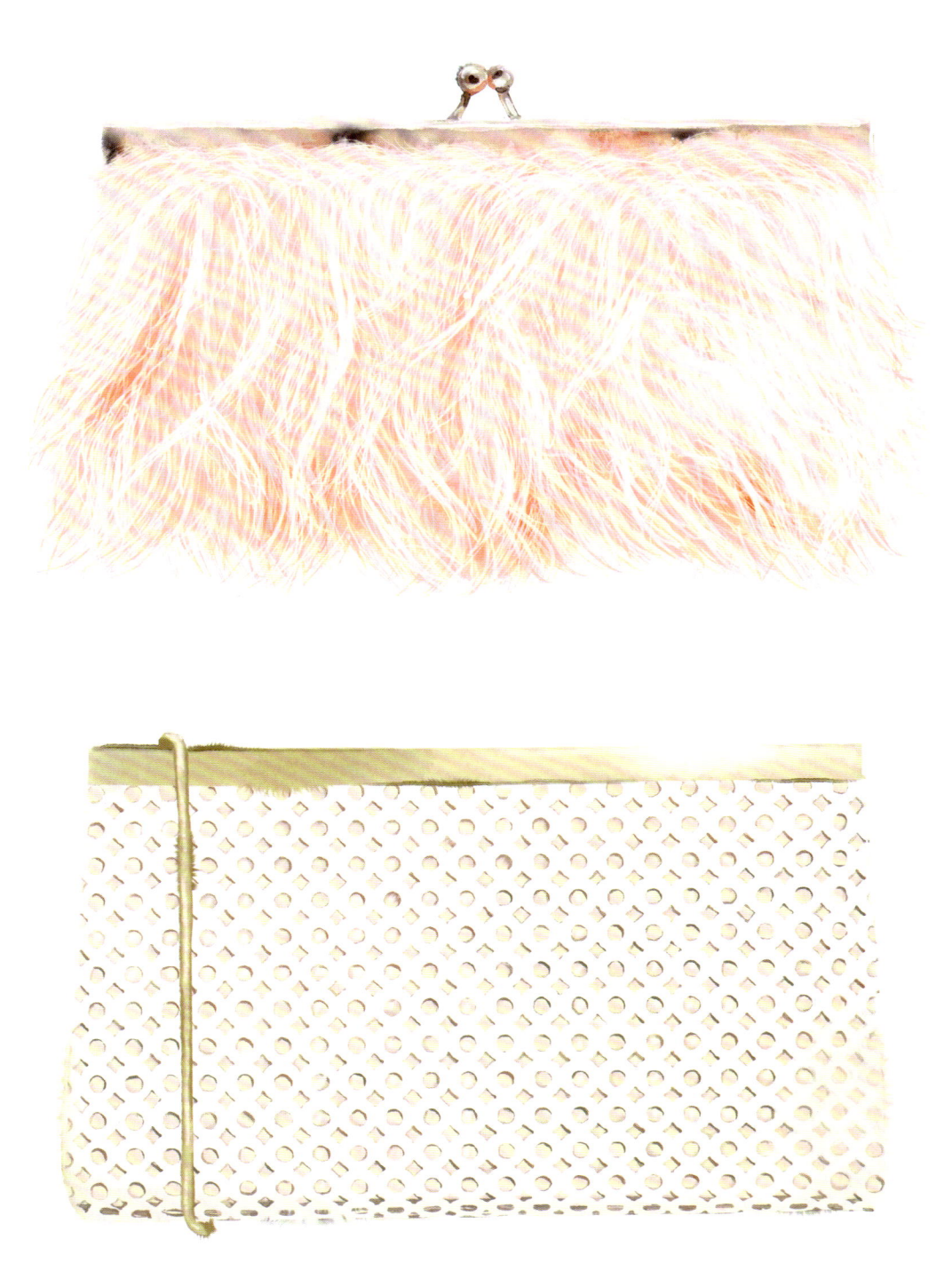

Dolce & Gabbana Jewel Bag

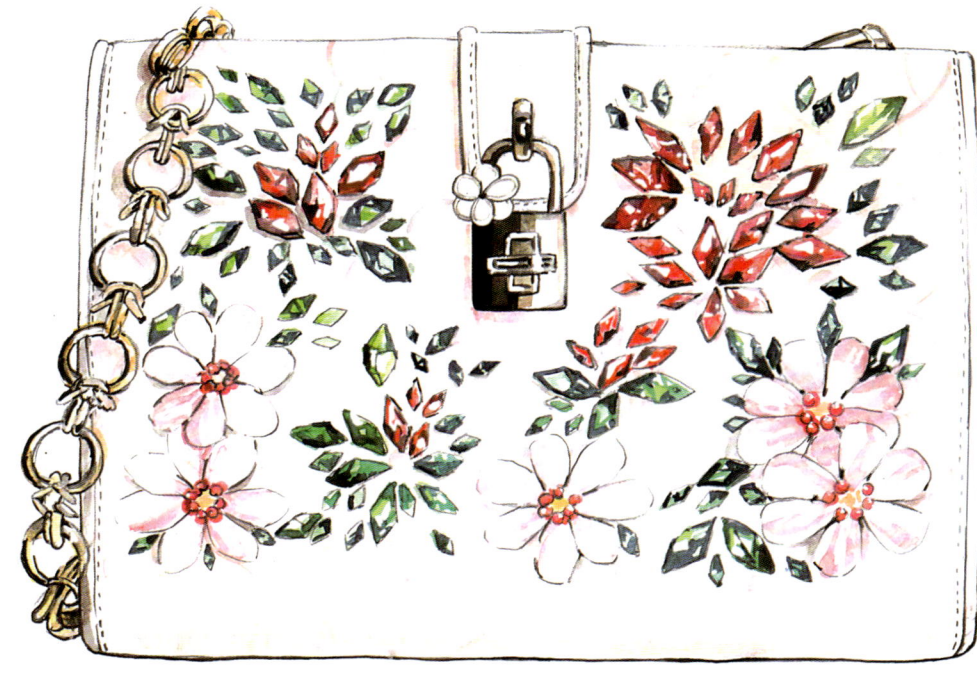

Illustration inspired by Dolce & Gabbana jewel bag, finished with pencil and watercolour.
Illustrator: Ricoho Country: China

Illustration inspired by Dolce & Gabbana weave bag, finished with pencil and watercolour.
Illustrator: Ricoho Country: China

Dolce & Gabbana Weave Bag

Index

A

Alena Lavdovskaya

Alicia Malesani

Anum Tariq

B

Barykina Anastasia

C

Carole Wilmet

Caroline Andrieu

Chidy Wayne

Cristina Alonso

E

Esra Roise

F

Floyd Grey

I

Irina Kaygorodova

K

Katerina Murysina

Kaznakova Olga

Kiara Tan

M

Maggie Ai

Margot Van Huijkelom

Mariana MARCHè

Mateja Kovac

Mélique Street

Mia Marie Overgaard

Mina K

N

Natalia Zamora

Natsuki Otani

Nicole Jarecz

Nina Mid

O

Olivia Au

P

Paula Blanche

Pelin Ozelmas

R

Rahel Guiragossian

Ricoho

S

Samantha Hahn

Sara Vera Lecaro

Stephanie Dellaportas

Svetlana Ikhsanova

T

Tania Santos

V

Veronica Kemsky

W

Will Bayum

Willa Gebbie

Gorffennol Llwyd a Dyfodol Duach

Atgofion un o Fwynwyr Ceredigion ar ddechrau'r ganrif ddiwethaf

A Grey Past and a Blacker Future

Reminiscences of a Cardiganshire Miner in the early 1900s

Golygydd/Editor: Megan Waring

Cedwir pob hawl. Ni chaniateir atgynhyrchu unrhyw ran o'r cyhoeddiad hwn mewn unrhyw fodd heb ganiatád y cyhoeddwyr ymlaen llaw.

All rights reserved. No part of this publication may be reproduced or transmitted in any form or by any means without the prior permission of the publishers

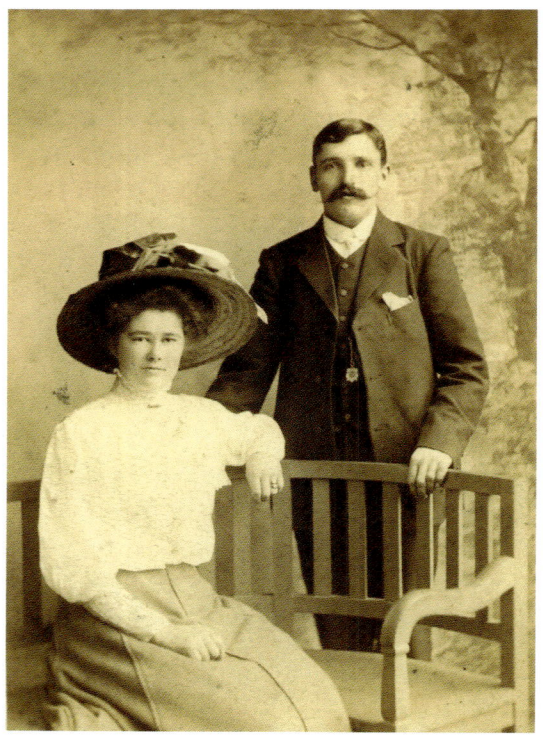

Priodas Elias a Hannah 1910
Elias and Hannah's Marriage 1910

Cyhoeddwyd gan Gannock Publishers, 2014
Published by Gannock Publishers, 2014

Argraffwyd a rhwymwyd gan Argraffwyr Cambrian Cyf., Aberystwyth..
Printed and bound by Cambrian Printers Ltd., Aberystwyth.
ISBN: 978-0-9930557-0-6

Cydnabyddiaethau

Yr wyf yn ddyledus i Sally Morris ac yn enwedig i Dai Jones sydd wedi fy helpu o'r cychwyn drwy eu cymorth wrth drawsgrifio'r dogfennau, rhoi cyngor ar gasglu a'u brwdfrydedd di-ffael. At hynny, ni fyddai'r cyhoeddiad wedi bod yn bosibl heb sgiliau y cyfieithu Dai, ei fab Llyr Jones, Hywel Wyn Jones a Gary Jones. Mae Dai a Hywel wedi bod yn arbennig o ddefnyddiol o ran gwneud yn siwr y bydd y darllenydd Cymraeg cyfoes yn deall arddull mwy hynafol y Gymraeg a ddefnyddiai Elias.

Diolch yn arbennig i fy ngŵr Tony, sydd wedi sganio a thrawsgrifio erthyglau a ffotograffau, rhoi cynllun y llyfr ar gyfrifiadur a bod yn brif weinyddwr y prosiect. Gyda'i gefndir fel daearegwr, mae wedi bod yn amhrisiadwy wrth chwilio mewn cylchgronau mwyngloddio a gwirio terminoleg.

Acknowledgments

I am indebted to Sally Morris and especially Dai Jones who have helped me from the start with their assistance in transcribing the documents, advice on compilation and unfailing enthusiasm. Furthermore, the publication would not have been possible without the skill in translation of Dai, his son Llyr Jones, Hywel Wyn Jones and Gary Jones. Dai and Hywel have been particularly helpful in making sure that the modern Welsh reader would understand the more archaic style of Welsh that Elias used.

Particular thanks goes to my husband Tony who has scanned and transcribed articles and photographs for the computer, planned the chapters and generally been the chief administrator of the project. With his background as a geologist he has been invaluable in contacting mining magazines and checking terminology.

Cynnwys

Yn y gyfrol hon fe osodir y 3 atgofion Cymraeg at y chwith a'r cyfieithiad Saesneg ar y dde. Os mai yn Saesneg yr ysgrifennwyd yr erthygl wreiddiol, megis erthyglau papurau newydd, nid yw'r rhain wedi'u trosi i'r Gymraeg. Mae'r Cymraeg gwreiddiol wedi ei olygu. Rhestrir y gyfres o atgofion a llythyron yn eu trefn amseryddol cyhyd ag sy'n bosibl.

Rhagair... vi
Map o'r lleoliadau... x

Atgofion

1. Hanes ac Atgofion Gwaith Frongoch 1948....................... 1
2. Atgofion am fywyd ardal yn Sir Aberteifi 1956.................. 25
3. Atgofion am Sir Forgannwg o Ebrill 18fed 1901 hyd Medi 1929... 79

Llythyron, Anerchiadau ac Erthyglau Papurau Newydd

4. Llythyr oddi wrth Emilio Invernizzi 1953......................... 95
5. Llythyr: Lead Mining or Fishing?.................................. 101
6. Anerchiad gan Elias Jones.. 105
7. Erthyglau Papurau Newydd.. 109

Erthyglau Eraill

8. Adroddiad ar Ddylanwad Mwyngloddiau Plwm Ceredigion ... 135
9. Lisburne Development Syndicate Ltd............................. 143
10. Trydydd Jiwbili Eglwys Fethodistaidd Bethel 165
11. Marwolaeth mwynwr Eidalaidd...................................... 177

Darluniau

12. Coeden Deuluol 179

Contents

The format of this book places the original 3 Welsh memoirs on one side where available and the English translation on the right. Where an original article was written in English, as in the newspaper articles, these have not been translated into Welsh. The original Welsh has also been edited. The series of memoirs and letters are listed as chronologically as possible.

Preface.. vii
Location Map... x

Memoirs
1 History and Reminiscences of the Frongoch Mine 1948……… 1
2 Reminiscences of an area of Cardiganshire 1956……………... 25
3 Reminiscences of Glamorganshire from 18th April 1901 to September 1929……………………………………………….. 79

Letters, Speeches and Newspaper Articles
4 Letter from Emilio Invernizzi 1953…………………………... 95
5 Letter: Lead Mining or Fishing? 101
6 Speech by Elias Jones…………………………………………. 105
7 Newspaper Articles……………………………………………. 109

Other Articles
8 Report on the Influence of the Lead Mines of Cardiganshire… 135
9 Lisburne Development Syndicate Ltd…………………………. 143
10 Third Jubilee of Bethel Methodist Chapel……………..………. 165
11 Death of Italian Miner………………………...…...................... 177

Illustrations
12 Family Tree……………………………………………………. 179

Rhagair

Ganed fy nhadcu, Elias Jones, ym mhentre Pontrhydygroes, Ceredigion yn 1881. Fel merch i deulu o Gymry a fagwyd yn Swydd Caer, fe dreuliais i'r rhan fwya o fy ngwyliau haf yno, ac mae gen i atgofion hudolus o fywyd pentre cefn gwlad yn y pumdegau a'r chwedegau. Mae fy atgofion o 'Nhadcu yn dyddio nôl i'r cyfnod hwn, wedi iddo fe ymddeol fel mwynwr ac iddo droi at ffermio defaid ar fryniau ei fro. Fe fu farw gartref yn 1965, yn 83 mlwydd oed.

Bu Elias yn fwynwr ers pan oedd yn dair ar ddeg oed, fel ei dad a'i frawd. Yn y rhan hon o ganolbarth Cymru, byddent yn cloddio am blwm, sinc ac arian, ond wedi i bris y plwm ddisgyn fe ymfudodd llawer o fwynwyr i'r gweithiau glo ym Morgannwg. Cadwodd llawer ohonynt eu tyddynnod a byddent yn dychwelyd adre adeg y cynhaeaf, ac adeg hau hadau'r tir. Roedd Elias yn berchen ar gartre'r teulu, Troedyrhiw, erbyn iddo briodi, ond roedd ei rieni'n dal i fyw yno. Fe gafodd ef a'i annwyl wraig Hannah dri o blant, ond fe'i gadawyd ef yn ŵr gweddw yn ifanc a bu'n byw ar ei ben ei hun am bron i ddeng mlynedd ar hugain. Roedd ganddo dri o blant: William a ddaeth yn rheolwr bysiau Crosville, Enid a oedd yn athrawes, ac Anne a fu'n Fetron ar Ysbyty Tregaron ac a urddwyd yn MBE. Bu'n rhaid i Enid, fy mam, fenthyca arian gan fodryb iddi er mwyn mynd i goleg hyfforddi athrawon gan na allai Elias fforddio talu ei ffioedd. Ym mhen amser fe ymddeolodd ef i fyw ym Mhontrhydygroes yng nghartre'r teulu gyda'i 19 cyfer lle gallai fugeilio defaid. Wedi ei farw yn 1965, dyma'i ferch iengaf, wedi symud nôl i Droedyrhiw, hen 'dŷ hir' fel yr oedd, yn dymchwel y tŷ a'i ail-adeiladu o'r newydd.

Wedi marw fy modryb yn 2008, mi ddes i o hyd i goflyfrau, dyddiaduron a ffotograffau mewn coffor gyda rhai llyfrau, peth ohonynt wedi llwydo yn y lleithder. Roedd hefyd hen lyfrau cownt, llythyron a phapurau am y tŷ a'r tir. Roedd ei ferch Anne eisoes wedi

Preface

My grandfather (Dadcu), Elias Jones was born in the village of Pontrhydygroes in mid Wales in 1881. As a child born to Welsh parents but brought up in Cheshire, I spent most of my summer holidays there and have idyllic memories of the village country life in the 1950s and '60s. My memories of Dadcu date back to this period when he had retired as a miner and was a hillside sheep farmer. He died aged 83 in 1965 in his house.

Elias was a miner from the age of 13, as were his father and brothers. In this area of mid Wales they mined for lead, zinc and silver, but when the price of lead fell many miners moved to Glamorgan to the coal mines. They often kept their smallholdings and would return home at harvest time or to sow seed. Elias owned the family home, Troedyrhiw, by the time he was married, but his parents lived there. He and his beloved wife Hannah had 3 children, but he was widowed early and lived alone for nearly 30 years. He had 3 children, William who became a manager of Crosville buses, Enid who was a school teacher and Anne, who was a Matron at Tregaron and later awarded the M.B.E. My mother Enid had to borrow money from an aunt to go to teacher training college as Elias could not afford her fees. He eventually retired in Pontrhydygroes to the family home with 19 acres of land and continued to rear sheep. After he died in 1965, his youngest daughter, who had moved back to Troedyrhiw, the Welsh ty unnos he describes, demolished and rebuilt the house.

After my aunt died in 2008, I found memoirs, diaries and many photos in a trunk with books, some covered with mould. There were also old account books, letters and papers about the house and land.

rhoi llyfrau cownt Capel Bethel, Pontrhydygroes i'r Llyfrgell Genedlaethol wedi i'r capel gau.

Dechreuais feddwl sut i drosglwyddo'r hanes yma i'm merch gan fod yr atgofion yn Gymraeg, iaith nad ydyn nhw yn ei siarad gan mai yn yr Alban y'u maged. Penderfynais gyhoeddi'r tair a sgrifennodd Elias wedi ymddeol am ei fywyd fel mwynwr a glowr, a chael cyfieithiad ohonynt. Dyn a oedd wedi addysgu ei hun oedd Elias, a chadwodd i ymgyfarwyddo ynghylch materion gwleidyddol y byd drwy ddarllen llyfrau fel *Herbert Morrison, H.G.Wells,* cyhoeddiadau'r blaid Lafur *a Soviet Russia as I saw it*, gan Sylvia Pankhurst. Roedd yn gynghorydd lleol, ac yn flaenor yng Nghapel Methodist Bethel y bu ei dad yn helpu i'w adeiladu. Roedd yn llwyr yn erbyn y Comisiwn Coedwigaeth yn planu coed ar dir ffermio, fel y cofnododd ar yr adeg pan ddaeth Enoch Powell A.S. i dalu ymweliad ag ef. Yn ddiweddarach fe osododd fy modryb y tir ar rent i ffermwr defaid cyfagos er mwyn gwneud yn siwr na fyddai hynny'n digwydd.

Fel llawer o fwynwyr a glowyr, roedd gan Elias ddaliadau politicaidd cryf, a byddai wrth ei fodd yn dadlau ar bynciau'r dydd. Bu'n undebwr selog, a chonsyrn mawr bob amser am amodau byw y gweithiwr cyffredin. Mae ei argyhoeddiad a'i bersonoliaeth gref yn amlwg, rwy'n tybio, yn ei gyfansoddiadau a'r erthyglau amdano.

Mae y llyfr hwn yn gyflwynedig i fy nhair merch Karen, Nerissa a Jacqueline sydd hefyd wrth eu bodd yn ymweld â Throedyrhiw. Byddai eu hen dad-cu yn falch iawn ohonynt.

Megan Waring
Hydref 2014

Other account books belonging to Bethel Chapel, Pontrhydygroes, had already been donated to the National library by his daughter Anne after the chapel closed.

I started thinking of how to pass this history on to my daughters as the memoirs are in Welsh, which they don't speak, having been brought up in Scotland. I decided to publish the 3 memoirs, which Elias had written in his retirement about his life as a miner and his political views and had them translated. He was self-educated and always kept himself informed about politics in the wider world through his reading material, which included *Herbert Morrison, H.G.Wells,* Labour party publications and *Soviet Russia as I Saw It* by Sylvia Pankhurst. He was a local councillor and Deacon of the Bethel Methodist Chapel, which his father had helped to build. He was very much against the Forestry Commission planting on farming land, as he mentions when Enoch Powell M.P. paid him a visit. My aunt later rented out the land to a sheep farmer to ensure that this did not happen.

As were many miners, Elias was very politically motivated and loved to debate the issues of the day. He was a strong unionist and was always concerned about the conditions of the working man. I think his strong personality and convictions come out through his writing and the newspaper articles about him.

This book is dedicated to my three daughters Karen, Nerissa and Jacqueline who also loved to visit Troedyrhiw. Their great Grandfather would be very proud of them.

Megan Waring
October 2014

Map o'r lleoliadau   Location Map

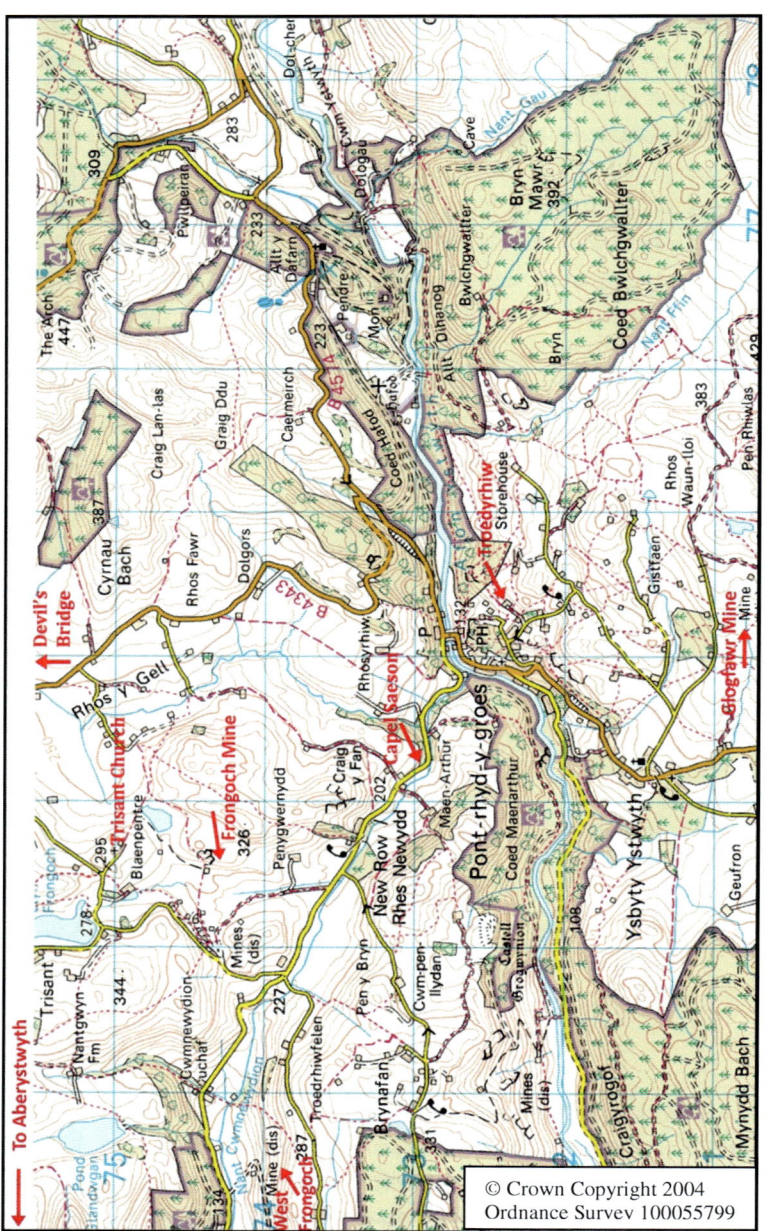

1
Hanes ac Atgofion Gwaith Frongoch
History and Reminiscences of the Frongoch Mine

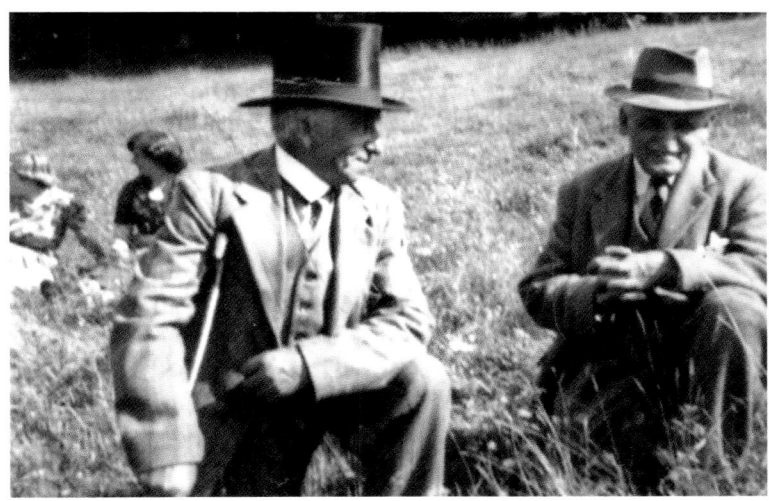

Elias a Dan, Hafodgau? (credir mae picnic Ysgol Sul ydyw)
Elias and Dan, Hafodgau? (thought to be a Sunday School picnic)

Nid yw'r ddwy gerdd Gymraeg wedi eu cyfieithu; y cyntaf gan Thomas Tudno Jones a'r ail gan Albert Evans-Jones (Cynan). Mae ei gerdd, 'Salaam' yn deyrnged i'r ffordd 'roedd Moslemiaid yn cael eu hystyried fel pobl heddychlon a chariadus.

The two Welsh poems have not been translated; the first by Thomas Tudno Jones in 1876, and the second by Albert Evans-Jones (Cynan). His poem, 'Salaam' is a tribute to the way in which Muslims were regarded as peace-loving people:

> I learned the greeting I love best
> When the sons of the east met the sons of the west.
> And the wish they share is my wish too
> May the Peace of God ever be with you.

Hanes ac Atgofion Gwaith Frongoch
3ydd Chwefror 1948

Dywedir i wraig Lot, pan edrychodd yn ei hol, droi'n golofn o halen. Tuedd ambell un trigain oed a siomwyd mewn bywyd yw troi'n ffiol o finegr. Buaswn yn euog o anniolchgarwch mawr pe trown yn finegr, canys bu fy nhaith gan mwyaf tros foroedd tawel a hyfryd.

Ni fu gennyf gyfoeth erioed, ac nis chwenychais; ni phrofais ychwaith dlodi; os yw'm hawl i bethau da'r ddaear yr un â phob un or ddwy fil miliynau sy byw heddyw (ac ni thybiais erioed fod gennyf hawl foesol i ragor) cefais fwy na'm rhan.

Dywedodd cyfaill i mi, a oedd wedi troi'r trigain, nad oedd yn cofio iddo ddihuno un bore heb deimlo fod ynddo ddigon o nerth i symud y ddaear. Ni chefais i mo'r fraint honno. Lawer i fore wrth godi teimlais yn amheus a allwn fynd trwy oruchwylion y dydd. Ni chefais er hynny ond ychydig salwch erioed ac ni roddais fawr o waith i feddygon.

Cefais gartref clyd a gofalus ar aelwyd dda nhad a mam. Mwynheais fywyd teuluol dymunol; breintiwyd fi â chyfeillion da a didwyll ac nid oes gennyf unrhyw gŵyn yn erbyn bywyd.

Nid peth hawdd yw cadw fy meddwl ar y gorffennol; myn amgylchiadau'r dydd sylw, yn wir yn y dyddiau helbulus hyn ar y byd tuedda'r meddwl i droi at drafferthion heddiw ac argoelion yfory.

Pan fo'r presennol yn gor-hawlio'r meddwl a'r dyfodol yn ddi-olau, af am dro, a dringaf i ben clogwyn uchaf Banc Troedyrhiw, yno syrth amser i gyfartaledd gwell, syllaf ar yr hen Afon Ystwyth a chlywaf sŵn murmur ei dŵr yn taro'r glannau fel pe'n dweud ei bod yn llifo'r ffordd yma ers oesoedd di-rif cyn geni Hitler, ac y bydd yn parhau i daro ei glannau pan fydd hwnnw a'i luoedd creulon wedi eu hir anghofio. "Do" meddai'r hen afon eilwaith, "rhoddais wasanaeth da i ddynolryw am yn agos i ddwy fil o flynyddoedd, gyrrais ei rhodau dŵr a golchais ei

History and Reminiscences of the Frongoch Mine
February 12th 1948

It is said that Lot's wife, on looking back, turned into a pillar of salt. I would be guilty of great ingratitude if I were to turn into vinegar, as my journey was, for the most part, over placid and lovely seas.

I never had wealth and never coveted it. Neither did I experience poverty. If my right to the good things of the earth is the same as that of the two thousand million people alive today (and I never believed that I had any moral right to a greater share) then I have had more than my share.

A friend who had just turned sixty told me that he never remembered waking up in the morning without feeling that he had the energy to move mountains. I never had that privilege. Many a morning on getting out of bed I doubted if I could get through the day's work. Even so, I have seldom been ill, and I didn't give my doctor much work.

I had a comfortable and caring home under the good care of my father and mother. I have enjoyed a pleasant family life. I have been blessed with good honest friends, and I have no complaint about life.

It's not easy to keep focussed on the past; the day's events need to be attended to, and indeed, in these troubled times the mind tends to turn to the problems of today and one's predictions for tomorrow.

When the mind is preoccupied by the present, and the future seems sombre, I go for a walk, climbing to the highest point of Banc Troedyrhiw. There I see time in a better perspective, looking at the dear old River Ystwyth and hearing the murmur of its waters lapping at the banks, as if to say that it has flowed this way for countless centuries, before Hitler was born and will still be lapping at its banks when he and his cruel forces will be long forgotten. "Yes" said the old river again

mwynau pan oedd y bobl yn rhoddi ffrwyn am fy mhen. Ond erbyn heddiw, does neb eisiau fy help, 'rydym yn byw yn yr Oes Haearn. Ond daw amser gwahanol eto pan ddeffroith plant y pentref o'u trwmgwsg hir."

Ar hyn troaf fy wyneb tua'r dwyrain a gwelaf dyddyn glas Hafodgau, yr aradr yn ymyl y clawdd yn dangos llafur boreuaf a diddiwedd dynolryw a Dan, fy hen gyfaill, yn y *plot cabbage* gorau'n y wlad. Tystia Dan bob amser fod plannu *cabbage* yn "paying game" a pha ryfedd, mae'n plannu naill flwyddyn ar ôl y llall, ond "always working to plan"; yn rhoddi ei "netting wire" amdanynt gan adael twll fan hyn a fan draw er mwyn hudo ysgyfarnogod i mewn i'w faglau liw nos, mae wedi crogi cannoedd ohonynt ar hyd y blynyddoedd. Mawr dda i'r hen gyfaill.

Troaf eto ac edrychaf i'r De Orllewin, gwelaf Eglwys Ysbyty Ystwyth a'r fynwent lle gorffwysa gwŷr a gwragedd a adwaenwn yn dda. Bydd yn rhaid i minnau eu dilyn i gyd ryw ddiwrnod. Yma bu'r hen a'r ieuanc yn addoli am ganrifoedd ac yn y fynwent hon y claddwyd gŵr o'r enw Shaci Troedyrhiw, am yr hwn byddaf yn sôn ychydig amdano nes ymlaen. Yr oedd gan Shaci fab o'r enw John Jones, Troedyrhiw, tad William Jones a dyma finnau, Elias, mab William.

Yn nhawelwch Banc Troedyrhiw y peth mwyaf naturiol yn y byd i mi yw edrych yn ôl dros yr hen amser gynt. Pleser puraf bywyd yw meddwl, ymgodymu â phroblemau, deall a moes; yn wahanol i lawer pleser arall, y maent yn ddigymysg. Gadawn dair cenhedlaeth o Shaci yn Mynwent Ysbyty Ystwyth, mae tair eto yn fyw, sef Elias, William a Clifford. Ond cyn gadael y meirw tu fewn i glawdd y fynwent, 'rwyf am ddarllen un o delynegion Tudno iddynt[1].

O hyn allan bydd yr hanes yn fwy llon a sionc. Dechreuais weithio yng ngwaith Frongoch yn Awst 1894, yr un diwrnod â thri arall o Bontrhydygroes sef Morgan Evans, Pantyrhedyn, William R. Jenkins, Bwlchyblaen a William Morgans.

"I've served humanity well for almost two thousand years, I've driven its water-wheels and washed its minerals when man chose to harness my powers long ago in the Iron Age. But a time will come again when the children of the village will awaken from their long sleep."

I then turn to look eastwards and see the verdant smallholding of Hafod-gau, the plough alongside the hedgerow demonstrating man's earliest and never-ending craft and my old friend Dan in the world's finest cabbage plot. Dan always swears that cabbage planting is a 'paying game' and no wonder – he plants them year in year out , always working to plan, laying netting wire around them but leaving gaps here and there to entice the hares into the nocturnal traps; he has strangled thousands of them over the years. Good luck to my old friend.

I turn and look towards the south-west and see Ysbyty Ystwyth church and the churchyard which is the resting place of men and women that I knew well. One day, I will have to follow them. For centuries, the young and old have worshipped here, and it is in this cemetery that Shaci Troedyrhiw lies buried; of whom I shall say more later. Shaci had a son called John Jones, Troedyrhiw, father of William Jones, and here I am – Elias, William's son.

For me the most natural thing to do on the peaceful slopes of Banc Troedyrhiw is to look back at the days of old. One of life's purest pleasures is thinking, dealing with problems, understanding morality; in contrast with many of life's other pleasures, these are pure. We will leave the three generations from Shaci in the Ysbyty Ystwyth churchyard; three are still alive – Elias, William and Clifford. But before I leave the dead within the confines of the cemetery wall I will recall and read to myself a lyrical poem by Tudno which dwells on bygone days[1].

I will now continue with the history in a more cheerful and lighter vein. I started working at the Frongoch mine in August 1894, the same day as three others from Pontrhydygroes, namely Morgan Evans, Pantyrhedyn, William R. Jenkins, Bwlch-y-blaen, and William Morgans.

Cawsom dâl am fis o waith ym mhen dau fis o amser a'r gyflog oedd naw ceinog y dydd, cofiaf y pae cyntaf yn dda, 17s 8d ar ôl cadw grot yn ôl i'r meddyg. Rhoddais y cyfan i Mam a theimlwn mai fi oedd tywysog y cwm. Cefais rot yn ôl gan Mam. Yn wir 'roedd calon dda ganddi. Yn awr am ychydig o hanes y gwaith a'i gychwyniad.

Shaci Troedyrhiw a ddarganfyddodd waith Frongoch yn y flwyddyn 1797 wrth iddo fynd heibio tŷ o'r enw Tan Dam sy'n adfeilion 'nawr, llithrodd ei droed a chododd dywarchen, ac o dan honno gwelodd fwyn yn disgleirio fel perlau a chododd les ar unwaith. Gweithiodd y mwyn ar y fan hynny, a chafodd arian i gloddio'r ffin sydd am Troedyrhiw ac hefyd i adeiladu y tŷ cyntaf yno. Nis gwn yn iawn pa hyd y bu'n codi'r mwyn hwnnw ond ni allai fod wedi cymeryd ond ychydig o amser. Gan fod gennyf lyfr hanes ac yn hwnnw mae hanes bonheddwr o'r enw J. Probert o'r Amwythig yn cychwyn gweithio gwaith Frongoch yn 1798, ac iddo ddarganfod gwaith Llwynwnwch dair blynedd yn ddiweddarach, sef 1801.

Saif adfeilion hynafol y gwaith yng nghysgod bryniau prydferth Ceredigion, rhyw ddeuddeg milltir i'r dwyrain o dref Aberystwyth yn ymyl y ffordd sydd yn arwain o bentref Trisant i bentref Pontrhydygroes. Fe'i hamgylchynir gan gaeau Frongoch ar yr ochr ogleddol a Banc Llettysynod ar yr ochr ddeau, Banc Llwynwnwch ar yr ochr ddwyreiniol, a Banc Blaenpentre – sydd wedi bod yn enwog am Gwrdd Gweddi'r Mynydd, ar yr ochr orllewinol iddo.

Nid oedd sôn am na gwaith nac adfeilion yma ers ychydig dros ganrif a haner yn ôl, ac ymborthai defaid ac ŵyn yma'n dawel ar y borfa las. Dichon na freuddwydiodd trigolion yr ardal yn y cyfnod hwnw am y cyfoeth a orchuddid ym mherfeddion y ddaear ond bodlon oeddynt i fyw ar log y diadelloedd defaid. Er symled a thaweled bywyd felly, nid oeddent heb wybod am chwerthin ac wylo, llawenydd a thristwch, ond

After working for two months, we were paid one month's wages, and the rate was nine pence a day; I will remember my first pay-packet, it was 17s 8d after four pence had been retained for the doctor. I gave it all to Mam and felt as if I was the prince of the valley. Mam gave me four pence back; she truly had a good heart. Now for a little about the mine's history and its origins.

Shaci Troedyrhiw discovered the Frongoch mine in 1797. As he was passing a house called Tan Dam, by now a ruin, his foot slipped and he turned over a sod of earth, under which he saw a shiny mineral; he immediately took out a lease. He worked the mineral, and he was given money to construct the boundary surrounding Troedyrhiw and build the first house there. I don't know exactly when he dug out this mineral, but it must have taken him only a small amount of time. I have in my possession a history book which relates the story of a gentleman called J Probert of Shrewsbury who started to mine minerals at Frongoch in 1798, and who discovered the Llwynwnwch mine three years later in 1801.

The ancient ruins of the mine can be seen in the shadow of Ceredigion's beautiful hills, some twelve miles to the east of Aberystwyth beside the road that runs from Trisant to Pontrhydygroes. It is bordered to the north by the fields of Frongoch and by Banc Lletysynod to the south. On the eastern side is Banc Llwynwnwch, to the west is Banc Blaenpentre, which was well known as the venue of the Mountain Prayer Meeting on its western slopes.

There was no mention of there being a mine or ruins here over a century and a half ago, and sheep and lambs grazed peacefully here on the rich pasture. In those days, the local inhabitants would surely not have dreamt of the riches hidden in the bowels of the earth, and they were content to live on the profits of rearing their stock or sheep. However simple and peaceful their way of life would have been, laughter and tears, happiness and sadness would have been theirs. But the past

mud yw'r gorffennol dros amser, ac erys ei ramant fwyaf gwir heb ei ddatguddio.

Casglodd y Bonheddwr Probert lawer o weithwyr ynghyd o'r ardaloedd cyfagos a than ei arweiniad ef suddwyd siafftau neu byllau rhyw dri ugain gwrhyd o ddyfnder, a chafwyd fod yn y dyfnder hwnw gyfran dda o fwyn, sinc ac arian. Codwyd y trysorau hyn drwy y siafftoedd mewn *skip* ac yna ei falu a'u golchi ar y "Floorings", ar ôl hynny ei gludo mewn wagenni i dref Aberystwyth, ei lwytho ar longau bychain a'i gludo ymaith i wahanol wledydd. Deunaw punt y dunnell oedd gwerth y mwyn yn y cyfnod hwnw. Gwerthodd Probert ei hawlfraint yn y flwyddyn 1834 i Mr Tailor a'u feibion, a gwnaethant welliannau enfawr i'r gwaith. Cyflogwyd cannoedd o ddynion o ardaloedd Pontarfynach, Trisant, Cnwch Coch, Llanafan, a Phontrhydygroes, ac adeilasant amryw o adeiladau cerrig. Hefyd suddwyd y shafftau yn ddyfnach sef i 152 fathom, lle'r oedd mwyn ardderchog i'w gael. Gorfu i'r cwmni hyn chwilo am rhagor o ddŵr at eu gwasanaeth a chawsant ef o lynnoedd Trisant ac o afon Prignant (Rhosygell).

Cynhyddodd nifer y tunnelli o ddeugain tunnell y mis i gan tunnell y mis yn y flwyddyn gyntaf. Cadwodd y cwmni hwn i gynhyrchu am flynyddoedd, ac yn ystod y tair blynedd ddiwethaf o'u hawlfraint hwy, sef o 1875 i 1878 gwerthasant 3,205 o dunelli o fwyn am £44,857, ond ar ôl talu y "Royalty" i'r tir-feddiannwr yr oedd y cwmni mewn dyled o £679.00. Felly gwerthasant y gwaith i Lord Lisburne, a gwerthodd yntau yn yr un flwyddyn, sef 1878, i Mr. John Kitto.

Parhaodd y gwaith i fod yn llwyddiannus iawn o dan lywyddiaeth Kitto a gwerthodd 2,850 o dunelli o'r mwyn yn y flwyddyn gyntaf. Cadwodd Kitto ei hawlfraint am ugain mlynedd ac yna yn y flwyddyn 1898 gwerthodd hwynt i gwmni o Belgium. Daeth cant ac ugain o Eidalwyr yn groes o'r Eidal i weithio i'r cwmni yma, Cyflogwyd rheolwr o'r Eidal or enw Nogara ag Almaenwr o'r enw Heini yn Gapten odditano, ac hefyd syrfewr o'r Eidal o'r enw Invernetsi, a chymaint â hynny ddwy waith wedyn o fân Gaptenaid o fryniau Ceredigion. Ychydig iawn a

becomes, over time, an unspoken word, and its truest romance remains undiscovered.

Mr Probert gathered together many workers from neighbouring areas and, under his direction, shafts or pits were sunk down to a depth of some sixty fathoms, and it was found that a substantial amount of mineral – zinc and silver – lay within this depth. These valuable minerals were brought to the surface in the shafts by means of a skip, and they were then crushed and washed on the 'floorings' and then transported by wagons to Aberystwyth to be loaded onto small boats, for export to various countries. In those days, the ore was valued at eighteen pounds a ton. In 1834, Probert sold his rights to Mr Taylor and sons, and they made substantial improvements to the mine. Hundreds of men from Devil's Bridge, Trisant, Cnwch Coch, Llanafan and Pontrhydygroes were employed, and several stone buildings were erected. Shafts were sunk to a greater depth of 152 fathoms, where excellent minerals were found. The company had to seek a greater supply of water, and they found this in the Trisant lakes and the Prignant River (Rhosygell).

The tonnage increased from 40 tons to 100 tons per month during the first year. This firm continued production for many years, and during the last three years of their lease, from 1875 to 1878, they sold 3205 tons of ore for £44,857, but after paying royalty dues to the landowners, the company found itself £679 in debt. So they sold the mine to Lord Lisburne, and in the same year, 1878, he sold it on to Mr John Kitto.

The mine continued to prosper under Kitto's direction, and 2850 tons of ore were sold during the first year. Kitto kept his rights for twenty years, and then in 1898 sold them to a Belgian company. One hundred and twenty Italians came over from Italy to work here. An Italian by the name of Nogara was appointed manager and a German called Heini was made captain to work under him. There was also an Italian surveyor called Invernetsi[2], and twice as many again from the hills of Ceredigion

wnaeth y cwmni hyn i agor a datblygu'r gwaith tanddaearol ond fe adeiladon beiriant golau trydan enfawr, y mwyaf yn Mhrydain ar yr adeg honno, a gallesid gweld golau Frongoch filltiroedd i ffwrdd. Gwariodd y cwmni yma swm enfawr o £130,000 ar beiriannau golchi a datblygiadau diweddaraf yr oes.

Arferai yr Eidalwyr addoli mewn lle a elwid yn 'Capel Saeson' sydd mwyach yn adfeilion, rhwng pentref New Row a Phontrhydygroes a thra buont yma bu un ohonynt farw, a chladdwyd ei weddillon ym mynwent Llantrisant gerllaw'r gwaith.

Ni fu'r gwaith yn llwyddiannus iawn o dan lywodraeth y cwmni yma ac wedi rhyw bum mlynedd o wario dychwelasant i'w gwlad eu hun ar ôl gwerthu'r cyfan o'r peirannau a'r offer, gan adael y gwaith yn nwylo y tirfeddianwr sef Lord Lisburne. Dywed hanes fod 50,669 o dunelli o *black zink*, 38,071 o dunelli o fwyn a 19,014 owns o arian wedi cael ei godi o waith Frongoch o'r flwyddyn 1845 i 1903 a dywedir mai cyfanswm yr arian a godwyd o'r gwaith hwn o 1798 hyd 1903 oedd 128,000 owns.

Wedi 1903 bu gwaith Frongoch yn segur hyd y flwyddyn 1929 pryd y gweithiwyd rhan ohono drachefn o dan lywodraeth Mr. Nancarrow, a dyma'r flwyddyn i minnau ddyfod yn ôl o Ddeheudir Cymru. Cychwynais weithio eto yn Braker Shafft, 'run shafft a gychwynais weithio ynddi pan oeddwn yn fachgen bach ifanc, ac ar y 10^{ed} o Dachwedd 1929 taniwyd y rownd dyllau olaf yn Frongoch gan ŵr o'r enw Elias Jones o'r un llinach â Shaci Troedyrhiw. Felly chwi welwch mai'r un hiliogaeth a'u cychwynodd ac a'u gorffennodd. Ar ôl hyn, gadawyd y gwaith i ddadfeilio a bu'n gartref cysurus i'r tylluanod, yr ystlumod a'r crogfrain.

Wedi deng mlynedd o lonyddwch, daeth rhyfel erchyll 1939, a phan gafodd y Gwarchodlu Cartref eu galw i amddiffyn eu gwlad, daeth gwaith Frongoch unwaith eto'n ddefnyddiol fel man ymarfer a pharatoi'r bechgyn, a byddai saethu a ffrwydro yn myned yn mlaen yno,

were appointed minor captains. This company did very little to open up and develop the underground workings but they built a huge electric light plant, the biggest in Britain at that time, and the lights of Frongoch were visible from miles away. The company spent the enormous sum of £130,000 on washing equipment and on the most modern facilities of the time.

The Italians worshipped in a place called 'Capel Saeson', which is by now a ruin, between New Row and Pontrhydygroes, and during their stay one of them died and was buried in Llantrisant cemetery, near to the mine[3].

The mine was not very successful under this company's management, and, after some five years of investment, they returned to their own country having sold off the machinery and equipment, leaving the mine in the hands of the landowner, Lord Lisburne. History tells us that 50,669 tons of black zinc, 38,071 tons of lead ore, and 19,014 ounces of silver were mined at Frongoch between 1845 and 1903, and it is said that the total amount of silver extracted from this mine between 1798 and 1903 was 128,000ounces.

After 1903, the Frongoch mine remained idle until 1929, when a part of it was again sold, under the control of Mr Nancarrow; that was the year that I returned from South Wales. Once more, I started working at the Braker shaft, which was the shaft at which I had worked as a young lad, and, on 10th November 1929, the final shot holes at Frongoch were fired by one Elias Jones who was a descendant of Shaci Troedyrhiw. Thereafter, the mine was abandoned, to deteriorate slowly and became the habitat of owls, bats and ravens.

After ten years of tranquillity, in 1939, the terrible war broke out and the Home Guard was called to provide defence for the country. Frongoch again became a useful place, as a training ground for the boys, and there was shooting and explosions from that minute on about once or twice

ryw unwaith neu ddwy bob wythnos. Erbyn heddiw mae'r Gwarchodlu Cartref wedi hen wasgaru, ond erys hen adfeilion Gwaith Frongoch.

Rhyw bryd ym mis Mawrth 1898 gorffennodd y cwmni newydd yma falu a golchi ar beiriannau Kitto ac aethant ati o ddifri i baratoi at adeiladu rhai newydd. Y gorchwyl cyntaf a gawsom ni, fechgyn y 'flooring', oedd cychwyn ar y trench dŵr newydd o Flaenpentre i Glandwgan.

Daeth deunaw o ferched oedd yn gweithio ar y *flooring* gyda ni i weithio i'r trench hwn. Merched glan a hardd ryfeddol oeddynt bob un, wedi eu gwisgo â phrydferthwch natur. Dim un o honynt wedi breuddwydio erioed am ddefnyddio na lipstic na phowdwr a phob un ohonynt yn ennill swllt y dydd fel cyflog. Beth feddyliai merched yr oes fodern hon am amgylchiadau or fath? Anfonodd y Cwmni lawer o'r chwarelwyr allan i weithio ar y trench a chawsom ninnau, y bechgyn a'r merched, ein dosbarthu fel bod mab a merch yn gweithio efo pob chwarelwr. Whîlo y berfeuau oedd gwaith y merched drwy'r dydd. Enwau rhai o'r chwarelwyr oedd Thomas Jones, Pantyrhedyn, Dafydd Davies, New Row, David Jones, Tanlanfedwen, John Phillips, Pontrhydygroes, ac amryw eraill. Trafodent bynciau dyrus yn aml. Credoau amrywiol oedd yno megis Methodistaid Calfinaidd hefo'i hetholedigaeth, Wesleyaid efo'u credo Arminaidd, yn grefyddwyr mawr heddiw a syrthio oddi wrth ras yfory. Yr oedd yno lawer o Eglwyswyr hefyd, cymerent hwythau ran yn y dadleuon ond cofiaf yn dda mai y pwyslais roddent hwy bob amser oedd ar y gwasanaeth ac nid ar y pynciau diwinyddol. 'Roedd yno hefyd un o'r Salvation Army ond ni dderbyniais fawr o wybodaeth ganddo yn werth ei gofnodi er ei fod yn gwaeddi "Come to Jesus" yn aml iawn. Ni welais yr un Bedyddiwr nac Annibynnwr chwaith. Codai'r dadleuon oddi amgylch y credoau hyn bob amser.

Yn ystod y cyfnod yma daeth dau ddyn canol oed 'nôl o Barnsley a oedd wedi cael eu magu yn Ysgol Sul Capel Saeson. Meibion Capten Paul Frongoch oeddynt, sef William a Philip Paul. William Paul oedd

every week. By today the Home Guard has long disbanded, but the ruins of the old Frongoch mine remain.

Sometime in March 1898, the new company ceased crushing and washing on the Kitto machinery, and they set about in earnest to prepare for the construction of new ones. The first task for us, the flooring boys, was to commence work on the new water conduit from Blaenpentre to Glanwgan.

We were accompanied, in the construction of this conduit, by eighteen girls who had been working with us on the flooring. They were all very attractive girls, blessed with a natural beauty. Not one of them had ever dreamt of using lipstick and powder, and each of them was paid a wage of one shilling per day. What would the girls of this modern age think of such circumstances? The company sent many of the miners out to work on the conduit and we, both boys and girls, were distributed so that one boy and one girl worked with each miner. The girls' task throughout the day was to wheel the barrows, day in day out. Here are the names of some of the quarrymen: Thomas Jones, Pantrhedyn, Dafydd Davies, New Row, David Jones, Tanlanfedwen, John Phillips Pontrhydygroes; there were many others. They and their fellow workers often discussed complex topics. You had there a mix of beliefs – Calvinistic Methodists with their belief in divine election, Wesleyans with their Armenian creed - as hugely religious men today who would fall out of grace tomorrow. There were also many Anglicans, they too would take part in the debates, but I well remember that they always emphasised the service rather than the theological aspects. There was one from the Salvation Army, but I hardly got any information from him that was worth recording, although he shouted out, "Come to Jesus" very frequently. I didn't see a single Baptist or Congregationalist. There were endless debates about these different creeds.

During this time, two middle-aged men came back from Barnsley. They had been nurtured at the 'Capel Saeson' Sunday school. They were the sons of Frongoch's Captain Paul, namely William and Philip Paul.

un o'r dynion mwyaf hyddysg yn yr ysgrythur a gwrddais erioed a dadleuwr da bob amser. Yr oedd ei gof wedi ei amharu gan ei fywyd afradlon yn ôl y sôn ond byddai bob amser yn medru adrodd cyfres o adnodau i brofi ei ochr ar bob pwnc. Cofiaf mai o'r Testament Newydd oeddent bron bob amser, megis o epistolau Paul at y Rhufeiniad a'r Corinthiaid ond bob amser y byddai William yn dweud eu bod i'w gweld yn yr Ysgrythur Lân, sef Llyfr Amos. Hoffem ni'r bechgyn glywed William yn cael goruchafiaeth ar y cewri eraill. Un diwrnod arbennig ym Mis Ebrill 'roeddem i gyd yn gweithio ar y trench uwchben Cwmnewydion Uchaf, a gwelem gawod drom yn dod i fyny'r cwm; rhedodd pawb am eu bywyd i hen dŷ Tan Dam. Cyrhaeddodd pawb yn sych ond am William Paul, a phan gyrhaeddodd William 'roedd y gawod drosodd ac yntau'n wlyb at ei groen, a dyma ddywedodd ar ben y drws:

"Arglwydd daear, maent yn dweud yn yr ysgrythur lân fod Duw yn trugareddu, lle mae trugaredd a William Paul wedi cael ei wlychu at ei groen efo'r gawod Ebrill ofnadwy yma, a rheumatism yn ei goesau oedd yn ei wahardd i redeg fel pawb arall."

Yn y cornel 'roedd dyn bach byr o'r enw John Lewis y Dŵr, 'roedd wedi colli ei wallt ar gorun ei ben ac a oedd bob amser ychydig yn groen denau, fel mae plant yr Arglwydd yn aml iawn. Dyma fe'n annerch William fel hyn:

"William Paul 'rwyt yn hela gwallt fy mhen i sefyll wrth dy glywed yn galw ar enw dy Dduw yn ofer," ar hynny nesaodd William yn nes ato. "John Lewis" meddai, "trueni na fuasai dy wallt wedi sefyll yn lle mynd i ffwrdd efo'r gwynt, a chofia hyn John Lewis, paid ti byth â cheryddu dyn heb dy fod yn sicr ei fod wedi troseddu; 'arglwydd daear' ddwedes i on' te, Lord Lisburne oedd gyda fi mewn golwg. Ef yw perchennog y tir yma'i gyd a fe sydd yn derbyn y 'royalties' bob mis; dyma'r lle cyntaf i mi glywed ac imi ddechrau meddwl am system mor anghyfiawn fod i ryw bersonau arbennig dderbyn 'royalties' am fwynau nad oeddynt

William Paul was one of the most learned men in the scriptures that I ever met, and he was always a good debater. His memory had been affected, so it was said, by his intemperate lifestyle, but he could always recite verses to prove his case, on any topic. They were almost invariably from the New Testament, such as from Paul's epistles to the Romans and Corinthians, but William always used to say that they were to be found in the Holy Scriptures, that is in the Book of Amos. We as young men enjoyed seeing William getting the better of the other stalwarts. One day in April, we were all working on the trench above Cwmnewydion Uchaf, and we could see a heavy shower making its way up the valley, and everyone ran for their lives to the old Tan Dam house. Everyone got there dry, except for William Paul, and when William arrived the shower had passed, and he was soaked to the skin, and this is what he said at the doorway:

"Lord of the earth, they say in the holy scriptures that God is merciful, but where is mercy with William Paul being soaked to the skin in this terrible April shower, and with rheumatism in his legs preventing him from running like everyone else".

In the corner there was a short little man called John Lewis y Dŵr, who had a bald patch at the top of his head, and who was always rather thin-skinned as the Lord's children often are. He addressed William with these words:

"William Paul, you make the hairs on my head stand up straight when I hear you call your God's name in vain".
With this, William came up close to him. "John Lewis," he said "what a pity your hair hadn't remained instead of being blown away by the wind, and remember this, John Lewis, don't you ever mock a man unless you're sure he has transgressed. 'Lord of the earth' is what I said wasn't it? It was Lord Lisburne I had in mind. He owns all this land and it is he who gets the royalties each month." This is the first time I had heard of and thought about a system that is so unjust as to enable certain people to receive royalties for minerals that they've never even seen.

wedi ei gweld erioed; mawr oedd ein llawenydd ni, y bobl ieuanc, fod William Paul wedi cael goruchafiaeth unwaith eto ar John Lewis y Dŵr.

Yn ystod yr Haf hwn cefais ddechrau gweithio fel chwarelwr efo Nhad yn 44 Braker Shafft. Bargen newydd oedd hon i Nhad, a'r gorchymyn gafodd oedd iddo fynd â'r offer i lawr ac y byddai'r Manager Nogara a'r Capten Heini yn ei ddilyn tua deg o'r gloch y bore. Wedi cyrraedd y lle dyma'r ymddiddan fu rhyngof â Nhad:

"Wel di Lei fe fydd hwn yn lle golew iti ddechrau gweithio ar y graig gan nad yw'n dir caled iawn. Mae'n debyg y byddant eisiau tair shifft ar hon a bydd hynny yn golygu rhagor o bris wyt ti'n deall, sef shifft y bore, prynhawn a'r nos, ac os câf chwech bunt y gwrgyd am ei dreifio fe enillwn arian fel brics."

Ac yna wedi i Nogara a Heini gyrraedd bu'r sgwrs rywbeth yn debyg i hyn:

Nogara: "Well William Jones, have you found the place? We want you to drive this level parallel with the fall and it will have to go about 80 fathom to reach the other end of the fall, and remember we want three shifts on it. For us to reach there as quick as possible."
Nhad yn ateb: "Three Shifts more price Mr. Nogara."
Nogara: "Yes quite so William. Now William what is the price?"
Nhad: "Well I'll leave it to you today. But mind you we are going to have very stiff ground here."
Nogara: "Well William, so long that you are willing for me to give the price £7.10.0 a fathom."
Capten Heini: "No, no, no too much, £7.0.0. is enough."
Nogara: "£7.10.0 - what say you William."
Nhad: "Well you are not far off the £8.0.0 I thought to ask. The Bargain settled."

A dyna ddiwedd y diwrnod cyntaf erioed imi fod tan y ddaear.

Great was our joy, as youngsters, that William Paul had once again had the upper hand over John Lewis y Dŵr.

During this summer, I started working as a miner with my father on 44 Braker Shaft. This was for my father a new bargain, and his orders were that he should take the equipment down and that the manager, Nogara, and Captain Heini would follow him around ten o'clock in the morning. When we got to the spot, this was the conversation I had with my father:

"See, Lei, this will be quite a good spot for you to start work on the rock, as it's not very hard rock. They'll probably want three shifts on this one, morning, afternoon and night - and that'll mean a higher price, you see. So if I get six pounds, a fathom for driving it forward we'll make money like bricks."

Then, after Nogara and Heini arrived, the conversation went something like this:-

Nogara: "Well, William Jones, have you found the place? We want you to drive this level parallel with the fall, and it will have to go about 80 fathom to reach the other end of the fall. And remember we want three shifts on it, for us to reach there as quick as possible."
Father replied: "Three shifts, more price, Mr Nogara."
Nogara: "Yes, quite so, William. Now William what is the price?"
Father: "Well I'll leave it to you today. But mind you we are going to have very stiff ground here."
Nogara: "Well William, so long that you are willing for me to give the price £7.10.0 a fathom."
Captain Heini: "No, no, no, too much; £7.0.0 is enough."
Nogara: "£7.10.0. What you say William."
Father: "Well you are not far off £8.0.0 I thought to ask. The bargain settled!"

And that was the end of my first day ever underground.

Ymhob ardal mae'r ifanc yn trafod a dadlau am ddigwyddiadau a phroblemau eu cyfnod. Cymerwch heddiw, mae pawb ifanc yn siarad a dadlau am "speed" mewn awyrlongau, neu foduron ac yn y blaen. Clywais yr wythnos o'r blaen am ddyn wedi marw'n sydyn iawn yn Sir Gaerfyrddin, a chyfaill i frawd yr ymadawedig yn cydymdeimlo ag ef:

"Bachgen", meddai "mi golloch eich brawd yn sydyn iawn."
"Do'n wir fachgen" atebodd, "ond dyna fe "speed" yw'r cwbwl 'nawr."

Ond tua 1900 dadlau 'roeddem ni'r bobl ifanc am geffylau y certwyr, mor ardderchog yr oeddent am dynnu eu pwysau dros Weingrach, Nantarthur, a Llettysynod, ond daliem ni fechgyn Pontrhydygroes mai ceffylau gorau'r wlad oedd rhai Seth Dolgroes; byddai'r dadleuon hyn yn cyrraedd pitsh go uchel yn aml. Un diwrnod daeth sôn am gaseg ifanc efo Thomas Langorslwyd a dynnai ei phwysau bob dydd a'i bod wedi ei magu a'i phorthi yn dda o'r cychwyn, byddaf yn sôn am hon eto nes 'mlaen. Sal oedd enw'r gaseg.

Testun pwysicaf y dydd o dan y ddaear yr adeg yma oedd y Rhyfel yn Ne Affrica. Mawr oedd y disgwyliad am bob dydd Iau pan fyddai Tom Williams, Cefngraig yn dod â'r *Faner ag Amserau Cymru* i'r gwaith. Eisteddem i lawr am amser mewn man llydan yn Lefel 44 yn gwrando ar Tom Williams yn darllen hanes y Rhyfel. Y nesaf at ochr Tom Williams bob amser fyddai James Oliver, Y Cnwc. 'Roedd yn syndod i mi bob amser mor hyddysg oedd James mewn Daearyddiaeth, gwyddai sawl troedfedd oedd pob bryn uwchlaw arwynebedd y môr. Fel Majuba Hill a Spion Kop ac yn blaen. Gwyddai amdanynt 'run fath â phe'n siarad am Pendrawsallt neu Bumlumon. Daeth newydd i'r gwaith fod Thomas Langorslwyd wedi gwerthu'r gaseg (Sal) i'r "Military Men", a'i bod wedi cael ei hanfon ar y llong i Dde Affrica. Ychydig o wythnosau ar ôl hyn cychwynodd y Frwydr Spion Kop a daeth gwybodaeth 'nôl yn fuan iawn mai Sal a dynnodd y Canon Du i ben Spion Kop ac i'r Prydeinwyr gael buddugoliaeth lwyr ar y Boeriaid. Tystiai Thomas fod

In every locality, young people have discussions and debates about the events and problems of the day. Take today – young people talk about the speed of aeroplanes, cars and so on. I heard the other week of a man who had died very suddenly in Carmarthenshire, and a friend of the deceased's brother commiserated with him:

"Well, my boy, you lost your brother very suddenly."
"Yes indeed" he replied "but there you are, speed is everything these days."

But around 1900, what we as young lads discussed was the carters' horses, how wonderful they were drawing loads over Waungrach, Nantarthur and Lletysynod. But we Pontrhydygroes boys swore that the best horses in the land were those of Seth Dolgroes; these debates often reached a high pitch. One day, news came of a young mare of Thomas Langorslwyd that could draw its own weight every day, that had been well fed and reared from the start. I shall mention her later. The mare's name was Sal.

The main topic of discussion underground at this time was the war in South Africa. We eagerly awaited each Thursday when Tom Williams, Cefngraig brought the *Baner* and *Amserau Cymru* newspapers to work. We would sit down in a wide space on Level 44 listening to Tom Williams reading out the reports of the war. James Oliver, Y Cnwc, would always sit next to Tom Williams. It always surprised me how well informed James was on geography; he knew the height above sea level of every hill - Majuba Hill and Spion Kop and so on. He knew about them as if he was talking of Pendrawsallt or Pumlumon. News arrived at the time that Thomas Langorslwyd had sold the mare (Sal) to the 'Military Men' and that it had been transported by ship to South Africa. A few weeks later, the Battle of Spion Kop started, and news came back that it was Sal that had pulled the Black Cannon to the summit of Spion Kop and that the British had had complete victory over

yr hanes yn ffaith a mwy na hynny fod Sal wedi dod i lawr a'r Canon Du gyda'r Kings Guards i Sgwâr Pretoria, lle 'roedd Cytundeb y Cadoediad yn cael ei arwyddo gan General Botha, General Smuts a Field Marshal Lord Roberts.

Hoffwn ofyn y cwestiwn yma i chi, sef faint o fudd i wareiddiad Prydain a'r Byd a wnaeth y digwyddiad i Shaci Troedyrhiw pan ddarganfyddodd y mwyn yn 1797? Pan edrychwn o gwmpas yr ardaloedd hyn a gweld yr ysgolion, capeli a'r bythynnod bychain a godwyd o gwmpas y gwaith ac hefyd o gofio am y rhestr enfawr o bregethwyr, offeiriaid, ysgolheigion gwych, ac hefyd bwysigion eraill y ganrif ynghyd â masiyniaid, gofaint a chrefftwyr eraill o bob math. Seiri coed fel Daniel Morgan a gododd rod fawr Frongoch, y fwyaf yn y byd yn ôl yr hanes. Codwyd un arall debyg iawn iddi ar Ynys Manaw ar ôl cael y patrwm gan Daniel Morgan.

Rhaid peidio anghofio'r gwragedd a'r mamau, 'Chancellors of the Exchequers' gorau a welodd Prydain erioed, wedi dysgu yn drwyadl y gelfyddyd 'o rannu angen un rhwng y naw'.

Terfynnaf mwyach, disgynnaf o Fanc Troedyrhiw i lawr o olwg mynwent Ysybyty Ystwyth a thelyneg Tudno. I ni y rhai byw, dyma delyneg Cynan i'n hatgoffa am bwysigrwydd dynoliaeth[4].

the Boers. Thomas swore that this was fact, and moreover that Sal had brought the Black Cannon back down with the King's Guards to Pretoria Square, where an Armistice Treaty was being signed by General Botha, General Smuts and Field Marshal Lord Roberts.

I would like to pose the following question: How much benefit to the civilisation of Britain and the world was Shaci Troedyrhiw's discovery of ore in 1797? When we look around these localities we see schools, chapels, little cottages which were built around the mine, and we remember the long list of fine preachers, priests, and scholars, and other key figures over the century - not forgetting the stonemasons, blacksmiths, and other craftsmen. There were carpenters like Daniel Morgan who built the great waterwheel at Frongoch, the biggest in the world or so it was said. Another one very similar to it was built in the Isle of Man after they got the blueprint from Daniel Morgan.

One must not forget the wives and mothers – the best 'Chancellors of the Exchequer' that Britain ever saw, and who had learnt from hard experience how to divide 'one person's share between many'.

I now come to a close, and step down from Banc Troedyrhiw, down from the Ysbyty Ystwyth churchyard. The poet Cynan wrote a lyrical poem 'Salaam' which recalls the practice of men of the East who blessed each other at the start of a long journey and which reminds us of the importance of humanity[4].

Troednodyn/Footnote 1 Cerdd/Poem:

<u>Adgofion Dyddiau Gynt</u>

Pan fyddo hwyrol wynt
Drwy'r ywen yn ochneidio
Daw cof o'r dyddiau gynt
Ac hen gyfoedion heibio,
Daw'r oll yn nol
Fel blodau'r ddol
O feddrod oer y gaeaf,
A llawer gwedd
Sydd yn y bedd
Geir eto'n gwenu arnaf.

Fel hyn tra'r hwyrol wynt
Drwy'r ywen yn ochneidio
Daw cof o'r dyddiau gynt
Ag hen gyfoedion heibio.

Wrth gofio llawer un
Sy 'nawr yn llwch a lludw,
Mor unig wyf fy hun
Am oriau gyda'r meirw,
Adgofion gant
Am lawen blant
A ddeuant yn ddiddiwedd,
A minnau'n hen
Heb hanes gwên
Ar riniog ei hoer annedd.

Fel hyn tra'r hwyrol wynt
Drwy'r ywen yn ochneidio
Daw cof o'r dyddiau gynt
Ag hen gyfoedion heibio.

Tudno

Troednodyn/Footnote 2: Gweler pennod/See Chapter 4:
Llythyr oddi wrth Emilio Invernizzi 1953/ Letter from Emilio Invernizzi 1953
(Sillafwyd fel 'Invernetsi' gan Elias /spelled 'Invernetsi' by Elias)

Troednodyn/Footnote 3: Gweler pennod/See Chapter 11:
Marwolaeth mwynwr Eidalaidd/ Death of Italian Miner

Troednodyn/Footnote 4 Cerdd/Poem:

Salaam

Ni wn i am un cyfarchiad gwell
Nag a ddysgais gan feibion y Dwyrain pell

Cyn ymadael dros dywod yr anial maith
Bendithiant ei gilydd ar ddechrau'r daith

Lle bynnag y crwydri er pelled y nen
Boed palmwydd Tangnefedd yn gysgod i'th ben

A phan ddelo Allah ar ddiwedd ein rhawd
Cawn yfed yn Ninas Tangnefedd, fy mrawd.

Ni wn i am un cyfarchiad gwell
Nag a ddysgais gan feibion y Dwyrain pell

A'u dymuniad hwy yw nymuniad i
Tangnefedd Duw a fo gyda chwi

Cynan

2
Atgofion am fywyd ardal yn Sir Aberteifi
Reminiscences of an area of Cardiganshire

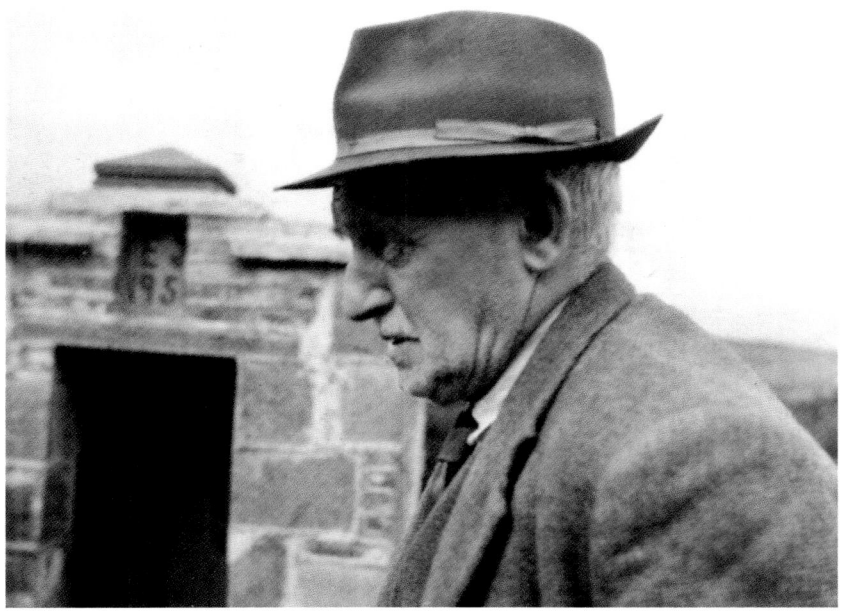

Elias tu allan i'w doiled yn Nhroedyrhiw, a adeiladwyd o gerrig a brynwyd oddi wrth Ystad Yr Hafod.
Elias outside his toilet at Troedyrhiw, built from stone bought from Hafod Estate.

Mae peth ail-adrodd yn '1 History and Reminiscences of the Frongoch Mine' ond mae hyn wedi cael ei gynnwys er mwyn cyflawnrwydd.

Some repetition with '1 History and Reminiscences of the Frongoch Mine' but this has been left in for completeness.

Atgofion am fywyd ardal yn Sir Aberteifi

Ganwyd fi yn ardal Pontrhydygroes yn y flwyddyn 1881, sef y 19fed o fis Mawrth, felly yno yr wyf wedi gadael fy 75 mlwydd oed. Nid yn y tŷ yr ydwyf yn byw ynddo yn awr ym ganwyd ond mewn tŷ arall sydd rhyw ddau can llath oddi wrtho. Brawd fy nhad oedd yn byw yma yn 1881 ond aeth i'r Amerig, ef a'i fab hynaf a thri arall o'r ardal hon, a chawsant waith yn Michigan, ar ôl iddo fethu â byw yma gan fod cyflog gwaith mwyn 'Lisburne Mines 'wedi mynd yn rhy isel. Ym mis Mai 1884 aeth y teulu cyfan allan i Michigan, sef ei wraig, tri mab a dwy ferch ar ei ôl, ac ym mis Mai daeth fy nhad a mam i fyw yn ôl i'r cartref hwn. Dyma'r cof cyntaf sydd gennyf. Cofiaf yn glir am fy ewythr a'i blant, ond nid oes gennyf ronyn o gof am y cartref ym ganwyd ynddo. Mae'r tair mlynedd a'r ddau fis yna yn angof bellach.

Felly, yr atgofion sydd gennyf o hyn ymlaen yw am ardal Pontrhydygroes, ond bydd yn rhaid i mi grwydro mor bell â Frongoch, Cwmystwyth a gwaith Bronberllan, gan fod y bobl 'rwyf am sôn amdanynt yn gweithio ar hyd yr amser yn rhai o'r gweithfeydd mwyn plwm hyn. Yr un cyntaf 'rwyf yn ei gofio yn dda yw Lisburne Mines yn cynnwys Glôg Fawr, Glôg Fach a Lefel Fawr, a'r cyfan yn cael eu talu yn swyddfeydd Lisburne Mines. Diwrnod pwysig oedd Dydd Sadwrn y talu, neu "Dydd Sadwrn 'sistance" fel 'roeddent yn ei alw, ac edrychwn ymlaen yn ifanc iawn am y dydd yma gan fod yno lawer o stondinau o bob math. Ond y stondin bwysicaf i ni'r plant oedd stondin Edward a Shani, Llanbadarn. Yr oedd ar werth bob amser ar y stondin hon fariau o India Roc, a chawsem un bob mis beth bynnag, a mawr oedd y boddhad.

Diwrnod pwysig arall oedd Dydd Llun cyntaf ar ôl Dydd Sadwrn y tâl. Dydd gŵyl oedd hwn bob amser gyda'r holl fwynwyr. Dyma'r dydd yr oeddent yn codi nwyddau am fis arall i bob bargen, sef canwyllau, powdwr, *caps* a *fuses*. Wedi imi dyfu yn rhyw ddeg oed cefais y fraint o gael mynd gyda nhad ar ôl dod adref o'r ysgol, tua pedwar o'r gloch y

Reminiscences of an area of Cardiganshire

I was born in the Pontrhydygroes area in the year 1881, on the 19th of March, and so tonight I have left my 75th year. I wasn't born in the house where I live now but in another about two hundred yards away. In 1881 my father's brother lived here, but he went to America with his eldest son and three others from the area, and they secured work in Michigan having failed to make a living here because wages at the Lisburne Mines lead works had become so low. In May 1884, the entire family followed him out to Michigan, that is, his wife, three sons and two daughters. In the same month my father and mother returned to live in this house. That is the first memory I have. I clearly remember my uncle and his wife and children, but I do not have the faintest memory of the home where I was born. I have forgotten completely those three years and two months spent there.

Therefore the memories I have from this point onward will be of the area around Pontrhydygroes, but I will have to wander as far as Frongoch, Cwmystwyth and Bronberllan works, as over the years the people hereabouts have worked in one or another of these lead mines. The first I remember well is Lisburne Mines, which included Glog Fawr, Glog Fach and Level Fawr, their wages all paid at the offices of Lisburne Mines, as they were called. Payday Saturday was an important day - 'sistance Saturday' they called it. I looked forward eagerly to this when I was young as there would be many stalls of every kind there, but the most important stall to us children was that of Edward and Shani, Llanbadarn. There were always bars of India Rock for sale on this stall, and we'd have a bar once a month no matter what, to our great enjoyment.

The other important day was the first Monday after Payday Saturday. It was always a festival day for all the miners. This was the day when they would pick up supplies for another month for every bargain, that is candles, powder, caps and fuses. When I was about ten years old I had the privilege of accompanying my father, after coming home from

prynhawn, i'w helpu i gario rhai o'r pethau hyn, canwyllau rhan amlaf oedd y baich. Nid oes rhyfedd mai mwynwr ydwyf wedi bod ar hyd fy oes; aeth yr ymarferiadau hyn i fy ngwaed yn gynnar, gynnar iawn.

Wel cychwynais fyned i'r ysgol yn Ysbyty Ystwyth ym mis Ebrill 1886, a chefais fy addysg yno o dan Mr. Jenkins, yr ysgolfeistr. Un o Ferthyr oedd y Jenkins hwn. Yna aeth i ffwrdd a daeth Mr. Jenkins arall o Gwmystwyth yn ei le, ac o dan ddisgyblaeth hwn yr oeddwn hyd ddiwedd Gorffennaf 1894. Yn Awst 1894 cychwynais weithio yng ngwaith mwyn Frongoch, sef ar y 'fflorin' – golchi mwyn, y fi a thri arall o'r un ysgol - a'r pedwar ohonom yr un oed, a mi yw'r unig ohonynt sy'n dal yn fyw. Bob mis, roeddent yn talu yn y gweithfeydd hyn ond yr oeddent yn cadw mis mewn llaw, felly cawsom ni y tâl cyntaf ymhen dau fis. Y tâl cyntaf a gawsom oedd yn ôl naw ceiniog y dydd, sef tâl am y mis cyntaf oedd 17s.8d. – pedair ceiniog wedi eu cadw 'nôl yn dâl i'r doctor. Yr oeddwn yn hynod foddhaol yn dod adref â'r cyflog gyntaf i Mam, a hithau'n canmol arnaf yn fawr ac yn rhoddi y bedair ceiniog 'nôl i mi yn arian poced.

Gadawaf yr ysgol a'r gwaith am ychydig nawr a cheisiaf roddi ychydig o hanes yr ardal. Yr oeddem yn myned i'r capeli a'r eglwysi bawb ohonom yn gyson. Cofiaf yn dda yr oedd arnom ofn nos yn ofnadwy hyd yn oed pan oeddem wedi cychwyn gweithio. Yr oedd amryw o bobl y pentref y dyddiau hynny yn gweled cymaint o olau cyffrous fel yr oedd arnom ofn myned allan o gwbl ar ôl gwrando arnynt – heb fod dau neu dri ohonom yn gwmpeini i'n gilydd. Diolch nad oes neb erbyn hyn yn yr ardal yn sôn am y fath erchyllterau.

Cofiaf yn dda am y sêl oedd ar grefydd yn y dyddiau cynnar hyn ac am yr Ysgol Sul, holi'r Pwnc, ac adrodd y Deg Gorchymyn efo'n gilydd – yr Ysgol Sul i gyd. Clywais gan rai o'r hynafwyr am faddeuant llwyr yn y pentref gyda dynes o'r enw Nancy Falant a gadwai'r siop ym Mhontrhydygroes. Mae'n debyg fod un o'r mwynwyr wedi mynd dipyn i'w dyled ac iddi ei rybuddio ar gyhoedd dydd Sadwrn y tâl os na dalai ei ddyled iddi y mis nesaf y byddai yn mynd ag ef i gyfraith. Addawodd

school at about four o'clock in the afternoon, to help him carry some of these things - a load of candles more often than not. It's no wonder that I've been a miner all my life. These practices entered my blood very, very early on.

I started attending Ysbyty Ystwyth School in April 1886, and was educated there by Mr Jenkins, the schoolmaster; this Jenkins was a man from Merthyr. Then he went away and another Mr Jenkins from Cwmystwyth took his place, and I was under his tutelage until the end of July 1894. In August 1894 I started working at Frongoch lead mines, on the 'flooring' washing the lead. As well as myself there were three others from the same school, the four of us of the same age, and they've all passed away now, apart from me. They paid monthly wages in these works, but kept a month's wages in hand, so we had our first pay packet after two months. Our first pay was at a rate of nine pence a day, which meant the first month's pay came to 17s. 8d. - four pence of which was kept back as payment for the doctor. It gave me great satisfaction to bring the first salary home to mam, with mam praising me highly and handing four pence back to me as pocket money.

I'll leave school and work for the time being and try to give a little of the area's history. All of us regularly went to the chapels and churches. I vividly remember that we were very afraid of the dark nights, even after we'd started working. In those days many of the villagers saw so many 'corpse candles' that, after listening to them, we'd be afraid to go out at all – without two or three of us to keep each other company. Thankfully, no one in the area speaks about such things any more.

I vividly remember the importance attached to religion in these early days, and to Sunday School, the catechism and the whole class reciting the Ten Commandments together. I heard from some of the elders about absolution in the village by a woman called Nancy Falant, who kept the first shop in Pontrhydygroes. It is said that one of the miners was in her debt and that she warned him publicly on 'sistance' Saturday that if he didn't pay his debt during the next month she'd take him to court. The

William, y dyledwr, y buasai yn gwneud ei oreu i wneud hynny. Yn y cyfamser bu priod Nancy farw, a chynhaliwyd gwylnos iddo. Yr oedd tri yn cymeryd rhan yn y gwasanaeth a William oedd yr olaf o'r tri. Mae'n debyg ei fod yn tynnu ar raffau yr addewidion yn gryf, a thorrodd Nancy Falant allan i weiddi

"Bendigedig – dal ati Wil bach, mae dy ddyled wedi ei maddau ers amser."

A dyna ni wedi cael maddeuant llwyr yn yr ardal yma beth bynnag – yn gyhoeddus i bawb.

Clywais gan fy nhad ac eraill mai yn 1870 yr aeth yr amser yn dlawd iawn, pan gwympodd pris y mwynau o tua wyth punt ar hugain y dunnell i wyth punt y dunnell. Cyn 1870 yr oedd mwynwyr oedd yn dreifio lefelau - a'r rhai oedd yn suddo siafftau a chodi codiadau - yn ennill tua chwech punt y mis a'r rhai oedd yn stopio, sef torri y mwnau i lawr, yn ennill pum punt y mis. Ond ar ôl 1870 daeth y cyflogau i lawr mor isel nes oeddent yn methu ennill digon o gyflog i dalu am sach o fflwr – pris y sach fflwr y pryd hynny oedd tair punt y sach. Yr oedd teuluoedd rhai o'r mwynwyr yn ddigon mawr a lluosog i fwyta sached bob mis. Teulu fel hynny oedd gan Elias Richards, Glannant, ef a'i wraig ac wyth o blant, ac yr oedd ef yn un o'r rhai aeth allan i Michigan, America, yn 1881. Y tâl olaf enillodd oedd dwy bunt a phedwar swllt ar ddeg. Mae'n debyg ei fod yn un o'r ysgolheigion gorau oedd yn gweithio yn y gwaith yn y cyfnod hynny, a chlywais ganddo ar ôl iddo ddyfod yn ôl o'r Amerig fod deg ar hugain o'r miners ar ben gwaith Glog Fawr un bore yn cynnal rhyw fath o gyfarfod ac iddynt basio fod yn rhaid anfon deisyfiad at y Rheolwr i ofyn am ychydig yn rhagor o gyflog a gofynnont i gyd i Elias Richards a fuasai ef yn ysgrifennu y deisyfiad.

"Gwnaf" meddai yntau. "Yn nawr pa un ohonoch sydd yn foddlon rhoddi ei enw gyntaf ar y daflen?"
Doedd dim un ohonynt yn fodlon gwneud hynny.

debtor, William, promised that he'd do his best to see that happened. In the meantime, Nancy's husband died and a wake was held in his honour. Three people took part in the service and William was the last of these. Apparently, he was passionately engaging with the Almighty when Nancy Falant shouted out,

"Fantastic – stick to it Wil Bach, your debt has long since been forgiven."

And we'd been completely forgiven in this area anyway – publicly, for everyone to hear.

I heard from my father and others that 1870 was the start of a very poor period, when the price of ore fell from around twenty eight pounds a ton to eight pounds a ton. Before 1870, the miners who were responsible for driving levels, sinking shafts and raising beams – their wage was six pounds a month, and those responsible for stoping, that is extracting the lead, their wage was five pounds a month. But after 1870 the wage came down so low that miners couldn't earn enough money to buy a sack of flour – the price of a sack of flour in those days was three pounds a sack. Some of the miners' families were large enough to eat a sackful a month. Elias Richards, Glannant, had just such a family which comprised himself, his wife and eight children, and he was one of those who went out to Michigan, America, in 1881. The final pay packet he received was worth two pounds fourteen shillings. He was probably one of the best scholars working in the mines at that time, and after he returned from America he told me that there were thirty miners at Glog Fawr works one morning holding some kind of meeting, and they passed a motion to petition the manager for higher wages, and everyone asked Elias Richards whether he'd write the petition.

"I will," he said, "now which one of you is willing to put your name to it first?"

None of them was willing to do so.

"Wel", meddai Elias Richards "'does bosibl eich bod yn disgwyl i mi roddi fy enw yn gyntaf – mae fy nheulu yn fwy lluosog na'r un ohonoch. Wel a ydyw pawb ohonoch yn fodlon rhoddi ei enw ar y deisyfiad ond i neb ohonoch fod yn gyntaf?"

Cytunodd pawb i hynny ac ysgrifennodd Elias Richards y deisyfiad yn gylch crwn – neb yn gyntaf nag yn olaf ond yr oedd y deg ar hugain â'u henwau i lawr yn gryno. Ni fuont ddim gwell o hynny; rywbryd yn 1879 oedd hyn. Wrth reswm ni ddaeth y Rheolwr i wybod am y cyfarfod nac hefyd i wybod pwy oedd wedi ysgrifennu y ddeisyfiad, a dyna y gosb oedd gwasgu digon arno nes gorfod iddo gilio o'i wlad, yn un o'r pump a aeth allan i'r Unol Daleithau yn 1881. Efe oedd yr hynaf o'r pump ar y pryd, sef pedair a deugain mlwydd oed.

Credaf mai fan yma dylwn ddweud am arferiad arall oedd yn cael ei arfer yn y gweithfeydd mwyn plwm, sef codi mwyn wrth y dunnell – arferiad oedd wedi gorffen yn llwyr cyn imi ddechrau gweithio. Nid oedd y *miners* yn cael bargen y dunnell pan fyddai cyflawnder da o fwyn i'w gael ar y cwrs (*lode*), ond ar rhyw wthïen fain yn torri allan o'r *lode*. Galwai rhai hon yn "fargen fenter" ac ambell i dro byddai rhai yn reit lwcus ar ôl dreifio ar ôl y wthïen am fisoedd lawer. Torrent i fewn o'r diwedd i boced dda y mwyn pur, pryd arall byddai yn hollol siomedig ar ôl hir weithio am ychydig iawn o fwyn plwm, byddent yn gorfod gadael y fargen a chael rhyw waith arall. Rhaid imi ddweud hyn, mai dyma y cyfnod gorau y codwyd y *miners* gorau hefyd, gan eu bod yn cymeryd cymaint o ddiddordeb mewn daeareg – yn wir yr oeddent yn gampwyr yn eu hardaloedd eu hun.

Clywais am un *miner* o'r enw Pryce wedi cymeryd bargen codi mwyn wrth y dunnell, a honno yn fargen go sâl ar y cychwyn. Rhyw hanner modfedd o drwch oedd y wthïen fwyn, a honno yn myned allan yn ddim yn aml iawn. £3.10.0. (tair punt a chweugen) y dunnell oedd yn ei gael am y mwyn ac yn aml iawn nid oedd ganddo hanner tunnell mewn dau fis. Ei fab oedd ganddo yn gweithio, ond dal ati oedd Pryce o un mis i'r llall er ei fod yn myned i ddyled mawr yn y siop fwyd, ac un diwrnod

"Well," said Elias Richards, "surely you don't expect me to put my name first – my family is larger than any of yours. Are you all willing to put your name to the petition but for none of you to be the first?"

Everyone agreed to that and Elias Richards drew up the petition in a circle – no one first and no one last, but the thirty names were all there neatly. They were no better for this – this was sometime in 1879. Of course the manager came to know about the meeting and also who had written the petition, and the punishment was to squeeze him enough that he had to leave his country, one of the five that went out to the United States in 1881, - he was the eldest of the five, being forty four years old at the time.

At this point I think I should mention another custom that was followed in the lead mines, that is raising ore by the ton – a custom that had come to an end entirely by the time I started working. The miners didn't receive a bargain per ton when there was an abundance of lead in the lode, but on some narrow veins breaking out of the lode. Some called this a 'venture bargain' and from time to time some of them would strike it quite lucky after driving the vein for months on end. Finally they'd break into a good pocket of pure ore, but other times would be bitterly disappointed after working for a long time for very little lead ore, and would have to leave the bargain and find other work. I must say this – that it was the best period that made the best miners too, as they took such an interest in geology – indeed they excelled in their fields.

I heard of one miner called Pryce who took a bargain to raise lead by the ton, and it was quite a poor bargain at the beginning, the vein was about half an inch wide and often tapered to nothing. He received £3.10.0 per ton for the ore, and often he wouldn't get half a ton in two months. He had his son working with him, but Pryce stuck to it from one month to the next even though he was running into great debt with the food shop,

dyma y swyddog, Captain Tyrrel, yn dod i mewn ato i'r gwaith ac yn dweud wrtho:

"Pryce, mae'n well iti roddi y fargen yma heibio neu ynteu yr ydwyt ti a'r bachgen yn sicr o glemio yma".
"Na", meddai Pryce, "mi ddalaf ati am ddau fis arall beth bynnag i gael gweled beth fydd fy lwc; credaf o hyd fod gobaith am boced o fwyn go dda yn nes ymlaen."

Yn y ddau fis nesaf torrodd Pryce i fewn i boced fawr o fwyn a mawr oedd ei lawenydd. Pen y ddau fis dyma y bargeinion yn cael eu rhoddi ar auction o dan y morthwyl.

Dyma fargen Pryce i fyny a'r gofyniad oedd "Beth ydyw dy bris heddiw Pryce?"
Atebodd Pryce "Tair punt a chweugen y dynnell - £3.10.0. *per ton.*"
Ac er syndod i bawb o'r miners dyma un miner arall yn gweiddi o'r dorf *"shilling less -* £3.9.0."
"Wyt ti yn clywed, Pryce, y cynnig olaf, beth ydyw dy gynnig di yn awr?"
Gwaeddodd Pryce unwaith eto "Tair a chweigen - £3.10.0."
gwaeddodd y *miner* arall eto *"shilling less* £3.9.0. - a chafodd y fargen am £3.9.0. y dunnell er syndod i'r holl *finers* y diwrnod hwnnw.

Nid oes eisiau dywedyd, torrodd Pryce ei galon ac ni fu byw yn hir ar ôl hyn.

Dyma hanes y fargen am y chwech mis canlynol. Y ddau fis cyntaf ennillodd saith cant o bunnau (£700.0.0). Y ddau fis nesaf un cant ar ddeg o bunnau (£1,100) a'r ddau fis olaf naw cant o bunnau, a gorffennodd y boced fwyn yn llwyr. Nid oes eisiau dweud wrthych mi gredaf – nid y *miner* a dorrodd y mwyn a gafodd yr arian yna i gyd o lawer. Dealltwriaeth rhyngddo â'r Manager oedd y cyfan ac mae'n debyg mae'r Manager gafodd y siâr fwyaf. Ni fuasai Pryce yn rhannu

and one day the officer, Captain Tyrrel, came over to him at the works and said to him:

"Pryce, you'd better leave this bargain or you and the boy are sure to starve here."

"No," said Pryce, "I'll stick to it for another two months whatever happens to see how my luck pans out, because I still believe that there's hope of striking a decent pocket of lead later on."

During the next two months Pryce broke into a large pocket of ore, and this made him very happy. At the end of these two months the bargains were put up for auction under the hammer.

Pryce's bargain came up and the question was "What's your price today Pryce?"
Pryce answered "£3.10.0 per ton."
Then, to the surprise of all the other miners another miner shouted from the crowd
"Shilling less - £3.9.0."
"Do you hear the last offer Pryce, what's your offer now?"
Pryce shouted once again "Three and ten shillings - £3.10.0."
The other miner again shouted "Shilling less - £3.9.0," and received the bargain for £3.9.0 a ton, to the surprise of all the miners present that day.

I don't need to tell you that Pryce's heart was broken, and he didn't live long after this.

This is the history of that bargain over the next six months. During the first two months it earned £700, the next two months £1,100 and the final two months £900, which finished off the pocket completely. Needless to say – it wasn't the miner who broke out that lead who received all the money, far from it, the whole thing was an understanding between himself and the manager, and the manager probably received the greatest share. Pryce wouldn't get to share a

dim, efe a aberthodd ac hefyd efe oedd y daearegwr a ddarganfyddodd y boced fwyn. Gorffenodd Lisburne Mines weithio tua 1892 ac aeth llawer o'r *miners* i ffwrdd tua Sir Forgannwg ag yno y sefydlodd llawer ohonynt am eu hoes, eraill yn gweithio yno a chadw eu teuluoedd yn ardal Pontrhydygroes a'r cylch, gan ddod adref rhyw ddwywaith neu dair yn y flwyddyn am ychydig ddyddiau. Yr oeddwn yn sylwi fod gwell graen ar y bobl hyn nag ar rhai oedd yn gweithio yn y gweithfeydd mwyn yma. Hawdd oedd dweud eu bod yn ennill gwell a mwy o arian, nes oeddwn yn penderfynu pan ddeiswn i yn ddigon mawr mai i Forgannwg yr aethwn innau.

Ond fel ag ydwyf wedi dweud eisioes, yn Frongoch y cychwynnais weithio yn 1894; Mr Kitto oedd perchennog y gwaith y pryd hyn. Cyflog y miners oedd tair punt y mis, a swllt y mis yn cael ei gadw yn ôl i dalu y doctor. Nis gwn pa fodd yr oeddent yn gallu byw, ond hyn sydd yn sicr yr oeddent yn gallu chwerthin o waelod eu bodolaeth y pryd hynny.

Wel gwaith digon diddorol oedd gwaith golchi y mwynau hyn ond gwaith trwm a digon caled, ond dal ati yr oeddem a chael ceiniog y dydd o godiad ar ôl rhoddi blwyddyn o wasanaeth i'r cwmni. Rhywbryd yn 1897 newidiais, ac euthum i weithio i waith Cwmnewidion o dan ddyn o'r enw Mr Murray, a chefais ddeunaw ceiniog y dydd o gyflog – gwella dipyn ar yr amgylchiadau, a'r gwaith rywbeth yn debyg i Frongoch. Yr oedd bachgen tua'r un oed â minnau yn gweithio ar fflorin olchi Mr. Murray o'r enw Evan Evans, Cwmnewidion Ganol. A phob dydd yr oedd yn dywedyd fod ganddo ferlod ifainc i'w gwerthu, a'r rhai hynny yn barod i waith. Mawr oedd fy awydd i ddod i berchen un o'r rhai hyn. Yr oeddwn innau hefyd wedi dechreu safio peth arian ac yr oedd gennyf erbyn hyn ddarn o arian, sef pisin coron, a'r pris oedd Evan yn dal am fferret, a honno yn *guarantee* i weithio, oedd pump swllt. Aeth yn fargen a phrynais y fferret am y pump swllt a chefais ddwy rwyd gan Evan i wella y fargen. Prynhawn dydd Sadwrn canlynol aethum i ffereta i Cwm Cell, a daliais bedair ar ddeg o wningod. Gwerthais ddeg ohonynt am chwech ceiniog yr un ac

thing, though it was he who sacrificed and he who was the geologist who discovered the pocket of ore. Lisburne Mines shut down about 1892 and many of the miners went away to Glamorgan, many of them setting themselves up there for life, others working there and keeping their families in the Pontrhydygroes area, coming home for a few days two or three times a year. I noticed that there was a better colour about these people than those working in the lead mines here. It was easy to tell that they earned more money, and I decided that when I was old enough, I'd go to Glamorgan.

But as I've already said, I started working at Frongoch in 1894, and the owner of the works at the time was Mr Kitto. The miners' wage was three pounds a month with a shilling kept back to pay the doctor. I don't know how they could survive, but what is certain is that, at that time, they could laugh from the depth of their souls.

The work of washing this ore was interesting enough, even though it was heavy and difficult, but we kept at it and were given a rise of a penny a day after a year's service. Sometime in 1897 I went to work at Cwmnewydion works under a man named Mr Murray, getting eighteen pence a day in wages – a considerable improvement on the circumstances for similar work to that at Frongoch. A boy about the same age as me worked on Mr Murray's 'flooring', whose name was Evan Evans of Cwmnewydion Ganol, and every day he said he had young ferrets to sell that were ready for work. I was very keen to own one of these. I had also started to save some money and by now had a bit of money, that is a crown, and the price Evan was asking for the ferret, which was guaranteed to work, was five shillings. We struck a deal, and I bought the ferret for five shillings and received two purse nets from Evan to sweeten the deal. The following Saturday afternoon I went ferreting in Cwm Cell and I caught fourteen rabbits. I sold ten of

euthum â phedair adref i Mam. Yr oeddwn yn ei gwneud yn go dda erbyn hyn; dyna feddyliwn beth bynnag.

Mi ddaeth prynder dŵr i olchi'r mwyn yng ngwaith Mr Murray, a chawsom ein stopio i gyd am beth amser. Yr oedd Nhad yn gweithio ar hyn o bryd yng ngwaith mwyn Bronberllan, Pontrhydfendigaid ac yn lodgio yn Dolybolion, ac wedi gweithio dau fis yno a chael tâl am un mis – sef pedair punt. Yr oedd rhyw ddeg ar hugain o *finers* yno yn gweithio. Draw â fi i Bronberllan at fy nhad, eisiau iddo chwilio gwaith i finnau yn awr i ddysgu bod yn *finer* ganddo.

"Cymer bwyll" meddai wrthyf, "mi dreiaf gael gwaith iti ymhen rhyw fis neu ddau."

Felly adref yr euthum drachefn ac ymhen y mis canlynol stopiodd gwaith Bronberllan yn llwyr a ni chafodd neb o'r *miners* yr un geiniog o gyflog byth am y ddau fis olaf hynny. Yr oedd ar fy nhad erbyn hyn ddau fis o lodging yn fferm Dolybolion, yn ôl deunaw ceiniog yr wythnos, felly gorfu iddo gael deueddeg swllt o fy nghyflog i dalu ar ei ôl. Erbyn hyn yr oedd digon o ddŵr i weithio gwaith Frongoch a Cwmnewidion a chafodd nhad waith yn awr yn Frongoch.

Ddechrau'r flwyddyn 1898 gwerthodd Mr. Kitto waith Frongoch i gwmni o Belgium. Daeth Manager o'r Eidal o'r enw Mr. Nogara ac Almaenwr o'r enw Mr. Heini yn Captain odano, a *surveyor* o'r Eidal o'r enw Mr. Invernetsi. Yn fuan iawn prynodd y Cwmni yma waith Cwmnewidion, oedd yn joino megis â Frongoch, a dyma'r cyfan yn nawr yn cychwyn gweithio yn un *combine*. Daeth 120 o *finers* o'r Eidal i chwyddo at y Cymry oedd yma yn barod. Parhaon i olchi y mwynau am ychydig o fisoedd ar hen beiriannau Mr. Kitto, ond yn fuan iawn dyma'r Cwmni yn cychwyn ar adeiliadu rhai newydd a mwy modern. Yr oedd y rhan fwyaf o'r gweithwyr yn gweithio yn awr ar y plan newydd hwn. Ychydig o'r *miners* oedd yn Gymry i rigo y shaft o'r newydd, a rhai ohonnynt yn dreifio levels i agor y gwaith, a'r Italians i gyd yn gwneuthur yr un pethau.

them for sixpence each and took four home to mam; I was doing quite well by now, I thought.

There was a shortage of water to wash the ore at Mr Murray's works, and all the work stopped for a while. At this time, my father was working at Bronberllan works in Pontrhydfendigaid, lodging at Dolebolion, and had been working there for two months receiving one month's pay – which was four pounds. There were about thirty miners working there. I went over to Bronberllan to my father, and I wanted him to find me work so that I could learn from him how to be a miner.

"Patience," he said, "I'll try to find you work in a month or two."

So I went back home and, at the end of the following month, Bronberllan works shut down completely and not one of the miners ever received a penny of their wages for those final two months. By now my father owed two months' lodging at Dolebolion farm, at a rate of eighteen pence a week, so he had to have twelve shillings of my wages to settle his account. By this time there was enough water at Frongoch and Cwmnewydion works, and my father found work at Frongoch.

At the beginning of 1898 Mr Kitto sold Frongoch to a company from Belgium. A Manager came from Italy called Mr Nogara, and a German called Mr Heini as Captain beneath him, and a Surveyor from Italy called Mr Invernetsi. Very soon this company bought Cwmnewydion works, combining it with Frongoch, and now they all started working as one unit. 120 miners came from Italy to swell the numbers of Welshmen already here. We continued to wash the lead for a few months on Mr Kitto's old machines, but soon the Company started building new, more modern ones. Most of the miners now worked according to this new plan. A few of the Welsh miners to rig the shaft anew, some to drive levels to open the works, and the Italians all doing the same tasks.

Yn awr am ychydig o hanes gwaith Frongoch a'i gychwyniad. John Jones, Troedyrhiw, a ddarganfyddodd waith Frongoch yn y flwyddyn 1797 wedi iddo fod yn myned heibio tŷ o'r enw Tan Dam, sydd yn adfeilion yn nawr. Llithrodd ei droed a chododd dywarchen ac o dan honno gwelodd fwyn plwm yn disgleirio fel perlau, a chododd *lease* ar unwaith a gweithiodd y mwyn plwm; y fan hynny cafodd arian i gloddio'r ffin sydd am dyddyn Troedyrhiw, ac hefyd i adeiliadu y tŷ cyntaf yno ar ôl y tŷ unnos. Nis gwn yn iawn pa hyd y bu codi y mwyn plwm hwnnw, ond ni allai fod wedi cymryd ond ychydig o amser. Cofiwch mai hanes o law i law ydyw'r hanes olaf yma.

Yn awr dyma hanes allan o lyfr sydd gennyf, ac yn hwnnw mae hanes boneddwr o'r enw J. Probert o'r Amwythig yn cychwyn gweithio gwaith Frongoch yn 1798, ac iddo ddarganfod gwaith Llwynwnwch dair blynedd yn ddiwerddarach, sef 1801. Saif adfeilion hynafol y gwaith yng nghysgod bryniau prydferth Ceredigion, rhyw ddeuddeg milltir i'r dwyrain o dref Aberystwyth, yn ymyl y ffordd sydd yn arwain o bentref Trisant i bentref Pontrhydygroes. Fe'u hamgylchynir gan gaeau Frongoch ar yr ochr ogleddol, Llwynwnwch ar yr ochr ddwyreiniol, a banc Blaenpentref (sydd wedi bod yn enwog am ei gwrdd gweddi'r mynydd) ar yr ochr orllewinol iddo, a banc Lletysynod ar yr ochr ddeheuol. Nid oedd sôn am na gwaith nac adfeilion yma ers ychydig dros ganrif a hanner yn ôl, ond ymborthai'r defaid a'r ŵyn yma yn dawel ar y borfa las. Dichon na freuddwydiodd trigolion yr ardal yn y cyfnod hwnnw am y cyfoeth a guddiai ym mherfeddion y ddaear, ond bodlon oeddent i fyw ar log diadelloedd y defaid. Er symled a thaweled bywyd felly, nid oedd heb wybod am chwerthin ac wylo, llawenydd a thristwch, ond mud yw'r gorffennol dros amser ac erys ei ramant fwyaf gwir heb ei ddatguddio.

Casglodd y boneddwr Probert lawer o weithwyr ynghyd o ardaloedd cyfagos, a than ei arweiniad ef sincwyd shaftau neu byllau rhyw dri ugain gwrhyd o ddyfnder a chafwyd fod yn y dyfnder hwnnw gyfran dda o fwyn, plwm, zinc a silver. Codwyd y trysorau hyn i fyny drwy y

Now for a little of the history of Frongoch and how it started. John Jones, Troedyrhiw, discovered Frongoch works in the year 1797 when he passed by a house called Tan Dam, which is now a ruin. His foot slipped and raised a sod of turf under which he saw lead ore shining like pearls, and he quickly obtained a lease to work the lead ore; thus he made the money to dig the boundary around the holding of Troedyrhiw, and also to build the first house there since the old 'tŷ unnos' - a cottage built within one day and a night. I don't really know for how long he mined that lead ore, but it can't have taken very much time. Remember that this last story is one passed from hand to mouth.

Now here's a story out of a book I have, and that is the story of a gentleman called J. Probert from Shrewsbury who started working at Frongoch in 1798 and who discovered Llwynwnwch works three years later in 1801. The old ruins of the works stand in the shadows of the beautiful hills of Ceredigion, about twelve miles east of the town of Aberystwyth, by the side of the road that leads from the village of Trisant to the village of Pontrhydygroes. They are surrounded by Frongoch fields to the north, Llwynwnwch to the east and Blaenpentre hill, which has been famous for its prayer meetings, to the west, and Lletysynod hill to the south. There were neither works nor ruins here until a little over a century and a half ago, but the sheep and the lambs grazed silently here on the green grass. The area's inhabitants at the time probably never dreamed of the riches which lay hidden in the depths of the earth but were content to live off the flocks of sheep. Despite the simplicity and peace of such a life, it wasn't without its laughter and weeping, its happiness and sadness, but the past falls silent over time, and its truest romance remains hidden.

The gentleman Probert gathered many workers together from neighbouring areas, and it was under his leadership that shafts or pits were sunk some sixty fathoms deep and, at that depth, lead, zinc and silver ore were found in good proportion. These treasures were brought

shaft mewn skip ac yna eu malu a'u golchi ar y fflorin, ac ar ôl hynny eu cludo mewn gwagenni i dref Aberystwyth i'w rhoddi ar fwrdd y llongau bychan i'w dwyn ymaith i wahanol wledydd. Deunaw punt y dunnell oedd gwerth y mwyn plwm yn y cyfnod hwnnw. Gwerthodd Probert ei hawlfraint yn y flwyddyn 1834 i Mri. Taylor a'i feibion, y rhai a wnaethant welliantau enfawr i'r gwaith. Cyflogasant gannoedd o ddynion o ardaloedd Pontarfynach, Trisant, Llanafan a Pontrhydygroes, ac adeiliasant amryw o adeiliadau cerrig. Hefyd sincwyd y shaftau yn ddyfnach, sef i 142 ffathom, lle yr oedd mwyn plwm ardderchog i'w gael yn y dyfnder hynny. Gorfu i'r Cwmni hwn chwilio rhagor o ddwr at eu gwasanaeth, a chawsant ef o lynnoedd Trisant ac o afon Prignant (Rhosygell). Codasant nifer y tunnelli i fyny o ddeugain tunnell y mis i gant tunnell y mis yn y flwyddyn gyntaf o'r gweithio. Cadwodd y Cwmni hyn yr *output* i fyny am flynyddoedd ac yn ystod y tair blynedd ddiwethaf o'i hawlfraint hwy, sef o 1875 i 1878, gwerthasant 3,205 o dunelli o fwyn plwm am £44,857.0.0 ond ar ôl talu y *royalty* i'r tirfeddiannwr, yr oedd y Cwmni mewn dyled o £679.0.0, felly gwerthasant y gwaith a'r cynllun i Lord Lisburne, a gwerthodd yntau hwynt yn yr un flwyddyn, sef 1878, i Mr. John Kitto. Parhaodd y gwaith i fod yn llwyddiannus iawn o dan lywyddiaeth Mr. Kitto, a gwerthodd 2,850 o dunnelli o'r mwyn yn y flwyddyn gyntaf. Cadwodd Mr. Kitto ei hawlfraint am ugain mlynedd ac yna yn y flwyddyn 1898 gwerthodd hwynt i gwmni o Belgium.

Rhywbryd yn mis Ebrill 1898 gorffennodd y Cwmni newydd yma falu a golchi ar hen *machinery* Mr. Kitto, ac aethant ati o ddifrif i baratoi popeth tuag at adeiliadu rhai newydd. Y gorchwyl cyntaf a gawsom ni fechgyn y fflorin ei wneuthur oedd cychwyn ar y trench dŵr newydd o Blaenpentre i Landwgan. Daeth tua dwsin o'r marched ag oedd yn gweithio ar y fflorin gyda ni i weithio i'r trench dŵr yma, - merched glan a hardd rhyfeddol oeddent bob yr un ohonynt, wedi eu gwisgo â phrydferthwch natur, dim un ohonynt wedi breuddwydio erioed i ddefnyddio na *lipstick* na phowdwr, a phob un ohonynt yn ennill swllt y dydd fel cyflog. Beth feddyliai merched yr oes fodern am amgylchiadau o'r fath. Anfonodd y Cwmni lawer o'r *miners* allan i weithio i'r trench

up through the shaft in a skip, ground and washed on the 'flooring', and after that taken in wagons to Aberystwyth to be put aboard small ships and taken away to different countries. In that period the lead ore was worth eighteen pounds a ton. Probert sold his rights in 1834 to Messrs Tailor and sons, who made great improvements to the works. They hired hundreds of men from Devil's Bridge, Trisant, Llanafan and Pontrhydygroes areas and built many stone buildings. The shafts were also sunk deeper, to a depth of 142 fathoms, where excellent lead ore was to be found. This Company had to find more water for the works and found it at Trisant lakes and the River Prignant (Rhosygell). They increased the output from forty tons a month to a hundred tons a month in the first year. The Company kept this up for years and during the final three years of their lease, between 1875 and 1878, sold 3,205 tons of iron ore for £44,857 but, after paying the royalties to the landowner, the Company was £679 in debt, so they sold the works and the plot to Lord Lisburne, who in turn sold them that same year, 1878, to Mr John Kitto. The works continued to be very successful under the management of Mr Kitto, and 2,850 tons of ore were sold in the first year. Mr Kitto kept his rights for twenty years and in the year 1898 sold it to a company from Belgium.

Sometime in April 1898 this new Company stopped crushing and washing using Mr Kitto's old machinery and began seriously preparing everything to build new ones. The first task given to us 'flooring' boys was to start on the new water trench from Blaenpentre to Llandwgan. About a dozen of the girls who worked on the 'floorings' came with us to work on this water trench, - decent and exceptionally pretty girls each one of them, dressed in nature's beauty, not one of them ever having dreamed of using lipstick or powder, and each of them earning a shilling a day in wages. What would modern day women make of such circumstances? The Company sent many of the miners out to work on

a chawsom ninnau, fechgyn a merched, ein dosbarthu, sef mab a merch i weithio efo pob *miner*. Whîlo y berfau oedd gwaith y merched drwy'r dydd. Enwau rhai o'r *miners* oedd Thomas Jones Pantrhedyn, David Davies New Row, David Jones Tanlanfedwen, ac amryw eraill. Trafodent bynciau dyrus yn aml iawn. Credoau amrywiol oedd yno, megis Methodistiaid Callfinaidd hefo eu hetholedigaeth, Wesleyaid efo'u credo Arminaidd, yn grefyddwyr mawr a selog heddiw a syrthio oddi wrth ras yfory. Yr oedd yno lawer o Eglwyswyr hefyd a'r rhai hynny yn selog, - cymerent hwythau ran yn y dadleuon, on cofiaf yn dda mai y pwyslais roddent hwy bob amser oedd ar y wasanaeth Eglwysig, ac nid ar y pynciau diwynyddol.

Yn yr amser yma daeth dau ddyn canol oed yn ôl o Barnsley a oedd wedi eu magu yn Ysgol Sul capel Wesleaidd Saesneg, oedd rhwng New Row a Pontrhydygroes; meibion oeddent i'r diweddar Captain Paul, Frongoch Mines – William a Phillip Paul oedd eu henwau. William Paul yma oedd un o'r dynion mwyaf hyddysg yn yr Ysgrythur Lân, sef llyfr y Proffwyd Amos. Hoffem ni y bechgyn bob amser glywed William yn cael goruchafiaeth ar y cewri eraill i gyd. Un diwrnod arbennig ym mis Ebrill, yr oeddem i gyd yn gweithio ar y *trench* uwchben Cwmnewidion Uchaf, a gwelem gawod o law drom yn dod i fyny drwy'r cwm ac yna rhedodd pawb am eu bywyd i lechu i'r hen dŷ Tan Dam. Cyrhaeddodd pawb yno yn sych ond William Paul – yr oedd y gawod heibio ac yntau yn wlyb at ei groen, a dyma ei ddywediad ar ben y drws,

"Arglwydd daear, maent yn dweud yn yr Ysgrythur Lân fod Duw yn Fod Trugarog; lle mae trugaredd a William Paul wedi cael ei wlychu at y croen efo'r *April shower* ofnadwy yma."

the trench and we, the boys and girls, were assigned, a boy and a girl to work with each miner. The girls were responsible for wheeling the barrows all day. Some of the miners were Thomas Jones - Pantrhedyn, David Davies - New Row, David Jones - Tanlanfedwen, and various others. They often discussed complicated subjects. They held various beliefs, such as Calvinist Methodists with their denominations, Wesleyans with their Arminian beliefs, greatly religious one day and falling from grace the next. There were also many devout Churchmen, - they took part in the debates as well, but I well remember that their emphasis was always on the Church service rather than theological subjects.

At this time two middle aged men came back from Barnsley who had been brought up at an English Wesleyan Chapel Sunday School between New Row and Pontrhydygroes, sons of the late Captain Paul, Frongoch Mines, - their names were William and Phillip Paul. This William Paul was one of the most learned in scripture that I ever heard, and was always an excellent debater. His mind had apparently been affected significantly through extravagant living. He would always be able to bring a series of biblical verses into play to back him up on any given subject; I remember that they were nearly always from the New Testament, such as the Epistles of St Paul to the Romans and Corinthians, but William would always say they were to be found in the Holy Scripture, that is the book of the Prophet Amos. We boys would always enjoy listening to William getting the better of all the other giants. One particular day in April, we were all working on the trench above Cwmnewydion Uchaf, when we saw a heavy rain shower coming up the valley and everyone ran for their lives to shelter in the old house called Tan Dam; everyone reached the house without getting wet apart from William Paul – the shower had passed and he was soaked to the skin, and this is what he said at the door,

"Lord of the earth, they say in the Holy Scripture that God is a Merciful Being, but where is the mercy when William Paul has been soaked to his skin by this terrible April shower."

Rheumatism yn ei goesau oedd yn ei stopio i redeg fel pawb arall. Yn y cornel yr oedd dyn bach byr o'r enw John Lewis (hwn oedd a gofal y *trench* mawr) ac oedd wedi colli ei wallt ar gorun ei ben, a phob amser dipyn yn groen-denau, a dyma ef yn annerch William fel hyn,

"William Paul, yr wyt yn hela gwallt fy mhen i sefyll wrth dy glywed yn galw ar enw dy Dduw yn ofer yn y fan yma". Ar hynny neshaodd William yn nes ato. "John Lewis" meddai, "trueni na fuasai dy wallt wedi sefyll yn lle ei fod wedi myned i ffwrdd efo'r gwynt, a chofia hyn, John Lewis, paid byth â cheryddu dyn heb dy fod yn sicr ei fod wedi troseddu. 'Arglwydd daear' ddywedais i onide – Lord Lisburne oedd gyda fi mewn golwg, efe yw perchennog y tir yma i gyd, a fe sydd yn derbyn y *royalties* yma bob mis."

Dyna'r lle cyntaf i mi glywed, ac i ddechreu meddwl, am system mor anghyfiawn ag i ryw bersonau arbennig dderbyn *royalties* am fwynau nad oeddent wedi eu gweled erioed, a mawr oedd ein llawennydd ni, y rhai ieuainc beth bynnag, fod William Paul wedi cael goruchafiaeth unwaith eto ar John Lewis, goruwchwyliwr y *trench* dŵr.

Rywbryd yr haf hwn cefais ddechrau gweithio fel *miner* efo Nhad yn 44 level yn y *braker shaft*. Bargen newydd oedd hon i Nhad a'r gorchymyn gafodd oedd am iddo fyned â'r *tools* i lawr, ac y byddai efe, y manager - Mr Nogara, a Captain Heini yn ei ddilyn tua deg o'r gloch y bore. Wedi cyrraedd y lle dyma'r ymddiddan a fu rhwng y tad a'r mab:

"Wel di Elias, bydd hwn yn lle go lew i ti i ddechre gweithio ar y graig am nad ydyw yn dir caled iawn. Mae'n debyg y byddant eisie gweithio tair shifft ar hon – bydd hynny yn golygu rhagor o bris, wyt ti yn deall, - shift y bore, prynhawn a'r nos. Os câf i chwech punt y gwrhyd am ei dreifio, fe ennillwn arian fel brics yma", a dyma y Manager Mr Nogara a'r Captain yn cyrraedd. Bu y sgwrs rhyngddynt yn debyg i hyn.

Rheumatism in his legs prevented him from running like everyone else. In the corner there was a little short man called John Lewis (who was in charge of the water trench) and he was bald on the crown of his head and always a little thin skinned, and he spoke to William as follows,

"William Paul, you make the hair on my head stand on end when I hear you taking your Lord's name in vain in this place."
At which point William approached him, "John Lewis," he said, "it's a shame that your hair hadn't stayed where it was instead of blowing away in the wind, and remember this John Lewis, don't ever rebuke a man without being certain that he has committed an offence. I said Lord of the Earth did I not – it was Lord Lisburne that I had in mind, he owns all this land and receives the Royalties every month."

That was the first time that I heard and started to think about what an unjust system it was that certain persons received Royalties for ore that they'd never set eyes upon, and it brought us youngsters great enjoyment that William Paul had once again bested John Lewis, supervisor of the water trench [commonly called a leat].

Sometime that summer I started working as a miner with my father at Level 44 in Braker Shaft. This was a new bargain for my father, and the order he was given was to take the tools down and that Mr Nogara, the Manager, and Captain Heini would follow about ten o'clock in the morning; when we reached the place this is the conversation between father and son:

"You'll see Elias, this will be a good place for you to start work on the rock as it isn't very hard ground. They'll probably want to work three shifts on this – that will mean a higher price you understand, - morning shift, afternoon shift and evening shift. If I get six pounds for each fathom I drive, we'll earn money like it's going out of fashion", and at that point Mr Nogara, the Manager, and the Captain arrived. The discussion between them went something like this:

Nogara – *"Well William Jones have you found the place? We want to drive this level parallel with the fall and it will have to go about 80 fathom to reach the other end of the fall, and we want three shifts on it so as to reach the other end as soon as possible."*
Nhad yn ateb – *"Three shifts more price Mr. Nogara".*
"Yes quite so William – now William what is your price?"
"Well I leave it to you today, but mind you we are going to have very stiff ground here."
"Well William, so long that you are willing for me to give the price, £7.10.0 a fathom."
"No, no, no - too much" meddai Captain Heini *"£7.0.0 is enough."*
Nogara – *"£7.10.0. What d'you say, William?"*
"Well you are not far off. £8.0.0 I thought to ask."
"The bargain is settled."

Dyma ddiwedd y diwrnod cyntaf erioed i mi fod tan y ddaear. Ar ôl iddynt fyned ymaith, gofynnais gwestiwn ar ôl cwestiwn i Nhad: paham oedd wedi dweud wrthyf os cawsai £6.0.0. y gwrhyd, y byddai yn gallu ennill arian fel brics, ac eto yn dweud wrthynt hwy mai £8.0.0 oedd wedi meddwl gofyn iddynt.

"O machgen i" meddai, "dyna'r *lesson* gyntaf i ti, bydd rhaid iti ddysgu llawer ohonynt cyn diwedd dy oes".

Gwir y dywedodd, bob ffordd. Buasem wedi gallu ennill cyflog go dda ar y chwech punt, ond yr oedd yn hawdd iawn gwneud hynny ar £7.10.0. Y gwir amdani oedd nad oeddent yn deall gwerth gweithio rhai tiroedd o gwbl. Yr oedd y tir yn amrywiol iawn. Gwae chwi os cawsech fargen mewn llawer o fannau lle'roedd y tir yn galed ofnadwy. Lle y dylech gael rhyw £18.0.0. y fathom dywedwch, buasent hwythau yn cynnig rhyw naw neu ddeg punt. Amhosibl fyddai ennill cyflog rhesymol ar eu pris hwy.

Mewn pob cyfnod ar yr ifanc, maent yn siarad a dadlau am bethau eu cyfnod, Cymerwch yr amser heddiw, mae pawb ifanc yn dadlau am

Nogara – "Well William Jones have you found the place? We want you to drive this level parallel with the fall, and it will have to go about 80 fathom to reach the other end of the fall, and we want three shifts on it so as to reach the other end as soon as possible."
My father answered – "Three shifts more price, Mr Nogara."
"Yes quite so William, - now William what is your price?"
"Well I leave it to you today, but mind you we are going to have very stiff ground here."
"Well William, so long that you are willing for me to give the price, £7.10.0. a fathom."
"No, no, no. too much", said Captain Heini, "£7.0.0. is enough."
Nogara – "£7.10.0. What d'you say William?"
"Well you are not far off - it was £8.0.0 I thought to ask."
"The bargain is settled."

That was the end of the first day I ever spent underground. After they'd gone away, I asked my father question after question; why had he told me if he had £6.0.0. a fathom that he could earn loads of money but then told them he'd thought to ask them for £8.0.0.?

"Oh my boy," he said, "that's your first lesson, you'll have to learn many of them before the end of your life."

He spoke the truth in every way. We could earn quite a good wage at six pounds, but it was very easy to do so at £7.0.0., - the truth was that they didn't understand the true value of working certain types of ground at all. The ground was extremely variable. Woe betide you if you had a bargain in one of the many places where the ground was very hard. Where you should get £18.0.0. a fathom, say, they would offer about nine or ten pounds. It would be impossible to earn a reasonable wage at their price.

In every era the young talk and argue about the things of their time. Take the present, for instance, every young person argues about the

speed mewn awyr-longau neu foduron ac yn y blaen. Clywais yr wythnos o'r blaen am ddyn wedi marw yn sydyn iawn a rhyw gyfaill i frawd yr ymadawedig yn cydymdeimlo ag ef.

"Bachgen" meddai "mi golloch eich brawd yn sydyn iawn."
"Do yn wir" meddai yntau "ond dyna fe, *speed* yw'r cwbl yn nawr."

On tua 1900 dadleu oeddem ni y rhai ifanc am y ceffylau a *waggoners*, rhai mor ardderchog oeddent am dynnu eu pwysau - 'Weingrach', 'Nantarthur' a 'Lletysynod', ond daliem ni fechgyn Pontrhydegroes mae ceffylau goreu y wlad oedd gyda Seth Dolgroes. Byddai y dadleuon hyn yn cyrraedd *pitch* go uchel yn aml. Un diwrnod daeth sôn am ryw gaseg ifanc efo Thomas Glangorslwyd, a dynnai ei phwysau bob dydd; ei bod wedi ei magu a'i phorthi yn dda o'r cychwyn, a byddaf yn sôn am hon eto ychydig yn nes ymlaen – 'Sal' oedd ei henw.

Mater pwysig y dydd efo'r *miners* o dan y ddaear yn nawr oedd y rhyfel yn *South Africa*. Mawr oedd y disgwyliad am bob dydd Iau. Dyna y diwrnod byddai Tom Williams, Cefngreigog, yn dod â'r 'Faner ac Amserau Cymru' i'r gwaith, a byddem yn eistedd i lawr am amser mewn lle llydan yn 44 level yn gwrando ar Tom Williams yn darllen hanes y rhyfel. Y nesaf at Tom Williams bob amser fyddai James Olliver, Y Cnwc, Ysbyty Ystwyth, yr hwn oedd y pryd hynny yn drigain mlwydd oed, a dyna oedd fy syndod mwyaf – mor hyddysg oedd James mewn daearyddiaeth. Gwyddai sawl troedfedd oedd pob bryn uwchlaw arwynebedd y môr, megis Majuba Hill a Spion Kop ac yn y blaen; gwyddai amdanynt 'run fath â phe bai yn siarad am Pendrawsallt neu ben Pumlumon. Yn y dyddiau hynny daeth newydd i'r gwaith fod Thomas Glangorslwyd wedi gwerthu y gaseg (Sal) i'r *military men*, a'i bod wedi cael ei hanfon efo llong am *South Africa*. Mewn ychydig o wythnosau ar ôl hyn cychwynnodd y *battle* fawr yn Spion Kop a daeth gwybodaeth yn ôl yn fuan iawn mai y gaseg Sal a dynnodd i fyny y cannon mawr i ben Spion Kop ac i'r Prydeinwyr gael buddugoliaeth lwyr ar y Boeriaid. Tystiai Thomas fod yr hanes yn ffaith, a mwy na hynny, fod Sal wedi dod i lawr â'r cannon mawr a'i fod efo'r Queen's

speed of airships or motors and so on. The other week I heard about a man who died very suddenly and that a friend of the departed's brother had commiserated with him,

"Boy," he said, "you lost your brother very suddenly."
"Yes indeed" answered the brother, "but there we go, speed is the 'be all and end all' these days."

But around the year 1900, we young people argued about the waggoners' horses, how excellent they were for pulling their weight, - 'Weingrach', 'Nantarthur' and 'Lletysynod', but we Pontrhydygroes boys insisted that the best horses in the country were to be found with Seth Dolgroes. These arguments would often reach quite a high pitch. One day we heard about some young mare in the possession of Thomas Glangorslwyd that pulled its weight every day as she'd been raised and fed well from the beginning. I'll come back to this mare a little later on – her name was 'Sal'.

The matter on everyone's lips underground now was the war in South Africa. There was great anticipation every Thursday. That was the day when Tom Williams, Cefngreigog, would bring '*Y Faner*' and '*Amserau Cymru*' to work, and we'd sit for a time at a wide spot on 44 level listening to Tom Williams reading about how the war was going. Sitting next to Tom Williams every time would be James Oliver, Y Cnwc, Ysbyty Ystwyth, who was sixty years old at the time, and what caused me the greatest surprise was how knowledgeable James was concerning geography. He knew how many feet each hill was above sea level, for instance Majuba Hill, Spion Kop and so on; he knew about them as though he was speaking about Pendrawsallt or the top of Pumlumon. In those days news reached the works that Thomas, Glangorslwyd, had sold the mare (Sal) to the military men and that she'd been put aboard a ship bound for South Africa. A few weeks later the great battle at Spion Kop began, and news soon reached us that it was Sal who pulled up the great canon to the top of Spion Kop, and that the British had won a complete victory over the Boers. Thomas attested

Guards ar Sgwâr Pretoria pan oedd y cytundeb y cadoediad yn cael ei seinio efo General Botha, General Smuts a Field Marshall Lord Roberts.

Ychydig iawn a wnaeth y Cwmni Belgian hyn i ddatblygu y gwaith tanddaearol, ond adeiliadon' nhw gynllun trydan enfawr. Gwariodd y Cwmni y swm rhyfeddol of £130.000 ar beiriannau golchi a phethau diweddaraf yr oes. Arferai yr Eidalwyr addoli yn hen gapel Wesle y Saeson, sydd heddiw yn adfeilion, rhwng pentref New Row a Phontrhydygroes, a thra y buont yma bu un ohonynt farw a chladdwyd ei weddillion ym mynwent Llantrisant gerllaw y gwaith.

Dywedaf hyn - cawsom amser digon terfysglyd y blynyddoedd hyn yn yr ardal – llawer streic go chwerw hefyd, gan nad oedd yr un math o undeb gyda'r *miners* – pob un yn myned ar ei hwc ei hun. Rhaid yw cydnabod mai hwy oedd y dosbarth mwyaf *backward* yng Nghymru y pryd hynny, gan fod y Gogledd a'r De a'u hundebau i gyd. Mae nofel "Y Chwalfa" gan T Rowland Hughes yn profi hynny am y Gogledd, a "How Green is my Valley" yn profi hynny am y De. Ond nid oedd gweithwyr Ceredigion wedi deffro i'w hangen o gwbl. Un o'r strikes gawsom oedd o achos yr Eidalwyr yn gweithio bob amser, sef prynhawn dydd Sadwrn a dydd Sul, ond gorfu iddynt ddyfod a gweithio yr un oriau gwaith â ninnau yng Nghymru. Costiodd hynny ymladdfa chwerw iawn rhwng yr Eidalwyr a'r Cymry ym Mhontrhydygroes, pryd y cafodd yr Eidalwyr eu curo yn arw iawn a'r Cymry wedi talu yn drwm am hynny.

Dywed hanes fod 50,669 o dunnelli o zinc, 38,071 o dunnelli o fwyn, a 19,014 owns o arian (*silver*) wedi cael eu codi o waith Frongoch o'r flwyddyn 1845 i 1903, a dywedir mai cyfanswm y *silver* a godwyd o'r gwaith hwn o 1798 hyd 1903 oedd 128,000 owns.

Yn awr gadawaf y broblem hon i rywun arall - sef faint o fudd i wareiddiad Prydain a'r byd a wnaeth y dygwyddiad i John Jones, Troedyrhiw, ddarganfod y mwyn yn 1797. Pan edrychwn o gwmpas yr ardaloedd hyn a gweled yr ysgolion, capeli, eglwysi a bythynnod

that the story was a fact, and more than that, Sal had brought the great cannon down and was with the Queen's Guards on Pretoria Square when the Ceasefire Agreement was signed with General Botha, General Smuts and Field Marshal Lord Roberts.

The Belgian Company did very little to develop the underground works, but they did build an enormous electrical plant. The company spent the incredible sum of £130,000 on machines for washing and the latest equipment. The Italians used to worship in the old English Wesleyan Chapel, which is now a ruin, between the villages of New Row and Pontrhydygroes, and while they were here one of them died and his remains buried at Llantrisant cemetery near the works.

I'll say this, we had a turbulent enough time in the area during these years – many a bitter strike too, as the lead miners had no trade union of any kind, - everyone had to look out for himself. It has to be admitted that they were the most backward class in Wales at that time, as the North and the South all had their own unions. The novel '*Y Chwalfa*' by T. Rowland Hughes proves that about the North, and '*How Green Was My Valley*' proves it about the South, but the workers of Ceredigion hadn't woken up to their need at all. One of the strikes was caused because the Italians were always working, that is Saturday afternoons and Sundays, but they had to change to work the same hours as us in Wales. That caused bitter fighting between the Italians and the Welsh in Pontrhydygroes, when the Italians received a severe beating for which the Welsh paid heavily.

History tells us that 50,669 tons of zinc, 38,071 tons of lead and 19,014 ounces of silver were extracted from Frongoch works between 1845 and 1903, and it is said that between 1798 and 1903 a total of 128,000 ounces of silver were extracted.

Now I'll leave this problem to someone else – that is how much good came to the civilisation of Britain and the world through the discovery of the ore in 1797 by John Jones, Troedyrhiw. When I look around these

bychain a godwyd o gwmpas yr hen weithfeydd mwyn plwm yma, a hefyd cofio am y rhestri enfawr o bregethwyr, offeiriaid, ysgolheigion gwych, pobl bwysig eraill yn y ganrif, sef masyniaid a ddysgodd codi welydd cryfion anferth. Ni fedraf gau fy llygaid un amser ar eu gwaith yn Frongoch, gofied oedd wedi dysgu gweithio gwaith trwm efo haearn mor rhagorol, seiri coed fel Daniel Morgan, a gododd rod ddŵr fawr Frongoch - y fwyaf yn y byd. Un arall a godwyd yn debyg iddi, a honno yn yr *Isle of Man*, wedi cael y patrwm oddi wrth Daniel Morgan. *Miners* eto a ddysgodd y gelfyddyd o drin y graig, pan oedd y cyfan megis yn *hammer and drill work* (sef tarad â morthwyl), ac ni fu eu gwell ar y ddaear erioed. Mamau rhagorol eto, *Chancellors of the Exchequer* gorau a welodd Prydain erioed – wedi dysgu yn drwyadl y gelfyddyd o rannu angen un rhwng y naw.

Wel yn nawr am ychydig o hanes pentref Pontrhydygroes ac Ysbyty, sydd yn aros yng nghwm afon Ystwyth, un o'r cwmydd prydferthaf ag ydwyf wedi eu gweled erioed. Yn niwedd y ganrif ddiwethaf, sef 1899, yr oedd yma bedwar tŷ tafarn, sef Star Inn, a Black Lion yn Ysbyty, a Lisburne Arms a'r Bear Inn ym Mhontrhydygroes, ac un hotel sef y Miners Arms Hotel, a llawer o fusnes yn cael ei wneuthur ym mhob un ohonynt. Clywais gan rai o'r tadau mai yn y Tumble y pryd hynny yn 1859 - dyna enw cyntefig y Miners Arms - y cychwynodd diwygiad Humphrey Jones a Dafydd Morgan y diwygiwr, mai yno yr aeth y ddau efo'i gilydd i gadw y cyfarfod cyntaf. Aeth llawer allan, a safodd y mwyafrif i mewn i uno yn y mawl. Erbyn heddiw, does yr un mewn busnes a dim ond un hotel, sef Miners Arms, sydd yn yr ardal. Ond pa ryfedd, does yma yr un dywydiant wedi dod i'r lle ar ôl i'r gweithfeydd mwyn sefyll yn llonydd. Y cyfan sydd o waith yn yr ardal ydyw coedwigoedd ar hyn o bryd. Yn nechrau y ganrif hon yr oedd rhyw bedwar o deilwriaid, rhyw chwech o gryddion, dau neu ragor o ofiaid gwlad, merched yn dysgu *dress-making*. Hefyd yr oedd pedair neu bump o siopau bwyd, dim ond dwy erbyn heddiw – a llawer o *vans* yn dod â nwyddau arbennig i'r lle. Pwy bynnag sydd yn gyfrifol, y cam mwyaf a wnawd erioed yn Sir Aberteifi oedd gwneud Gogledd y Sir

areas and see the schools, the chapels, the churches and the little cottages built around the old lead ore works, and also remember the great lists of preachers, clergymen, great scholars and other important people of the century, such as masons who learnt to raise large, strong walls, I can't close my eyes to their work at Frongoch. Then there were blacksmiths who'd learnt to work heavy metals such as iron so skilfully, carpenters such as Daniel Morgan, who built the great Frongoch water wheel (the largest in the world – only one other similar wheel was built on the Isle of Man, which took its design from Daniel Morgan). It was also miners who learned the art of handling rock, when everything was hammer and drill work, and the world never saw their like. And then there were great mothers, the best Chancellors of the Exchequer Britain ever saw – who learned the art of sharing the needs of one between nine.

Now for a little of the history of Pontrhydygroes and Ysbyty [Ystwyth], which are located in the valley of the River Ystwyth, one of the most beautiful valleys I have ever seen. At the end of the last century, in 1899, there were four taverns here, which were the Star Inn and the Black Lion in Ysbyty, the Lisburne Arms and the Bear Inn in Pontrhydygroes and also one hotel, the Miners Arms Hotel, with all of these doing a roaring trade. I heard from some of the fathers that it was at that time in 1859 in Tumble, that the revival led by Humphrey Jones and Dafydd Morgan began, that they both went there to hold the first meeting. Many went out and many stayed inside to join in the worship. By now, none of the taverns remain in business and only the hotel, the Miners Arms, is still a going concern in the area and no wonder, because no industry has come to the place since the time of the lead works. The only work in the area now is forestry work. At the beginning of the century there were about four tailors, six cobblers, two or more country blacksmiths, girls learning the trade of dress-making; there were also four or five food shops, but only two survive today, - but many vans came on to the place on special days. Whoever is responsible, the greatest injustice ever done in Cardiganshire was to make the northern part of the county a non-industrial area, and no area

yma yn *non-industrial area*, a does yr un ardal wedi cael ei bwrw yn waeth nag Ysbyty Ystwyth, Pontrhydygroes, i fyny i Gwmystwyth.

'Roeddwn i a chyfaill i mi yn cyfri tri ugain a deg o gartrefi ym mhlwyf Ysbyty wedi myned i lawr yn *ruins* o fewn ein cof ni. Mae yn wir hefyd ein bod wedi cael deg o dai newydd yn y blynyddoedd olaf yma ym Mhontrhydygroes, ac hefyd buom yn ffodus i gael *electricity* i gyfran helaeth o blwyf Ysbyty. Yr ydym hefyd wedi cael *scheme* ddŵr i'r ran fwyaf o'r trigolion.

Yn awr yn diwedd mis Mawrth 1901, cafodd y rhan fwyaf o'r gweithwyr eu stopio yn Frongoch, a'r gweddill a gafodd eu cadw er mwyn cychwyn tynnu'r cyfan i lawr; gorffennwyd hynny yn 1903. Yr oeddwn i a'm brawd efo llawer eraill yn y rhai cyntaf, ac ar y 18ed o Ebrill 1901 aethom i lawr i Abercynon, Morgannwg, i edrych am waith yn y pwll glo. Llwyddom i gael gwaith, ac ar y dydd Llun cyntaf o fis Mai, sef dydd yr Wyl Lafur, aethom i ben Carreg Siglo, Pontypridd, lle oedd yr Wyl Lafur yn cael ei chynnal. William Abraham (Mabon) oedd y prif siaradwr y diwrnod hwnnw. Yr oedd torf o bobl yno – rhyw ugain mil neu ragor. Dyma fel y cychwynnodd Mabon ar ei araith: meddai

"Fechgyn, pwy ddaeth â lampau rhyddion ag olew ynddynt i chwi at eich gwaith?"
a dyma'r dorf yn gweiddi ag un llef "Mabon."
"Pwy ddaeth â choed i chwi at eich gwaith?"
"Mabon" gwaeddai'r dorf.
"Mor wir â bod Mabon yn sefyll ar y garreg sigledig yma heddiw, mi ddaw Mabon ag wyth awr i chwi i weithio, wyth awr i chwi i chwarae, wyth awr i chwi gysgu ac wyth swllt y dydd."
"Hear Hear", meddai'r crowd.
Yn fy ochr yr oedd dyn o golier, canol oed mi dybiwn, a dyma fe yn dywedyd, "Beth mae ef yn siarad mor ffol, - yr ydym yn methu ag ennill bywoliaeth mewn deg awr a hanner."

has suffered worse than Ysbyty Ystwyth, Pontrhydygroes and up to Cwmystwyth.

I and a friend of mine have counted seventy homes in the parish of Ysbyty that have been reduced to ruins during the time we can remember. It is also true that we have had ten new homes over the last few years here in Pontrhydygroes, and we have also been lucky enough to have electricity in most of the parish of Ysbyty. We have also had a water scheme for the majority of residents.

At the end of March 1901, most of the workers at Frongoch were laid off, and those who were kept on were tasked with starting to take the whole lot down; that was finished in 1903. My brother and I and many others were among the first group, and on the 18th of April 1901 we went down to Abercynon, Glamorganshire, to look for work in the coal pit. We succeeded in finding work, and on the first Monday in May, that is Labour Day, we went down to the Rocking Stone in Pontypridd where the Labour Day celebrations were held, - William Abraham (Mabon) was the main speaker that day. There was a crowd of people there – about twenty thousand or more. This is how Mabon began his speech, he said

"Boys, who brought you free lamps with oil for your work?"
And the crowd shouted as one "Mabon."
"Who brought wood for your work?"
"Mabon" shouted the crowd.
"As true as Mabon stands here on this rocking stone today, Mabon will bring eight hours for you to work, eight hours for you to play, eight hours for you to sleep and eight shillings a day."
"Hear Hear," said the crowd.
At my side there was a collier, about middle aged by my reckoning, and he said, "Why is he talking such nonsense, - we can't earn a living on ten and a half hours."

Hyn sydd yn ffaith - erbyn 1908 yr oedd wedi dod yn ddeddf y wlad erbyn hynny, ac unais innau â'r 'Miners Federation' yn mis Mai 1901 a pharheais yn undebwr selog ar hyd fy oes. Yn mis Medi o'r un flwyddyn, euthum i Gwmaman, Aberdâr i weithio, a chyfarfyddais â dyn yno o Gwmystwyth o'r enw John Lloyd, Pantygorlan, yr hwn oedd yn *finer* gwaith plwm da ac wedi bod yn agor chwareli slât cerrig mynydd i doi llawer o fythynod y plwyf yma. Ni welais ef erioed ond clywais lawer amdano, yr adeg yma yr oedd yn wael iawn ac un diwrnod cyfarfyddais ar yr heol â John Lloyd, Colerado a meddai wrthyf

"Fachgen, mae'r hen Jac yn myned i'w hedfan hi nawr" – "O ydyw" meddai
"Mi aiff yr hen Jac i Barawys yn *allright* – wyddost ti y peth cyntaf a wnaiff yno – cael gafael ym mynydd Sinai ac yna bydd wrth ei fodd yn chwilio am gerrig *slates* i doi tai, ac yna chwilio am gwrs mwyn plwm."

Gorffennais yng Nghwmaman ddechrau mis Medi 1902, ac euthum adref i Bontrhydygroes. Yr oedd Nhad a brawd i mi yn gweithio yng ngwaith mwyn plwm Cwmystwyth ac yn lodgio mewn *barracks* coed yno, - myned bob dydd Llun ac adref ddydd Sadwrn. Aethom yno i weithio fore dydd Llun – cawsom fyned i weithio i adeiliadu y dam ochr uchaf i Flaencwm. Yr oedd y Cwmni yn caniatáu awr o amser i ni gerdded i fyny a 'run peth i ni ddyfod yn ôl. Rywbryd yn y prynhawn, gwelsom fŵg mawr yn dyfod i fyny a llanw'r cwm o un ochr i'r llall; ni ddaeth i feddwl neb ohonom beth oedd wedi digwydd. Cychwynsom yn ôl tua'r *barracks,* ac er mawr syndod, wedi i ni ddyfod i lawr yr oedd y *barracks* coed wedi llosgi yn llwyr i'r llawr, a deuddeg ar hugain o lodgers wedi colli y cyfan oedd ganddynt yno, sef bwyd wythnos a'u dillad newid. Collais innau'r un peth – dillad newidiaeth, pâr o esgidiau newydd sbon a siwt o ddillad a hanner sofren felen a dau hanner coron a oedd yn fy mhoced. Cefais yr hanner sofren yn dalp bach fel marblen a chefais saith a chwech amdani gan *jeweller*. Dyna hanes y dydd cyntaf

What is a fact is that by 1908 this had become the law of the land, and I joined the Miners' Federation in May 1901 and remained a zealous unionist my whole life. In September of the same year I went to Cwmaman, Aberdare to work, and met a man there from Cwmystwyth called John Lloyd, a man of genius who'd been out to Montana and Colorado – in fact, he was known to everyone as John Lloyd, Colorado. There was another family living there from Ysbyty Ystwyth, that is John Lloyd, Pantygorlan, who was a good lead miner and had opened mountain slate quarries for the roofs of many a cottage in this parish. He'd also been prospecting a lot for lead courses. I never saw him but heard a lot about him; at this time he was very ill and one day I met John Lloyd, Colorado, on the road and he said to me:

"My boy, old Jack is going to leave us now."
"Yes he is" I said, "old Jack will get to Paradise alright - and d'you know the first thing he'll do there – find Mount Sinai, and there he'll enjoy nothing more than to look for slate to roof houses, and then search for lead ore courses."

I finished in Cwmaman at the beginning of September 1902, and went home to Pontrhydygroes. My father and a brother of mine were working at Cwmystwyth lead ore works, lodging in a wooden barracks there - going up every Monday and coming back home on Saturday. We went there to work on Monday morning – we were sent to work building the dam on the upper side of Blaencwm. The Company allowed us an hour to walk up and the same to come back. Sometime in the afternoon, we saw a great deal of smoke coming up and filling the valley from one side to the other; it didn't occur to any of us what had happened. In time we started back for the barracks, and to our great surprise, when we returned, the wooden barracks had burned to the ground completely and thirty two lodgers had lost everything they had there, that is a week's worth of food and change of clothes. I lost the same things - change of clothes, a brand new pair of shoes and a suit of clothes, a golden half sovereign and two half-crowns that were in my pocket. I found the half sovereign as a small marble-like lump, and a

yng ngwaith y Cwm. Gorfu inni gerdded adref ryw chwech milltir arall yn nawr i gael pryd o fwyd. Ni chawsom ddim *compensation* am y golled yna chwaith. Gorffennwyd mewn rhyw bythefnos o amser a dyma fi yn nawr yn gweithio ar y mwynau efo cewri'r Cwm, a chredwch fi, yr oeddent yn gewri ar lawer o bynciau, a diddorol iawn i ddyn ifanc oedd cael cymdeithasu â hwy, - amryw ohonnynt yn ddaearegwyr lled dda.

Mae *fault lode* fawr yn rhedeg trwy Cwmystwyth, mae yn cychwyn yn Grogwynion ac yn rhedeg allan i Cwm Elan. Diddorol iawn rhyw fore ar ôl cawod go drom o eira oedd clywed a gwrando ar John Roberts, Pen Cnwch, Cwmystwyth yn traco y *fault* ar hyd ochr y mynydd yn yr eira, gan fod yr eira yn toddi yn fwy cyflym ar hyd y f*ault lode*. Erbyn heddiw yr ydwyf yn sicr ei fod yn iawn, gan for O. T. Jones, M.A., D.Sc., *Professor of Geology and Mineralogy*, yn dweud yr un peth yn ei *special reports on the Mineral Resources of Great Britain*. Hefyd yr oedd llawer ohonynt yn selog rhyfeddol efo crefydd, a holi yn aml ar fore Llun am y pregethu 'roeddem wedi gwrandaw arnynt y Sul cynt, ac yr oedd yn rhaid i chwi fod yn go sicr o'r pwyntiau i gyd neu mi fyddent yn siwr o'ch cael i lawr. Clywais hanes am un ohonynt, ar adeg diwygiad 1904, - yr oeddent yn deulu mawr, tad a mam, pedwar o feibion a'u mamgu, (yr hon oedd dros ei phedwar ugain mlwydd oed). Yr oedd yr holl deulu yn awr wedi ymuno yn aelodau capel Methodistiaid y Cwm, ond un, sef y bachgen hynaf - a hwn oedd ffefryn yr hen wraig. Ac un noswaith dyma hi yn dweud,

"Yn wir" meddai, "pe buasai Tom yn ymuno â dod i mewn i'r gorlan, byddwn yn fodlon marw wedyn."
A meddai tad y meibion wrthi, "mae yn well i chwi ddweud wrth Tom ei hunan, Mam".
Pan ddaeth Tom adref dyma'r hen wraig yn dweud ei dymuniadau ac fel y byddai yn llawenychu o'i weled tu fewn i'r gorlan cyn iddi ymadael â'r fuchedd hon.
"Ie, Mamgu" meddai Tom, "faint ydyw eich oed yn nawr – pedwar ugain onide?"

jeweller gave me seven and six for it. That was my first day at Cwm works. We had to walk home about another six miles now for a meal. We never had any compensation for what we lost either. We finished in about a fortnight, and then I was working on the ore with the 'giants of the Cwm' and, believe me, they were giants on many a subject, and it was very interesting for a young man to be in their company, - many of them were quite good geologists.

The great Fault Lode runs through Cwmystwyth, starting at Grogwynion and running out to the Elan Valley. One morning after quite a heavy snow shower, it was very interesting to hear and listen to John Roberts, Pen Cnwch, Cwmystwyth, tracking the lode along the mountainside in the snow, as the snow melted quicker along the Fault Lode. By now I'm sure he was right, as O.T. Jones, M.A., D.Sc., Professor of Geology and Mineralogy, says the same thing in his special reports on the Mineral Resources of Great Britain. Many of them were also incredibly zealous in religion, and, on Monday mornings, often asked about the sermon's I'd listened to the previous Sunday, and you'd have to be quite sure of all the points or they'd surely bring you to task. I heard a story about one of them at the time of the Revival of 1904 - they were a large family, father and mother, four sons and their grandmother (who was over eighty years old). The whole family had now become members of the Cwm Methodist Chapel, all apart from one – the eldest son, who was the old woman's favourite, and one night she said:

"Truly," she said, "if Tom would join and come into the fold I'd be happy to die then."
And the father told her, "you'd better tell Tom yourself, mam."
When Tom came home the old woman told him of her wishes and how she'd rejoice in seeing him in the fold before she left this life.
"Yes, grandma," Tom said, "how old are you now – eighty isn't it?"
"Yes, my son."

"Ie machgen i", "Wel yn nawr Mamgu, faint sydd er pan ddysgoch chwi eich pader?"

Yn wir nid oedd hi yn sicr, ond ei bod yn ei wybod cyn ei bod yn chwech oed.

"Wel da rhagorol" meddai Tom, "yn nawr Mamgu, pan fyddwch wedi croesi, Pedr fydd yn eich cyfarfod, ar cwestiwn cyntaf a ofynith i chwi, 'Mary Davies, buest yn ffyddlon iawn efo crefydd Iesu o Nasareth ar hyd dy oes, dywedaist dy bader am yn agos i bedwar ugain mlynedd, yr ydwyf am iti ei ddweud tuag yn ôl heddiw'. Beth amdani Mamgu, ydych chwi yn meddwl y gellwch wneud hynny?"

Wel dyna rai o gymeriadau y Cwm.

Clywais hanes diddorol efo John Roberts yma am un cymeriad arall o'r Cwm, sef Thomas y Pentref, ag oedd wedi myned am dro i Lundain, ac wrth gwrs wedi cael pâr o ddillad newydd o frethyn cartref, a'r teilwr oedd yn y Cwm ar y pryd wedi eu gwneud i fesur, gan wneud y trowser yn dynn rhyfeddol o'r ben lin i lawr i ben yr esgid. Ar ôl iddo ddod nôl, dyma'r cymdogion yn ei holi am ryfeddodau y Brifddinas ac am y rhyfeddod fwyaf a welodd yno.

"Wel wir", meddai, "Dwn i ddim, ond yr ydwyf yn sicr mai y rhyfeddod fwyaf a welodd pobl Llundain oedd gweled Thomas y Pentref yn cerdded strydoedd y ddinas yn ei drowser tyn o waith Isaac y Teilwr. Bobl ar y ddaear, yr oedd miloedd yn cerdded ar fy ôl ym mhobman yr aethwn."

Wel ar ôl gweithio am ryw flwyddyn a thri mis yn y Cwm, daeth amser i ymadael eto â'r lle digon difyrus, efo cymdeithas mwynwyr y Cwm, gan iddynt stopio llawer iawn o ddynion am ryw amser beth bynnag, a rhesymol iawn mai ni o'r ardaloedd cyfagos oedd y rhai cyntaf. Beth bynnag, yr oeddwn i a brawd imi yn rhai ohonynt, ac nid oedd dim i wneud unwaith eto ond myned am dramp i Forgannwg. Yn Mountain

"Well now grandma, how long has it been since you learnt to say the Lord's Prayer?"

And indeed she wasn't sure, except that she knew it before she was six years old.

"Well that's excellent," said Tom, "now grandma, when you cross over, you'll be met by Peter, and the first question he'll ask you will be, 'Mary Davies, you've arrived and you've been very faithful to Jesus of Nazareth's religion all your life, you've said the Lord's Prayer for almost eighty years, and today I want you to recite it backwards', - how about it grandma, do you think you can do that?"

These are some of the characters to be found in the Cwm.

I heard an interesting story from this John Roberts about another of the Cwm's characters, that of Thomas, Pentref, who had gone on a trip to London, and of course he'd bought himself a pair of new clothes of homespun cloth, and the tailor who was in the Cwm at the time had measured him for size, making the trousers very tight from the knee down to the top of the shoe. When he came back, the locals asked him about the wonders of the capital city and the greatest wonder he saw there.

"Well really," he said, "I don't know, but I'm sure that the greatest wonder the people of London saw was Thomas Pentref, walking the city streets in his tight trousers crafted by Isaac the Tailor. People there were following my footsteps in their thousands, everywhere I went."

Well after working for about a year and three months in the Cwm it was time to take my leave again of the companionship of the miners there, as they had lain off many men from working for some time, and it was very reasonable that it was us from the neighbouring areas who were the first to go. Anyway, I and one of my brothers were among them, and there was nothing for it but to tramp down to Glamorgan once again.

Ash y llwyddom i gael gwaith a sefydlais i lawr yn y De hyd y flwyddyn 1929. Ym mis Medi o'r flwyddyn 1929 daethum yn ôl i fy hen gartref cyntefig ym Mhontrhydygroes. Erbyn hyn yr oedd fy nhad wedi marw ers rhyw flwyddyn ynghynt, a finnau erbyn hyn, fel pob dyn call arall, wedi cael gwraig, - a thri o blant ganddom. Bydd yn rhaid imi adael yr hanes y blynyddedd hyn allan o'r ysgrif hon a cheisio dod yn ôl o hyn i'r diwedd i'r ardal yma.

Cefais waith efo Mr. Nancarrow yr wythnos gyntaf wedi imi gyrraedd yn ôl ym Mhontrhydygroes, sef y nawfed o Fedi 1929; yn Frongoch unwaith eto ac i lawr i'r un shafft, sef *Braker Shaft*, yr un shafft a gychwynais weithio ynddi pan yn fachgen ifanc, ac yn '24 level' yr oeddwn yn gweithio y tro hwn. Rhyw ddeg o *finers* oedd yno i gyd yn gweithio, - wyth ar shifft y bore, a dau ar shifft y prynhawn, sef fi a John Jones o'r Porth, ac ar y ddegfed o fis Tachwedd 1929 tanwyd y rownd dyllau olaf o dyllau yn y Frongoch gan ŵr o'r enw Elias Jones, o'r un llunach â Shaci Troedyrhiw. Felly chwi welwch mai'r un hiliogaeth o bobl a'i cychwynnodd ac a'i gorffennodd. Ar ôl hyn, gadawyd yr hen waith i ddadfeilio, a bu yn gartref cysurus i'r tylluanod, ystlumod a'r crogfrain.

O hyn ymlaen, am y ddeng mlynedd nesaf, dyma y blynyddoedd mwyaf cythreulig yn hanes gweithwyr Cymru i gyd, mi gredaf. Yr oeddent yn ddigon i dorri calon unrhyw ddyn neu wraig. Os byddech yn ddigon lwcus i gael gwaith am ychydig fisoedd, dywedwch, yna seinio ar y *dole*, ac os byddech chwech mis neu fwy, byddech yn cael y *MeansTest*. Yr oeddech yn cael eich dysgu i ddweud celwydd yn ofnadwy, neu byddech yn cael eich cropio yn isel rhyfeddol yn y tâl wythnosol. Gobeithio na ddygwyddith hyn byth mwy i weithwyr Cymru. Mae edrych yn ôl dros y ddeg mlynedd hyn yn hela dynion yn sâl. Hoffwn yn fawr eu hanghofio, ond fedraf fi byth.

Wedi deng mlynedd o lonyddwch daeth rhyfel erchyll 1939, a phan gafodd y Gwarchodlu Cartref ei galw i amddiffyn eu gwlad, daeth

We managed to find work in Mountain Ash, and I stayed down in the south until 1929. In September 1929 I came back to my primitive old house in Pontrhydygroes. By this time my father had been dead about a year, and I, like every other sensible man, had found myself a wife, - and we had three children. I'll have to leave the history of these years out of this account and try to return at last to speaking about this area.

I found work with Mr Nancarrow the first week I arrived back in Pontrhydygroes, that is the ninth of September 1929, in Frongoch once again and down the same shaft, that is Braker Shaft, and this time I was working on the 24 Level. In all there were about ten miners working there, - eight on the morning shift and two on the afternoon shift, myself and John Jones from Porth, and on the tenth of November 1929 the last round of holes were fired in Frongoch at half past nine in the evening by a man called Elias Jones, of the same lineage as John Jones, Troedyrhiw. So as you see, a descendent of those who started it all off also brought it to an end. After this, the old works were allowed to fall into ruin, and it became a cosy home for owls, bats and jackdaws.

The next ten years I believe were the most fiendish years in the history of the workers of Wales. They were enough to break the hearts of any man or woman. If you were lucky enough to have work for a few months say, and then you'd sign on the dole and, if you were on the dole six months or more, you'd have a means test. You were taught to tell terrible lies or your weekly pay would be cropped severely. I hope this never happens again to the workers of Wales. Looking back over these ten years is enough to make people ill; I'd greatly like to forget them, but I'll never be able to.

After ten years of peace came the abominable war of 1939, when the Home Guard were called to defend their country. Frongoch works

gwaith Frongoch unwaith eto yn ddefnyddiol fel rhyw fath o gae brwydr i'r bechgyn, a byddai saethu a ffrwydro yn myned ymlaen yno ryw unwaith neu ddwy bob wythnos. Erbyn hyn mae'r Gwarchodlu Cartref wedi hen wasgaru, ond sefyll a wna adfeilion hen waith Frongoch.

Daeth amser gwell o lawer i'r gwaith yn 1939 trwy i'r Rhyfel Fawr dorri allan. Peth ofnadwy oedd fod yn rhaid cael rhyfel cyn i ddynion gael gwaith cyson a cyflog rhesymol amdano, ond dyna y gwirionedd. Yr ydwyf am orffen efo'r blynyddoedd hyn gan ddweud fy mod yn sicr na chafodd bron neb siwt o ddillad newydd am y cyfnod yn yr ardaloedd hyn, ond pawb yn prynu rhyw ddillad ail law. Fel trowseri ar ôl y *railway men* neu ynteu ar ôl y *policemen*. Ond o hyn ymlaen mae llawer iawn gwell graen ar bawb a phopeth, pawb yn yr ardal yn gwisgo fel y dylent, a phleser ydyw gweled pobl ar ddiwrnod unrhyw ŵyl neu ffair a dyddiau eisteddfod, dywedwch. Mae yn well hefyd ar yr hen bobl, neb megis yn trengi fel ag yn yr amseroedd cynt. Cofiaf yn dda, yn fy amser ysgol, am yr hen wragedd yn myned i fyny i Ysbyty Ystwyth i mofyn y tâl plwyf. Hanner coron yr wythnos oedd y tâl, ac os byddai un ohonynt wedi cael ffedog newydd, mawr fyddai yr holi yn lle oedd wedi ei chael, ac efallai gostwng ychydig ar y tâl wythnosol am gwpwl o droeon. Os byddai gan rai o'r hen wragedd hyn fab neu ddau, byddai yn rhaid iddynt gyfrannu tuag at y tâl o hanner coron. Hen wraig fel hynny oedd Mamgu, sef mam fy nhad. Gorfod iddo ef dalu dau swllt yr wythnos ar hyd yr amser tuag ati, allan o dair punt y mis yr oedd yn ei ennill. Nod y plwyf oedd ar Mamgu a phawb arall oedd yn derbyn a chael yr un nod. Fodd bynnag, cefais lawer i geiniog gan Mamgu y dyddiau hynny, a mawr oedd fy niolch.

Wel dyma'r wawr yn torri, sef fod Hafod Estate wedi cael ei werthu i ddyn o'r enw Mr. Tarrant, a dyma ninnau i gyd ag oedd yn seinio'r Dole yn *Post Office* Pontrhydygroes, rhyw chwech ugain ohonom, yn cael gorchymyn nad oedd neb ohonom y diwrnod hwnnw i gael seinio'r Dole heb yn gyntaf fyned i fyny i'r Hafod i ofyn am waith, ac i fyny â ni yn fintau gref. Gwelsom y gŵr Tarrant ynghyd â'i *foreman*. Dyn o'r enw Prichard. Cawsont ddychryn ofnadwy wrth weled cymaint

became useful once again as some kind of battle field for the boys, and there'd be shooting and explosions going on there once or twice a week. The Home Guard were disbanded a long time ago, but the ruins of the old Frongoch works still stand.

Much better times came in 1939 when the Great War broke out. It was terrible that we had to have a war before men could have consistent work for a reasonable wage, but that's the truth. I'll finish with these years by saying I'm sure almost no one had a new suit of clothes in this area during that period, but everyone bought second hand clothes - like trousers off the railway men or policemen. But from this time onward everyone and everything were in a much better state, everyone in the area dressing as they should, and it's a pleasure to see people on the day of any festival or fair or eisteddfod, for example. It's also better for the elderly, and no one perishes like in previous years. I well remember in my school years the old women used to go up to Ysbyty Ystwyth to ask for parish charity. This was worth half a crown a week and, if anyone had a new apron, there'd be a lot of curiosity about where she'd had it, and maybe a reduction in the weekly pay for a couple of weeks. If any of these old women had a son or two, they'd have to contribute towards the pay of half a crown. My grandmother, my father's mother, was just such a woman. He had to pay her two shillings a week the whole time, - out of the three pounds he earned every month. Grandmother and several others were also receiving parish charity. However, I was given many a penny by my grandmother in those days, and I was very grateful.

The dawn broke, and the Hafod Estate was sold to a Mr Tarrant, and all of us who signed on the dole at the Post Office in Pontrhydygroes, about one hundred and twenty of us, were told that not one of us would be allowed to sign on without first going up to Hafod to ask for work, and up we went in a great troop. We saw Mr Tarrant and his foreman, - a man by the name of Prichard. They had a terrible fright to see so many

ohonom. Yr oedd rhyw hanner dwsin wedi cychwyn gweithio y bore hynny o ardal Pontarfynach a Chwmystwyth. Gofynnodd rhai ohonom iddynt am *start,* ond chafodd neb ohonom y diwrnod hwnnw. Dywedsont wrthom am i ryw ddau ddwsin ddyfod i fyny tua hanner yr wythnos; y byddent wedi cael amser i drefnu pethau erbyn hynny. Felly y bu, ac mewn ychydig o wythnosau yr oedd pawb wedi cael gwaith, a bendith rhyfeddol oedd hynny. Dyma'r amser gorau a welodd trigolion yr ardaloedd hyn yng nghof neb sydd yn fyw.

Gwaith trwm a chaled ydoedd, ond yr oedd pawb yn ennill cyflog resymol dda, a'r ardaloedd cyfagos yma o flwyddyn i flwyddyn yn edrych yn fwy llewyrchus o lawer. Parhawyd i dorri coed am ryw naw neu ddeg mlynedd, ac ar ôl hynny mae y *Forestry Commission* yn plannu eto, a dyna'r cyfan o waith sydd yn yr ardal hon ar hyn o bryd. Yn yr amser o dorri y coed, rhannwyd hwy yn dair rhan, sef y coed mwyaf o faintioli i William Evans, rhan arall i'r *Board of Trade,* a'r rhan arall i Mr. Tarrant ei hun. Syrthiodd i'm rhan yn awr o gael myned i gwympo coed i'r *Board of Trade* ac yn y fan honno y bûm am fisoedd. Yn y misoedd hyn daeth Mr. Tarrant i wybod fy mod i a Nhad wedi bod yn cynnig am *lease* ar Hafod Estate yn 1917 i chwilio am fwyn plwm, a dyma ef yn dod ataf ryw brynhawn dydd Sadwrn – eisiau gwybod manylion megis a oeddwn yn meddwl a oedd yna 'prospect'. Dywedais wrtho y deuwn â mwyn plwm iddo o dir yr Hafod yr wythnos ganlynol. Y nos Fawrth ar ôl hynny, mi es i chwilio am blwm a daethum a baged o *lead ore* rhyfeddol o dda iddo. Anfonodd ef i Lundain ac yn fuan dyma ef yn cael gwybod y byddai *'experts'* yn dod i lawr i weled y lle. Yn awr dyma Mr. Tarrant yn gofyn i'r *Board of Trade* a fyddent cystal ag i fi gael dod yn rhydd am ryw dri diwrnod i gyfarfod â'r bobl hyn. Caniataon nhw i'r cais, a dyma finnau ar fy mhraw o flaen *Manager* ag oedd wedi dod yn ôl o Czechoslovakia o'r enw Mr. Jackson, a *geologist* o'r enw Dr. Williams, a oedd yn Gymro pur. Aeth popeth ymlaen yn bur dda a phenderfynnodd y ddau fod yn rhaid i Mr. Tarrant gael fy rhyddhau o'r *Board of Trade* yn gyfan gwbl, er mwyn i mi fod at eu gweithfeydd Plynlimon, sef gwaith Brynrafar, a phedwar arall o *finers* a oedd yn lodgo yn Nantymoch, dau arall yn

of us. About half a dozen had started work that morning from Devil's Bridge and Cwmystwyth areas. Some of us asked for a start, but none of us were given one that day. They said that about two dozen of us should return about the middle of the week, - they'd have had some time to sort things out by then. And that's how it was, and in a few weeks everyone had work, and that was a great blessing. That was the best time the people of this area ever saw – in living memory.

It was heavy and difficult work, but everyone earned a reasonably good wage, and the neighbouring areas looked more prosperous year after year. We continued felling trees for about nine or ten years, and after that the Forestry Commission would plant again, and that is the only work in this area at the moment. When the trees were felled, they were shared in three parts, that is the largest trees to Wm. Evans, another share to the Board of Trade, and the other to Mr Tarrant himself. I was now given the task of going to fell trees for the Board of Trade, and that's where I was for months. During these months Mr Tarrant came to know that my father and I had been trying for a lease on Hafod Estate in 1917 to search for lead ore, and he came to me one Saturday afternoon - wanting to know whether I thought there was a 'prospect'. I told him that I'd bring him lead ore from Hafod land the following week. And that was how it was, - the following Tuesday night I went looking and found a bagful of excellent lead ore for him. He sent it to London and before long he was told that experts would be coming down to see the place. Now Mr Tarrant asked the Board of Trade would they be willing to release me for about three days to meet with these people. They agreed to the request and I was put to the test in front of a manager who had returned from Czechoslovakia called Mr Jackson, and a geologist called Dr Williams (a Welshman through and through). Everything went very well and the two of them decided that Mr Tarrant had to have the Board of Trade release me completely, so that I could be at their service. So I went with them to the Plynlimon works, that is Brynrafar works, and another four miners – two of them lodging at Nantymoch, another

Llynaidde, Ponterwyd a finnau yn myned i fyny bron bob dydd. Buom hefyd yn agor gwaith Llwynllwyd, Ffair Rhos, ac yn amryw o lefydd eraill. Pan nad oeddwn yn gweithio ar y *mining* yma byddwn yn gweithio i Mr. Tarrant yn gwneud gwhanol *jobs*. Fi ac un arall o'r enw David Evans ag sydd byw heddiw.

Dyn digon dymunol oedd Mr. Tarrant gennyf, ond yr oedd oriau rhyfedd arno weithiau. Un prynhawn dywedodd wrthyf ei fod eisiau i mi a David Evans weithio a phlannu blodau *dahlias* iddo o flaen *mansion* yr Hafod.

"Or gorau" meddwn innau wrtho, a dyma ef yn galw ar Mrs. Tarrant ac yn gofyn iddi pa sut oedd am eu plannu.
Hithau yn ateb "*I do not know Wally, anyhow I don't want them in rows. Perhaps Jones will show us.*"
Meddwn innau, "*What about the horizontal way?*"
"*Very good idea,*" meddai Mrs Tarrant.
"*Carry on,*" meddai yntau Mr Tarrant.
"*Elias*" meddai, "*if I won't be in the office tomorrow morning; ring me up will you.*"
"*I will sir*" meddwn, a ffwrdd ag ef yn ei fotor car i Aberystwyth.

Bore drannoeth, eithum i a David Evans i'r office ond nid oedd Mr. Tarrant yno. Mae'n debyg ei fod yn potio yn drwm weithiau yn y nos, ac mi gredaf mai dyna oedd wedi digwydd y noson cynt. Dyma fi yn ringo cloch drws ffrynt y *mansion* ac mewn ychydig dyma fe yn dyfod allan atom ar hyd y corridor. Gwyddwn pan welais ef nad oedd yr hwyl yn dda o gwbl. Yr oedd yn edrych fel cythraul. Beth oedd yn ei flino yn arw iawn bob amser oedd clywed Lord Haw Haw ar y *wireless*, a dyma ef yn cyrraedd atom i ddrws y ffrynt, a meddwn

"*Good Morning Mr Tarrant.*"
"*Good morning men. Have you got your tools with you. Where are they?*"
"*Here they are.*"

two in Llynaidde, Ponterwyd, and I went up there nearly every day. We also opened Llwynllwyd works, Ffair Rhos, and a number of other places. When I wasn't doing this mining work I'd be working for Mr Tarrant – doing various jobs, myself and another called David Evans who is still alive today.

Mr Tarrant was a pleasant enough man, but he'd go into strange moods sometimes. One afternoon he told me he wanted me and David Evans to plant dahlias for him in front of Hafod mansion.

"Very well," I said, and he called on Mrs Tarrant and asked her how she wanted them planted.
She answered, "I do not know Wally, anyhow I don't want them in rows; perhaps Jones will show us."
I said, "What about the horizontal way?"
"Very good idea," Mrs Tarrant said.
"Carry on," said Tarrant then.
"Elias," he said, "if I won't be in the office tomorrow morning ring me up will you?"
"I will, sir," and off he went in his motor car to Aberystwyth.

Next morning, I went with David Evans to the office, but Mr Tarrant wasn't there (apparently he sometimes drank heavily during the evening, and I think that's what had happened the night before). I rang the mansion's front door bell and in a while he came out along the corridor. I knew when I saw him that he wasn't in a good mood at all - he looked like the devil, and what always irked him greatly was listening to Lord Haw Haw on the wireless, and when he got to the front door I said:

"Good morning Mr Tarrant."
"Good morning men, have you got your tools with you? Where are they?"
"Here they are."

Gofynnodd *"Where are your picks and shovels?"*
"We have no picks and shovels. We have not been using such tools for many months."
"Here you are Elias Jones, you are no different from every other Welshman. Coming to me and begging for work and you have no tools."

Cynhyrfais i waelod fy modolaeth, a dyma fi yn ei annerch fel hyn.

"Mr Tarrant, I beg to differ with you. In the first place you are wrong because I never asked you for work. You came to me when I was working with the Board of Trade and begged me to come and work with you when you had the Mining Engineers around here. What have you got to say about the Welshman? Look here, Mr Tarrant, over a thousand pits have been sunk in Glamorgan and Monmouthshire in the last hundred years, and all of them were sunk by Cardiganshire miners. You never turned out their equal in Surrey. I know we've got our faults, but we have got our virtues. Don't you read your papers nowadays. Didn't you see in your paper that they drove ten miles of tunnel in the rocks of Gibraltar for the Defence of the Realm and all of it was driven by 85% of Welsh miners and a good percentage of them had their roots in the hills of Cardiganshire. Now, Mr Tarrant, I make a gamble with you today. Whatever our faults, Wales will never turn out a Lord Haw Haw."
Chwarddodd allan a dywedodd, *"That's worth a pot of ale any time"*, a nôl ag ef drwy'r *hall,* a dyma ef yn dod a llond jwg o *ale* i fi ac yntau a David Evans.

Cawsom ymgom go dda o hynny ymlaen am wahanol bethau oedd arno eisiau gwneud. Beth bynnag, ar ôl hyn nid ydwyf yn credu fy mod wedi cael yr un gair croes ganddo tra bu byw, ac yr oedd hynny yn rhai blynyddoedd beth bynnag. Gwyddai Mrs Tarrant, ei wraig, y cyfan am y storm bore hwnnw. Gwyddai hefyd ei fod yn barchus ryfeddol ohonof ar ôl hyn, ac wedi iddo farw yn sydyn iawn un noson, nid oedd neb ond

"Where are your picks and shovels?"

"We have no picks or shovels, we have not been using such tools for many months."

"Here you are Elias Jones, you are no different from every other Welshman, - coming to me and begging for work and you have no tools."

This agitated me to the core, and I addressed him as follows:

"Mr Tarrant, I beg to differ with you. In the first place you are wrong because I never asked you for work. You came when I was working with the Board of Trade and begged me to come and work with you when you had the mining engineers around here. What have you got to say about the Welshman? Look here, Mr Tarrant, over a thousand pits have been sunk in Glamorgan and Monmouthshire in the last hundred years, and all of them were sunk by Cardiganshire miners. You never turned out their equal in Surrey. I know we've got our faults, but we've got our virtues. Don't you read your papers nowadays – didn't you see in your paper that they drove ten miles of tunnel in the rocks of Gibraltar for the Defence of the Realm and all of it was driven by 85% of Welsh miners and a good percentage of them had their roots in the hills of Cardiganshire? Now, Mr Tarrant, I make a bet with you today, - whatever our faults, Wales will never turn out a Lord Haw Haw."

And he laughed out loud and said, "that's worth a pot of ale anytime", and back along the hall he went and came out with a jug full of ale for me and him and David Evans.

We had a good conversation from then on in about different things he wanted to do. Anyway, after this I don't think I had one cross word with him while he lived, and that was a few years at least. Mrs Tarrant, his wife, knew everything about the fuss that morning; she also knew that he had great respect for me after this, and after he died very

y fi i dorri ei fedd mewn craig ym mynwent Eglwys Newydd yr Hafod. Wel heddwch i'w llwch bellach.

Cyn tynnu i derfyn yr ysgrif hon, rhaid imi dalu teyrnged i rai o bethau gorau a gefais ar ddwylaw a gofalon eraill, sef y cefais gartref clyd a gofalus ar aelwyd Nhad a Mam. Mwynheais fywyd teuluol dymunol. Breintiwyd fi â chyfeillion di-rif a didwyll. Nid oes gennyf gŵyn yn erbyn bywyd.

Eto pan aethum yn ŵr, credaf i mi gael cymar mewn gwraig orau a allwn feddwl amdani, a dwynodd ein plant i fyny yn ofn yr Arglwydd, ac er fy mod wedi ei cholli ers pedair blynedd ar bymtheg, teimlaf golled o'i chwmni heno gymaint ag erioed. Er hynny mae gennyf fab a dwy ferch sydd wedi myned oddi cartref cyn marw eu mam, ond eto sydd â'u gofal yn fawr iawn amdanaf ar hyd yr amser maith yma. Nid peth hawdd ydyw cadw fy meddwl ar y gorffennol fel ag ydwyf wedi ei wneud yr wythnosau diweddar yma – myn amgylchiadau'r dydd sylw; yn wir yn y dyddiau helbulus hyn ar y byd, tuedda'r meddwl i ganoli ar drafferthion heddiw ac argoelion yfory. Pan fo'r presennol yn gorhawlio'r meddwl a'r dyfodol yn ddi-olau, âf am dro a dringaf i ben clogwyn uchaf y banc yma. Yno syrth amser i gyfartaledd gwell. Syllaf ac edrychaf i'r De Orllewin a gwelaf eglwys plwyf Ysbyty. Yng nghladdfa'r Eglwys gorffwys gwyr a gwragedd a adwaenwn yn dda. Atgofia'r cerrig beddau fi y bydd yn rhaid i minnau hefyd ddilyn y llu a aeth ymlaen. Yn nhawelwch y bryniau teimlaf hi yn naturiol i edrych yn ôl. Pleser puraf bywyd yw meddwl, ac ymgodymu â phroblemau deall a moes. Yn wahanol i lawer pleser arall, y mae'n ddigymysg.

Llawer iawn o bethau eraill a gofiaf yn yr ardal, sef y felin i falu blawd, y *factory* wlân a'r gwehydd. Hefyd clywais ddweud mai i'r Hafod y daeth yr aradr haearn cyntaf. Peth arall, mai yn Dologau y gwelwyd y ci defaid cyntaf yn yr ardal. Peth pwysig arall yr ydwyf wedi ei adael allan yw bywyd yr hen *finers,* a rhai mor gynnil oeddent efo llosgi canhwyllau. Byddent yn cael pedwar pwys o ganhwyllau rhwng pob dau *finer,* ond pan fyddent yn tyllu tyllau byddent bob amser yn

suddenly one night, there was no one but me to cut his grave in rock in Eglwys Newydd Cemetery at Hafod. May he rest in peace.

Before drawing this essay to a close, I must pay tribute to some of the best things in my life, I had a cosy home on my mother and father's hearth; I enjoyed a pleasant family life, and had the privilege of having many a true and honest friend. I have no complaints about my life.

Again when I became a husband, I believe I found a partner in my wife who was the best I could imagine, and she brought up our children in fear of the Lord, and though I have lost her these last nineteen years, I feel the loss of her company tonight as much as ever. Even so, I have a son and two daughters who left home before their mother's death, but who have taken great care of me all this time. It hasn't been easy to keep my mind on the past as I have done these last weeks – the affairs of the present day preoccupy my mind, - indeed during these turbulent times for the world the mind tends to focus on today's troubles and tomorrow's portents. When the present is forefront in the mind and the future dark, I go for a walk and climb to the top of the highest crag on this hill, - there time falls into better proportions – I stare and gaze towards the south west and see Ysbyty Parish Church; in the church graveyard rest men and women I knew well, and the gravestones remind me that I too will have to follow the host who proceeded onward. In the silence of the hills it feels natural to look back, - thinking is life's greatest pleasure, grappling with the problems of understanding and morality, - and unlike many another pleasure, it's pure.

I remember many other things about the area, such as the mill to grind flour, the woollen mill and the weavers. I also heard it said that the first iron plough came to the Hafod, and another that the first sheep dog in the area was seen in Dologau. Another important thing I've left out of the life of the old miners is how thrifty they were when it came to burning candles, - they would have four pounds of candles between every two miners, but when they dug holes they'd always do so by the

gwneud hynny wrth olau un gannwyll, fel ac y byddent yn gallu safio rhyw bwys neu ragor i'w rhannu rhyngddynt i fyned â hwy adref i oleuo eu tai.

Dyma fi heno, gan fod yr amserau wedi newid gymaint, yn ysgrifennu y nodion hyn yn y bwthyn hwn wrth ddigon o oleuni trydan.

Mawr yw fy mraint. 'Rwyf yn ddiolchgar am y cyfan.

light of a single candle, so that they'd be able to save about a pound or more to share between them to take home to light their homes.

Times have changed so much that here I am tonight, writing these notes in this cottage with plenty of electric light.

Great is my privilege. I am grateful for it all.

3
Atgofion am Sir Forgannwg o Ebrill 18fed 1901 hyd Medi 1929
Reminiscences of Glamorganshire from 18th April 1901 to September 1929

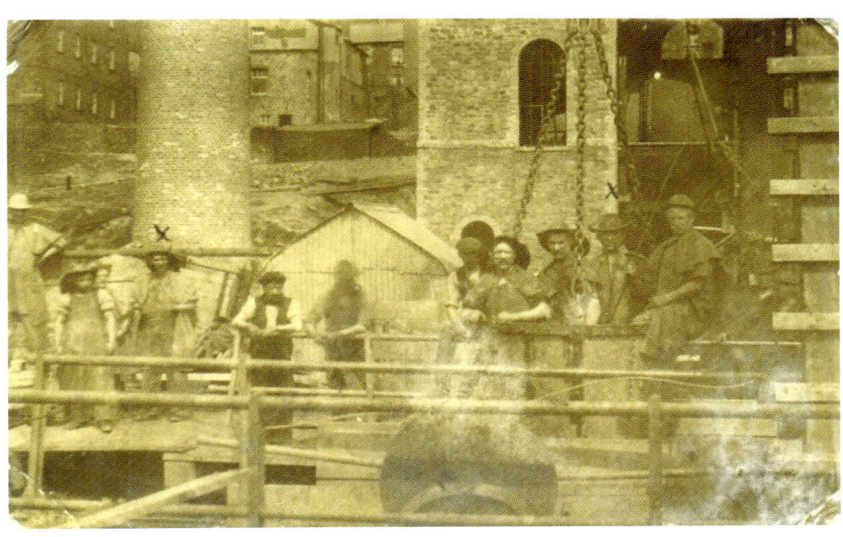

Cerdyn post oedd yn perthyn i Elias ar y chwith. Ar y cefn 'Morgan Jones a minnau sydd dan y groes'.

Postcard belonging to Elias on left. On the back 'Morgan Jones under the cross and myself'.

Nid yw'n ymddangos fod Elias wedi cwblhau'r cofiant hwn gan ei fod yn gorffen tua 1905.

Elias does not seem to have completed this memoir as it finishes around 1905.

Atgofion am Sir Forgannwg o Ebrill 18fed 1901 hyd Medi 1929

Gan mai 'Atgofion unrhyw ardal yn Sir Aberteifi' oedd testun yr atgofion a ysgrifennais o'r blaen, gorfod imi adael rhyw gwarter canrif allan, sef o 1901 hyd 1929. Cychwynnaf bellach ar Ebrill 8fed 1901. Dyma'r tro cyntaf imi a'm brawd, oedd ddwy flynedd a hanner yn iau na mi, adael cartref. Cofiaf yn dda gynghorion fy nhad cyn inni gychwyn; meddai "cofiwch fod yn fechgyn da a dilynwch gwmni fyddwch yn credu eu bod yn well na chi, yn rhoi eu hunain i bethau rhinweddol a da. Mynychwch y Capel yn gyson fel y byddwch yn ddiogel. Gwnewch yn siwr eich bod yn bwyta'n dda neu ddaliwch chi ddim ohoni, fe gewch gymaint ag a allwch ei wneud o waith, fydd dim amser segur o'r cychwyn hyd ddiwedd y 'turn ", a gwir oedd hynny bob gair.

Cawsom 'lodging' rhagorol gyda gŵr a gwraig o Ferthyr. Wedi cael gwaith ym Mhwll Glo Abercynon a mynd â'n bocs dillad i'n cartref newydd a'i agor i gael gafael yn ein dillad gwaith, beth oedd yng ngwaelod y bocs ond dau Destament Newydd newydd sbon, wedi cael eu rhoddi yno gan ein hannwyl fam heb ddweud yr un gair amdanynt wrthym. Credwch fi, mi lynodd hynny wrthyf weddill fy mywyd.

Cychwynsom weithio yr un bore ond ni chawsom fynd i'r un ardal, ein dau yn mynd i wahanol gyfeiriad. Cefais i fynd efo dyn o'r enw Richard Evans a oedd yn wreiddiol o Quaker's Yard, dyn gofalus rhyfeddol ydoedd ohonof, bob amser yn fy rhybuddio am beryglon y "top".

Un bore ymhen rhyw wythnos pan aethom at ein gwaith 'roedd yno gwymp go fawr yn ein disgwyl a dyma ni ati o ddifri i'w glirio mor fuan ag oedd bosibl er mwyn i'r coliers gael drams i lanw'r glo. Yr oedd lle i dair dram gael eu llanw ar yr un pryd ac 'roedd chwech ohonom yn eu llenwi. Dywedodd Richard Evans wrthyf am newid lle ag ef a mynd i lanw dram arall am ei bod yn saffach i mi lanw honno, ac y llanwe fe yr un oeddwn i wedi cychwyn gan fod y top ddim yn rhyw saff iawn wrth

Reminiscences of Glamorganshire from 18th April 1901 to September 1929

As the subject of my previous Article was 'Reminiscences of an area of Cardiganshire', I was obliged to omit a period of more than a quarter century, from 1901 to 1929. I therefore start on 8th April 1901, which was when I and my brother, who was two and a half years younger, left home for the first time. I well remember my father's advice before our departure, which was "remember to be good boys and keep company with those you believe to be better than yourselves, and who adhere to good and virtuous ways. Attend chapel regularly, so as to keep yourselves safe. Make sure you eat well or else you won't be able to keep going; you'll find as much work as you can manage, there will be no time for idleness from the start to finish of each shift" – and how true were his words.

We had excellent lodgings with a husband and wife from Merthyr. After finding work at Abercynon colliery, and after taking our box of clothes to our new home and opening it to take out our working clothes, what we found at the bottom of the box were two brand-new New Testaments, placed there by our dear mother without her mentioning it. Believe me that left an impression with me for the rest of my life.

We both started work the same morning, but rather in two different directions. I was sent with a man by the name of Richard Evans who was originally from Quakers' Yard; he took great care of me, always reminding me of the dangers of the "top", or roof.

One morning, after a week or so, when we came to work we came face to face with a substantial rock-fall, and we had to set about clearing it as soon as possible in order that the colliers could have their drams to fill them with coal. There was space for loading three drams at the same time, and six of us worked together to load them. Richard Evans told me to change places with him and to load another of the drams as it would be safer for me, and he would carry on where I'd started, as the

ben honno, a dyna fuodd. Pawb 'nawr yn llanw â'u holl egni a phan oeddem bron â gorffen llanw'r ddram gyntaf dyma Richard Evans yn gweiddi am i bawb gilio 'nôl, a dyna wnaed. Pan welais Richard wedyn 'roedd yr ochor arall i'w ddram ac 'roedd carreg fawr wedi disgyn ar ei droed a'i thorri yn glir i ffwrdd tu ôl i fysedd ei droed. Y gorchwyl nesaf oedd cael yr ambiwlans i stopio ei waed a mynd ag ef adref i Quaker's Yard. Mi fu bron i minnau ddianc adref am fy mywyd hefyd i Sir Aberteifi.

Dynion fel Richard Evans a welais bron bob amser ar hyd fy nhaith yng Nglofeydd Morgannwg. Ni allaf dystio eto i mi hoffi bod yn Abercynon, er fod yno ddynion cyfeillgar a doniol. Cyn hir ar ôl y digwyddiad hwn, cefais fynd i weithio efo dyn o'r enw John Double Power ac yn wir roedd yn enw ardderchog arno gan ei fod yn ddyn nerthol rhyfeddol ac yn grefyddol iawn, yn or-dduwiol efallai.

Un Saboth ym mis Gorffennaf euthum i gyfarfod pregethu'r Bedyddwyr yng nghwmni llawer eraill i wrando ar y genadwri , ac yno gwelais John Jones yn mwynhau ei hun yn fawr, gallwn feddwl. Y dydd Llun canlynol yn y pwll glo, a llawer ohonom gyda'n gilydd yn bwyta tamaid o fara a chaws ar y 'Parting Dwbwl', yn eistedd nesaf at John Jones roedd dyn o Nelson o'r enw Shoni Wasgod Felfed. Dyn canol oed a thipyn yn rheglyd hefyd. Ymhen ychydig dyma John Jones Double Power yn dweud wrthyf "gwelais di yng Nghapel y Bedyddwyr brynhawn ddoe Elias; beth oedd dy farn am y bregeth dwed". Minnau yn ei ateb fy mod yn credu ei bod yn bregeth ragorol iawn, "Wel oedd fachgen", meddai John Jones Double Power, "yr oedd yn fendigedig a theimles fy hun yn cael bendith o dan y genadwri." A dyma Shoni Wasgod Felfed yn ei ateb "dim cyn bod ei heisiau arnoch chi, John Jones." Llawer o ddynion tebyg i hynna oedd ym Mhwll Glo Abercynon. Ni allaf ddweud imi hoffi bod yn y lofa eto, a phan ddaeth mis Awst adref yr aethom ein dau, mi a'm brawd i helpu fy nhad efo'r cynhaeaf gwair.

roof wasn't too safe at that end - and that's what happened. Each one loading for all their might, and when we had almost finished loading the first dram, Richard Evans shouted out for everyone to take cover, and that's what we did. When I next saw Richard he was the other side of the dram and a large boulder had fallen on his foot and had severed it at the base of his toes. The next task was to get the ambulance to stop the bleeding and to take him home to Quakers' Yard. That almost caused me to flee for my life, back home to Cardiganshire.

It was men like Richard Evans that I came across, almost without exception, during my time in the Glamorgan collieries. I can't say that I liked being in Abercynon, although the men there were friendly and humorous. Soon after that incident, I was put to work with a man called John Double Power, and it was indeed a most appropriate nickname as he was a remarkably strong man, and was very religious - perhaps too godly.

One Sunday in July, I went to a special preaching service with the Baptists, along with a number of others, to listen to the sermon, and there I saw John Jones, enjoying himself immensely or so it seemed to me. The following Monday in the pit, whilst many of us sat together in the 'double parting', sitting next to John Jones was a man from Nelson known as Shoni Wasgod Felfed (*which means Shoni Velvet Waistcoat*) a middle-aged man who swore quite a lot. In a short while, John Jones Double Power said to me "I saw you in the Baptist Chapel yesterday afternoon, Elias. What did you think of the sermon?" I answered that I thought it an excellent sermon. "Well yes, boy", said John Jones Double Power "it was wonderful and I felt myself getting a blessing from the message given." And Shoni Wasgod Felfed came in like a shot: "and not a minute too soon for you John Jones." There were many characters like that at Abercynon Colliery. I can't say that I liked being down the pit and when August came, back home we went, my brother and I, to help our father with the hay harvest.

Cychwynodd fy mrawd weithio efo nhad yng ngwaith Cwmystwyth ac euthum innau yn ol i'r De, i Gwmaman, Aberdâr y tro hwn. Yr oeddwn wedi meddwl cael gwaith efo John Lloyd, Colorado, gan ei fod â chontract dreifio 'heading' caled.

Roedd tair shifft ar bob 'heading' a phedwar o ddynion yn gweithio ar bob shifft. Euthum i weld John Lloyd a gofyn iddo am waith ond 'roedd yn anobeithiol gan fod ganddo un-ar-ddeg o weithwyr, ac yntau yn eu gwneud yn ddeuddeg. Doedd dim gobaith o gwbwl meddai "ond paid â phryderu dim, machgen i" meddai, "mae heding caled arall wedi cychwyn ers wythnos efo John Jones Cardi Byr, mi âf â thi yno nawr i'w weld". Ac aethom ein dau i dŷ John Jones a dyma John Lloyd yn gofyn iddo am waith i mi, a rhoddi iddo fy mhedigri i gyd gan ddweud na fuodd gwell fy nhad a'i deulu am handlo arfau tir caled erioed.

"O", meddai John Jones "mi fydd yn dda gennyf ei ddechrau, Lloyd, ond cychwyn un shifft arno ydym eto; ymhen tair wythnos byddwn yn barod i gychwyn dwy shifft arall arno a bydd yn dda gennyf ei ddechre y pryd hynny; mae'n edrych yn ddyn ifanc cryf." "Wel mae'n rhaid iddo gael gwaith yn rhywle am y tair wythnos hyn." "Dere fyny gyda fi i ben y pwll, Elias, mi welwn y manager neu'r under-manager rwy'n siwr." Ac i fyny â ni.

Nid anghofiaf yr hanner awr hynny tra byddaf byw, Thomas Isaac yr under-manager a welsom, a dyma John Lloyd yn dweud wrtho yn syth ei fod am iddo roddi gwaith imi am dair wythnos, hyd nes byddai Cardi Byr yn barod i ddechrau tair shifft ar yr heading caled, ac yna y buaswn yn cychwyn ar un o'r shiffts hynny. Tybiodd Lloyd nad oedd yr under-manager yn rhoi fawr o sylw i'r hyn oedd yn ei ofyn, a dyma fe'n rhoddi tipyn o hanes fy nhad a hyd yn oed fy mamgu, hen wraig mor ragorol oedd wedi bod iddo ef pan oedd yn gweithio yn hogyn deuddeg oed yng ngwaith Lisburne Mines ac yntau yn lodjo ganddi. Bob nos cyn mynd i'r gwely, meddai, yr oeddwn yn cael llond *glass* mawr o laeth *fresh* o'r fuwch,

My brother went to work with my father in the Cwmystwyth Mine, and I returned to the south, this time to Cwmaman, Aberdare. I had thought of finding work with John Lloyd, Colorado, as he had a contract for driving a 'hard heading'.

There were three shifts on each heading, and four men working on each shift. I went to see John Lloyd to ask him for work but it was hopeless, as he already had eleven men and he himself made up the twelve. There was no chance, he said, but "don't worry my boy, another hard heading has opened up a week ago with John Jones Cardi Byr (*meaning 'Short Cardi'*) and I'll take you to see him." We both went to John Jones' house and John Lloyd went about asking him for work for me, giving him my pedigree and saying that there was never anyone better than my father and my family for handling implements for cutting hard surfaces.

"Oh" said John Jones "I'll be glad to give him a start, Lloyd, but we're only starting one shift at the moment. We'll be ready to start two shifts in three weeks' time and I'll be happy to take him on then. He looks a strong lad. Well, he's got to have some work somewhere for these three weeks, so come up to the pit-head with me, Elias, and I'm sure we'll see the manager or the under-manager." And up we went.

I'll never forget that half-hour. We saw Thomas Isaac the under-manager, and John Lloyd told him straight away that he wanted to give me work for three weeks, until Cardi Byr was ready to start three shifts on the hard heading, when I would be able to work on one of those shifts. Lloyd thought the under-manager was hardly paying any attention to what he was asking, so he gave him a bit of my father's history and even my grandmother's, who had been so good to him when he was lodging with her as a twelve year old lad working in the Lisburne Mines.

"Ddyn" meddai "rwy'n bownd o gael gwaith i'r dyn ifanc 'ma."
"Fachgen, Lloyd", meddai, "yr wyt yn haerllug ofnadwy."
"Wel", meddai Mr Isaac wedyn "oes rhaw gennyt?"
"Nagos" meddwn inne.
"Wel bydd rhaid i ti brynu rhaw a starto bore fory. Mae gennyf waith iti ar waelod y pwll, ac aros ar y gwaelod nes dof i lawr"
"O'r gore!" meddwn inne.
"Thomas" meddai Lloyd wedyn, "bydd yn rhaid i ti dalu hwn gyflog tir caled o'r cychwyn ac nid arian labrwr cofia."
"Wel fachgen", meddai Thomas, "'rwyt ti'n hynod o feiddgar heno, gawn ni weld."

Cychwynais fore drannoeth a chefais waith ar waelod y Pwll i dorri lle i'r pibau, ar ôl pedwar o'r gloch y prynhawn roedd *fitters* yn dod i'w cysylltu a minnau'n gweithio 'mlaen wedyn bob nos efo nhw a chael hanner "turn" yn ychwanegol a chyflog y buaswn yn ennill yn yr "Heading Caled", a hynny trwy i John Lloyd Colorado siarad mor uchel amdanaf. Ymhen wythnos gorffensom y gwaith efo'r pibau ar waelod y Pwll a chefais orchymyn i fynd efo dyn o'r enw Ioan Isaac, mab i'r Dirprwy Reolwr, Thomas Isaac. Gwaith hollol ddieithr imi, sef rhannu'r awyr i wahanol gyfeiriadau o'r gwaith. Yr oedd yn ddiddorol dros ben a dysgais lawer a fu'n help mawr imi am flynyddoedd wedyn.

Wedi i'r pythefnos ddod i ben cychwynais weithio ar yr 'heading caled' gyda dyn o Ysbyty Ystwyth o'r enw Richard Lewis, Maesybeudy, a bu'n ofalus iawn ohonof. 'R oedd yno dair shifft gyfan yn awr, pedwar o ddynion ar bob shifft a phob shifft yn newid â'u gilydd yng ngwyneb yr *heading* i mewn ddwy filltir o waelod y pwll. Gwaith hanner awr o gerdded i mewn ac hanner awr arall i ddod allan. Shiffts wyth awr oeddent yn eu galw ond yr oeddent yn naw awr bob un gan ein bod yn cerdded am awr. Rhaid cyfaddef er hynny fy mod wedi mwynhau'n

"Every night before going to bed", he recalled "I had a large glass of milk from the cow." " Look man" he said "I must find work for this young man."

"Lloyd my boy" said Mr Isaac "you're being very forward."
Then he said to me "Have you got a shovel?"
"No" I replied.
"Well, you'll have to buy a shovel and start tomorrow morning. I've got work for you at the bottom of the pit, and stay at the bottom till I come down."
"Fine" I said.
"Thomas" said Lloyd afterwards, "don't forget you'll have to pay this boy for cutting hard rock, and not just a labourer's wage."
"Well boy," said Thomas "you're chancing it tonight aren't you? We'll have to see."

I started the next morning and had work at the bottom of the pit, cutting a rut for pipes. After four o'clock in the afternoon the fitters came to connect them, and I then worked along with them every night, getting an extra half-shift and earning the wage I would have got in the hard heading, because John Lloyd Colorado had spoken so highly about me. Within a week, we had finished the work on the pipes at the bottom of the pit, and I was ordered to go with a man called Ioan Isaac, the son of the Deputy Manager, Thomas Isaac. The work was new to me; it involved diverting the air to different sections of the pit. It was very interesting, and I learnt a lot that stood me in good stead for the years that followed.

After a fortnight, I started working on the 'hard heading' with a man from Ysbyty Ystwyth - Richard Lewis, Maesybeudy, who took great care of me. There were by now three full shifts, four men on each shift, and each shift changing over on the face of the heading, some two miles in from the bottom of the pit shaft. It took us half an hour to walk in and another half-hour to come back out. They were called eight-hour shifts, but each took us nine hours as we spent an hour walking to the coal-face and back. Nevertheless, I must admit that I very much

fawr yn y gwaith glo. Yr oeddwn wedi arfer digon efo nhad mewn gwaith mwyn plwm, sut i drin yr offer, 'roeddwn yn teimlo ac yn gwybod mai fi oedd y meistr arnynt erbyn hyn. Roeddwn hefyd yn dechrau deall y ddaear lo a deall sut i osgoi'r peryglon ac ar yr un pryd hefyd dod i adnabod 'shonis' Morgannwg. Dynion brawdgarol iawn oeddynt a theimlwn yn hollol gartrefol yn eu cwmni.

Aeth Richard Lewis, Maesybeudy, adref yn y Gwanwyn i hau hâd ar y tyddyn bach ac fe syrthiodd i'm rhan innau gymeryd y flaenoriaeth yn lle Richard ar y shifft hynny, a llenwais ei le yn ogoneddus; mawr oedd llawenydd John Lloyd Colorado fod ei broffwydoliaeth wrth ofyn am waith imi wedi ei gwireddu. Dysgais lawer iawn yn ystod y cyfnod hwn. Dysgais gymaint gyda John Lloyd mewn gwerth gwahanol strata o'r tir wrth setlo am bris nes 'roeddwn yn sicr bob amser fy mod ar yr ochr iawn, a dilynodd yr athrawiaeth hon a ddysgais gan John Lloyd fi hyd ddiwedd fy amser yn y gwaith glo.

Gorffenwyd yr 'heading caled' yn nechrau'r mis Awst canlynol ac euthum adref i helpu fy nhad i gael ei gynhaeaf i ddiddosrwydd, dyma'r adeg y dechreuais weithio yng ngwaith Cwmystwyth; 'rwyf wedi rhoddi'r hanes hynny mewn pennod arall.

Ar ôl gorffen yng Nghwm Ystwyth ym mis Rhagfyr 1903 euthum i a David, fy mrawd, i ffwrdd unwaith eto am y De. Ar ôl teithio yn hir llwyddasom o'r diwedd i gael gwaith yn Clydach Vale. Nid oedd yn waith da iawn a'r gyflog yn bur isel ac fe benderfynsom ein dau symud i Aberdâr tua diwedd mis Mawrth a chawsom waith yno ar dir caled. Gweithiem o dan ddau gontractor a chael y gyflog uchaf a oedd yn cael ei thalu mewn unrhyw fan, a hynny o fewn pythefnos o gychwyn yn Aberdâr.

Cofiaf y newyddion yn dod fod "explosion" fawr wedi digwydd yn Clydach Vale yn y pwll lle'r arferem ein dau weithio ynddo. Draw â ni i weld beth oedd wedi digwydd gan fod amryw o bobol o'r gymdogaeth hon yn gweithio yno ar y pryd, a balch oeddem o ganfod fod pawb

enjoyed being in the colliery. I was used to working with my father in the lead-mine, learning how to use the implements, so I felt that I could by now master them. I was also getting to understand the coal-face and how to avoid the dangers, whilst also getting to know the Glamorganshire characters, whom we call 'Shonis'. They were very brotherly, and I felt very comfortable in their company.

Richard Lewis, Maesybeudy, returned home in the spring to sow seeds on his smallholding, and it fell to me to take the lead role on the shifts in place of Richard. I filled his shoes honourably, and John Jones Colorado was delighted that I had fulfilled the prophecy he made when pleading for work for me. I learnt much during this time. I learnt so much with John Lloyd about the differing values of each strata of ground when settling a price, to the extent that I was always confident of being right, and this expertise that I learnt from John Lloyd remained with me throughout my time in the colliery.

The 'hard 'heading' was completed at the beginning of the following August, and I returned home to help my father get the hay harvested. This was the time I began work up at the Cwmystwyth mine, as I've recorded in another chapter.

After finishing at Cwmystwyth in December 1903 I, together with my brother David went away again to the south. After a long journey, we managed to get work in Clydach Vale. It wasn't very good work, and the pay was poor, so we both decided to move to Aberdare towards the end of March and had work on Hard Ground. We worked for two contractors and received the highest wage paid anywhere at the time, and all that within a fortnight of starting at Aberdare.

I remember receiving news that a huge explosion had taken place in Clydach Vale, in the pit where we had been working. Off we went to see what had happened, as several people from this community were working there at the time, and we were very glad to find that all of them

ohonynt wedi dod allan yn ddiogel y tro hwn. Roedd tua 24 o ddynion aeth lawr yn y caets cyntaf wedi eu lladd ac Edgar Davies, ein "fireman" wedi ei losgi'n golsyn. Yn drwm iawn ein traed yr aethom yn ôl i Aberdâr.

Hoffais fy ngwaith yn fawr o dan y ddau gontractor hyn, tua thrigain a deg ohonom i gyd. Eu henwau oedd William Davies oedd yn enedigol o Bontrhydfendigaid, a Richard Davies yn enedigol o Lanidloes, dau ddyn digon teilwng o'r cyfrifoldeb oedd wedi disgyn arnynt.

Gweithiai'r rhan fwyaf ohonom ar waelod y pwll yng ngwythien naw, lle erchyll, a'r gwythiennau hynny yn bump troedfedd ar hugain yn y clir a llathed o waith masiynaid cerrig reit o gwmpas. Roedd yna lawer o ddaear yn cael ei symud i bob naw troedfedd i bob *arch*. Buom yno am rai blynyddoedd ac yn ffodus ddigon ni chafodd unrhyw un ei anafu.

Un gŵyn fawr oedd gennyf yn erbyn y gwaith oedd yr arferiad o dalu cyflogau bob pythefnos, a thalu pawb yn y Dyffryn Vaults Hotel, casgenni cwrw bob ochor a'r ddiod yn dod mewn jwgiau swllt. Cychwyn talu am hanner dydd bob yn ail ddydd Sadwrn. Gallaf eich sicrhau na yfais yr un dafn o ddiod erioed yn y Vaults beth bynnag, er nad oeddwn yn llwyr ymwrthodwr ar y pryd. Gwelais lawer o'r gweithwyr tua chwech neu saith o'r gloch wedi yfed trwy'r prynhawn nes oeddynt yn feddw chwil ac wedi gwario llawer o'u cyflogau. Gorfod i'r 'Miners Federation' gymryd y mater i fyny, ac mewn blynyddoedd rai, llwyddasant i wneud yr arferiad hynny yn anghyfreithlon drwy basio deddf seneddol. Yn dilyn hynny bu'n rhaid talu ar ben y pwll a rhoddi *paysheet* a stamp y Cwmni i bawb ar ei diced.

Roedd 1904 yn flwyddyn bythgofiadwy yn hanes Cymru, y flwyddyn y torrodd Diwygiad Evan Roberts allan. Cafodd Aberdâr ran ohono fel pob ardal arall, cyfarfodydd fore a hwyr a barhaodd hyd ddiwedd 1905. Bum yn bresennol yn y rhan fwyaf ohonynt a mwynhau fy hun yn fawr, ond ni allaf ddweud imi deimlo dim rhagor o deimladau crefyddol nad oeddwn wedi eu teimlo lawer o weithiau ynghynt. Nid fy lle i yw eu

had escaped safely on this occasion. Around 24 men who had gone down the first pit-cage had been killed, and Edgar Davies, our fireman, had been burnt to a cinder. It was with heavy hearts that we returned to Aberdare.

I greatly enjoyed my work under these two contractors; there were around seventy of us in all. Their names were William Davies, a native of Pontrhydfendigaid, and Richard Davies who came from Llanidloes, two men who were well worthy of the responsibility placed upon them.

Most of us worked at the bottom of the pit on coal-seam nine, a horrible place, and those seams had a clearance of twenty-five feet, with a yard of masonry surrounding it. There was much rubble to be moved, with a length of nine foot to each arch. We worked there for some years and we were very fortunate that no-one was injured.

One of my great complaints against the work was the practice of paying wages every fortnight, and everyone being paid them at the Dyffryn Vaults Hotel, with beer-barrels on each side and drinks being served in shilling jars. Payments were handed out at midday, every other Saturday. I can assure you that I never drank a single drop at the Vaults, although I was not a teetotaller at the time. I saw many of the workmen who had been drinking throughout the afternoon, until they were drunk by six or seven in the evening, having spent a good part of their wages. The Miners' Federation had to take the matter in hand, and some years later they managed to make this practice illegal by an Act of Parliament. Thereafter, payments had to be made at the pit-head, and every worker given a pay sheet and the company's stamp imprinted on their dockets.

1904 was an unforgettable year in the history of Wales, the year when Evan Roberts' Revival started. Aberdare experienced it, as did other areas, with morning and evening services which went on until the end of 1905. I attended most of them and enjoyed myself immensely, but I can't say that I felt any more religious than I had felt on many occasions previously. It's not for me to judge.

barnu. Roeddwn wedi deall cyn hyn nad oedd gan yr "Hen Grefyddwyr" selog fawr iawn o sêl tuag at y "Miners' Federation" fel y cyfryw, a'r prynhawn yma darllenais dipyn ar gofiant Edward Mathews, Ewenni, gan J. J. Morgan yr Wyddgrug gynt, ac ym mhennod XXIX (tudalen 378) mae'n beirniadu, ergydio a gwawdio'r "Miners' Federation".

Dyma Mabon, ebe William Abraham wrth Mathews,
"O chi yw awdur 'Mabon's Days'"
"Ie" atebodd Mabon,
"Devil's Day" ebe Mathews, a throdd ei gefn arno. Cyfeirio oedd at y dydd Llun cyntaf yn y mis yr hwn a enillwyd yn ddydd gorffwys i'r glowyr.

Wel dyna ddigon, mi gredaf fy mod wedi barnu'n deg am yr hen grefyddwyr selog gynt. Credaf fod y diwygiad yma, sef 1904-1905 wedi newid dipyn ar ôl hyn gan i lawer roddi cefnogaeth i'r Miners' Federation er cael pasio'r Act of Parliament.

I had understood before then that the old brigade of ardent religious leaders had very little to say for the Miners' Federation as such, and I read this afternoon some of the biography of Edward Mathews Ewenny, by J J Morgan, Mold, in which he criticises, attacks and mocks 'the Miners' Federation in chapter XXIX (page 378).

"Here's Mabon", said William Abraham to Mathews.
"Oh, you're the instigator of the Mabon's Days?"
"Yes" replied Mabon.
"Devil's Day" said Mathews, and turned his back to him. He was referring to the first Monday in the month, which had been secured as a rest day for coal miners.

I'll leave it there. I think I've given fair judgement on the ardent old religious leader. I believe attitudes to this 1904-1905 revival did change somewhat in the years that followed, as many did give their support for a Miners' Federation with a view to getting the Act of Parliament passed.

4
Llythyr oddi wrth Emilio Invernizzi
Letter from Emilio Invernizzi

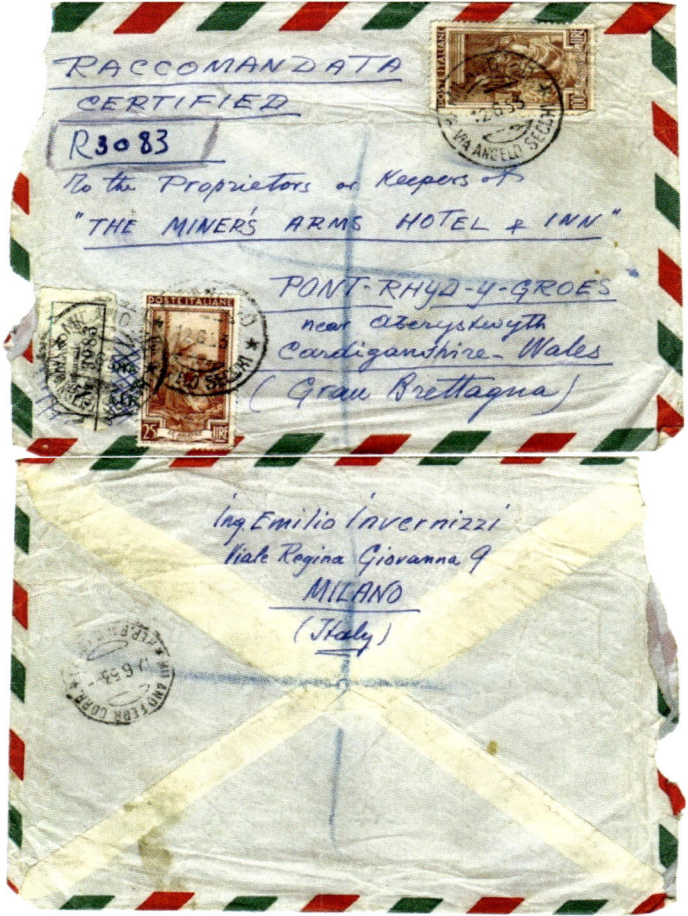

Llythyr a gafwyd ynghanol eiddo Elias oddi wrth beiriannydd Eidalaiddd a fu'n gweithio o dan Nogora ym Mhwll Frongoch.

Letter found in Elias' belongings from an Italian engineer who worked under Nogora at the Frongoch Mine.

ING. Emilio INVERNIZZI MILAN (Italy) June 10ᵗʰ 1953
Viale Regina Giovanna 9

(I would advise you to begin reading the Second sheet !!)

Messrs. The present Proprietors or Keepers of "MINER'S ARMS HOTEL & INN.
PONTRHYD-Y-GROES
(near Aberystwyth — WALES
(Cardiganshire)

Dear Sirs,

in the "ancient times" of Queen Victoria, the Boer-War etc. (from January 1899 to August 1902). I lodged at the "Miners' Arms", which was then the property of Mr. Lloyd and the two daughters Mary and Peggy (these Ladies, in 1901, moved to Aberystwyth (Caerwys Terrace), and the Hotel was afterwards managed by Mr. Hepburn, a Scottish Gentleman, formerly "Keeper" of Hafod-Park, close to Pontryd-y-Groes.

(*) who kept also the POST-OFFICE and a SHOP.—

(Devil's Bridge)

I was, at that time, a very fresh & young Engineer, working under the direction of Eng.ʳ Nagara at the FRONGOCH Mine: and we had the help of about 100 italian workmen, apart from the very sympathetic welsh-miners, under the management of old "Captain Owen". (good singers!)

In consequence, for more than 3½ years, I rode every day (on horseback and afterwards with a Humber bycicle!) back and fro to the Mine.

I have a vivid recollection of these journeys, in winter with frost and snow, in summer, and particularly in the beautiful welsh springs —

Especially, I remember with relish the sweet-bitter perfume of the white bunches of flowers of "haw-thorns" (or "white-thorns), i.e. the thorny bushes of the hedges, particularly at the border of the road climbing up the hill and reaching the "ROW" of miners-lodging and a certain "Store" kept by a very simpathetic old welsh Lady, who was "very proud" of "her meat", meaning her "home-cured hams" (..!!)

Now, after more than 50 years (at the age of 78!) I feel a very keen longing for the sweet-bitter perfume of those thorny bushes, and I would pay anything if I could grow some bushes in the small garden that surrounds my little country-house near Varese.

./.

ING. Emilio INVERNIZZI   Milan (Italy) June 10th 1953
                          Viale Regina Giovanna 9
(I would advise you   Mssrs The present Proprietors or
to begin reading the   Keepers of "MINER'S ARM'S
Second Sheet!)   HOTEL & INN"
                          PONTRHYDYGROES
                          (near Aberystwyth, WALES,
                          Cardiganshire)

Dear Sirs,
    in the "Ancient Times" of Queen Victoria, the Boer War etc. (from January 1899 to August 1902), I lodged at the "Miner's Arms, which was then the property of Mrs. Lloyd and the two daughters, Mary and Peggy*. These ladies, in 1901, moved to Aberystwyth (Caeryng Terrace), and the hotel was afterwards managed by Mr Hepburn, a Scottish Gentleman, formerly "keeper" of Hafod-Park, close to Pontrhyd-y-groes.
    I was, at that time a very fresh & young engineer, working under the direction of Eng err(?) Nogora at the FRONGOCH Mine and we had the help of about 100 Italian workmen, apart from the very sympathetic Welsh miners (good singers!), under the management of old, "Captain Owen".
    In consequence, for more than 3½ years, I rode every day (on horseback and preferably with a Humber bicycle!) back and for to the mine.
    I have a vivid collection of the journeys in winter with frost and snow, in summer, and particularly in the beautiful welsh springs.
    Especially I remember with relish the sweet, bitter perfume of the white bunches of little flowers of "hawthorns" (or "white thorns") i.e. the thorny bushes of the hedges, particularly at the border of the road climbing up the hill and reaching the "ROW" of miners-lodging and a certain "store" kept by a very sympathetic old welsh lady, who was "very proud" of her meat", meaning her "home-cured lamb" (!!)
    Now, after more than 50 years (at the age of 78!), I feel a very keen longing for the sweet-bitter perfume if I could grow some bushes in the small garden that surrounds my little country-house near Varese.

If you, Gentlemen, have had the patience of reading so far (and the possibility of understanding by bad, half-forgotten English!), you will guess the purpose of this letter. —

Would it be possible for you to let me send (in the proper season) some sound branches (or roots) of haw-thorn (white-thorn), or seeds (if feasible), so that I could replant them in my Varese garden? — Perhaps a local gardener could advise the best way to follow.

Of course, any expense you should incur into I would be very glad to recognise and pay through a Bank or postal-order. —

I hope you will be so kind to forgive my "cheek" and the trouble I cause to you —

Thanking you in advance for a kind answer, I remain

yours truly

η. Emilio Turbinizzi

Post-Scriptum. I always lived in the big corner-room of the first floor, at the left of the front of the Hotel. How many nights I passed in the private drawing room downstairs, *poking the open fire-grate and* singing with Misses Lloyd the songs of the Boer-War (... I pass the hat, for your credit's sake, and pay, pay, pay!!" — (xx)
During my stay in Wales both your Great Queen Victoria and our King Umberto passed to a better World!
The Jonpsch. Mine is still working? or, has it been abandoned?? —
If working, the Management is British or foreign??

Excuse the trouble —

E.

If you, Gentlemen, have had the patience of reading so far (and the possibility of understanding my bad, half-forgotten English!), you will guess the purpose of this letter.

Would it be possible for you to let me send (in the <u>proper season</u>) some <u>sound branches or roots</u> of haw-thorn (white-thorn), or <u>seeds</u> (if feasible), so that I could replant them in my Varese garden? Perhaps a local gardener could advise the best way to follow?

<u>Of course, any expense</u> you should incur into, <u>I would</u> be very glad to recognise <u>and pay</u> through a Bank or postal-order.

I hope you will be so kind to forgive my "cheek" and the trouble I cause to you.

Thanking you in advance for a kind answer,

I remain
yours truly,
Sr Emilio Invernizzi

Post Scriptum

I always lived in the big corner-room of the first floor, at the left of the front of the Hotel. Howe many nights I passed in the private drawing room downstairs poking" the open fire-grate and lingering with Misses Lloyd the songs of the Boer-War (.. pass the hat for your credit's sake, and pay, pay, pay!!**

During my stay in Wales both your <u>Great Queen Victoria</u> and our <u>King Umberto</u> passed to a better World! <u>The Frongoch Mine</u> is still working? Or has it been abandoned? If working, the management is British or Foreign? Excuse the trouble, Ing

About 1933, Miss Peggie (married to Mr Graham King of "<u>Walkover Shoe</u>" came to Italy and was our guest in <u>Milan</u> – but I have lost her direction in London!

*who kept also the POST-OFFICE and a shop (Devil's Bridge)
** We also used to sing, often "Daisy, Daisy give me an answer do, I can't afford a carriage but you look so nice upon the seat of a bicycle built for two!"

5
Llythyr: Lead Mining or Fishing?
Letter: Lead Mining or Fishing?

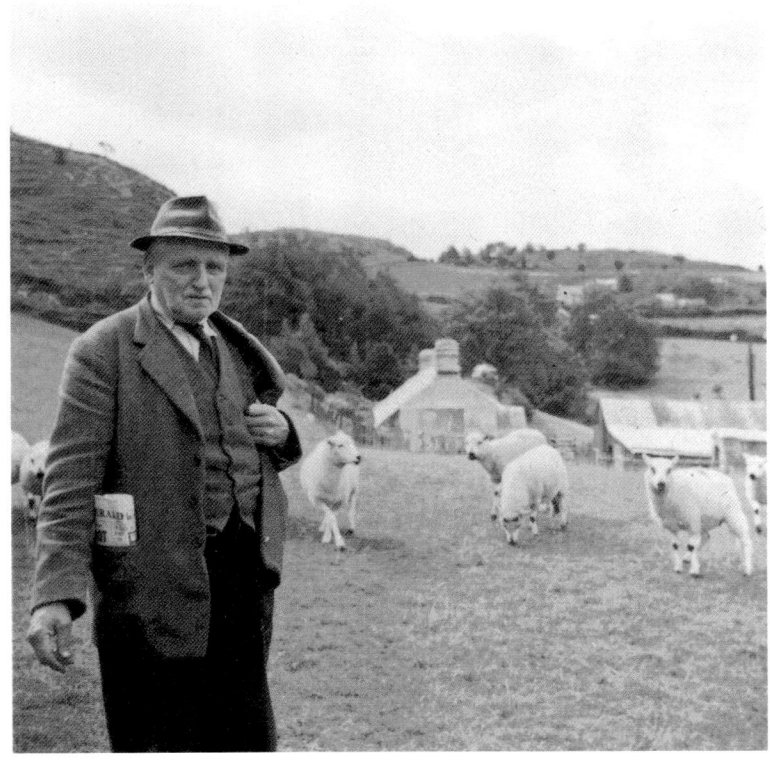

Elias gyda'i ddefaid yn Nhroedyrhiw
Elias with his sheep at Troedyrhiw

Llythyr gan Elias Jones a gyhoeddwyd gan y Welsh Gazette, Dydd Iau, Gorffennaf 13eg, 1944.

Letter by Elias Jones published by the Welsh Gazette, Thursday July 13th 1944.

To the Editor of the 'Welsh Gazette.'

Sir, - I was pleased to read the letter on "Lead Mining or Fishing?" by Mr. John Jones, Wandsworth Common. I agree with everything he said. I started my career as a miner, as a young lad, under my father's supervision at Frongoch Mine in 1894 under Mr. Kitto, and I continued under then Belgian company which took over in 1898 and until 1901. Also I came back to work under Mr. Nancarrow in 1929, and happened to blast the last round of holes in November of that year, in the very shaft where I had started to work as boy. I also worked 18 months at Cwmystwyth Mines during the years of 1902-03.

If I had my time over again, I would not wish for any other work than mining. But I should like to see the conditions of work improved, such as ventilation and improvement in wages. I am convinced that the early deaths in the district were due to these two factors – bad ventilation and poor wages, rather than to anything inherently evil in lead mining itself, as your correspondent "Son of a Lead Miner" seems to suggest. By the way, I worked in a certain place at Cwmystwyth for six weeks, and had I continued for six months in the same place I would have been in my grave 40 years ago, but I was sensible enough to leave it for the coal mines. The majority of places in Cwmystwyth mines were not fit for any human being to work in, as the levels were dead ends, with no ventilation.

I can trace my family back on both sides to about 1785, when they were working at the Lisburne mines, and they all lived to a decent age. My father worked 54 years as a lead miner and died at the age of 80 without suffering any ill-effects from lead mining. But I always considered him a very wise person. I cannot recollect seeing him returning to examine the result of the blasting, as many young miners did, coughing for hours afterwards as a result of the smoke.

I consider that I have a right to speak on mining as a career, having had practical experience of both lead and coal mining. I still work every day

in quarrying stone, and I feel myself strong both mentally and physically, and able to hold my own easily with younger men.

Now we come to face the issue, and I hope that at the end of this war we will be leaving the iron age for the age of reason, and bury the past, and start a new world. Whatever we do, let us give men a chance to work for their living in their native land, whether on the soil, or on the banks of a river, or in the bowels of the earth. The latter can be made quite as healthy as the first two.

I am sure that if there is wealth in North Cardiganshire, i.e., north of a line drawn from Talybont and through Llanafan, that it lies in the possibility of finding great deposits of lead ore and blende ore for generations to come. I tried my utmost, with Mr. Tarrant, of Hafod Estate, in 1941 and 1942, to draw the attention of the government to this possibility and we were successful in getting Dr. Williams the eminent geologist, and Mr. Jackson, a mining engineer, and other government engineers to investigate the district from Hafod to Plynlimon. Mr. Tarrant and Clr. D. J. Davies also interviewed Mr. D. O. Evans, M.P. on the matter.

The Art of Mining

I myself would rather work again till the end of my days in mining, than to be left to the mercies of the Means Test system. In my estimation the Means Test system killed more in the last 25 years than lead mining did in a century. It should be remembered that mining is in itself a very fine art, well worth preserving. Cardiganshire miners have done well in the last century. Every pit that was sunk in South Wales and Monmouthshire, and they were well over 300, was sunk with about 85 per cent Cardis. The remainder were North Walians from the slate quarries. All of them were skilled men in mining, it should be remembered that Cardiganshire men have done well all over the world. Men from Pontrhydygroes and Cwmystwyth and Goginan explored the first lead ore in Bute, Montana. One of them was my uncle on my mother's side.

Now to come nearer home. I read in 1942 of how 10 miles of tunnelling was driven through the Rock of Gibraltar for the defence of the Realm. This work was properly ventilated, and furthermore 85 per cent, of the workmen were South Wales miners, the majority of whom I believe had their roots in Cardiganshire.

Whatever we do in the future, let us destroy nothing that is good. Let the rivers be kept clean so that the trout and other fish live until the angler comes around with his rod and line. But also let the lead mines be opened out all over the county. I believe there is plenty of brain in the land to work them economically with proper ventilation, as the collieries have been ventilated in the last quarter of a century and without polluting the rivers. Also I think we ought to educate some of the young men in mining, so that some of them could go in for mining engineering and be professors of geology and mineralogy, so that young miners of the future could serve under men of their own country, instead of having foreigners like Heine and Nogara and Invernezzi, etc. I hope the young men of the future will demand progress of this kind, instead of being driven to Labour Exchanges for another 25 years.

– Yours, etc., ELIAS JONES. Troedyrhiw, Pontrhydygroes.

6
Anerchiad gan Elias Jones
Speech by Elias Jones

> Mr Chairman,
>
> I never intended to speek a word in this meeting to day. But my mind have gone back this evening after (hearing) listing to all the speehis, to about 60 years ago I was talking to and old gent, just my age now, and watching a child learning to crawl, and the old gent said, We shall only begin to walk when we have plenty of Railways. You dont realise how true that is. I couldnt understand at first what

Anerchiad mewn llaw-ysgrifen a ddarganfuwyd ymysg eiddo Elias, ynglyn â'r angen am drydan ym Mhontrhydygroes.

Hand written speech found in Elias' belongings on the need for electricity in Pontrhydygroes.

Mr Chairman,

I never intended to speak a word in this meeting today, but my mind has gone back this evening after (hearing) listening to all the speeches, to about 60 years ago. I was talking to an old gent, just my age now, and watching a child learning to crawl, and the old gent said, 'We shall only begin to walk when we have plenty of railways'. You don't realise how true that is. I could not understand at first what the old gent meant, but he explained after that railways were essential to the progress of the Country. By today we can't grumble about our railways and road transport. But again we are in mid Wales lacking much behind in power, and we can't go on with the work that is to be done in the future. We are only learning to crawl instead of going along and doing the work as we ought to in this modern age, and today I am going to appeal to you, Sir David, to help Wales with all your might to give us power in this part of our old Country.

We have work and will work but begging we are ashamed of. To prove to you Sir David that there is work in our bones, an old pal of mine who is two years older than what I am had come down one night to an inn in our village to have a glass or two. So he thought by putting spirits down, that his spirits would rise up and by going home that night which was about two miles from the inn. His pals had walked faster than him and they turned back to see where he was. And there was Jack talking to a wooden post and asking what sort of a place was Heaven and answering himself. They do say that they'll be playing the harp to all eternity, I won't like at all because I am not much of a musician. Will they be mowing down hay with scythe, will they be cutting peat there, if not, I don't want to go there at all. So there you are, that proves to you that there is plenty of work like old Jack in us all. So all I ask you Sir David, stick to us.

So all I ask you Mr H… is do your utmost to extend the electricity power to Ffair Rhos and Pontrhydygroes which are old mining districts and ought to be explored once again and before they will be explored

we must have power and, believe me, I believe that there is as much mineral ore in the bowels of the old hills of Ffair Rhos and Pontrhydygroes as ever that was mined in the last 200 years, and I can prove to you from the records of the mines that mountains of lead and silver went from these two villages and the top price per ton that was paid for this ore was only about £28 a ton. Why not try again when the ore is so scarce in the world today and the price today is over £120. Give us power so that somebody will come along and do some prospecting work again. They are walking round now and again already. A company of three men came to me at the end of September last to see about the mineral rights of Hafod Estate. They told me that they were coming again and what was worrying them that day was where was the electric power of the village. So I ask you today Mr ……., do something for the sake of the young people and perhaps for the yet unborn.

7
Erthyglau Papurau Newydd
Newspaper Articles

7.1   Development at Pontrhydygroes
7.2   Speech Night at Pontrhydygroes: Two Opening Ceremonies
7.3   Minister arrives in a Jeep
7.4   Views on Water Supplies
7.5   The Minister called at the Ty-Un-Nos
7.6   Ninepence for a nine-and-half-hour day – a grey past and a blacker future

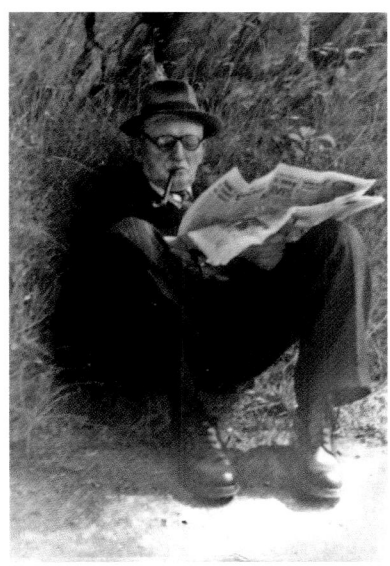

Elias

Hen erthyglau papurau newydd a ddarganfuwyd ymysg eiddo Elias, sy'n rhoi blas o fywyd ardal Pontrhydygroes yn y gorffennol.

Old newspaper articles found in Elias' possessions, which give a flavour of the life in Pontrhydygroes in the past.

7.1 Development at Pontrhydygroes
Cambrian News, Friday 4th June 1954

NEW HOUSES AND ELECTRICITY SUPPLY

Clr. Richard Ebenezer, chairman of the Tregaron Rural District Council, officially opened the new Maesyderi Housing Estate at Pontrhydygroes last Friday evening. In a short speech he referred to the good work of the local member, Clr. John Jones on the Council, and added that many difficulties had been overcome He was glad that the land had been obtained without a compulsory purchase order. The houses, he said, were an asset to the village and a credit to the Council. He hoped that the families who came to live in the ten houses would make them into real homes. He thought that the general deterioration in the homes of Britain was responsible for the problems facing the country at present. Mr. Ebenezer paid tribute to the work of the housing contractors (Richard Davies and Son, Llanfarian).

The Vicar, the Rev. W. M. Davies, offered prayer.

GRAND TRADITION

Mr. Roderic Bowen Q.C., M.P., said he was glad the houses had been built In the middle of the village and in the shadow of the Chapel. Congratulating the Tregaron R.D.C. he said he was glad they had a sharp enough scissors in the Tregaron Office to cut through the red tape. Mr. Bowen referred to the grand tradition of the village and said that here the homes were homes in the true sense of the word

Mr. W S P. Cotterrel, the Architect, thanked the Tregaron R.D.C for its patience towards him and his staff.

The speakers were introduced by Mr. Elwyn Howells, clerk to the Tregaron R.D.C.

After Clr. Ebenezer had unlocked the door of number nine, Maesyderi, and declared the estate open, those present inspected this three-bedroomed type house.

A £14,000 SCHEME

Later the same evening Mr. Roderic Bowen pressed a button In Bethel Wesleyan Chapel, and the light came on. He was opening officially the electric light supply to the district. As he pressed the switch, Mr. Bowen said he would welcome the opportunity to perform a similar function in other villages in the near future. He did not want people to waste electricity but he appealed to them to make full use of it, and not to switch on just to light the oil lamp or on Sundays only as one old man of his acquaintance was in the habit of doing. He paid tribute to the local craftsmen and said that the electrical industry should attract more Welsh boys than it does.

The Rev. D. Lewis Evans offered prayer.

Clr. R. Ebenezer also appealed to those who had electricity to make full use of it.

Cir. John Thomas, vice-chairman of the Tregaron R.D.C., said that the inhabitants of Pontrhydyroes should honour their local member, Clr. John Jones, as he had done much for them.

Mr. J Holloway, Aberaeron district commercial manager of the South Wales Electricity Board, revealed that it had cost some £14,000 to bring electricity supplies to the village, and he hoped the people would make full use of it.

Mr. C. Thomas, assistant district manager stressed that the Board ran a free advisory service and gave free demonstrations to all who requested them. He also stated that there was a scheme where electrical appliances could be paid for over a number of years.

Mr. Gareth Jones, assistant engineer also spoke.

NEED FOR INDUSTRY

Last of the speakers was Mr. **Elias Jones**, Troedyrhiw, oldest member of the local Parish Council. Mr. Jones doubted if the present generation with electricity would see as much as their fathers did with the reed candle. The speaker, a former lead miner said that electricity brought power as well as light He stressed the need for work in the area and suggested that Pontrhydygroes should invite the light engineering works that Aberystwyth had rejected.

The meeting was presided over by Mr. J T. Owen, M.A., Aberaeron, a native of Ysbyty Ystwyth. He said that he was glad to be back in the area and that he still took a great interest in the people. Mr. Owen touched on the problem of rural depopulation and said that no answer could be found to it unless amenities were brought to rural areas. It was a loss that so many brilliant pupils left the county to take up work elsewhere, and he was glad when he found some of them returning to the land.

A vote of thanks was proposed by CIr. T. Caradog Edwards and seconded by Clr. John Jones. The ladies of the village provided refreshments to those invited.

7.2 Speech Night at Pontrhydygroes

Eight – The Cambrian News and Welsh Farmers' Gazette, Friday 4th June 1954

TWO OPENING CEREMONIES

FRIDAY night was ceremony night at Pontrhydygroes. Roderic Bowen, Q.C., M.P., was there to see the official opening of the Council houses and to officially "switch-on" the national electricity supply.

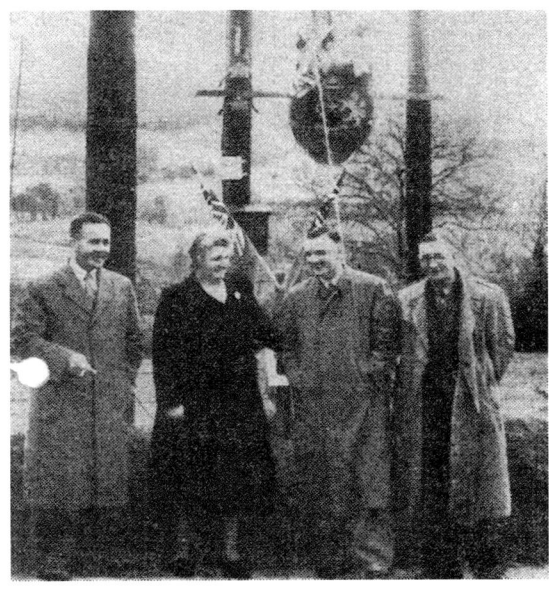

Low clouds frequently dropped light rain, but the folk showed their interest in civic events by lining the roadway overlooking the Council houses four deep. And then flocked up to Bethel Chapel, where they listened respectively to an hour of eulogistic speeches. The Clerk to Tregaron Rural

Mrs. Elizabeth Jane Jones, Tynporth, Ysbytty Ystwyth, with Officials of the South Wales Electricity Board, at the handing over by her of the private electricity undertaking she had conducted for the last twenty-six years.

In the picture (from left to right): Mr. D.C. Gwyn, Tenby, sub-area manager; Mrs. Elizabeth Jane Jones; J. Holloway, Aberaeron, district commercial manager, and Cllr. F. R. Gregg, Lampeter, district engineer.

Council (Mr. Elwyn Howells), the housing authority for Pontrhydygroes, presided outside No. 9, Maesyderi, the house that was officially opened by the Chairman (Cllr. Richard Ebenezer). There were no slip-ups here, he was given the right key by Mr. Howells and the front door swung open easily.

Speaking in Welsh from the doorstep Cllr. Ebenezer could be heard clearly by the people 40 ft. away on the road, for the empty house behind him was a sound box and echoed his words to the crowd

No C.P.O.

Pontrhydygroes people, he said, owed many thanks to their local member, Cllr. John Jones, who was largely responsible for having the houses built there. Cllr. Ebenezer was glad too, that it had not been necessary to compulsory purchase the site. He hoped the tenants of the houses would keep them in good condition, for he thought the condition of homes was deteriorating which was a reflection of the state of the world today. He congratulated the contractors. Mr. Richard Davies and Son, Llanfarian, for the workmanship in the houses

The Council's Architect (Mr. W. P. Cotterell) thanked all for their co-operation, and said most people wanted to know why could not more houses be built. Although this was a free country, he said the answer was the red-tape that was slowing down housing progress. Mr. Cotterell suggested that Mr. Roderic Bowen visit the Council Chamber to see the red-tape himself.

Sharp Scissors

Mr. Bowen congratulated the local member on his efforts to get houses built in Pontrhydygroes. His answer to the red-tape problem was that the Tregaron Rural Council should sharpen the scissors in their offices.

Prayer was offered by the Rev. W. M. Davies, Ystrad Meurig and Ysbyty Ystwyth, and then the councillors inspected the house. All

trapesed through the house admiring design and workmanship, leaving their muddy footmarks all over the clean floors. Miss Blodwen Evans, the tenant-to-be of the house, did not seem to mind. "I'll soon clean it up," she said.

Quite leisurely everyone walked up the hill to Bethel, where Mr. J. T. Owen, headmaster of Aberayron Secondary School, and a native of Ysbytty Ystwyth, presided.

Clamour

Thanking the Ysbytty Parish Council for inviting him to preside, Mr. Owen said nothing gave him more pleasure than to hear of the success of a local boy or girl.

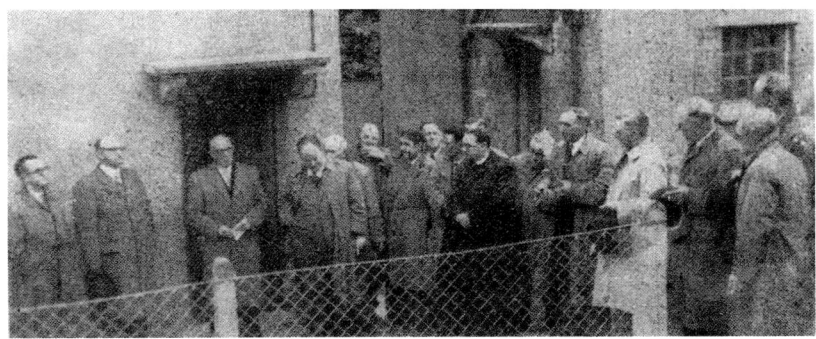

A "Cambrian News" picture of the official opening of the Tregaron Rural Council's housing site at Maesderi, Pontrhydygroes. The chairman (Mr. Rd. Ebenezer) is seen in the doorway, and also in the picture are Mr. Roderic Bowen, Q.C., M.P., and officials and members of the Council including the clerk (Mr. Elwyn Howells) on the extreme left.

He said those present were about to witness the switching on of the electricity, an act for which scores of rural areas were clamouring. On rural depopulation, he said unless the necessary amenities were provided they could not expect young people to remain.

Mr. Roderic Bowen said the electricity authority itself provided employment for young folk as did the forestry, but the proportion of Welsh who took up such careers was lamentable. He paid tribute to the improvement of electrification in the county, but added that it was not at a rate commensurate with the problem of depopulation

The button and the sack

He urged the people in the newly electrified area to make use of the electricity. He told of one consumer who only used the electric light to see to light the oil-lamp!

Pressing a button on a little black box in front of him he said: "If nothing happens now somebody is going get the sack!"

But no-one did, for the chapel was lit at the touch of the button.

Cllr. Rd. Ebenezer also appealed to people to use more electricity. Cllr. J. Thomas, vice-chairman of Tregaron Council, told the audience to honour their local member who had done much for them.

Cost of £14,000

Mr. S. Holloway (district commercial officer, South Wales Electricity Board) disclosed that it had cost about £14,000 to bring the supply to Pontrhydygroes.

Urging more use of the facility, he told the story of the consumer who tried unsuccessfully for a week to blow the light out! Mr. C. T. Thomas (assistant district manager) explained the S.W.E.B. home-visiting advisory service

Others who spoke were Mr. Gareth Jones (assistant engineer) and Mr. **Elias Jones**, Troedyrhiw, the oldest member of the Parish Council, whose suggestion to stop the rural drift was that Pontrhydygroes should

invite to the district the engineering firms that had been refused premises in Aberystwyth.

Shook hands

All were thanked by County Councillor T. Caradoc Edwards and Cllr. John Jones.

Catering by the ladies of the chapel had been done on a generous scale and there were platesful of food left over. Mr. Bowen stayed long enough to have a hasty snack before he left for the Mayor-making ceremony at Lampeter. He shook hands all round, almost, not forgetting a word for the hard working ladies in the kitchen.

7.3 Minister arrives in a Jeep
Source unknown but after 12th September 1956

Visitors to Cardiganshire by Government official and ministers are not new. In fact quite a number have visited us during the past year or two but, Mr. J. Enoch Powell, Parliamentary Secretary to the Ministry of Housing, did it the hard way on Wednesday. He bumped his way into Cardiganshire in a jeep along the little-used mountain road from Abergwesyn to Tregaron allowing his visit to Llanwrtyd Wells.

He was accompanied, among others, by Mr. F. Blaise Gillie, Under Secretary to the Welsh Office of the Ministry, and Mr. G. Ryle, Director, Forestry Commission.

Mr. Powell said he was on a "fact-finding tour" of Rural Wales to see the countryside for himself and discuss with local Councils, housing, water and general problems of finance.

At Pontrhydygroes he made an unscheduled stop at a cottage he had spotted oil the hillside - Troedyrhiw. He had a long chat with the occupier, Mr. **Elias Jones**, on living conditions in the area, and complimented him on the excellent way in which he had renovated the cottage.

He passed through Hafod, Devil's Bridge and Ponterwyd on his way to Aberystwyth to have an informal discussion at the County Offices with officials and representatives of the County, Town and Rural Councils.

Mr. Powell told "The Cambrian News" after the meeting that he had learned a lot from his visit to Cardiganshire and that talks had been very informative.

Area of special need

After saying that the complex problem of the county's finances had been put to him, he said the Government were carrying out a review of local government finance and it was hoped, under the new system, that the special circumstances and needs of an area would be taken into account when allocating Government grants.

The outline of the main proposals for reform of local government finances would be communicated to local authority Associations within the next few months.

It is understood that Mr. Powell had been told during his talks with Council officials that Cardiganshire has been particularly hard hit under the new assessment revaluation and the loss of exchequer equalisation grants (a total loss in the region of £180,000). Aggravating the problem in Aberystwyth was the fact that all the large buildings connected with the University College and also the National Library of Wales have been exempted from paying the new assessments. Cardiganshire, Cambridgeshire and Caernarvonshire are the only three counties in the country which are suffering in this respect.

Improvement Grants

Emphasising the use of improvement grants, Mr. Powell said it may well be in the scattered rural area the use of these grants for improving standard housing conditions would avoid the necessity of demolition. Quite a number of houses now deemed temporarily unfit could be saved by improvement grants.

Combined schemes

He said Cardiganshire was an interesting county from another point of view. It was the example of the way in which water undertakings had been regrouped. There were nine county districts in the county, and seven had recently grouped themselves into a single Water Board and

were going ahead with a joint water scheme. At a time when capital expenditure had to be strictly limited, the suitability and competence of the bodies spending the money on new work on water supply was a matter of public importance. "Money must not be sunk in local schemes where larger and better schemes would be produced by regrouping," said Mr. Powell, and added that a new Ministry circular on the advantages of regrouping was to be issued this week. He hoped Aberystwyth Borough and Rural Councils would find it possible to combine in a water scheme in the same way as had been done in the south of the county.

Later in the day Mr. Powell visited Dolgelley, and before returning to London on Thursday met Ald. Huw Edwards, chairman of the Council for Wales and Monmouthshire at Corwen.

7.4 Views on Water Supplies

Cambrian News, Friday September 14th 1956

RE-GROUPING ADVOCATED

Mr. ENOCH POWELL, Parliamentary Secretary to the Ministry of Housing and Local Government, who made a three-day tour of Wales last week, visited the Mid-Wales area which was recently the subject of a survey by the Welsh Agricultural Land Sub-Commission.

On Wednesday last he travelled from Llanwrtyd to Aberystwyth where, at a Press conference in the evening, he referred to the essential dove-tailing of certain policies in with what was going to be the economic future of Cardiganshire and other Mid-Wales counties.

IN STEP

The "big three" on the Government side in future development activities would be the Heads in Wales of the Ministries of Housing and Local Government and of Agriculture Fisheries and Food, and also of the Forestry Commission in Wales. It was important that they and local government authorities should keep in step in this problematic area of Mid-Wales.

VERY INTERESTING

Referring to his meeting with the representatives of the Aberystwyth Rural and Borough Council and of the Cardiganshire County Council, Mr. Powell said: "We went over the field pretty well." One point emerged from the discussion which he felt was very interesting and encouraging and that was the emphasis which was placed on the use of housing improvements grants. It could well be, said the Minister that in a scattered rural area the use of these grants for improving the standard of houses would avoid the necessity for demolition and replacement. And that quite a number of houses technically unfit could be dealt with

more satisfactorily and more economically by means of the improvement grants, "and the figures given to me were quite encouraging," he added.

GOOD EXAMPLE

Cardiganshire, he said, was an interesting county from another point of view. It was a good example of the way in which water undertakings have been regrouped. There were nine county districts in Cardiganshire and seven of those had recently been grouped into a single Joint Water Board and were going ahead with a joint water scheme.

That was the policy that the Minister was very keen on and a circular urging this policy generally was being issued in the next few days. This system was obviously of particular importance at a time when capital expenditure was to be strictly limited and when it came for the Minister to decide whether or not he could sanction a proposed water scheme. He had obviously got to look at the organisation which was going to carry out the work and maintain the water schemes afterwards. It was often forgotten that it was not only a matter of carrying out the schemes, but of maintaining and running it afterwards for periods that could be anything from twenty, thirty or forty years

MINISTER'S HOPE

Therefore, said Mr. Powell, it was increasingly important that we should see the re-grouping of water undertakings which would provide a better basis for modern works. "I must say," he added, "I hope that the Aberystwyth Borough and the Aberystwyth Rural Councils will find it possible in some form to combine in the same way, because there are water problems for them as well as South Cardiganshire.

FINANCIAL TALK

Mr. Powell said he and the representatives of the local authorities had talked a good deal about housing subsidies, rates of interest, and he had

pointed out to the representatives that the case of each housing authority was looked at on its own merit and its own financial circumstances, And that there was a provision in the Act passed this year where a housing authority encountered exceptional difficulty in money special aid could be provided

GRANTS

The review of local government finance, now in progress, with the position of Cardiganshire in that context had also been discussed. The Exchequer Grant (Equalisation Grant) which Cardiganshire received this financial year had automatically fallen as a result of the new assessments. He had pointed out that this was a matter which was obviously involved in the review of local government finance and any construction of central grants must take into account a county like Cardiganshire affected by a sparsity of population.

In reply to a question, Mr. Powell said that it was hoped the result of the local government finances review would be communicated to the local authority association during the next few months.

Although this was Mr. Powell's first visit to Wales and Aberystwyth as a Minister, he has spent several holidays at Aberystwyth. He is of Welsh extraction and learnt the Welsh language in his undergraduate days at Cambridge.

CALLED AT COTTAGE

On his way on Wednesday he made an unscheduled visit to a retired miner's cottage near Pontrhydygroes. He said that the **occupier** of the cottage had carried out a lot of work on the building and he had clearly loved the work. Whilst it was difficult to generalise as to the housing conditions, Mr. Powell said that this cottage, for instance, had it gone to the hands of some people, could have become derelict, but instead, the present occupier had made it a most interesting dwelling and provided good accommodation.

Mr. Powell left Aberystwyth on Thursday morning for Dolgelley and afterwards met Mr. Huw Edwards, chairman of the Council for Wales and Mon. in the Corwen area before returning to London.

7.5　The Minister called at the Ty-Un-Nos

Page Ten – The Cambrian News and Welsh Farmers' Gazette, Friday September 21st 1956

Story: Harry Pugh   Pictures: Ken Hankey

WEDNESDAY, Sept. 12th, 1956, is a date that **Elias Jones** will not forget. For a very strange thing happened to him as he sat smoking his pipe in his Ty-un-nos home that morning. He had a caller, Mr. Enoch Powell, M.P. for Wolverhampton South, Parliamentary Secretary to the Minister of Housing.

The Minister was making a tour of Wales with V.I.P's from his Welsh Office. He happened to be passing through Pontrhydygroes when he spotted the two-in-one cottage where Elias lives.

The visit was not on the schedule, but he decided to call. He was greeted by the barking of a sheep dog and by Elias himself, who, not expecting any callers that morning, was wearing old corduroys and a battered old jacket.

Let Elias go on: "I heard the clatter, went outside and saw two jeeps pulling up. I can tell you I was scared I don't get many visitors and I wondered who it could be.

BARKING

"Floss, my dog, was barking. I told her to shut up and went to see who had come. I recognised one of the party as an official of the Forestry Commission. I didn't half get stuck into them. 'You're not going to have any of my land for your trees,' I told them.

"They convinced me eventually that they had not come to look for new forestry preserves and introduced themselves. I cooled off and invited the eight of them inside.

"Mr. Powell was very interested to know all about me and the house. I gave him all the history."

Elias has lived at Troedyrhiw on and off since his birth in 1881. His family has occupied the house since the 17th century when his great-great-grandfather built it as a Ty-un-nos.

The Ty-un-nos (one night house) is not uncommon in Cardiganshire. They are so called because they had actually to be built in a night. Any man who took a pile of building materials on a common land and transformed it, between sunset and dawn, into a house with smoke coming from the chimney, could live in it rent free.

FIGHTS

What, in fact, usually happened was that, to comply with the law which was repealed in the last century, the builder would construct just the chimney and light a fire beneath it. The rest of the house could be finished at any time; but with smoke coming from the chimney, the site was his.

Elias is an ex-miner. He went to Ysbyty Ystwyth school until he was 13, then to work in the lead mines. He was first of all at Frongoch, and he has some grand stories to tell about the fights between the Welsh and the imported Italian miners.

In 1920 he went to the collieries of South Wales. But he returned to Cardiganshire mines, and worked at Cwmystwyth. He went again to South Wales and worked all over Glamorgan.

RUMOUR

A rumour that work was going to begin on the Cwmystwyth-Rhayader coach road brought him back to Cardiganshire. But it never materialised. "And it is still only a rumour," he adds.

He worked for a while longer in the lead mines, then gave up. The price of lead - £4/10/0 a ton compared to £104 today – was not sufficient to pay the men's wages and most of the mines were closing.

Then came years of odd periods of work alternating with the dole. At one time there were 21 men on the dole in the district. But many at them - like Elias – got work at the outbreak of war in the Hafod forests.

What most impressed the Minister was the condition of Elias's home. He said at Aberystwyth, "This is sort of place that could quite easily be a hovel in somebody else's hand."

THE HOUSE ELIAS BUILT

But it will never be one while Elias is there. Since he retired in 1948 he has been working almost every day on the house.

Troedyrhew was condemned once because dampness was seeping in from a bank against which leaned the back of the house. Elias toiled for six was weeks and cleared the bank. Now it's as dry as a cork.

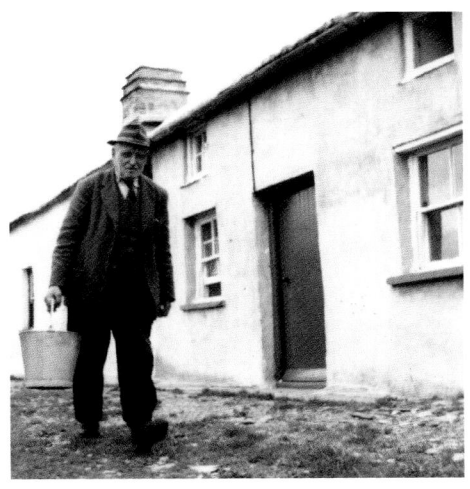

COWSHED

He used to live in the house but decided to convert the

Elias Jones leaves his home swinging a bucket to fetch water. His house has electricity but, as yet, no water laid on.

cow shed next door and make it habitable as a sort of study-cum-kitchen. It was here that he entertained Mr. Powell and party.

He has roofed the house and proofed the walls with liquid cement. Everything is ship-shape. And the inside of the house, neat and dustless as a surgery, would make any housewife house-proud.

He has built a lavatory that looks like a small chapel. He purchased the stone from the remains of Hafod mansion. "Cost me £25," he says, "but it's a good strong lavatory."

And he has built himself a well. "I'm going to put an inscription over it," he told me. "'Come all ye thirsty. This water is crystal clear!'"

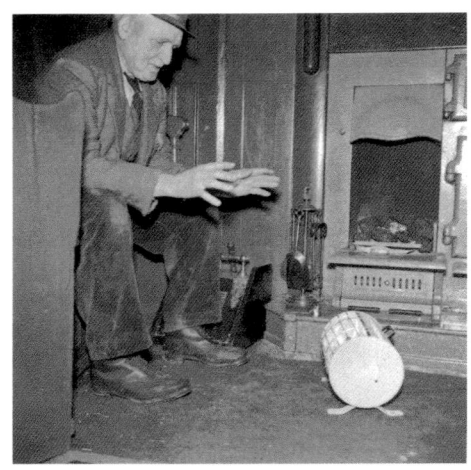

He warms his hands at the electric fire. His home, which was built in the 17th century, is spotless.

PENSION

Since his wife died 19 years ago, Elias has done all his own cooking and most of his housework. He lives on his £2 a week pension and the little he makes from keeping a few sheep.

But his wants are simple. He likes reading and his home is crammed with books. "Reading too much, I am," he said. "That's why I'm so awkward to live with!" And he likes to sit smoking his pipe.

One of the things he wants in life is to have as much as his father had: His father made 30/- a week; he makes, a little more than £2:

"My father liked his quarter of tobacco and so do I. The only difference is it was 1/2d. in his day and now it's 16/4d."

Elias Jones blew a cloud of blue smoke towards the hob on which two black kettles were comfortably stood.

He seems to have to have found what many of us are searching for – peace.

7.6 Ninepence for a nine-and-half-hour day – a grey past and a blacker future

Cambrian News, Friday December 27th, 1963

Today the picture is one of complete desolation – it could be a Flanders battlefield, a scene from the blitz. The buildings are still there but disused, they crumble slowly, the massive wooden beams rotting and collapsing under the heavy stonework, the gaping windows look out over mounds of rubble and twisted, rusting machinery. It could be any one of the 50 or so lead mines now disused that dot Cardiganshire - this one is Frongoch, one of the largest and most productive.

In its heyday, during the latter part of the last century, it employed around 150 workers - some of them women. Most of them were miners working in shafts of varying depths - some of them as far down as 800 feet. The land was owned by Lord Lisburne and in 1853 the mines in the area produced over 250,000 tons of lead ore and about 330,000 tons of mixed ores. Some of the mines, as did Frongoch, also produced silver.

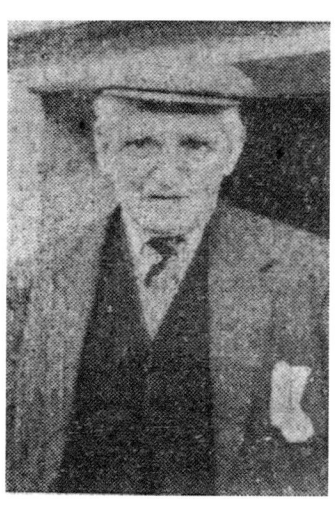

ELIAS JONES his fore father started it all

It is difficult now to picture the mines when they were in production. But one man who remembers it vividly is 83-year-old **Elias Jones**, of Troed-yr-Rhiw, Pontrhydygroes who worked in many of the lead mines in the Frongoch area. One of his forefathers, a lead miner himself, discovered the Frongoch lead deposits and sank the first shaft in 1795. Mr. Jones entered the mines in 1890, at the age of 13 and started on the dressing floors washing the lead ore for 9d a nine-and-a-hour day.

He left the area to live in South Wales and worked as a miner in many Glamorgan coal mines before returning to the Frongoch mine in 1929. The mine had ceased production, to all intents and purposes in 1903 but an attempt was made to revive it in 1922. Elias Jones saw the end of this attempt and blasted the last holes in November, 1929, when the mine closed completely. So the wheel had turned the full circle and Elias Jones saw the end of the mine which had been discovered by his great grandfather.

The Frongoch mine had been taken over by J. Probert of Shrewsbury in 1798. In 1834, Frongoch and the neighbouring Llwynwnwch mine was acquired by Messrs. Taylor and Sons when the deepest shaft then was just over 200 feet. The output from all the Lisburne mines at that time was 40 tons a month - in the first year under Taylor's management it rose to 100 tons a in month. Ten levels were operated varying from depths of 200 to just over 800 feet. In 1878 the Taylors sold the mine and plant to the Earl of Lisburne and it was then taken over by a Mr. John Kito. It then passed into the ownership of a Belgian mining company before it closed in 1903.

Referring to the reasons for the closure of the mine, Professor O.T. Jones, of Manchester University wrote in 1922; "The causes which led to the abandonment of the mine are worthy of examination. There is no known geological cause to account for the impoverishment in depth, for the base of the Frongoch mine is probably about 3,000 feet below the surface and there is therefore no reason to suspect the influence of the Gwestyn shales. When Messrs. Taylor gave over the mine in 1879 it was returning over 1,000 tons of galena (lead sulphide) per annum but the expense of keeping the bottom levels dry and of raising the ore was greater than the value of the produce. The quantity of water appears to have keen considerable and the lode from 90 fathoms downwards is described as being extremely hard which added to the cost of breaking ground. Owing to frosts in winter and droughts in summer water wheels could not be relied on for pumping and a steam engine was required necessitating the transport of coal."

He adds; "There is little doubt that there are reserves of galena and probably even larger reserves of blende below the 90 fathom level but the expense or re-opening from the surface would probably be greater than the value of the ore, even with an enhanced price."

Since those words were written the price of lead has risen steadily from the £4/16/0 a ton when Elias Jones worked at Frongoch to today's highest peace time price of around £75 a ton.

Is there still a future for Cardiganshire's lead mines? Elias Jones believes there is and there are some who will agree with him. Ten years ago Elias Jones was back on the lead mines, this time helping a local business man to map and assay the best seams. Over a period of six months they worked their way down from Dylife in Montgomeryshire to Ffair Rhos. The samples they collected were highly promising but the businessman died and the venture died with him.

Recently Mr. M. M. Dandrick who owns the mineral rights of the North Cardiganshire mines told a public inquiry that a mine in Cwm Rheidol was sure to open in the near future. There are also unconfirmed reports that there could be similar developments at Ffair Rhos next year.

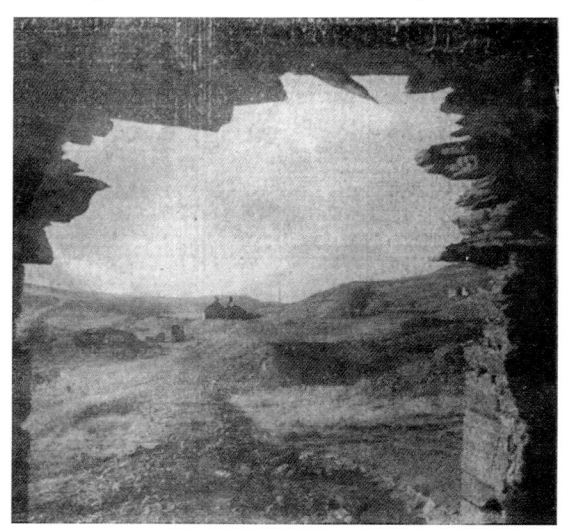

Frongoch - a scar of busier times

But although some isolated attempts may be made to re-work the lead tips in the area, Frongoch, one of the most promising of the disused mines, is unlikely to relive the Klondyke days of the past.

Mr. W. J. Lewis, a member of the staff of the U.C.W., Aberystwyth, who has been working on a book of Cardiganshire's mines, said that during the war when lead was at a premium, a Ministry geologist surveyed the mines and came to the conclusion that it would be uneconomical to reopen them. Mr. Lewis' estimates that it would cost a $\frac{1}{4}$m to transport and install modern machinery.

In meantime the mines, continue to scar the Cardiganshire countryside – the grey of the tips and tottering buildings brooding over an ugly reminder of the past.

Pictures and story by G. Ll Thomas

8
Adroddiad ar Ddylanwad Mwyngloddiau Plwm Ceredigion
Report on the Influence of the Lead Mines of Cardiganshire

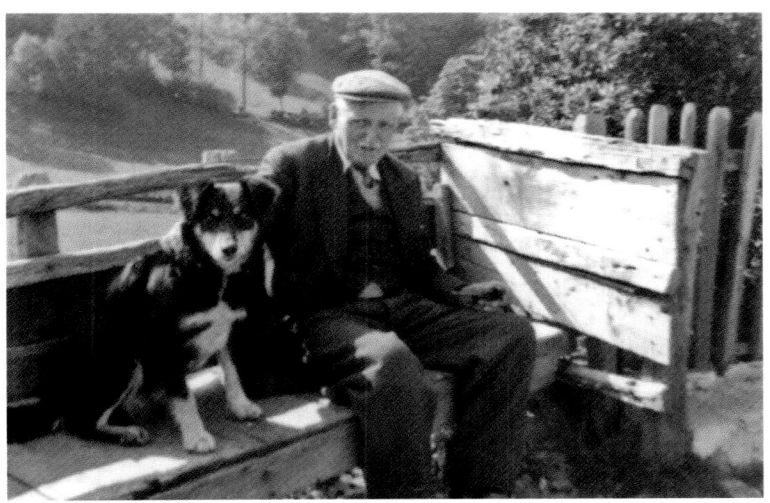

Elias tu allan i'w dŷ gyda Floss.
Elias outside his house with Floss

Darganfuwyd y dogfennau teipiedig isod ymysg eiddo Elias.

Cyhoeddwyd drwy garedigrwydd Archifau Ceredigion, Cyngor Sir Ceredigion.

Typed document found in Elias' possessions. Original is named: "Cardiganshire C.C.: Report on the Influence of the Lead Mines of Cardiganshire on the Health and Welfare of the People". Ernest Jones, Co. M.O.H., January 1938

Published by kind permission of Ceredigion Archives, Ceredigion County Council.

Report on the Influence of the Lead Mines of Cardiganshire on the health and Welfare of the People

Of the large number of mines which up to 50 years ago flourished in North Cardiganshire, four were at work as late as 1926. These were Esgairmwyn near Pontrhydfendigaid, Gwaith Coch above Pont Llanafan, the Cwmystwyth mine and Erwtomau near Devil's Bridge.

Conditions in the different groups of mines varied very little. The miners of Esgairhir and Camdwrmawr lived in the villages of Talybont, Taliesin and Tre'rddol. Every Monday morning they left their homes at 5.30 o'clock with the week's supply of food in their wallets and lived for the remainder of the week in barracks near the mines. Those who worked in the Lisburne, Pontrhydygroes, Frongoch, Esgairmwyn and Cwmystwyth mines returned daily to their cottages of small holdings.

Life in the Barracks

The men slept two in a bed with six beds in the room. The bedclothes were grey or coloured blankets which were rarely washed. The men did their own cooking.

The Miners' Homes

These were small houses, often damp and often badly ventilated. Usually, there were only one or two bedrooms to each house, and more often than not, the tuberculous miner slept in the same room as some of the children.

Food

Those miners who lived in barracks took with them each Monday morning a large loaf of bread, tea and sugar, a pound of butter and a small supply of bacon. This fare lasted them a week. Those who lived at home fed on tea, bread and butter, bacon and "cawl cig moch".

Sometimes on Sunday, fresh meat was eaten, but eggs, cheese, milk, fruit and vegetables, apart from those used in the cawl, were for the most part missing from the diet. The food taken by the miners to their work was just bread and butter and cold tea in a tin bottle. The children were no better fed than the parents; it was not uncommon for them to have nothing better at mid-day than a basin of bread with hot tea poured over it – a concoction known as "siencin".

Conditions of Work

The mines were worked in eight hour shifts, two shifts and even three in a day. When one shift followed on another, there was no time to ventilate the workings and the newcomers had to work in the dust and smoke created by the blasting and drilling of the first shift. The ventilation varied from mine to mine. In some, it was particularly bad, and it is stated that at times a candle would not burn. The dust created by the drilling was largely silica, and though no investigations on silicosis in Cardiganshire have been carried out, it must be assumed that this disease was very prevalent amongst the workers. Sometimes, the men were wet through from un-pumped water and drippings from the roof.

Length of life of the lead miner

From the Registrar General's figures of mortality from consumption in males, the following comparisons can be made. The figure 1,000 is taken as representing the consumption death rate for the whole of the male population of the country:-

Ministers of religion	42.2
Farmers	67.7
Doctors	75.6
Railwaymen	75.8
Coal Miners	112.2
Slate Quarries	260.6
Masons and stonecutters	332.0
Tin Copper and lead miners	2,061.3

The Cardiganshire miner rarely lived beyond the age of 45. Those who lived to 55 looked old men. They owed the longer lease of life to the fact that only part of their working life had been below ground.

Character of the Men

All accounts agree that the Cardiganshire miners, as a class, were intelligent, sober and religious. They spent whatever leisure they had in political, religious and philosophical study and male voice singing. Thus, alcohol and venereal disease can be ruled out as influences in their ill health.

Pay

The miner's earnings were £3.0.0 a month. Sometimes they were a little more, but seldom did they reach £4.0.0. Some of the miners had small holdings, on each of which a cow might be kept. But from all accounts they were not usually expert gardeners and thus vegetables were not available in sufficient quantities for their needs.

Conditions of the Present Inhabitants of the Mining Areas

This part of Cardiganshire is a distressed area, and has been for nearly 50 years. In 1920 an enquiry was made into housing conditions, and in 1926 into food and habits of feeding. The 1926 enquiry revealed the fact that food has changed very little from the mining days. The main diet is tea and bread and butter. Sunday is the only day when fresh meat appears on the table. Country products, such as milk, eggs, garden vegetables and fruit, enter very little into the diet of the people, and the milk-oatmeal foods, once so characteristic of Welsh farm life, are rarely seen even in outlying farms. The garden and its produce are fallen into neglect, and the art of vegetables cooking has largely disappeared. In many villages milk cannot be obtained at any price.

The monotonous starchy diet, revealed by this enquiry must have lowered the resistance to tuberculosis. Not only is it wanting in calcium

and vitamins - so necessary to the tuberculosis patient – but it actually leads to a loss of calcium, because it lacks the balancing effect of butter, milk and green vegetables. As things are, a cottager, to feed himself and his family, must grow his own vegetables and keep his own cow or goat. To buy vegetables is beyond his means, and it is quite out of the question for his family to consume a pint of milk per head per day, for that would cost 10/- a week. The consumption of fabricated foods and drinks is therefore very common, and a very large section of the population is living on a diet which is short of those ingredients that protect the body from disease and decay. Some of this bad feeding is due to lack of skill in cooking, some to ignorance of the true nature of much that is advertised as food, and some to the mistaken belief that to keep a cow, or to cultivate a garden, is to disqualify oneself from unemployment benefit or help from other funds.

Influence of the Lead Mines on the Fertility of the Land and the Condition of the Animals

Several reports have been made on the evil effects of the lead mines on farm pasture land of the county. In 1815 Gwallter Mechain reported that the waters from the mines spread sterility over the adjacent fields, poisoned farm animals and killed the fish in the rivers. In 1874 the Rivers Pollution Commissioners recorded the large extent of damage done to land and livestock by the lead mines of Cardiganshire and Montgomeryshire, and specially mentioned the valleys of the Ystwyth, Rheidol and Clarach. The report of the Rural Commission on Land in Wales, issued in 1896, contains evidence of animals dying after grazing on land which had recently been flooded by mine water.

A little over 20 years ago a detailed investigation into the influence of mines upon land and livestock in Cardiganshire was carried out by Professor J. J. Griffith[1] of the University College of Wales, Aberystwyth. The information below is taken from his report.

Most of the lead mines are situated in the hills on the upper reaches of the rivers, the waters of which were commonly used in the separation of

the lead sulphide in the crushed ore. The separation was never complete. Much lead remained in the waste. With weathering this lead became soluble and therefore dangerous to plants and animals. Left in heaps on the river banks, or on the hillside, the 'slime', as the mine waste was called, is carried away by flood water or blown about by wind.

Thus, swollen rivers in flood and dry east winds of winter are repeatedly added damage to that already done. At every big flood, slime is carried from the slime heaps and distributed over miles of riverside land, from the upper valleys down to the sea.

A large meadow, damaged apparently for all time, can be seen close to Aberystwyth, miles away from the offending refuse heaps. A sample of soil from a field at Talybont yielded 0.11% of lead brought there by an overflowing river.

In winter the action of the east winds in spreading poisonous dust is plain to the eye, for the dust descends and discolours the fallen snow. Chemical analysis of the soils in the neighbourhood of the mine dumps at Cwmsymlog and Mynyddgorddi showed the action of wind by revealing a high lead content in the soil to the west of a dump and little to the east.

Where the effect of mine dust is great, grass will not grow, pasturage is destroyed, and when the plants are killed, the soil is washed away, for there remains nothing to bind it together.

Professor Griffith's report, illustrated by photographs, the widespread desolation thus brought about, and gives a list of modes by which lead poison is conveyed from the mines to land and animals:

1. Surface drainage from mine debris during the heavy rains. Near the heaps the poisoned land is fenced to keep off farm animals.

2. Mine waste used for road repairs.
3. Water from hillside leats overflowing on to the land below.
4. Water from poisoned rivers diverted to turn water wheels.
5. Water running directly out of the old levels, as at Cwmystwyth
6. Mine waste used as compost or for making mortar.

Taking all forms of damage into account, a conservative estimate gives 3,000 acres as the area of land involved.

Influence on Crops

Much of the lead-poisoned land yields nothing. Valauble grasses will not grow; cereals germinate, but soon wither. Even where the degree of poisoning is so slight that some plants contrive to survive, the poisoned places can be detected by the skilled eye marking the inferior type of herbage growing there.

Influence on Farm Animals

It is this partly poisoned land that is so dangerous. By grazing it, especially after a flood, farm animals have died in large numbers. Thus in 1912, one hundred and seventy sheep were lost to one farmer, and four horses to another.

Certain animals suffer more than others. Sheep abort, horses have diarrhoea and die before they are four years old, whilst poultry are paralysed by lead gravel they pick up.

So formidable is the lead poisoning of animals that it has been the subject of a special investigation by the veterinary surgeon Mr Edward Morgan (see "Plumbism in North Cardiganshire").

In words quoted by Gwallter Mechain in 1815, "The lead and silver mines are not sources of wealth to the county. Rather are they a curse. They enrich a person or two in an age and entail poverty on hundreds for generations to come". These words refer to property, not persons.

The population of the lead mining area, as is shown above, suffered not from lead poisoning but from tuberculosis. The mines, however, share with bad housing, poor feeding, and dangerous habits of living, the blame for the magnitude of this disease. But there is another aspect; bad housing, poor feeding and unhygienic living are associated with poverty. An industry introduced into the district would help to banish this and in so doing would remove one main factor in tuberculosis morbidity. Lead mining is an industry unhealthy in itself. The tuberculosis mortality of lead miners is twenty times that of coal miners and thirty times that of farmers. It is said that at the peak of the mining prosperity, the total annual profit from all the mines was only £53,000.

1. J. J. Griffith, Influence of mines upon land and livestock in Cardiganshire, The Journal of Agricultural Science, V7, Issue 4, October 1

9
Lisburne Development Syndicate

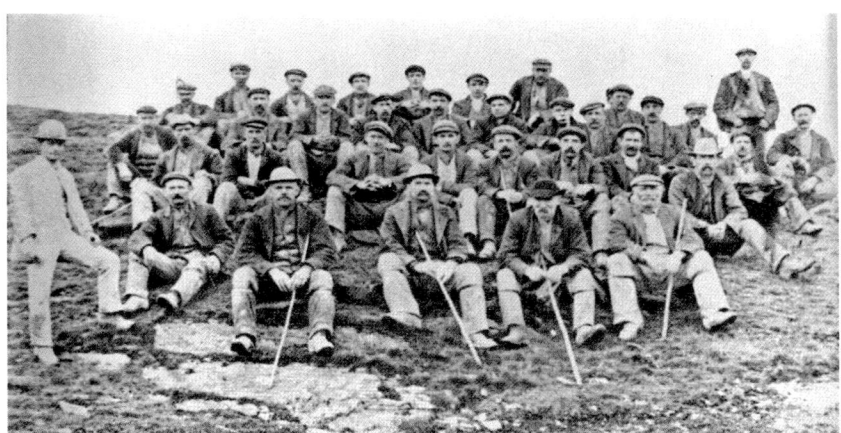

Mwynwyr Glogfawr tua 1912. Ar y chwith, Mr R. R. Nancarrow, y goruchwyliwr. Sylwer ar y math o "hetiau celyd" a wisgid dan y ddaear.
Glogfawr mine around 1912. On the left, Mr R. R. Nancarrow, the manager. Look at the types of "flat caps" that they wore underground.

NB Gorwedd Mwynglawdd Glogfawr i'r de-ddwyrain o Frongoch, ger Ysbyty Ystwyth.
NB Glogfawr mine lies to the southeast of Frongoch, near Ysbyty Ystwyth.

Ffynhonnell anhysbys oedd yn rhan o eiddo Elias. Mae'r fformat a'r sillafu wedi cael eu diweddaru a'u cywiro.

Source unknown but part of Elias's belongings. Format and spelling have been updated and corrected.

Lisburne Development Syndicate Ltd.,
Pontrhydygroes,
Ystrad Meurig,
CARDIGANSHIRE.
November 10th, 1919.

Précis of Evidence on Cardiganshire Mining to be given before The Committee of Enquiry appointed to investigate the Non Ferrous Mining Industry.

---

1. Though the two fundamental factors which form the basis of any mining industry are:-
    1. Occurrence of the ore.
    2. Price of the produce.

   There are two other factors which might almost be said to rank in equal importance with them viz:
    3. Efficient and economical administration of the mines.
    4. Efficiency of labour to give the maximum output and the co-operation of that labour with the management of the mines.

   All four factors are essential to-day for the welfare of the Industry. The absence of any one of these factors on a mine renders the others futile and imperils the success of that particular mine.

   1. <u>Occurrence of the Ore.</u>

2. In dealing with occurrence of the mineral ores in Cardiganshire, here I may say I use the word in a broad sense, I propose to show by a very brief historical sketch that large quantities of lead and zinc ores have, in the past, been found in the County.

3. Cardiganshire has for several centuries, but more especially for the past two, been noted for its silver lead and zinc ore mines.

True from time to time small quantities of copper ore and iron pyrites have been found but, so far, the production of these ores has been so limited in comparison with the silver lead and zinc ores that I hardly think it is necessary to go into details beyond mentioning the presence of these ores in the county and to further state that I have seen some good specimens of copper ore taken from a small mine near Ystrad Meurig, which I am told was worked entirely for copper by a few miners themselves about the year 1840. Silver lead ore occurs in the County mainly in the form of argentiferous galena – the sulphide of lead – containing from 2 or 3 oz. of silver per ton to, as in the case of Cwmsymlog Mine, 70 oz. silver per ton. The zinc ore is principally seen in conjunction with the lead ore in the form of a high grade zinc blende – the sulphide of zinc – both ores are found in or close proximity to fissure veins.

4. While tradition reports that the mines were worked for silver previous to the advent of the Romans, and though it is very probable the mining operations were carried out before and during Henry VII's reign, yet but little attention appears to have been given to the mines in Cardiganshire until the third year of Queen Elizabeth's reign. That Queen sent to Germany for some experienced miners and at a later date – in 1568 – established a corporation of 96 persons under the title of the "Society of the Mines Royal". Under this corporation the mines at Cwmsymlog, the Darren Hills, Goginan, Talybont, Cwmystwyth, Rhosfawr were worked for some years. There are no records of the quantity of ore raised by this Company. It is however stated by Sir John Pettus that they wrought several mines with great success. These mines were eventually let for an annual rental of £400.

5. The mines of Cardiganshire became, during the latter half of the 16th and the beginning of the 17th century, the property of Sir Hugh Middleton, who worked them somewhat deeper than the German miners appear to have done and was successful in finding

very rich ore. It is said that the ore of one mine, (probably Cwmsymlog) yielded 100 oz. of silver to a ton of lead, this may be exaggerated or probably refers only to selected samples. It is from his speculation in Cardiganshire Mines. A clear profit of £2000 a month is stated to have been derived from Cwmsymlog and the neighbouring mines. On the proceeds of these mines he undertook to bring the New River from Ware to London for which accomplishment King James 1 conferred on him the honour of knighthood and afterwards a baronetcy.

6. After Sir Hugh Middleton we find the Cardiganshire mines were worked very successfully by a Mr. Thomas Bushell, Secretary to Sir Francis Bacon, who worked the mines at a greater depth than Sir Hugh Middleton and in 1647 established a mint at Aberystwyth.

7. In 1690 the Gogerddan Mines were discovered. The ore is said to have outcropped to surface. These mines have been amongst the largest producers in the county and were worked almost continuously for 200 years. It was at these mines that we hear of mine bargains being set. Robert Hunt describes the process of setting these bargains in the following words:-

"When the Steward of the Mines has a bargain to set out he comes into the field, and there openly and publicly proclaims to the Miners the taking of such bargain, and he or they that comes to the lowest rate have the bargain granted to them."

Subsistence money was paid every week, and they made a clear profit every six weeks. This system of setting bargains or tribute pitches was in vogue until about 30 years ago.

8. It is recorded by Mr. Waller that 10 mines were working about the year 1700 four producing argentiferous galena carrying 44 ozs silver per ton of lead ore. From this date to 1810, when Sir

Samuel Rush Meyrick published a list of 30 mines in active working, it is difficult to obtain any authentic account of the progress of the industry in the County. It is interesting however to note that three of these mines are in operation today, viz: Ystumtuen, Cwmystwyth, and Esgair Mwyn.

9. Sir Warrington Smyth in his notes on the mining industry of Cardiganshire and Montgomeryshire gives a list of 120 mines which came under the notice of the Geological Survey 1846-7. Of these 120 mines, the following are the returns given for 20 mines during the years 1845-6 and for 15 mines in 1847.

Year	No. of Mines from which returns were available	Tons of Lead Ore Produced	Tons Lead	Tons Zinc Blende Produced	Available Returns from 11 Mines No of persons employed
1845	20	5726	3711	130	1343
1846	20	5711 ¾	3712¾		
1847	15	4899	3176½		

10. From 1847 to 1872 the mines of Cardiganshire enjoyed quite a period of prosperity. Sir Lionel Phillips in his report dated 1st March, 1918, of the Mineral Resources in the United Kingdom states that in the year 1856 there were 33 mines operating in the County which produced 8560 tons of lead ore and 35,751 ozs of silver. The Home Office records for 1878 show 1844 persons engaged in or about the mines, which that year produced:-
      5846 tons of lead ore.
      308 tons of zinc ore.
      306 tons of copper ore.

11. Mr. Absalom Francis, a noted Mining Engineer, who practised in the County during the middle of the last century, stated in his diagram of the mines in the County dated 1878 that the known

output of the Cardiganshire lead and zinc ore mines to that date amounted to eleven million pounds sterling.

12. In the Tables Nos. 1 and 2 appended I have given the output and value of the mines every six years from 1887 to 1918, and also the number of persons employed in or about the mines at various recent dates.

13. The serious decline of the industry in the county during the past 40 years is in my opinion a large measure due to lack of development. It is a known fact that, when the mines were rich and good dividend payers and when the ore was to be had in abundance, the companies were content to rest on their oars and merely developed the ore shoots or ore zones in existence, without energetically prospecting along the outcrop of the lode nor sufficiently testing the barren zones between the known payable shoots. When the price of lead fell from £24 per ton in 1856 to £9.11.6 per ton in 1894, the mines not only found themselves faced with a low price for their produce but with their developed ore reserves almost exhausted and not sufficient reserve capital to enable them to make up the "leeway" of development work.

14. In order to fully appreciate the manner in which real exploration work has been neglected in the past it is necessary to go into the mode of occurrence a little more closely. The average strike of the main lodes is about 20 North of East and the great ore producers, e.g. Frongoch and Loggylas which have each produced ores to the value of over a million pounds sterling underlie South. The notable exceptions to this occurrence are the Esgair Mwyn and Glogfawr lodes both of which underlie north. The ore in the lodes occurs either in well-defined chutes or zones, often in the latter case one finds "a lens" formation with ore both on the footwall and on the hanging, - a pillar "or horse" of barren ground between - sometimes the payable portion of the lode is only found

on the footwall, other times on the hanging making continual crosscutting advisable.

15. Whether the ore occurs in zones or shoots continual development, both laterally and in depth, is essential. It is a remarkable fact that not a single new ore body has been discovered in the county during the past 80 years. All the ore which has been produced since say 1840, indeed one might venture to say 1820, has been won from ore bodies which has been discovered before that date. True, since then the ore bodies have at various periods pinched but subsequent development either by a drive or a short crosscut have only proved that the ore had left the footwall for the hanging or vice versa. After careful enquiry I have failed to ascertain that any mining company has discovered a new ore body for the past eighty years. In fact I have failed to discover when that last ore body was found. By this I do not refer to bunches which have been located from time to time, though even with these small pockets they are simply the continuation of the main ore zones or chutes which our predecessors worked in the early part of the last century. To me it is inconceivable to believe that all the ore zones or bodies have been discovered. For instance, the Loggylas lode, a big south underlier which varies in width from 4 to 20 feet and has been traced for over 12 miles in length has only been worked in two places, i.e. the Lisburne Mines and Cwmystwyth. In each case it produced tens of thousands of tons of lead ore. I find it difficult to believe that such a lode is only productive at those two mines which are 4 miles apart. Again the Frongoch Series, which also underlie South, can be traced for a distance of six or seven miles and though they were found productive at Frongoch, Bodcoll, Tygwyn and Dolwen, yet no trials have been made on that lode except at those places named, and with the exception of the Frongoch Mine which produced over 50,000 tons of Lead Ore and 60,000 tons of Zinc Ore the workings of the other mines on this lode cannot in anyway be termed extensive. There are thousands of yards on "the Strike" of this lode which have never

been proved or even prospected. The same remarks can be passed about the Rheidol, Penrhiw, Castell and Van Series. This Series extends for a distance of over 15 miles and contains several miles of entirely virgin ground.

16. I am of the opinion that had the mines in the County when they were at their zenith done some exploration work, either by long drives along the most favourable horizon or by some prospecting shafts say 300 feet deep from surface, it is my belief that their developed ore reserves would have been sufficient to have enabled them by increasing their output to carry them over the lean years when the price of their produce was low.

17. Another remarkable feature of Cardiganshire lead and zinc ore mines is that there is not a mine in the County which has reached the vertical depth of 900 feet, and this even though the dip of the lodes from the horizontal is roughly 55 and 70°. In fact there are only a very few mines which extended their workings more than 600 feet from the surface. One would naturally come to the conclusion that the reason the mines have only been worked at comparatively shallow depths was because the lodes had pinched out. But that is not the case. Speaking generally the lodes are as strong at the bottom of the mines as they are when only 400 feet from surface, but they have impoverished in value. It must not be supposed that the impoverishment has taken place at one fixed horizon, that is not so, for the mines varying in depth from 450 feet to say 900 feet. Without in anyway wishing to belittle the work of the previous companies in the County we cannot shut our eyes to the fact that when their mines were rich their work was too concentrated on the ore bodies discovered. They sunk so long as the ore lasted then said the mine was bottomed. Another reason the mines have not been tested in depth is that there was hardly a mine equipped for deep sinking. With the permission of the Committee I should like to quote Sir Warrington Smyth on the probability of the occurrence of ore in depth in Cardiganshire. In

his notes on the Mining District of Cardiganshire and Montgomeryshire he writes about the former county as follows:-

"Still more hopeless appeared to be the condition of Goginan, when taken in hand by the Messrs Taylor and Company. The previous adventurer, whose excavations extended to a depth of 30 to 40 fathoms, repeatedly assured them that it was in vain to expect anything there, for that after many years' experience he was so satisfied that no more remained in the lode, that he would undertake to carry on his back to Aberystwyth all that they would ever extract. And yet, in spite of predictions the mine has for years produced upwards of 1500 tons of silver lead ore per annum.

Among the miners of this part of Wales, a prejudice, somewhat modified of late, by the example of the above mines is prevalent, that lead ore is not continuous in depth, and that 30, 40, or 50 fathoms is the limit below which it will not extend; and, in support of the argument, they adduce instances of lodes several fathoms wide at the surface, which at 40 fathoms have dwindled away a few feet, as Esgair-hir; and of others which, very productive in the shallow workings, have presented a mere thread, when opened at greater depth, as at Talybont. We might at once give credence to such an opinion, did the geological features of this district resemble those of Durham, of Derbyshire or Flintshire, where the ore bearing strata are of known and moderate thickness; but with the deep clay-slates of the lower Silurian and Cambrian systems, the same reasoning will not hold, and cases such as those above cited may probably be explained by a local change in the character of the rock, or, in fact, are to be classed among those "nips" or "squeezes" (etranglements) to which all lodes are more or less subject, both in their strike and dip. How rarely has a vein been systematically opened, as in Cornwall or in Saxony, to a depth of 200 or more fathoms, without several of these interruptions to its thickness; and how common to see a lode

of six feet wide, after being reduced to a mere rib and for a considerable distance, open again to its former size."

"That lead ore is not contracted in its vertical range, coeteris paribus, than copper, appears to be satisfactorily proved in districts where due perseverance has been applied. In the Harts, many of the Mines are from 200 to 300 fathoms deep; at Andreasburg (Andreasberg in the Harz Mountains?), in the same mountains, the vein of the Sampson Shaft is still productive at 410 fathoms from the surface. Around Freiburg, in Saxony most of the Mines are from 150 to 250 fathoms in depth, and the lodes continue downwards with undiminished thickness, the principal falling off being in the proportion of silver."

18. Sir Warrington Smyth then goes on to enumerate the depths of other European silver lead mines which met with rich ore at depths far below the deepest Cardiganshire mines, but we need not leave these islands to prove that lead ore veins are productive between 1000 feet and 2000 feet from surface.

One has only to think of Great Laxey lead hills and Waenlockhead Mines which have all been highly productive below the depth of a thousand feet. Sir Warrington Smyth concludes with the following paragraph which sums up Cardiganshire Mining in depth.

"How insignificant after this do mining trials appear which, after penetrating some 40 or 50 fathoms, have been abandoned, because a diminution of size or contents led to the hypothesis that the lode was drawing to a termination".

19. I have brought plans and sections of two of the Lisburne mines to illustrate the foregoing remarks and shall be pleased to answer, to the best of my ability, any questions the Committee may desire to ask.

2. Price of Produce.

20. I understand the matter of price of our production has already been brought before the Committee, but I would like to also emphasize the fact that while the price of the produce – lead ore – of Glogfawr Mine, the property of the Lisburne Development Syndicate, where I am manager, and which is situated in the Parish of Ysbytty Ystwyth, Cardiganshire, was controlled by the Government for 2 years during 1917 & 1918, there was no control on the price of our mining stores. The advance in the price of the latter was over double the rise in the price of our produce. Not only so, but the Government were purchasers of imported lead at a much higher figure than the controlled price. Further, soon after the Armistice when the control on lead was removed, we found the Government placing their accumulated stocks, which were obtained from Foreign Countries at a higher figure than what the 'Home Mines' were allowed for their produce, on the market at a much lower figure than the original controlled price. In other words the Government controlled the price of lead produced at 'Home' at £30 per ton. They purchased foreign lead at a much higher figure, over £40 per ton. They accumulated large stocks. Then removed the controlled price of £30 per ton and sold from their stocks under £30 per ton even as low as £23 per ton.

21. The partial control certainly had an adverse effect on Glogfawr and against all the mines in the County. I know in our case we very reluctantly had to curtail the footage of our unpayable development in our lower levels, which in Glogfawr is always a dangerous proceeding, but more so at that time when our payable ore reserves were low and getting lower every month.

22. If the lead and zinc ore mining industry in the County ever revives, it can only do so through the restoration of public confidence in the mines. I know of no other way of obtaining that confidence except through dividends. Bearing in mind the present

position of the mines in Cardiganshire, with their developed ore reserves at a very low ebb, in order to bring the ordinary mining proposition in the County into the dividend list the prices of lead and zinc ore to the mines must be in the same proportion as the mining costs in 1914.

23. If the Government acting for the interests of the whole state found it expedient to resort to such measures which inadvertently penalised the lead and zinc ore mining industry of this country during the past three years, I suggest that now the war is over, it should not hesitate in the interests, not only of the Industry but in the interests of the state as a whole, to make ample reparation to the industry not only for a period equal to the time during which the industry was penalised, but for at least two years longer. This would enable the Industry to re-establish itself. The form which that reparation should take I will deal at the end of the précis.

3. Efficient and Economical Administration of the Mines.

24. In the great majority of the mines in the county the local physical features are very favourable for economical working. The sides of the mountains often make it possible to intersect the lode at a depth of several hundred feet from surface by a crosscut of moderate length, thus greatly facilitating drainage problems, for such adits not only form a means of exit for the water but in many cases tap most of the surface waters. In some cases it is even possible to commence driving on the lode almost from the hillside and soon obtain considerable height on the back of the lode, e.g. the western section of the Rheidol Mines.

25. Very few mines troubled with water, 250 gallons per min. are looked upon as being an exceptionally wet mine, while in the majority of cases the water under the adit is, I think I am quite safe in stating, less than 100 gallons per min.

26. There is ample timber for all mining purposes within the County, in fact nearly all the mines can obtain within 6 miles from their works good Scotch Fir @ 9½d. Larch @ 1/3 and Oak @ 1/3 per cub. foot felled in the wood.

27. Power. While some mines have sufficient water for power purposes for 12 months in the year, most of the mines have sufficient for 10 or 11 months. Mines which are entirely dependent on steam, gas, or coal are very rare. Should, however, we see a revival of the industry in the County the River Rheidol should be harnessed and a central power station erected near Devil's Bridge. This matter has already been investigated, and it is estimated that it is possible to obtain with an expenditure of between £250,000 and £300,000, six thousand horse power the whole year round, as all the mines are within a radius of 10 miles from Devil's Bridge. This, with the installations already in the mines, would not only be sufficient for many years to come but would also be of invaluable assistance to the mines which have sufficient water for the twelve months, but would be the means of other mines being opened up in the County.

28. Transit of produce to the nearest railway station is, in some cases, a serious item, both motor tractors and horse drawn carts or waggons are used. The cost being from 8/ - to 17/6 per ton. There are however two mines viz. the Rheidol and Erwtomau, which are situated near the railway, the former delivers its ore into bins on the railway, by means of a ropeway thrown across the valley, while the latter tram their ore sacks from the ore house, a distance of a few yards, into the railway truck. Most of the mines, through paying rates to the local authorities, have to attend to the roads leading from the mines to the main district or county roads. In as much as the mines are local rate payers I would respectfully suggest that, if the Committee of Enquiry thought wise to make a special minute of this fact, it might be of great assistance to such mines as Esgair Mwyn, Glogfawr and Bwlchglas.

29. The railway freights on our produce are by no means low, ranging from 9/- to 19/- per ton according to the geographical position of the station to which ore is consigned. Taking for sake of argument an average of say 14/- per ton railway freight and adding to this cost of transport from the mine to the station say 11/- per ton, we see that the overall cost of transport from the mine to the consignment station is 25/- per ton on our produce, which on a 5% recovery proposition works out at 1.25 shillings per ton milled. This, I consider, far too high for any mining proposition in the County, and I believe could be reduced by mines in the same district co-operating in the transport of their produce to the station. There should also be a reduction of the railway freights.

30. It will be gathered, from the suggestion that mines might bring down their transport charges by co-operating in the transit of their produce to the railway station, that their output is low and that the mines are worked on a small scale. And here we have one of the principal drawbacks to the economical working of the mines. All our mines are worked on such a small scale that the standing charges are heavy in proportion to the working costs of the mines. The reason of this is principally due to lack of development before the commencement of milling operations owing to shortage of working capital. Some mines suffer from over capitalisation. Cardiganshire to-day suffers from the reverse. True I will admit that during the past twenty years, four or five mining companies have come into the County and have each spent over £20,000 some more than £40,000; one I am informed over £80,000 and, after working a matter of five or six years, have suspended operations. Certainly this is not encouraging, but the reason of their failure is easy to understand. Money, which should have been spent underground, was utilised on surface equipment, when the mills and mine offices were completed they found that their predecessors had not left sufficient developed ore reserves behind to enable them to run the new mills to their economical capacity.

They thus found themselves owners of large mills and very little ore to put through them and no available capital for further underground development.

31. Though I am strongly of the opinion that there is as good an opportunity in this field for profitable mining as ever there was. Yet I am convinced that anyone coming into the County to-day and commences to open up an ordinary Cardiganshire proposition by first erecting a large mill is only courting disaster which ultimately reflects on the rest of the mining industry of the County.

32. The position of the Cardiganshire mines to-day is that their underground developed ore reserves are practically exhausted. By this please do not misunderstand me. I do not wish to infer that there is no ore in sight, far from it. Most of the mines have either ore in their lowest levels or in the drives, but they need capital to open them out. During the past eleven years to my knowledge most of the mines have working on ore which was left behind in the old workings by previous companies. Adequate development has been curtailed through lack of capital.

33. A wholesale amalgamation of Cardiganshire mines or mining companies would not, in my opinion, benefit the individual mines nor advance the Industry as a whole. The distance between the mines and the variation of the ores of the different mines making it doubtful whether any company would be effected by putting the ores through three or four central mills, especially when one considers that a mill capable of treating 10 tons per hour of lead and zinc ore can be erected for the same expenditure as 2½ miles of an aerial ropeway. Further the milling costs of lead and zinc proposition are so low, that very little saving could be expected by utilising a central mill. While the disadvantages would be mixing of high grade silver ores with ores carrying small quantities of silver. Clean blende ores with ores containing certain quantities of

pyrites. Clean galena ores with other galena ores containing small quantities of blende of copper pyrites. Further any accident, and accidents do happen in mines, on a central mill causing the mill to be rendered idle for a number of hours or days would be far more serious than an accident in a mill at one of the mines. But while I am opposed to a wholesale amalgamation I believe amalgamation in at least one district of the County would be of the greatest value. I refer to the mines on the Rheidol Penrhiw Series. Here we have at least three mining setts, Rheidol, Penrhiw and Bwlchgwyn, which adjoin, none of them at present are very extensive. Their ores are of similar character. A deep adit from the Rheidol would afford drainage for the whole group. Further the mines on the top of the hill, i.e. Penrhiw and Bwlchgwyn have only sufficient water for six or seven months in the year, while at the Rheidol Mines there is ample power for the whole group. Here we have an ideal proposition for an amalgamation.

34. Speaking for the Lisburne Development Syndicate we already have mining rights over 8000 acres, which are known to contain six payable lodes. These run right through the sett for a distance of four miles. We have sufficient water to generate at one station 500 B.H.P. at another 200 B.H.P. On the south of the Ystwyth our lodes only contain a clean galena ore. On the north they produce more blende than galena. Should the capital be forthcoming to enable us to open out on these lodes and if success attended our efforts. The 500 B.H.P. central power station would be first erected and two mills, one for the lead ore south of the Ystwyth, the other for the zinc lead ore mines north of the Ystwyth. Speaking from a mining standpoint I do not think an amalgamation of our mines with others would benefit either party.

35. Co-operation amongst the mines has until recent years been sadly missing in Cardiganshire and even to-day there is ample room for closer co-operation. Broadly speaking the interests of the mines are identical and I cannot help feeling that, if the managers and

officials of the various mines could occasionally meet at one of the mines in the district or outside the district, we should not only get to know each other better, but the Industry would benefit by the interchange of the ideas.

36. In as much as the great majority of the mines in the county are to-day really development propositions, a detailed plan of every district in the County showing the workings of the various mines, the outcrop of lodes all main faults and cross courses and any other peculiar geological feature in the district would be of invaluable assistance. Such a plan should be made and kept up to date by the Government, the mines to have a copy of such a plan on payment of a moderate fee.

37. I stated just now that the physical features of the metalliferous zone of the County, which extends roughly for a distance of say 16 miles in length and continues into the adjoining counties by a width of say 20 miles at its widest part, lend themselves favourable for economical mining. Appended is a list of tables showing our working costs at Glogfawr since 1911. Bearing in mind that we have hydraulic power for 10 months in the year and that most our work was above the deep adit, these costs are somewhat high, the reason being due to the limited scale of our operations. In a new mining proposition which my directors are now contemplating working, we hope, if the lode maintains its present size and value, to be able to bring down our costs over all to about 16/6 per ton milled on a tonnage of 720 tons per week.

4. Efficiency of Labour to give the Maximum Output and the Co-operation of that Labour with the Management of the Mines.

38. Most of our labour is obtained locally from the mountain villages, a large percentage of men come from mining families. The decline of the mining industry was followed by an exodus of a very large number of men, the consequence being that there is a

scarcity in certain branches of skilled men especially good Timber-men, rock-drillers, shaft-sinkers, and mine carpenters.

39. Roughly three quarters of the mine employers have small holdings of their own or rent a few fields, where they keep a cow, pig and a few sheep. While there is a certain advantage in this class of labour, namely that one does not experience the difficulties attending "floating" labour, there is also a serious disadvantage, as in some cases, true, as far as our mines are concerned, they are in the minority, but there is a marked tendency on the part of a few to regard the small farm as their real occupation and the mine the place where to put in their spare time. For this reason a second shift underground during harvest time is not always satisfactory, while the more night shift that can be avoided the better both for the management and the men.

40. Appended are tables numbered 7 and 8 giving the average rate of pay on day work and contract, together with the amount of work done per man per shift during years 1911 to 1919. While it may seem at first sight that our rates of pay were low in 1914, it is only fair to state that they were above the rates paid to other forms of labour in the County during the same period, i.e. road men were only 2/6 to 2/9 per day and agricultural labourers even less.

41. On the whole our labour was fairly satisfactory until the end of 1917. About this time a workman's union was formed in the district, which included mine employees, Government workmen, engaged in timber felling, estate employees, etc. etc. At union meetings all, whether they were woodmen or estate workers, voted and still do on questions affecting the working of the mines. I regret to state that owing to outside agitation by men who were neither miners nor workmen nor up to that date trade unionists, that a good deal of discontent was created amongst a section of our employees. This had for several months a very serious adverse effect on the work of the mine, but I am pleased to state that

owing to our older employees, who showed a willingness to co-operate with me, a saner spirit eventually prevailed. I have no fear of the future so long as our employees continue to realise their responsibility.

42. If our Labour is to advance and we sincerely hope it will, the men must accept their responsibilities. There can be no real advancement of the industry in the County or in the conditions of mine employees without hard work. Money does not grow on apple trees nor does it fall from the skies. Money which after all forms the chief stepping stones by which our workmen can attain better living conditions must be earned. The harder he works the more money he should get. And here we come to the most important factor in our industry viz. output. A mine may have a rich lode and a high price for its produce yet will fail to return the capital outlay, let alone the interest unless the worker puts forth his best energies to give an adequate output. Maximum output is as vital to a mine as the price of its produce, or the occurrence of its ore. That being so it is no encouragement to our workmen to suggest at any time, even if the present price of foodstuffs fall, a reduction of wages. But high wages without a corresponding amount of work is finally fatal.

43. On every contract underground I would suggest a bonus which should be within the reach of the contractor. Often I have heard it said by men that have been miners that the only economical method of working a mine is by contract. Obviously that is so, yet in Cardiganshire to-day there is the greatest difficulty in getting the men to work on contract. Men who, before the war and even much later before the advent of the Workmen's Union, invariably asked for a contract now can only be persuaded and that with great difficulty to take a contract. I cannot help feeling that there is some sinister influence behind the men urging them to have a flat rate throughout the mines.

44. Men who advocate a flat rate can know nothing and care less of the local mining industry and the real welfare of the men. A flat rate throughout the mine is an evil and an abominable system. It is a premium on laziness and inefficiency. It discourages the worker in his work and encourages the slacker in his slackness. What Mining Industry can thrive under such conditions? What possibility is there to get an adequate output when all are brought to the level of the lowest?

45. <u>OUTPUT</u>. Output is the keystone of the industry. No effort should be spared either by the workmen or anyone else to obtain the maximum output. We are dependent on the men for output, which is the life of the mine. The men are dependent on the mine for means whereby to live. Surely the interests of the two are, identical. Yet how few act as if they realised it.

46. <u>Co-operation</u>. Co-operation between the management and the men to-day is essential for the output of the mine. I use the word co-operation in its true sense. May I first explain what in my opinion co-operation is not. Some workmen are under the impression that co-operation merely means a number of their representatives sitting round the table with management. That may be the outward sign of co-operation. But that is worse than useless unless it is carried into the mine work. It is no co-operation for men to sit round a table with us and the following day or week discourage their fellow workmen to take contracts, and I will go further and say pull their fellow workmen up because they make a certain footage or fathomage in the mine.

47. Co-operation should mean that, if the men have a voice through their Pit Committee – a committee which personally I am only too glad to have to-day – on matters affecting the working of the mine, they should individually and collectively do their utmost to increase the output of the mine.

48. Another serious factor which I am afraid is sometimes not fully appreciated which must effect our output is, in a good many cases, the very poor housing conditions of our men. It surprises me sometimes, after calling to see one of our men at his home, and having been invited inside and seeing a whole family in a small kitchen, and a leaky kitchen at that, with clothes drying by an open hearth that the men work so well as they do, especially when one remembers that the living room is used in many cases as a bedroom by some of the members of the family, and a dark loft close under the roof, which is reached by means of a ladder or narrow staircase affords the only sleeping accommodation for the remainder of the family. The reports of the various medical officers of health year after year call attention to the serious conditions of housing in the mining areas of Cardiganshire. Probably the condition in these areas is worse than in any other part of Wales, and is responsible for more phthisis, which is rampart in the district, than the actual nature of the men's employment underground. I consider this is a most serious factor in the working of our mines. A man to do good day's working day after day must have a decent dry house in which to live and bring up his family. How better housing conditions for Cardiganshire miners can be obtained is a problem which must be faced and solved should a revival of the Industry take place. The actual solving of this problem may not come within the scope of the committee, but with utmost deference I would respectfully suggest that this matter be brought to the notice of the Ministry of Health.

49. Finally I would welcome any machinery which would break down any mistrust and suspicion between the management and the men, such mistrust can only lead to misunderstandings and a dislocation of work.

50. In conclusion without in anyway wishing to minimise the very serious conditions of the lead and zinc ore mining industry in

Cardiganshire to-day, this industry which, at one time, had correct records been kept, must have employed three for four thousand men is not dead but can be revived by the importation of working capital, good administration, efficient labour and co-operation of that labour with the management of the mines. For we have the vital factors – the existence of the Ore – with us. To encourage capital coming into the C ounty and also the present mine owners, now in existence, to develop the mines, I would suggest that the Government make a twofold grant for the five years dating from June 30th last.

(a) A bonus of 7/3 a foot on all development work approved by a 'Ministry of Mines' to be set up by the Government.
(b) A minimum price for the produce set in relation to the advance of the mining costs since 1914 or a bonus on output.

If this is done a word of warning may not be out of place. Envious eyes should not be cast on the owners' profits either by the Government or by labour. For after all it is the mine owner who takes the risk and only by dividends is proportion to that risk can the industry thrive.

10
Trydydd Jiwbili Eglwys Fethodistaidd Bethel
Third Jubilee of Bethel Methodist Chapel

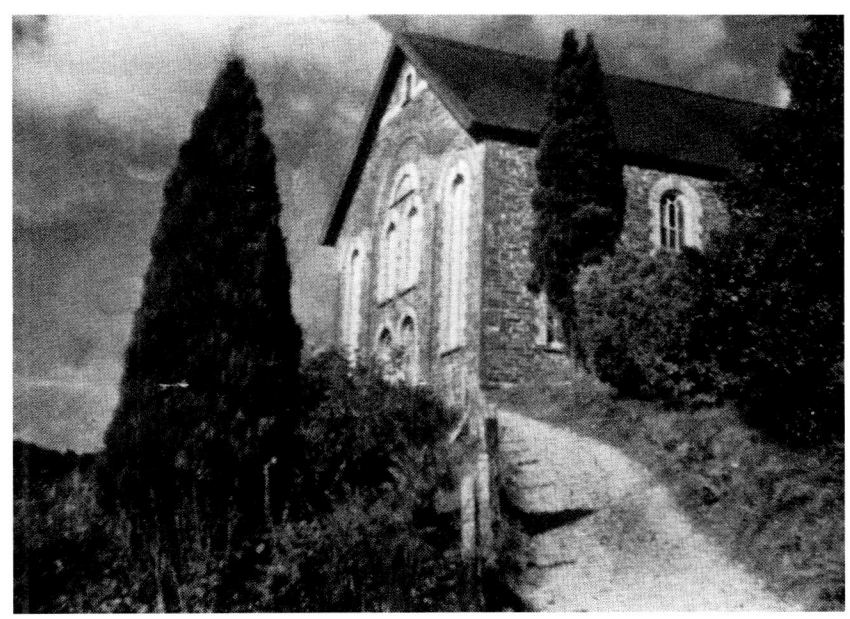

Eglwys Bethel
Bethel Chapel

Bu Willam Jones, tad Elias yn cynorthwyo i adeiladu Eglwys Bethel. Daeth Elias yn ddiacon yn yr Eglwys.

Willam Jones, Elias' father helped to build Bethel chapel. Elias became an elder of the chapel.

1810-1960

TRYDYDD JIWBILI BETHEL
Yr Eglwys Fethodistaidd
PONTRHYDYGROES

Awst 16 a 17, 1960

NOS FAWRTH am 7 o'r gloch: PREGETH gan y Parch. CLIFFORD ROBERTS, Ystumtuen.
DYDD MERCHER am 2.30 o'r gloch: CYFARFOD DATHLU.
Llywydd: Y Parch. CLIFFORD ROBERTS.
Y Parch. JOSEPH JENKINS, Blaenau Ffestiniog.
Anerchir gan: **Mr. JOHN JONES.**
Mr. ELIAS JONES a
Miss FLORRIE JONES.

Am 7 o'r gloch, PREGETH gan y Parch. D. LLEWELYN JONES, B.A., Llanidloes (Cadeirydd y Dalaith).
Estynnwn groeso cynnes i chwi ymuno gyda ni yn y cyfarfodydd uchod.
DISGWYLIR CASGLIAD TEILWNG

Darperir te prynhawn dydd Mercher.
"Yr Arglwydd a wnaeth i ni bethau mawrion."

Awst, 1960   CLIFFORD ROBERTS.

Cambrian News, Cyf., Aberystwyth

1810-1960

THIRD JUBILEE BETHEL
The Methodist Church
PONTRHYDYGROES

August 16 a 17, 1960

TUESDAY EVENING at 7 o'clock: SERMON by the Revd. CLIFFORD ROBERTS, Ystumtuen.
DYDD MERCHER at 2.30 o'clock': CELEBRATION MEETING.
President: Revd. CLIFFORD ROBERTS.

Address by:
Revd. JOSEPH JENKINS, Blaenau Ffestiniog.
Mr. JOHN JONES.
Mr. ELIAS JONES and
Miss FLORRIE JONES.

At 7 o'clock, SERMON by Revd. D. LLEWELYN JONES, B.A., Llanidloes (Chairman of the Province).
We extend a warm welcome to you to join us in the above meetings.

·

EXPECT A DESERVED COLLECTION

Tea will be provided on Friday afternoon.
"The Lord made great things for us."

August 1960   CLIFFORD ROBERTS.

Cambrian News, Cyf., Aberystwyth

Braslun o Hanes yr Achos

Ychydig o fanylion am gychwyn yr Achos ym Mhontrhydygroes sydd gennym. Dywedir i Mr. E. Jones, Bathafarn, a W. Davies, Croesefa, ymweled â'r lle yn gymharol gynnar, ond ni wyddom gan bwy, nac ymhle y sefydlwyd y Gymdeithas. Yn ôl Taflen y Capelau, ymddangosodd yn yr Eurgrawn, adeiladwyd y capel cyntaf yn 1810, ond yr oedd yn un bychan ac annhymig, gyda tho brwyn neu welit. Safai yn y lle y mae adfeilion yr ail gapel. Arferai David Jones, Hafod y Gau ddweud, fod £40 o ddyled yn aros arno, a digon tebyg fod hynny yn golygu yr holl draul; ac yr oedd yn rhwystr i lwyddiant y gwaith, am ei fod yn rhy fychan i'r rhai a gyrchai iddo. Penderfynwyd symud y ddyled gyda chyfarfod te, trwy i'r cyfeillion roddi y defnyddiau. Yr oedd cyfarfod o'r fath yn newyddbeth yn yr ardal, a daeth nifer fawr ynghyd er mwyn gweled pa fath gyfarfod ydoedd. Llwyddwyd yn yr ymgais, a chliriwyd y ffordd i godi capel newydd capel llawer helaethach, ac oriel arno. Codwyd tŷ capel yr un pryd, osodwyd i un Mrs. Hughes, oedd i groesawu y pregethwyr fel rhan o'r ardreth; ond aeth tu cefn i'r swyddogion, a thalodd hanner-coron o ardreth i'r tirfeddiannwr, a thrwy wneud hynny collwyd yr hawl o'r tir, o'r ffordd uchaf hyd yr isaf. Y swyddogion cyntaf oedd Mri. John Richard, W. Ishmael, John Jones, D. Davies, T. Morgan, Jacob Edwards, David Jones, E. Jenkins, J. Richard, T. Jones, Jonathan Davies, E. Jones y Gof, S. Davies, T. Edwards a W. Jones.

Cyfarfu J. Richard, Glannant, â'i ddiwedd trwy ddamwain yn y gwaith, ond parhaodd ei weddw a'i blant yn ffyddlon i'r Achos, a daeth John ac Elias y meibion yn swyddogion eglwysig defnyddiol. Bu W. Ishmael yn bregethwr defnyddiol a llafuriodd lawer yn y gylchdaith. Marw yn 42 mlwydd oed o'r darfodedigaeth wnaeth John Jones, wedi iddo fod yn flaenor am flynyddau. (Efo oedd tad y Parch. Thomas Jones). Yr oedd David Davies yn gerddor a chanwr rhagorol. Gallai ysgrifennu yn fedrus, ond ni wyddai neb pa fodd y dysgodd. Magodd deulu lluosog a fu yn ffyddlon iawn gyda'r Achos, Jonathan, y mab hynaf yn bregethwr cynorthwyol. Dyn tawel, hynod grefyddol oedd Thomas Morgan, ac fe

Outline History of the Cause

We have a few details of the beginning of the cause in Pontrhydygroes. It is said that Mr. E. Jones, Bathafarn, and W. Davies, Croesefa visited the place comparatively early on but we don't know who established the society or where. According to the chapel's pamphlet which appeared in the Eurgrawn, the first chapel was built in 1810, but it was a small and unsuitable one with a thatch or straw roof. It would stand in the place of the ruins of the second chapel. David Jones, Hafod y Gau would say that £40 of debt remained on it and more than likely this meant the whole expense; and it was an obstacle to the success of the work and too small for those who attended it. It was resolved to remove the debt by holding a tea party with friends of the chapel making donations. This type of event was new to the area and large numbers came to see what sort of event it was. The attempt was successful and cleared the way to build a new chapel, a much roomier chapel with a gallery attached. A chapel house was erected at the same time and let to Mrs. Hughes, who was to make the visiting preachers welcome as part of her duties; but she went behind the backs of the officials and paid half a crown of the rent to the to the landowner, and through doing that the rights over the land were lost, from the upper road to the lower. The first officials were Messrs John Richard, W. Ishmael, John Jones, D. Davies, T. Morgan, Jacob Edwards, David Jones, E. Jenkins, J. Richard, T. Jones, Jonathan Davies, E. Jones y Gof, S. Davies, T. Edwards a W. Jones

J. Richard, Glannant, met his end through an accident at work, but his widow and children remain faithful to the cause and his two sons John and Elias became useful officials of the chapel. W. Ishmael became a useful preacher, and he preached a great deal in the locality. John Jones died at the age of 42 from TB having been an elder for many years (he was the father of the Rev Thomas Jones). David Davies was a deacon and excellent singer. He was able to write ably but no one knows how he learnt to do so. Several family members were brought up who were very faithful supporters of the cause, Jonathan, the eldest son becoming assistant preacher. Thomas Morgan was a quiet man but very religious,

ddilynodd y plant ôl y tad, Mathew y mab, yn Abercynon, ac Anne y ferch yn Nhreorci. Pentewyn wedi ei achub o'r tân oedd Jacob Edwards, ond cafodd afael ar rym duwioldeb, ac fe efelychodd ei blant ef. Gofalodd T. Morgan, Creigiau Bach, geisio crefydd yn ieuanc, gan ei weithio allan yn holl gylchoedd bywyd. Efo oedd tad y Parch. H.P. Morgan fu yn gynorthwywr yr Eglwys Bach ym Mhontypridd, ac yn weinidog amlwg wedyn gyda'r Annibynnwyr yn America. David Jones, Hafod y Gau, fu y golofn amlygaf gyda'r Achos am lawer o flynyddoedd. Yr oedd yn well ysgolor na'r cyffredin, a chyda bod yn flaenor rhagorol, bu yn bregethwr cynorthwyol cymeradwy, ac yn oruchwyliwr y gylchdaith. Cynrychiolai y gylchdaith yn y Cyfarfod Taleithiol, a'r Dalaith yn y Gynhadledd. Daeth ei feibion yn flaenoriaid ac yn swyddogion, a rhai yn bregethwyr cynorthwyol. Bu Thomas Herbert yn bregethwr cynorthwyol, ac yr oedd yn ddyn o allu uwchraddol. Ymddangosodd cofiant iddo yn Eurgrawn 1878, td. 265. Gwnaeth W. Davies wasanaeth fel athraw a cherddor, a meibion iddo oedd y Parchn. William ac Evan Davies. Llanwodd Morgan Ishmael le mawr fel cerddor ac athraw, ond aeth i'w fedd yn gynnar.

Costiodd y capel presennol, godwyd yn 1873, £1,400, a'r ddyled wedi ei chlirio, gwaith orffennwyd gan y Parch. W. J. Arter. Penodwyd deunaw o Ymddiriedolwyr Chwefror, 27, 1904. Samuel Davies, William Davies, Thomas Morgan, Edward Jones, John Richards, Thomas Jones, Jonathan Davies, Evan Jenkins, David Ishmael, John Richard Jones, Thomas Hughes, Morgan Ishmael, David Morgan; William Jones, Thomas Edwards, Daniel Jones Davies, William Hopkins (ieu) a Thomas Rees.

Aeth wyth o feibion yr Eglwys i'r weinidogaeth. **William Davies** (D) aeth i'r weinidogaeth yn 1873, ac a fu farw yn Llangollen, Gorffennaf 12, 1888, yn 37 mlwydd oed. **Evan Davies** ei frawd a ddechreuodd deithio yn 1878 ac a fu farw yng Nghorwen, Chwefror 7, 1897, yn 39 mlwydd oed. Cafodd y brodyr hyn eu magu ym Mwlchyblaen. **Thomas Jones** ddechreuodd deithio yn 1876, ac a fu farw yn Mhontrhydygroes, Mawrth 22, 1937, yn 85 mlwydd oed. **David Meurig Jones**

and the children took after their father, Matthew the son, in Abercynon, and the daughter, Anne in Treorchy. Jacob Edwards was a firebrand rescued from the fires of hell but piety took hold of him and his children followed him. T. Morgan, Creigiau Bach, sought religion at a young age by acting out his beliefs in all walks of life. He was the father of Rev H.P. Morgan who was an assistant of the small church in Pontypridd and then a minister with the Independents in America. David Jones, Hafod y Gau, became the most prominent supporter of the cause for many years. He was a better than average scholar and with being an excellent elder, became an approved assistant preacher and supervisor of the circuit. He would represent the circuit in the provincial meeting and the province at the conference. His sons became elders and officials and also assistant preachers. Thomas Herbert became an assistant preacher and was a man of superior ability. A tribute was paid to him in the Eurgrawn (religious journal) in 1878 at page 265.W. Davies served as a teacher and musician, and his sons were the Reverand W and Evan Davies. Morgan Ishmael filled a big void as an elder and teacher but he went to an early grave.

The cost of the present chapel, built in 1873, was £1400 having cleared the debt, and was completed by the Rev W. J. Arter. 18 trustees were appointed on 27 February 1904. . Samuel Davies, William Davies, Thomas Morgan, Edward Jones, John Richards, Thomas Jones, Jonathan Davies, Evan Jenkins, David Ishmael, John Richard Jones, Thomas Hughes, Morgan Ishmael, David Morgan; **William Jones**, Thomas Edwards, Daniel Jones Davies, William Hopkins (the younger) and Thomas Rees.

Eight of the sons of the church went into the ministry. **William Davies** went into the ministry in 1873 and died in Llangollen on 12th of July 1888 aged 37. **Evan Davies**, his brother, started on the circuit in 1878 and died in Corwen on 7 February 1897 aged 39. The brothers were brought up in Bwlchyblaen. **Thomas Jones** started preaching in 1876 and died in Pontrhydygroes on 22nd of March 1937 aged 85. **David**

ddechreuodd deithio yn 1895 ac a fu farw yn Abergele, Mawrth 10, 1950, yn 84 mlwydd oed. **Thomas Oliver** ddechreuodd deithio yn 1904, ac a fu farw yng Nghaersws, Medi 14, 1946 yn 70 mlwydd oed. **Joseph Jenkins,** ddechreuodd deithio yn 1913. Aeth yn Uwchrif yn 1959 ac ar hyn o bryd y mae yn byw ym Mlaenau Ffestiniog. **Rhys Jones, a** fu yn weinidog gyda'r Annibynnwyr ac a fu farw yn Nhaliesin, a H. P. **Morgan,** fu yn cynorthwyo Eglwys Bach ac yn weinidog gyda'r Annibynnwyr yn yr America.

Yn 1912 a'r Parch. T. Gabriel Hughes yn weinidog ar y pryd, adeiladwyd Festri hardd tu ôl i'r Capel. Ar achlysur ei agor pregethwyd ac anerchwyd gan y Parch. Thomas Jones. Yn 1924, dathlwyd hanner can-mlwyddiant y capel presennol gyda the a chyfarfod dathlu, pryd yr anerchwyd gan nifer o frodyr. Cyhoeddwyd yn y cyfarfod hwn fod y capel yn ddi-ddyled. Yn 1932, ffurfiwyd rhestr newydd o ymddiriedolwyr. Wele yr enwau, Samuel Davies, Edward Jones, David Morgan, Thomas Edwards, David J. Davies, David Jenkins, David Lloyd Jones, John Jones, Evan Jones, William Thomas Jones, Thomas Caradoc Edwards, Joseph Thomas Davies, Thomas Rees, William John Rees, **Elias Jones**, Daniel Jones, Edward Lewis Davies, a David Rhys Jones. Yn 1957, ffurfiwyd rhestr newydd eto, a dyma ymddiriedolwyr y capel ar hyn o bryd. John Jones, William John Rees, Thomas Caradoc Edwards, Thomas Rees, **Elias Jones**, William John Davies, David John F. Richards, Samuel Gerwyn Davies, John Davies, Daniel I. Edwards, John Goronwy 0. Davies, David Gwynfryn Jones, Morgan John Rees, David Gwyn Jones ac Edward Lloyd Jones.

Diddorol eto ydyw sylwi ar restrau'r blaenoriaid. Yn gyntaf oll cawn Thomas Morgan, Jonathan Davies, Evan Jenkins, Thomas Jones, Pantyrhedyn, a John Richards. Yna wedyn cawn David Morgan, John R. Jones, John Jenkins (tad y Parch. Joseph Jenkins), Joseph Davies, David J. Davies, Thomas Rees a Morgan Ishmael (Blaenor y Gân). Yna yn ddiweddarach ychwanegwyd atynt enwan Edward Jones a Samuel Edwards, Penbanc. Wedi iddynt ddychwelyd i'r hen ardal cawn y Parch. Thomas Jones, David Lloyd Jones ac Evan Jones yn flaenoriaid. Yn

Meurig Jones became a minister in 1895 and died in Abergele on 10 March 1950 at the age of 84. **Thomas Oliver** started preaching in 1904 and died in Caersws on 14 September 1946 aged 70. **Joseph Jenkins,** started on the circuit in 1913. He became a supernumerary in 1959 and now lives in Blaenau Ffestiniog. **Rhys Jones** ,became a minister with the Annibynwyr (independents) and died in Taliesin, while **H. P. Morgan** was assistant at Eglwys Bach and became a minister with the Independents in America.

In 1912, at the time Rev T. Gabriel Hughes was minister, a beautiful vestry was built behind the chapel. On the occasion of its opening Rev Thomas Jones preached and addressed the congregation. In 1924, the present chapel celebrated its half-century with tea and a celebration meeting, addressed by a number of the brethren. In 1932 a new list of trustees was formed. Note the names, Samuel Davies, Edward Jones, David Morgan, Thomas Edwards, David J. Davies, David Jenkins, David Lloyd Jones, John Jones, Evan Jones, William Thomas Jones, Thomas Caradoc Edwards, Joseph Thomas Davies, Thomas Rees, William John Rees, **Elias Jones,** Daniel Jones, Edward Lewis Davies, a David Rhys Jones. In 1957 a new list was formed and here are the chapel trustees at present. John Jones, William John Rees, Thomas Caradoc Edwards, Thomas Rees, **Elias Jones**, William John Davies, David John F. Richards, Samuel Gerwyn Davies, John Davies, Daniel I. Edwards, John Goronwy 0. Davies, David Gwynfryn Jones, Morgan John Rees, David Gwyn Jones ac Edward Lloyd Jones.

It was interesting to note the list of elders. First of all came Thomas Morgan, Jonathan Davies, Evan Jenkins, Thomas Jones, Pantyrhedyn, and John Richards. Then came David Morgan, John R. Jones, John Jenkins (father of the Rev Joseph Jenkins), Joseph Davies, David J. Davies, Thomas Rees a Morgan Ishmael (the song elder). Then subsequently were added the names of Edward Jones and Samuel Edwards, Penbanc. Then the Rev Thomas Jones arrived in the area with David Lloyd Jones and Evan Jones as elders.

1940, gwnaethpwyd John Jones yn flaenor ac yn 1948, Mri. **Elias Jones**, Richard Hughes a Miss Florrie Jones. Y blaenoriaid ar hyn o bryd ydynt John Jones, **Elias Jones** a Miss Florrie Jones a (Eleanor Jones, 1958).

Magwyd nifer o bregethwyr cynorthwyol yn yr Eglwys. Cyfeiriwyd at rhai ohonynt eisoes. Dyma eraill ohonynt, Elias Lloyd Jones, David Lloyd Jones, D. Rhys Jones, Samuel Edwards ac R. D. Jenkins (brawd i'r Parch. Joseph Jenkins). Y mae yn byw yn Nhrefor, Sir Fôn, ar hyn o bryd). Rhoddodd y brodyr wasanaeth mawr a gwerthfawr i Bethel ac i'r gylchdaith. Diddorol ydyw sylwi ar aelodaeth yr Eglwys yn ystod y deugain mlynedd olaf. Yn 1920, yr oedd 90 o aelodau, yn 1938, yr oedd 92, yn 1945, yr oedd yn 110. Dyna'r penllanw yn rhif yr aelodaeth yn ystod y deugain mlynedd olaf. Er 1945, aeth yr aelodaeth i lawr yn raddol, rhif yr aelodau yn 1960 ydyw 62.

Derbyniodd yr Eglwys roddion gwerthfawr o bryd i'w gilydd. Defnyddiwyd cymunrodd o £60 gan John T. Davies i brynu piano i'r Festri er côf amdano. Llynedd rhoddodd Miss Elinor Jones, B.A., organ hardd i'r capel er cof am ei thad a'i mam. Mr. a Mrs. Evan Jones, a'i hewyrth, Mr. Daniel Jones. Llynedd hefyd cafwyd cymunrodd o £25 er cof am y diweddar Mr. Samuel Moreton, Croesoswallt. Yn ystod yr wythnosau diwethaf derbyniwyd cymunrodd o £500 gan y diweddar Elias Lloyd Jones, y pregethwr cynorthwyol a'r swyddog eglwysig ffyddlon a garai Bethel mor angherddol.

Yn y cyfarfodydd hyn byddwn yn ail-agor y capel yn swyddogol ar ôl ei atgyweirio a'i lanhau, gwaith yr oedd mawr angen ei wneud. Aeth y gost i wneud y cyfan oll yn £1000. Penderfynodd yr Ymddiriedolwyr agor cronfa ynglŷn a'r cyfarfodydd dathlu. Carwn apelio at bawb sydd yn dal unrhyw gysylltiad a'r Achos ym Methel gofio yn hael am y drysorfa hon. Anfonwch eich rhoddion i'r Gweinidog, Y Parch. Clifford Roberts, Glan Tuen, Ystumtuen, Aberystwyth, Cards., neu i Mr. John Jones, Lisburne House, Pontrhydygroes, Ystrad Meurig, Cards. Derbynnir pob rhodd a estynnir i ni yn ddiolchgar.

In 1940 John Jones was made an elder and in 1948 Messrs **Elias Jones**, Richard Hughes a Miss Florrie Jones. The elders at present are John Jones, **Elias Jones** and Miss Florrie Jones and (Eleanor Jones, 1958).

Lots of assistant preachers were brought up in the church. Reference has previously been made to some of them. Here are some others, Elias Lloyd Jones, David Lloyd Jones, D. Rhys Jones, Samuel Edwards ac R. D. Jenkins (brother of the Rev Joseph Jenkins) who lives in Trefor, Anglesey at present. The brethren gave great and valuable service to Bethel and the immediate circuit. It is interesting to note the church membership in the last 40 years. In 1920 there were 90 members, in 1938 there were 92 and in 1945 110. That was as high as the membership got in the last 40 years. Since 1945, the membership gradually reduced until in 1960 it was 62.

The church receives some worthwhile donations from time to time. A bequest of £60 from John T. Davies was used to buy a piano for the vestry in his memory. Last year Miss Elinor Jones, B.A., donated a beautiful organ to the chapel in memory of her mother and father, Mr and Mrs Evan Jones and her uncle Mr. Daniel Jones. Last year a bequest for £25 was also received in memory of the late Mr Samuel Morton, Croesoswallt (Oswestry). During the last few weeks a bequest of £500 by the late Elias Lloyd Jones, the assistant preacher and faithful church officer who loved Bethel so deeply.

In these meetings, the chapel will be officially reopened after being refurbished and cleaned, work which was badly needed. The total cost of all the work was £1000. The trustees resolved to open a fund relating to the celebration meetings. An appeal is made to everyone who has a connection with the cause in Bethel to remember to give generously to the fund. Donations may be given to the minister, Rev Clifford Roberts, Glan Tuen, Ystumtuen, Aberystwyth, Cards., or Mr. John Jones, Lisburne house, Pontrhydygroes, Ystrad Meurig, Cards.. Each donation offered to us will be gratefully received.

11
Marwolaeth mwynwr Eidalaidd
Death of Italian miner

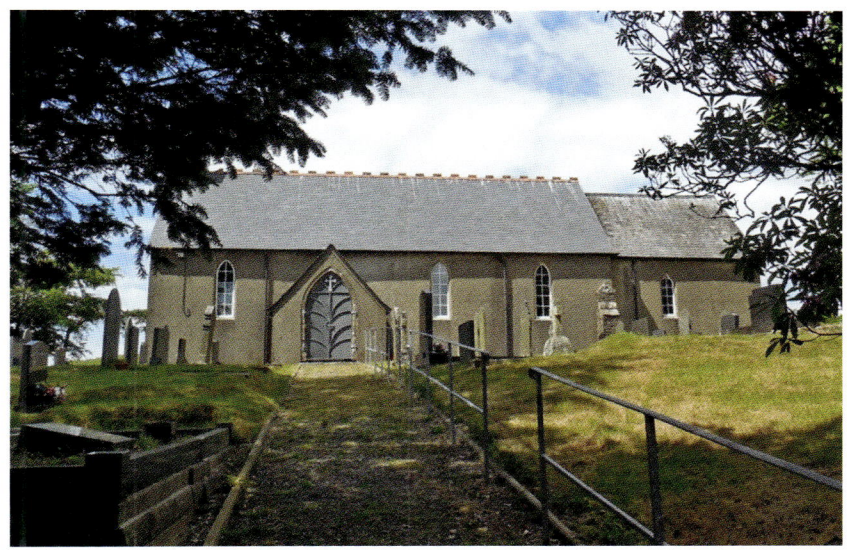

Eglwys Trisant
Trisant Church

Methwyd darganfod bedd y mwynwr Eidalaidd, Vanni Ferdinando, sy'n cael ei grybwyll yn yr atgofion ond dangosir llun o'i Dystysgrif Marwolaeth.

Unable to locate the grave of Italian miner, Vanni Ferdinando, who is mentioned in memoirs but a copy of his Death Certificate is illustrated.

Tystysgrif Marwolaeth — **Death Certificate**

CERTIFIED COPY of an ENTRY OF DEATH
COPI DILYS O GOFNOD MARWOLAETH
Pursuant to the Births and Deaths Registration Act 1953

WHDU342UU

Registration District: Aberystwyth
Sub-district: Rheidol, in the County of Cardigan

No.	When and where died	Name and surname	Sex	Age	Occupation	Cause of death	Signature, description and residence of informant	When registered	Signature of registrar
208	Fifth December 1900, New Row, Llanfihangel Upper R.D.	Vanni FERDINANDO	Male	37 Years	Lead Miner	Gastritis 1 month, Congestion of liver, Oedema of legs 2 months. Certified by Jno Morgan MRCS	x the mark of Magri Gatone Present at the death New Row Llanfihangel Upper	Eighth December 1900	Thos Morgan Deputy Registrar

Certified to be a true copy of an entry in a register in my custody.

R Pugh, Superintendent Registrar / Cofrestrydd Arolygol
Date: 22nd July 2014

WARNING: A CERTIFICATE IS NOT EVIDENCE OF IDENTITY.
RHYBUDD: NID YW TYSTYSGRIF YN PROFI PWY YDYCH CHI.

CAUTION: THERE ARE OFFENCES RELATING TO FALSIFYING OR ALTERING A CERTIFICATE AND USING OR POSSESSING A FALSE CERTIFICATE. ©CROWN COPYRIGHT
GOFAL: MAE YNA DROSEDDAU YN YMWNEUD Â FFUGIO NEU ADDASU TYSTYSGRIF NEU DDEFNYDDIO TYSTYSGRIF FFUG NEU WRTH FOD AG UN YN EICH MEDDIANT. ©HAWLFRAINT Y GORON

12
Coeden Deuluol
Family Tree

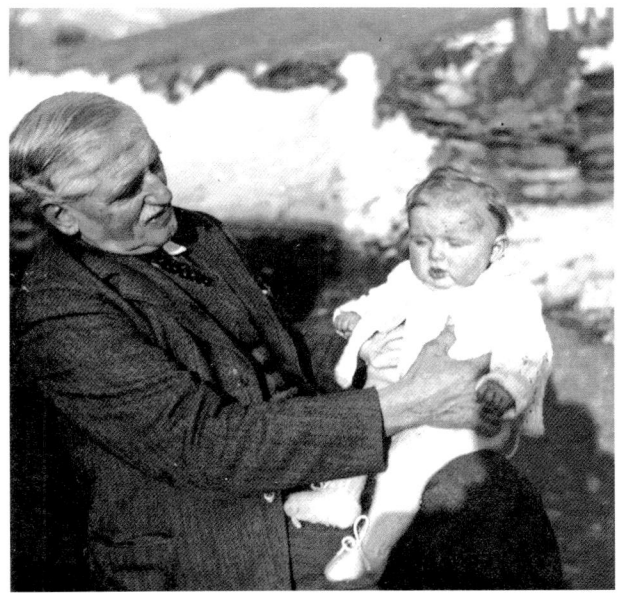

Elias a minnau yn fabi
Elias and myself as a baby

Dywed Elias i'w hen hen daid adeiladu Ty Unnos Troedyrhiw ond mewn erthygl arall dywed mai Shaci (Siaci) oedd yr adeiladwr. Mae'r enw Shaci (Siaci) yn ffurf gyfarwydd anffurfiol o Jack neu John, yn enwedig yng Ngorllewin Cymru. Mae Elias hefyd yn defnyddio 'Shacci' (dwy c). Credaf mewn gwirionedd fod y sillafiad 'Siaci' yn fwy naturiol a chywir.

....

Elias says that his great great grandfather, John, built the Ty Unnos, Troedyrhiw and, in another article, states that Shaci built it. The name Shaci (Siaci) is a common 'familiar'/ informal form of Jack/John, particularly in West Wales. Elias also uses 'Shacci' (2 'c's) but really it is more natural and correct to use the spelling Siaci.

Coeden Deuluol   **Family Tree**

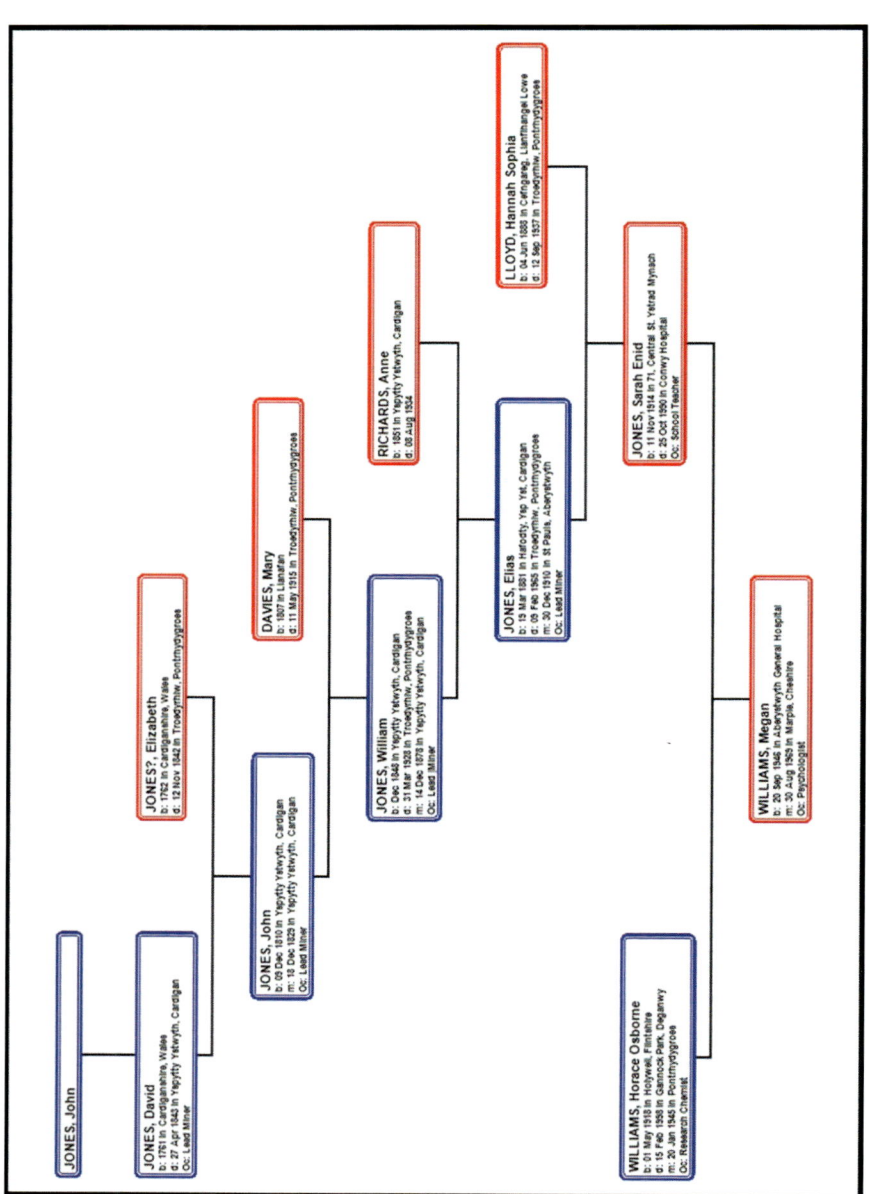

180